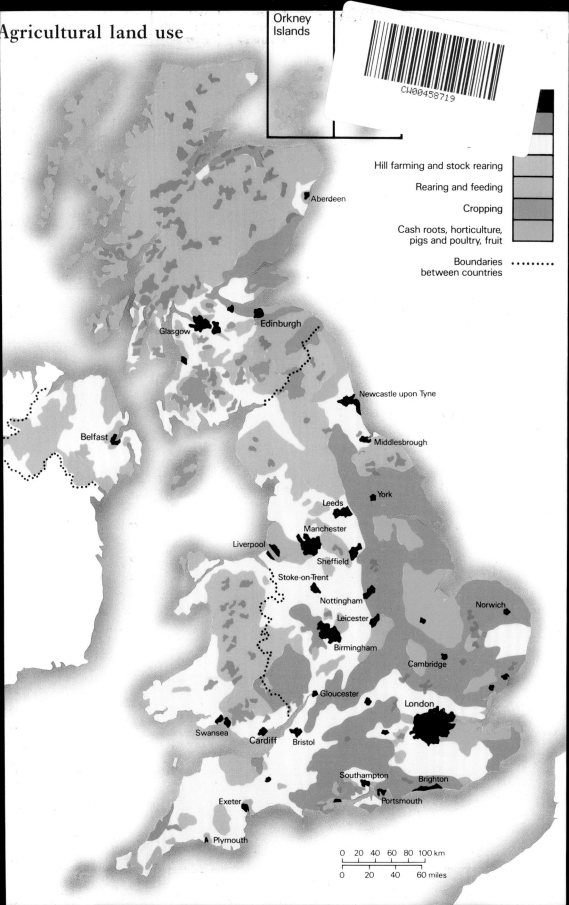

BRITAIN
1992
AN OFFICIAL HANDBOOK

BRITAIN
1992
AN OFFICIAL HANDBOOK

Prepared by the Central Office of Information
London: HMSO

ISBN O 11 701638 1

Contents

Diagrams

Maps

Photographs

Introduction

Britain 1992 is the forty-third handbook in the series. Prepared by the Central Office of Information and published by HMSO, it is widely known in Britain and overseas as an established work of reference and is an important element of the information service provided by diplomatic posts. It is sold by Her Majesty's Stationery Office throughout the world.

Britain 1992 describes many features in the life of the country, including the workings of the Government and other major institutions. It does not attempt an analytical approach to current events.

Care should be taken when studying British statistics to note whether they refer to England, to England and Wales (considered together for many administrative and other purposes), to Great Britain, which comprises England, Wales and Scotland, or to the United Kingdom (which is the same as Britain, that is, Great Britain and Northern Ireland) as a whole.

The factual and statistical information in *Britain 1992* is compiled with the co-operation of other government departments and agencies, and of many other organisations. Sources of more detailed and more topical information (including statistics) are mentioned in the text and a guide to official sources is given in Appendix 2.

The text, generally, is based on information available up to August/September 1991.

Reference Services
Central Office of Information

1   Land and People

Introduction

Britain comprises Great Britain (England, Wales and Scotland) and Northern Ireland, and is one of the 12 member states of the European Community. Its full name is the United Kingdom of Great Britain and Northern Ireland.

Physical Features

Britain constitutes the greater part of the British Isles. The largest of the islands is Great Britain. The next largest comprises Northern Ireland and the Irish Republic. Western Scotland is fringed by the large archipelago known as the Hebrides and to the north east of the Scottish mainland are Orkney and Shetland. All these have administrative ties with the mainland, but the Isle of Man in the Irish Sea and the Channel Islands between Great Britain and France are largely self-governing, and are not part of the United Kingdom.

With an area of some 242,500 sq km (93,600 sq miles), Britain is just under 1,000 km (some 600 miles) from the south coast to the extreme north of Scotland and just under 500 km (some 300 miles) across in the widest part.

The climate is generally mild and temperate. Prevailing winds are south-westerly and the weather from day to day is mainly influenced by depressions moving eastwards across the Atlantic. It is subject to frequent changes but to few extremes of temperature. It is rarely above 32°C (90°F) or below -10°C (14°F). The average annual rainfall is more than 1,600 mm (over 60 inches) in the mountainous areas of the west and north but less than 800 mm (30 inches) over central and eastern parts. Rain is fairly well distributed throughout the year, but, on average, March to June are the driest months and September to January the wettest. During May, June and July (the months of longest daylight) the mean daily duration of sunshine varies from five hours in northern Scotland to eight hours in the Isle of Wight; during the months of shortest daylight (November, December and January) sunshine is at a minimum, with an average of an hour a day in northern Scotland and two hours a day on the south coast of England.

Historical Outline

The word 'Britain' derives from Greek and Latin names probably stemming from a Celtic original. Although in the prehistoric time-scale the Celts were relatively late arrivals in the British Isles (following cultures which had produced such notable monuments as the stone circles of Avebury and Stonehenge), only with them does Britain emerge into recorded history. The term 'Celtic' is often used rather generally to distinguish the early inhabitants of the British Isles from the later Anglo-Saxon invaders.

England and Wales

Roman rule lasted for over 300 years from AD 43. The final Roman withdrawal in 408 followed a period of increasing disorder during which the island began to be raided by Angles, Saxons and Jutes from northern Europe. It is from the Angles that the name 'England' derives. In the next two centuries the raids turned into settlement and a number of small kingdoms were established. The Britons maintained an independent existence in the areas now known as Wales and Cornwall. Among these kingdoms, more powerful ones emerged, claiming overlordship over the whole country, first in the north (Northumbria), then in the midlands (Mercia) and finally in the south (Wessex). However, further raids and settlement by the Vikings from Scandinavia occurred, although in the tenth century the Wessex dynasty defeated the invading Danes and established a wide-ranging authority in England.

In 1066, the last successful invasion of England took place. Duke William of Normandy defeated the English at the Battle of Hastings. Normans and others from France came to settle. French became the language of the nobility for the next three centuries and the legal and, to some extent, social structure was influenced by that prevailing across the Channel.

Wales had remained a Celtic stronghold, although often within the English sphere of influence. However, with the death in battle in 1282 of Prince Llywelyn, Edward I launched a successful campaign to bring Wales under English rule. Continued strong Welsh national feeling was indicated by the rising led by Owain Glyndŵr at the beginning of the fifteenth century. The Acts of Union of 1536 and 1542 united England and Wales administratively, politically and legally.

Scotland

Scotland was mainly inhabited by the Picts. In the sixth century, the Scots from Ireland (or 'Scotia') settled in what is now Argyll. Lothian was populated by the English, while Welsh Britons moved north to Strathclyde. During the ninth century, the various parts of Scotland united in defence against the Vikings. The powerful monarchy which now existed in England threatened Scottish independence throughout the Middle Ages.

The eventual unification of England and Scotland showed that religious differences were now more important than old national antagonisms. In England, Elizabeth I was succeeded in 1603 by James VI of Scotland (James I of England). Even so, England and Scotland remained separate during the seventeenth century, apart from an enforced period of unification under Oliver Cromwell.

In 1707, both countries, realising the benefits of closer political and economic union, agreed on a single parliament for Great Britain. Scotland retained its own system of law and church settlement. The Union became strained during the reigns of the Protestant Hanoverians George I and George II, when two Jacobite risings attempted to restore the Catholic Stuarts.

Ireland

A number of kingdoms had emerged in Ireland before the Christian era. Ireland, however, did not escape the incursions of the Vikings, who dominated the country during the tenth century.

In 1169 Henry II of England launched an invasion of Ireland. He had been granted its overlordship by the English Pope Adrian IV, who was anxious to bring the Irish church into full obedience to Rome. Although a large part of the country came under the control of Anglo-Norman magnates, little direct authority was exercised from England during the Middle Ages.

The Tudor monarchs showed a much greater tendency to intervene in Ireland. During the reign of Elizabeth I, a series of campaigns was waged against Irish insurgents. The main focus of resistance was the northern province of Ulster. With the collapse of this resistance and the flight of its leaders in 1607, Ulster became an area of settlement by immigrants from Scotland and England.

The English civil wars (1642–52) led to further risings in Ireland, which were crushed by Cromwell. There was more fighting after the deposition of James II in 1688.

During most of the eighteenth century there was an uneasy peace; towards its end various efforts were made by British governments to achieve stability. In 1782 the Irish Parliament (dating from medieval times) was given legislative independence; the only constitutional tie with Great Britain was the Crown. The Parliament represented, however, only the privileged Anglo-Irish minority and Catholics were excluded from it. An abortive rebellion took place in 1798

Some dates in British history

122-38
Hadrian's Wall built

832-60
Scots and Picts merge under Kenneth Macalpin to form what is to become the kingdom of Scotia

860s
Danes overrun East Anglia, Northumbria and East Mercia

871-99
Reign of Alfred of Wessex

1016-35
Cnut, king of Denmark, also king of England

1086
Domesday survey

1215
King John signs Magna Carta, to protect feudal rights against royal abuse

1296-1336
Anglo-Scottish wars

1337
Hundred Years War between England and France begins

1348-49
Black Death (bubonic plague) wipes out a third of England's population

1381
Peasants' Revolt in England

1455-87
Wars of the Roses, between Lancastrians and Yorkists

1534-40
English Reformation: Henry VIII breaks with the papacy and dissolves the monasteries

1547-53
Protestantism becomes official religion in England under Edward VI

1553-58
Catholic reaction under Mary I

1558-1603
Reign of Elizabeth I. Moderate Protestantism established

1587
Execution of Mary Queen of Scots at Elizabeth's hands

1588
Defeat of Spanish Armada

c1590-c1613
Plays of Shakespeare written

1649
Execution of Charles I

1653-59
Republic of Oliver Cromwell

1688
Glorious Revolution: Accession of William III and Mary II

1756-63
Seven Years War settles rivalry between Britain and France in America and India in Britain's favour

c1760s-c1830
Industrial Revolution

1767
James Hargreaves's spinning jenny invented

1769
James Watt's steam engine patented

1785-87
Edmund Cartwright's power-loom patented

1825
Stockton to Darlington railway built

1831
Michael Faraday discovers magneto-electricity

1776
Adam Smith's *Wealth of Nations*, written in Kirkcaldy in Scotland, published

1800-15
Napoleonic Wars

1829
Catholic emancipation

1832
First Reform Act extends franchise and redistributes parliamentary seats

1837-1901
Reign of Victoria

1940
Battle of Britain

1973
Britain enters European Community

and in 1801 Ireland was unified with Great Britain.

The 'Irish question' continued as one of the major problems of British politics during the nineteenth century. In 1886 the Liberal Government introduced a Home Rule Bill which would have given an Irish Parliament authority over most internal matters while reserving to Britain control over external affairs. This led to a split in the Liberal Party and the failure of the Bill. In 1914 Home Rule was enacted by the Government of Ireland Act. Its implementation was prevented by the threat of armed resistance on the part of the Protestant majority in Ulster and by the outbreak of the first world war.

Although a nationalist rising in Dublin in 1916 was suppressed, a guerrilla force known as the Irish Republican Army (IRA) began operations against the British administration at the end of the first world war. The Government of Ireland Act 1920 provided for the establishment of two Home Rule parliaments, one in Dublin and the other in Belfast. The Act was implemented in 1921 in Northern Ireland, when six of the nine counties of the province of Ulster received their own Parliament and remained represented in, and subject to the supreme authority of, the British Parliament. In the South the IRA continued to fight for independence from the British administration. After the signature of a truce in June, the Anglo-Irish Treaty of December 1921 established the Irish Free State, which became a republic in 1949.

Channel Islands and Isle of Man

Although the Channel Islands and the Isle of Man are not part of the United Kingdom, they have a special relationship with it. The Channel Islands were part of the Duchy of Normandy in the tenth and eleventh centuries. The Isle of Man was under the nominal sovereignty of Norway until 1266, and eventually came under the direct administration of the Crown in 1765. Today the territories have their own legislative

Table 1.1: General Statistics

	England	Wales	Scotland	Northern Ireland	United Kingdom
Population[a] ('000)	46,161	2,799	4,957	1,570	55,487
Area (sq km)	130,478	20,768	77,167	14,121	242,534
Population density (persons per sq km)	354	135	64	111	229
Gross domestic product (per head, 1989)	7,717	6,372	7,021	5,758	7,666
Employees in employment ('000, June 1990)	19,356	993	1,973	530	22,852
Percentage of employees (June 1990) in:					
services	69·6	66·6	68·5	70·1	69·4
manufacturing	22·8	23·8	20·2	19·8	22·5
construction	4·5	4·8	6·7	4·9	4·8
energy and water supply	1·8	2·5	3·0	1·5	2·0
agriculture, forestry and fishing	1·2	2·0	1·5	3·7	1·3
Unemployment rate (per cent, seasonally adjusted, June 1991)	8·0	8·8	9·0	13·8	8·1

[a]Based on preliminary figures from the census held on 21 April 1991. These will be replaced by final figures in 1992.

assemblies and systems of law. The British Government is responsible for their defence, their international relations and, ultimately, their good government.

The Four Lands

In the following pages there are brief separate descriptions of aspects of social, economic and political life for England, Wales, Scotland and Northern Ireland, with some additional material on the political situation in Northern Ireland.

ENGLAND

England is predominantly a lowland country, although there are upland regions in the north (the Pennine Chain, the Cumbrian mountains and the Yorkshire moorlands) and in the south west in Cornwall, Devon and Somerset. Central southern England has the downs—low chalk hill ranges. The greatest concentrations of population are in London and the south east, the West Yorkshire and north-west industrial cities, the Midlands conurbation around Birmingham, the north-east conurbations on the rivers Tyne and Tees, and along the Channel coast.

The Church of England, which was separated from the Roman Catholic Church at the time of the Reformation, is the Established Church; the Sovereign must always be a member of the Church and appoints its two archbishops and 42 other diocesan bishops.

The English language is descended from the German tongue spoken by the Anglo-Saxons in the fifth and sixth centuries. This was subsequently influenced by Latin and Norse vocabulary. The language was transformed with the settlement by the Normans from France.

Government

England has no government minister or department exclusively responsible for its central administration in domestic affairs, in contrast to Wales, Scotland and Northern Ireland. Instead, there are a number of government departments, whose responsibilities in some cases also cover aspects of affairs in Wales and Scotland.

There are 523 Members of Parliament for England in the House of Commons, and arrangements are made for the discussion of regional affairs. Of the two major political parties, the Conservatives find their support chiefly in suburban and rural areas and have a large majority of the parliamentary seats in the southern half of England and in East Anglia, while the Labour Party derives its main support from urban industrialised areas. In June 1991 England had 353 Conservative Members of Parliament, 157 Labour, 9 Liberal Democrat, 3 Social Democrat and the Speaker of the House of Commons.

Local government is administered through a two-tier system of counties subdivided into districts. There are 32 single-tier borough authorities in London and six metropolitan counties in other parts of England.

The English legal system comprises on the one hand a historic body of conventions known as 'common law' and 'equity', and, on the other, parliamentary and European Community legislation.

In the formulation of common law since the Norman Conquest, great reliance was placed on precedent. Equity law derives from the practice of petitioning the King's Chancellor in cases not covered by common law.

The Economy

In the later eighteenth and nineteenth centuries Britain became the first industrialised country, basing its wealth on coalmining, on the manufacture of iron and steel, heavy machinery and textiles, on shipbuilding and on trade.

In the twentieth century a second period of industrialisation changed the broad pattern of development in England. In the 1920s and 1930s the northern industrial centres saw their traditional manufactures weakened owing to fluctuations in world trade and competition from other industrialising

Britain

Shetland Islands

Orkney Islands

SCOTLAND

SCOTLAND

0   50   100   150 km

0   50   100 miles

International boundaries

Country boundaries

County boundaries
(regional boundaries
in Scotland)

Hebrides

Western Isles

Outer

Inner Hebrides

Highland

Grampian

Tayside

Fife

Central

Edinburgh

Lothian

Borders

Strathclyde

Northumberland

Dumfries and
Galloway

Tyne and Wear

Cumbria

Durham

Cleveland

Atlantic
Ocean

North Sea

NORTHERN
IRELAND

Belfast

North Yorkshire

Isle of Man

Lancashire

West
Yorkshire

Humberside

ENGLAND

Irish Sea

Merseyside

1

South
Yorkshire

Derbyshire

Lincolnshire

IRISH
REPUBLIC

Clwyd

Cheshire

2

Gwynedd

Staffordshire

Leicester

Norfolk

3

WALES

4

Cambridge

Suffolk

Powys

5

6

Hereford and
Worcester

7

Dyfed

9

8

Essex

Gwent

Gloucestershire

Oxford

10

London

11

12

Berkshire

Cardiff

13

Avon

Wiltshire

Surrey

Kent

1. Greater Manchester
2. Nottinghamshire
3. Shropshire
4. West Midlands
5. Warwickshire
6. Northamptonshire
7. Bedfordshire
8. Hertfordshire
9. Buckinghamshire
10. Greater London
11. West Glamorgan
12. Mid Glamorgan
13. South Glamorgan

Hampshire

West
Sussex

East
Sussex

Strait of Dover

BELG

Somerset

Devon

Dorset

Isle of Wight

FRANCE

Cornwall

English Channel

Isles of Scilly

Channel Islands

countries, and, in some cases, from substitute products. The south east and the west Midlands generally benefited from the newer industries such as pharmaceuticals, artificial fibres, electrical equipment, car manufacture and a wide range of consumer goods.

In the second half of the century, jobs in service industries have accounted for an increasing share of total employment, expansion being particularly marked in financial and business services. In addition, there has been a rise in self-employment.

London is one of the world's leading centres of banking, insurance and other financial services. Many high technology industries in the surrounding regions have also developed. There has been an increase in retailing activity, with a trend towards large shopping developments on the outskirts of towns, designed for shoppers with cars. London is also the main English media centre; the national press is published there, and the national radio and television networks have their headquarters there.

London and the neighbouring counties account for half of central government services and a significant proportion of non-food wholesale distribution in England. After London and the South East (where about three-quarters of employees are engaged in the service sector), the South West has the next highest concentration of service industries.

East Anglia has been the fastest-growing English region in both population and employment since the 1960s. Although largely agricultural, high-technology industry has in recent years developed throughout the region. One significant example is the Cambridge Science Park. It contains a number of science-based companies and research organisations, which have close collaborative links with the University.

Greater London and the industrial cities of the West Midlands, the North West, Yorkshire and Humberside, and the North continue to represent the largest concentrations of manufacturing industry. A number of industrial areas (in the North, the North West, Yorkshire and Humberside, and the West Midlands) which suffered as a result of the decline in traditional manufacturing employment are benefiting

from the Government's regional industrial policy. This aims to reduce regional disparities in job opportunities by making investment incentives available in the areas of greatest need, especially those which have been dependent on declining industries. The objective of the Enterprise Initiative, launched in 1988 and aimed particularly at small and medium-sized businesses, is to increase competitiveness by improving management skills.

In agriculture, dairying is most common in the west of England; sheep and cattle are reared in the hilly and moorland areas of the North and South West. Arable farming, pig and poultry farming and horticulture are concentrated in the east and south. Horticulture is also important in the West Midlands. The principal fishing ports are on the east coast and in the South West.

England has plentiful energy resources in its coalfields and has access to offshore oil and gas reserves. Important mineral deposits include sand, gravel and crushed rock used by the construction industry; industrial minerals include clay, salt from the North West, china clay from Cornwall and gypsum from the midlands, North and South East.

The motorway network comprises four long-distance routes linking London and the cities of the Midlands, the North and North West and the South West, the London orbital route, and over 30 shorter motorways.

Considerable investment is being made in the railways, both to improve inter-city services and to provide new rolling-stock for local services. The cross-Channel railway tunnel will link Britain with the European rail system and also provide a vehicle shuttle service on specially designed trains. Services through the tunnel are planned to start in 1993.

The major airports are Heathrow (the busiest international airport in the world) and Gatwick, both serving London; and Manchester, Luton and Birmingham. Stansted is being developed as London's third airport.

Tourism and the leisure industries have expanded considerably in recent years. Over half of expenditure by overseas visitors in Britain takes place in London, although areas elsewhere, encouraged by government policies to expand tourism in the regions, are becoming increasingly popular with overseas tourists. The South West is the most popular region for domestic tourism.

Cultural and Social Life

London has an extraordinary concentration of cultural features (including four major art galleries and a dozen renowned museums) and theatrical, opera, ballet and concert venues. Much the same broad range of cultural interests is reflected in other major cities and towns. Many theatres outside London are used for touring by the national theatre, dance and opera companies.

Of the many tourist attractions in England, the most popular of those charging for admission in 1990 were Madame Tussaud's waxworks in London, the Tower of London and Alton Towers (Staffordshire), with 2·5, 2·3 and 2·1 million visitors respectively.

The English love of gardens and landscapes is associated with a tradition of sightseeing visits to country houses, gardens and unspoilt rural and coastal areas. There are seven National Parks, six forest parks, 34 designated 'areas of outstanding natural beauty', ten environmentally sensitive areas, almost 200 country parks approved by the Countryside Commission, over 6,000 conservation areas, 800 km (500 miles) of designated heritage coastline, and about 2,000 historic buildings and over 3,000 gardens open to the public. There are also safari and wildlife parks, and 'theme' parks, all offering family activities and entertainment. Many regions and towns have associations with great English writers and artists, such as William Shakespeare (Stratford-upon-Avon), William Wordsworth (Lake District), Arnold Bennett (Stoke-on-Trent), the Brontë sisters (Yorkshire), Thomas Hardy (Dorset) and John Constable (Essex and Suffolk).

WALES

Wales is a country of hills and mountains, the highest of which are in Snowdonia in the north west; the tallest peak is Snowdon (1,085 m, 3,560 ft). Two-thirds of the population lives in the southern valleys and the lower-lying coastal areas. The chief urban centres are Cardiff, Swansea, Newport and Wrexham. Wales is a principality; Prince Charles, the heir to the throne, was invested by the Queen with the title of Prince of Wales at Caernarfon Castle in 1969, when he was 20.

Latest figures suggest that about one-fifth of the population speaks Welsh, a language of Celtic origin.

Welsh speakers are concentrated in the rural north and west. The Welsh name of the country is Cymru. Welsh has equal validity with English in law courts, bilingual education in schools is encouraged, and there has been an extended use of Welsh for official purposes and in broadcasting. Welsh-language television programmes are transmitted in Wales by Sianel 4 Cymru (Channel 4 Wales). A Welsh Language Board advises on matters relating to the Welsh language.

There is no established church, the Anglican church having been disestablished in 1920 following decades of pressure from adherents of the Methodist and Baptist churches. Methodism in particular spread rapidly in Wales in the eighteenth century, assuming the nature of a popular movement among Welsh speakers and finding strong support later in industrial communities.

Government

The country returns 38 Members of Parliament and there are special arrangements for the discussion of Welsh affairs. For the last 60 years the industrial communities have tended to support the Labour Party in elections, ensuring a Labour majority of seats. Wales has 26 Labour Members of Parliament, 6 Conservative, 3 Plaid Cymru (Welsh Nationalist) and 3 Liberal Democrat.

The Secretary of State for Wales, who is a member of the Cabinet, has wide-ranging responsibilities relating to the economy, welfare services and the provision of amenities. The headquarters of the administration is the Welsh Office in Cardiff, which also has an office in London. Local government is exercised through a system of elected authorities similar to that in England, and the legal system is identical with the English one.

The Economy

In the nineteenth century the Welsh economy was mainly based on coal, iron, steel and tinplate. It contracted sharply during the 1920s and 1930s, resulting in severe unemployment and substantial emigration.

In the past 30 years contraction of the older heavy industries has continued. Practically all the coal mines have been closed. Wales produces about 10 per cent of British opencast coal production, including all of its anthracite. Although Wales still accounts for 31 per cent of British steel production, it is now an important centre for electronics and several new high-technology businesses in related industries have been established. Significant investment by overseas companies accounts for about 27 per cent of jobs in manufacturing. Financial and business services are expanding rapidly; some large companies have relocated major parts of their operation to Wales, providing support for industrial development. Government relocation has also benefited employment.

Although south Wales remains the principal industrial area, new industries and firms have been introduced in north-east Wales and light industry attracted to the towns in mid- and north Wales rural areas. A development corporation was set up in 1987 to stimulate the regeneration of the Cardiff Bay area. Regional aid for the south Wales valleys has created and safeguarded about 18,000 jobs. The Welsh Development Agency has invested about £65 million in factory building, and a total of 620 hectares (1,550 acres) of derelict land in the valleys has been cleared. A £14 million investment in environmental improvement schemes was announced by the Government in 1990.

Agriculture occupies about 80 per cent of the land area, the main activities being sheep and cattle rearing in the hill regions and dairy farming in the lowlands. Wales accounts for over 20 per cent of the Forestry Commission's timber production.

The biggest pumped-storage power station in Europe is at Dinorwig in Gwynedd. Good communications exist in the south, with motorway links across the Severn Bridge to southern England and the Midlands, and high-speed rail services to a number of destinations in England. A second road crossing of the Severn is planned. Flights to New York leave from Cardiff-Wales airport.

There has been expansion in the tourist and catering trades and in some areas of public administration. With its coastal resorts, and three National Parks (Snowdonia, the Brecon Beacons and the Pembrokeshire Coast), as well as other areas of picturesque hill, lake and mountain country, Wales attracts many tourists, especially for outdoor holidays.

Cultural and Social Life

Welsh literature is one of the oldest and richest in Europe, and there is a national library. The Welsh people also have strong musical traditions; the country is well known for its choral singing and the Welsh National Opera has an international reputation. Special festivals, known as *eisteddfodau*, encourage Welsh literature and music. The largest is the annual Royal National Eisteddfod, consisting of competitions in music, singing, prose and poetry entirely in Welsh. The town of Llangollen includes artists from all over the world in the annual International Musical Eisteddfod. An active local press includes a number of Welsh language publications.

The education system is similar to that in England, except for the use of Welsh in some schools, particularly in the Welsh-speaking, largely rural, areas. The collegiate University of Wales, founded in 1893, comprises six member institutions.

Among many sporting activities, there is particular interest in rugby union football, which has come to be regarded as the Welsh national game.

SCOTLAND

Just over half of Scotland consists of the sparsely populated highlands and islands in the north. Three-quarters of the population and most of the industrial towns are in the central lowlands. Scotland contains large areas of unspoilt and wild landscape, with internationally significant concentrations of plants and animals. It contains the majority of Britain's highest mountains—nearly 300 peaks over 913 m (3,000 ft). The highest are the Grampians in the central highlands, with Ben Nevis (1,343 m, 4,406 ft) the tallest peak. The southern uplands, which contain a number of hill ranges, border on England. The chief cities are Edinburgh (the capital), Glasgow, Aberdeen and Dundee.

The established Church of Scotland is a Protestant church which is Presbyterian in form; it is governed by a hierarchy of church courts, each of which includes lay people.

Government

There are special arrangements for the conduct of Scottish affairs within the British system of government and separate Acts of Parliament are passed for Scotland where appropriate. In August 1991 the 72 Scottish seats in the House of Commons were represented by 48 Labour Members of Parliament, 10 Conservative, 9 Liberal Democrat and 5 Scottish National.

Scottish administration is the responsibility of the Secretary of State for Scotland, a member of the Cabinet, working through the Scottish Office, which has its headquarters in Edinburgh and an office in London.

Local government generally operates on a two-tier basis broadly similar to that in England and Wales. The three islands councils (for Orkney, Shetland and the Western Isles) are single-tier authorities. The principles and procedures of the Scottish legal system (particularly in civil law) differ in many respects from those of England and Wales; these differences stem, in part, from the adoption of elements of other European legal systems, based on Roman law, during the sixteenth century.

The Economy

Scotland has experienced the same pressure on its traditional industries as the north of England and Wales. However, over the past decades its economy has been transformed, with a developed oil and gas industry, and investment by overseas companies making significant contributions to the growth of modern, technologically based industries.

The electronics industry, which includes many of the world's leading companies in this field, provides 12 per cent of jobs in manufacturing and 20 per cent of output and investment. Between 1979 and 1989 Scottish electronics output quadrupled. By mid-1990 about 210 plants were employing some 47,000 workers, one of the biggest concentrations of the electronics industry in Western Europe.

Scotland accounts for more than half of Britain's output of integrated circuits and for over 10 per cent of European output.

Since the early 1970s the Scottish economy has also benefited from industries related to the discovery of oil and gas under the northern North Sea. Up to about 100,000 jobs are estimated to have arisen directly or indirectly as a result of North Sea activities.

Traditional industries, such as coal, steel and shipbuilding, have experienced a long-term decline in employment. Others, such as high-quality tweeds and other textiles, and food and drink products, remain important. The Scotch whisky industry had exports of over £1,700 million in 1990.

The disadvantage and decay to be found in some areas, particularly housing estates on the periphery of cities and towns, are being tackled through comprehensive renewal projects designed to solve the economic, social and physical problems which have arisen.

Scotland has about one-third of Britain's agricultural land, but 70 per cent consists of rough grazing (including common grazing) for cattle and sheep. About 11 per cent of the agricultural area is used for crops, and 53 per cent of this is under barley. Scotland accounts for nearly half of Britain's forest area and for over one-third of timber production; the bulk of new planting in Britain takes place in Scotland, most of it in the upland and mountain areas. Fishing remains an important activity; more than 75 per cent of total landings of fish in Britain are made at Scottish ports.

Nuclear and hydro-electric generation supply a higher proportion of energy than in any other part of Britain. With the two Advanced Gas-cooled Reactor stations at Torness (Lothian) and Hunterston (Strathclyde) in full production, some 50 per cent of Scotland's electricity comes from nuclear power. Hydro-power and other renewables contribute a further 12 to 15 per cent, the remainder coming from low-sulphur Scottish coal and (from 1992) North Sea gas.

Communications, both domestic and international, have improved in many areas, particularly in the north and north east, owing to the stimulus of the offshore oil industry, of road- and bridge-building programmes and of the improvement of ferry links to the Scottish islands. The offshore oil industry has also encouraged expansion in the traditionally strong financial and business services, which are one of the fastest-growing sectors of the Scottish economy. Tourism makes a significant contribution to the overall economy, and the tourism and leisure industries directly provide about 154,000 jobs —8 per cent of Scottish employment.

Cultural and Social Life

A vigorous cultural life has as its highlight the annual Edinburgh International Festival, one of the world's leading cultural events. Notable performing arts bodies are the Royal Scottish Orchestra, Scottish Opera, Scottish Ballet, Scottish Chamber Orchestra, Scottish Baroque Ensemble and the BBC Scottish Symphony Orchestra. Scotland possesses excellent collections of the fine and applied arts, notably in the National Galleries of Scotland, the Royal Museums of Scotland and the City of Glasgow Museum and Art Galleries (including the Burrell collection, opened in 1983). The Government intends to fund the construction in Edinburgh of a new Museum of Scotland.

Gaelic, a language of ancient Celtic origin, is spoken by some 80,000 people, mainly in the islands and north west.

An active press includes six national daily morning newspapers, six local evening newspapers and four national Sunday newspapers. Television programmes are produced by BBC Scotland and by three independent companies, covering the highland, lowland and border regions. BBC Radio Scotland covers most of the population.

The educational tradition has been particularly strong, helping many Scots to positions of eminence in the arts and sciences. There are eight universities, of which four (St Andrews, Glasgow, Aberdeen and Edinburgh) were established in the fifteenth and sixteenth centuries, while the other four have been established since 1964.

Over 57 per cent of Scotland's housing has been built since 1945, a higher proportion than in either England or Wales. The tenure pattern is very different from that in the rest of Britain, with 42 per cent of housing rented from the public sector, compared with 25 per cent for Great Britain as a whole. As in the rest of Britain, there has been a noticeable growth in owner-occupied housing in recent years.

The sport of golf originated in Scotland, and courses at St Andrews, Gleneagles, Turnberry, Muirfield, Troon and Prestwick are internationally renowned. There are also winter sports centres at Aviemore, Glenshee, Glen Coe, Aonach Mhor and the Lecht.

NORTHERN IRELAND

Northern Ireland is at its nearest point only 21 km (13 miles) from Scotland. It has a 488-km (303-mile) border in the south and west with the Irish Republic. At its centre lies Lough Neagh, Britain's largest freshwater lake (381 sq km, 147 sq miles). Many of the principal towns lie in valleys leading from the Lough, including the capital, Belfast, which stands at the mouth of the river Lagan. The Mourne Mountains, rising sharply in the south east, include

Slieve Donard, Northern Ireland's highest peak (852 m, 2,796 ft).

Just under two-thirds of the population are descendants of Scots or English settlers who crossed to north-eastern Ireland mainly in the seventeenth century; most belong to the Protestant faith, and support the maintenance of the union with Great Britain. The remainder, over a third, are Irish in origin and mainly Roman Catholic; many of them are nationalist in political opinion, favouring union with the Irish Republic.

Government

Background to Civil Disturbances

For 50 years from 1921 Northern Ireland had its own devolved Parliament in which the mainly Protestant Unionists consistently formed the majority and therefore constituted the Government after successive elections. Nationalists resented this domination and their effective exclusion from political office.

An active and articulate civil rights movement emerged during the late 1960s. Reforms were made but sectarian disturbances developed, which required the introduction of the Army in 1969 to support the police in keeping the peace. Subsequently, sectarian divisions were exploited by the actions of terrorists from both sides, but most notably by the Provisional Irish Republican Army, who claimed to be protecting the Roman Catholic minority.

From 1969 the Northern Ireland Government enacted reforms aimed at securing the minority's right to an effective voice in public bodies. A police authority representative of all sections of the community was created. Commissioners became responsible for investigating complaints of maladministration, including discrimination, against government departments and local authorities. A central housing executive became responsible for all public sector house-building and the allocation of houses according to need. Local government was restructured and electoral law, including the franchise and

the arrangements for reviewing electoral boundaries, was reformed.

Direct Rule and Political Initiatives

Despite this reform programme, the inter-communal violence continued, this leading to a decision by the British Government to take over responsibility for law and order in 1972. The Northern Ireland Government resigned in protest against this decision and direct rule began. Northern Ireland continues to be governed by direct rule under legislation passed in 1974. This allows the Parliament in London to approve all laws for Northern Ireland and places its government departments under the direction and control of the Secretary of State for Northern Ireland, who is a Cabinet minister.

Legislation passed in 1973 and 1982 provides for a measure of devolved government in Northern Ireland. This arrangement was last in force in January 1974, following agreement between the Northern Ireland political parties to form a power-sharing Executive. The Executive, however, collapsed in May 1974 and there has been no devolution since.

Attempts have been made by successive British governments to find a means of restoring a widely acceptable form of devolved government to Northern Ireland. A 78-member Assembly was elected by proportional representation in 1982. Four years later this was dissolved after it ceased to discharge its responsibilities to make proposals for the resumption of devolved government and to monitor the work of the Northern Ireland government departments. One of the reasons for the Assembly's dissolution was in part the Unionists' reaction to the signing of the Anglo-Irish Agreement between the British and Irish governments in November 1985.

The objectives of the Agreement are to:
- promote peace and stability in Northern Ireland;
- create a new climate of friendship and co-operation between the peoples of Britain and the Irish Republic; and
- improve co-operation in combating terrorism.

The Agreement commits the British and Irish governments to the principle that Northern Ireland shall remain part of Britain for so long as that is the wish of a majority. It recognises that at present a majority in Northern Ireland wishes to remain as part of Britain. Both governments have undertaken that, should a majority in Northern Ireland formally consent to the establishment of a united Ireland, they would introduce and support the necessary legislation. The Agreement binds both governments to these commitments in international law. The Agreement also established an Inter-governmental Conference through which the Irish Government can put forward views and proposals on specified matters affecting Northern Ireland affairs. This only applies where these matters are not the responsibility of a devolved administration in Northern Ireland and where cross border co-operation can be promoted in the interests of both countries. There is no derogation from the sovereignty of either the British or the Irish Government as a result of the Agreement; each retains full responsibility for decisions and administration within its own jurisdiction.

Despite the dissolution of the last Assembly the Government remains committed to finding a means by which substantial power and responsibility might be transferred to local elected representatives on a widely acceptable basis. In January 1990 the Government invited the leaders of the four constitutional parties—the Alliance Party, the Social Democratic and Labour Party, the Ulster Unionist Party and the Ulster Democratic Unionist Party—to enter into a dialogue with it about the possibility of holding round-table talks. It soon became clear that the agenda which the parties wished to address would require the involvement of the Irish Government and it too became involved in this process of 'talks about talks'. It was agreed that the talks should take place on the basis of three strands:

- Strand One, involving the constitutional parties and the Government, would look at relationships within Northern Ireland, including that between any new institutions there and the British Parliament at Westminster;

- Strand Two, involving the four parties and the British and Irish governments, would look at relationships between the people of the island of Ireland; and

- Strand Three, involving the two governments, would look at the relationship between the peoples of the British Isles.

To allow an opportunity for such wider political dialogue, the two governments agreed not to hold any meetings of the Anglo-Irish Intergovernmental Conference between two prespecified dates (subsequently identified as 26 April and 16 July 1991).

The talks began on 30 April with a series of bilateral meetings between the Government and the political parties to discuss practical and procedural issues. Plenary sessions began on 17 June. By 3 July it had become clear that it would not be possible to launch Strands Two and Three in the time available, and that this was likely to inhibit further progress in Strand One. It was therefore agreed that the talks should end in an orderly manner.

The final statement issued by the participants affirmed that the talks had been valuable and had produced genuine dialogue. The British Government hopes that they will provide a firm foundation for future dialogue and that further exchanges with the parties and the Irish Government will produce a basis for fresh talks.

Northern Ireland returns 17 members to the United Kingdom Parliament. In the last general election in 1987 the seats (and votes) were distributed as follows: Ulster Unionist 9 (37·8 per cent), Democratic Unionist 3 (11·7 per cent), Ulster Popular Unionist 1 (2·5 per cent), Social Democratic and Labour 3 (21·1 per cent), and Sinn Fein 1 (11·4 per cent); the Sinn Fein member has not taken his seat. The Alliance Party received 10 per cent of the votes but no seats.

Human Rights

The Government is committed to the protection of human rights in Northern Ireland. Britain is a signatory to the European Convention on Human Rights and allows individual petition. Legislation passed in 1973 outlaws discrimination by public bodies, including the Government, on the grounds of religious belief or political opinion. It also set up the independent Standing Advisory Commission on Human Rights, which advises the Government on the effectiveness of anti-discrimination legislation and on other human rights issues. In 1987 a central community relations unit was established within the Government to advise on the impact of government policies and programmes on community relations and to bring forward ideas on future action.

Direct and indirect discrimination in employment by public and private employers is also illegal. Legislation passed in 1976 made discrimination on the grounds of religion or politics unlawful and established a Fair Employment Agency to promote equal opportunities and work towards the eradication of discrimination.

New legislation came into effect in 1990. It strengthened the 1976 measures by requiring employers to:

● monitor the religious composition of their workforce and job applicants;

● take firm action, where necessary, to provide for a fair distribution of jobs between the two communities; and

● review their employment practices every three years.

The legislation also provides for criminal fines and economic sanctions against employers found guilty of bad practice.

Two new bodies have been established. The Fair Employment Agency was renamed the Fair Employment Commission. It has increased powers and resources to enable it to investigate employment practices, prescribe affirmative measures and offer advice and guidance. The new Fair Employment Tribunal determines individual complaints of alleged discrimination and appeals by employers against directions of the Commission.

The effectiveness of the legislation is being continuously evaluated and will be formally reviewed after five years.

Security Policy

While terrorism continues, certain emergency powers are in force. These include special powers of arrest in respect of certain serious crimes, non-jury courts to try those offences, and the banning of terrorist organisations. The powers are balanced by specific safeguards; the measures are temporary, need annual renewal by Parliament and are subject to annual independent review.

Most traditional rights, including freedom from persecution and freedom of speech, remain in force. The Government has, however, banned the broadcasting of direct statements by representatives of terrorist organisations or their supporters.

The security forces are accountable to the law; if they break it, their members are liable to prosecution like any other members of the community. An independent police complaints commission supervises police investigations into more serious complaints and, at its discretion, the investigation of others. Northern Ireland's legal system, and the safeguards it enshrines, are broadly similar to those in England and Wales.

The use of violence as a means of overcoming political differences has been condemned by the overwhelming majority of people living in Northern Ireland and, although terrorism continues, the overall level of violence is lower than in the early 1970s. Since 1969 some 3,000 people have been killed as a result of terrorist campaigns. The police take the primary role in maintaining order; the Army's task is one of assisting the civil authorities, and the number of soldiers on service has been considerably reduced. Terrorists are brought to justice through the courts and are tried for criminal offences, not political beliefs.

The Economy

Population and industry are concentrated on the eastern seaboard, while the rest of Northern Ireland remains predominantly rural and reliant mainly upon agriculture for its livelihood. Since the end of the second world war employment in shipbuilding, linen and agriculture has declined. However, there has been fast growth in the numbers seeking work, reflecting the relatively high rate of natural increase of the population, which is only partly offset by emigration. Unemployment is therefore higher than in any other British region. The unemployment rate fell from 17·1 per cent in June 1987 to 13·8 per cent in June 1991.

There has been a switch in emphasis from agriculture and manufacturing towards services. However, agriculture (predominantly livestock and livestock products) still accounts for three times the proportion of civil employment in Britain as a whole. Belfast has one of Britain's largest shipyards, and aerospace engineering is one of Northern Ireland's biggest manufacturing industries. Other industrial activities include the manufacture of a wide range of engineering products and clothing, vehicle components, oil-well equipment, electronics, telecommunications equipment, carpets, synthetic rubber, and food processing and packaging.

Manufacturing output increased by 13 per cent between 1985 and 1990, while output per employee hour rose by 15 per cent over this period. Living standards, as measured by gross domestic product per person, are lower than in Britain as a whole, standing at 75 per cent in 1989. Average earnings in 1990 were around 86 per cent of those in Great Britain. Governments have offered more generous incentives than are available in the rest of Britain to encourage new investment.

In 1990 the Government published a document which concluded that long-term growth could only be generated by improvements in competitiveness led by the private sector. Government policy is to:

- ensure that future assistance tackles obstacles preventing Northern Ireland industry becoming internationally competitive;

- target areas with growth potential in partnership with the private sector;

- intensify the drive for inward investment;

- build up management and workforce skills;

- target programmes on areas of social and economic deprivation and on the needs of the long-term unemployed;

- stimulate the development of entrepreneurs; and

- change the emphasis from promotion of new jobs to the strengthening of industry's competitive position, from which more jobs can result in the medium term.

In 1988 the Making Belfast Work initiative was launched to address the economic, educational, social and environmental problems in the most disadvantaged areas of Belfast. During the period 1988–94 an additional £123·6 million is being allocated to projects designed to create jobs and businesses, and to improve levels of skill, the physical environment, and health and living conditions in the areas.

Northern Ireland has parity with England, Scotland and Wales on taxation and services. To maintain social services at the level of those in Great Britain, to meet the cost of security measures and to compensate for the natural disadvantages of geography and lack of resources, the British Government's subvention to Northern Ireland in 1990–91 was just over £2,000 million.

In 1986 the British and Irish governments signed an agreement setting up the International Fund for Ireland and donations have been received from the United States, Canada, New Zealand and the European Community. The Fund finances projects covering business enterprise, tourism, urban development, agriculture and fisheries, science and technology, and community relations. Two investment companies, one on each side of the border, provide venture capital to new businesses. Three-quarters of the Fund is being spent in Northern Ireland and the rest in the Irish Republic's border counties.

Cultural and Social Life

Northern Ireland's landscape and natural features, cultural traditions and festivals continue to offer special attractions; it received nearly 1·2 million visitors in 1990.

15

The annual Belfast Festival at Queen's University is among the most important international festivals in Britain. The story of Ulster emigrants' contributions to American life, the history of Northern Ireland, and other aspects of its culture, including its dialects and strong literary tradition, are recorded in the Ulster-American Folk Park, the Ulster Museum and the Ulster Folk and Transport Museum.

The Government provides financial support for arts and cultural activities related to the Irish language. Over 20,000 secondary school pupils currently study Irish; full degree courses and research programmes are available at Northern Ireland's two universities, which have well developed links with industry.

Health and personal social services correspond fairly closely to those in the rest of Britain, although the administrative framework is different.

Although publicly maintained schools must be open to children from all religions, in practice Roman Catholic and Protestant children are for the most part educated in separate schools. In recent years a small number of integrated schools have been established with government support to provide education for Protestant and Roman Catholic children together. Successive governments have encouraged such schools where there is sufficient parental demand.

In the last ten years the housing stock in Northern Ireland has increased by about 12 per cent and owner-occupation from 51 per cent to more than 60 per cent.

Major town centre developments are taking place in Belfast, Londonderry and other towns, providing greatly improved shopping facilities.

Local television and radio programmes are broadcast and there is a local press; national radio and television networks are also received, and the national press is sold widely.

The Social Framework

The underlying causes of the changing lifestyle in Britain in the second half of the twentieth century include a lower birth rate, longer life expectancy, a higher divorce rate, wider educational opportunities, technological progress and a higher standard of living.

POPULATION

According to preliminary results of the April 1991 census, Britain's population is 55·5 million. It ranks seventeenth in the world in terms of population. Population figures are derived from the census of population (taken every ten years), with allowance for subsequent births and deaths (obtained from compulsory registration) and migration. The latest census included for the first time a question on ethnic grouping. The results are being published in stages from mid-1991.

The British population is expected, on mid-1989 based projections, to be 59·2 million in 2001 and 60 million in 2011.

Birth Rates

In 1990 there were 798,600 live births, 21,300 more than in 1989. Births outnumbered deaths (641,800) by 156,800. The total period fertility rate (an indication of the average family size) remains below 2·1, the level leading to the long-term replacement of the population, although it is projected to increase from 1·8 in 1989 to 2 for women born in or after 1980.

Contributory factors to the relatively low birth rate in recent years (13·9 live births per 1,000 population in 1990) include:

- the trends towards later marriage and towards postponing births, which have led to an increase in the average age of women having children—provisionally 27·5 years in 1990 compared with 26·7 in 1980;

- the current preference for smaller families than in the past, which has led to a significant decline in the proportion of families with four or more children. In 1990, 21 per cent of households in Great Britain consisted of a married couple with one or two children only, compared with 4 per cent of households consisting of a married couple with three or more children; and

● more widespread and effective contraception, making it easier to plan families. Voluntary sterilisation of men and women has also become more common. Of all pregnancies in England and Wales in 1989, 42·3 per cent were conceived outside marriage and of these 36·4 per cent were terminated by legal abortion.

Mortality

At birth the expectation of life for a man is about 72 years and for a woman 78 years, compared with 49 years for men and 52 years for women in 1901. There has only been a small increase in life expectancy in the older age groups.

The general death rate has remained roughly the same for the past 40 years, at about 12 per 1,000 population, although in 1990 it fell to 11·2. However, there has been a decline in mortality at most ages, particularly among children. The infant mortality rate (deaths of infants under one year old per 1,000 live births) was 7·9 in 1990; neonatal mortality (deaths of infants under four weeks old per 1,000 live births) was 4·5 in 1990; and maternal mortality is about 0·07 per 1,000 total births. The decline in mortality reflects better nutrition, rising standards of living, the advance of medical science, the growth of medical facilities, improved health measures, better working conditions, education in personal hygiene and the smaller size of families. Deaths resulting from infectious diseases (notably tuberculosis) have virtually disappeared.

Deaths caused by circulatory diseases (including heart attacks and strokes) now account for nearly half of all deaths, and mortality from heart disease in Britain remains high compared with that of other developed countries. The next largest cause of death is cancer, which is responsible for nearly one-quarter of deaths.

Cigarette smoking is the greatest preventable cause of illness and death in Britain. However, there has been a significant decline in the incidence of smoking, with 33 per cent of adult males and 30 per cent of adult females smoking cigarettes in 1988, as against 52 and 41 per cent respectively in 1972.

The Government is pursuing a comprehensive strategy against drug misuse in Britain. Initiatives are aimed at reducing both the supply of, and demand for, drugs. A number of government priorities, to support the overall aims of improving the country's health and providing high-quality care for those who need it, have been listed.

Marriage and Divorce

In 1989 there were 392,042 marriages in Britain, of which 36 per cent were remarriages of one or both parties. Some 34 per cent of all marriages in 1989 were remarriages where one or both parties had been divorced. Of the population aged 16 or over in England and Wales in 1989, 59 per cent were married, 26 per cent single, 9 per cent widowed and 6 per cent divorced. The average age for first marriages in England and Wales is now 26·3 for men and 24·2 for women.

In 1989 about 12·7 decrees of divorce were made absolute for every 1,000 married couples in England and Wales. The rates are lower in Scotland and Northern Ireland. In 1989, 150,872 divorces were granted in England and Wales; the proportion granted to wives was 71·6 per cent. The average age of people at the time of divorce in England and Wales is now about 38·3 for men and 35·7 for women.

Another feature, common to many other Western European countries, has been an increase in cohabitation. Over one-quarter of women in Great Britain marrying during the period 1980 to 1984, where the marriage was the first for both parties, had lived with their husbands before marriage (compared with 7 per cent for those married in the early 1970s). About 21 per cent of non-married women aged 18 to 49 were cohabiting during 1988. Cohabitation occurs more frequently for separated or divorced women than for single women.

There is some evidence of a growing number of stable non-married relationships. Half of all births outside marriage (which now account for 28 per cent of live births in Britain) are registered by both parents giving a single address as their place of residence.

Age and Sex Structure

The total population has remained relatively stable over the last decade. The proportion of young people aged under 16 fell steadily in the early 1980s, but numbers in this age group have increased slightly in the last two years. The proportion of elderly people, especially those aged 85 and over, has continued to increase. The age distribution of the British population in mid-1990 was estimated as follows:

- 20·2 per cent under 16 years of age;

- 64·1 per cent between 16 and 64 years; and

- 15·7 per cent aged 65 and over.

Some 18 per cent of the population were over the normal retirement ages (65 for men and 60 for women), compared with 15 per cent in 1961.

There is a ratio of about 105 females to every 100 males. There are about 5 per cent more male than female births every year. Because of the higher mortality of men at all ages, there is a turning point, at about 50 years of age, beyond which the number of women exceeds the number of men. This imbalance increases with age so that there are many more women among the elderly.

Distribution of Population

The population density is about 229 inhabitants per sq km, which is well above the European Community average of about 145 per sq km. Of the four lands, England is the most densely populated with 354 people per sq km. Scotland is the least densely populated with 64 people per sq km. Wales and Northern Ireland have 135 and 111 people per sq km respectively.

Since the nineteenth century there has been a trend, especially in London, for people to move away from congested urban centres into the suburbs. There has also been a geographical redistribution of the population from Scotland and the northern regions of England to the South East, East Anglia, the South West and the East Midlands in recent decades. An increase in the rate of retirement migration has also occurred, the main recipient areas (where in some towns the retired constitute over one-quarter of the population) being the south coast of England and East Anglia.

Table 1.2: Size and Population of the Main Urban Areas, Mid-1991

	Area		Population[a]
	sq km	sq miles	(thousands)
Greater London	1,579	609·7	6,377·9
Birmingham	266	102·6	934·9
Leeds	562	217·0	674·4
Glasgow	202	78·0	645·5
Sheffield	368	141·9	499·7
Bradford	367	141·5	449·1
Liverpool	113	43·6	448·3
Manchester	116	44·9	406·9
Edinburgh	261	100·8	421·2
Bristol	110	42·3	370·3
Coventry	97	37·3	292·5
Belfast	121	46·7	281·0
Cardiff	120	46·4	272·6

[a] Based on preliminary figures from the census held on 21 April 1991. These will be replaced by final figures in 1992.

Migration

From 1984 to 1988 some 998,000 people left Britain (excluding the Channel Islands and the Isle of Man) to live abroad and about 1·1 million came from overseas to live in Britain, so that net immigration increased the population by about 114,000. (These figures exclude migration to and from the Irish Republic.)

In 1989 the total inflow of people intending to stay in Britain was 250,000, 16 per cent higher than in 1988. The outflow of people leaving to live abroad, at 205,000, was 13 per cent lower than in 1988 and slightly below the average for the last ten years.

Of the 205,000 departing residents in 1989:

- 27 per cent left for Australia, Canada or New Zealand;
- 16 per cent for other Commonwealth countries;
- 22 per cent for other European Community countries;
- 15 per cent for the United States;
- 6 per cent for the Middle East; and
- 3 per cent for South Africa.

Of the 250,000 new residents in 1989:

- 19 per cent came from Australia, Canada or New Zealand;
- 23 per cent from other Commonwealth countries;
- 22 per cent from other European Community countries;
- 13 per cent from the United States;
- 5 per cent from the Middle East; and
- 5 per cent from South Africa.

Nationality

Under the British Nationality Act 1981 there are three main forms of citizenship:

- British citizenship for people closely connected with Britain, the Channel Islands, and the Isle of Man;

- British Dependent Territories citizenship for people connected with the dependencies; and
- British Overseas citizenship for those citizens of the United Kingdom and Colonies who did not acquire either of the other citizenships when the 1981 Act came into force.

British citizenship is acquired automatically at birth by a child born in Britain if his or her father or mother is a British citizen or is settled in Britain. A child adopted in Britain by a British citizen is a British citizen. A child born abroad to a British citizen born, adopted, naturalised or registered in Britain is a British citizen by descent. The Act safeguards the citizenship of a child born abroad to a British citizen in Crown service, certain related services, or in service under a European Community institution.

British citizenship may also be acquired:

- by registration of certain children, including those born in Britain who do not automatically acquire such citizenship at birth or who have been born abroad to a parent who is a citizen by descent;
- by British Dependent Territories citizens, British Overseas citizens, British subjects under the Act (three very limited categories), and British National (Overseas) and British protected persons after five years' residence in Britain (except for people from Gibraltar, who may be registered without residence); and
- by naturalisation for Commonwealth citizens, citizens of the Irish Republic, and foreign nationals aged 18 or over.

Naturalisation is at the Home Secretary's discretion: it requires five years' residence, good character, sound mind, the intention to have one's home in Britain thereafter and sufficient knowledge of English, Welsh or Scottish Gaelic, except for the spouse of a British citizen, who needs only three years' residence and no language or future intentions qualification.

Legislation passed in 1983 conferred

British citizenship on those Falkland Islanders who did not acquire it under the 1981 Act. Special arrangements covering the status of British Dependent Territories citizens connected with Hong Kong when the territory returns to the People's Republic of China in 1997 are made by the Hong Kong (British Nationality) Order 1986. Under this, such citizens are entitled, before 1997, to acquire a status known as British National (Overseas) and to hold a passport in that status. In addition, the British Nationality (Hong Kong) Act 1990 made provision for the registration as British citizens before 30 June 1997 of up to 50,000 persons who are able to meet certain criteria and who are recommended by the Governor.

In 1990, 55,693 people acquired citizenship by naturalisation or registration in Britain.

Immigration

Immigration into Britain is controlled under the Immigration Rules made in accordance with legislation passed in the 1970s and 1980s.

British citizens under the British Nationality Act 1981 and those Commonwealth citizens who had the right of abode before 1 January 1983 (when the 1981 Act came into force) maintain the right of abode and are not subject to immigration control. Those who do not have this right require permission to enter and remain in Britain; this is given in accordance with the Immigration Rules, which are subject to the scrutiny of Parliament and which set out the requirements to be met by those seeking entry.

The nationals of specified countries require prior entry clearance before they can enter Britain. Other nationals subject to immigration control require entry clearance when coming to work or to settle in Britain. Visas and other entry clearances are normally obtained from the nearest British diplomatic post in a person's home country.

In accordance with Britain's obligations under the Treaty of Rome, European Community nationals do not require entry clearances, nor are they subject to restrictions on their freedom to take or seek work in Britain. Britain similarly respects its obligations under the United Nations Convention and Protocol relating to the Status of Refugees. These include granting refugees the right of access to courts and the right to work, to education, to social security and to freedom of religion.

In 1990, 9·2 million foreign and Commonwealth nationals were admitted to Britain (excluding European Community nationals) and 52,400 persons were accepted for settlement.

THE ECONOMIC AND SOCIAL PATTERN

The average size of households in Great Britain has fallen from over four people in 1911 to 3·09 in 1961 and 2·46 in 1990. The fall reflects a greater number of people living on their own (11 per cent), or in one-parent families, the increasing number of old people (more of whom are living alone) and the preference for smaller families.

Housing, Transport and the Environment

A large proportion of households, 66 per cent, own or are buying their own homes. Owner-occupation is higher among married couples than for single, divorced or widowed household heads. The number of owner-occupied dwellings rose from over 4 million in 1951 to over 15 million in 1990. Four-fifths of British households live in houses rather than flats.

An important influence on the planning of housing and services has been the growth of car ownership; in 1990, 67 per cent of households had the use of at least one car or van, including 23 per cent with the use of two or more. Greater access to motorised transport and the construction of a network of modern trunk roads and motorways have resulted in a considerable increase in personal mobility and changed leisure patterns. Most detached or semi-detached houses in new suburban estates have garages, and out-of-town shopping centres, often including large supermarkets and do-it-yourself stores, are usually planned with the motorist in mind.

Availability of Certain Durable Goods

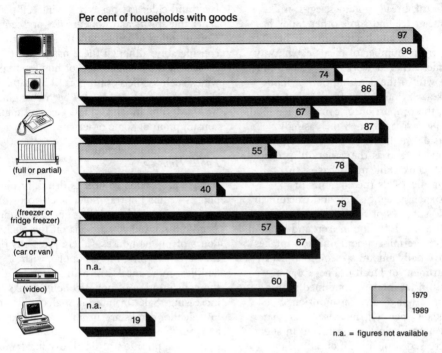

Per cent of households with goods

	1979	1989
television	97	98
washing machine	74	86
telephone	67	87
central heating (full or partial)	55	78
deep freezer (freezer or fridge freezer)	40	79
car (car or van)	57	67
video	n.a.	60
computer	n.a.	19

n.a. = figures not available

Source: *General Household Survey*

The growth in car ownership has brought great benefits but also a number of problems, notably, in many towns and cities, increased congestion, noise and air pollution arising from motor vehicle emissions. Cars, taxis and motor cycles accounted for 86 per cent of all passenger transport in Great Britain in 1989, compared with 55 per cent in 1961. To relieve road congestion, the Government regards carefully targeted improvements to the road system as essential. With the aim of shifting traffic from road to rail, however, it put forward in 1991 measures to help railways achieve a greater share of traffic.

Living Standards

Economic Growth

Marked improvements in the standard of living have taken place during the twentieth century. According to a United Nations report on human development published in 1991, Britain ranked eleventh out of 160 countries on a human development index that combines life expectancy, education levels and basic purchasing power. Britain has also performed well economically. Although gross domestic product (GDP) per head fell in the early 1980s, Britain then experienced an economic recovery and had eight successive years of sustained growth at an annual average rate of over 3 per cent. Growth since 1980 has been among the highest in the European Community. By the late 1980s, however, Britain's growth rate had slowed, in common with that of other major industrialised countries. By September 1991 there were indications that the recession in Britain was close to its trough.

Eating and Drinking Habits

The general level of nutrition remains high. Over the last 25 years there have been substantial rises in the consumption of poultry, instant coffee and processed vegetables and fruit, while home consumption per person of mutton and lamb, beef and veal, bread, potatoes, eggs, milk, butter, sugar, tea and some other foods has fallen. However, another feature has been an increase in the number of meals eaten away from home, either at work or in restaurants, and a growth in the consumption of food from 'take-away' and 'fast-food' shops. In addition, the proportion of convenience foods eaten has grown as women increasingly work outside the home and have less time to prepare meals, and as the variety of prepared foods and 'cook-chill' meals has risen.

During the 1980s the amounts of nutrients such as energy, fat and calcium in household supplies of food declined, and there was a small decline in iron and vitamin C. But average mineral and nutrient intakes were above daily amounts recommended by the Department of Health. There was a steady fall in fat intakes, combined with a decline in carbohydrate consumption. Such factors as a 17 per cent increase in low fat milk consumption, a 7 per cent fall in sugar sales, increased expenditure on all major vegetable groups, and a rise in consumption of fresh fruit and fruit juice between 1988 and 1989 reinforce evidence that health considerations influence food consumption. The Government encourages the widest availability of wholesome food, while giving high priority to consumer safety.

The Food Safety Act 1990 covers all of Great Britain. It

- strengthens the enforcement of existing law;
- gives powers for immediate closure of food premises when the public health is at risk;
- extends controls throughout the food chain;
- enables detailed legislation to be introduced to keep pace with new technology; and
- increases the penalties for food safety offences.

There was little change in alcohol consumption between 1979 and 1989. Beer, lager (now estimated to account for over half of beer sales) and cider are the most popular drinks among male drinkers. Women's alcohol consumption is mostly made up from beer, lager and cider (31 per cent), wine (29 per cent) and spirits and liqueurs (28 per cent). Consumption of light (table) wine has grown considerably, although there has been little change in the consumption of higher strength wines such as sherry and port. The pattern of spirits consumption has also been changing, with a decline in whisky and gin, and higher consumption of some other spirits.

Public Houses

A high proportion of beer is drunk in public houses ('pubs'), a traditional social centre for many people, and in clubs. The Licensing Act 1988 relaxed restrictions on the opening hours of public houses. There are signs that they are becoming more popular with families: more meals are being served and the consumption of non-alcoholic drinks is increasing. Sales of more non-alcoholic and low-alcohol drinks are promoted, helped by a favourable excise duty structure and rigorous application of drink-driving laws.

The Workforce and Earnings

The proportion of the resident population in the workforce, 63 per cent in 1988, is the second highest in the European Community. Some 89 per cent of men of working age, 70 per cent of married women and 74 per cent of non-married women were economically active in 1989. The educational standards of adults have risen, with 14 per cent of men and 7 per cent of women aged 25–29 in Great Britain holding a degree or equivalent qualification in 1989, compared with 10 per cent and 3 per cent respectively of those aged 50–59. The average size of classes has fallen in recent years, in both primary and secondary schools.

Earnings from employment are the main source of income for most people; in 1989 wages and salaries accounted for 59 per cent of household income. The distribution of pre-tax income has remained relatively stable over a long period, the lower 50 per cent of income earners accounting for some 22 to 24 per cent of pre-tax income since 1949. The combined effect of the tax system and the receipt of benefits is to redistribute incomes on a more equal basis.

Distribution of Wealth

Wealth is less evenly distributed, with the richest 1 per cent of the population aged 18 or over owning 17 per cent of marketable wealth in 1988, and the richest 10 per cent having 53 per cent. The inclusion of 'non-marketable' rights in occupational and state pension schemes reduces these shares substantially, to 10 and 36 per cent respectively. Since the mid-1970s there has been little change in the distribution of marketable wealth or in that of marketable wealth plus occupational and state pension rights. The proportion of net wealth held in shares declined up to 1984, but has since increased. The Government's privatisation programme has had a major effect on the pattern of share ownership. In 1990 nearly one-quarter of the adult population in Great Britain owned shares, compared with one in 13 people in 1979.

Women

The economic and domestic lives of women have been transformed in the twentieth century. These changes are due partly to the removal of almost all sex discrimination in political and legal rights. At the heart of women's changed role has been the rise in the number of women, especially married women, at work. With later marriages and the availability of effective contraception there has been a decline in family size. Women are involved in childbearing for a shorter time and this, together with technological advances which have made housework less onerous and time-consuming, has made it possible for women with children to combine child-rearing with paid employment. The growth of part-time and flexible working patterns, and training and retraining schemes, allows more women to take advantage of employment opportunities.

Women make up more than two-fifths of the workforce. The proportion of married women working outside the home has increased to two-thirds of those between the ages of 16 and 59, a quarter of the total labour force, compared with only 4 per cent in 1921. Married women are most likely to be in full-time work if they are aged 16 to 29 with no children. Over two-fifths of all women in employment work part-time, representing almost nine-tenths of all part-time workers.

By the mid-1990s the numbers of young people entering the labour market will have declined substantially and it is expected that the resulting shortfall in the labour force will be met to a considerable extent by the recruitment of more married women.

There is still a significant difference between men's and women's earnings, but the equal pay legislation which came into force in 1975 has helped to narrow the gap; in 1990 women's average hourly earnings were only 77 per cent of men's, despite a progressive rise in women's hourly rates over the last three years. Women's wages remain relatively low because they tend to work in the lower-paid sectors of the economy and work fewer hours than men (the latter because of their domestic commitments). A major reform in the taxation of women came into effect in 1990, when their earnings began to be taxed separately rather than being treated as part of their husbands' income for tax purposes.

Equal Opportunities

The Sex Discrimination Acts 1975 and 1986 make discrimination between men and women unlawful in employment, education, training and the provision of housing, goods, facilities and services. Discriminatory job recruitment advertisements are also unlawful. In most cases complaints of discrimination are dealt with by industrial tribunals since they concern employment; others are taken before county courts in England and Wales or the Sheriff Court in Scotland. Under the Equal Pay Act 1970, as amended in 1984, women in Great Britain are entitled to equal pay with men when doing work that is the same or broadly similar, or work which is of equal value. Parallel legislation on sex discrimination and equal pay is in operation in Northern Ireland.

The Equal Opportunities Commission, set up in 1975 (1976 in Northern Ireland under separate laws), has powers to enforce the Sex Discrimination and Equal Pay Acts. Its statutory duties are to work towards eliminating sex discrimination and to promote equality of opportunity. The Commission advises people of their rights under the Acts and may give financial or other assistance to help individuals conduct a case before a court or tribunal. It is empowered to carry out investigations and issue notices requiring discriminatory practices to stop. The Commission also keeps legislation under review and submits proposals for amending it to the Government.

Ethnic and National Minorities

For centuries people from overseas have settled in Britain, either to escape political or religious persecution or in search of better economic opportunities.

The Irish have long formed a large section of the population. Jewish refugees who came to Britain towards the end of the nineteenth century and in the 1930s were followed by other European refugees after 1945. Substantial immigration from the Caribbean and the South Asian sub-continent dates principally from the 1950s and 1960s. There are also sizeable groups from the United States and Canada, as well as Australians, Chinese, Greek and Turkish Cypriots, Italians and Spaniards. More recently people from Latin America, Indo-China and Sri Lanka have sought refuge in Britain.

In 1987–89, according to the results of a sample survey, the ethnic minority population of Great Britain numbered about 2·6 million (some 4·8 per cent of the total population), of whom 46 per cent were born in Britain. Some 45 per cent of the ethnic minority population was of Indian, Pakistani or Bangladeshi origin; about one-fifth was of Afro-Caribbean ethnic origin; and one in five was of mixed ethnic origin.

The sample survey also indicated that the proportion of men of working age in Great Britain who were economically active was higher among the white population and the Afro-Caribbean group than among those from other ethnic groups. Among women the variation was greater: 73 per cent of those from the Afro-Caribbean ethnic group were economically active, compared with 69 per cent in the white group, 57 per cent in the Indian group and only 20 per cent in the Pakistani/Bangladeshi group.

Alleviating Racial Disadvantage

Although many members of the black and Asian communities are concentrated in the inner cities, where there are problems of deprivation and social stress, progress has been made over the last 20 years in tackling racial disadvantage in Britain.

Many individuals have achieved distinction in their careers and in public life and the proportion of ethnic minority members occupying professional and managerial positions is increasing. In law, for example, an estimated 6 per cent of practising barristers are of ethnic minority origin. There are at present four ethnic minority Members of Parliament, and the number of ethnic minority councillors in local government is growing. There has also been an expansion of commercial enterprise, and numerous self-help projects in ethnic minority communities have been established. Black competitors have represented Britain in a range of sporting activities, and ethnic minority talents in the arts and in entertainment have increasingly been recognised.

The principal means of combating disadvantage is through the economic, environmental, educational and health programmes of central government and local authorities. There are also special allocations, mainly through Home Office grants and the Urban Programme, which channel extra resources into projects of specific benefit to ethnic minorities. These include, for example, the provision of specialist teachers for children needing English language tuition, business support services and measures to revive local economies and improve the inner city environment. Cultural and recreational schemes and the health and personal social services also take account of the particular needs of ethnic minorities.

The Government is encouraging the development of black businesses in inner city areas through the Ethnic Minority Business Initiative. It is also promoting equal opportunities for ethnic minorities through training programmes, including greater provision for unemployed people who need training in English as a second language.

Ethnic Minorities and the Police

In recognition of the tensions that can arise between the police and ethnic minorities, there is statutory consultation between the police and the community. In addition, liaison work is undertaken in schools.

Police training in race relations has received particular attention. A specialist unit, launched in 1989 and run by an independent company, provides police forces with practical help and support in community and race relations training.

Campaigns are run by the police to encourage the recruitment of officers from the ethnic minority communities and racially discriminatory behaviour by officers has been made an offence under the police discipline code.

Race Relations Act 1976

Equal opportunities policies are backed up by legislation against racial discrimination. The Race Relations Act 1976, which strengthened previous legislation passed in the 1960s, makes discrimination unlawful on grounds of colour, race, nationality or ethnic or national origin in the provision of goods, facilities and services, in employment, in housing and in advertising. The 1976 Act also gave complainants direct access to civil courts and, in the case of employment complaints, to industrial tribunals.

It is a criminal offence to incite racial hatred under the provisions of the Public Order Act 1986.

Commission for Racial Equality

The Commission for Racial Equality was established by the 1976 Act. It has power to investigate unlawful discriminatory practices and to issue non-discrimination notices, requiring such practices to cease. It has an important educational role and has issued codes of practice in employment, education and rented housing. It also provides the main advice to the general public about the Race Relations Act and has discretion to assist individuals with their complaints about racial discrimination. In 1990 the Commission registered almost 14,000 applications for assistance and handled successfully 85 litigation cases. It can also undertake or fund research.

The Commission supports the work of over 80 race equality councils, which are autonomous voluntary bodies set up in most areas with a significant ethnic minority population to promote equality of opportunity and good relations at the local level. It helps pay the salaries of the race equality officers employed by the councils, most of whom also receive funds from their local government authorities, and gives grants to ethnic minority self-help groups and to other projects run by or for the benefit of the minority communities.

Leisure Trends

Agreed hours of full-time work are usually from 35 to 40 hours a week, although many people actually work longer because of voluntary overtime.

On average between 15 and 16 per cent of total household expenditure went on leisure in 1989. The most common leisure activities are home-based, or social, such as visiting relatives or friends. Television viewing is by far the most popular leisure pastime, and nearly all households have a television set, with 93 per cent in 1990 having a colour set. Average viewing time for the population aged four and over is nearly 25 hours a week. In 1990 more than half of households had at least one video recorder; 38 million pre-recorded videotapes were bought by the general public. The proportion of households with videos rose from 60 per cent to 64 per cent. Over 40 million compact discs (CDs) were sold in 1989. For the first time, sales of CDs exceeded sales of long-play albums. In 1989 people made on average 1·5 visits to the cinema (compared with 23 in 1959).

Other popular pursuits include: listening to radio, reading, do-it-yourself home improvements, gardening and going out for a meal or for a drink. About half of households have a pet, the most common being dogs and cats, of which there are thought to be roughly 7 million of each in Britain.

Many people give up free time to work for voluntary organisations, of which there are over 250,000 in England and Wales. It is estimated that about one-quarter of the population is involved in some way in voluntary work in Britain. Fund-raising is the most frequently mentioned activity. Voluntary environmental organisations, for example, have experienced consistent growth since 1971.

Holidays

In 1989, 91 per cent of full-time manual employees were entitled to more than four weeks paid holiday; in 1961, 97 per cent were entitled to only two weeks. A significant proportion of all employees have at least 24 days leave. In 1990, 59 per cent of the adult population took at least one long holiday of four or more nights away from home. The number of long holidays taken by British residents was 52·5 million in 1990 (compared with 48 million in 1978), of which 32·5 million were taken in Britain. The most frequented free attraction in 1990 was Blackpool Pleasure Beach (Lancashire). The most popular destinations for summer holidays are the West Country, Scotland and Wales. British residents also took 20·5 million holidays overseas in 1990, of which 56 per cent involved 'package' arrangements. The most popular destinations were Spain, France and Greece, and 77 per cent of all holidays abroad were taken in Europe. The proportion of adults taking two or more holidays a year was 15 per cent in 1990.

2 Government

The British constitution, unlike that of most other countries, is not set out in any single document. Instead it is made up of statute law, common law and conventions. It can be altered by Act of Parliament, or by general agreement to alter a convention. The constitution is thus readily adaptable to changing political conditions.

The organs of government overlap but can be clearly distinguished. Parliament is the *legislature* and the supreme authority. The *executive* consists of:

- the Government—the Cabinet and other ministers responsible for national policies;
- government departments, responsible for national administration;
- local authorities, responsible for many local services; and
- public corporations, responsible for operating particular nationalised industries or other bodies, subject to ministerial control.

The *judiciary* determines common law and interprets statutes, and is independent of both legislature and executive.

The Monarchy

The British people look to the Queen not only as their head of State, but also as the symbol of national unity. The monarchy is the most ancient secular institution in Britain. During the last thousand years its continuity has only once been broken, by the establishment of a republic which lasted from 1649 to 1660. Despite interruptions in the direct line of succession, the hereditary principle upon which it was founded has always been preserved.

The form of the royal title varies in the other Commonwealth countries of which the Queen is head of State.[1] Other member states are republics or have their own monarchies.

The royal title in Britain is: 'Elizabeth the Second, by the Grace of God of the United Kingdom of Great Britain and Northern Ireland and of Her other Realms and Territories Queen, Head of the Commonwealth, Defender of the Faith'.

The seat of the monarchy is in Great Britain. In the Channel Islands and the Isle of Man the Queen is represented by a Lieutenant-Governor. In the other member nations of the Commonwealth of which the Queen is head of State, her representative is the Governor-General, appointed by her on the advice of the ministers of the country concerned and completely independent of the British Government.

In British dependencies the Queen is usually represented by governors, who are responsible to the British Government for the administration of the countries concerned.

Succession, Accession and Coronation

The title to the Crown is derived both from statute and from common law rules of descent. Only Protestant descendants of a granddaughter of James I of England and VI of Scotland (Princess Sophia, the Electress of Hanover) are eligible to succeed. The order of succession can be altered only by common consent of the countries of the Commonwealth.

[1] The other Commonwealth countries of which the Queen is head of State are: Antigua and Barbuda, Australia, Bahamas, Barbados, Belize, Canada, Grenada, Jamaica, Mauritius, New Zealand, Papua New Guinea, Saint Christopher and Nevis, Saint Lucia, Saint Vincent and the Grenadines, Solomon Islands and Tuvalu.

The Royal Family

From the reign of Queen Victoria to August 1991

QUEEN VICTORIA 1819–1901
m. Prince Albert of Saxe-Coburg and Gotha (Prince Consort)

KING EDWARD VII 1841–1910
m. Princess Alexandra of Denmark
(**QUEEN ALEXANDRA** 1844–1925)

Princess Alice 1843–1878
m. Grand Duke Louis of Hesse
3 brothers and 4 sisters

Princess Victoria 1863–1950
m. Marquess of Milford Haven
2 brothers and 4 sisters

Princess Alice 1885–1969
m. Prince Andrew of Greece
2 brothers and 1 sister

Philip, Duke of Edinburgh b. 1921
m. princess Elizabeth (**QUEEN ELIZABETH II**)
4 sisters

KING GEORGE V 1865–1936
m. Princess Mary of Teck (**QUEEN MARY** 1867–1953)
2 brothers and 3 sisters

Duke of Windsor 1894–1972
KING EDWARD VIII (abdicated 1936)
m. Wallis Simpson

KING GEORGE VI 1895–1952
m. Lady Elizabeth Bowes-Lyon
(**QUEEN ELIZABETH** The Queen Mother)

Mary, **Princess Royal** 1897–1965
m. Earl of Harewood
2 sons

Henry; **Duke of Gloucester** 1900–1974
m. Lady Alice Montagu Douglas Scott

George, **Duke of Kent** 1902–1942
m. Princess Marina of Greece

Prince John 1905–1919

QUEEN ELIZABETH II b. 1926
m. Philip, Duke of Edinburgh

Princess Margaret b. 1930
m. Antony, Earl of Snowdon (divorced 1978)

Prince William 1941–1972

Richard, **Duke of Gloucester** b. 1944
m. Birgitte van Deurs

Edward, **Duke of Kent** b. 1935
m. Katharine Worsley

Princess Alexandra b. 1936
m. Hon. Angus Ogilvy

Prince Michael b. 1942
m. Baroness Marie-Christine von Reibnitz

Charles, **Prince of Wales** b. 1948
m. Lady Diana Spencer

Anne, **Princess Royal** b. 1950
m. Captain Mark Phillips

Andrew, **Duke of York** b. 1960
m. Sarah Ferguson

Prince Edward b. 1964

David Viscount Linley b. 1961

Lady Sarah Armstrong-Jones b. 1964

Prince William of Wales b. 1982

Prince Henry of Wales b. 1984

Peter Phillips b. 1977

Zara Phillips b. 1981

Princess Beatrice of York b. 1988

Princess Eugenie of York b. 1990

Alexander, **Earl of Ulster** b. 1974

Lady Davina Windsor b. 1977

Lady Rose Windsor b. 1980

George, **Earl of St. Andrews** b. 1962
m. Sylvana Tomaselli

Lady Helen Windsor b. 1964
m. Edward, **Baron Downpatrick** b. 1988

Lord Nicholas Windsor b. 1970

James Ogilvy b. 1964
m. Julia Rawlinson

Marina b. 1966
m. Paul Mowatt

Zenouska b. 1990

Lord Frederick Windsor b. 1979

Lady Gabriella Windsor b. 1981

Order of Succession to the Throne

The Prince of Wales
Prince William of Wales
Prince Henry of Wales
The Duke of York
Princess Beatrice of York
Princess Eugenie of York
The Prince Edward
The Princess Royal
Peter Phillips
Zara Phillips
The Princess Margaret, Countess of Snowdon
Viscount Linley
Lady Sarah Armstrong-Jones
Earl of Ulster
Lady Davina Windsor
Lady Rose Windsor
The Duke of Kent
Baron Downpatrick
Lord Nicholas Windsor
Lady Helen Windsor
Lord Frederick Windsor
Lady Gabriella Windsor

Dates Relating to Queen Elizabeth II

Marriage:	20 Nov. 1947
Accession to throne:	6 Feb. 1952
Coronation:	2 June 1953
Birthday:	21 April
Official Birthday Celebration:	During June

Sons of the Sovereign have precedence over daughters in succeeding to the throne. When a daughter succeeds, she becomes Queen Regnant, and has the same powers as a king. The consort of a king takes her husband's rank and style, becoming Queen. The constitution does not give any special rank or privileges to the husband of a Queen Regnant, although in practice he fills an important role in the life of the nation, as does the Duke of Edinburgh.

The Sovereign succeeds to the throne as soon as his or her predecessor dies: there is no interregnum. He or she is at once proclaimed at an Accession Council, to which all members of the Privy Council are summoned. The Lords Spiritual and Temporal (see p 31), the Lord Mayor and Aldermen and other leading citizens of the City of London are also invited.

The Sovereign's coronation follows the accession after a convenient interval. The ceremony has remained essentially the same for over a thousand years, even if details have often been changed to suit the customs of the time. It takes place at Westminster Abbey in London, in the presence of representatives of the Houses of Parliament and of all the great public organisations in Britain. The Prime Ministers and leading members of the other Commonwealth nations and representatives of other countries also attend.

The Monarch's Role in Government

The Queen personifies the State. In law, she is head of the executive, an integral part of the legislature, head of the judiciary, the commander-in-chief of all the armed forces of the Crown and the 'supreme governor' of the established Church of England. As a result of a long process of evolution, during which the monarchy's absolute power has gradually declined, the Queen acts on the advice of her ministers. Britain is governed by Her Majesty's Government in the name of the Queen.

Within this framework, and in spite of a trend during the past hundred years towards giving powers directly to ministers, the Queen still takes part in some important acts of government. These include summoning, proroguing (discontinuing until the next session without dissolution) and dissolving Parliament; and giving Royal Assent to Bills passed by Parliament. The Queen also formally appoints many important office holders, including government ministers, judges, officers in the armed forces, governors, diplomats, bishops and some other senior clergy of the Church of England. She is also involved in conferring peerages, knighthoods and other honours;[2] and pardoning people convicted of crimes. An important function is appointing the Prime Minister: by convention the Queen invites the leader of the political party which commands a majority in the House of Commons to form a government. In international affairs the Queen, as head of State, has the power to declare war and make peace, to recognise foreign states and governments, to conclude treaties and to annex or cede territory.

With rare exceptions (such as appointing the Prime Minister), acts involving the use of 'royal prerogative' powers are nowadays performed by government ministers. The ministers are responsible to Parliament and can be questioned about particular policies. Parliamentary authority is not required for the exercise of these prerogative powers, although Parliament has the power to restrict or abolish such rights.

The Queen continues to play an important role in the working of government. She holds meetings of the Privy Council, gives audiences to her ministers and other officials in Britain and overseas, receives accounts of Cabinet decisions, reads dispatches and signs state papers. She must be consulted on every aspect of national life, and she must show complete impartiality.

The significance attached to these royal functions is such that provision has been made to appoint a regent to perform them should the Queen be totally incapacitated. The regent would be the Queen's eldest son, the Prince of Wales, then those, in order of

---

2 Although most honours are conferred by the Queen on the advice of the Prime Minister, a few are granted by her personally—the Order of the Garter, the Order of the Thistle, the Order of Merit and the Royal Victorian Order.

succession to the throne, who are of age. In the event of the Queen's partial incapacity or absence abroad, the Queen may delegate certain royal functions to the Counsellors of State (the Duke of Edinburgh, the four adults next in line of succession, and the Queen Mother). However, Counsellors of State may not, for instance, dissolve Parliament (except on the Queen's instructions), nor create peers.

Ceremonial and Royal Visits

Ceremonial has always been associated with the British monarchy, and, in spite of changes in the outlook of both the Sovereign and the people, many traditional ceremonies continue to take place. Royal marriages and royal funerals are marked by public ceremony, and the Sovereign's birthday is officially celebrated in June by Trooping the Colour on Horse Guards Parade. State banquets take place when a foreign monarch or head of State visits Britain; investitures are held at Buckingham Palace and the Palace of Holyroodhouse in Scotland to bestow honours; and royal processions add significance to such occasions as the state opening of Parliament.

Each year the Queen and other members of the royal family visit many parts of Britain. Their presence at scientific, artistic and industrial events of national and local importance attracts nationwide interest and publicity. They are also closely involved in the work of many charities. The Queen pays state visits to foreign governments, accompanied by the Duke of Edinburgh. She also undertakes lengthy tours in the other countries of the Commonwealth. Other members of the royal family pay official visits overseas, occasionally representing the Queen, or often in connection with an organisation or a cause with which they are associated.

Royal Income and Expenditure

The expenditure incurred by the Queen in carrying out her public duties is financed from the Civil List and from government departments (which meet the cost of, for example, the Royal Yacht and the Queen's Flight). All such expenditure is approved by Parliament. In January 1991 Civil List payments were fixed at £7·9 million a year for ten years. About three-quarters of the Queen's Civil List provision is required to meet the cost of staff. These deal, among other things, with state papers and correspondence, the organisation of state occasions, visits and other public engagements undertaken by the Queen in Britain and overseas. The Queen's private expenditure as Sovereign is met from the Privy Purse, which is financed mainly from the revenue of the Duchy of Lancaster;[3] her expenditure as a private individual is met from her own personal resources.

Under the Civil List Acts, other members of the royal family also receive parliamentary annual allowances to enable them to carry out their public duties. The Prince of Wales, however, receives no such allowance, since as Duke of Cornwall he is entitled to the income of the estate of the Duchy of Cornwall. (He voluntarily surrenders a quarter of this revenue to the Government.) The Queen pays the Government each year a sum equivalent to that provided by Parliament for certain members of the royal family.

Parliament

Parliament is the supreme legislative authority. Its three elements, the Queen, the House of Lords and the elected House of Commons, are constituted on different principles. They meet together only on occasions of symbolic significance such as the state opening of Parliament, when the Commons are summoned by the Queen to the House of Lords. The agreement of all three elements is normally required for legislation.

Parliament can legislate for Britain as a whole, or for any part of the country. It can also legislate for the Channel Islands and the Isle of Man, which are Crown dependencies

---

[3] The Duchy of Lancaster is an inheritance which, since 1399, has always been enjoyed by the reigning Sovereign; it is kept quite apart from his or her other possessions and is separately administered by the Chancellor of the Duchy.

and not part of Britain. They have subordinate legislatures which make laws on island affairs.[4]

As there are no legal restraints imposed by a written constitution, Parliament may legislate as it pleases. It can make or change any law; and can overturn established conventions or turn them into law. It can even prolong its own life beyond the normal period without consulting the electorate.

In practice, however, Parliament does not assert its supremacy in this way. Its members bear in mind the common law and normally act in accordance with precedent. The validity of an Act of Parliament, once passed, cannot be disputed in the law courts, but no Parliament would be likely to pass an Act which it knew would receive no public support. The House of Commons is directly responsible to the electorate, and in this century the House of Lords has recognised the priority of the elected chamber. The system of party government helps to ensure that Parliament legislates with its responsibility to the electorate in mind.

As a member of the European Community, Britain recognises the various types of Community legislation and wider policies. It sends 81 elected members to the European Parliament.

The Functions of Parliament

The main functions of Parliament are:
- to pass laws;
- to provide, by voting taxation, the means of carrying on the work of government;
- to scrutinise government policy and administration, including proposals for expenditure; and
- to debate the major political issues of the day.

In carrying out these functions Parliament helps to bring the relevant facts and issues before the electorate. By custom, Parliament

is also informed before all important international treaties and agreements are ratified. The making of treaties is, however, a royal prerogative exercised on the advice of the Government and is not subject to parliamentary approval.

The Meeting of Parliament

A Parliament has a maximum duration of five years, but in practice general elections are usually held before the end of this term. The maximum life has been prolonged by legislation in rare circumstances such as the two world wars. Parliament is dissolved and writs for a general election are ordered by the Queen on the advice of the Prime Minister.

The life of a Parliament is divided into sessions. Each usually lasts for one year—normally beginning and ending in October or November. There are 'adjournments' at night, at weekends, at Christmas, Easter and the late (English) Spring Bank Holiday, and during a long summer recess starting in late July or early August. The average number of 'sitting' days in a session is about 168 in the House of Commons and about 150 in the House of Lords. At the start of each session the Queen's speech to Parliament outlines the Government's policies and proposed legislative programme. Each session is ended by prorogation. Parliament then 'stands prorogued' for about a week until the new session opens. Prorogation brings to an end nearly all parliamentary business: in particular, Bills which have not been passed by the end of the session are lost.

The House of Lords

The House of Lords consists of the Lords Spiritual and the Lords Temporal. The Lords Spiritual are the Archbishops of Canterbury and York, the Bishops of London, Durham and Winchester, and the 21 next most senior diocesan bishops of the Church of England. The Lords Temporal consist of:
- all hereditary peers and peeresses of England, Scotland, Great Britain and the United Kingdom;

---

[4] The legislatures of the Channel Islands (the States of Jersey and the States of Guernsey) and the Isle of Man (the Tynwald Court) consist of the Queen, the Privy Council and the local assemblies. It is the duty of the Home Secretary, as the Privy Council member primarily concerned with island affairs, to consider each legislative measure before it is submitted to the Queen in Council.

- life peers created to assist the House in its judicial duties (Lords of Appeal or 'law lords');[5] and
- all other life peers.

Hereditary peerages carry a right to sit in the House (with certain exceptions), provided holders establish their claim and are aged 21 years or over. However, anyone succeeding to a peerage may, within 12 months of succession, disclaim that peerage for his or her lifetime. Disclaimants lose their right to sit in the House but gain the right to vote and stand as candidates at parliamentary elections.

Peerages, both hereditary and life, are created by the Sovereign on the advice of the Prime Minister. They are usually granted in recognition of service in politics or other walks of life or because one of the political parties wishes to have the recipient in the House of Lords. The House also provides a place in Parliament for people who offer useful advice, but do not wish to be involved in party politics.

In mid-1991 there were 1,191 members of the House of Lords, including the two archbishops and 24 bishops. The Lords Temporal consisted of 762 hereditary peers who had succeeded to their titles, 20 hereditary peers who have had their titles conferred on them (including the Prince of Wales), and 383 life peers, of whom 18 were 'law lords'. Of the total, 84 peers did not receive a writ of summons and some 137 peers were on leave of absence from the House.[6] Holders of Irish peerages are not entitled to membership of the House of Lords, but some peers of Ireland sit in the House of Lords as holders of English, Scottish, Great Britain or United Kingdom peerages.

Not all peers with a right to sit in the House of Lords attend the sittings. Peers who attend the House (the average daily attendance is some 320) receive no salary for their parliamentary work, but can claim for expenses incurred in attending the House (for which there are maximum daily rates) and certain travelling expenses.

Officers of the House of Lords

The House is presided over by the Lord Chancellor, who takes his place on the woolsack[7] as ex-officio Speaker of the House. In his absence his place is taken by a deputy speaker, a deputy chairman or, if neither is present, by a speaker chosen by the Lords present. The first of the deputy speakers is the Chairman of Committees, who is appointed at the beginning of each session and normally chairs all committees. The Chairman and the Principal Deputy Chairman of Committees are Lords, but receive salaries as officers of the House.

The permanent officers of the House include the Clerk of the Parliaments, who is responsible for the records of proceedings and for promulgating Acts of Parliament. He is the accounting officer for money voted to the House, and is in charge of the administrative staff of the House, known as the Parliament Office. The Gentleman Usher of the Black Rod, who is also Serjeant-at-Arms in attendance upon the Lord Chancellor, is responsible for security, accommodation and services in the House of Lords' part of the Palace of Westminster. The Yeoman Usher is Deputy Serjeant-at-Arms and assists Black Rod in his duties.

The House of Commons

The House of Commons is elected by universal adult suffrage and consists of 650 Members of Parliament (MPs). At present there are 44 women, one Asian and three black MPs. Of the 650 seats, 523 are for England, 38 for Wales, 72 for Scotland, and 17 for Northern Ireland. (At the next general election the number of seats will rise to 651, with the creation of an additional seat for Milton Keynes in England.)

---

[5] The House of Lords is the final court of appeal for civil cases in Britain and for criminal cases in England, Wales and Northern Ireland.
[6] Some hereditary peers do not establish their claim to succeed and so do not receive a writ of summons entitling them to sit in the House. Lords may apply for leave of absence for the duration, or for the remainder, of a Parliament.

[7] The woolsack is a seat in the form of a large cushion stuffed with wool from several Commonwealth countries; it is a tradition dating from the medieval period, when wool was the chief source of the country's wealth.

General elections are held after a Parliament has been dissolved and a new one summoned by the Queen. When an MP dies or resigns,[8] or is given a peerage, a by-election takes place. Members are paid an annual salary of £28,970 (from January 1991) and an office costs allowance of up to £27,166. There are also a number of other allowances, including travel allowances, a supplement for London members and, for provincial members, subsistence allowances and allowances for second homes. (For ministers' salaries see p 44.)

Officers of the House of Commons

The chief officer of the House of Commons is the Speaker, elected by MPs to preside over the House. Other officers include the Chairman of Ways and Means and two deputy chairmen, who act as Deputy Speakers. They are elected by the House on the nomination of the Government but are drawn from the Opposition as well as the government party. They, like the Speaker, neither speak nor vote other than in their official capacity. Overall responsibility for the administration of the House rests with the House of Commons Commission, a statutory body chaired by the Speaker.

Permanent officers (who are not MPs) include the Clerk of the House of Commons, who is the principal adviser to the Speaker on its privileges and procedures. The Clerk's departmental responsibilities relate to the conduct of the business of the House and its committees. The Clerk is also accounting officer for the House. The Serjeant-at-Arms, who waits upon the Speaker, carries out certain orders of the House. He is also the official housekeeper of the Commons' part of the building, and is responsible for security. Other officers serve the House in the Library, the Department of the Official Report (*Hansard*), the Administration Department and the Refreshment Department.

---

[8] An MP who wishes to resign from the House can only do so by applying for an office under the Crown as Crown Steward or Bailiff of the Chiltern Hundreds, or Steward of the Manor of Northstead. These are ancient offices which disqualify the holder from membership of the House but which carry no salary and have no responsibilities.

Parliamentary Electoral System

For electoral purposes Britain is divided into constituencies, each of which returns one member to the House of Commons. To ensure fair representation four permanent Parliamentary Boundary Commissions, one each for England, Wales, Scotland and Northern Ireland, review the constituencies periodically. They recommend any adjustment of seats that may seem necessary in the light of population movements or other changes. Elections are by secret ballot.

Who May Vote

British citizens, together with citizens of other Commonwealth countries and citizens of the Irish Republic resident in Britain, may vote provided they are aged 18 or over, included in the annual register of electors for the constituency and not subject to any disqualification. People not entitled to vote include members of the House of Lords, patients detained under mental health legislation, sentenced prisoners and people convicted within the previous five years of corrupt or illegal election practices. Members of the armed forces and their spouses, Crown servants and staff of the British Council employed overseas (together with their wives or husbands if accompanying them) may be registered for an address in the constituency where they would live but for their service. The Representation of the People Act 1989 extended the right to vote for British citizens living abroad by increasing from 5 to 20 years the period during which they may apply to be registered to vote.

Voting Procedures

Each elector may cast one vote, normally in person at a polling station. People entitled to an absent vote may vote by post or by proxy, although postal ballot papers cannot be sent to addresses outside Britain. Overseas electors and electors who are physically incapacitated or unable to vote in person because of the nature of their work may vote either by post (unless they are abroad at the time of the election) or by proxy for an indefinite period. Under the 1989 Act, electors whose circumstances on polling day are such that they cannot reasonably be expected to vote in person at their local polling station—for example, electors away on holiday—may apply for an absent vote at a particular election.

Voting is not compulsory; 74·6 per cent of a total electorate of 43·6 million people voted in the general election in June 1987. The simple majority system of voting is used. Candidates are elected if they have more votes than any of the other candidates (although not necessarily an absolute majority over all other candidates).

Candidates

British citizens and citizens of other Commonwealth countries, together with citizens of the Irish Republic, may stand for election as MPs provided they are aged 21 or over and are not disqualified. Those disqualified include undischarged bankrupts; people sentenced to more than one year's imprisonment; clergy of the Church of England, Church of Scotland, Church of Ireland and Roman Catholic Church; peers; and holders of certain offices listed in the House of Commons Disqualification Act 1975. The latter include holders of judicial office, civil servants, some local government officers, members of the regular armed forces, police officers, some members of public corporations and government commissions, and British members of the legislature of any country outside the Commonwealth. A candidate's nomination for election must be proposed and seconded by two electors registered as voters in the constituency and signed by eight other electors. Candidates do not have to have party backing. A candidate must also deposit £500, which is returned if he or she receives 5 per cent or more of the votes cast.

The maximum sum a candidate may spend on a general election campaign is £4,144, plus 3·5 pence for each elector in a borough constituency or 4·7 pence for each elector in a county constituency. Higher limits have been set for by-elections in order to reflect the fact that they are often regarded as tests of national opinion in the period between general elections. The maximum sum is £16,577, plus 14·1 pence for each elector in borough seats and 18·6 pence for each elector in county seats. A candidate may post an election address to each elector in the constituency, free of charge. All election expenses, apart from the candidate's personal expenses, are subject to the statutory limit.

The Political Party System

The party system, which has existed in one form or another since the eighteenth century, is an essential element in the working of the constitution.

The present system depends upon the existence of organised political parties, each of which presents its policies to the electorate for approval. The parties are not registered or formally recognised in law, but in practice most candidates in elections, and almost all winning candidates, belong to one of the main parties.

For the last 150 years a predominantly two-party system has existed.

Since 1945 either the Conservative Party, the origins of which go back to the eighteenth century, or the Labour Party, which emerged in the last decade of the nineteenth century, has held power. A new party—the Liberal Democrats (formally known as the Social and Liberal Democrats)—was formed in 1988 when the Liberal Party (which could trace its origins to the eighteenth century) merged with the Social Democratic Party (formed in 1981). Other parties include two nationalist parties, Plaid Cymru (founded in Wales in 1925) and the Scottish National Party (founded in 1934). In Northern Ireland there are a number of parties. They include the Ulster Unionist Party, which was formed in the early part of this century; the Democratic Unionist Party, founded in 1971 by a group which broke away from the Ulster Unionists; and the Social Democratic and Labour Party, founded in 1970.

Since 1945 seven general elections have been won by the Conservative Party and six by the Labour Party; the great majority of members of the House of Commons have belonged to one of these two parties. The percentages of votes cast for the main political parties in the last general election of June 1987 and the resulting distribution of seats in the House of Commons are shown in Table 2.1.

The party which wins most seats (although not necessarily the most votes) at a general election, or which has the support of a majority of members in the House of Commons, usually forms the Government. By tradition, the leader of the majority party is asked by the Sovereign to form a government. About 100 of its members in the House of Commons and the House of Lords receive ministerial appointments (including appointment to the Cabinet—see p 44) on the advice of the Prime Minister. The largest minority party becomes the official Opposition, with its own leader and 'shadow cabinet'.

The Party System in Parliament

Leaders of the Government and Opposition sit on the front benches of the Commons with their supporters (the backbenchers) sitting behind them.

Similar arrangements for the parties also apply to the House of Lords; however, Lords who do not wish to be associated with any political party may sit on the 'cross-benches'.

The effectiveness of the party system in Parliament rests largely on the relationship between the Government and the opposition parties. Depending on the relative strengths of the parties in the House of Commons, the Opposition may seek to overthrow the Government by defeating it in a vote on a 'matter of confidence'. In general, however, its aims are to contribute to the formulation of policy and legislation by constructive criticism; to oppose government proposals it considers objectionable; to seek amendments to government Bills; and to put forward its own policies in order to improve its chances of winning the next general election.

Table 2.1: Percentages of Votes Cast, and Members Elected, in the 1987 General Election

Party	% of votes cast	Party	Members elected
Conservative	42·3	Conservative	375
Labour	30·8	Labour	229
Liberal–Social		Liberal	17
Democratic Alliance[a]	22·6	Social Democratic	5
Others	4·3	Scottish National	3
		Plaid Cymru (Welsh Nationalist)	3
		Ulster Unionist (Northern Ireland)	9
		Democratic Unionist (Northern Ireland)	3
		Social Democratic and	
		Labour (Northern Ireland)	3
		Ulster Popular Unionist (Northern Ireland)	1
		Sinn Fein (Northern Ireland)[b]	1
		Speaker[c]	1
		Total	650

[a] The former Liberal and Social Democratic Parties (see p 34) entered into an electoral alliance in 1981 and contested the general elections of 1983 and 1987 with a joint programme.
[b] The member of Sinn Fein (the political wing of the Provisional IRA) has not taken his seat.
[c] The Speaker's candidacy was as 'Mr Speaker seeking re-election'. (He was, before his election as Speaker, a Conservative MP.)
Note: In mid-September 1991 the state of the parties (excluding the Speaker and his three deputies) was as follows: Conservative 368; Labour 227; Liberal Democrats 21; Social Democratic 3; Scottish National 5; Plaid Cymru (Welsh Nationalist) 3; Ulster Unionist 9; Democratic Unionist 3; Social Democratic and Labour 3; Ulster Popular Unionist 1; Sinn Fein 1; there were 2 vacancies.

Government business arrangements are settled, under the direction of the Prime Minister and the Leaders of the two Houses, by the Government Chief Whips in consultation with the Opposition Chief Whips. The Chief Whips together constitute the 'usual channels' often referred to when the question of finding time for a particular item of business is discussed. The Leaders of the two Houses are responsible for enabling the Houses to debate matters about which they are concerned.

Outside Parliament, party control is exercised by the national and local organisations. Inside, it is exercised by the Chief Whips and their assistants, who are chosen within the party. Their duties include keeping members informed of forthcoming parliamentary business, maintaining the party's voting strength by ensuring members attend important debates, and passing on to the party leadership the opinions of backbench members. The Whips indicate the importance their party attaches to a vote on a particular issue by underlining items of business (once, twice or three times) on the notice sent to MPs. Failure to comply with a 'three-line whip' (the most important) is usually seen as a rebellion against their party. Party discipline tends to be less strong in the Lords than in the Commons, since Lords have less hope of high office and no need of party support in elections.

The formal title of the Government Chief Whip in the Commons is Parliamentary Secretary to the Treasury. Of the other Government Whips, three are officers of the Royal Household (one of these is Deputy Chief Whip), five hold titular posts as Lords Commissioners of the Treasury and five are Assistant Whips. Salaries are also paid to the Opposition Chief Whips in both Houses and to two of the Opposition Assistant Whips in the Commons. The Government Whips in the Lords hold offices in the Royal Household; they also act as government spokesmen.

Annual assistance from public funds helps opposition parties carry out their parliamentary work at Westminster. It is limited to parties which had at least two members elected at the previous general

election or one member elected and a minimum of 150,000 votes cast. The amount is £2,550 for every seat won, plus £5·10 for every 200 votes.

Parliamentary Procedure

Parliamentary procedure is based on custom and precedent. The system of debate is similar in both Houses. The subject starts off as a proposal or 'motion' by a member. When a motion has been moved, the Speaker proposes the question for debate. At the end of each debate the question may be decided without voting, or by a simple majority vote. The main difference between the two Houses is that the Speaker of the Lords has no authority to curtail debate. Such matters are decided by the general feeling of the House. In the Commons the Speaker has full authority to enforce the rules of the House and must guard against the abuse of procedure or infringements of minority rights. The Speaker has discretion on whether to allow a motion to end discussion so that a matter may be put to the vote and has powers to put a stop to irrelevance and repetition in debate, and to save time in other ways. In cases of grave disorder the Speaker can adjourn or suspend the sitting. The Speaker may order members who have broken the rules of behaviour of the House to leave the Chamber or he or she can initiate their suspension for a period of days.

The Speaker supervises voting in the Commons and announces the final result. In a tied vote the Speaker gives a casting vote, without expressing an opinion on the merits of the question. The voting procedure in the House of Lords is similar to that in the Commons, except that the Speaker or chairman has an ordinary vote.

The Commons has a public register of MPs' financial interests. Members with a financial interest in a matter before the House must declare it when taking part in a debate. To act as a disqualification from voting the interest must be direct, immediate and personal. In other proceedings of the House or in dealings with other members, ministers or civil servants, MPs must also disclose any relevant financial interest. There is no register of financial interests in the Lords, but Lords speaking in a debate in which they have a direct interest are expected to declare it.

Proceedings of both Houses are normally public. The minutes and speeches (*Hansard*) are published daily.

The records of the Lords from 1497 and of the Commons from 1547, together with the parliamentary and political papers of certain past members of both Houses, are available to the public through the House of Lords Record Office.

The proceedings of both Houses of Parliament may be broadcast on television and radio, either live or, more usually, in recorded or edited form.

Legislative Proceedings

The law undergoes constant reform in the courts as established principles are clarified or reapplied to meet new circumstances. Fundamental changes are the responsibility of Parliament and the Government through the normal legislative process.

Draft laws take the form of parliamentary Bills. Most are public Bills involving measures relating to public policy. Private Bills deal with matters of individual, corporate or local interest. Hybrid Bills are public Bills which may affect private rights. The passage of private Bills and hybrid Bills through Parliament is governed by special procedures which allow those affected to put their case. Public Bills can be introduced, in either House, by a government minister or by an ordinary member. Most public Bills that become law are sponsored by the Government.

Before a government Bill is drafted, there is normally considerable consultation with professional bodies, voluntary organisations and other agencies interested in the subject. These include major interest and pressure groups which seek to promote specific causes. Proposals for legislative changes are sometimes set out in government 'White Papers', which may be debated in Parliament

before a Bill is introduced. From time to time consultative documents, sometimes called 'Green Papers', set out government proposals which are still taking shape and seek comments from the public.

Bills must normally be passed by both Houses. Government Bills likely to raise political controversy usually go through the Commons before being discussed in the Lords, while those of a technical but non-political nature often pass through the Lords first. A Bill with a mainly financial purpose is nearly always introduced in the Commons, and a Bill involving taxation must be based on resolutions agreed by that House, often after debate, before it can be introduced. If the main object of a Bill is to create a public charge, it must be introduced by a minister in the Commons or, if brought from the Lords, be taken up by a minister. This gives the Government considerable control over financial legislation.

Private Members' Bills

At the beginning of each session private members of the Commons ballot (or draw lots) for the opportunity to introduce a Bill on one of the Fridays specially allocated; the first 20 are successful. Private members may also present a Bill after question time (see p 40). They may also seek to introduce a Bill under the 'ten minute rule'. This allows two speeches, one in favour of and one against the measure, after which the House decides whether to allow the Bill to be brought in. Private members' Bills do not often proceed very far, but a few become law each session. If one secures a second reading, the Government usually introduces any necessary money resolution. Private members' Bills may be introduced in the House of Lords at any time, but the time that can be given to them in the Commons is limited.

Passage of Public Bills

The process of passing a public Bill is similar in both Houses. The Bill receives a formal first reading on introduction and is printed. After between one day and several weeks, depending on the nature of the Bill, it is given a second reading after a debate on its general principles. In the Commons a non-controversial Bill may be referred to a second reading committee for its second reading debate. After a second reading in the Commons, a Bill is usually referred to a standing committee for detailed examination (see p 39). If the House so decides, the Bill may be referred to the whole House sitting in committee. The committee stage is followed by the report stage, during which further amendments may be considered.

At the third reading a Bill is reviewed in its final form and may be debated again. The House may vote to limit the time devoted to examining a Bill by passing a government timetable motion, commonly referred to as a 'guillotine'.

After the third reading a Commons Bill is sent to the Lords. After the second reading in the Lords, a Bill is considered by a committee of the whole House, unless the House takes the rare decision to refer it to a Public Bill Committee. It is then considered on report and read a third time; at all these stages amendments may be made. A Bill which starts in the Lords and is passed by that House is then sent to the Commons for all its stages there. Amendments made by the second House must generally be agreed by the first, or a compromise reached, before a Bill can become law.

Most government Bills introduced and passed in the Lords pass through the Commons without difficulty. However, a Lords Bill which was unacceptable to the Commons would not become law. The Lords, on the other hand, do not generally prevent Bills insisted upon by the Commons from becoming law, though they will often amend them and return them for further consideration by the Commons. In practice, the Lords pass Bills authorising taxation or national expenditure without amendment. Under the Parliament Acts 1911 and 1949, a Bill that deals only with taxation or expenditure must become law within one month of being sent to the Lords, whether or not they agree to it, unless the Commons directs otherwise. If no agreement is reached between the two Houses on a non-financial Commons Bill the Lords can delay the Bill

for a period which, in practice, amounts to at least 13 months. Following this the Bill may be submitted to the Queen for Royal Assent, provided it has been passed a second time by the Commons. The Parliament Acts make one important exception: any Bill to lengthen the life of a Parliament requires the full assent of both Houses in the normal way.

The limits to the power of the Lords, contained in the Parliament Acts, are based on the belief that nowadays the main legislative function of the non-elected House is to act as a chamber of revision, comple- menting but not rivalling the elected House.

When a Bill has passed through all its parliamentary stages, it is sent to the Queen for Royal Assent, after which it is part of the law of the land and known as an Act of Parliament. The Royal Assent has not been refused since 1707.

Private Bills

Private Bills are promoted by people or organisations outside Parliament (often local authorities) to give them special legal powers. They go through a similar procedure to public Bills, but most of the work is done in committee, where procedures follow a semi- judicial pattern. The promoter must prove the need for the powers sought and the objections of opposing interests are heard. Both sides may be legally represented.

Delegated Legislation

In order to reduce pressure on parliamentary time, much legislation gives ministers and other authorities the power to regulate administrative details by making 'delegated legislation'. To minimise the risk that powers given to the executive might undermine parliamentary government, they are normally delegated to authorities directly responsible to Parliament. Moreover, the Acts of Parliament concerned often provide for some measure of parliamentary control over the delegated legislation, by giving Parliament the right to affirm or annul it. Certain Acts also state that the organisations affected must be consulted before rules and orders can be made.

A joint committee of both Houses reports on the technical propriety of these 'statutory instruments'. In order to save time on the floor of the House, the Commons also uses standing committees to debate the merits of instruments; actual decisions are taken by the House.

Parliamentary Committees

Committees of the Whole House

Either House may pass a resolution setting itself up as a committee of the whole House to consider Bills in detail after their second reading. This permits unrestricted discussion: the rule that an MP or Lord may speak only once on each issue does not apply in committee.

Standing Committees

House of Commons standing committees formally debate public Bills at the committee stage and, in certain cases, at the second reading stage. They also include two Scottish standing committees, and the Scottish and Welsh Grand Committees. Ordinary standing committees do not have names as such but are referred to simply as Standing Committee A, B, C, and so on; the members are separately appointed to consider each Bill. Each committee has between 16 and 50 members, with a party balance reflecting as far as possible that in the House as a whole. The Scottish Grand Committee, which comprises all 72 Scottish members (and may be convened in Edinburgh), considers the principles of Scottish Bills referred to it at second reading stage. It also debates Scottish estimates and other matters concerning Scotland only which may be referred to it. The Welsh Grand Committee, with all 38 Welsh members and up to five others, considers Bills referred to it at second reading stage, and matters concerning Wales only. There is also provision for a Northern Ireland committee to debate matters relating specifically to Northern Ireland.

The Lords' equivalent to a standing committee, a Public Bill Committee, is rarely used.

Select Committees

Select committees are appointed, normally for the duration of a Parliament, to examine subjects by taking written and oral evidence. After private discussion they report their conclusions and recommendations. Some select committees may be appointed to help Parliament with the control of the executive by examining aspects of public policy and administration. These include the 14 committees established by the House of Commons to examine the expenditure, administration and policy of the main government departments and related bodies. The Foreign Affairs Committee, for example, 'shadows' the work of the Foreign & Commonwealth Office. The committees are constituted on a party basis, in approximate proportion to party strength in the House. Select committees also cover the internal workings of Parliament.

Other regular Commons committees include those on European Legislation, Public Accounts, Members' Interests, and the Parliamentary Commissioner for Administration. The Committee of Selection and the Standing Orders Committee have duties relating to private Bills, and the Committee of Selection also chooses members to serve on standing and select committees. A Liaison Committee considers general matters relating to select committees. On rare occasions a parliamentary Bill is examined by a specially appointed select committee, in addition to the usual legislative process: this occurs, for example, every few years for the Armed Forces Bill.

In their scrutiny of government policies and administration, the committees question ministers, senior civil servants and interested bodies and individuals. Through hearings and published reports, they bring before Parliament and the public a body of fact and informed opinion on many issues, and build up considerable expertise in their subjects of inquiry.

In the House of Lords, besides the Appeal and Appellate Committees, in which the bulk of the House's judicial work is transacted, there are two major select committees, with several sub-committees, on the European Communities and on Science and Technology. There are also select committees on House of Lords' Offices, Hybrid Instruments, Leave of Absence and Lords' Expenses, Personal Bills, Private Bill Standing Orders, Privileges, Procedure, Selection and Broadcasting.

Joint Committees

Joint committees, with a membership drawn from both Houses, are appointed in each session to deal with Consolidation Bills and delegated legislation. The two Houses may also agree to set up joint select committees on other subjects.

Party Committees

In addition to the official committees of the two Houses there are several unofficial party organisations or committees. The Conservative and Unionist Members' Committee (the 1922 Committee) consists of the backbench membership of the party in the House of Commons. When the Conservative Party is in office, ministers attend its meetings by invitation and not by right. When the party is in opposition, the whole membership of the party may attend meetings and the leader appoints a consultative committee, which acts as the party's 'shadow cabinet'.

The Parliamentary Labour Party comprises all members of the party in both Houses. When the Labour Party is in office a parliamentary committee, half of whose members are elected and half of whom are government representatives, acts as a channel of communication between the Government and its backbenchers in both Houses. When the party is in opposition the Parliamentary Labour Party is organised under the direction of an elected parliamentary committee, which acts as the 'shadow cabinet'.

Other Forms of Parliamentary Control

The effectiveness of parliamentary control of the Government is a subject of continuing discussion, both inside and outside

Parliament. In addition to the system of scrutiny by select committees, the House of Commons offers a number of opportunities for the examination of government policy by both the Opposition and the Government's own backbenchers. These include:

1. Question time, when for an hour on Monday, Tuesday, Wednesday and Thursday, ministers answer MPs' questions. The Prime Minister's question time is on Tuesday and Thursday. Parliamentary questions are one means of seeking information about the Government's intentions. They are also a way of raising grievances brought to MPs' notice by constituents. MPs may also put questions to ministers for written answer; the questions and answers are published in *Hansard*, the official report.

2. The right of MPs to use motions for the adjournment of the House to raise constituency cases or matters of public concern. There is a half-hour adjournment period at the end of the business of the day, while immediately before the adjournment for each recess (Parliament's Christmas, Easter, spring and summer breaks) a full day is spent discussing issues raised by private members. In addition, an MP wishing to discuss a 'specific and important matter that should have urgent consideration' may, at the end of question time, seek leave to move the adjournment of the House. If the Speaker accepts the terms of the motion, the MP asks the House for leave for the motion to be put forward. Leave can be given unanimously, or it can be given if 40 or more MPs support the motion or if fewer than 40 but more than ten support it and the House (on a vote) is in favour. Once leave has been given, the matter is debated for three hours, usually on the following day.

3. The 20 Opposition days each session, when the Opposition can choose subjects for debate. Of these days, 17 are at the disposal of the Leader of the Opposition and three at the disposal of the second largest opposition party.

4. Debates on the occasion of the passage, three times a year, of Consolidated Fund or Appropriation Bills, when members can exercise their traditional right of 'raising grievances' on matters for which any minister is responsible. This takes place after voting the necessary supplies (money) for the Government.

5. Debates on three days in each session on details of proposed government expenditure recommended for consideration by the Liaison Committee (see p 39).

Procedural opportunities for criticism of the Government also arise during the debate on the Queen's speech at the beginning of each session, during debates on motions of censure for which the Government gives up part of its own time, and during debates on the Government's legislative proposals.

Opportunities for criticism and examination of government policy are provided in the House of Lords at daily question time and during debates on general motions. Other opportunities include 'unstarred' questions (which can be debated) at the end of the day's business and debates on proposed legislation.

The main responsibilities of Parliament, and more particularly of the House of Commons, in managing the revenue of the State and payments for the public service, are to authorise the raising of taxes and duties and the various objects of expenditure and the sum to be spent on each. It also has to satisfy itself that the sums granted are spent only for the purposes which Parliament intended. No payment out of the central government's public funds can be made and no taxation or loans authorised, except by Act of Parliament. However, limited interim payments can be made from the Contingencies Fund. The Finance Act is the most important of the annual statutes which authorise the raising of revenue. The legislation is based on the Chancellor of the Exchequer's Budget statement, normally made in March or April each year. It includes a review of the public finances of the previous year, and proposals for the estimated expenditure of the coming year.

Scrutiny of public expenditure is carried out by House of Commons select committees (see p 39).

To keep the two Houses informed of European Community developments, and to enable them to scrutinise and debate Community policies and proposals, there is a select committee in each House (see p 39). Ministers also make regular statements about Community business.

The final control is the ability of the House of Commons to force the Government to resign by passing a resolution of 'no confidence'. The Government must also resign if the House rejects a proposal for legislation which the Government considers so vital to its policy that it has made it a 'matter of confidence' or if the House refuses to vote the money required for the public service.

Parliamentary Commissioner for Administration

The Parliamentary Commissioner for Administration (the 'Parliamentary Ombudsman') investigates, independently, complaints of maladministration when asked to do so by MPs on behalf of members of the public. Powers of investigation extend to administrative actions by central government departments and certain executive and non-departmental bodies. They do not include policy decisions (which can be questioned in Parliament) and matters affecting relations with other countries. Complaints by British citizens arising from dealings with British diplomatic posts overseas are open to investigation in some circumstances. The Commissioner has access to departmental papers and reports the findings to the MP who presented the complaint. The Commissioner is required to report annually to Parliament. He or she also publishes details of selected investigations at quarterly intervals and may submit other reports where necessary. A Commons select committee oversees the Commissioner's work.

Parliamentary Privilege

Each House of Parliament has certain rights and immunities to protect it from obstruction in carrying out its duties. The rights apply collectively to each House and individually to each member.

For the Commons the Speaker formally claims from the Queen 'their ancient and undoubted rights and privileges' at the beginning of each Parliament. These include freedom of speech; freedom from arrest in civil actions; exemption from serving on juries, or being compelled to attend court as witnesses; and the right of access to the Crown, which is a collective privilege of the House. Further privileges include the rights of the House to control its own proceedings (so that it is able, for instance, to exclude 'strangers'[9] if it wishes); to decide upon legal disqualifications for membership and to declare a seat vacant on such grounds; and to punish for breach of its privileges and for contempt.

The privileges of the House of Lords are broadly similar to those of the House of Commons.

The Privy Council

The Privy Council was formerly the chief source of executive power in the State. As the system of Cabinet government developed, however, the Privy Council became less prominent. Many powers were transferred to the Cabinet as an inner committee of the Council, and much of its work was handed over to government departments, some of which were originally committees of the Privy Council.

Nowadays the main function of the Privy Council is to advise the Queen to approve Orders in Council, including those made under prerogative powers, such as Orders approving the grant of royal charters of incorporation, and those made under statutory powers. Responsibility for each Order, however, rests with the minister answerable for the policy concerned, regardless of whether he or she was present at the meeting where approval was given.

The Privy Council also advises the Crown on the issue of royal proclamations, some of which are prerogative acts, such as

summoning or dissolving Parliament. The Council's own statutory responsibilities, which are independent of the powers of the Sovereign in Council, include supervising the registering bodies for the medical and allied professions.

Cabinet ministers must be Privy Counsellors and are sworn in on first assuming office. Otherwise membership of the Council (retained for life, except for very occasional removals) is accorded by the Sovereign, on the recommendation of the Prime Minister, to eminent people in Britain and the independent monarchies of the Commonwealth. There are about 400 Privy Counsellors. A full Council is summoned only on the accession of a new Sovereign or when the Sovereign announces his or her intention to marry.

Committees of the Privy Council

There are a number of advisory Privy Council committees. These include prerogative committees, such as those dealing with legislation from the Channel Islands and the Isle of Man, and with applications for charters of incorporation. Committees may also be provided for by statute, such as those for the universities of Oxford and Cambridge and the Scottish universities.

The Judicial Committee of the Privy Council is the final court of appeal for certain independent members of the Commonwealth, the British dependencies, the Channel Islands and the Isle of Man. It also hears appeals from the disciplinary committees of the medical and allied professions and certain ecclesiastical appeals.

Administrative work is carried out in the Privy Council Office under the Lord President of the Council, a Cabinet minister.

Her Majesty's Government

Her Majesty's Government is the body of ministers responsible for the administration of national affairs. The Prime Minister is appointed by the Queen, and all other ministers are appointed by the Queen on the recommendation of the Prime Minister. Most ministers are members of the

---

[9] All those who are not members or officials of either House.

Commons, although the Government is also fully represented by ministers in the Lords. The Lord Chancellor is always a member of the House of Lords.

Composition

The composition of governments can vary both in the number of ministers and in the titles of some offices. New ministerial offices may be created, others may be abolished, and functions may be transferred from one minister to another.

Prime Minister

The Prime Minister is also, by tradition, First Lord of the Treasury and Minister for the Civil Service. The head of the Government became known as the Prime Minister during the eighteenth century. The Prime Minister's unique position of authority derives from majority support in the House of Commons and from the power to appoint and dismiss ministers. By modern convention, the Prime Minister always sits in the House of Commons.

The Prime Minister presides over the Cabinet, is responsible for the allocation of functions among ministers and informs the Queen at regular meetings of the general business of the Government.

The Prime Minister's other responsibilities include recommending to the Queen a number of appointments. These include:

● Church of England archbishops, bishops and deans and some 200 other clergy in Crown 'livings';
● high judicial offices, such as the Lord Chief Justice;
● Privy Counsellors; and
● Lord-Lieutenants.

They also include certain civil appointments, such as Lord High Commissioner to the General Assembly of the Church of Scotland, Poet Laureate, Constable of the Tower, and some university posts; and appointments to various public boards and institutions, such as the British Broadcasting Corporation (BBC), as well as various royal and statutory commissions.

Recommendations are likewise made for the award of many civil honours and distinctions and of Civil List pensions (to people who have achieved eminence in science and the arts and are in financial need). The Prime Minister also selects the trustees of certain national museums and institutions.

The Prime Minister's Office at 10 Downing Street (the official residence in central London) has a staff of civil servants who assist the Prime Minister. The Prime Minister may also appoint special advisers to the Office from time to time to assist in the formation of policies.

Departmental Ministers

Ministers in charge of government departments are usually in the Cabinet; they are known as 'Secretary of State' or 'Minister', or may have a special title, as in the case of the Chancellor of the Exchequer.

Non-Departmental Ministers

The holders of various traditional offices, namely the Lord President of the Council, the Chancellor of the Duchy of Lancaster, the Lord Privy Seal, the Paymaster General and, from time to time, Ministers without Portfolio, may have few or no departmental duties. They are thus available to perform any duties the Prime Minister may wish to give them.

Lord Chancellor and Law Officers

The Lord Chancellor holds a special position, as both a minister with departmental functions and the head of the judiciary. The four Law Officers of the Crown are: for England and Wales, the Attorney General and the Solicitor General; and for Scotland, the Lord Advocate and the Solicitor General for Scotland.

Ministers of State

Ministers of State usually work with ministers in charge of departments. They normally have specific responsibilities, and are sometimes given titles which reflect these functions. More than one may work in a department. A Minister of State may be given a seat in the Cabinet and be paid accordingly.

Junior Ministers

Junior ministers (generally Parliamentary Under-Secretaries of State or, where the senior minister is not a Secretary of State, simply Parliamentary Secretaries) share in parliamentary and departmental duties. They may also be given responsibility, directly under the departmental minister, for specific aspects of the department's work. The Parliamentary Secretary to the Treasury and other Lords Commissioners of the Treasury are in a different category as Government Whips (see p 36).

Ministerial Salaries

The salaries of ministers in the House of Commons range from £42,272 a year for junior ministers to £59,914 for Cabinet ministers. In the House of Lords salaries range from £36,066 for junior ministers to £48,381 for Cabinet ministers. The Prime Minister receives £72,533 and the Lord Chancellor £91,500.

The Cabinet

The Cabinet is composed of about 20 ministers (the number can vary) chosen by the Prime Minister and may include departmental and non-departmental ministers.

The functions of the Cabinet are initiating and deciding on policy, the supreme control of government and the co-ordination of government departments. The exercise of these functions is vitally affected by the fact that the Cabinet is a group of party representatives, depending upon majority support in the House of Commons.

Cabinet Meetings

The Cabinet meets in private and its proceedings are confidential. Its members are bound by their oath as Privy Counsellors not to disclose information about its proceedings, although after 30 years Cabinet papers may be made available for inspection in the Public Record Office at Kew, Surrey.

Normally the Cabinet meets for a few hours once or twice a week during parliamentary sittings, and rather less often when Parliament is not sitting. To keep the workload of the Cabinet within manageable limits, a great deal of work is carried on through the committee system. This involves referring issues either to a standing Cabinet committee or to an ad hoc committee composed of the ministers directly concerned. The committee then considers the matter in detail and either disposes of it or reports upon it to the Cabinet with recommendations for action.

The present Cabinet has four standing committees: a defence and overseas policy committee and an economic strategy committee, both chaired by the Prime Minister; a home and social affairs committee chaired by the Lord Privy Seal; and a legislation committee chaired by the Lord President of the Council. Sub-committees of the standing committees may be established. The membership and terms of reference of all Cabinet committees are confidential. Diaries published by several former ministers have given the public insight into Cabinet procedures in recent times.

Non-Cabinet ministers may be invited to attend meetings on matters affecting their departments, and may be members of Cabinet committees. Where appropriate, the Secretary of the Cabinet and other senior officials of the Cabinet Office attend meetings of the Cabinet and its committees.

The Cabinet Office

The Cabinet Office, headed by the Secretary of the Cabinet (who is also Head of the Home Civil Service), under the direction of the Prime Minister, comprises the Cabinet Secretariat, the Office of the Minister for the Civil Service and the Historical Section.

The Cabinet Secretariat serves ministers collectively in the conduct of Cabinet business, and in the co-ordination of policy at the highest level.

The Office of the Minister for the Civil Service is responsible for implementing the Next Steps policy (see p 53). Other tasks include the provision of services in the field of recruitment, training and occupational health; policies for the management and development of staff; and equal opportunities.

The Historical Section of the Cabinet Office recently completed the official histories of the second world war; it is now responsible for preparing official histories of certain peacetime events.

Ministerial Responsibility

'Ministerial responsibility' refers both to the collective responsibility which ministers share for government policy and actions and to ministers' individual responsibility for their departments' work.

The doctrine of collective responsibility means that the Cabinet acts unanimously even when Cabinet ministers do not all agree on a subject. The policy of departmental ministers must be consistent with the policy of the Government as a whole. Once the Government's policy on a matter has been decided, each minister is expected to support it or resign. On rare occasions, ministers have been allowed free votes in Parliament on government policies involving important issues of principle.

The individual responsibility of ministers for the work of their departments means that they are answerable to Parliament for all their departments' activities. They bear the consequences of any defect of administration, any injustice to an individual or any aspect of policy which may be criticised in Parliament, whether personally responsible or not. Since most ministers are members of the House of Commons, they must answer questions and defend themselves against criticism in person. Departmental ministers in the House of Lords are represented in the Commons by someone qualified to speak on their behalf, usually a junior minister.

Departmental ministers normally decide all matters within their responsibility. However, on important political matters they usually consult their colleagues collectively, either through the Cabinet or through a Cabinet committee. A decision by a departmental minister binds the Government as a whole.

On assuming office ministers must resign directorships in private and public companies, and must ensure that there is no conflict between their public duties and private interests.

Government Departments

Government departments are the main instruments for giving effect to government policy when Parliament has passed the necessary legislation, and for advising ministers. They often work alongside local authorities, statutory boards, and government-sponsored organisations operating under various degrees of government control.

A change of government does not necessarily affect the number or general functions of government departments, although major changes in policy may be accompanied by organisational changes.

The work of some departments (for instance, the Ministry of Defence) covers Britain as a whole. Other departments (such as the Department of Employment) cover England, Wales and Scotland, but not Northern Ireland. Others, such as the Department of the Environment, are mainly concerned with affairs in England. Some departments, such as the Department of Trade and Industry, maintain a regional organisation, and some which have direct contact with the public throughout the country (for example, the Department of Employment) also have local offices.

Departments are usually headed by ministers. Certain departments in which questions of policy do not normally arise are headed by permanent officials, and ministers with other duties are responsible for them to Parliament. For instance, ministers in the Treasury are responsible for HM Customs and Excise, the Inland Revenue, the Central Statistical Office, the National Investment and Loans Office and a number of other departments as well as executive agencies such as the Central Office of Information,

HMSO and the Royal Mint. Departments generally receive their funds directly out of money provided by Parliament and are staffed by members of the Civil Service.

Non-Departmental Public Bodies

A number of bodies with a role in the process of government are neither government departments nor part of a department (in April 1990 there were 1,539). Known as non-departmental public bodies, they are of three kinds: executive bodies, advisory bodies and tribunals.

Executive Bodies

Executive bodies normally employ their own staff and have their own budget. They are public organisations whose duties include executive, administrative, regulatory or commercial functions. They normally operate within broad policy guidelines set by departmental ministers but are in varying degrees independent of government in carrying out their day-to-day responsibilities. Examples include the Arts Council of Great Britain, the British Council, the Commonwealth Development Corporation and the Commission for Racial Equality.

Advisory Bodies

Many government departments are assisted by advisory councils or committees which undertake research and collect information, mainly to give ministers access to informed opinion before they come to a decision involving a legislative or executive act. In some cases a minister must consult a standing committee, but usually advisory bodies are appointed at the discretion of the minister.

The membership of the advisory councils and committees varies according to the nature of the work involved, and will usually include representatives who belong to relevant interests and professions.

In addition to the standing advisory bodies, there are committees set up by the Government to examine specific matters and make recommendations. For certain important inquiries Royal Commissions, whose members are chosen for their wide experience, may be appointed. Royal Commissions examine evidence from government departments, interested organisations and individuals, and submit recommendations. The Government may accept the recommendations in whole or in part, or may decide to take no further action or to delay action. Inquiries may also be undertaken by departmental committees.

Tribunals

Tribunals are a specialised group of judicial bodies, akin to courts of law. They are normally set up under statutory powers which also govern their constitution, functions and procedure. Tribunals often consist of laypeople, but they are generally chaired by someone who is legally qualified. They tend to be less expensive, and less formal, than courts of law. Independently of the executive, tribunals decide the rights and obligations of private citizens, and of government departments and local authorities. Important examples are industrial tribunals, rent tribunals and social security appeal tribunals. Tribunals usually consist of an uneven number of people so that a majority decision can be reached. Members are normally appointed by the minister concerned with the subject. Tribunals and advisory bodies do not normally employ staff or spend money themselves, but their expenses are paid by the government departments concerned.

Government Information Services

Each of the main government departments has its own information division, public relations branch or news department. These are normally staffed by professional information officers responsible for communicating their department's activities to the news media and the public (sometimes using publicity services provided by the Central Office of Information—see p 48). They also advise their departments on the public's reaction.

As press adviser to the Prime Minister, the Prime Minister's Press Secretary and other staff in the Prime Minister's Press Office have direct contact with the parliamentary press through regular meetings with the Lobby correspondents. The Lobby correspondents are a group of political correspondents who have the special privilege of access to the Lobby of the House of Commons where they can talk privately to government ministers and other members of the House. The Prime Minister's Press Office is the accepted channel through which information about parliamentary business is passed to the media.

Functions of Government Departments

An outline of the principal functions of the main government departments and executive agencies is given below. Arrangement is in alphabetical order, except for the Scottish and Northern Ireland departments and agencies, which are grouped at the end of the section, and the Cabinet Office, described on p 44.

MAIN AREAS OF RESPONSIBILITY OF DEPARTMENTS

The work of many of the departments and agencies listed on pp 47–49 covers Britain as a whole. Where this is not the case, the following abbreviations are used:

- (GB) for functions covering England, Wales and Scotland;
- (E, W & NI) for those covering England, Wales and Northern Ireland;
- (E & W) for those covering England and Wales; and
- (E) for those concerned with England only.

Ministry of Agriculture, Fisheries and Food

Policies for agriculture, horticulture, fisheries and food; responsibilities for related environmental and rural issues (E); food policies.

Office of Arts and Libraries

General promotion of arts (GB); library and information services (E with advice to W and NI); national museums (E); public libraries and local museums (E); British Library; national heritage.

Crown Prosecution Service

The prosecution of criminal offences, in which its decisions are independent of Government; headed by the Director of Public Prosecutions, who is superintended by the Attorney General (E & W).

HM Customs and Excise

Collecting and accounting for revenues of Customs and Excise, including value added tax; agency functions including controlling certain imports and exports and compiling trade statistics.

Ministry of Defence

Defence policy and control and administration of the armed services.

Department of Education and Science

Policies for education, sport and recreation (E); the Government's relations with universities (GB); promoting civil science in Britain and internationally.

The Office of Electricity Regulation (OFFER)

Promotion of competition in the generation and supply of electricity; ensuring that all reasonable demands for electricity are satisfied; protection of consumer interests (GB).

Department of Employment

The Employment Service, employment policy and legislation; training policy and legislation; health and safety at work; industrial relations, wages councils, equal opportunities; small firms and tourism; statistics on labour and industrial matters (GB); the Careers Service (E); international representation on employment matters.

Department of Energy

Policies for all forms of energy, including its efficient use and the development of new sources; the Government's relations with the energy industries.

Department of the Environment

Policies for planning and regional development, local government, new towns, housing, construction, inner city matters, environmental protection, water, the countryside, conservation, historic buildings and ancient monuments (E); and Property Services Agency (GB).

ECGD (Export Credits Guarantee Department)

Provision of insurance for exporters against the risk of not being paid for goods and services, and access to bank finance for exports; insurance cover for new investment overseas.

Foreign & Commonwealth Office

Conduct of Britain's overseas relations; provision of consular facilities to British citizens overseas.

Office of Gas Supply

Monitoring of British Gas as the sole public gas supplier, ensuring compliance with its statutory obligations, and granting authorisations to other suppliers of gas through pipes; development of competition in the industrial market.

Department of Health

National Health Service, personal social services provided by local authorities, and certain aspects of public health, including hygiene (E).

Home Office

Administration of justice; criminal law; treatment of offenders, including probation; the prison service; the police; crime prevention; fire and civil defence services; licensing laws; scrutiny of local authority by-laws; control of firearms and dangerous drugs; electoral matters (E & W). Gaming and lotteries (GB). Regulation of broadcasting; passports, immigration and nationality; race relations and sex discrimination. Responsibilities relating to the Channel Islands and the Isle of Man.

Central Office of Information

Providing publicity material and other information services for government departments and publicly funded organisations.

Board of Inland Revenue

Administration and collection of direct taxes; valuation of property (GB).

The Law Officers' Departments

Provision of advice to the Government on English law and representation of the Crown in appropriate domestic and international cases, both civil and criminal, by the Law Officers of the Crown for England and Wales—the Attorney General and the Solicitor General (E & W). The Attorney General, who is also Attorney General for Northern Ireland, oversees the Treasury Solicitor's Department, the Crown Prosecution Service (E & W), the Serious Fraud Office (E, W & NI) and the Director of Public Prosecutions for Northern Ireland (NI).

The Lord Chancellor's Department

Administration of the Supreme Court (Court of Appeal, High Court, Crown Court) and the county courts (E & W), together with certain other courts and tribunals, and all work relating to judicial and quasi-judicial appointments. Responsibility for civil and criminal legal aid, the Public Trust Office and the Official Solicitor's Department. Promotion of general reforms in the civil law. (The Home Office has important responsibilities for the criminal law.)

Ordnance Survey

Official surveying, mapping and associated scientific work covering Great Britain and some overseas countries.

Overseas Development Administration

Administration of financial aid and technical co-operation to developing countries.

Parliamentary Counsel

Drafting of government Bills (except those relating exclusively to Scotland); advising departments on parliamentary procedure (E, W & NI).

Paymaster General's Office

Provision of banking services for government departments other than the Boards of Inland Revenue and Customs and Excise, and the payment of public service pensions.

Office of Population Censuses and Surveys

Administration of the Marriage Acts and local registration of births, marriages and deaths; population estimates and projections; compilation of health statistics; Census of Population (E & W). Surveys for other government departments (GB).

HM Procurator General and Treasury Solicitor's Department

Provision of a common legal service for a large number of government departments. Duties include instructing Parliamentary Counsel on Bills and drafting subordinate legislation; providing litigation and conveyancing services; and giving general advice on interpreting and applying the law (E & W).

Serious Fraud Office

Investigating and prosecuting serious and complex fraud under the supervision of the Attorney General (E, W & NI).

Department of Social Security

The social security system (GB). Three executive agencies cover the main aspects of the Department's work: the Information Technology Services Agency; the Benefits Agency; and the Contributions Agency. A fourth agency, the Resettlement Agency, runs residential units designed to help single homeless people.

HMSO (Her Majesty's Stationery Office)

Providing stationery, printing and related services to Parliament, government departments and other public bodies; and publishing and selling government documents.

Central Statistical Office

Preparing and interpreting key economic statistics needed for government policies; collecting and publishing business statistics; publishing annual statistical digests.

Office of Telecommunications (OFTEL)

Monitoring of BT (formerly British Telecom), Mercury, and other telecommunications operators; enforcing competition legislation and representing users' interests.

Department of Trade and Industry

Industrial and commercial policy, promotion of enterprise and competition, information about new methods and opportunities, investor and consumer protection. Specific responsibilities include industrial innovation policy; regional industrial policy and inward investment promotion; management development and business/education links; international trade policy; commercial relations and export promotion; competition policy; company law; insolvency; radio regulation; patents and copyright protection (GB).

Department of Transport

Land, sea and air transport; sponsorship of the nationalised London Transport and British Rail; domestic and international civil aviation; international transport agreements; shipping and the ports industry; marine pollution; oversight of road transport (GB); motorways and trunk roads; road safety; and oversight of local authority transport (E).

HM Treasury

Broad economic strategy with particular responsibilities for public finance and expenditure, including control of staffing and pay in the Civil Service.

Office of Water Services (OFWAT)

Monitoring the activities of companies appointed as water and sewerage undertakers (E & W); regulation of prices and representing customers' interests.

Welsh Office

Many aspects of Welsh affairs, including health and personal social services; education, except for terms and conditions of service, student awards and the University of Wales; the Welsh language and culture; agriculture and fisheries; forestry; local government; housing; water and sewerage; environmental protection; sport; land use, including town and country planning; countryside and nature conservation; new towns, ancient monuments and historic buildings; roads; tourism; a range of matters affecting the careers service and the training activities of the Department of Employment in Wales; selective financial assistance to industry; the Urban Programme in Wales; the operation of the European Regional Development Fund in Wales and other European Community matters; non-departmental public bodies; civil emergencies; all financial aspects of these matters including Welsh revenue support grant; and oversight responsibilities for economic affairs and regional planning in Wales.

SCOTLAND

Scotland has its own system of law and wide administrative autonomy. The Secretary of State for Scotland, a Cabinet minister, has responsibility in Scotland (with some exceptions) for policy relating to agriculture and fisheries, education, law and order, environmental protection and conservation of the countryside, land-use planning, local government, housing, roads and certain aspects of transport services, social work and health.

The Secretary of State also has a major role in the planning and development of the Scottish economy, and important functions relating to industrial development, with responsibility for financial assistance to industry. He or she is also responsible for Scottish Enterprise, Highlands and Islands Enterprise and new town development corporations and for the Scottish Tourist Board. The Secretary of State plays a full part in determining energy policy, particularly in relation to the electricity supply industry in Scotland. He or she is also responsible for government involvement in a range of other functions from fire services to sport and for overseeing many non-departmental public bodies.

The Secretary of State has overall responsibility for legal services in Scotland and is advised by the two Scottish Law Officers, the Lord Advocate and the Solicitor General for Scotland (see below).

The distinctive conditions and needs of Scotland and its people are reflected in separate Scottish legislation on many domestic matters. Special provisions applying to Scotland alone are also inserted in Acts which otherwise apply to Britain generally.

The Secretary of State's responsibilities are discharged principally through the Scottish Office's five departments (which include two executive agencies), supported by Central Services (see p 51). There are also four smaller departments: the Registers of Scotland (an executive agency), the Scottish Record Office, the General Register Office for Scotland and the Scottish Courts Administration.

British government departments with significant Scottish responsibilities have offices in Scotland and work closely with the Scottish Office. The British headquarters of several government departments are located in Scotland.

An outline of the functions of the main Scottish departments is given below.

FUNCTIONS OF DEPARTMENTS

Scottish Office Agriculture and Fisheries Department

Promotion of the agricultural and fishing industries; enforcement of fisheries laws and regulations through the Scottish Fisheries Protection Agency.

Scottish Office Environment Department

Environment, including environmental protection, nature conservation and the countryside; land use planning; water supplies and sewerage; local government;

housing; building control; protection and presentation to the public of historic buildings and ancient monuments through Historic Scotland, an executive agency.

Scottish Office Education Department

Education (excluding universities); student awards; the arts, libraries, museums and galleries, Gaelic language; sport and recreation; the arts.

Scottish Office Home and Health Department

Central administration of law and order (including police service, criminal justice, legal aid and penal institutions); the National Health Service; fire, home defence and civil emergency services; social work services.

Scottish Office Industry Department

Industrial and regional economic development matters; training; energy; tourism; urban regeneration; new towns; roads and certain transport functions.

Central Services

Services to the five Scottish departments. These include the Office of the Solicitor to the Secretary of State, the Scottish Office Information Directorate, Personnel, Management and Organisation Divisions.

Lord Advocate's Department and Crown Office

Provision of legal advice to the Government on issues affecting Scotland and the principal representation of the Crown for litigation in Scotland by the Law Officers of the Crown for Scotland (the Lord Advocate and the Solicitor General for Scotland); control of all prosecutions in Scotland.

NORTHERN IRELAND

Since the British Government's assumption of direct responsibility for Northern Ireland in 1972 (see p 12), the Secretary of State for Northern Ireland has been the Cabinet minister responsible for Northern Ireland affairs. Through the Northern Ireland Office the Secretary of State has direct responsibility for constitutional developments, law and order, security, and electoral matters. The work of the Northern Ireland departments, whose functions are listed below, is also subject to the direction and control of the Secretary of State.

FUNCTIONS OF DEPARTMENTS

Department of Agriculture for Northern Ireland

Development of agricultural, forestry and fishing industries; rural areas; veterinary, scientific and advisory services; administration of European Community and other support arrangements; education and training.

Department of Economic Development for Northern Ireland

Development of industry and commerce, as well as administration of government policy in relation to tourism, energy, minerals, industrial relations, employment equality, consumer protection, health and safety at work and company legislation; administration of an employment service and labour training schemes through the Training and Employment Agency and assistance to industry, through the Industrial Development Board for Northern Ireland.

Department of Education for Northern Ireland

Control of the five education and library boards and education as a whole, youth services, sport and recreation, cultural activities and community services and facilities, including the improvement of community relations.

Department of the Environment for Northern Ireland

Housing; planning; construction and maintenance of roads; transport and traffic management, and motor taxation; water and sewerage; environmental protection; ordnance survey; collection of rates; harbours; historic monuments and buildings; maintenance of public records; and certain controls over local government.

Department of Finance and Personnel

Control of public expenditure; liaison with HM Treasury and the Northern Ireland Office on financial matters, economic and social planning and research; Ulster Savings; charities; Valuation and Lands Service; policies for equal opportunities and personnel management; and general management and control of the Northern Ireland Civil Service.

Department of Health and Social Services for Northern Ireland

Health and personal social services; social security; social legislation; and the Office of the Registrar-General.

The Civil Service

The Civil Service is concerned with the conduct of the whole range of government activities as they affect the community. These range from policy formulation to carrying out the day-to-day duties of public administration.

Civil servants are servants of the Crown. For all practical purposes the Crown in this context means, and is represented by, the Government of the day. There are special cases in which certain functions are conferred by law upon particular members or groups of members of the public service. However, in general the executive powers of the Crown are exercised by, and on the advice of, Her Majesty's Ministers, who are in turn answerable to Parliament. The Civil Service as such has no constitutional responsibility separate from that of the duly constituted Government of the day. The duty of the individual civil servant is first and foremost to the Minister of the Crown who is in charge of the Department concerned. A change of minister, for whatever reason, does not involve a change of staff. Ministers sometimes appoint special advisers from outside the Civil Service. The advisers are normally paid from public funds, but their appointments come to an end when the Government's term of office finishes, or when the Minister concerned leaves the Government or moves to another appointment.

The number of civil servants has fallen from 732,000 in April 1979 to 554,000 in April 1991, reflecting the Government's policy of controlling the cost and size of the Civil Service and of improving its efficiency. About half of all civil servants are engaged in the provision of public services. These include paying sickness benefits and pensions, collecting taxes and contributions, running employment services, staffing prisons, and providing services to industry and agriculture. Around a quarter are employed in the Ministry of Defence. The rest are divided between: central administrative and policy duties; support services; and largely financially self-supporting services, for instance, those provided by the Department for National Savings and the Royal Mint. The total includes about 64,000 'industrial' civil servants, mainly manual workers in government industrial establishments. Four-fifths of civil servants work outside London.

The Government is committed to achieving equality of opportunity for all its staff. In support of this commitment, the Civil Service is actively pursuing policies to increase employment and career opportunities for women, ethnic minorities and people with disabilities. The number of black and Asian people now employed in the Civil Service is proportionate to their representation in Britain's population.

Reforms of the management of government departments are being implemented to ensure improved management performance, in particular through the increased accountability of individual managers, based on clear objectives and responsibilities. These reforms include performance-related pay schemes and other incentives.

Executive Agencies: Next Steps Initiative

The Next Steps Initiative, launched in 1988, is intended to improve management in the Civil Service and the efficiency and quality of services provided to the public and to customers within government. This has involved setting up, as far as practicable, separate units or agencies to perform the executive functions of government. Agencies remain part of the Civil Service but they enjoy greater delegation on financial, pay and personnel matters. Agencies are headed by chief executives who are personally responsible for the performance of the agency. By July 1991 a total of more than 50 agencies had been set up, together with 30 executive units covering 95 per cent of Customs and Excise. Over 210,000 civil servants work in organisations run on Next Steps lines. It is expected that this programme will have been applied to at least half the Civil Service in the course of 1992.

Efficiency Measures

Savings in public expenditure are being sought by competitive tendering and by contracting out to the private sector services carried out by government departments when this leads to better management and value for money. By April 1990 savings of around £54 million net a year had been achieved.

Citizen's Charter

Government proposals to raise standards in the public services were set out in a White Paper, *The Citizen's Charter*, published in July 1991. The proposals involve more privatisation, wider competition, further contracting-out and pay more closely related to performance. They also include requirements for comprehensive information on standards achieved, more effective complaints procedures, better redress for the citizen when things go wrong, and tougher and more independent inspectorates and auditing. All public services are expected to take action: the Government intends to publish separate charters for specific services, for example, taxation (see p 343) and education (see p 144).

Executive agencies will fully comply with the principles of *The Citizen's Charter*. The Government will introduce legislation to remove obstacles to the delegation of decisions to civil servants. Performance-related pay will be introduced for most staff.

Central Management and Structure

Responsibility for central co-ordination and management of the Civil Service is divided between the Treasury and the Cabinet Office (Office of the Minister for the Civil Service). In addition to its other functions, the Treasury is responsible for the structure of the Civil Service. It is also responsible for recruitment policy and for controlling staffing, pay, pensions and allowances. The Office of the Minister for the Civil Service, which is under the control of the Prime Minister, as Minister for the Civil Service, is responsible for the organisation, non-financial aspects of personnel management and overall efficiency of the Service. The function of official Head of the Home Civil Service is combined with that of Secretary to the Cabinet.

At the senior levels, where management forms a major part of most jobs, there are common grades throughout the Civil Service. These unified grades 1 to 7 are known as the Open Structure and cover grades from Permanent Secretary level to Principal level. Within the unified grades each post is filled by the person best equipped in terms of skills, ability and experience, regardless of the occupational group to which he or she previously belonged.

Below this the structure of the non-industrial Civil Service is based on a system of occupational groups, which are the basic groupings of staff for the purposes of personnel management. These include the Administration, Economist, Information Officer, Lawyer, Librarian, Professional and Technical (which includes architects, surveyors, and electrical and mechanical engineers), Secretarial, Science and Statistician Groups. These groups, together with the Inland Revenue's administration and typing grades, account for about 65 per cent of non-industrial staff. Work requiring specialist skill is always done by qualified individuals.

Personnel management policies encourage the deployment of staff so that talent can be used to the best advantage. Higher posts are open to people of outstanding ability, whatever their specialist background or original method of entry into the Service. This ensures that people with the necessary qualities can gain suitably wide experience to fit them for posts at the highest levels. The exchange of staff between the Civil Service and industry is also encouraged.

The Diplomatic Service

The Diplomatic Service, a separate service of some 6,600 or so people, provides the majority of the staff for the Foreign & Commonwealth Office and at British diplomatic missions and consular posts abroad. Its functions include:

● advising on policy;

● negotiating with overseas governments and conducting business in international organisations;

● promoting British exports and trade generally;

● administering aid;

● presenting British ideas, policies and objectives to the people of overseas countries;

● administering the remaining dependent territories; and

● protecting British interests abroad and British nationals overseas.

The Service has its own grade structure, linked for salary purposes with that of the Home Civil Service. Conditions of work are in many ways comparable, but take into account the special demands of the Service, particularly of postings overseas. Members of the Home Civil Service and the armed forces, and individuals from the private sector, may also serve in the Foreign & Commonwealth Office and at overseas posts on loan or attachment.

Recruitment and Training

Recruitment is based on the principle of selection on merit by open competition. Independent Civil Service Commissioners are responsible for selecting people for appointment to the higher levels and to the fast-streams of the Home Civil Service and the Diplomatic Service. Recruitment of middle ranking and junior staff is the responsibility of departments and executive agencies; it is monitored by the Commissioners. Departments and agencies can choose whether to undertake the recruitment work themselves, to employ a private sector recruitment agency or to use the Recruitment and Assessment Services Agency (an executive agency) to recruit on their behalf.

People from outside the Civil Service may be recruited directly to the higher levels in the open structure (at and above Grade 7 level), particularly to posts requiring skills and experience more readily found in the private sector.

For the Administration Group, there are three main levels of entry. They broadly relate to the academic achievements of: a first or second class honours degree; GCE Advanced level; and GCSE Grade A, B or C. For entry at the first of these levels (the fast-stream administration entry) applicants must succeed in a one-day qualifying test, followed by two days of tests and interviews at the Civil Service Selection Board and an interview by the Final Selection Board. For the GCE Advanced entry (Executive Officer) selection normally involves a qualifying test followed by an interview. For the GCSE entry (Administration Officer/Assistant) selection is usually by interview for those who hold the required educational or vocational qualifications, or who pass specially designed job-related tests.

Entrants to the Professional and Technology Group must usually have relevant qualifications, ranging from membership of an architectural, engineering or related professional institution to technical qualifications. New graduates are offered a structured training programme leading to membership of an appropriate professional institution.

Entrants to the Science Group must normally have appropriate qualifications in science, engineering or mathematical subjects. Relevant experience is required before appointment to the more senior levels (Higher and Senior Scientific Officer). There are opportunities for accelerated career development for honours graduates through the Science Management Trainee scheme. School leavers with GCSE Grade A, B or C qualifications may join the Science Group as Assistant Scientific Officers.

Many government departments and agencies employ training officers and tutors to help identify staff training needs and organise training by the most effective method. The Civil Service College provides a wide range of training courses in both management and specialist skills. Considerable use is also made of external institutions.

Civil servants under the age of 18 may continue their general education by attending courses, usually for one day a week ('day release' schemes). All staff may be entitled to financial support to continue their education, mainly in their own time. There are also opportunities for civil servants to obtain fellowships for research and study in areas of interest to them and to their department or agency.

Promotion

Departments are responsible for promotion up to and including Grade 4. Normally promotion is from grade to grade, but there can be accelerated promotion for staff who show exceptional promise. Promotion or appointment to Grades 1 and 2 and all transfers between departments at these levels are approved by the Prime Minister, who is advised by the Head of the Home Civil Service. Promotions and appointments to Grade 3 are approved by the Cabinet Office.

Political and Private Activities

Civil servants are required to perform loyally the duties assigned to them by the Government of the day, whatever its political persuasion. It is essential that ministers and the public should have confidence that the personal views of civil servants do not influence the performance of their official duties, given the role of the Civil Service in serving successive governments of different political complexions. The aim of the rules which govern political activities by civil servants is to allow them, subject to these fundamental principles, the greatest possible freedom to participate in public affairs consistent with their rights and duties as citizens. The rules are therefore concerned with political activities liable to give public expression to political views rather than with privately held beliefs and opinions.

The Civil Service is divided into three groups for the purposes of deciding the extent to which individuals may take part in political activities. Those in the 'politically free' group, consisting of industrial staff and non-office grades, are free to engage in any political activity, including adoption as a candidate for the British or the European Parliament (although they would have to resign from the Service if elected). Those in the 'politically restricted' group, which comprises staff in Grade 7 and above as well as Administration Trainees and Higher Executive Officers (D), are debarred from national political activities but may apply for permission to take part in local political activities. The 'intermediate' group, which comprises all other civil servants, may apply for permission to take part in national or local political activity, apart from candidature for the British or the European Parliament.

Where required, permission is granted to the maximum extent consistent with the Civil Service's reputation for political impartiality and the avoidance of any conflict with official duties. A code of discretion requires moderation and the avoidance of embarrassment to ministers.

Generally, there are no restrictions on the private activities of civil servants, provided that these do not bring discredit on the Civil Service, and that there is no possibility of conflict with official duties. For instance, a civil servant must comply with any departmental instruction on the need to seek authority before taking part in any outside activity which involves the use of official experience, or before accepting a directorship in any company holding a contract with his or her department.

Security

As a general rule the political views of civil servants are not a matter of official concern. However, no one may be employed in connection with work which is vital to the security of the State if they have been involved in, or associated with, activities threatening national security. Certain posts are not open to persons who fall into this category, or to anyone whose reliability may be in doubt for any other reason.

Each department is responsible for its own internal security, advised as necessary by the Security Service. The Security Commission may investigate and report on breaches of security in the public service and advise on changes in security procedure, if requested to do so by the Prime Minister after consultation with the Leader of the Opposition.

Local Government

Many public services, such as school education and personal social services, are provided by democratically elected local authorities throughout Britain.

Local authorities' powers and duties are conferred on them by Parliament, or by measures taken under its authority. Administration is the responsibility of the local authority. In the case of certain services, however, ministers have powers to secure some national uniformity in standards in order to safeguard public health or to protect the rights of individual citizens. For some services the minister concerned has wide powers of supervision; in other cases the minister's powers are strictly limited.

The main link between local authorities and central government in England is the Department of the Environment, although other departments such as the Department of Education and Science and the Home Office are concerned with various local government functions. In the rest of Britain the local authorities deal with the Scottish and Welsh Offices and the Department of the Environment for Northern Ireland.

Principal Types of Local Authority

England and Wales (outside Greater London) are divided into 53 counties, sub-divided into 369 districts. All the districts and 47 of the counties—the 'non-metropolitan' counties—have locally elected councils with separate functions. County councils provide large-scale services, while district councils are responsible for the more local ones (see p 58).

Greater London—with a population of some 6·4 million—is divided into 32 boroughs, each of which has a council responsible for local government in its area; in addition there is the Corporation of the City of London. In the six metropolitan counties there are 36 district councils; there are no county councils. A number of services, however, require a statutory authority over areas wider than the individual boroughs and districts. These are waste regulation and disposal (in certain areas); the police and fire services, including civil defence, and public transport (in all metropolitan counties); and the fire service, including civil defence (in London). All are run by joint authorities composed of elected councillors nominated by the borough or district councils.

In addition to the two-tier local authority system in England, there are over 10,000 parish councils or meetings. They provide and manage local facilities such as allotments and village halls. They also provide a forum for discussion of local issues. In Wales community councils have similar functions.

On the mainland of Scotland local government is on a two-tier basis: nine regions are divided into 53 districts, each of which has an elected council. There are three virtually all-purpose authorities for Orkney, Shetland and the Western Isles. Provision is also made for local community councils: although these have no statutory functions they can draw attention to matters of local concern.

The areas and electoral arrangements of local authorities are kept under review by the Local Government Boundary Commissions for England, Wales and Scotland.

In Northern Ireland 26 district councils are responsible for local environmental and certain other services. Statutory bodies, such as the Northern Ireland Housing Executive and area boards, are responsible to central government departments for administering other major services (see below).

Proposed Reforms to the Structure and Internal Management of Local Government

In April 1991 the Government began consultations on the structure of local government in England. The Government has stated that it believes there should be a move towards unitary, all-purpose authorities to replace the existing two-tier structure. In July 1991 consultation began on the internal management of local authorities in England. Consultation on these subjects is also taking place in Scotland and Wales.

Election of Councils

Local authority councils consist of elected unpaid councillors. Councillors may, however, be entitled to a basic flat rate allowance and to certain expenses when attending meetings or taking on special responsibilities. Parish and community councillors cannot claim allowances for duties undertaken within their own council areas.

In England, Wales and Northern Ireland each council elects its presiding officer and his or her deputy annually. Some districts have the ceremonial title of borough, or city, both granted by royal authority (in Northern Ireland, by the Secretary of State). In boroughs and cities the presiding officer is normally known as the Mayor. In the City of London and certain other large cities, he or

she is known as the Lord Mayor. In Scotland the presiding officer of the district council of each of the four cities is called the Lord Provost. No specific title is laid down for those of other councils; some are known as conveners, while others continue to use the old title of 'provost'.

Councillors are elected for four years. All county councils in England and Wales, London borough councils, and about two-thirds of non-metropolitan district councils are elected in their entirety every four years. In the remaining districts (including all metropolitan districts) one-third of the councillors are elected in each of the three years between county council elections. In Scotland local elections are held every two years, alternately for districts and for regions and islands authorities. Each election covers the whole council so that councillors are elected for four years at a time.

Anyone is entitled to vote at a local government election in Britain provided he or she is:

- aged 18 years or over;

- is a citizen of Britain or another Commonwealth country, or a citizen of the Irish Republic;

- is not subject to any legal incapacity; and

- is on the electoral register.

To qualify for registration a person must be resident in the council area on the qualifying date. In Northern Ireland there are slightly different requirements.

A candidate for election as councillor normally stands as a representative of one of the national political parties, although there are some independent candidates, and some represent local interests. Candidates must be British citizens, other Commonwealth citizens or citizens of the Irish Republic, and aged 21 or over. In addition, they must either:

- be registered as local electors in the area of the local authority to which they seek election; or

- have lived in or occupied (as owner or tenant) land or other premises in that area during the whole of the 12 months preceding the day on which they are nominated as candidates; or,

- have had their main or only place of work in the area throughout this 12-month period.

No one may be elected to a council of which he or she is an employee, and there are some other disqualifications. All candidates for district council elections in Northern Ireland are required to make a declaration against terrorism.

Counties in England and Wales are divided into electoral divisions, each returning one councillor. Districts in England, Wales and Northern Ireland are divided into 'wards', returning one councillor or more. In Scotland the electoral areas in the regions and islands areas are called electoral divisions, each returning a single member; the districts are divided into wards, similarly returning a single member. For parish or community council elections in England and Wales, each parish or community, or ward of a parish or community, elects one member or more.

The procedure for local government voting in Great Britain is similar to that for parliamentary elections. In Northern Ireland local government elections are held on the basis of proportional representation, and electoral wards are grouped into district electoral areas.

Functions and Services

In England county councils are responsible for strategic planning, transport planning, highways, traffic regulation, education, consumer protection, refuse disposal, police, the fire service, libraries and the personal social services. District councils are responsible, for instance, for environmental health, housing, decisions on most local planning applications, and refuse collection. They may also provide off-street car parks subject to the consent of the county council. Both tiers of local authority have powers to provide facilities like museums, art galleries and parks; arrangements depend on local agreement.

In the metropolitan counties the district councils are responsible for all services apart from the police, the fire service and public transport and, in some areas, waste

regulation and disposal (see p 56). In Greater London the boroughs and the City Corporation have similar functions but London's metropolitan police force is directly responsible to the Home Secretary. Responsibility for public transport lies with London Transport.

In Wales the division of functions between county and district councils is much the same as that between county and district councils in non-metropolitan areas of England.

Local authorities in England and Wales may arrange for any of their functions to be carried out on their behalf by another local authority, other than those relating to education, police, the personal social services and national parks.

In Scotland the functions of regional and district authorities are divided up in a similar way to the counties and districts in England and Wales. Because of their isolation from the mainland, Orkney, Shetland and the Western Isles have single, virtually all-purpose authorities; they take part in wider-scale administration for their police and fire services, however, and rely on the mainland for assistance in the more specialised aspects of education and social work.

In Northern Ireland local environmental and certain other services, such as leisure and the arts, are administered by the district councils. Responsibility for planning, roads, water supply and sewerage services is exercised in each district through a divisional office of the Department of the Environment for Northern Ireland. Area boards, responsible to central departments, administer education, public libraries and the health and personal services locally. The Northern Ireland Housing Executive, responsible to the Department of the Environment, administers housing.

Internal Organisation of Local Authorities

Local authorities have considerable freedom to make arrangements for carrying out their duties. The main policies are decided by the full council; other matters concerning the various services are the responsibility of committees composed of members of the council. A council may delegate to a committee or officer any function except those concerned with raising loans, levying local taxes or making financial demands on other local authorities liable to contribute. These powers are legally reserved to the council as a whole. Some councils have policy advisory or co-ordinating committees which originate policy for implementation by the full council. The powers and duties of local authority committees are usually laid down in formal standing orders. Parish and community councils in England and Wales are often able to do their work in full session, although they appoint committees from time to time as necessary.

Following an independent inquiry into the conduct of local authority business, legislation was passed in 1989 to strengthen the democratic functioning of local authorities. Under its provisions, committees have to reflect the political composition of the council. In England and Wales people who are not members of the council may be appointed to decision-making committees and are able to speak and take part in debates; they cannot normally vote. The legislation also prevents senior officers and others in politically sensitive posts from being members of another local authority or undertaking public political activity. Some of these provisions have not been introduced in Northern Ireland.

Public Access

The public (including the press) are admitted to council, committee and sub-committee meetings, and have a right of access to agendas, reports and minutes of meetings and certain background papers. Local authorities may exclude the public from meetings and withhold these papers only in limited circumstances specified by legislation.

Officers and Employees

Almost 3 million people are employed by local authorities in Great Britain. These include administrative, professional and technical staff, teachers, firefighters, those engaged on law and order services, and manual workers.

Nearly half of all local government workers are employed in the education service.

Although a few appointments must be made by all the authorities responsible for the functions concerned, councils are individually responsible within national policy requirements for determining the size and duties of their workforces. In Northern Ireland each council must by law appoint a clerk of the council as its chief officer.

As a general rule, employees are of three kinds: heads of departments or chief officers; administrative, professional, clerical and technical staff; and manual workers. Senior staff appointments are usually made on the recommendation of the committee or committees involved. Most junior appointments are made by heads of departments, who are also responsible for engaging manual workers. Pay and conditions of service are generally a matter for each council, although there are scales recommended by national negotiating machinery between authorities and trade unions.

Authorities differ in the degree to which they employ their own permanent staff to carry out certain functions or use private firms under contract. The Government's policy of promoting value for money is encouraging the use of private firms where savings can be made. Authorities are required to expose to competition the following services: refuse collection, street cleaning, school and general catering, vehicle maintenance, ground maintenance and building cleaning, sport and leisure management, construction and building maintenance and highways work.

Local Authority Finance

In the past 30 years or so the gradual expansion of local government led to a steady rise in local government expenditure which now accounts for about a quarter of public spending. The Government has sought to check this growth as part of a general policy of controlling the growth of public expenditure. Under the community charge system, introduced in 1990–91, the Government has the power to restrain excessive budgets by setting caps or maximum limits.

In 1990–91 expenditure by local authorities in Britain amounted to £57,300 million, over one-quarter of general government expenditure. Current expenditure amounted to £46,800 million, and capital expenditure, net of capital receipts, was £5,300 million and debt interest £5,200 million.

System of Finance

Local authorities in Great Britain raise revenue through a community charge, which is set by each charging local authority and payable by almost all resident adults. There is also a grant system, which compensates for differences in the cost of providing a standard level of service between authorities. Finally, in England and in Wales, there are uniform business rates (single rates per pound of rateable value of business property applying throughout England and throughout Wales), the proceeds of which are distributed to authorities in proportion to the number of people registered to pay the community charge. In Scotland progress is being made towards a uniform business rate. In Northern Ireland there is, instead of the community charge, a system of domestic rates (local property taxes).

In 1991 the Government announced a change in the balance between central and local financing of local authority expenditure. Local domestic taxpayers would in future be asked to meet a reduced proportion of such expenditure. In the longer term the community charge would be replaced by a council tax, payable by every household. The new system could be in place in 1993–94.

Current Expenditure

In 1990–91 education accounted for 44 per cent of local authorities' current expenditure

in England, Scotland and Wales. Most of the remainder was spent on roads and transport; housing and other environmental services; law, order and protective services; and personal social services.

Capital Expenditure

Local government capital expenditure is financed primarily by borrowing and from capital receipts from the disposal of land and buildings. These sources are supplemented mainly by capital grants and contributions from central government.

Control of Finance

Local councils normally have a finance committee to keep their financial policy under constant review. Their annual accounts must be audited by independent auditors appointed by the Audit Commission in England and Wales, or by the Commission for Local Authority Accounts in Scotland. In Northern Ireland this role is exercised by a local government audit section appointed by the Department of the Environment for Northern Ireland.

Local Government Complaints System

Citizens' allegations of injustice resulting from local government maladministration may be investigated by independent statutory Commissions for Local Administration. The English Commission has three local commissioners (or local ombudsmen) and the Welsh, one. In Scotland there is a single commissioner.

A report is issued on each complaint investigated and, if injustice caused by maladministration is found, the local ombudsman normally suggests a remedy. The council must consider the report and tell the commissioner what action it proposes to take.

In Northern Ireland a Commissioner for Complaints deals with complaints alleging injustices suffered as a result of maladministration by district councils and certain other public bodies.

3 Overseas Relations

Britain's main foreign policy objectives are to maintain its security and prosperity through global peace and economic growth.

It has worldwide interests, including responsibility for 14 dependent territories and for 6 million British citizens who live overseas. It imports over one-third of its food and over one-half of its raw materials. Exports account for over a quarter of gross national product (GNP). Britain's overseas investments are among the largest in the world.

Britain believes that its security and economic interests can best be protected by working with other countries. It has diplomatic or consular relations with 168 countries and is a member of some 120 international organisations, including the United Nations, the North Atlantic Treaty Organisation (NATO) and the European Community (EC).

Britain has close links with many developing countries, notably within the Commonwealth, which links 50 independent countries. Commonwealth members have a language in common and close professional, academic and commercial ties. In all, Britain provides development assistance to over 120 independent countries as well as to its dependencies.

Britain also has strong links with the United States, including a common language and similar political and cultural traditions.

Administration

The Foreign and Commonwealth Secretary is responsible for the conduct of overseas relations. He is supported by four Ministers of State and the staff of the Foreign & Commonwealth Office (FCO).

Britain has embassies and high commissions in nearly 130 countries and missions at ten international organisations. Other posts include consulates-general and consulates. All are staffed by members of the Diplomatic Service and locally engaged people. About 30 per cent of staff are involved in commercial work, 24 per cent in consular services, 18 per cent in political and economic work and 9 per cent in information. Other departments concerned with overseas relations include the Ministry of Defence, the Department of Trade and Industry, the Treasury and the Overseas Development Administration (ODA), which is part of the FCO.

When other departments are involved, the FCO makes policy in consultation with them. The department with the main interest usually takes the lead, particularly in European Community matters and international economic policy. The FCO co-ordinates EC policy through the Cabinet Office.

The British Overseas Trade Board and the ECGD (Export Credits Guarantee Department) provide export services to industry.

Crown Agents helps to arrange purchases from British aid funds; it also provides purchasing and management services to overseas governments and institutions.

The British Council

The principal agent for British cultural relations overseas is the British Council which is represented in 90 countries. Its main activities are:

- helping people to study and train in Britain;
- enabling British specialists to teach in other countries;
- teaching English and promoting its use;
- the provision of library and information services in other countries;
- the promotion of British education, science and technology; and

● financing overseas tours by British theatre and dance companies, orchestras and authors.

The Council is financed partly by a grant from the FCO. Another important source of income is the training and education programmes organised by the Council on behalf of the ODA and the FCO. The Council's own earnings bring in about a quarter of its income.

Membership of the European Community

Britain is an active member of the European Community. The 1957 Treaty of Rome sets out the Community's objectives, which are to establish:

● a common internal market and closer union between the peoples of Europe;

● common economic and trade policies; and

● a framework of Community law.

The 12 member states have agreed to complete the free internal market by the end of 1992. The Community, which acts for member states in international trade negotiations, accounts for a fifth of world trade.

Half of Britain's trade is with the other member states of the European Community.

Overseas countries having special links with the Community are accorded preferential treatment in aid and the development of trade.

Community Institutions

Council of Ministers

Policy decisions are taken by the Council of Ministers, on which member states are represented by ministers. Most Council decisions are taken on the basis of a proposal made by the European Commission. Depending on the treaty article being used, some may be decided by majority or qualified majority, with votes weighted according to each country's size. In other cases the Council proceeds on the basis of

The European Community

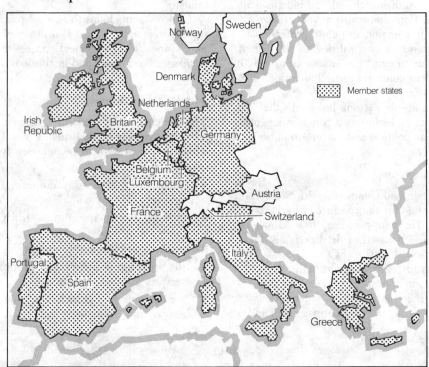

unanimity. The Single European Act 1986 provided for increased use of qualified majority voting, particularly on internal market measures.

Heads of Government usually meet twice a year as the European Council, which discusses Community policies and world affairs generally and provides guidance on major issues.

European Commission

The European Commission puts forward policy proposals, executes decisions taken by the Council of Ministers and ensures that Community rules are correctly observed. It is composed of 17 Commissioners (two from Britain), nominated by member governments and appointed by common agreement, and is pledged to act independently of national or sectional interests.

European Parliament

The 518 members of the European Parliament are directly elected by the people in member states at five-yearly intervals; 81 members come from Britain. Members sit in party political groups and not national ones. The most recent election took place in 1989.

The Parliament is consulted on a wide range of issues before final decisions are taken by the Council of Ministers. The Single European Act 1986 increased the Parliament's legislative powers. On certain proposed legislation, such as that relating to the internal market, it can voice an opinion on the Commission's proposal and on the common position adopted by the Council of Ministers. The latter is done at a second reading, which allows Parliament to make amendments. The Commission then reconsiders the proposal and may take account of the Parliament's amendments before the Council makes a final decision. There is a strict timetable on these consultation procedures in order to speed decision making.

The Parliament adopts the Community's annual budget in agreement with the Council.

New applications for Community membership must receive the assent of an absolute majority of the Parliament, as must the conclusion of agreements establishing an association with other countries involving reciprocal agreements.

The Commission can be removed from office as a whole by a two-thirds majority of all members of the Parliament in a vote of censure. Members may also put questions to the Council of Ministers and the Commission.

Court of Justice

The Court of Justice, consisting of 13 judges, adjudicates on the meaning of the treaties and on any measures taken by the Council of Ministers and the Commission. It also hears complaints and appeals brought by or against Community institutions, member states or individuals and gives preliminary rulings on cases referred by courts in the member states. It is the final authority on Community law.

There is also a Court of First Instance, created to relieve the Court of Justice of some of its workload.

Court of Auditors

The Court of Auditors examines all Community revenue and expenditure to see that it has been legally received and spent, and to ensure sound financial management.

Policy Implementation

Community policies are implemented by:

- regulations which are legally binding on all member states;

- directives which are binding on member states to which they are addressed but which allow national authorities to decide on methods of implementation;

- decisions which are binding on those to whom they are addressed such as member states, firms or individuals; and

- recommendations and opinions which have no binding force.

The Council of Ministers can also indicate a general policy direction through resolutions.

Intergovernmental Conferences

Two intergovernmental conferences are considering economic and monetary union and reform of the Community's political institutions. Work began in December 1990 and this is expected to conclude in December 1991. Britain is taking an active part.

Finance

The Community is financed by:

● a system of levies on agricultural imports;

● customs duties;

● contributions from member states based on value added tax (VAT) levied on a harmonised base; and

● contributions from member states based on gross national product (GNP).

These are known as 'own resources'.

When it first joined the Community, Britain made a net contribution to the Community substantially in excess of that justified by its share of GNP. Following negotiations to put this right, Britain has received since 1984 an annual abatement of its contribution equal to two-thirds of the gap between its share of VAT contributions and its share of expenditure in the previous year.

Internal Policies

The Single Market

In Britain's view, completion of a genuine single market for goods and services should reduce business costs and stimulate increased efficiency.

The Single European Act commits member states to establish a genuine single market by the end of 1992, and 70 per cent of the programme is now agreed. It covers, for example, the liberalisation of capital movements, the mutual recognition of professional qualifications and the opening up of public procurement markets. Britain's current priorities include achieving further progress in the liberalisation of financial services, public procurement and transport.

Transport

Britain fully supports the further liberalisation of transport in the Community, for example the 1988 regulation to remove quotas on the movement of road haulage between member states by 1993 and a 1991 regulation increasing access to the market for air cargo operators licensed by member states. Britain is pressing for more competition in transport. The completion of the Channel Tunnel in 1993 will improve Britain's links with other member states.

Monetary Policy

Britain is a full participant in the European Monetary System, which consists of an exchange rate mechanism (ERM), the European Currency Unit (ECU) and enlarged short- and medium-term credit facilities. The ECU is based on a 'basket' of the Community currencies, the value of which is recalculated daily.

In 1989 the European Council approved the first stage of a plan for Economic and Monetary Union (EMU) drawn up by a committee of governors of central banks. This stage, implementation of which began in July 1990, envisages:

● improved economic and monetary policy co-ordination;

● the completion of the single market;

● the strengthening of competition policy; and

● all member states joining the ERM on equal terms.

Britain is fully committed to stage one but has some reservations about full monetary union.

During Community discussions on monetary policy, Britain has suggested the creation of a European Monetary Fund

(EMF) to manage the ERM, to co-ordinate exchange rate intervention with external currencies and to promote use of the ECU. Britain believes that the Fund could issue ECU bank notes for general circulation alongside member states' currencies, backed by EMF holdings of various Community currencies.

Research and Development

Community industrial collaboration is promoted primarily through a five-year Framework Programme for the period between 1990 and 1994, which defines priorities and sets out the overall level of funding.

British firms and other organisations have secured about 20 per cent of the funding and participate in between 50 per cent and 80 per cent of funded projects, depending on subject area; this gives good access to the results of the research.

The British Government played a large role in negotiations on the current Programme by ensuring that its objectives reflect the needs of British industry and that they complement other national and international programmes. British industry is expected to receive some £100 million from Community funds in 1991.

Under the current Programme, priority is being given to information technology (ESPRIT), telecommunications (RACE) and industrial materials and technologies (BRITE/EURAM). However, there are other important programmes covering the environment, biotechnology, agriculture, health and energy, along with new funding for the application of information technology—the Telematics programme. There is also a scheme for the exchange of researchers.

Together with a number of other European states and the European Commission, Britain participates in the EUREKA initiative, which encourages projects in high technology. EUREKA is concerned with the commercial exploitation of research and development and with removing barriers to commercial success.

Structural Funds

The main objectives of the Community's three Structural Funds, administered by the Commission, are to:

- promote economic development in poorer regions;
- convert regions seriously affected by industrial decline;
- combat long-term unemployment;
- find jobs for young people; and
- promote development in rural areas.

Infrastructure projects and productive investments are financed by the European Regional Development Fund. The European Social Fund supports training and employment measures for the long-term unemployed and young people. The European Agricultural Guidance Fund supports agricultural restructuring and some rural development measures.

Other Community programmes aim to assist the development of new economic activities in regions affected by the restructuring of the steel and coal industries.

In 1990 Britain received 15 per cent of lending within the Community by the European Investment Bank. As a non-profit-making institution, the Bank lends at competitive interest rates to public and private capital projects. Lending is directed towards:

- less favoured regions;
- transport infrastructure;
- protection of the environment; and
- improving industrial competitiveness.

The Bank also provides loans to small and medium-sized enterprises.

Employment and Social Affairs

Britain believes that Community social policy should concentrate on creating new jobs by encouraging competition within the internal market. The Government fully supports Community action on such issues as health and safety, equal opportunities and freedom of movement.

The Environment

Community environment policy is concerned with such issues as water and air pollution and the disposal of wastes. A regulation establishing the European Environment Agency was adopted by the Community in 1990; this is designed to bring together environmental information from existing bodies for the use of member states and the Commission.

In 1988 Britain and its Community partners agreed to reduce emissions of sulphur dioxide and nitrogen oxide from power stations, refineries and other industrial plants and to set stringent emission standards for new plants. Sulphur dioxide emissions are to be reduced by 60 per cent of 1980 levels by 2003, and nitrogen oxide emissions by 30 per cent of 1980 levels by 1998.

Member states are also taking action on car exhaust pollution; under these measures emissions of nitrogen oxide, carbon monoxide and hydrocarbons from each new car are being reduced by about 60 per cent. In addition, lead-free petrol is widely available throughout the Community.

In 1987 the Community signed the Montreal Protocol to the Vienna Convention for Protection of the Ozone Layer. In June 1990 an international conference in London, attended by nearly 60 developed and developing countries, agreed to phase out chlorofluorocarbons (CFCs) by 2000. It also agreed to phase out halons by 2000, except for agreed essential uses. Controls on other ozone-depleting chemicals—carbon tetrachloride and methyl chloroform—were also agreed; the use of the former will be phased out completely by 2000 and the latter by 2005. Britain believes that CFCs should be banned by 1997 and is pressing the Community to ensure that member states do this.

At the Third North Sea Conference in 1990, Britain, six other Community member states, Norway and Sweden agreed to phase out and destroy all remaining identifiable uses of polychlorinated biphenyls (PCBs) by 1999, to end incineration at sea by 1991 and to protect wildlife such as dolphins and porpoises. The Community has banned the import of harp and hooded seal pup skins and products. In June 1989 Britain banned imports of ivory from the African elephant, as did the Community in August 1989.

Agriculture

The Common Agricultural Policy (CAP) is designed to secure food supply and to stabilise markets. It has also, however, created overproduction and unwanted food surpluses, placing an increasing burden on the Community budget.

Britain is one of the main advocates of reform of the CAP. In 1988 it persuaded its partners to agree a limit on overall agricultural spending and measures under which automatic cuts are made in prices for a commodity if agreed production levels are exceeded. Britain is insisting on maintaining CAP budgetary discipline and wants more CAP reform.

Fisheries

Britain has a particular interest in the control of Community fishing, since a sizeable proportion of the total Community catch comes from British waters. It therefore takes an active role in Community fisheries policy negotiations on:

● access to coastal waters;

● conservation of fish stocks;

● the allocation of quotas among member states within each year's total allowable catch;

● enforcement; and

● measures to promote the adaptation and development of the Community's fishing fleet.

Political Co-operation

Member states form common positions on foreign policy questions. As the result of a British initiative, the Single European Act placed this political co-operation on a treaty basis. Member states are considering how to move towards a common foreign and security policy to replace political co-operation.

Eastern Europe and the Soviet Union

The twelve member states have welcomed the establishment of democracy in former Communist-ruled states in Central and Eastern Europe and the political and economic reforms in the Soviet Union. They are committed to helping these states in the change from centrally planned economies to market economies. The Twelve have welcomed the return to constitutional rule following the attempted coup in the Soviet Union in August 1991. They also recognised the independence of the Baltic states. The Twelve have also co-operated in the search for a peaceful solution to the crisis in Yugoslavia. They favour a secure and stable balance of forces in Europe at lower levels.

The Middle East

Community member states believe that a lasting solution to the Arab-Israeli dispute should be based on UN Security Council resolutions 242 and 338, which call for Israeli withdrawal from territories occupied in 1967 in exchange for security within guaranteed borders. The Twelve support the right of the Palestinian people to self-determination and the convening of a properly prepared international peace conference on the Middle East when the time is right. The Community has a development programme for the Arab territories occupied by Israel in 1967 and has adopted measures to allow direct exports of agricultural and industrial products from them to the Community market.

The Twelve condemned Iraq's invasion of Kuwait in August 1990 and urged Iraq to comply with UN Security Council resolution 660 calling for a withdrawal of its troops. They supported all subsequent Security Council resolutions against Iraq, including the imposition of economic sanctions and the authorisation of force to achieve Iraqi withdrawal from Kuwait.

Britain and France contributed ground, sea and air forces to a coalition led by the United States and Saudi Arabia which expelled Iraq from Kuwait in 1991 when peaceful means failed to secure Iraq's withdrawal. Other member states contributed warships or aircraft to this effort.

South Africa

The Twelve have welcomed reforms in South Africa which have abolished the core of statutory racial discrimination. The major changes announced since February 1990 have met many of the demands the Twelve have made, notably the release of Mr Nelson Mandela and other political prisoners, the lifting of the ban on the African National Congress and other organisations and the repeal of apartheid legislation. Regular meetings have taken place between representatives of the South African Government and the African National Congress. The Twelve have supported this process and expressed the hope that full constitutional negotiations may begin soon. To encourage more reforms and to help prevent the process being undermined by economic recession, the Twelve have lifted their 1986 ban on new investment and decided in principle to lift the bans on imports of iron and steel and gold coins. The Community has also substantially increased aid programmes to assist the victims of apartheid.

There is a voluntary code of conduct for EC companies with subsidiaries in South Africa which aims to improve conditions for black employees.

Terrorism and Crime

Member states have sought to act jointly against the threat posed by international and other terrorism. They have agreed not to export arms or other military equipment to countries clearly implicated in supporting terrorist activity and to take steps to prevent such material being diverted for terrorist purposes.

The Twelve believe that there should be no concessions made under duress to terrorists or their sponsors and that every effort should be made to prevent terrorism and to bring the guilty to justice. Counter-terrorist measures include a secure communications link between police forces and arrangements for regular assessments and analyses of terrorist threats to member states.

Regular meetings of ministers responsible for criminal justice take place to discuss common measures directed at terrorists and other criminals. Britain believes that, with the completion of the single market in 1992, some frontier checks will need to be retained to ensure that such people do not enjoy unlimited freedom to move throughout the Community.

Measures against Drug Trafficking

The Twelve attach great importance to co-operation against drug trafficking. Discussions on law enforcement, international co-operation, assistance to developing countries, education and health take place regularly. A committee co-ordinates anti-drugs work within the Community and the international aspects are dealt with by a political co-operation working group. Member states fully support the work of the United Nations in combating drug abuse. They also participate in regular meetings of the Council of Europe's Pompidou Group, which is concerned with anti-drugs measures. In June 1990 member states decided to set up a European drugs intelligence unit.

Trade

Under the Treaty of Rome, the European Commission negotiates on behalf of the Community in major international trade negotiations. The Community is seeking to extend the world open trading system on which member states depend for future growth and jobs and to defend the interests of its members against protectionist measures.

One of the Community's priorities is the successful conclusion of the Uruguay Round of trade negotiations launched in 1986. The negotiations seek to:

- strengthen the rules and disciplines of the General Agreement on Tariffs and Trade (GATT);

- liberalise trade in services and investment;
- improve protection of intellectual property;
- negotiate multilateral tariff reductions; and
- establish a fair and market-oriented system for agricultural trade.

The Community is negotiating an agreement with the European Free Trade Association (EFTA) under which the common internal market would be extended to EFTA members in January 1993.

The Community has association and co-operation agreements with all countries with a Mediterranean coastline (except Albania and Libya) and with Jordan; these give preferential access to Community markets. Non-preferential co-operation agreements have also been made with individual countries in South Asia and Latin America as well as with the People's Republic of China, the Association of South East Asian Nations, the Andean Pact and the Central American states. Trade relations with the developing countries of Africa, the Caribbean and the Pacific are governed by the Lomé Conventions (see p 80). Trade and co-operation agreements have been signed with Bulgaria, Czechoslovakia, Hungary, Poland, Romania, the Soviet Union and Yugoslavia. Building on these, association agreements are being negotiated with Czechoslovakia, Hungary and Poland.

The Community's Generalised System of Preferences grants tariff-free access to the Community market for most industrial goods from developing countries and varying degrees of preferential access for their agricultural produce (mainly processed) and textiles. The scheme concentrates benefits on the poorer producers and countries. Very few categories of exports from the more competitive producers are excluded.

The Commonwealth

The Commonwealth is a voluntary association of 50 independent states with a combined population of some 1,300 million, nearly a quarter of the world total. Commonwealth members include some of the richest and poorest nations of the world community and also some of the largest and smallest. Their peoples are drawn from practically all the world's main races, from all continents and from many faiths. Britain participates fully in all Commonwealth activities.

The members are Antigua and Barbuda, Australia, Bahamas, Bangladesh, Barbados, Belize, Botswana, Britain, Brunei, Canada, Cyprus, Dominica, The Gambia, Ghana, Grenada, Guyana, India, Jamaica, Kenya, Kiribati, Lesotho, Malawi, Malaysia, Maldives, Malta, Mauritius, Namibia, Nauru, New Zealand, Nigeria, Pakistan, Papua New Guinea, Saint Christopher and Nevis, Saint Lucia, Saint Vincent and the Grenadines, Seychelles, Sierra Leone, Singapore, Solomon Islands, Sri Lanka, Swaziland, Tanzania, Tonga, Trinidad and Tobago, Tuvalu, Uganda, Vanuatu, Western Samoa, Zambia and Zimbabwe. Nauru and Tuvalu are special members, entitled to take part in all Commonwealth meetings and activities, with the exception of Commonwealth Heads of Government meetings.

The Queen is recognised as head of the Commonwealth; she is also head of State in 17 of these countries.

Nearly all the Commonwealth countries were British territories to which independence was gradually granted, starting with the older territories such as Australia, Canada and New Zealand where European settlement had occurred on a large scale. The modern Commonwealth, comprising republics and national monarchies as well as monarchies under the Queen, became possible when it was agreed in 1949 that India, on becoming a republic, could continue to be a member. Since then, almost all of Britain's former dependent territories have attained their independence and have voluntarily joined the Commonwealth.

Consultation

Consultation between Commonwealth member states takes place through:

- meetings of heads of Government;
- specialised conferences of other ministers and officials;
- diplomatic representatives known as high commissioners;
- non-governmental organisations; and
- other international discussions.

Heads of Government meet every two years. Proceedings are held in private, facilitating a frank and informal exchange of views on international issues. No votes are taken, decisions being reached by consensus. Common views are set out in the communiqués issued at the end of the meetings. Occasionally, separate declarations are made on particular issues.

The apartheid system in South Africa has been a major concern for Commonwealth countries for many years. Now that apartheid is being abolished, Britain hopes that the Commonwealth will join in building the new society by helping to restore growth to the South African economy, and by drawing on the Commonwealth's experience with education and training programmes. Britain would support any application by the post-apartheid South Africa to rejoin the Commonwealth.

The Commonwealth has expressed concern about the security and development of the many small states among its members. Britain supports regional co-operation and provides economic aid and technical assistance. It is also British policy to consult with other Commonwealth states in the event of aggression against small member nations and to involve the UN Security Council where appropriate.

The Commonwealth Secretariat

The Commonwealth Secretariat promotes consultation and co-operation, disseminates information on matters of common concern, and organises heads of Government meetings, ministerial meetings and other conferences. It also administers the Commonwealth Fund for Technical Co-operation. Because of its neutral position the Secretariat has been able to make its good offices available in cases of dispute and has carried out, on request, special assignments requiring demonstrable impartiality. The Secretariat is financed by all member governments on an agreed scale, with Britain contributing 30 per cent of the total.

The Secretary General is elected by Commonwealth Heads of Government.

Technical Co-operation

Britain contributes 30 per cent of the income of the Commonwealth Fund for Technical Co-operation, which provides technical assistance for economic and social development in Commonwealth developing countries. The Fund helps to raise levels of technical, industrial, managerial and other skills, and makes wide use of expertise and training facilities within developing member countries for the benefit of other developing countries. It promotes industrial and export market development in poor countries.

Expenditure by Britain on bilateral technical co-operation with Commonwealth developing countries in 1990 was £201 million, the greater part being spent on financing staff for service with Commonwealth governments and in funding training places in Britain. The British Government also finances students from Commonwealth developing countries. Other assistance includes sending volunteers to serve overseas, consultancy services, the supply of training and research equipment, and advice given by British scientific and technical institutions. (About 70 per cent of Britain's gross bilateral aid goes to Commonwealth countries, including Britain's remaining dependencies—see below).

Commonwealth Organisations

Commonwealth Foundation

The Commonwealth Foundation, financed by member governments, promotes closer co-operation among professional and other non-governmental organisations within the Commonwealth. It has assisted over 30 Commonwealth professional associations,

and has helped in the creation and growth of many national ones; it has also supported 16 multidisciplinary professional centres. It is encouraging the strengthening of information links through the establishment of liaison units in each Commonwealth country.

The Commonwealth Institute

The Commonwealth Institute in London promotes the Commonwealth, its countries and its peoples to the British public. Funded mainly by the British Government, it has galleries of permanent exhibitions and a changing programme of temporary exhibitions, conferences and performances. Its education service runs an extensive programme of teaching about the Commonwealth in schools around Britain. A wide range of books and other materials can be borrowed.

The Commonwealth Trust

The Commonwealth Trust is a centre for study and discussion, its library in London housing one of the largest collections on the Commonwealth. The Trust has branches in many countries.

Other Organisations

Many unofficial organisations, professional bodies and voluntary societies are vehicles for co-operation. They include the Commonwealth Parliamentary Association, which organises an annual conference of parliamentarians, the Commonwealth Press Union, the Association of Commonwealth Universities, the Commonwealth Games Federation and the English Speaking Union of the Commonwealth.

DEPENDENCIES

Britain's 14 dependent territories have a combined population of about 6 million, of whom 5·8 million live in Hong Kong. Most territories have considerable self-government, with their own legislature and civil service.

ARCHITECTURE

Embankment Place is an office development which utilises the 'air rights' above the railway tracks at Charing Cross Station, London. Most of the superstructure hangs from arches assembled at roof level.

The international passenger terminal at Stansted Airport in Essex was officially opened by the Queen in March 1991. Inside, 36 columns support lightweight roof domes with triangular windows, allowing maximum daylight. Each column houses heating, lighting and air-conditioning and is the site for passenger information.

The President of Poland, Lech Walesa, and his wife, Danuta, with the Queen, the Duke of Edinburgh and the Queen Mother at Windsor Castle.

From the flightdeck of his ship HMS *Campbeltown* the Duke of York points out some of the sights at Portsmouth Harbour to the Queen, the Duke of Edinburgh and the Duchess of York.

The Prince and Princess of Wales at a tree-planting ceremony during their 1991 visit to Brazil.

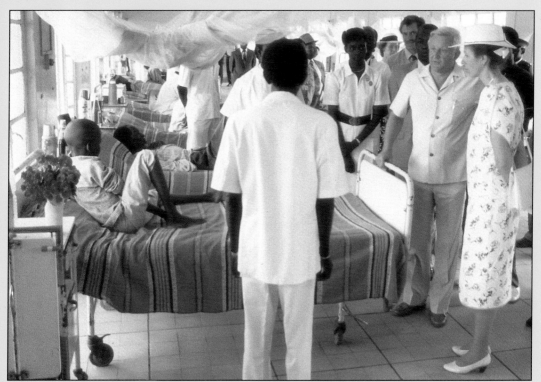

The Princess Royal visits the Royal Victoria Hospital in Banjul, Gambia, in her capacity as President of the Save the Children Fund.

JUSTICE AND THE LAW

Procession of the Lord Justices of Appeal at the House of Lords, Palace of Westminster, London.

Patricia Scotland, Britain's first black woman Queen's Counsel, after being sworn in at the House of Lords.

Britain is generally responsible for defence, internal security and foreign affairs. The territories are:

- Anguilla;
- Bermuda;
- British Antarctic Territory;
- British Indian Ocean Territory;
- British Virgin Islands;
- Cayman Islands;
- Falkland Islands;
- Gibraltar;
- Hong Kong;
- Montserrat;
- Pitcairn, Ducie, Henderson and Oeno;
- St Helena and St Helena Dependencies (Ascension and Tristan da Cunha);
- South Georgia and the South Sandwich Islands; and
- Turks and Caicos Islands.

Few are rich in natural resources, and some are scattered groups of islands. There are no permanent inhabitants in the British Antarctic Territory, British Indian Ocean Territory, South Georgia or the South Sandwich Islands.

Britain's policy is to give independence to those dependencies that want it and where it is practicable to do so.

The Falkland Islands are the subject of a territorial claim by Argentina but the inhabitants wish to retain the link with Britain. The Government is committed to the defence of the Islanders' right to live under a government of their own choosing. The Islanders' right of self-determination is set out in the 1985 Falkland Islands Constitution.

Gibraltar is the subject of a territorial claim by Spain. Britain wishes to see the development of practical co-operation between Gibraltar and Spain to the benefit of both peoples and remains committed to honouring the wishes of the people of Gibraltar as to their future, as set out in the 1969 Gibraltar Constitution.

Hong Kong

In 1984 an agreement was signed between Britain and the People's Republic of China on the future of Hong Kong, which is leased from China until 1997. Under the Sino-British Joint Declaration, which was ratified by the two governments in 1985, Britain is responsible for the administration of Hong Kong until 30 June 1997. Hong Kong will then become a Special Administrative Region (SAR) of China, but its capitalist system and lifestyle will remain unchanged for at least 50 years. With the exception of foreign affairs and defence, the Hong Kong SAR will enjoy a high degree of autonomy and its government and legislature will be composed of Hong Kong people.

In February 1990 the British Government announced that the Hong Kong Government would introduce 18 directly elected seats into the Legislative Council in 1991. Elections to these seats took place in September 1991. The ultimate aim is the election of all members of the Legislative Council by universal suffrage.

In April 1990 legislation was passed to give British citizenship to 50,000 key people in Hong Kong and their dependants without their having to leave the territory in order to qualify. Its purpose is to persuade these people to remain in Hong Kong so that the territory can remain stable and prosperous up to and beyond 1997.

International Peace and Security

Britain is pledged to maintain effective defence while seeking to reduce tension in the world. Since 1949 its defence has been based on membership of the North Atlantic Treaty Organisation (NATO), a defensive alliance based on the principle of collective security. In July 1990 NATO members reaffirmed their commitment to contribute towards the development of peaceful and friendly international relations.

East–West Relations

Britain has welcomed the recent progress made in East–West relations, the reforms being made in the Soviet Union, the recent replacement of Communist dictatorships by democratically elected governments in Eastern and Central Europe, and the unification of Germany. Britain is committed to increasing its official and unofficial contacts with the Soviet Union and the new governments in Eastern and Central Europe. Improvements in East–West relations include the agreement signed by 22 European and North American states in 1990 limiting the number of conventional weapons in Europe. Others include greater co-operation on regional issues— for example, Southern Africa—and the improved human rights provisions of the 1989 agreement signed by the countries participating in the Conference on Security and Co-operation in Europe (CSCE).

Economic Assistance

Britain recognises the magnitude of the task now being undertaken by the Soviet Union and the new governments in Central and Eastern Europe in transforming their centrally planned economies into market-based ones. The British Government's 'Know How' Fund is helping them by providing training in such areas as management and financial services, banking and accountancy, and commercial law. The Fund also finances the provision of advice on the running of a free media, democratic political parties and an independent judiciary. Britain is also supporting debt-rescheduling schemes being negotiated by the International Monetary Fund with several Eastern European countries. In addition, it is participating in other multilateral assistance plans, including World Bank loans and European Community agreements liberalising trade, aimed at encouraging the development of market economies.

Conference on Security and Co-operation in Europe

Britain welcomes the recent and significant improvements in the implementation of the provisions of the 1975 Helsinki Final Act. This established a large number of important political commitments and a code of behaviour for a more normal and open relationship between both governments and peoples in East and West. In order to achieve these goals, the signatories of the Final Act made undertakings about security, respect for human rights, and co-operation in economic, humanitarian and other matters. These commitments were developed at follow-up meetings, notably the Vienna meeting in November 1989, which agreed new commitments on human rights.

Meeting in Paris in November 1990, CSCE states agreed to the formal end of the Cold War. The Charter of Paris for a New Europe expressed commitment to democratic principles and to the principle of enshrining human rights and fundamental freedoms in a society based on the rule of law. States also agreed on a regular pattern of ministerial and summit meetings, supported by a permanent secretariat. A conflict prevention centre was established, as was an office to exchange information on democratic elections. A CSCE parliamentary assembly is also being established.

In June 1991 CSCE states agreed to a procedure allowing for special meetings to discuss emergency situations arising from a violation of one of the principles of the Final Act or as the result of incidents endangering peace, security or stability. These meetings would not require prior consensus of the participating states.

In 1986 participating states signed the Stockholm Document on confidence- and security-building measures designed to bring about a greater degree of openness and predictability in military activities. It provides for advance notification and observation of planned military manoeuvres (above specified thresholds) and the provision of detailed information on their purpose and size. Verification takes place in the form of on-site challenge inspections. In November 1990 CSCE states endorsed further measures, including detailed exchange of information on armed forces.

Arms Control

Together with its NATO allies, Britain is committed to the search for significant, balanced and verifiable measures of arms control. NATO priorities are further reductions as appropriate in United States and Soviet strategic nuclear arsenals, an agreement on short-range nuclear forces in Europe, a global ban on chemical weapons, and the elimination of conventional imbalances in Europe.

Nuclear Weapons

Britain strongly supported talks between the United States and the Soviet Union which led to the signature of the strategic arms reduction talks (START) treaty in July 1991. Britain fully shares the agreed objective of limiting and reducing nuclear arms and strengthening strategic stability.

Britain has welcomed the reciprocal decisions of the United States and the Soviet Union to eliminate unilaterally some of their nuclear weapons.

Nuclear Deterrent

Britain's strategic nuclear deterrent is the minimum necessary for credible deterrence and is very small in comparison with Soviet nuclear forces. It will continue to be a minimum force even after the replacement of the submarine-launched Polaris force by the modernised Trident missile system.

Britain believes that reductions should first take place in the arsenals of the United States and the Soviet Union. It does not exclude the possibility of British involvement in strategic arms control talks at some stage. However, even after the START treaty is implemented, the size of Britain's nuclear forces would in no way be comparable with those of the two superpowers.

Non-Proliferation

Britain is a party to the 1968 Non-Proliferation Treaty designed to stop the spread of nuclear weapons by ensuring that nuclear materials in non-nuclear-weapon states are not used for explosive purposes. It also protects the right of all countries to use nuclear energy for peaceful purposes.

Britain was the first nuclear-weapon state to conclude a voluntary agreement with the International Atomic Energy Agency for the application of safeguards to some nuclear installations. It has also undertaken not to use nuclear weapons against non-nuclear-weapon states which are parties to the Treaty or to other internationally binding commitments not to manufacture or acquire nuclear explosive devices. This undertaking would not apply in the case of an attack on Britain, its dependent territories, its armed forces or its allies by such a state in alliance with a nuclear-weapon state.

Nuclear Tests

Because of the need to preserve nuclear deterrence, there is a continuing requirement to conduct underground nuclear tests to ensure that Britain's nuclear weapons remain effective and up to date. Britain has welcomed the ratification by the United States and the Soviet Union of the 1974 Threshold Test Ban Treaty and the 1976 Peaceful Nuclear Explosions Treaty, which set ceilings on the yield of nuclear tests. Protocols on verification were signed by both countries in 1990. A comprehensive test ban remains a long-term goal, progress on which is dependent on improving prospects for effective verification as well as progress elsewhere in arms control and the attitude of other states.

Nuclear-Weapon-Free Zones

The Government thinks that the establishment of nuclear-weapon-free zones in certain parts of the world could contribute to regional security, to non-proliferation and to disarmament in general, provided that nuclear weapons do not already feature in the security of the region involved and that the balance of security is maintained.

Chemical and Biological Weapons

Britain is working towards a comprehensive and effectively verifiable worldwide ban on chemical weapons, having abandoned its own chemical weapons in the late 1950s. The negotiations for such a treaty take place at the Conference on Disarmament in Geneva, where Britain has presented a number of proposals, particularly, on the question of verification.

Pending achievement of a global ban, Britain and some other Western nations have imposed export controls on certain chemicals which may be used to produce chemical weapons in order to curb further proliferation of such weapons.

The Government has welcomed the US pledge to destroy all its chemical weapons stocks within ten years of a convention entering into force.

Biological weapons are already prohibited under a 1972 convention.

Conventional Weapons

Conventional weapons are by far the largest component of national armouries. In 1990 Britain and 21 other states signed an agreement (the CFE Treaty) covering reductions in conventional armed forces in Europe from the Atlantic to the Urals mountains.

The Treaty is designed to establish a balance of conventional forces at lower levels, while eliminating the danger of surprise attacks. It establishes limits on tanks, artillery, armoured combat vehicles, attack helicopters and combat aircraft. In addition, there is provision for a rigorous and intrusive verification regime. Britain played a major role in the negotiations.

The Gulf war demonstrated the danger of a nation building up an arsenal far beyond its legitimate defensive requirements. Britain believes that more openness is needed in this sphere, and proposed to the European Council in April the establishment of a UN

register of conventional arms transfers. This led to the Twelve adopting a declaration in which they stated that they would table a UN resolution setting up a register. Britain believes that this would introduce greater transparency in the arms trade, allow the scale of arms build-up in any one country to be monitored, and discourage destabilising sales to regions of tension.

Britain and the United Nations

Britain is fully committed to the principles of the United Nations and its Charter and believes that all member states should ensure that the organisation functions as effectively as possible to maintain peace, assist developing countries and protect human rights and freedoms. Britain is the sixth largest contributor to the UN budget, contributing nearly $45 million in 1991.

Keeping the Peace

Britain believes that the United Nations should seek to resolve disputes which threaten international peace and stability. As a permanent member of the Security Council, Britain has sought to develop and improve its role in the peaceful settlement of disputes.

Britain is the major contributor to the UN peacekeeping force in Cyprus and has provided logistic support to the UN Interim Force in Lebanon. It is also contributing personnel to the United Nations observer unit set up to monitor a demilitarised zone between Iraq and Kuwait, following the expulsion of Iraqi forces from Kuwait early in 1991 and has sent a contingent of observers to the western Sahara to participate in the monitoring operation established there.

Human Rights

Britain has consistently supported United Nations efforts to promote human rights through the establishment of internationally accepted standards. The UN Charter states that one purpose of the United Nations is to achieve international co-operation in promoting and encouraging respect for human rights and for fundamental freedoms for all. Britain believes that human rights are a legitimate matter for international concern. UN members pledge themselves to take joint and separate action in co-operation with the UN to promote universal respect for, and observance of, human rights and fundamental freedoms without distinction as to race, sex, language or religion.

Fundamental human rights provisions are set out in the Universal Declaration of Human Rights proclaimed by the General Assembly in 1948, and in the two International Covenants (one on Economic, Social and Cultural Rights and the other on Civil and Political Rights) which impose legal obligations on those who ratify them and which came into force in 1976. Britain has ratified both Covenants.

Britain is also a party to international conventions on:

- the elimination of racial discrimination;
- the elimination of all forms of discrimination against women;
- prevention of genocide;
- the abolition of slavery;
- the status of refugees and stateless persons;
- the political rights of women; and
- consent to marriage.

In 1988 Britain ratified the UN Convention against Torture, which had been adopted with British support by the General Assembly in 1984. Britain has signed the Convention on the Rights of the Child and intends to ratify it shortly.

Britain continues to support the idea of appointing representatives of the UN Commission on Human Rights to investigate human rights abuses. In 1991, Britain was elected to the Commission for a three-year term starting in 1992.

In 1985 Britain withdrew from the United Nations Educational, Scientific and Cultural Organisation (UNESCO). Although Britain supports the ideals and objectives contained in UNESCO's constitution, it has major doubts about the effectiveness with which the Organisation has pursued them. After a detailed review of UNESCO activities, Britain announced in 1990 that the reforms carried out were not yet sufficient to merit rejoining the Organisation. The funds saved from the withdrawal are allocated to a number of educational, scientific and cultural programmes in developing countries.

Britain's contributions to UN aid programmes for developing countries are described on p 79.

Other International Organisations

Britain is a member of many other international organisations, including the International Monetary Fund, established in 1945 (along with the World Bank) to regulate the international financial system and to provide a source of credit for member countries facing balance-of-payments problems.

Britain is also a member of the Organisation for Economic Co-operation and Development (OECD), an instrument for intergovernmental co-operation among 24 industrialised countries. The basic objectives of the OECD arc to promote the economic growth of its members, to help less developed countries within and outside its own membership and to encourage worldwide trade expansion.

Other organisations to which Britain belongs or extends support include the regional development banks in Africa, the Caribbean, Latin America and Asia and specialist technical, agricultural and medical institutions.

Britain is a founder member of the Council of Europe, which is open to any European parliamentary democracy accepting the rule of law and the protection of fundamental human rights and freedoms. The 26 member states co-operate on culture, education, sport, social questions, legal affairs, health, crime and drug prevention, youth affairs and the improvement of the environment.

The Council was responsible for the adoption in 1950 of the European Convention on Human Rights, which Britain was the first to ratify in 1951. Britain recognises the right of individual petition and the compulsory jurisdiction of the European Court of Human Rights.

Development Co-operation

The British aid programme for poor countries is designed to reduce poverty and promote sustainable economic and social development. Its main objectives include:

- supporting economic reform programmes which many countries are pursuing;

- promoting more open and accountable government;

- helping to lessen the pressure of excessive population growth;

- helping to protect the environment and conserve natural resources; and

- ensuring that poor people, and in particular women, share the benefits of development.

Gross public expenditure on the aid programme was £1,722 million in 1990. About 76 per cent of Britain's bilateral aid is directed to the poorest countries of the world. The Overseas Development Administration (ODA), responsible for Britain's aid policy, ensures that aid is correctly targeted and efficiently administered. Individual projects are carefully appraised before approval, monitored and then assessed on completion. British aid takes account of the recipient country's development priorities, the activities of other donors and the contribution that Britain can make in expertise, goods and services.

Economic Reform and Debt Rescheduling

Britain has taken a number of measures to assist the poorest and most heavily indebted countries pursuing policies of economic reform. These include:

- the cancellation of about £1,000 million of old concessional aid loans; and

- the giving of all new aid on grant terms.

Britain was the first major creditor to offer debt reduction on non-concessional debts owed to export credit agencies. This proposal led to agreement at the 1988 Toronto Economic Summit under which government creditors offered concessional debt reschedulings to the poorest countries pursuing economic reform. Twenty countries have benefited.

Britain is the largest contributor to the interest subsidy account of the IMF's Enhanced Structural Adjustment Facility, which lends on highly concessional terms to the poorest countries pursuing economic reforms.

At the Commonwealth Finance Ministers Meeting in September 1990, Britain proposed that the debts of the poorest countries to governments should be reduced by two-thirds with the balance payable over 25 years. This proposal is still under discussion.

Wider Effort

Britain's aid represents part of a wider Western effort to help developing countries. In 1990 total net official development assistance disbursed by the 18 countries belonging to the OECD's Development Assistance Committee amounted to $54,077 million.

Private Sector

In addition to official aid, the British private sector provides investment, technology and management expertise, and assists the development of indigenous resources and skills in developing countries. In 1990 estimated investment by British companies in developing countries amounted to £1,500 million. Trade, too, is important, developing countries providing over 12 per cent of British imports in 1990.

Official and Other Flows

In 1990 total official flows[1] of aid amounted to some £1,838 million net, of which £1,485 million represented official development assistance and £353 million other official flows.

Bilateral Aid

In 1990, about £839 million of gross public expenditure on overseas aid went to individual countries. Some 70 per cent of that directly allocated to countries went to the Commonwealth and to Britain's remaining dependencies. Total aid of £1,042 million was disbursed regionally as follows:

- Africa   £389 million
- Asia   £312 million
- Latin America and the Caribbean   £93 million
- Pacific   £28 million
- Middle East   £18 million
- Europe   £5 million
- Not allocable by continent   £197 million

Major recipients included Bangladesh, India, Kenya, Malawi, Zambia, Tanzania, Mozambique, Pakistan, Uganda and Indonesia.

Financial Aid

Gross bilateral financial aid in 1990 totalled £534 million. Aid for individual projects totalled £385 million. The main sectors supported were:

- Agriculture, fisheries and forestry   £63 million
- Manufacturing   £45 million
- Energy   £90 million
- Mining   £37 million
- Transport and communications   £70 million
- Social and community services   £28 million

Other financial aid totalled £150 million; of this £73 million was for programme aid, £37 million for debt relief, £21 million for disaster relief, £12 million for food aid and £6 million for budgetary aid.

Some 94 per cent of the ODA's bilateral financial aid in 1990 was provided in grants. Development aid to the poorest countries is on grant terms which also apply to the majority of recipients of British financial aid. There are simplified loan terms for those countries still not qualifying for grants.

Most financial aid—54 per cent in 1990 —is tied to the purchase of goods, equipment and services from Britain, although there may be a substantial element for local costs and foreign content in contracts financed from tied aid in appropriate cases. Commitments can be untied, if the recipient agrees, to enable goods to be purchased from the poorest developing countries as well as from Britain.

Aid Projects

More resources (£250 million) are being committed to the sustainable development of forestry. Britain is co-operating with Brazil to solve environmental problems, including schemes to manage and conserve the Amazon rain forest.

In 1989 Britain and India signed a £35 million aid agreement to improve primary education in the state of Andhra Pradesh in southern India; over 4,000 new classrooms will be built and over 1,100 teachers' centres upgraded, mostly in remote rural areas. It is also giving £50 million for Indian energy efficiency projects.

Direct British support is being given to over 200 community projects and to a private sector scheme designed to build new, low-cost owner-occupied homes in South Africa for the black population. Some £10 million of British aid was given to independent Namibia in 1990.

[1] 'Total official flows' is an international reporting concept. Its main component—official development assistance—is defined as official flows for development purposes with a grant (concessional) element of 25 per cent or more. The main British reporting concept is 'public expenditure on overseas aid', which excludes certain British flows which benefit developing countries but are not considered developmental, and by recording some contributions to multilateral agencies at a different time. All concepts can be measured before (gross) or after (net) deducting capital repayments.

Other British projects include:

- a major water and sanitation scheme in Karachi;
- the building of a power station in south-west Pakistan;
- the repair and maintenance of road bridges in Sierra Leone, Cameroon and Zaire;
- the rehabilitation of the Limpopo rail link between Zimbabwe and Maputo in Mozambique; and
- major repairs to the Maputo power station.

Aid and Trade Provision

The Aid and Trade Provision is designed to match the mixed credit practices of other donors by providing aid in combination with export credits to support sound investment projects offering commercial opportunities to British exporters. Expenditure under this provision amounted to £74 million in 1990.

Commonwealth Development Corporation

The Commonwealth Development Corporation (CDC) is empowered to invest in Commonwealth developing countries, in British dependencies and, with ministerial approval, in other developing countries.

By the end of 1990, the Commonwealth Development Corporation (CDC) had total commitments of £1,248 million in Africa, Asia, the Caribbean and Latin America, and the Pacific Islands. The main areas in which CDC investment took place were:

- **Basic development: £391 million;**
- **Primary production and processing: £601 million; and**
- **Industry and commerce: £256 million.**

Disaster Relief and Food Aid

Britain responds to disasters throughout the world by providing food, medical equipment, blankets, shelters and clothing, power generators, boats, bridges and other vital supplies. Britain is setting up an emergency aid procedure which will allow it to respond promptly and effectively to disasters.

British emergency aid was sent to Iran in 1990 following a severe earthquake. In sub-Saharan and southern Africa, Britain continued its contribution to disaster relief and food aid to help combat drought and famine. In addition to its multilateral aid contributions to UN agencies and the European Community (see pp 79–80), Britain gave £129 million in bilateral disaster relief in 1990. Bilateral and multilateral food aid by Britain amounted to £123 million.

Many African countries suffering from famine are also victims of locusts. Britain and three other countries are financing research on the biological control of locusts.

Britain also helps refugees and people displaced by famine, political upheaval, civil war and invasion. Since 1980, for instance, over £70 million has been contributed to assist Afghan refugees. Over £40 million was given to assist Iraqi refugees after April 1991; British forces were also committed by the Government to provide a safe haven in northern Iraq to which many Kurdish refugees returned.

Technical Co-operation

Expenditure on the transfer of specialised knowledge and skills was £452 million, nearly 43 per cent of gross bilateral aid, in 1990. The distribution was as follows:

- Expert personnel and volunteers   £91 million
- Students and trainees   £85 million
- Other education and training   £55 million
- Consultancy services   £78 million
- Research and development   £35 million
- Equipment and supplies   £27 million

At the end of 1990 there were nearly 1,500 people financed by Britain (other than volunteers or consultants) working in developing countries. In terms of person-years worked, 36 per cent were engaged in education, 19 per cent agriculture and related areas, and 8 per cent in health services.

In addition, there were nearly 1,437 volunteers, mainly qualified people with some relevant work experience, working in developing countries, about half in education. Recruitment, training and placing overseas are undertaken by voluntary bodies. The four main agencies are the Catholic Institute for International Relations, International Voluntary Service, United Nations Association International Service and Voluntary Service Overseas. More than 80 per cent of their costs are met by the Government.

Britain receives large numbers of students and trainees from developing countries. Approximately 15,000 were financed in 1990 under a variety of award schemes.

The ODA's scientific agency, the Natural Resources Institute, collaborates with developing countries on increasing the productivity of their renewable natural resources. The Government provides support for many other institutions, including overseas units/divisions of the Transport and Road Research Laboratory, the Building Research Establishment, the British Geological Survey, the Overseas Surveys Directorate of the Ordnance Survey, and of Hydraulics Research Ltd. These organisations provide specialist information, advice and experts for service overseas, and undertake field and laboratory research investigations.

International Agencies

Some 40 per cent of British aid is channelled through international agencies.

The United Nations

The UN system is the largest single source of technical assistance for developing countries.

In 1990 Britain contributed £20 million to the World Health Organisation and £9·6 million to the Food and Agriculture Organisation. British contributions to the UN's voluntary funds, which help developing countries and provide emergency and relief aid, including help to refugees, are as follows:

- UN Development Programme £27·0 million
- UN High Commissioner for Refugees £19·5 million
- UN Relief and Works Agency for Palestinian Refugees £5·6 million
- UN Children's Fund £9·3 million
- UN Population Fund £3·0 million
- World Food Programme £4·2 million

Britain is the largest source of expertise and the second largest of fellowships and equipment provided under the UN Development Programme.

Britain encourages the deployment of UN resources towards the poorest countries and the poorest communities in the developing world. It also seeks to promote the most efficient use of UN development funds and improvements in the co-ordination, control and effectiveness of the system.

World Bank Group

Britain is a major subscriber to the World Bank group of institutions which includes the International Bank for Reconstruction and Development and the International Development Association (IDA).

The resources of the IDA, which provides interest-free loans to developing countries unable to service loans on conventional terms, are replenished at three-year intervals. The British commitment to its Ninth Replenishment, covering the three years starting in 1991, is £619 million towards a total of US$17,000 million.

Britain has welcomed the creation by the International Monetary Fund of facilities to provide special assistance to developing countries experiencing financial or trading difficulties.

European Community

Almost half of British multilateral aid goes to European Community aid programmes. The largest of these is the Lomé Convention which governs aid, trade and co-operation between the Community and 69 developing countries in Africa, the Caribbean and the Pacific (ACP).

Under the current Convention—the fourth in a series—which was signed in 1989, Britain's commitment to Community aid over the next five years is £1,300 million out of a total of £8,500 million. The Convention will run for ten years with provision for review after five years; there will be two European Development Funds, each lasting five years.

The Convention provides for aid totalling over £7,700 million for the first five years and up to £850 million in loans from the European Investment Bank over the same period. It also covers emergency industrial and agricultural co-operation. There is a scheme designed to help stabilise the agricultural and commodity export earnings of the ACP countries and assistance for ACP producers of certain products whose output and income suffer from temporary disruptions beyond their control. There is a special allocation of £810 million for countries undertaking economic reform. In addition, the Convention offers duty-free access to the Community for ACP exports of most agricultural goods, including special arrangements for sugar, bananas, rum and beef and industrial products satisfying the rules of origin.

All British dependent territories (with the exception of Bermuda, Gibraltar and Hong Kong), together with the overseas territories of other Community members, are formally associated with the Community under provisions parallel to those of the Lomé Convention.

The Community's aid programme for developing countries in Asia and Latin America not covered by the Lomé Convention or having any other special relationship with the Community will be worth some £1,925 million for the period between 1991 and 1995. Priority is given to rural development and agricultural production in the poorest countries, most of which are in Asia, and economic co-operation with the better-off countries.

Co-operation and association agreements with individual countries and regional groupings also include provision for development aid. In 1987, for instance, new five-year financial protocols were agreed with most of the Community's Mediterranean partners. These provide for £430 million of Community aid and £706 million in loans from the European Investment Bank.

The Community's food aid programme is designed to be an effective instrument of development policy. In 1990 it spent some £349 million on food aid, of which Britain's share was £77 million, much of which went to Africa.

Other Bodies

Britain contributes to the Asian Development Bank, the Inter-American Development Bank, the Caribbean Development Bank and the African Development Bank.

Voluntary Agencies

Voluntary agencies raise funds for use in developing countries in such areas as agriculture, health and nutrition, education projects, and emergency relief operations.

There are more than 200 agencies, including church and missionary societies. Among the best known are Oxfam, Christian Aid, the Save the Children Fund, and the Catholic Fund for Overseas Development. The funds are raised through regular donations and collections, legacies and trading activities. Special funds are set up to cope with emergencies. The Government meets half the cost of about 1,260 selected development projects undertaken by the agencies and aimed at helping the poorest people; over £20 million was contributed by the Government in 1990–91. In 1989–90 the Government gave over £65 million to the activities of voluntary agencies.

4 Defence

The primary objectives of Britain's defence policy are to ensure the country's security, to preserve peace with freedom, and to enable it to pursue its legitimate interests both within Britain and overseas. Britain's policy is based on membership of the North Atlantic Treaty Organisation (NATO), a defensive alliance whose collective strength continues to provide each of its members[1] with far greater security than any could achieve alone.

Britain supports the new democratic governments in Eastern Europe and welcomes the quickening pace towards democracy in the Soviet Union and its republics. It believes that British security can best be protected by the continuing maintenance of collective defence with its NATO allies. At the same time, Britain and its NATO partners have recognised the need to readjust their military structure and strategy to the new security position arising from these developments and have outlined ways in which this will be done.

Most of the defence budget goes, directly or indirectly, towards carrying out Britain's main defence roles in NATO, to which the majority of its armed forces are committed. In recent years the structure and balance of these forces have been improved to increase their combat effectiveness. As a result of these improvements Britain also has the flexibility to respond quickly and effectively to challenges to its interests outside the NATO area.

Changes in Europe

There have been important and welcome political and military changes in the Soviet Union and Eastern Europe in the past few years. These include:

- the unification of Germany as a sovereign state within NATO;
- the break-up of the Warsaw Pact as a military alliance;
- the withdrawal of all Soviet forces from Hungary and Czechoslovakia;
- the withdrawal by 1994 of Soviet forces from Germany; and
- the collapse of Communism in the Soviet Union.

NATO is, however, still needed to provide continuing stability and security during a period of great political uncertainty in Europe. Britain also believes that NATO provides the most effective forum for transatlantic political co-operation and consultation on security and arms control, for co-ordinating the implementation of arms control agreements and for establishing the basis for further negotiations.

NATO Policy

NATO is a political and military alliance of countries sharing a common commitment to peace, democracy and the rule of law. Its aims are:

- to prevent war and maintain the security of its members at the lowest possible levels of forces;
- to deter potential aggression by maintaining a balanced mix of nuclear and conventional forces, based in Europe and kept up to date as necessary; and
- to provide a transatlantic forum for allied consultation.

In a joint declaration in July 1990, the allies reaffirmed their commitment to defend

---

[1] NATO's 16 member countries are Belgium, Britain, Canada, Denmark, France, Germany, Greece, Iceland, Italy, Luxembourg, the Netherlands, Norway, Portugal, Spain, Turkey and the United States.

the territory of all NATO members. However, they also recognised that, as Europe was changing militarily and politically, the Alliance should alter its structure and strategy to meet the new security environment. Alliance strategy in future will include:

- the deployment of smaller, highly mobile forces;
- more multinational units; and
- reduced reliance on nuclear weapons.

NATO leaders also agreed to develop further the Alliance's political dimension, initiating, for example, measures to achieve closer relations with the former Warsaw Pact countries.

Britain plays a full part in the Alliance's efforts to negotiate balanced and verifiable arms control agreements. NATO seeks:

- the ratification and full implementation of the 1990 Conventional Armed Forces in Europe (CFE) agreement;
- a new agreement to limit armed forces' personnel to restrain further offensive capabilities in Europe; and
- additional confidence- and security-building measures to create greater openness.

Britain is playing a leading part in work aimed at establishing a United Nations register of arms transfers to promote greater transparency and confidence. It also participates in negotiations at the Conference on Disarmament in Geneva. The most important issue under discussion is a global ban on chemical weapons.

The NATO allies have acknowledged that Western interests outside the NATO area may be threatened and they recognise the need, in the last resort, for those members with the means to do so to take action in consultation with their allies.

Britain's NATO Contribution

Britain's contribution to NATO is concentrated in areas where it can best help to maintain Alliance security, principally NATO's strategic nuclear deterrent and the defence of the European mainland, the

Eastern Atlantic and English Channel, and the British 'home' base and its immediate approaches.

Because of the changes in the European security situation, Britain is reducing the forces it commits to NATO, although it will continue to make a substantial contribution in each of these areas.

Britain's strategic forces, equipped with improved Polaris missiles (to be replaced by a Trident force from the mid-1990s), provide an independent and European centre of decision-making within the Alliance, thereby guarding against any misconception that Europe's defence is ultimately dependent on the US nuclear guarantee. Britain has also committed its other nuclear systems to NATO.

Virtually all of the Royal Navy (RN) is committed to the Alliance. Permanent contributions are made to NATO's two standing naval forces, in the Atlantic and the Channel, and to its Mediterranean force when activated. The British Army of the Rhine (BAOR) and Royal Air Force (RAF) Germany are being restructured.

Nearly all the RAF's combat and support aircraft are assigned to NATO. RAF Germany's squadrons of combat aircraft and helicopters are equipped for strike/attack, reconnaissance, close support, air defence and air transport roles. RAF Strike Command, which is based in Britain, provides forces for these and for the maritime patrol and anti-submarine warfare roles.

Britain also contributes ships and commando units to a British–Dutch amphibious force, ground and air units for the Allied Command Europe Mobile Force, and several squadrons for NATO's Strategic Air Reserve.

RN and RAF units are stationed at Gibraltar, which, positioned at the western entry to the Mediterranean, is an important base for NATO.

Britain's Defence for the 1990s

Because of the reduction in East–West tension in Europe and progress in arms control negotiations, the Government has proposed changes in Britain's defence structure. The strategic deterrent and a sub-strategic nuclear force, provided by dual-capable aircraft, will be retained. The air defence of Britain will be undertaken by seven Tornado F3 squadrons, supplemented by Hawk fighters. Airborne early warning will be the task of Boeing aircraft. Home defence forces and the fleet of mine counter-measures vessels will be maintained at a substantial level.

Although Britain will continue to play a full part in the defence of Europe, British forces stationed in Germany will be reduced to half their existing strength by the mid-1990s. When reinforced, Britain's land contribution to the defence of mainland Europe will comprise two divisions rather than four as at present. These forces will represent Britain's main contribution to the new Allied Command Europe Rapid Reaction Corps. In addition, Britain will provide the commander for this new corps.

RAF Germany will be reduced to six fixed-wing squadrons, and two of the four RAF bases in Germany will close. There will be a reduced force of support helicopters. An amphibious force will be retained to reinforce NATO's northern region, as will the ability to provide air support to defend that area. One of the two divisions assigned to the Rapid Reaction Corps will also be able to undertake a range of operations beyond the NATO area.

The Government proposes that Britain's maritime contribution to NATO should continue to include three aircraft carriers, a force of destroyers and frigates (reduced to about 40), nuclear-powered and conventional submarines, and Nimrod maritime patrol aircraft.

These changes will mean a reduction of 20 per cent in the strength of the armed forces to around 55,000 in the Royal Navy and the Royal Marines; 116,000 in the Army; and 75,000 in the Royal Air Force. The number of headquarters staff and civilian personnel employed by the Ministry of Defence will be similarly reduced.

Europe and the Alliance

Britain's contribution to NATO is part of the wider effort which the European allies make to Alliance defence. The European allies provide the majority of NATO forces, as well as communications, transport and military facilities for United States forces.

Britain and its European allies play a full part in the Independent European Programme Group, which promotes arms co-operation among European allies, and in the Conference of National Armaments Directors, the forum for defence equipment collaboration across the Atlantic. They also work together in the Eurogroup to improve their contributions to the Alliance and to achieve better use of available resources. In addition, the Western European Union (WEU)[2] provides further impetus towards European defence and security co-operation. The WEU helped to co-ordinate contributions by member countries in mine clearance operations in the Gulf during the Iran–Iraq war in the late 1980s; in 1990–91 WEU members agreed to co-ordinate their participation in the multinational campaign in the Gulf (see p 84).

Britain believes that the WEU can provide a focus for a more coherent European defence identity and act as a bridge between NATO and the foreign and security policies of the 12 members of the European Community.

Outside the NATO Area

Britain maintains the ability to operate outside the NATO area to protect its interests without diminishing its commitment to the Alliance. It has an airborne brigade which can be deployed to trouble spots should the need arise. Under the new force structure Britain will have the ability to deploy parachute, airmobile and mechanised formations outside the NATO area as necessary.

Britain provides the largest national troop contingent to the United Nations Force in

---

2 WEU members are Belgium, Britain, France, Germany, Italy, Luxembourg, the Netherlands, Portugal and Spain.

Cyprus, as well as giving support for the United Nations Interim Force in Lebanon; it also contributes a detachment to the Multinational Force and Observers in Sinai. Britain contributed significant contingents to the multinational force deployed in the Middle East after the invasion of Kuwait by Iraq in 1990–91; it also made contributions to the UN force in southern Iraq and to the military force providing protection to Iraqi refugees in northern Iraq.

Considerable effort is devoted to the provision of military assistance and training to about 30 countries outside NATO, and Britain deploys its forces on visits and exercises in important areas.

British garrisons are maintained in Belize, Brunei, Cyprus, the Falkland Islands and, until 1997, Hong Kong.

Northern Ireland

The armed forces continue to support the Royal Ulster Constabulary (RUC) in the fight against terrorism in Northern Ireland. The Army provides ten regular units and nine battalions of the Ulster Defence Regiment (UDR). The Government has announced plans to merge the UDR with another regiment. The RN, which carries out patrols to prevent arms smuggling, and the RAF also make substantial contributions; the Royal Marines support Army and Navy operations.

THE ARMED FORCES

Personnel

On 1 April 1991 the strength of the regular armed forces, all volunteers, was about 298,100: 62,100 in the Royal Navy and the Royal Marines, 147,600 in the Army and 88,400 in the Royal Air Force. The Ministry of Defence employed about 140,200 civilians (based in Britain) at the same date.

The 18,600 female personnel in the nursing and women's services (4,100 in the Royal Navy, 7,200 in the Army and 7,200 in the RAF) serve alongside servicemen in Britain and overseas.

Commissioned Ranks

Commissions, either by promotion from the ranks or by direct entry based on educational and other qualifications, are granted for short, medium and long terms. All three Services have schemes for school, university and college sponsorships.

Commissioned ranks receive initial training at the Britannia Royal Naval College, Dartmouth; the Royal Military Academy, Sandhurst; or the Royal Air Force College, Cranwell. This is followed by specialist training, often including degree courses at Service establishments or universities.

Higher training for officers is provided by the Royal Naval College, Greenwich; the Army Staff College at Camberley; and the Royal Air Force Staff College at Bracknell. Selected senior officers and civilian officials from Britain attend the Joint Services Defence College, Greenwich, and the Royal College of Defence Studies, London, which is also attended by officers and officials from other countries. These provide the wider background necessary for those destined to fill higher appointments.

Non-commissioned Ranks

Engagements for non-commissioned ranks range from three to 22 years, with a wide choice of length and terms of service. Subject to a minimum period of service, entrants may leave at any time, at 18 months' notice (12 months for certain engagements). Discharge may also be granted on compassionate grounds, by purchase, or on grounds of conscience.

Throughout their Service careers non-commissioned personnel receive basic training supplemented by specialist training. Study for educational qualifications is encouraged and Service trade and technical training lead to nationally recognised qualifications.

Reserve Forces

Trained reserve and auxiliary forces supplement the regular forces on mobilisation and are able immediately to take their places either as formed units or as individual reinforcements. They are also a link between the Services and the civil community. Some members of these forces become reservists following a period of regular service (regular reserve); others are volunteers who train in their spare time. Volunteer reserve forces include the Territorial Army (TA), whose role is to reinforce the ground forces committed to NATO and to help maintain a secure home base in Britain. Set up in 1985, a Home Service Force, linked to the TA and with a current strength of about 3,200, would on mobilisation assist in guarding important civilian and military installations.

Other volunteer forces include the Royal Naval and Royal Marines Reserves, the Royal Naval Auxiliary Service, the Royal Auxiliary Air Force and the Royal Air Force Volunteer Reserve. All, except the Royal Naval Auxiliary Service, have been expanded substantially in recent years or are planned to increase in strength in the near future. The Ulster Defence Regiment (see p 84) is also a reserve force.

At the beginning of 1991 regular reserves totalled 257,000 and volunteer reserves and auxiliary forces 90,200. The strength of the cadet forces, which make a significant contribution to recruitment to the regular forces, was 130,200.

COMBAT FORCES

Strategic Nuclear Forces

The Royal Navy's Polaris force comprises four nuclear submarines, each of which can remain on underwater patrol for long periods and is capable of carrying 16 nuclear-armed Polaris missiles. The missile system, incorporating improvements designed to penetrate anti-ballistic missile defences, will maintain the force's effectiveness until it is replaced from the mid-1990s by four Trident nuclear submarines. They will extend Britain's independent nuclear deterrent into the twenty-first century.

The Trident programme, which will cost an estimated £9,863 million (at 1990–91 prices), is expected to account on average for less than 3 per cent of the defence budget (and less than 6 per cent of the equipment budget) during its procurement period. It is also estimated that about 70 per cent of the money for the project will be spent in Britain.

Three of the submarines designed to carry Trident missiles are under construction; the invitation to tender for the fourth was issued in 1991.

Royal Navy Combat Forces

Britain's naval forces, while capable of operating throughout the world when required, are concentrated in the Eastern Atlantic and in the Channel, where they constitute the majority of naval forces immediately available to NATO. Their primary role is anti-submarine warfare. The Royal Navy includes:

- three Invincible-class anti-submarine warfare carriers, deploying Sea King anti-submarine and airborne early warning helicopters, Sea Harrier aircraft, and Sea Dart air defence missiles;

- 14 nuclear-powered attack submarines (with another one on order), equipped with torpedoes and anti-ship missiles; and

- six diesel-electric-powered submarines, including the more powerful Upholder class, the first two of which have entered service.

In addition to the four ballistic missile submarines, Britain's submarine force will be reduced to about 16 vessels by the mid-1990s, three-quarters of which will be nuclear powered.

The Royal Navy also has 46 destroyers and frigates (including the first three of the new Type 23 frigate) for air defence, anti-submarine and general purpose duties. These are to be reduced to about 40. Most of these vessels have weapon-carrying helicopters, and their armaments include surface-to-surface, air defence, and anti-ship missiles. There are also Royal Marines forces, specialist amphibious shipping and supporting vessels. Other ships include mine counter-measures vessels, and offshore patrol vessels for protecting fishing interests and oil and gas installations.

In future Britain's contribution to NATO's maritime defence will be made up of nuclear-powered attack submarines and advanced diesel-electric conventional submarines; the Type 23 frigate (of which a further seven have been ordered and tenders invited for up to three more); and Nimrod maritime patrol aircraft, equipped with Searchwater radar and armed with Harpoon anti-ship missiles and Stingray anti-submarine torpedoes. In addition, the surface fleet has been strengthened by 14 multi-role Type 22 frigates and by the new Sandown class of minehunter, of which two are in service and a further three on order.

New or improved weapons will include the Harpoon missile for the last four Type 22 and for the new Type 23 frigates, the Sea Eagle anti-ship missile, Goalkeeper rapid firing guns, and, for submarines, the Spearfish torpedo. The Sea Wolf and Sea Dart air defence missiles are also being developed or improved. The Type 23 frigate, which is to be armed with the ship- or air-launched Stingray torpedo, is planned to deploy the EH101 helicopter when that enters service later in the decade. The Navy's Sea Harriers are being updated.

Army Combat Forces

The three armoured divisions currently in BAOR include 12 armoured regiments; five of these are equipped with Chieftain tanks while the other seven have the more modern Challenger. From the mid-1990s when there will be one British armoured division based in Germany, Chieftain will be replaced by the new Challenger 2 tank. The mobility and fire power of the armoured infantry is being enhanced by the continued introduction of the Warrior mechanised infantry combat vehicle. Deployment also continues of the

SA80 rifle and the light anti-tank weapon, LAW80, which have markedly improved the infantry's firepower.

The multiple launch rocket system is entering service; it will be enhanced by rockets able to lay anti-tank mines at long range. A new attack helicopter will be ordered for the Army. In the meantime improvements are being made to the Lynx anti-tank helicopter, more of which are being acquired.

Major improvements to the Army's air defences are planned for the 1990s, including the introduction of the Starstreak missile, the next generation of Rapier missiles and a new air defence command and control system. The need for other types of sophisticated command, control and communications systems is being met by the PTARMIGAN secure communications, the WAVELL computerised battlefield information and the BATES artillery targeting systems, among others.

Royal Air Force

Following the withdrawal from service of Phantom aircraft by mid-1993, seven squadrons of Tornado F3 aircraft—together with Rapier surface-to-air missiles and Oerlikon guns directed by Skyguard radar—will provide Britain's air defence. They will be assisted by seven Boeing airborne early warning (AEW) aircraft which are entering service, and the ground radars and command, control and communication systems of the improved United Kingdom Air Defence Ground Environment. In addition, a number of Hawk trainer aircraft have been equipped with air-to-air missiles and cannon for local air defence. The strike/attack fleet is equipped with the Tornado GR1; a variant of this aircraft is replacing some Jaguars to provide reconnaissance. Close air support for ground troops is provided by the Harrier GR5/GR7 and Jaguar aircraft.

Nimrod maritime aircraft form part of Britain's anti-submarine warfare force, and also undertake long-range surveillance operations against surface ships, as well as providing offshore surveillance and fishery protection. The Buccaneer currently employed in an anti-ship role will be replaced by Tornado GR1s armed with the Sea Eagle missile.

Victor, TriStar and VC10 aircraft are used as tankers for in-flight refuelling. Tactical transport is provided by VC10 and Hercules aircraft, while Chinook, Puma and Wessex helicopters provide tactical support to ground forces. Sea King and Wessex helicopters perform search and rescue duties around the British Isles. Weapons in service include Skyflash, Sparrow, Sidewinder, Martel and Sea Eagle missiles, and guided and cluster bombs.

Improvements to Britain's air defence include the modernisation of the Tornado F3 radar, better communications and control systems and the introduction of the Boeing AEW aircraft. The ability of the Tornado GR1 to attack at night will be enhanced; the new Harrier GR5 is also being upgraded to a night-attack version, GR7, the first squadron of which became operational in 1991. All strike/attack and offensive support aircraft will be fitted with advanced electronic warfare equipment to increase their ability to survive. The Tornado GR1, already equipped with the British JP233 airfield attack weapon, will have the ALARM anti-radiation missile. It is expected that the European Fighter Aircraft, which is being developed by Britain, Germany, Italy and Spain, will complement the Tornado F3. Air-to-air refuelling capacity is being increased by converting more VC10 aircraft into tankers; a force of 13 aircraft is planned. The Chinook helicopter fleet is being updated.

Finance and Management

The defence budget for 1991–92 is over £24,000 million. Britain remains one of the highest contributors to NATO, with about £670 per capita spent on defence in 1990; 4 per cent of gross domestic product was devoted to defence expenditure, a proportion only exceeded in NATO by Greece, Turkey and the United States.

Increased competition in the letting of contracts has improved both quality and value for money. About 39 per cent of Britain's defence expenditure is devoted to the purchase of equipment.

Organisation and Management

Within the Ministry of Defence a military–civilian Defence Staff is responsible for defence policy and strategy, operational requirements and commitments. An Office of Management and Budget handles budgets and resources. Each Service Chief of Staff reports through the Chief of Defence Staff to the Secretary of State on matters related to the fighting effectiveness, management, efficiency and morale of his Service. The management of the three services is exercised through executive committees of the Service Boards, which are chaired by their respective Chiefs of Staff and act in accordance with centrally determined policy objectives and budgets. The Procurement Executive deals with the purchase of equipment, including equipment collaboration with allies and friendly nations.

Under a new system of budgeting, military and civilian managers are allowed greater discretion in the most efficient use of their allocated resources. This new approach is designed to promote better value for money, and to provide clear direction for local managers.

Defence Procurement

About £9,271 million is being spent on defence equipment in 1991–92, making the Ministry of Defence British industry's largest customer. Contracts are awarded by open international competition where possible, and strict guidelines ensure that companies are given the maximum incentive to perform efficiently.

Research and Development

Research is undertaken by the Ministry's research establishments and under contract in industry and the universities.

Nearly all design and development of defence equipment is carried out by industry. The Ministry seeks to involve industry in the research programme and to promote civil applications. As part of the Government's policy of improving the strength of Britain's science base, the Ministry, together with the research councils, makes joint grants to academic institutions in areas of research relevant to defence. In order to obtain better value for money, the Ministry's four main non-nuclear research and development establishments were combined into the Defence Research Agency, which began operating in 1991. Another research organisation—the Chemical and Biological Defence Establishment—was launched as a Defence Support Agency in 1991.

Around £425 million is expected to be spent on defence research and £2,500 million on development in 1991–92.

Alliance Co-operation

International co-operation has been a feature of armaments procurement for over 20 years, and Britain was one of its pioneers in programmes such as the British-French Jaguar aircraft and the Lynx, Puma and Gazelle helicopters; the FH70 towed howitzer developed jointly with Germany and Italy; and the successful Tornado aircraft developed and produced with the same two partners. Britain also worked with the United States on the Harrier GR5.

In order to make better use of limited resources, Britain plays an active role in NATO's Conference of National Armaments Directors, and the Independent European Programme Group. In the latter, ten member countries are following Britain and France in publishing bulletins of contract opportunities, so helping to open up the European defence equipment market.

Major new collaborative programmes under way include:

- the EH101 helicopter (with Italy);
- the new European Fighter Aircraft (with Germany, Italy and Spain);
- the multiple-launch rocket system (with France, Germany, Italy and the United States); and

- anti-tank guided weapons (with France and Germany).

Civil Defence

Civil defence arrangements are based on the extended and adapted use of the peacetime resources of government departments, local authorities, emergency services and nationalised industries, supplemented by the efforts of voluntary organisations and individual volunteers. Civil defence regulations require local authorities to make and keep up to date plans for a range of essential functions in the event of war; to arrange training and exercises for civil defence staff and volunteers; and to provide suitable emergency centres for the direction of civil defence in wartime. Following legislation in 1986, local authorities may use their civil defence resources in responding to peacetime emergencies.

Expenditure on civil defence has been growing steadily and was about £129 million in 1990–91. This is being used to:

- improve the quality and readiness of central and local government planning;
- increase training opportunities arranged by the Home Office on staff college lines at the Emergency Planning College, Easingwold;
- help local authorities to plan for better community involvement in civil defence; and
- improve the emergency system for decentralised government control and communications.

Improvements are also being made in the communications, equipment and administrative facilities of the United Kingdom Warning and Monitoring Organisation. This includes the civilian Royal Observer Corps, which is organised to provide public warning of an attack, of the location and strength of nuclear explosions, and of the distribution and level of radioactive fall-out.

5 Justice and the Law

England and Wales, Scotland and Northern Ireland all have their own legal systems, with considerable differences in law, organisation and practice. However, a large volume of modern legislation applies throughout Britain.

The main sources of law are government legislation, common law and European Community law. Common law is the ancient law of the land deduced from custom and interpreted by judges; it has never been precisely defined or codified but forms the basis of the law except when superseded by legislation. European Community law is confined mainly to economic and social matters; in certain circumstances it takes precedence over domestic law. It is normally applied by the domestic courts, but the most authoritative rulings are given by the Community's Court of Justice.

Certain changes to United Kingdom law have been made following rulings of the European Court of Human Rights. These arose where domestic law was in breach of the Council of Europe's Convention for the Protection of Human Rights and Fundamental Freedoms, to which Britain is a party.

Criminal Justice

The aims of the criminal justice system are:

- to prevent and reduce crime where possible;

- to help victims;

- to deal fairly, justly and without delay with those suspected, accused or convicted of offences;

- to convict the guilty and acquit the innocent; and

- to punish suitably those found guilty.

Public expenditure on the criminal justice system has increased in real terms by 50 per cent since 1979, and in 1990–91 it stood at £11,120 million. Extra spending has taken place on the police, the probation service and prison building. More than two-thirds of expenditure is initially incurred by local government authorities, with the help of central government grants, mainly on the police.

Crime Statistics

Differences in the legal systems, police recording practices and statistical classifications in the countries of Britain make it impracticable to analyse in detail trends in crime for the country as a whole. Nevertheless, it is clear that, as in Western Europe generally, there has been a substantial increase in crime since the early 1950s. However, annual official statistics cover only crime recorded by the police and can be affected by changes in the proportion of crimes which are undiscovered or unreported.

Table 5.1 gives the crime figures for England and Wales.

The Scottish police recorded 959,000 crimes and offences, of which 32 per cent were cleared up. In Northern Ireland just over 57,000 crimes were recorded, of which 38 per cent were cleared up. Crime tends to be concentrated in inner cities and deprived areas; the risk of burglary can be as high as one in ten houses a year in inner city areas, compared with one in 100 in rural areas. Rising affluence has provided more opportunities for casual property crime. In 1957, for example, car crime was only 10 per cent of total crime but this has risen to over 25 per cent.

89

Table 5.1: Notifiable Crimes Recorded by the Police[a] in England and Wales 1990

Offence group	Crimes recorded	Crimes cleared up
Violence against the person	184,665	141,694
Sexual offences	29,044	22,041
Burglary	1,006,813	255,887
Robbery	36,195	9,574
Theft and handling stolen goods	2,374,409	709,848
Fraud and forgery	147,909	89,831
Criminal damage	553,466	120,527
Other	31,131	30,021
Total	**4,363,632**	**1,379,423**

Source: Home Office.
[a] Excludes criminal damage of £20 and under.

Most crime is committed by young males, is opportunist and is not planned by hardened professional criminals, although these do exist. Only a small proportion of young male offenders go on to become serious repeat offenders.

Crime Prevention

National publicity campaigns, such as the current Crack Crime campaign, are a regular feature of the Government's programmes. The Home Office's Crime Prevention Unit encourages local agencies to design and implement preventive measures and to assess the results. Other government departments are brought together with the Home Office to formulate crime prevention strategies. The Department of the Environment's programmes are designed to encourage improvements in the design, layout and management of housing estates. Gas and electricity suppliers have speeded up their programme of replacing domestic prepayment meters by cashless or 'token' meters, so removing a prime target for burglaries.

Crime Concern, a national independent organisation, encourages local initiatives and business participation in crime prevention.

Local crime prevention panels—each one assisted by the police—identify crime problems and try to tackle them through publicity, marking goods and equipment, and fund-raising to buy security devices. The police have been closely involved in setting up 92,000 neighbourhood watch schemes in England and Wales. There are some 1,700 watch schemes in Scotland.

In 1986 five local projects were set up with government support to see how crime and the fear of crime could be reduced through action by local government, private businesses, the police and voluntary agencies. As part of the Government's Safer Cities projects, this model has been adapted for use in 20 inner city areas in England and Wales. Each project is led by a committee, drawn from local agencies and supported by a co-ordinator funded by the Home Office. Four projects are also being established in Scotland. Similar projects are being funded by the Government in Northern Ireland.

Strengthening the Law

A number of measures to strengthen the criminal justice system have been taken in recent years. The courts now have powers to trace, freeze and confiscate the proceeds of drug trafficking. A court can issue an order requiring the offender to pay an amount equal to the full value of the proceeds arising from the trafficking. The laundering of illegal money associated with trafficking is unlawful. Because of the international nature of the problem, restraint and confiscation orders made by courts can be enforced against assets held overseas, and vice versa; these arrangements apply to countries with which mutual enforcement agreements have been concluded.

A court may also make a confiscation order against the proceeds arising from offences such as robbery, fraud, blackmail and insider dealing in shares.

The Serious Fraud Office has wide powers to investigate and prosecute serious or complex fraud in England, Wales and Northern Ireland. Fraud in Scotland is investigated and prosecuted under the direction of the Lord Advocate.

A law has been passed to increase controls on firearms. The private ownership of certain highly dangerous types of weapon such as high-powered self-loading rifles and burst-fire weapons is banned. The police have increased powers to regulate the possession, safekeeping and movement of shotguns and other firearms. Similar legislation applies in Northern Ireland.

Under 1988 legislation it is unlawful to manufacture, sell or import certain weapons such as knuckledusters or, in England and Wales, to carry a knife in a public place without good reason.

The Criminal Justice Act 1991 has made a number of reforms to the criminal law in England and Wales. These mainly concern sentencing and the system for early release of prisoners.

Helping the Victim

Consideration is given to the needs of victims of crime. There are, for instance, more than 350 victim support schemes, covering 96 per cent of the population in England and Wales, with over 6,000 trained volunteer visitors. They are co-ordinated by a national organisation, Victim Support, which receives a government grant. The Government also finances local schemes to meet either the salaries of co-ordinators or running costs. Victim Support is also established in Northern Ireland.

In February 1990 the Government published its Victims' Charter, setting out for the first time the standards of service that victims of crime are entitled to expect from criminal justice agencies.

Victims of violent crime in Britain, including foreign nationals, may apply for compensation under the Criminal Injuries Compensation Scheme administered by a Board. Compensation is based on common law damages and is a lump-sum payment. In Northern Ireland there is separate, statutory provision in certain circumstances for compensation to be paid from public funds for criminal injuries, and for malicious damage to property, including the resulting loss of profits.

In February 1990 Britain ratified a European Convention under which mutual arrangements for compensation apply to citizens of those countries in which the Convention is in force.

Measures to Combat Terrorism

The Government has certain exceptional powers for dealing with and preventing terrorist activities. These take account of the need to achieve a proper balance between the safety of the public and the rights of the individual.

Northern Ireland

The security forces in Northern Ireland have special powers to search, question and arrest. The maximum period for which the police can hold a suspected terrorist on their own authority has been reduced from 72 to 48 hours, although he or she can be held for up to a further 5 days with the consent of the Secretary of State. Legislation allows terrorist organisations to be banned by the Government. Terrorist offences are tried by a judge sitting alone without a jury because of the possibility of jurors being intimidated by terrorist organisations. Statements obtained by the use or threat of violence are inadmissible in court.

Nobody can be imprisoned for political beliefs; all prisoners, except those awaiting trial, have been found guilty in court of criminal offences. The legislation is reviewed annually by an independent person whose reports are presented to Parliament.

Other Legislation

Other legislation applies throughout Britain and is renewable annually by Parliament. It provides for the exclusion from Great Britain, Northern Ireland or the United Kingdom of people connected with terrorism related to Northern Ireland affairs and for the banning of terrorist organisations in Great Britain. It also gives the police powers to arrest suspects without warrant and hold them for 48 hours and, with ministerial approval, for up to a further five days. This provision also applies to suspected international terrorists.

It is a criminal offence to finance terrorism or receive funds for use in the furtherance of terrorism. Police can apply for a court order to freeze a suspect's assets once he or she has been charged. Funds can be confiscated if a person is convicted. The legislation allows for reciprocal enforcement agreements with other countries.

The Government believes that there should be no concessions to terrorist demands and that international co-operation is essential in tracking down terrorists and impeding their movement from one country to another.

THE POLICE SERVICE

Organisation

There are 52 police forces in Britain, mainly organised on a local basis. The Metropolitan Police Force and the City of London force are responsible for policing London. At the end of 1990 police strength in Britain was just over 149,000, of which the Royal Ulster Constabulary numbered over 8,200. Each force has an attachment of volunteer special constables who perform police duties in their spare time, without pay, acting mainly as auxiliaries to the regular force. In Northern Ireland there is a 4,600-strong part-time and full-time paid reserve.

Police forces are maintained in England and Wales by committees of local county councillors and magistrates, and in Scotland by regional and islands councils. The Home Secretary is responsible for London's Metropolitan Police Force. In Northern Ireland the police force is responsible to a body appointed by the Government.

Chief constables are in charge of their police forces and are responsible for the appointment, promotion and discipline of all ranks below assistant chief constable. They are generally answerable to the police authorities on matters of efficiency, and must submit an annual report.

The police authorities appoint the chief constable and other top officers. They also fix the maximum permitted strength of the force and provide buildings and equipment.

In the Metropolitan Police area the commissioner of police and his immediate subordinates are appointed on the recommendation of the Home Secretary.

The police service is financed by central and local government.

Central Authorities

The Home Secretary and the Secretaries of State for Scotland and Northern Ireland approve the appointment of chief, deputy and assistant chief constables. Where necessary they can:

- require a police authority to retire a chief constable in the interests of efficiency;
- call for a report from a chief constable on matters relating to local policing; and
- institute a local inquiry.

These ministers can also make regulations covering:

- qualifications for appointment, promotion and retirement;
- discipline;
- hours of duty, leave, pay and allowances; and
- uniform.

Some of these regulations are first negotiable within the Police Negotiating Board for the United Kingdom. The Board consists of an independent chairman and representatives of the police authorities, police staff associations and the home departments.

All police forces (except the Metropolitan Police) are inspected by inspectors of constabulary reporting to central government. On request, the inspectorate also undertakes inspections of selected parts of the Metropolitan Police.

Members of the police service may not belong to a trade union, nor may they withdraw their labour in furtherance of a trade dispute. All ranks, however, have their own staff associations to represent their interests.

Co-ordination of Police Operations

Several common services are provided by central government and by arrangements between forces. In England and Wales the most important of these cover telecommunications and central and provincial criminal records. In Scotland the main common services are centralised police training, the Scottish Crime Squad and the Scottish Criminal Record Office.

Certain special services such as liaison with the International Criminal Police Organisation (Interpol) are provided for other British forces by the Metropolitan Police. The National Drugs Intelligence Unit assists police forces and the Customs service throughout Britain. A new National Criminal Intelligence Service is to be set up in 1992 to co-ordinate and analyse intelligence; it will bring together a number of units, including the National Drugs Intelligence Unit and the Interpol Bureau.

The services of the Fraud Squad, which is run jointly by the Metropolitan Police and City of London Police to investigate company frauds, are available in England and Wales.

Regional crime squads, co-ordinated at national level in England and Wales, deal with serious crimes, such as drug trafficking, and are used whenever operations cannot be dealt with by individual police forces alone.

In all areas of police work the use of scientific aids is widespread. A national police computer helps to rationalise records and speed up the dissemination of information.

Police Discipline

A British police officer may be sued or prosecuted for any wrongful act committed in carrying out duties. Police discipline codes are designed to prevent any abuse of police powers and to maintain public confidence in the impartiality of the service.

The independent Police Complaints Authority has powers to supervise the investigation of any serious complaint against a police officer in England and Wales. In Scotland complaints against police officers involving allegations of any form of criminal conduct are investigated by an independent procurator fiscal service.

In Northern Ireland the Independent Commission for Police Complaints is required to supervise the investigation of a complaint regarding death or serious injury and has the power to supervise that of any other complaint if it so wishes. In certain circumstances, the Secretary of State may direct the Commission to supervise the investigation of matters that are not the subject of a formal complaint.

Community Relations

Virtually all forces have liaison departments designed to develop closer contact between the force and the community. Almost all areas have police/community consultative groups. Particular efforts are made to develop relations with young people through greater contact with schools; school governing bodies and head teachers are under an obligation to describe in their annual reports the steps they take to strengthen their schools' links with the community, including the police.

Emphasis is placed on improving relations with ethnic minorities. The Government believes that all police officers should receive a thorough training in community and race relations. The Home Office sponsors national courses in these subjects for community liaison officers and police managers. There is also a national specialist support unit which makes a valuable contribution to improving community and race relations training for the police. Discriminatory behaviour by police officers is an offence under the Police Discipline Code. The Home Office organises recruitment advertising campaigns in the press in order to encourage black and Asian recruits to the police. In December 1990 there were 1,418 ethnic minority police officers in England and Wales.

Police Powers

Officers in Great Britain do not normally carry firearms, although in an emergency they can be issued quickly on the authority of a senior officer. In Northern Ireland police officers are issued with firearms for personal protection and other firearms are available for duty purposes.

Under legislation passed in 1985, the Government can authorise interception of postal and telephone services by the police in order to prevent and detect serious crime, or, in some cases, national security. The other ground for interception is the safeguarding of Britain's economic well-being. Any interception outside these procedures is a criminal offence.

A police officer in England and Wales has a general power of stop and search if he or she has reasonable grounds for suspicion that a person is carrying stolen goods, offensive weapons or implements that could be used for theft, burglary and other offences. The officer must, however, state and record the grounds for taking this action and what, if anything, was found.

Arrest

In England and Wales the police have wide powers to arrest suspects with or without a warrant issued by a magistrate. For serious offences, known as 'arrestable offences', a suspect can be arrested without a warrant; this covers all offences for which a maximum period of five years' imprisonment can be imposed on conviction. Arrest without a warrant also applies to people suspected of committing 'serious arrestable offences' such as murder, rape and kidnapping. For lesser offences, arrest without warrant exists only when certain criteria are met, for instance, if it is not possible or appropriate to send out a summons to appear in court.

Detention, Treatment and Questioning

A statutory code of practice issued by the Government regulates detention, treatment and questioning of suspects by the police in England and Wales. Failure to comply with its provisions can render a police officer liable to disciplinary proceedings. Evidence obtained in breach of the code may be ruled inadmissible in court.

An arrested person has a statutory right to consult a solicitor and to ask the police to notify a relative or other named person likely to take an interest in his or her welfare. Where a person has been arrested in connection with a serious arrestable offence, but has not yet been charged, the police may delay for up to 36 hours the exercise of these rights in the interests of the investigation if certain strict criteria are met.

The police must caution a suspect before any questions are put for the purpose of obtaining evidence. The caution informs the suspect that he or she is entitled to refuse to answer questions—the so-called 'right to silence'. Questions relating to an offence may not normally be put to a person after he or she has been charged with that offence or informed that he or she may be prosecuted for it.

The length of time a suspect is held in police custody before charge is strictly regulated. For lesser offences this may not exceed 24 hours. A person suspected of committing a serious arrestable offence can be detained for up to 96 hours without charge but only beyond 36 hours if a warrant is obtained from a magistrates' court. Reviews must be made of a person's detention at regular intervals—six hours after initial detention and thereafter every nine hours as a maximum—to check whether the criteria for detention are still satisfied. If they are not, the person must be released immediately.

The tape recording of interviews with suspected offenders at police stations will become standard practice by the end of 1991. A code of practice governing these tape recordings has been approved by Parliament.

A person who thinks that the grounds for detention are unlawful may apply to the

High Court for a writ of habeas corpus against the person who detained him or her, requiring that person to appear before the court to justify the detention. Habeas corpus proceedings take precedence over others.

A similar remedy is available to anyone who is unlawfully detained in Scotland.

Charging

Once there is sufficient evidence for a charge, the police have to decide whether to charge the person with the offence. As an alternative to charging immediately, they can, for example, decide to defer charging or to take no further action and release the person with or without bail. They may also issue a caution, which is a warning that prosecution is likely for a second offence.

If charged with an offence, a person may be kept in custody if there is a risk that he or she might fail to appear in court or might interfere with the administration of justice. A young person may also be detained for his or her protection. When no such considerations apply, the person must be released on or without bail. Where someone is detained after charge, he or she must be brought before a magistrates' court quickly. This is usually no later than the next working day.

Time Limits

There are time limits on the period a defendant may be remanded in custody awaiting trial in England and Wales. In cases tried before a magistrates' court these are 56 days from first appearance to trial or 70 days between first appearance to committal for trial (see p 98) in the Crown Court. The limit in Crown Court cases is 112 days from committal to taking of the plea. When a time limit expires, the defendant is entitled to bail unless the court extends the limit; it can only do this if satisfied that there is a good and sufficient reason, and that the prosecution has acted expeditiously.

Bail

Most accused people are released on bail pending trial. They are not remanded in custody except where strictly necessary. In England and Wales, the court decides whether a defendant should be released on bail. Unconditional bail may only be withheld if the court has substantial grounds for believing that the accused would:

- abscond;
- commit an offence;
- interfere with witnesses; or
- otherwise obstruct the course of justice.

A court may also impose conditions before granting bail. If bail is refused, the defendant may apply to a High Court judge or to the Crown Court for bail. An application can also be made to the Crown Court for conditions imposed by a magistrates' court to be varied.

In some cases a court may grant bail to a defendant on condition that he or she lives in an approved bail or probation/bail hostel.

The probation service has developed bail information schemes which provide the Crown Prosecution Service with verified information about a defendant. This assists the Service to decide whether to oppose bail and enables the courts to take an informed decision on whether to grant bail.

Scotland

In Scotland the police may detain and question a suspected person for a period of up to six hours. After this period the person must either be released or charged. Once a person has been charged with a criminal offence, only voluntary statements will normally be allowed in evidence at the trial. The court will reject statements unless satisfied that they have been fairly obtained. In many areas interviews with suspects in police stations are tape recorded. Anyone arrested must be brought before a court with the least possible delay (generally not later than the first day after being taken into custody), or—in less serious cases—liberated by the police, often on a written undertaking to attend court.

Where an accusation of a more serious offence is to be made, the accused is brought before the sheriff in private to be committed, either for further examination or until liberated in due course of law. A judicial examination may take place. A maximum of eight days may elapse between committal for further examination and committal for trial.

Anyone accused of a crime, except murder or treason, is entitled to apply for release on bail. Even in cases of murder or treason, bail may be granted at the discretion of the Lord Advocate or a quorum of the High Court.

There is a right of appeal to the High Court by the accused person against the refusal of bail, or by the prosecutor against the granting of bail, or by either party against the conditions imposed.

If a person charged with a more serious offence has been kept in custody pending trial, the trial must begin within 110 days of the date of full committal. The trial of a person charged with a summary offence and held in custody must begin within 40 days of the date of first appearance in court.

CRIMINAL COURTS

Prosecution

England and Wales

Once the police have decided to charge a person with a crime, the Crown Prosecution Service, headed by the Director of Public Prosecutions, assumes control of the case and decides whether to prosecute. The Service is divided into 31 areas, each of which is run by a locally based Chief Crown Prosecutor appointed by the Director. The Service provides prosecution lawyers for the magistrates' courts and briefs barristers to appear in the Crown Court.

Although the decision to prosecute is generally delegated to the lawyers in the area offices, some especially sensitive or complex cases are dealt with by the headquarters of the Service, including terrorist offences and breaches of the Official Secrets Acts.

Scotland

Discharging his duties through the Crown Office and Procurator Fiscal Service, the Lord Advocate is responsible for prosecutions. The permanent adviser to the Lord Advocate on prosecution matters is the Crown Agent, who is head of the Procurator Fiscal Service and is assisted in the Crown Office by a staff of legally qualified civil servants.

Prosecutions in the High Court of Justiciary are prepared by procurators fiscal and Crown Office officials. They are conducted by the Lord Advocate, the Solicitor General for Scotland (the Lord Advocate's ministerial deputy) and advocate deputes, who are collectively known as Crown Counsel.

Crimes tried before the sheriff and district courts are prepared and prosecuted by procurators fiscal. The police and other law enforcement agencies investigate crimes and offences and report to the procurator fiscal, who decides whether to prosecute, subject to the directions of Crown Counsel.

When dealing with minor crime, the procurator fiscal increasingly makes use of alternatives to prosecution such as formal warnings and fixed penalties. The offender is not obliged to accept such an offer but if he or she does so the prosecution loses the right to prosecute.

Northern Ireland

The Director of Public Prosecutions for Northern Ireland prosecutes all offences tried on indictment, and may do so in summary cases of a serious nature. Other summary offences are prosecuted by the police.

Prosecutions for Fraud

The Serious Fraud Office investigates and prosecutes the most serious and complex cases of fraud in England, Wales and Northern Ireland. Investigations are conducted by teams of lawyers, accountants, police officers and other specialists. In Scotland the Crown Office Fraud Unit investigates and prepares—in co-operation with the police and other agencies—prosecutions against fraud.

Courts in England and Wales

Very serious offences such as murder, manslaughter, rape and robbery are tried on indictment only by the Crown Court, where all contested trials are presided over by a judge sitting with a jury.

Summary offences—the least serious offences and the vast majority of criminal cases—are tried by unpaid lay magistrates or by a few paid stipendiary magistrates; both sit without a jury.

A third category of offences (such as theft, burglary or malicious wounding) are known as 'either way' offences; they can be tried either by magistrates or by jury in the Crown Court, depending on the circumstances of each case and the wishes of the defendant.

All those charged with offences to be tried in the Crown Court must first appear before a magistrates' court, which decides whether to commit them to the Court for trial.

A magistrates court, which is open to the public and the media, usually consists of three lay magistrates—known as justices of the peace—who are advised on points of law and procedure by a legally qualified clerk or a qualified assistant.

There are nearly 28,000 lay magistrates. The few full-time, legally qualified stipendiary magistrates may sit alone and usually preside in courts in urban areas where the workload is heavy.

Cases involving people under 17 (soon to be 18) are heard in juvenile courts (to become youth courts). These are specialist magistrates' courts which either sit apart from other courts or are held at a different time. Restrictions are placed on access by ordinary members of the public, and media reports must not identify a young person appearing either as a defendant (unless a judge directs otherwise) or a witness.

Where a young person under 17 is charged jointly with someone of 17 or over, the case is heard in an ordinary magistrates' court or the Crown Court. If the young person is found guilty, the court may transfer the case to a juvenile court for sentence unless satisfied that it is undesirable to do so.

The Crown Court sits at about 90 centres and is presided over by High Court judges, full-time 'circuit judges' and part-time recorders.

In cases of serious or complex fraud, full committal proceedings in magistrates' courts may be bypassed at the discretion of the prosecution. The accused can apply to the Crown Court to be discharged on the ground that there is no case to answer.

Appeals

A person convicted by a magistrates' court may appeal to the Crown Court against sentence if he or she has pleaded guilty. The appeal may be made against both conviction and sentence if a not guilty plea has been made.

If convicted by the Crown Court, the defendant can appeal to the Court of Appeal against both conviction and sentence imposed.

The House of Lords is the final appeal court, but it will only consider cases that involve a point of law of general public importance.

The Attorney General may seek the opinion of the Court of Appeal on a point of law which has arisen in a case where a person tried on indictment is acquitted; the Court has power to refer the point to the House of Lords if necessary. The acquittal in the original case is not affected.

The Attorney General may refer a case to the Court of Appeal if he considers that a sentence passed by the Crown Court is over-lenient. This only applies to a case triable exclusively in the Crown Court. If the Court of Appeal agrees, it may increase the sentence within the statutory maximum laid down by Parliament for the offence.

Scotland

The High Court of Justiciary, which sits in Edinburgh and other major towns and cities, tries the most serious crimes and has exclusive jurisdiction in cases involving murder, treason and rape. The sheriff court is concerned with less serious offences and the district court with minor offences.

Criminal cases are heard either under solemn procedure, when the judge sits with a jury of 15 members, or under summary procedure, when the judge sits without a jury.

All cases in the High Court and the more serious ones in sheriff courts are tried by a judge and jury. Summary procedure is used in the less serious cases in the sheriff courts, and in all cases in the district courts. District court judges are lay justices of the peace. In Glasgow there are also stipendiary magistrates who are full-time lawyers with the same criminal jurisdiction in summary procedure as the sheriff.

Children under 16 who have committed an offence are normally dealt with by children's hearings (see p 106).

All appeals are dealt with by the High Court. In both solemn and summary procedure, an appeal may be brought by the accused against conviction, or sentence, or both. The Court may authorise a retrial if it sets aside a conviction. There is no further appeal to the House of Lords. In summary proceedings the prosecutor may appeal on a point of law against acquittal or sentence. The Lord Advocate may seek the opinion of the High Court on a point of law which has arisen in a case where a person tried on indictment is acquitted. The acquittal in the original case is not affected.

Northern Ireland

Cases involving minor summary offences are heard by magistrates' courts presided over by a full-time, legally qualified resident magistrate. Young offenders under 17 are dealt with by a juvenile court consisting of the resident magistrate and two lay members (at least one of whom must be a woman) specially qualified to deal with juveniles. Appeals from magistrates' courts are heard by the county court, as are appeals on a point of law.

The Crown Court deals with criminal trials on indictment. It is served by High Court and county court judges. Proceedings are heard before a single judge, and all contested cases, other than those involving offences specified under emergency legislation, take place before a jury.

Appeals from the Crown Court against conviction or sentence are heard by the Northern Ireland Court of Appeal. Procedures for a further appeal to the House of Lords are similar to those in England and Wales.

Those accused of terrorist offences are tried in non-jury courts. The onus remains on the prosecution to prove guilt beyond reasonable doubt and the defendant has the right to be represented by a lawyer of his or her choice. The judge must set out in a written statement the reasons for convicting and there is an automatic right of appeal against conviction and sentence. In 1990 some 43 per cent of defendants who pleaded not guilty to all charges in the non-jury courts were found not guilty.

Trial

Criminal trials in Britain have two parties: the prosecution and the defence. Since the law presumes the innocence of an accused person until guilt has been proved, the prosecution is not granted any advantage over the defence.

An accused person has the right to employ a legal adviser and may be granted legal aid from public funds (see p 111). If remanded in custody, he or she may be visited by a legal adviser to ensure a properly prepared defence.

In England, Wales and Northern Ireland the prosecution has the duty to disclose information to the defence; it must, for example, inform the defence of witnesses whose evidence may help the accused and whom the prosecution does not propose to call. In Scotland the prosecution must give to the defence advance notice of the witnesses it will call.

The defence or prosecution may suggest that the defendant's mental state renders him or her unfit to be tried. If the jury (or in Scotland, the judge) decides that this is so, the defendant is admitted to a specified hospital.

Criminal trials are normally in open court

and rules of evidence, which are concerned with the proof of facts, are rigorously applied. If evidence is improperly admitted, a conviction can be quashed on appeal.

During the trial the defendant has the right to hear and cross-examine witnesses for the prosecution, normally through a lawyer. He or she can call his or her own witnesses who, if they will not attend voluntarily, may be legally compelled to do so. The defendant can also address the court in person or through a lawyer, the defence having the right to the last speech at the trial before the judge sums up. The defendant cannot be questioned without consenting to be sworn as a witness in his or her own defence. When he or she does testify, cross-examination about character or other conduct may be made only in exceptional circumstances; generally the prosecution may not introduce such evidence. In Northern Ireland the judge can draw inferences from a refusal by a defendant to give evidence.

In England and Wales the judge in complex fraud cases may order a preparatory open Crown Court hearing to be held. This is done to give him or her an opportunity to settle questions regarding admissibility of evidence and any other points of law relating to the case. The law on evidence has been changed to make it possible for courts to have before them a wider range of written evidence in the form of business documents which could be relevant to a successful prosecution.

The Jury

In jury trials the judge decides questions of law, sums up the evidence for the jury, and discharges the accused or passes sentence. In England, Wales and Northern Ireland the jury is responsible for deciding whether a defendant is 'guilty' or 'not guilty', the latter verdict resulting in acquittal. If the jury cannot reach a unanimous verdict, the judge may direct it to bring in a majority verdict provided that, in the normal jury of 12 people, there are not more than two dissenters.

In Scotland the jury's verdict may be 'guilty', 'not guilty' or 'not proven'; the accused is acquitted if either of the last two verdicts is given. The jury consists of 15 people and a verdict of 'guilty' can only be reached if at least eight members are in favour. As a general rule no one may be convicted without corroborated evidence from at least two sources.

If the jury acquits the defendant, the prosecution has no right of appeal and the defendant cannot be tried again for the same offence. The defendant, however, has a right of appeal to the appropriate court if found guilty.

A jury is independent of the judiciary. Any attempt to interfere with a jury once it is sworn in is a criminal offence. Potential jurors are put on a panel before the start of the trial. The prosecution and the defence may challenge individual jurors on the panel, giving reasons for doing so. In Scotland the prosecution or defence may challenge up to three jurors without reason.

People between the ages of 18 and 65 (70 in England, Wales and Northern Ireland) whose names appear on the electoral register, with certain exceptions, are liable for jury service and their names are chosen at random. Ineligible people include, for example, judges and people who have within the previous ten years been members of the legal profession or the police, prison or probation services. People convicted of certain offences within the previous ten years cannot serve on a jury. Anyone who has received a prison sentence of five years or more is disqualified for life.

Coroners' Courts

Coroners in England and Wales investigate violent and unnatural deaths or sudden deaths where the cause is unknown. An inquest is, however, not necessary if a sudden death was due to natural causes. The coroner must hold an inquest if the deceased died a violent or unnatural death or died in prison or in other specified circumstances. (In Northern Ireland the coroner investigates the matter to decide whether an inquest is necessary). It is the duty of the coroner's court to establish how, when and where the deceased died. A coroner may sit alone or, in certain circumstances, with a jury.

In Scotland the local procurator fiscal inquires privately into all sudden and suspicious deaths and may report the findings to the Crown Office. In a minority of cases a fatal accident inquiry may be held before the sheriff; this is mandatory in cases of death resulting from industrial accidents and of deaths in custody.

TREATMENT OF OFFENDERS

The Government's aim is to ensure that convicted criminals are punished justly and suitably according to the seriousness of their offences. It believes that those who commit very serious crimes, particularly crimes of violence, should receive long custodial sentences, but that many other crimes can best be punished within the community through compensation and reparation. These principles are contained in the Criminal Justice Act 1991.

Legislation sets the maximum penalties for offences, the sentence being entirely a matter for the courts, subject to these maxima. The Court of Appeal issues guidance to the lower courts on sentencing issues when points of principle have arisen on individual cases which are the subject of appeal.

Custody

The Government believes that custody should be used only for offenders convicted of serious criminal offences or where the public needs to be protected from serious harm from a violent or sexual offender. The Court of Appeal has stated that sentencers in England and Wales should ensure that terms of custody are as short as possible, consistent with the courts' duty to protect the public and to punish the criminal.

The Criminal Justice Act 1991 will require a court in England and Wales, before giving a custodial sentence, to be satisfied that the offence is serious enough to merit custody. The court will also have to give reasons if it considers a custodial sentence to be necessary. Longer custodial sentences— within the statutory maxima—will be available for persistent violent and sexual offenders in order to protect the public from serious harm.

A magistrates' court in England and Wales cannot impose a term of more than six months' imprisonment for an individual offence tried summarily; it can impose consecutive sentences for 'either way' offences (see p 97), subject to an overall maximum of 12 months' imprisonment. If an offence carries a higher maximum penalty, the court may commit the offender for sentence at the Crown Court.

The Crown Court may impose a custodial sentence for any term up to life, depending on the gravity of the sentence and the maximum penalty available.

In trials on indictment in Scotland the High Court may impose a sentence of imprisonment for any term up to life, and the sheriff court any term up to three years. The latter may send any person to the High Court for sentence if the court considers its powers are insufficient. In summary cases, the sheriff may normally impose up to three months' imprisonment or six months' for some repeated offences. The district court can impose a maximum term of imprisonment of 60 days.

In Northern Ireland the position is generally the same as for England and Wales. A magistrates' court, however, cannot commit an offender for sentencing at the Crown Court if it has tried the case.

In all three legal systems there is a mandatory sentence of life imprisonment for murder. Life imprisonment is also the maximum penalty for a number of serious offences such as robbery, rape, arson and manslaughter.

The Death Penalty

The death penalty remains on the statute book for the offences of treason, piracy with violence and some other treasonable and mutinous offences. It has, however, not been used for any of these offences since 1946.

Non-custodial Treatment

The Government believes that more offenders, particularly those convicted of property crimes and less serious cases of violence, should be punished in the community. In its view this should involve fines levied on the offender and compensation to the victim, probation, community service, a new combined order linking probation and community service, or a new curfew order to be used by itself or with other orders.

Fines

Roughly 80 per cent of offenders are punished with a fine. There is no limit to the fine (unless set by statute) which may be imposed on indictment; on summary conviction the maximum limit is usually £2,000 in England, Wales and Northern Ireland, and in Scotland £2,000 in the sheriff court and £1,000 in the district court.

The Criminal Justice Act 1991 will enable fines to be more closely related to ability to pay. The court's penalty will be given in units which will then be translated into monetary values according to the offender's disposable weekly income. The maximum fine usually available on summary conviction will be increased to £5,000.

Probation

The locally organised probation service supervises offenders in the community under direct court orders and after release from custody. It also provides offenders in custody with help and advice.

A probation order, which can last between six months and three years, can only be made by a court with the consent of the offender, who may be sentenced for the original offence if he or she fails to comply with the order or commits another offence while on probation.

A probation order requires the offender to maintain regular contact with the probation officer. Special conditions attached to the order may require the offender to attend a day centre for up to 60 days. Although intended as a punishment, the time spent by offenders under supervision in the community offers an opportunity for constructive work to reduce the likelihood of reoffending.

In England and Wales the probation service also administers supervision orders, the community service scheme and supervises those released from prison on parole.

National standards are to be introduced for a wide range of probation work.

Community Service

Offenders aged 16 or over (17 in Northern Ireland) convicted of imprisonable offences may, with their consent, be given community service orders. The court may order between 40 and 240 hours' unpaid service to be completed within 12 months; for 16-year-olds the maximum in England and Wales is 120 hours. Examples of work done include decorating the houses of elderly or disabled people and building adventure playgrounds.

The Criminal Justice Act will introduce a new court order in England and Wales which will combine community service and probation. The maximum term for the probation element will be the same as a probation order and the maximum period of community service will be 100 hours.

Curfew Order

Under the Criminal Justice Act 1991 courts in England and Wales will be empowered to issue a curfew order confining offenders to their homes at certain times to prevent them going to places which may be associated with their offending. It can also be combined with probation, community service or the new order linking probation and community service.

Compensation and Reparation

The courts may order an offender to pay compensation for personal injury, loss or damage resulting from an offence. In England and Wales courts are required to give reasons for not awarding compensation to a victim. Compensation takes precedence over fines.

Courts may order the confiscation of proceeds gained by a criminal from drug trafficking and other offences such as robbery, fraud, blackmail and insider dealing in shares.

Other Measures

A court in England and Wales may discharge a person if it believes that punishment should not be inflicted and a probation order is not appropriate. If he or she is conditionally discharged, the offender remains liable to punishment for the offence if convicted of another offence within a period specified by the court (not more than three years).

The Crown Court can require an offender to keep the peace and/or be of good behaviour. If this requirement is not complied with, the offender may be brought before the court and dealt with for the original offence. Alternatively a sum of money may be forfeited if conditions stated by the court are not met.

In Scotland there is a system of deferral of sentence until a future date. During this period the accused is required to be of good behaviour and to meet any other conditions stipulated by the court. The court may also warn the offender or grant an absolute discharge.

Police cautions are used particularly for young offenders; the caution is a form of warning and no court action is taken.

Prisons

The Government aims to provide a humane and efficient prison service. The average inmate population in 1990 was about 45,600 in England and Wales, 4,724 in Scotland and 1,750 in Northern Ireland.

Prisoners may be housed in accommodation ranging from open prisons to high security establishments. In England, Scotland and Wales sentenced prisoners are classified into groups for security purposes. There are separate prisons for women.

There are no open prisons in Northern Ireland, where the majority of offenders are serving sentences for terrorist offences.

People awaiting trial in custody are entitled to privileges not granted to convicted prisoners. Those under 21 are, where possible, separated from convicted prisoners.

Building on the recommendation of the Woolf Report on the 1990 prison disturbances, a White Paper, published in September 1991, set out a programme of reforms for the prison service in England and Wales, focusing on the main areas of custody, care and justice.

The Government is seeking to foster greater private sector involvement in the prison system of England and Wales. Under the Criminal Justice Act 1991 competitive tenders will be invited from the private sector for the operation of new remand centres and for the work of escorting prisoners to and from courts and safeguarding them at court.

Many prisons in Great Britain were built in the nineteenth century and require major repairs to bring them up to modern standards. In order to ensure that all prisoners are housed in decent conditions, a major programme of improvement is in progress in England and Wales which will, for example, eliminate by 1994 cells without access to integral sanitation. Overcrowding is being relieved by a prison building programme; by March 1994 over 7,000 places at new prisons will have been added in England and Wales, and about 3,000 new places at existing establishments.

In Northern Ireland there is no overcrowding in the six prison establishments, five of which have been built since 1970.

Remission of Sentence

Most prisoners in Great Britain are eligible for remission of one-third of their sentence. Prisoners serving a sentence of 12 months or less in England and Wales are entitled to half remission. Release on remission does not involve any official supervision in the community. It may be forfeited for serious misconduct in prison.

Northern Ireland

In Northern Ireland prisoners serving a sentence of more than five days are eligible for remission of half their sentence. A prisoner serving a sentence of more than 12 months who is given remission is liable to be ordered to serve the remainder of this sentence if convicted of fresh imprisonable offences during this period.

The rate of remission for those convicted of terrorist offences and serving sentences of five years or more is one-third. Any released prisoners convicted of another terrorist offence before the expiry of the original sentence must complete that sentence before serving any term for the second offence.

Parole

In England and Wales prisoners serving sentences of more than 12 months can be conditionally released on parole when they have served one-third of the sentence, or six months, whichever expires the later. In Scotland they qualify after 12 months.

The first stage in England and Wales is consideration by a local review committee attached to each prison. This is followed by scrutiny by Home Office officials, who refer the more difficult and complex cases to the Parole Board, which makes recommendations for release on parole. Home Office ministers take the final decision on whether to accept the recommendation. Less serious cases are dealt with by the Home Office without reference to the Board on the basis of the local review committee recommendation. A similar procedure operates in Scotland, where there is a separate Parole Board.

Of those cases reviewed in England and Wales each year, three-quarters of prisoners serving sentences of less than two years receive parole; the corresponding figure for those serving two years or more is about a half. Parole is only granted in exceptional circumstances, or for a few months at the end of a sentence, for those serving sentences of over five years for violence, arson, sexual offences or drug trafficking. The parole licence remains in force until the date on which the prisoner would otherwise have been released from prison. It prescribes the conditions, including contact with a supervising officer, with which the offender must comply.

Parole is not available in Northern Ireland, which has more generous remission terms.

New Legislation

The Criminal Justice Act 1991 is designed to reform the remission and parole systems in England and Wales. Remission will be abolished, as will parole, for prisoners serving under four years; instead, they will spend half their sentence in custody and then be released. All prisoners sentenced to a year or more will be supervised on release until three-quarters of their sentence has passed. Certain sex offenders may be supervised to the end of their sentence.

For the remainder there will be a selective system of parole based on clear and published criteria. Prisoners sentenced will become eligible for parole halfway through their sentence. If convicted of another offence punishable with imprisonment and committed before the end of the original sentence, a released prisoner will be liable to serve all or part of the original sentence outstanding at the time the fresh offence was committed.

Similar changes are to be made in Scotland.

Life Sentence Prisoners

The release of prisoners serving life sentences is at the discretion of the Home Secretary or the Secretary of State for Scotland, subject to a favourable recommendation by the relevant parole board and after consultation with the judiciary. The Secretaries of State do not, however, have to accept such a recommendation for release, nor are they bound by the views of the judiciary.

People serving life sentences for the murder of police and prison officers, terrorist murders, murder by firearms in the course of robbery and the sexual or sadistic murder of children are normally detained for at least 20 years. At the end of 1990 there were about 2,700 life sentence prisoners detained in prisons in England and Wales, of whom about 270 had been detained for over 15 years. The equivalent figures in Scotland were 437 and 31 respectively.

On release, life sentence prisoners remain on licence for the rest of their lives and are subject to recall should their behaviour suggest that they might again be a danger to the public.

In Northern Ireland the Secretary of State reviews life sentence cases on the recommendation of an internal review body.

Repatriation

Sentenced prisoners who are nationals of countries which have ratified the Council of Europe Convention on the Transfer of Sentenced Persons or similar international arrangements may apply to be returned to their own country to serve the rest of their sentence there.

Independent Oversight of the Prison System

The Secretary of State appoints a board of visitors, as representatives of the local community, to act as voluntary independent observers at every establishment. Boards report to him annually and whenever any matter of particular concern arises. Members see that prisoners are treated fairly and that the prison is properly administered. They can go to any part of the prison and interview any inmate at any time.

Prison Industries, Physical Education and Education

Prison industries aim to give inmates work experience which will assist them when released and to secure a return which will reduce the cost of the prison system. The main industries are clothing and textile manufacture, engineering, woodwork, laundering, farming and horticulture. Most production caters for internal needs and for other public services. A few prisoners are employed outside prison, some in community service projects. Inmates are paid at pocket money rates for work done; in some prisons incentive payment schemes provide an opportunity for higher earnings on the basis of output and skill.

Education is financed by the prison service and staffed by local education authorities. Full-time education of 15 hours a week is compulsory for young offenders below school leaving age. For older offenders it is voluntary. Some prisoners study for public examinations, including those of the Open University. Library facilities are available in all establishments. Voluntary vocational training courses are taught by prison and civilian instruction officers in order to assist prisoners to get a job after release.

Physical education is voluntary for adult offenders but compulsory for young offenders. Practically all prisons have physical education facilities, some of which are purpose built. Opportunities are given for inmates to obtain proficiency awards issued by governing bodies of sport. Inmates also compete against teams in the local community.

Medical and Psychiatric Care

The prison medical service has a general responsibility for the physical and mental health of all those in custody. Most establishments have accommodation for sick people and some have surgical facilities. Patients can also be transferred to National Health Service hospitals. Psychiatric care is available.

Privileges and Discipline

Prisoners may write and receive letters and be visited by relatives and friends, and those in some establishments may make telephone calls. Privileges include a personal radio, books, periodicals and newspapers, and the opportunity to make purchases from the canteen with money earned in prison. Depending on facilities, prisoners may be granted the further privileges of dining and recreation in association, and watching television.

Breaches of discipline are dealt with by the prison governor, or by the boards of visitors, who have power to order forfeiture of remission.

Welfare

Prison officers deal with welfare matters and are supported in this by probation staff (in Scotland, social workers), who use their own professional skills to help individual prisoners understand more about the nature of their offending behaviour.

Religion and Spiritual Care

Anglican, Church of Scotland, Roman Catholic and Methodist chaplains provide opportunities for worship and spiritual counselling. They are supported by visiting ministers of other denominations and faiths as required. In a multi-faith and multicultural society particular attention is given to the needs of those of non-Christian faiths and ethnic minorities.

Preparation for Release

Many medium- and long-term prisoners in the later parts of their sentences may be granted home leave for periods of between two and five days. Its purpose is to give the prisoner the opportunity to maintain links with family and friends, and, where leave is taken near the end of the sentence, to contact prospective employers and make firm plans for release.

The Pre-Release Employment Scheme provides an opportunity for selected long-term prisoners to spend their last six months before release in one of eight hostels, which are attached to prisons, to help them re-adapt to society. Hostellers work in the outside community and return to the hostel each evening. Frequent weekend leave allows hostellers to renew ties with their families.

In Northern Ireland arrangements exist for prisoners serving fixed sentences to have short periods of leave near the end of their sentences and at Christmas. Life-sentence prisoners are given a nine-month pre-release programme which includes employment outside the prison.

Aftercare

Professional social work support is given to offenders following their release. Most young offenders under the age of 22, adult offenders released on parole and those released on licence from a life sentence receive a period of compulsory supervision from the probation service.

Young Offenders

England and Wales

If charged with a criminal offence, children aged between 10 and 16 are brought before a juvenile court which will be renamed as the youth court. If the child is found guilty, the court may:

- grant a conditional or absolute discharge;
- order payment of compensation;
- impose a fine which the parents can be ordered to pay;
- impose a supervision order or attendance centre order;
- impose a community service order (for 16-year-olds) for up to 120 hours; or
- in some cases, pass a custodial sentence.

A court can also issue a care order under which the child becomes the responsibility of local government social services. From October 1991, however, care orders in criminal proceedings will be abolished and juvenile courts will no longer hear care proceedings.

Under a supervision order (which may remain in force for not more than three years) a child normally lives at home under the supervision of a social worker or a probation officer. The order can be used to provide for a programme of constructive and remedial activities by means of a short residential course or, more usually, attendance at a day or evening centre.

The terms of an attendance centre order mean that the offender has to spend a total of up to 24 hours of his or her Saturday leisure time (up to three hours on any one occasion) at an attendance centre.

Boys aged between 14 and 16, for whom a non-custodial sentence would not be appropriate, may be sent to a young offender institution; for those aged 14 the maximum period is four months and for those aged 15 or 16 it is 12 months. This sentence is also available for girls from the age of 15. In the case of a very serious crime, detention in a place approved by the Home Secretary may be ordered, and must be ordered in the case of murder.

The custodial sentence for those aged between 17 and 20 years is also detention in a young offender institution. The use of custody for this group has dropped by 40 per cent since 1985. Alternative penalties include fines and compensation, attendance centre orders (for up to 36 hours) and community service orders (for between 40 and 240 hours).

When the Criminal Justice Act 1991 enters into force, it will make major changes in the arrangements for dealing with young offenders. In future, 17-year-olds will be dealt with in the juvenile or youth court. For 16-year-olds the maximum length of a community service order will be extended to 240 hours, and that for an attendance centre order to 36 hours—in line with the arrangements for 17-year-olds. In addition, probation orders, supervision orders and the new combination and curfew orders will be available for 16- and 17-year-olds. Detention in a young offender institution for 14-year-olds is being abolished.

Scotland

Children under 16 who have committed an offence or are considered to be in need of care and protection may be brought before a children's panel which consists of three lay people. This children's hearing determines in an informal setting whether compulsory measures of care are required and, if so, the form they should take. An official 'reporter' decides whether a child should come before a hearing. If the grounds for referral are not accepted by the child or parent, the case goes to the sheriff for proof. If he finds the grounds established, the sheriff remits the case to the reporter to arrange a hearing. The sheriff also decides appeals against any decision of a children's hearing.

Custody is available to the courts for young people aged between 16 and 21; as in England and Wales they serve their sentence in a young offender institution. Remission of part of the sentence for good behaviour, release on parole and supervision on release are available.

Northern Ireland

Those aged between 10 and 16 who are charged with a criminal offence will normally be brought before a juvenile court. If found guilty of an offence punishable in the case of an adult by imprisonment, the court may order the child or young person to be placed in care, under supervision or on probation. The offender may also be required to attend a day attendance centre, be sent to a training school or committed to custody in a remand home. Non-custodial options are the same as in England and Wales.

Offenders aged between 17 and 21 who receive custodial sentences of less than three years serve them in a young offenders' centre.

Civil Justice

The Civil Law

The civil law of England, Wales and Northern Ireland covers business related to the family, property, contracts and torts (non-contractual wrongful acts suffered by one person at the hands of another). It also includes constitutional, administrative, industrial, maritime and ecclesiastical law. Scottish civil law has its own, broadly similar, branches.

CIVIL COURTS

England and Wales

The limited civil jurisdiction of magistrates' courts extends to matrimonial proceedings for custody and maintenance orders, adoption orders, guardianship orders and family protection orders. The courts also have jurisdiction regarding public health and the recovery of local taxes.

The jurisdiction of the 286 county courts covers:

- actions founded upon contract and tort;
- trust and mortgage cases;
- action for the recovery of land;
- adoption and divorce cases;
- cases involving disputes between landlords and tenants;
- complaints about race and sex discrimination; and
- from October 1991, child care cases.

There are special arbitration facilities and simplified procedures for small claims not exceeding £1,000. The judge normally sits alone although, in exceptional cases, a trial may be with a jury.

The High Court deals with the more complicated civil cases. Its jurisdiction covers civil and some criminal cases, and it also deals with appeals. The Family Division is concerned with jurisdiction affecting the family, including that relating to wardship, adoption and guardianship. The Chancery Division deals with the interpretation of wills and the administration of estates. Maritime law and commercial law are the responsibility of admiralty and commercial courts of the Queen's Bench Division.

In the event of overlapping jurisdiction between the High Court and the County court, cases of exceptional importance, complexity or financial substance are reserved for trial in the High Court. County courts are no longer restrained by an upper financial limit in cases, except for some specialist business such as chancery matters.

New court rules have been introduced to reduce delay, encourage openness between parties and cut the cost of litigation.

Appeals

Appeals in matrimonial, adoption and guardianship proceedings heard by magistrates' courts go to the Family Division of the High Court. From October 1991 appeals on child care cases will also be dealt with by the High Court. Appeals from the High Court and county courts are heard in the Court of Appeal (Civil Division),

and may go on to the House of Lords, the final court of appeal in civil and criminal cases.

The judges in the House of Lords usually sit as a group of five. Lay peers do not attend the hearings of appeals, which normally take place in a committee room, but peers who hold or have held high judicial office may also sit. The president of the House in its judicial capacity is the Lord Chancellor.

Scotland

The main civil courts are the Court of Session and the sheriff court. The sheriff court has jurisdiction over most civil litigation. Although there is no upper monetary limit, it considers all cases with a value of less than £1,500. Appeals may be made to the sheriff principal or directly to the Court of Session. This does not apply where the value of the case is under £1,500, when an appeal must first be made to the sheriff principal, who may sanction an appeal to the Court of Session on a point of law only.

The Court of Session sits in Edinburgh, and in general has jurisdiction to deal with all kinds of action. It is divided into the Outer House, a court of first instance; and the Inner House, mainly an appeal court. Appeals to the Inner House may be made from the Outer House and from the sheriff court. From the Inner House an appeal may go to the House of Lords.

The Scottish Land Court deals exclusively with matters concerning agriculture. Its chairman has the status and tenure of a judge of the Court of Session and its other members are lay specialists.

Northern Ireland

Civil cases up to a limited and specified monetary value are dealt with in county courts, though magistrates' courts also deal with certain limited classes of civil case. The superior civil law court is the High Court of Justice, from which an appeal may be made to the Court of Appeal. The House of Lords is the final civil appeal court.

Civil Proceedings

England and Wales

In England and Wales civil proceedings are started by the aggrieved person. Actions in the High Court are usually begun by a writ served on the defendant by the plaintiff, stating the nature of the claim. Before the case is set down for trial in the High Court, documents (pleadings) setting out the scope of the dispute are filed with the court; the pleadings are also served on the parties. County court proceedings are initiated by a summons usually served on the defendant by the court. From October 1991, child care cases will be initiated by an application.

In order to encourage parties to confine the issues in dispute, the High Court and the county courts have power to order pre-trial exchange of witness statements in most cases. Courts may impose penalties in costs on parties who unreasonably refuse to admit facts or disclose documents before trial.

A decree of divorce must be pronounced in open court, but a procedure for most undefended cases dispenses with the need to give evidence in court and permits written evidence to be considered by the district judge.

Civil proceedings, as a private matter, can usually be abandoned or ended by settlement between the parties at any time. Actions brought to court are usually tried without a jury, except in defamation, false imprisonment, or malicious prosecution cases, when either party may apply for trial by jury. The jury decides questions of fact and determines damages to be paid to the injured party; majority verdicts may be accepted. Under recent legislation the Court of Appeal would be able to increase or reduce damages awarded by a jury if it considered them inadequate or excessive.

In civil cases heard by a magistrates' court, the court issues a summons to the defendant setting out details of the complaint and the date on which it will be heard. Parties and witnesses give their evidence at the court hearing. Domestic proceedings are normally heard by not more than three lay justices, including, where practicable, a woman; members of the public are not allowed to be present. The court may order provision for custody, access and supervision of children, as well as maintenance payments for spouses and children.

The law has been changed recently to speed up civil proceedings in magistrates' courts by allowing written statements, expert opinions and hearsay evidence to be accepted in court without the presence of the witness unless the evidence is disputed and the disputing party requests the presence of the witness.

Most judgments are for sums of money and may be enforced, in cases of non-payment, by seizure of the debtor's goods or by a court order requiring an employer to make periodic payments to the court by deduction from the debtor's wages. Other court remedies may include an injunction restraining someone from performing an unlawful act. Refusal to obey a court order may result in imprisonment for contempt. An arrest under an order of committal may be effected only on a warrant.

Normally the court orders the costs of an action to be paid by the party losing it, but, in the case of family law maintenance proceedings, a magistrates' court can order either party to pay the whole or part of the other's costs.

Scotland

In Scotland proceedings in the Court of Session or ordinary actions in the sheriff court are initiated by serving the defender with a summons (an initial writ in the sheriff court). A defender who intends to contest the action must inform the court; if he or she does not appear, the court grants a decree in absence in favour of the pursuer. Where a case is contested, both parties must prepare written statements. Time is allowed for either party to readjust their statement in the light of what the other has said. The court then hears the case.

In summary cases (involving small sums) in the sheriff court the statement of claim is incorporated in the summons. The procedure is designed to enable most actions to be carried through without the parties involved having to appear in court. Normally they (or their representatives) need appear only when an action is defended. A new small claims procedure was introduced in 1988.

Northern Ireland

There are a number of differences between proceedings in Northern Ireland and those in England and Wales, for example, procedures regarding divorce or pre-trial disclosure.

Restrictive Practices Court

The Restrictive Practices Court is a specialised United Kingdom court dealing with monopolies and restrictive trade practices. It comprises five judges and up to ten other people with expertise in industry, commerce or public life.

Administrative Tribunals

Administrative tribunals exercise judicial functions separate from the courts and tend to be more accessible, less formal and less expensive.

Some tribunals decide disputes between private citizens—for example, industrial tribunals have a major role in employment disputes. Others, such as those concerned with social security, resolve claims by private citizens against public authorities. A further group (including tax tribunals) decide disputed claims by public authorities against private citizens, while others decide cases concerning immigration into Britain.

In the case of many tribunals, a two-tier system operates, with an initial right of appeal to a lower tribunal and a final right of appeal, usually on a point of law, to a higher one. Appeals from some of the higher tribunals on a point of law only may be made to the High Court in England and Wales, to the Court of Session in Scotland, and to the Court of Appeal in Northern Ireland. There are a few exceptions including, for example, immigration appeals, where there is no right of appeal directly from the Immigration Appeals Tribunal to the courts.

The independent Council on Tribunals exercises general supervision over many tribunals, advising on draft legislation and rules of procedure, monitoring their activities and reporting on particular matters. A Scottish Committee of the Council exercises the same function in Scotland.

Administration of the Law

GOVERNMENT RESPONSIBILITIES

Administration of justice rests with the Lord Chancellor, the Home Secretary, the Attorney General and the Secretaries of State for Scotland and Northern Ireland. The highest judicial appointments are made by the Queen on the advice of the Prime Minister. The judiciary is independent, its adjudications not being subject to ministerial direction or control.

England and Wales

The Lord Chancellor is the head of the judiciary. He is concerned with court procedure and is responsible for the administration of all courts other than magistrates' and coroners' courts, and for a number of administrative tribunals. He recommends all other judicial appointments to the Crown and appoints magistrates. He has general responsibility for the legal aid and advice schemes and for the administration of civil law reform.

The Home Secretary is concerned with the criminal law, the police service, prisons, and the probation and after-care service. He has general supervision over magistrates' courts and approves the appointment of justices' clerks. He appoints a board of visitors to each prison establishment (see p 104). He is advised by the Parole Board on the release of prisoners on licence. The Home Secretary is also responsible for advising the Queen on the exercise of the royal prerogative of mercy to pardon a person convicted of a crime or to remit all or part of a penalty imposed by a court.

The Attorney General and the Solicitor General are the Government's principal advisers on English law, and they represent the Crown in appropriate domestic and international cases. They are senior barristers, elected members of the House of Commons and hold ministerial posts. The Attorney General is also Attorney General for Northern Ireland. As well as exercising various civil law functions, the Attorney General has final responsibility for enforcing the criminal law. The Solicitor General is, in effect, the deputy of the Attorney General. As head of the Crown Prosecution Service, the Director of Public Prosecutions is subject to superintendence by the Attorney General, as are the Director of the Serious Fraud Office and the Director of Public Prosecutions for Northern Ireland.

Scotland

The Secretary of State for Scotland recommends the appointment of all judges other than the most senior ones, appoints the staff of the High Court of Justiciary and the Court of Session, and is responsible for the composition, staffing and organisation of the sheriff courts. District courts are staffed and administered by the district and islands local authorities.

The Secretary of State is also responsible for the criminal law of Scotland, crime prevention, the police, the penal system and legal aid; he is advised on parole matters by the Parole Board for Scotland.

The Lord Advocate and the Solicitor General for Scotland are the chief legal advisers to the Government on Scottish questions and the principal representatives of the Crown for the purposes of litigation in Scotland. Both are government ministers. The Lord Advocate is closely concerned with legal policy and administration, and is responsible for the Scottish parliamentary counsel. He must exercise an independent discretion when prosecuting crime.

Northern Ireland

The administration of all courts is the responsibility of the Lord Chancellor, while the Northern Ireland Office, under the Secretary of State, deals with the criminal law, the police and the penal system. The Lord Chancellor has general responsibility for legal aid, advice and assistance.

THE PERSONNEL OF THE LAW

The courts of the United Kingdom are the Queen's Courts, since the Crown is the historic source of all judicial power. The Queen, acting on the advice of ministers, is responsible for all appointments to the judiciary.

Judges

Judges are normally appointed from practising barristers, advocates (in Scotland), or solicitors (see below).

Lay magistrates in England and Wales need no legal qualifications but are trained to give them sufficient knowledge of the law, including the rules of evidence, and of the nature and purpose of sentencing.

The Scottish district court justices of the peace need no legal qualifications, but they too must take part in training.

In Northern Ireland members of a lay panel who serve in juvenile courts undertake training courses; resident magistrates are drawn from practising solicitors or barristers.

The Legal Profession

The legal profession is divided into two branches: barristers (advocates in Scotland) and solicitors.

Barristers are known collectively as the 'Bar', and collectively and individually as 'counsel'.

Solicitors undertake legal business for individual and corporate clients, while barristers advise on legal problems submitted through solicitors and present cases in the higher courts. Certain functions are common to both, for example, presentation of cases in the lower courts. Although people are free to conduct their own cases, most people prefer to be legally represented in the more serious cases.

Recent legislation is designed to increase the provision of good quality legal services for clients in Great Britain by lifting restrictions on who can provide these services. Solicitors will be eligible to appear in the higher courts. Building societies, banks and other financial organisations can offer conveyancing services under a scheme providing important new safeguards to clients. People in England and Wales wanting to take legal action will be able, like those in Scotland, to negotiate a form of 'no win, no fee' agreement, in personal injury cases, with their legal advisers.

The system of complaints against legal practitioners has been strengthened by the creation of a Legal Services Ombudsman able to investigate how the professional bodies handle these complaints. Similar proposals regarding legal services in Northern Ireland are being considered.

LEGAL AID

A person in need of legal advice or legal representation in court may qualify for help with the costs out of public funds, either free or with a contribution according to means under the various legal aid schemes.

Green Form Scheme

People whose income and savings are within certain limits are entitled to help from a solicitor on legal matters (with the exception of conveyancing and, in some cases, the making of a will in England and Wales). Such help includes advice on the relevant law, writing letters on the client's behalf, and taking the opinion of a barrister or advocate. In England, Wales and Northern Ireland it may be extended to cover representation in civil proceedings in the magistrates' court, Mental Health Review Tribunal hearings and certain disciplinary proceedings before prison boards of visitors.

In England and Wales the scheme provides for initial work to be done up to a limit of three hours' worth of work for matrimonial cases where a petition is drafted and two hours' worth for other work. There are cost limits in Northern Ireland.

Legal Aid in Civil Proceedings

Legal aid, which covers representation before the court, may be available for most civil proceedings to those who satisfy the financial eligibility conditions. An applicant for legal aid must also show not only that he or she has reasonable grounds for taking or defending proceedings—or being a party to proceedings—but also that it is reasonable that he or she should receive legal aid. If legal aid is granted, the case is conducted in the normal way; in England and Wales all payments to lawyers are made through the Legal Aid Fund administered by the Legal Aid Board.

In certain limited circumstances the successful unassisted opponent of a legally aided party may recover his or her costs in the case from the Legal Aid Fund. Where the assisted person recovers or preserves money or property in the proceedings, the Legal Aid Fund will usually have a first charge on that money or property to recover money spent on the assisted person's behalf.

Legal Aid in Criminal Proceedings

In criminal proceedings in England, Wales and Northern Ireland a legal aid certificate may be granted by the court if it appears to be in the interests of justice and if a defendant is considered to require assistance in meeting his or her costs. A certificate must be granted (subject to means) when a person is committed for trial on a murder charge or where the prosecutor appeals or applies for leave to appeal from the Court of Appeal to the House of Lords. No person who is unrepresented can be given a custodial sentence for the first time unless given the opportunity to apply for legal aid.

The Legal Aid Board in England and Wales makes arrangements for duty solicitors to be present at magistrates' courts to provide initial advice and representation to unrepresented defendants. Solicitors are available, on a 24-hour basis, to give advice and assistance to suspects at police stations. The services of a solicitor at a police station and the duty solicitor at court are free.

In Scotland there is a duty solicitor scheme for accused people in custody in sheriff and district court cases. An 'interests of justice' and 'means' test applies only in summary cases, where decisions on applications for legal aid are taken by the Scottish Legal Aid Board.

In Northern Ireland a voluntary duty solicitor scheme has been introduced at the principal magistrates' court in Belfast.

Legal aid for criminal cases in Scotland and Northern Ireland is free.

Law Centres

In a number of urban areas law centres provide free legal advice and representation. Financed from various sources, often including local government authorities, they usually employ full-time salaried lawyers and many have community workers. Much of their time is devoted to housing, employment, social security and immigration problems.

Free advice is also available in Citizens Advice Bureaux, consumer and housing advice centres and in specialist advice centres run by various voluntary organisations.

LAW REFORM

In England and Wales the Law Commission is responsible for reviewing the law and making recommendations for its simplification and modernisation. The Lord Chancellor also occasionally refers specific topics to the Law Reform Committee, nominating as members experts in the particular field of law involved. In criminal law matters the Home Secretary acts similarly with the Criminal Law Revision Committee. Any changes in the law are a matter for legislation.

Law reform in Scotland is the responsibility of the Scottish Law Commission, which reports to the Lord Advocate. In Northern Ireland the Law Reform Advisory Committee, which reports to the Secretary of State, reviews certain aspects of the civil law and makes recommendations for reform.

6   Social Welfare

The British social welfare system comprises the National Health Service (NHS), the personal social services and social security. The NHS provides a full range of medical services which are available to all residents, regardless of their income. Local authority personal social services and voluntary organisations provide help and advice to the most vulnerable members of the community. These include elderly, physically disabled, mentally ill and mentally handicapped people and children in need of care. The social security system is designed to secure a basic standard of living for people in financial need by providing income during periods of inability to earn (including periods of unemployment), help for families and assistance with costs arising from disablement.

Central government is directly responsible for the NHS, administered by a range of health authorities and boards throughout Britain acting as its agents, and for the social security system. Personal social services are administered by local authorities but central government is responsible for establishing national policies, issuing guidance and overseeing standards. Joint finance and planning between health and local authorities aims to prevent overlapping of services and to encourage the development of community services.

Planned spending on social welfare in 1991–92 is: health nearly £31,000 million and social security benefits over £60,000 million, while the standard spending assessment for personal social services is some £4,800 million.

Spending on the health service has increased substantially in real terms since 1980, and is planned to grow further over the next two years. More patients are being treated than ever before. Spending on social security is rising because of increased numbers of beneficiaries, especially retirement pensioners, and the long-term sick and disabled. The value of retirement and most other long-term benefits has also increased in real terms since 1980. Spending on the personal social services is determined by local authorities. Central government has restricted the total expenditure of individual local authorities, but spending has risen substantially in real terms since the late 1970s, reflecting the priority given to this sector.

National Health Service and Community Care Act 1990

The National Health Service and Community Care Act 1990 has introduced wide-ranging reform in management and patient care in the health and social care services. The NHS reforms came into effect in April 1991. Their aim is to give patients, wherever they live in Britain, better health care and greater choice of service. (For fuller details see pp 115, 117 and 118.) The reforms in community care provision, which take effect between April 1991 and April 1993, establish a new financial and managerial framework which aims to secure the delivery of good quality services in line with national objectives. They are intended to enable vulnerable groups in the community to live as normal a life as possible in their own homes, and to give them a greater say in how they live and how the services they need should be provided. (For fuller details see p 130.)

National Health Service

The NHS is based upon the principle that there should be a full range of publicly provided services designed to help the individual stay healthy. The services are intended to provide effective and appropriate treatment and care where necessary while making the best use of available resources. All taxpayers, employers and employees contribute to its cost so that those members of the community who do not require health care help to pay for those who do. Some forms of treatment, such as hospital care, are provided free; others (see p 115) may be charged for.

Growth in real spending on the health service is being used to meet the needs of increasing numbers of elderly people, to take full advantage of advances in medical technology and to remedy shortfalls in areas such as renal services. It is also used to provide more appropriate types of care, often in the community rather than in hospital, for priority groups such as the elderly, the mentally ill and people with mental handicaps. Increased spending is, in addition, intended to combat the growing health problems arising from alcohol and drug misuse; and to remedy disparities in provision between the regions of Britain.

The Government emphasises the importance of preventive health services, and the responsibility of individuals for their own health. While great progress has been made in eliminating infectious diseases such as poliomyelitis and tuberculosis, there has been less success in controlling the major causes of early death and disability—heart disease, cancer and stroke. Most recently the threat of AIDS (see p 125) has proved a serious problem for public health services.

Because of the close link between such diseases and individual behaviour, emphasis is placed on helping people to adopt healthier ways of living. In June 1991 the Government published a consultation paper containing proposals for a health strategy for England. Entitled *The Health of the Nation*, this outlines plans to reduce preventable diseases which lead to ill health and early death.

The Government stresses the need for a partnership between the public and private health sectors and for improving efficiency in order to secure the best value for money and the maximum patient care. Measures to achieve more effective management of resources in the NHS have included:

● appointing at regional, district and unit levels general managers drawn from inside and outside the health service;

● improving the accountability of health authorities for the planning and management of their resources;

● increasing the proportion of total staff who provide direct patient care, such as doctors and nurses; and

● introducing a range of programmes to provide services at lower cost.

Considerable savings have been made through the policy of competitive tendering for hospital cleaning, portering, catering and laundry services. Economies are also made in prescribing by restricting the use of expensive branded products in favour of cheaper but equally effective equivalent medicines.

ADMINISTRATION

The Secretary of State for Health in England and the Secretaries of State for Scotland, Wales and Northern Ireland are responsible for all aspects of the health services in their respective countries. The Department of Health is responsible for national strategic planning in England. The Scottish Office Home and Health Department, the Welsh Office and the Department of Health and Social Services in Northern Ireland have similar responsibilities.

District health authorities in England and Wales and health boards in Scotland are responsible for planning and operational control of all health services in their areas. England, because of its greater size and population, also has regional authorities responsible for regional planning, resource allocation, major capital building work and certain specialised hospital services. The authorities and boards co-operate closely with local authorities responsible for social work, environmental health, education and other services. Family health services authorities (health boards in Scotland) arrange for the provision of services by doctors, dentists, pharmacists and opticians, and administer their contracts. Community health councils represent local opinion on the health services provided. (In Scotland this function is exercised by local health councils.)

In Northern Ireland health and social services boards are responsible for all health and personal social services in their areas. The representation of public opinion on these services is provided for by area health and social services councils.

Major Reforms in Management

Under the National Health Service and Community Care Act 1990 a number of major reforms in organising and financing the NHS have been introduced.

1. Health authorities have been given a new role as purchasers of health care on behalf of their local residents, responsible for assessing local health care needs and ensuring that those needs are met within existing resources.

2. Each health authority is funded to buy health care for its local residents through arranging contracts with hospitals and other health service units—in either the public or private sectors. Under this system hospitals compete to sell their treatments to the health authorities. For the first time hospitals are directly funded for the number of patients they treat, making it easier for family doctors (general practitioners or GPs) to refer patients outside their area if treatment elsewhere is faster and better. Powers exist for allocating resources where the urgent need for treatment does not allow NHS contracts to be arranged in advance.

3. The contracts agreed between health authorities and hospitals set out the quality, quantity and cost of the services to be delivered during the year. The contracts secured by each health authority are based on wide consultation with all local GPs.

4. Hospitals may apply to become self-governing NHS trusts (see p 118), independent of local health authority control, but remaining within the NHS, accountable

to the relevant health department and funded largely through general taxation.

5. Family doctors from larger medical practices may apply to join the general practitioner fundholding scheme (see p 117), under which they receive an annual budget directly from the health authority, enabling them to buy certain hospital services for their patients.

Broadly similar changes have been introduced in Northern Ireland under separate legislation.

Finance

Nearly 80 per cent of the cost of the health service in Great Britain is paid for through general taxation. The rest is met from the NHS contribution paid with the National Insurance contribution and from the charges towards the cost of certain items such as drugs prescribed by a family doctor, and dental treatment. Health authorities may raise funds from voluntary sources. Certain hospitals increase their revenue by taking private patients who pay the full cost of their accommodation and treatment.

Around 75 per cent of medical prescription items are supplied free. Prescription charges do not apply to the following: children under 16 years (or students under 19 and still in full-time education); expectant mothers and women who have had a baby in the last year; women aged 60 and over and men aged 65 and over; patients suffering from certain medical conditions; war and armed forces disablement pensioners ; people who are receiving income support or family credit (see p 140); and families with low incomes.

There are proportional charges for all types of general dental treatment including dental examination. However, women who are pregnant or who have had a baby in the last year, anyone under the age of 18 (or 19 if in full-time education), people receiving income support or family credit, and families on low incomes do not have to pay. Sight tests are free to children, those on low incomes and certain other priority groups. Some disadvantaged groups receive help for the purchase, repair and replacement of spectacles.

Family practitioners (doctors, dentists, opticians and pharmacists) are self-employed and have contracts with the NHS. Family doctors are paid by a system of fees and allowances designed to reflect responsibilities, workload and practice expenses. Dentists providing treatment in their own surgeries are paid by a combination of capitation fees for treating children, continuing care payments for adults registered with the practice, and a prescribed scale of fees for individual treatments. Pharmacists dispensing from their own premises are refunded the cost of the items supplied, together with professional fees. Ophthalmic medical practitioners and ophthalmic opticians taking part in the general ophthalmic service receive approved fees for each sight test made.

Staffing

The NHS is one of the largest employers in the world, with a workforce of nearly 1 million people. Staff costs account for two-thirds of total NHS expenditure and three-quarters of current expenditure on hospitals and community health services. Between 1981 and 1989:

- the number of nursing and midwifery staff, who make up 51 per cent of the workforce, increased by 4·1 per cent;
- the number of medical and dental staff by 13·8 per cent; and
- the number of scientific, professional and technical staff by 25 per cent.

Health Service Commissioners

There are three posts of Health Service Commissioner (one each for England, Scotland and Wales) for dealing with complaints from members of the public about the health service. The three posts are held by the same person, who is also the Parliamentary Commissioner for Administration (Ombudsman), who reports annually to Parliament. The Health Service Commissioner can investigate complaints that a health authority or family health services authority has not carried out its statutory duties, has provided an inadequate service or, through maladministration, has caused injustice or hardship. Complaints about clinical judgment, personnel matters and the use of a health authority's discretionary powers lie beyond the Health Service Commissioner's jurisdiction, and separate procedures exist for these. In Northern Ireland the Commissioner for Complaints has a similar role.

FAMILY HEALTH SERVICES

The family health services are those given to patients by doctors, dentists, opticians and pharmacists of their own choice. Family doctors provide the first diagnosis in the case of illness and either prescribe a suitable course of treatment or refer a patient to the more specialised services and hospital consultants.

About four-fifths of family doctors in Britain work in partnerships or group practices, often as members of primary health-care teams. The teams also include health visitors and district nurses, and sometimes midwives, social workers and other professional staff employed by the health authorities. About a quarter of family doctors in Great Britain and over half in Northern Ireland work in modern and well-equipped health centres, where medical and nursing services are provided. Health centres may also have facilities for health education, family planning, speech therapy, chiropody, assessment of hearing, physiotherapy and remedial exercises. Dental, pharmaceutical and ophthalmic services, hospital outpatient and supporting social work services may also be provided.

There have been substantial increases in primary health care staff in recent years. For example, in England between 1978 and 1989, the number of family doctors increased by 22 per cent (to 25,600) and average patient list size fell by 15 per cent (to 1,970), while the number of family dentists increased by 28 per cent (to 15,000). Practice staff have increased by 95 per cent since 1978, and within that total the number of practice nurses has grown by 425 per cent.

Special funds have been earmarked by the Government for improving the quality of primary health care in inner city areas. Efforts have also been made to improve health services for black and ethnic minority groups. These include new health projects in Britain's Chinese communities, and increased central funding for health information material to be produced in many minority languages.

Eye Services

Only ophthalmic opticians and ophthalmic medical practitioners may test sight. Entitlement to free NHS sight tests is restricted to people on low incomes, children and those with particular medical needs. Spectacles are supplied by registered ophthalmic and dispensing opticians but unregistered retailers may also sell spectacles to adults under carefully prescribed conditions. Children, people on low incomes and those requiring certain complex lenses receive a voucher to put towards the cost of their spectacles.

Recent Developments

GP Fundholders

Under the 1990 Act GP practices with 9,000 patients or over may apply for fundholding status. They then become responsible for their own NHS budgets, enabling them to buy certain non-urgent hospital services. Prescription charges and part of the cost of running the practice are also covered. Fundholders may negotiate directly with hospitals from both public and private sectors in any district or regional health authority. By March 1991 over 300 practices—covering nearly 4 million people or 7·5 per cent of the population—were awaiting final approval as fundholders.

Contracts

A new performance-related contract for GPs came into effect in April 1990. It is designed to raise standards of care, extend the range of services available to patients and improve patient choice. The changes are intended to make it easier for patients to see their GP at times convenient to them and easier for patients to change doctors; and to encourage doctors to practise more preventive medicine.

A new contract for dentists was introduced in October 1990. As a result NHS dental care now includes preventive care as well as restorative treatment. Under the contract patients are offered continuing care, and dentists are encouraged to practise more preventive dentistry for children. There are also incentives for dentists to undertake further training.

Medical Audit

Medical audit systems, which are intended to enable doctors at all levels in the health service to review the quality of the medical care they give to their patients, have been introduced in all health authorities. In 1991–92 the Government is allocating £46 million to continue to develop medical audit in the hospital and community health services.

Health Visitors, District Nurses and Midwives

Health visitors are responsible for the preventive care and health education of families, particularly those with young children. They work closely with GPs, district nurses and other professions. District nurses give skilled nursing care to people at home or elsewhere outside hospital; they also play an important role in health promotion and education. Although almost all babies are born in hospital, some antenatal care and most postnatal care is given in the community by midwives and GPs, who also care for women having their babies at home. Midwives are responsible for educating and supporting women and their families during the child-bearing period.

HOSPITALS AND SPECIALIST SERVICES

A full range of hospital services is provided by district general hospitals. These include treatment and diagnostic facilities for in-patients, day-patients and outpatients;

maternity departments; infectious disease units; psychiatric and geriatric facilities; rehabilitation facilities; convalescent homes and all forms of specialised treatment. There are also specialist hospitals or units for children, people suffering from mental illness or mental handicaps, and elderly people, and for the treatment of specific diseases. Examples of these include the world-famous Hospital for Sick Children, Great Ormond Street, and the Brompton Heart and Chest Hospital in London. Hospitals designated as teaching hospitals combine treatment facilities with training medical and other students, and research work.

Many of the hospitals in the NHS were built in the nineteenth century; some, such as St Bartholomew's and St Thomas' in London, trace their origins to much earlier charitable foundations. Much has been done to improve and extend existing buildings and many new hospitals have been or are being opened. Since 1979 in Great Britain 580 health building schemes, each costing £1 million or more, have been completed. A further 225 schemes are at various stages of development.

Recent policy in England and Wales has been to provide a balanced hospital service centred around a district general hospital, complemented as necessary by smaller, locally based hospitals and facilities.

The world's first low-energy nucleus hospital, which is expected to use less than half the energy of a conventional nucleus hospital, opened on the Isle of Wight in late 1990, and another is being built in Northumberland.

The latest development in hospital planning in England and Wales is the nucleus hospital. This is designed to accommodate a full range of district general hospital facilities and is capable of being built in self-contained phases or as an extension to an existing hospital. By mid-1991, 70 nucleus hospitals had been completed. A further 57 are at various stages of development. Those already open have proved economical to build and are providing high-quality and cost-effective services to patients.

The hospital service is now treating more patients a year than ever before. Between 1978 and 1989–90 lengths of stay for in-patients declined and the number of people treated as day patients more than doubled. Over 1 million cases are now dealt with in this way. Newer forms of treatment and diagnosis are being made more widely available. These include kidney dialysis, hip replacements, laser treatment for certain eye conditions, and body scanning.

In 1986 the Government launched a drive to reduce hospital waiting lists and times. In 1991–92 the Government is investing £35 million in a variety of projects, including mobile operating theatres, to improve waiting times for patients.

Community services such as the psychiatric nursing service, day hospitals, and local authority day centres have expanded so that more patients remain in the community and others are sent home from hospital sooner.

Self-governing NHS Trusts

Under the National Health Service and Community Care Act 1990 hospitals and other health service units may apply to become independent of health authority control and establish themselves as self-governing NHS trusts. These are run by boards of directors, and are free to employ their own staff, conduct research and provide facilities for medical education and other forms of training. Self-governing NHS trusts derive their income mainly through NHS contracts to provide services to health authorities and GP fundholders. The trusts may treat private patients. All trusts must provide annual reports, and annual accounts modelled on commercial accountancy practices. By August 1991, 57 NHS trusts had been established.

Private Medical Treatment

The Government's policy is for the NHS and the independent sector to co-operate in meeting the nation's health needs. It believes that this will benefit the NHS by adding to the resources devoted to health care and offering flexibility to health authorities in the delivery of services. Some health authorities share expensive facilities and equipment with private hospitals, and NHS patients are sometimes treated (at public expense) in the private sector to reduce waiting lists.

The scale of private practice in relation to the NHS is, however, small. There are 113,000 beds in the independent health care sector, while approximately 3,000 beds in health service hospitals in England are authorised for private patients.

It is estimated that about three-quarters of those receiving acute treatment in private hospitals or NHS hospital pay-beds are covered by health insurance schemes which make provision for private health care in return for annual subscriptions. Over 3 million people subscribe to such schemes, half of them within group schemes, some arranged by firms on behalf of employees. Subscriptions often cover more than one person (for example, members of a family) and the total number of people covered by private medical insurance in Britain is estimated at over 6 million. The Government has introduced tax relief on private health insurance premiums paid by people aged 60 and over to encourage the increased use of private health facilities.

Many overseas patients come to Britain for treatment in private hospitals and clinics, and Harley Street in London is an internationally recognised centre for medical consultancy.

There is a growing interest in alternative therapies such as homoeopathy, osteopathy and acupuncture, which are mainly practised outside the NHS.

Organ Transplants

Over the past 25 years there have been significant developments in transplant surgery in Britain. The United Kingdom Transplant Support Service Authority provides a centralised organ matching and distribution service. Around 8,000 people in Britain were living with functioning kidney transplants, and during 1990 over 1,800 kidney transplants were performed. A similar service exists for corneas, and in 1990, over 2,000 were transplanted.

Heart transplant operations have been conducted at Papworth Hospital in Cambridgeshire and Harefield Hospital in London since 1979. There are five other heart transplant centres in England, while Scotland's first unit is scheduled to open in Glasgow in late 1991.

A programme of combined heart and lung transplants is in progress and in 1990, over 280 heart and 94 heart-lung transplants were performed. The world's first combined heart, lungs and liver transplant operation was carried out at Papworth in 1987. Over 350 liver transplants were also performed in 1990.

A voluntary organ donor card system enables people to indicate their willingness to become organ donors in the event of their death. Commercial dealing in organs intended for transplant is illegal.

Blood Transfusion

The blood transfusion service in England and Wales collects over 2 million donations of blood and over 130,000 donations of plasma each year from voluntary unpaid donors; in Scotland the figures are over 330,000 and over 15,000 respectively. Regional transfusion centres recruit donors and organise donor sessions in towns and villages, factories and offices, and within the armed forces. Donors are normally aged between 18 and 65. The centres are also responsible for blood grouping and testing, maintaining blood banks, providing a consultancy service to hospitals, teaching in medical schools, and instructing doctors, nurses and technicians.

The Central Blood Laboratories Authority is responsible for the manufacture of blood products as well as for research. There is also increasing emphasis on the most effective use of blood and, in particular, its separation into components such as plasma for specific uses. A laboratory at Elstree, Hertfordshire, was opened in 1987 with the aim of meeting the needs for all blood products in England and Wales. Facilities in Scotland are being expanded to cope with rising demand.

Ambulance Services

The health authorities provide free transport by ambulance for accident and emergency patients and urgent maternity cases. Transport is also provided for some people needing non-emergency outpatient treatment at hospitals, clinics and day hospitals. In some areas voluntary organisations using their own vehicles or volunteers using their own cars help with non-urgent cases. In 1991 fast-response pilot schemes were introduced in London, the West Midlands area, and in four Scottish cities, in which paramedics use cars and motorcycles to reach emergency cases. In Scotland an air ambulance service is available in the islands and in the remoter parts of the mainland. Helicopter ambulances also serve several parts of England.

Rehabilitation

Rehabilitation begins at the onset of illness or of injury and continues throughout, with the aim of helping people to adjust to changes in life-style and to live as normally as possible. Rehabilitation services are available for elderly, young, disabled, mentally ill and mentally handicapped people who need such help to resume life in the community. These services are offered in hospitals, centres in the community and in people's own homes through co-ordinated work by a range of professional workers.

Medical services may provide free artificial limbs and eyes, hearing aids, surgical supports, wheelchairs, and other appliances. Following assessment, very severely physically handicapped patients may be provided with environmental control equipment which enables them to operate devices such as alarm bells, radio and television, telephones, and heating appliances. Nursing aids may be provided on loan for use in the home.

Local authorities may provide a range of facilities to help patients in the transition from hospital to their own homes. These include the provision of aids, care from home helps, and professional help from occupational therapists and social workers. Voluntary organisations also provide help, complementing the work of the statutory agencies and widening the range of services.

Hospices

A number of hospices provide care for the terminally ill (including children) either directly in in-patient or day care units or through nursing and other assistance in the patient's own home. Control of symptoms and psychological support for patients and their families form central features of the modern hospice movement, which started in Britain and is now worldwide. Some hospices are administered entirely by the NHS; the remainder are run by independent charities, some receiving support from public funds.

The Government is seeking to provide a level of public funding for the hospice movement which matches voluntary donations. In 1991–92, £17 million was allocated to health authorities to enable them to offer increased support to hospices and similar organisations, while a further £3·2 million was allocated to enable them to arrange for drugs to be supplied to hospices without charge. The Government has also provided an initial £150,000 to support research into standards of palliative care.

Parents and Children

Special preventive services are provided under the health service to safeguard the health of expectant mothers and of mothers with young children. Services include free dental treatment, dried milk and vitamins; health education; and vaccination and immunisation of children against certain infectious diseases (see p 126). Pregnant women receive antenatal care from their family doctor and hospital clinics, and women in paid employment have the right to visit the clinics during working hours. Some 99 per cent of women have their babies in hospital, returning home shortly afterwards to be attended by a midwife or health visitor and, where necessary, the family doctor. The Government attaches great importance to improving the quality of maternity services, and to making them more sensitive to the needs and wishes of mothers and their families. The perinatal mortality rate (the number of stillbirths and deaths in the first week of life) has fallen in England and Wales from 14·6 per 1,000 births in 1979 to 8·1 per 1,000 births in 1990. A similar reduction has occurred in Scotland and Northern Ireland.

A comprehensive programme of health surveillance is provided for pre-school children in clinics run by the community health authorities, and increasingly by family doctors. This enables doctors, dentists and health visitors to oversee the physical and mental health and development of pre-school children. Information on preventive services is given and welfare foods are distributed. The school health service offers health care and advice for schoolchildren, including medical and dental inspection and treatment where necessary.

Child guidance and child psychiatric services provide help and advice for children with psychological or emotional problems.

In recent years special efforts have been made to improve co-operation between the community-based child health services and local authority social services for children. This is particularly important in the prevention of child abuse and for the health and welfare of children in care.

Human Fertilisation and Embryology

The world's first 'test-tube baby' was born in Britain in 1978, as a result of the technique of *in vitro* fertilisation. This opened up new horizons for helping with problems of infertility and for the science of embryology. The social, ethical and legal implications were examined by a committee of inquiry under Baroness Warnock, which reported in 1984. Legislation implementing the main recommendations of this report was passed in 1990. The Human Fertilisation and Embryology Act, which came into effect in August 1991, provides for:

- The establishment of the Human Fertilisation and Embryology Authority (HFEA) to regulate certain infertility treatments and human embryo research centres.
- Research to be conducted on embryos for up to 14 days after fertilisation.
- The legal status and rights of children born as a result of the new treatments.
- The clarification of the legal position on surrogate motherhood (the practice where one woman bears a child for another).

The HFEA is responsible for issuing a code of practice for such centres and must report annually to Parliament.

These provisions constitute one of the most comprehensive pieces of legislation on assisted reproduction and embryo research in the world.

Legislation to ban commercial surrogacy agencies, and advertising of or for surrogacy services, was passed in 1985.

Family Planning

Free family planning advice and treatment are available to women from family doctors and from health authority family planning clinics, which also make services available to men.

Abortion

The Abortion Act 1967 allows the ending of pregnancy by a doctor if two doctors consider that continuing the pregnancy would be more damaging to the well-being of the woman (or to any existing children in the family) than having an abortion. An abortion may also be allowed if two doctors consider there is a substantial risk that if the child were born it would have a severe physical or mental handicap. In 1990 amendments to the Act introduced a 24-week time limit for abortions, but stipulated no time limit where there is risk of grave permanent injury to the health of the woman, or substantial risk of serious foetal handicap.

Abortions are carried out in NHS hospitals or in private premises approved for the purpose by the Secretary of State. Over half of the legal abortions to women resident in England and Wales in 1990 were performed in private hospitals and clinics; in Scotland, 97 per cent of abortions take place in NHS hospitals.

The Act does not apply in Northern Ireland.

Drug Misuse

The misuse of dangerous drugs, such as heroin, cocaine and amphetamines, is a serious social and health problem, and the Government has made the fight against such misuse a major priority. Its strategy comprises action to reduce the supply of illicit drugs from abroad; to promote more effective law enforcement by the police and Customs services; and to maintain tight controls on medicinal drugs that can be misused. It also includes action to maintain effective deterrents against misuse; to develop effective programmes to treat and rehabilitate misusers; and to prevent people who are not misusers from starting, by means of educational programmes and publicity campaigns.

Research on various aspects of drug misuse is funded by several government departments. The Government is advised on a wide range of matters relating to drug misuse and connected social problems by the Advisory Council on the Misuse of Drugs.

Prevention

The Government has set up a drugs advisory service to advise district health authorities on the development of facilities in their areas. It continues to make funds available for local education authorities in England and Wales to appoint staff to promote and co-ordinate preventive work in their areas, especially for anti-drug-misuse work in schools. As part of the National Curriculum (see p 152), children in primary and secondary schools receive education on the dangers of drug misuse. Since 1986 the Government has supported expenditure of over £14 million to drugs education.

The Government's Drug Prevention Initiative has provided funding for the establishment of local drug prevention teams in 20 areas in England, Scotland and Wales. Their task is to strengthen community resistance to drug misuse. Separate measures have been introduced in Scotland to discourage drug misuse through publicity campaigns and action in the education service and the community.

Publicity Campaigns

As part of its prevention policy, the Government began a major publicity campaign in 1985 to persuade young people not to take drugs, and to advise parents, teachers and other professional staff on how to recognise and combat the problem. Subsequent phases of the campaign have warned of the dangers of heroin misuse and of the risks of transmitting HIV (human immunodeficiency virus), the virus which causes AIDS (see p 125), through the sharing of injecting equipment. In 1990 the Government launched a further £3·8 million campaign to promote awareness of the dangers of drug misuse among young people. In 1991–92 the campaign is focusing on local drugs problems and local methods of prevention.

Treatment and Rehabilitation

A total of £17·5 million over the three years 1988–89 to 1990–91 was spent on the development of services for drug misusers. Additional sums have been made available since 1986–87 through the health authorities in England for the expansion of services for drug misusers, rising to nearly £16·5 million in 1991–92. A further grant of £2 million in 1991–92 is intended to help local authorities to develop voluntary sector services for drug as well as alcohol misusers. Similar projects are in progress in Wales and in Scotland, where over £2 million is made available annually to health boards for the support of drug misuse services. To reduce the spread of AIDS a number of trial schemes are in progress, offering drug misusers counselling and the exchange of clean for used syringes and needles.

Treatment for drug dependence is provided mainly on an outpatient basis. Many hospitals provide specialist treatment for drug misusers, mainly in psychiatric units, or have special drug treatment units. An increasing number of family doctors also treat drug misusers, but only certain specialist doctors are licensed to prescribe heroin, cocaine and dipipanone (Diconal). All doctors must notify the authorities of any patient they consider to be addicted to certain controlled drugs, and guidelines on good medical practice in the treatment of drug misuse have been issued to all doctors in Great Britain. The Home Secretary has statutory powers for dealing with doctors found to have prescribed irresponsibly.

Other Sources of Provision

A number of non-statutory agencies work with and complement the health service provision. Advice and rehabilitation services including residential facilities, for example, are provided mainly by voluntary organisations. Support in the community is provided by the probation service and local social services departments.

Solvent Misuse

Action is also being taken by the Government to curb the problem of solvent misuse (the breathing in of vapour from glue, lighter fuel and other substances) by young people. In England and Wales it is an offence to supply such substances to children under 18 if the supplier knows or has reason to believe they are to be used to cause intoxication. Information and guidance material have been distributed to retailers, parents, teachers and other professional workers to help them educate young people on the dangers of the habit and warn them against experimenting. Work in these areas is increasing in 1991–92. In Scotland the misuse of a solvent is a ground for referral to a children's hearing (see p 106).

Smoking

Cigarette smoking is the greatest preventable cause of illness and death in Britain. It accounts for around 110,000 premature deaths and 30 million lost working days each year, and costs the NHS an estimated £500 million a year for the treatment of diseases caused by smoking (for example, heart disease, lung cancer and bronchitis). In addition, smoking by pregnant women can cause low birth weight in infants. The Government is following an active health education policy supported by voluntary agreements with the tobacco industry aimed at reducing the level of smoking.

Health Education

The Government aims to reduce adult smoking from the present level of 32 per cent to 21 per cent among women and 22 per cent among men by the year 2000. A further aim is to reduce smoking by young people by one-third by 1994. A £2 million a year campaign directed at those aged 11 to 15 started in late 1989 and is planned to last until 1994. In late 1991 the Government will launch a £1 million campaign over two years to alert women to the dangers of smoking during pregnancy.

Education on the harmful effects of smoking is included in the National Curriculum for all pupils in publicly maintained schools in England and Wales.

The Government also supports the work of the voluntary organisation Action on Smoking and Health (ASH), whose services include a workplace services consultancy, offering advice and help to employers in formulating smoking policies. The Government encourages the restriction of smoking on public transport and in public buildings. Health authorities have been asked to promote non-smoking as the normal practice in health service buildings and to give help and advice to people who want to give up smoking. The Independent Scientific Committee on Smoking and Health estimates that 'passive smoking', especially in the workplace and the home, may cause several hundred deaths through lung cancer every year.

Voluntary Agreements

Voluntary agreements between the Government and the tobacco industry regulate the advertising and promotion of tobacco products, and sports sponsorship by the industry. The agreement on tobacco advertising provides for the use of six different health warnings about the dangers of smoking and contains measures to protect groups at particular risk, such as children, young people and women in early child-bearing years. In September 1991 a new agreement was signed, under which the tobacco industry is to reduce shopfront advertising by 50 per cent by 1996. The voluntary agreement on sports sponsorship covers levels of spending, restrictions on sponsorship of events chiefly for spectators under 18 years and controls over the siting of advertising at televised events.

Legislative Measures

It is illegal to sell any type of tobacco product to children. Cigarette advertising is banned on television and radio, and cigar advertisements are to be banned on television from October 1991. The Government proposes to replace some aspects of the voluntary system relating to health warnings on tobacco products and tar yield by legislation in 1992.

Alcohol Misuse

The far-reaching effects of alcohol misuse in terms of illness, family break-ups, inefficiency at work, loss of earnings, accidents and crime are widely acknowledged. The Government considers that the reduction of such misuse requires a range of action by central and local government, voluntary and community bodies, the health professions, business and trade unions. It believes that emphasis should be placed on policies to prevent alcohol misuse and continues to seek better information about the causes of problem drinking. It also seeks to encourage healthier life-styles, and to provide earlier help for the problem drinker.

Treatment and rehabilitation include in-patient and outpatient services in general and psychiatric hospitals and specialised alcoholism treatment units. Primary care teams (GPs, nurses and social workers) and voluntary organisations providing hostels, day centres and advisory services also play an important role.

There is close co-operation between statutory and voluntary organisations. The national voluntary agency, Alcohol Concern, which is receiving a government grant of £583,000 for 1991–92, plays a prominent role in the prevention of misuse, training for professional and voluntary workers, and improving the network of local voluntary agencies and their collaboration with statutory bodies. In 1990 Alcohol Concern launched a workplace advisory service with initial government funding of £100,000 as part of a campaign to persuade companies that alcohol misuse is an industrial as well as a social problem. From 1990–91 to 1993–94 a total government contribution of £4 million will be allocated to Alcohol Concern for improving and extending the network of advisory and counselling services. The Scottish Council on Alcohol undertakes similar work in Scotland. Research and surveys on various aspects of alcohol misuse are funded by several government departments.

In 1987 the Government established an interdepartmental group to develop strategy for combating the misuse of alcohol. Measures taken include legislative changes as well as steps to secure better health education and more effective action by local services and organisations. Legislation came into force in 1988 to strengthen the law banning the sale of alcohol to people under 18 years. At the same time, stricter controls on alcohol advertising were introduced. People appearing in advertisements must now be seen to be over 25 years of age; excessive drinking is not to be encouraged, shown or implied; and alcohol is not to be advertised alongside aggressive or anti-social behaviour. Independent television restricts the advertising of alcohol in programmes aimed at young people.

In 1989 the Government announced

increased funding for the Health Education Authority's expanded alcohol education programme. This aims to reduce the harm caused by the misuse of alcohol by promoting sensible drinking as part of a healthy way of life. It also seeks to develop a climate of opinion which favours appropriate measures to prevent alcohol-related harm. Alcohol misuse co-ordinators have been appointed in each of the 14 regional health authorities in England with the aim of developing strategies to counter the misuse of alcohol.

AIDS

The number of cases of AIDS reported in Britain continues to rise: by the end of June 1991 there were 4,758 cases, of whom 2,747 (58 per cent) had died. Recent statistics show a steady increase in the number of AIDS cases among injecting drug users and people infected through heterosexual intercourse.

Government measures to limit the spread of AIDS have included measures to maintain the safety of blood and blood products through publicity aimed at blood donors, the screening of blood donations, the treatment of blood products for haemophiliacs, and the development of public education campaigns at national and local level.

Public Education Campaigns

The first major public education campaign on AIDS was launched in 1987. This comprised television, radio, cinema and poster advertising, the establishment of a free national telephone advisory service and the delivery of leaflets to all households in Britain. Subsequent campaigns and educational work have been directed at the general population and specific groups including students and young people, women, homosexual and bisexual men, people travelling overseas, and at drug misusers who risk contracting AIDS through sharing infected needles and syringes. By the end of 1990–91 the Government had allocated over £50 million to this work. Separate educational packages have also been prepared for particular groups of people,

including prison staff and prisoners, schoolchildren, and employers. National campaigns are now being supplemented by local HIV prevention initiatives run by health and local authorities and the voluntary sector. The Government has asked each district to appoint an HIV prevention co-ordinator to lead this work for which additional funds have been provided. The Government continues to spend more on HIV/AIDS health education than on any other single health education programme.

Funding for Services

The Government continues to make additional funding available to health authorities and local authorities for treatment and advisory services, needle exchange schemes for drug misusers (see p 123) and training staff. In 1991–92, £137 million is being provided to health authorities and £10 million to local authorities towards the costs of providing HIV-related services. Government grants of £76 million have been allocated to the Macfarlane Trust to help haemophiliacs in Britain who have become infected with HIV as a result of treatment with infected blood products. The anonymous and voluntary named screening tests for HIV began in January 1990. The first results of anonymised testing carried out in sexually transmitted disease clinics and in antenatal clinics indicated a high incidence of HIV in the London area. In response to this in May 1991 the Government set up an AIDS Action Group to reinforce prevention initiatives in areas with high incidence of AIDS.

Research

In 1987 a £31 million research programme was launched with the aim of developing both a vaccine to prevent HIV infection and drugs to treat people already infected. A new drug, 'Retrovir' (zidovudine—AZT), which can improve the health of some people with AIDS, has been developed by a British pharmaceutical company.

Voluntary Agencies

A number of voluntary agencies receive financial support from the Government (some £1·9 million in 1991–92). Among them, the Terrence Higgins Trust, London Lighthouse and the Scottish AIDS Monitor promote knowledge about the disease and help people with AIDS and HIV. Both London Lighthouse and the Mildmay Mission Hospital provide hospice care and community support.

International Co-operation

Britain gives high priority to international efforts to reduce the spread of HIV and AIDS. The Government fully supports the work of the World Health Organisation (WHO) in leading and co-ordinating international action, and has committed £21 million to the WHO's Global Programme on AIDS, which is helping developing countries to establish and develop national AIDS control programmes. Britain has also pledged £7·5 million in support of WHO-co-ordinated national programmes in Africa and the Caribbean.

Other assistance includes a grant of nearly £3 million over six years to the International Planned Parenthood Federation for AIDS-related activities; about £0·9 million for small AIDS projects jointly funded by non-governmental organisations and some £3 million for research into the demographic, behavioural, social and economic aspects of AIDS in the developing world.

The European Community allocated about £23·3 million to AIDS projects through its Development Fund in 1987–91, of which Britain's attributed share was £4·7 million.

Infectious Diseases

District health authorities (health boards in Scotland) carry out programmes of immunisation against diphtheria, measles, rubella (for women of child-bearing age and girls only), poliomyelitis, tetanus, tuberculosis and whooping cough. A new combined vaccine against measles, mumps and rubella was introduced in 1988 to replace that for measles for children in the second year of life. A new programme for immunisation, which is designed to provide earlier protection for children, was introduced in 1990. Immunisation is voluntary, but parents are encouraged to protect their children. The proportion of children being vaccinated has been increasing since the end of 1978. In 1990 the Government introduced special payments to GPs who achieve targets of 70 and 90 per cent uptake of child immunisation. The response to these targets has been encouraging in many areas.

The Public Health Laboratory Service provides a network of bacteriological and virological laboratories throughout England and Wales which conduct research and assist in the diagnosis, prevention and control of communicable diseases. Microbiological work in Scotland and Northern Ireland is carried out mainly in hospital laboratories.

Cancer Screening

Breast cancer accounts for some 13,000 deaths in England each year. To help combat this, the Government is setting up a nation-wide breast cancer screening service for all women aged between 50 and 64. The aim of the programme is to reduce breast cancer deaths among women invited for screening by 25 per cent by 2000. The service is now available in most areas, and all eligible women in England and Wales should have their mammography screening invitations by 1993 (and in Scotland and Northern Ireland by 1994).

About 1,700 women die each year in England from cancer of the cervix. The cervical screening programme aims to reduce such deaths by inviting women at risk to be screened regularly. All district health authorities in England have computerised call and recall systems, which enable all women aged between 20 and 64 to be invited regularly for cervical cancer screening. Similar arrangements apply in Wales, Scotland and Northern Ireland. Special payments are made to GPs who achieve uptake targets of 50 and 80 per cent.

Health Education

In England health education is promoted by the Health Education Authority, a part of the NHS with the major executive responsibility for public education in Britain about AIDS (see p 125). In addition, in England the Authority's functions are:

- to advise the Government on health education;
- plan and carry out health education programmes in co-operation with health authorities and other bodies; and
- sponsor research and evaluation.

It also assists the provision of training, and provides a national centre of information and advice on health education. Major campaigns carried out by the Authority include those that focus on coronary heart disease (represented by the Look After Your Heart initiative), smoking and alcohol misuse.

In Wales these functions are undertaken by the Welsh Health Promotion Authority. The Health Education Board for Scotland and the Northern Ireland Health Promotion Agency are responsible for health education in their areas.

Almost all health authorities have their own health education service, which works closely with health professionals, health visitors, community groups, local employers and others to determine the most suitable local programmes. Increased resources in the health service are being directed towards health education and preventive measures.

Healthier Eating

There has been growing public awareness in recent years of the importance of a healthy diet. Following recommendations issued by the Committee on Medical Aspects of Food Policy (COMA), the Government has advised people to reduce their intake of fats, particularly saturated fats, sugar and salt, since this could help to reduce the possibility of cardiovascular disease.

Nutritional labelling indicating the energy, fat, protein and carbohydrate content of food is being encouraged on a voluntary basis. Some supermarket chains have already introduced voluntary labelling schemes.

To help people reduce their fat intake, the Government has issued guidelines on the labelling of food to show nutrient content in a standard format.

Current work by COMA includes a review of the relationship between diet and cardiovascular disease; and matters relating to the nutrition of infants, children and the elderly. In 1989 the Committee issued a report on the role of dietary sugars in human disease and on the diets of British schoolchildren. In July 1991 it published a major report containing comprehensive information on recommended personal intakes of food energy and nutrients.

The four health promotion departments in Britain have all run public information campaigns promoting healthy eating.

ENVIRONMENTAL HEALTH

Environmental health officers employed by local authorities are responsible for the control of air pollution and noise, and food hygiene and safety. Their duties also cover the occupational health and safety aspects of a variety of premises, including offices and shops; the investigation of unfit housing; and in some instances refuse collection and home safety. Doctors who specialise in community medicine and are employed by the health authorities advise local authorities on the medical aspects of environmental health, infectious diseases and food poisoning. They may also co-operate with the authorities responsible for water supply and sewerage. Environmental health officers at ports and airports carry out duties concerned with shipping, inspection of imported foods and disease control. In Northern Ireland district councils are responsible for noise control; collection and disposal of refuse; clean air; and food composition, labelling and hygiene.

Safety of Food

It is illegal to supply food unfit for human consumption or to apply any treatment or process to food which makes it harmful to health. Places where food or drink is prepared, handled, stored or sold must conform to certain hygiene standards. Environmental health officers may take for examination samples of any food on sale or being distributed. Special regulations control the safety of particular foods such as milk, meat, ice-cream and shellfish.

The Food Safety Directorate was established within the Ministry of Agriculture, Fisheries and Food in 1989, to maintain the safety and quality of Britain's food supplies. A consumer panel created in the same year gives consumers a direct means of conveying their views on food safety and consumer protection issues to the Government.

The independent Advisory Committee on the Microbiological Safety of Food assesses the risks to human health from micro-organisms in food and drink and recommends action where appropriate.

The Food Safety Act 1990 emphasises food safety and consumer protection throughout the food chain. The Act applies to England, Wales and Scotland, introducing more effective powers and greatly increased penalties for offenders. Food companies must demonstrate that they have taken all reasonable precautions in manufacture, transport, storage and preparation. Special regulations govern the temperatures at which foods such as cooked meats should be stored. Separate legislation exists in Northern Ireland.

SAFETY OF MEDICINES

The health and agriculture ministers are responsible for licensing the manufacture, marketing and import of medicines for human and veterinary use. The Medicines Commission advises the ministers on policy regarding such products. The Committees on Safety of Medicines, on Dental and Surgical Materials and on the Review of Medicines advise on the safety, quality and effectiveness of medicinal products. The Committee on Safety of Medicines also monitors adverse reactions to drugs. Legislation also controls the advertising, labelling, packaging, distribution, sale and supply of medicinal products.

RESEARCH

In 1990–91 the health departments spent about £26·5 million on health research, in addition to expenditure by the Medical Research Council (the main government agency for the support of biomedical and clinical research). Priority areas include research into AIDS, primary health care, community care and child care, the NHS and personal social services staffing, public health and the NHS acute sector.

For England and Wales the Director of Research and Development at the Department of Health advises health ministers on the direction of centrally supported research, and, as a director of the NHS Management Executive, oversees research in the NHS. In Scotland the directly funded programme is administered by the Chief Scientist of the Scottish Office Home and Health Department.

In 1991 the Government announced a major research and development strategy for the NHS. Its aim is to use scientific research to identify the best and most cost-effective methods of health care. The strategy will set national priorities for research, which will be carried out by the regional health authorities. It is intended that up to 1·5 per cent of NHS expenditure will be used for research and development.

The Department of Health is involved in international research and development, and takes part in the European Community's medical and public health research programme.

THE HEALTH PROFESSIONS

Doctors and Dentists

Only people on the medical or dentists' registers may practise as doctors or dentists in the NHS. University medical and dental schools are responsible for teaching; the NHS provides hospital facilities for training. Full registration as a doctor requires five or six years' training in a medical school and hospital, with a further year's experience in a hospital. For a dentist, four or more years' training at a dental school is required. The regulating body for the medical profession is the General Medical Council and for dentists, the General Dental Council. The main professional associations are the British Medical Association and the British Dental Association.

Nurses

The minimum period of training required to qualify for registration as a first level nurse in general, mental health or mental handicap, or children's nursing is normally three years. Midwifery training for registered general nurses takes 18 months, and for other student midwives in England three years. Health visitors are registered general nurses with midwifery or approved obstetric experience who have completed a one-year course in health visiting. District nurses are registered general nurses who practise within the community. They must complete a six-month course followed by a period of supervised practice in district nursing.

Project 2000 is a scheme to reform the education of nurses, designed to make training more attractive and to give nurses a broader based education, enabling them to work in hospitals or the community without extensive further training. In 1991–92 the Government is allocating £71 million to fund the scheme in 14 colleges of nursing in England, while comparable arrangements are being made in other parts of Britain.

The United Kingdom Central Council for Nursing, Midwifery and Health Visiting is responsible for regulating and registering these professions.

Pharmacists

Pharmacists in general practice and in hospital must be registered with the Pharmaceutical Society of Great Britain or the Pharmaceutical Society of Northern Ireland. A three-year degree course approved by the Pharmaceutical Society followed by a year's approved training is necessary before registration. Most medicines can be supplied to customers only by, or under the supervision of, a registered pharmacist.

Opticians

The General Optical Council regulates the professions of ophthalmic optician and dispensing optician. Only registered ophthalmic opticians (or registered ophthalmic medical practitioners) may test sight. Training of ophthalmic opticians takes four years, including a year of practical experience under supervision. Dispensing opticians take a two-year full-time course with a year's practical experience or follow a part-time day-release course while employed with an optician.

Other

State registration may also be obtained by chiropodists, dietitians, medical laboratory scientific officers, occupational therapists, orthoptists, physiotherapists and radiographers. The governing bodies are seven boards, corresponding to the professions, under the general supervision of the Council for Professions Supplementary to Medicine. Training lasts one to four years and only those who are state registered may be employed in the NHS and some other public services.

Dental therapists (who have taken a two-year training course) and dental hygienists (who have taken a training course of about a year) may carry out some simple dental work under the supervision of a registered dentist.

In mid-1990 a new group of NHS staff— health care assistants—began work in hospitals and the community. They are intended to support the work of more highly qualified staff.

ARRANGEMENTS WITH OTHER COUNTRIES

The member states of the European Community have special health arrangements under which Community nationals resident in a member state are entitled to receive any treatment, either free or at a reduced cost, during visits to other Community countries. There are also arrangements to cover people who go to work or live in other Community countries. In addition, there are reciprocal arrangements with some other countries under which medical treatment is available to visitors if required immediately. Visitors are generally expected to pay if the purpose of their visit is to seek medical treatment. Visitors who are not covered by reciprocal arrangements must pay for any medical treatment they receive.

Personal Social Services

Personal social services assist elderly people, disabled people and their carers, children and young people, and families. Major services include skilled residential and day care, help for people confined to their homes and the various forms of social work. The statutory services are provided by local government social services authorities in England and Wales, social work departments in Scotland and health and social services boards in Northern Ireland. Alongside these providers are the many and varied contributions made by independent voluntary services. Much of the care given to elderly and disabled people is provided by families and self-help groups.

Demand for these services is rising because of the increasing number of elderly people and the fact that groups such as the elderly, the disabled and mentally ill or handicapped people can lead more normal lives in the community, given suitable support and facilities.

New policies regarding community care in England, Wales and Scotland are being implemented under the National Health Service and Community Care Act 1990. In April 1991 the rights of people using the personal social services were strengthened with the introduction of a complaints procedure. From April 1992 local authorities will be obliged to produce community care plans after wide consultation with the NHS and other interests. New procedures for

assessing individuals' care needs and commissioning services to meet them will be introduced in April 1993. Local authorities will then become responsible for the financial support of people in residential or nursing homes.

Elderly People

Services for elderly people are designed to help them live at home whenever possible. Only about 5 per cent of those aged 65 or over live in residential homes. These services may include advice and help given by social workers, domestic help, the provision of meals in the home, sitters-in, night attendants and laundry services as well as day centres, luncheon clubs and recreational facilities. Adaptations to the home can overcome a person's difficulties in moving about, and a wide range of aids is available for people with difficulties affecting their hearing or eyesight. Alarm systems have been developed to help elderly people obtain assistance in an emergency. In some areas 'good neighbour' and visiting services are arranged by the local authority or a voluntary organisation.

Many local authorities provide free or subsidised travel to elderly people within their areas. Social services authorities also provide residential home care for the elderly and those in poor health, and register and inspect homes run by voluntary organisations or privately.

As part of their responsibility for public housing, local authorities provide homes designed for elderly people; some of these developments have resident wardens. Housing associations and private builders also build such accommodation.

Disabled People

Britain has an estimated 6 million adults with one or more disabilities, of whom around 400,000 (7 per cent) live in communal establishments. Local social services authorities help with social rehabilitation and adjustment to disability. They are required to establish the number of disabled people in their area and to publicise services, which may include advice on personal and social problems arising from disability, as well as occupational, educational, social and recreational facilities, either at day centres or elsewhere. Other services provided may include adaptations to homes (such as ramps for wheelchairs, and ground-floor toilets); the delivery of cooked meals; and help in the home. In cases of special need, help may be given with installing a telephone or a television. Local authorities and voluntary organisations may provide severely disabled people with residential accommodation or temporary facilities to allow their carers relief from their duties. Specially designed housing may be available for those able to look after themselves.

Some authorities provide free or subsidised travel for disabled people on public transport, and they are encouraged to provide special means of access to public buildings. Special government regulations cover the provision of access for disabled people in the construction of new buildings.

The Independent Living Fund was set up in 1988 to provide financial help to very severely disabled people who need paid domestic support if they are to live in their own homes. The Fund, for which the Government is providing over £62 million in 1991–92, will run for five years.

In March 1991 the Government committed £3 million for a pilot scheme— the national disability information project— designed to improve information services for disabled people and their carers.

People with a Mental Handicap

The Government's policy is to encourage the development of local services for people with a mental handicap and their families through mutual co-operation between health and local authorities and voluntary and other organisations.

Services provided by social services authorities include short-term care, support for families in their own homes, provision for accommodation in ordinary housing and various types of day care. The main aims of the services are to ensure that as far as possible people with mental handicaps can lead full lives in their communities and that no one should be admitted to hospital unless it is necessary on health grounds.

Social services departments now provide most community services for people with a mental handicap. Specialised residential health provision, which may consist of small units in the community, is also provided for people with special needs, as is specialist health service support for those living elsewhere.

The transfer of children with a mental handicap living in institutions to more ordinary living arrangements remains a priority.

Mentally Ill People

Arrangements made by social services authorities for providing preventive care and after care for mentally ill people in the community include day centres, social centres and residential care. Social workers help patients and their families with problems caused by mental illness. In some cases they can apply for a mentally disordered person to be compulsorily admitted to and detained in hospital. The rights of such patients were extended by legislation in 1983, and a Mental Health Act Commission was set up to provide better safeguards. Corresponding legislation has also been introduced for Scotland and Northern Ireland.

In 1989 the Government announced a number of measures to improve the provision of services for mentally ill people. These include requiring district health authorities (health boards in Scotland) to plan individual health care programmes for all patients leaving hospital and a code of practice for compulsorily admitting and treating patients in hospital. Other measures include a review of public funding of voluntary organisations concerned with mental health and a new grant to local authorities to help meet the social care needs of patients.

There are many voluntary organisations concerned with mental illness and mental handicap, and these play an important role in the provision of services for both of these groups of people.

Help to Families

The Government believes in the central importance of the family to the well-being of society and considers that stable adult relationships are needed to support and enhance family life. Social services authorities, through their own social workers and others, give help to families facing special problems. This includes services for children at risk of injury or neglect who need care away from their own families, and support for family carers who look after elderly and other family members in order to give them relief from their duties. They also help single parents, including unmarried mothers. There are now many refuges run by local authorities or voluntary organisations for women, often with young children, whose home conditions have become intolerable. The refuges provide short-term accommodation and support while attempts are made to relieve the women's problems. Many authorities also contribute to the cost of social work with families (such as marriage guidance) carried out by voluntary organisations.

The Self-help and Families Project provides funding for nine voluntary agencies to assist groups of families to help themselves.

The Government launched a three-year initiative in 1989 to increase voluntary sector provision in England for disadvantaged families with children under five. With funds of £2 million, it is enabling voluntary organisations to research and develop day care services, particularly for single parents and families living in temporary accommodation.

Child Care

Day care facilities for children under five are provided by local authorities, voluntary agencies and privately. In allocating places in their day nurseries and other facilities, local authorities give priority to children with special social or health needs. Local authorities also register childminders, private day nurseries and playgroups in their areas and provide support and advice services for them.

The authorities can offer advice and help to families in difficulties to promote the welfare of children. The aim is to act at an early stage to reduce the need to put children into care or bring them before a court.

Child Abuse

Cases of child abuse are the joint concern of many authorities, agencies and professions, and local review committees provide a forum for discussion and co-ordination and draw up policies and procedures for handling these cases. The Government established a central training initiative on child abuse in 1986. This consists of a variety of projects, including training for health visitors, school nurses, and local authority social services staff. Training packs have been drawn up for those concerned with implementing the Children Act 1989 (see below).

In England, Wales and Northern Ireland children under the age of 14 in child abuse cases are able to give evidence to courts through television links, thus sparing them from the need to give evidence in open court.

Children in Care

Local government authorities must receive into their care any child under the age of 17 who has no parent or guardian, who has been abandoned or whose parents are unable to provide for him or her. The local authority promotes the welfare of the children in its care.

Under the Children Act 1989, which comes into effect in England and Wales in October 1991, parents of children in care retain their parental responsibilities but act as far as possible as partners with the authority. There is a new requirement to prepare a child for leaving the local authority's responsibility and for continuing to advise him or her up to the age of 21. The legislation requires local authorities to have a complaints procedure with an independent element to cover children in their care.

In England and Wales a child may be brought before a family proceedings court if he or she is neglected or ill-treated, exposed to moral danger, beyond the control of parents or not attending school. The court can commit the child to the care of a local authority under a care order. Under the Children Act 1989 certain preconditions have to be satisfied to justify an order. These are that the child is suffering or is likely to suffer significant harm because of a lack of reasonable parental care or is beyond parental control. However, an order will be made only if the court is also satisfied that this will positively contribute to the child's well-being and be in his or her best interests. In court proceedings the child will be entitled to separate legal representation and the right to have a guardian to protect his or her interests.

All courts have to treat the welfare of the child as the paramount consideration when reaching any decision about his or her upbringing. The family proceedings court consists of specially trained magistrates with power to hear care cases as well as all other family and children's cases.

In Scotland children in trouble or in need may be brought before a children's hearing, which can impose a supervision requirement on a child if it thinks that compulsory measures are appropriate. Under these requirements most children are allowed to remain at home under the supervision of a social worker but some may live with foster parents or in a residential establishment while under supervision. Supervision requirements are reviewed at least once a year until ended by a children's hearing or by the Secretary of State. A review of child care legislation in Scotland has been conducted and its results are under consideration.

In Northern Ireland the court may send children in need or in trouble to a training school, commit them to the care of a fit person (including a health and social services board), or make a supervision order. Children in trouble may be required to attend an attendance centre or may be detained in a remand home. New child care legislation is being prepared in Northern Ireland. Where appropriate it will reflect the changes introduced in England and Wales and will make a distinction between the treatment of children in need of care and young offenders.

Fostering and Community Homes

When appropriate, children in care are boarded out with foster parents, who receive payments to cover living costs. Alternatively, the child may be placed in a children's home, voluntary home or other suitable residential accommodation. In Scotland local authorities are responsible for placing children in their care in foster homes, in local authority or voluntary homes, or in residential schools. In Northern Ireland there are residential homes for children in the care of the health and social services boards; training schools and remand homes are administered separately. Regulations concerning residential care and the boarding out of children in care are made by central government.

Adoption

Local authorities are required by law to provide an adoption service, either directly or by arrangement with a voluntary organisation. Agencies may offer adoptive parents an allowance if this would help to find a family for a child. Adoption is strictly regulated by law, and adoption societies must be approved by the Government. The Registrars-General keep confidential registers of adopted children. Adopted people may be given details of their original birth record on reaching the age of 18, and counselling is provided to help them understand the circumstances of their adoption. An Adoption Contact Register enables adopted adults and their birth parents to be given a safe and confidential way of making contact if that is the wish of both parties. A person's details are entered only if they wish to be contacted.

Custodianship

A person who has cared for a child for some time (for example, a foster parent, step-parent or relative) may apply to a court for a custodianship order giving him or her legal custody of the child. This gives the custodian most of the rights and duties of a natural parent and enables him or her to make decisions about a child's day-to-day care and upbringing in the same way as a parent. Unlike an adoption order, a custodianship order may be revoked. The custodianship provisions do not extend to Northern Ireland.

Social Workers

The effective operation of the social services depends largely on professionally qualified social workers. Training courses in social work are provided by universities, polytechnics (in Scotland, central institutions) and colleges of further education. The length of courses depends on educational qualifications and experience and can extend from one to four years. The Central Council for Education and Training in Social Work is the statutory body responsible for social work training and offers advice to people considering entering the profession. The Council has proposed a range of improvements to the system of qualifying training.

Professional social workers (including those working in the NHS) are mainly employed by the social services departments of local authorities. Others work in the probation service, the education welfare service, or in voluntary organisations.

Voluntary Social Services

There is a long tradition in Britain of voluntary service to the community, and the partnership between the voluntary and statutory sectors is encouraged by the Government. It has been estimated that about a quarter of all adults take part in some form of voluntary work during the course of a year. Local and health authorities plan and carry out their duties taking account of the work of voluntary organisations. Voluntary provision enables these authorities to continue the trend towards local community care rather than institutional care for the elderly, and for mentally ill and mentally handicapped people. Funding voluntary organisations also provides opportunities to try out new approaches to services which, if successful, can be included in mainstream statutory provision.

Various government schemes assist almost 3,000 local voluntary projects to enable unemployed volunteers to help disadvantaged groups in the community. Voluntary organisations also take part in several other government schemes, including the Employment Training programme and Youth Training.

Co-ordination of government interests in the voluntary sector throughout Britain is the responsibility of the Home Office Voluntary Services Unit.

Voluntary Organisations

Funding

Voluntary organisations receive income from several sources, including contributions from individuals, businesses and trusts, central and local government grants, and earnings from commercial activities and investments. They also receive fees (from central and local government) for those services which are provided on a contractual basis. Some 500 bodies receive government grants. Tax changes in recent budgets have helped the voluntary sector secure more funds from industry and individuals. The Gift Aid scheme introduced in 1990, for example, provides tax relief on gifts of between £600 and £5 million in any one year. Employees can now make tax-free donations to charity from their earnings. The Payroll Giving Scheme provides tax relief on such donations of up to £50 a month (£600 a year). Voluntary organisations benefit not only from direct donations from the private sector but also from gifts of goods, sponsorship, secondments and joint promotions.

REGIONAL INDUSTRY

A worker at the new Mourne Mill in Northern Ireland, Europe's first new linen spinning mill for 25 years, which supplies linen to countries throughout the world.

Andromeda operates from converted barns in Oxfordshire, preparing the text and layout of illustrated reference books for publishers and printers as far away as the United States, France, Spain, Finland and Japan.

COASTLINES

Loch Carron, Plockton, in the Highlands of Scotland.

Bedruthan Steps, Cornwall.

The Antrim coast
near Dunluce,
Northern Ireland.

Porthdafarch Beach,
Holyhead, in
Gwynedd, Wales.

CONSERVATION SCIENCE

The RV *Corystes*, the latest research vessel of the Directorate of Fisheries Research, carries equipment such as this plankton sampler to monitor marine life and the constantly changing environment of the sea.

A conservation scientist from the National Trust Statuary Workshop removes a sample of loose surface material from an eighteenth century statue, using a stereo binocular microscope. With X-rays and ultrasonic scanning the state of the stone can be established and a programme of clearing and consolidation formulated.

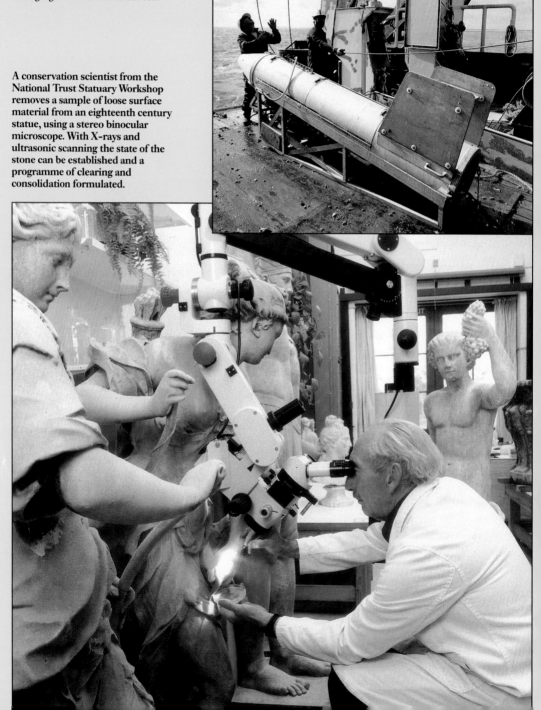

Charities

Over 171,000 voluntary organisations are
registered as charities. In England and Wales
the Charity Commission gives advice to
trustees of charities on their administration.
The Commission also maintains a register of
charities, gives consent to land transactions
by charities and holds investments for them.
Organisations may qualify for charitable
status if they are established for purposes
such as the relief of poverty, the
advancement of education or religion or the
promotion of certain other purposes of
public benefit. These include good
community relations, the prevention of racial
discrimination, the protection of health and
the promotion of equal opportunity.
Legislation to strengthen the powers of the
Charity Commissioners and improve the
supervision of charities is proposed.

The Charities Aid Foundation, an
independent body, is one of the main
organisations that aid the flow of funds to
charity from individuals, companies and
grant-making trusts.

Co-ordinating Bodies

The National Council for Voluntary
Organisations is the main co-ordinating body
in England, providing central links between
voluntary organisations, official bodies and the
private sector. It also protects the interests
and independence of voluntary agencies, and
provides them with advice, information and
other services. Councils in Scotland, Wales
and Northern Ireland perform similar
functions. The National Association for
Councils for Voluntary Service is another
network providing resources, with over 200
local councils for voluntary service throughout
England encouraging the development of local
voluntary action, mainly in urban areas. The
rural equivalent is Action with Rural
Communities in England, representing 38
rural community councils.

Types of Voluntary Organisations

There are thousands of voluntary
organisations concerned with health and
social welfare, ranging from national bodies
to small local groups. 'Self-help' groups have
been the fastest expanding area over the last
20 or so years—examples include bodies
which provide playgroups for pre-school
children, or help their members to cope with
a particular disability. Groups representing
ethnic minorities and women's interests have
also developed in recent years. Many
organisations belong to larger associations or
are represented on local or national co-
ordinating councils or committees. Some are
chiefly concerned with giving personal
service, others with influencing public
opinion and exchanging information. Some
perform both functions. They may be staffed
by both professional and voluntary workers.

Personal and Family Problems

Specialist voluntary organisations concerned
with personal and family problems include
family casework agencies such as the Family
Welfare Association, Family Service Units
and the National Society for the Prevention
of Cruelty to Children. They also include
marriage guidance centres affiliated to Relate:
National Marriage Guidance; Child Care (the
National Council of Voluntary Child Care
Organisations); the National Council for One
Parent Families; Child Poverty Action
Group and the Claimants' Union, which
provide advice on social security benefits;
and the Samaritans, which helps lonely,
depressed and suicidal people.

Health and Disability

Voluntary service to both sick and disabled
people is given by—among others—the
British Red Cross Society, St John
Ambulance, the Women's Royal Voluntary
Service and the Leagues of Hospital Friends.
Societies which help people with disabilities
and difficulties include the Royal National
Institute for the Blind, the Royal National
Institute for the Deaf, the Royal Association
for Disability and Rehabilitation, the
Disabled Living Foundation, the
Disablement Income Group, MIND
(National Association for Mental Health),
MENCAP (Royal Society for Mentally

Handicapped Children and Adults), the Spastics Society, Alcoholics Anonymous, Age Concern, Help the Aged and their equivalents in Wales, Scotland and Northern Ireland.

Other Organisations

National organisations whose work is religious in inspiration include the Salvation Army, the Church Army, Toc H, the Board of Social Responsibility of the Church of Scotland, the Church of England Children's Society, the Church of England Council for Social Aid, the Young Men's Christian Association, the Young Women's Christian Association, the Catholic Marriage Advisory Council, the Jewish Welfare Board and the Church's Urban Fund.

Community service of many kinds is given by young people, often through organisations such as Community Service Volunteers, Scouts and Girl Guides, and the 'Time for God' scheme run by a group of churches.

A wide range of voluntary personal services is given by the Women's Royal Voluntary Service. These include bringing 'meals on wheels' to housebound invalids and old people, providing flats and residential clubs for the elderly, help with family problems, and assistance in hospitals and during emergencies.

Over 1,300 Citizens Advice Bureaux advise people on their social and legal rights. Some areas have law centres and housing advisory centres.

The Volunteer Centre

The Volunteer Centre UK provides information and research on voluntary work. Its Scottish counterpart is Volunteer Development Scotland. There are many local volunteer bureaux, some part-time, which direct volunteers to opportunities in both the voluntary and statutory sectors.

Social Security

Nearly a third of government expenditure is devoted to the social security programme, which provides financial help for people who are elderly, sick, disabled, unemployed, widowed, bringing up children or on very low incomes.

Some benefits depend on the payment of contributions by employers, employees and self-employed people to the National Insurance Fund, from which benefits are paid. The Government also contributes to the Fund. The other social security benefits are non-contributory and are financed from general taxation; some of these are income-related. Appeals about claims for benefits are decided by independent tribunals.

Administration

The Department of Social Security's Benefits Agency is responsible for paying the majority of social security benefits in Great Britain; in Northern Ireland they are administered by the Social Security Agency.

Administration of National Insurance contributions is the task of the Department's National Insurance Contributions Agency.

The Information Technology Services Agency is responsible for computerising the administration of social security; once this is completed, there will be 20,000 terminals in over 500 locations. This will enable service to the public to be improved.

The housing benefit scheme is administered mainly by local government authorities, which recover most of the cost from the Government.

Advice about Benefits

The demand for advice about benefits is partly met by the Freeline Social Security Service, which handled over 1 million calls between April 1989 and March 1990. A complementary service, the Social Security Advice Line for Employers, provides advice on social security for employers and the Ethnic Freeline Service provides information on social security in Urdu, Punjabi and Chinese.

CONTRIBUTIONS

Entitlement to National Insurance benefits such as retirement pension, sickness and invalidity benefit, unemployment benefit, maternity allowance and widow's benefit is dependent upon the payment of contributions. There are four classes of contributions. Class 1 contributions are related to earnings subject to an upper limit and are paid by employees and employers. The contribution is lower if the employer operates a 'contracted-out' occupational pension scheme (see below). Self-employed people pay a flat rate Class 2 contribution and may have to pay a Class 4 contribution which is assessed as a percentage of profits or gains within certain limits; they are not eligible for unemployment and industrial injuries benefits. Voluntary Class 3 contributions are made by people wanting to safeguard rights to some benefits.

Employees who work after pensionable age (60 for women and 65 for men) do not pay contributions but the employer continues to be liable. People earning less than a certain amount do not pay contributions; neither do their employers. Self-employed people with earnings below a set amount may apply for exemption; those over pensionable age do not pay contributions.

BENEFITS

For most benefits there are two contribution conditions. First, before benefit can be paid at all, a certain number of contributions have to be paid. Secondly, the full rate of benefit cannot be paid unless contributions have been made up to a specific level over a set period. Benefits are increased annually in line with percentage increases in retail prices. The main benefits (payable weekly) are summarised below. The rates given are those effective from April 1991 until April 1992.

Retirement Pension

A state retirement pension is payable, on making a claim, to women at the age of 60 and men at the age of 65. The Sex Discrimination Act 1986 protects employees of different sexes in a particular occupation from being required to retire at different ages. This, however, has not affected the payment of state retirement pensions at different ages for men and women. The state pension scheme consists of a basic weekly pension of £52 for a single person and £83·25 for a married couple, together with an additional earnings-related pension. Pensioners may have unlimited earnings without affecting their pensions. Those who have put off their retirement during the five years after state pension age may earn extra pension. A non-contributory retirement pension of £31·25 a week is payable to people over the age of 80 who meet certain residence conditions, and who have not qualified for a contributory pension. People whose pensions do not give them enough to live on may be entitled to income support ranging from £13·75 to £18·45 a week for a single person and £20·90 to £26·20 a week for a couple.

Rights to basic pensions are safeguarded for mothers who are away from paid employment looking after children or for people giving up paid employment to care for severely disabled relatives. Men and women may receive the same basic pension, provided they have paid full-rate National Insurance contributions when working.

From the year 2000 the earnings-related pension scheme will be based on a lifetime's revalued earnings instead of on the best 20 years. It will be calculated as 20 per cent rather than 25 per cent of earnings, to be phased in over ten years from 2000. The pensions of people retiring this century will be unaffected.

Occupational and Personal Pensions

Employers are free to 'contract out' their employees from the state scheme for the additional earnings-related pension and to provide their own occupational pension instead. Their pension must be at least as good as the state additional pension. The State remains responsible for the basic pension.

Occupational pension schemes cover about half the working population and have over 11 million members. The occupational pension rights of those who change jobs before pensionable age, who are unable or who do not want to transfer their pension rights, are now protected against inflation up to a maximum of five per cent. Workers leaving a scheme have the right to a fair transfer value. Pension funds and other pension schemes have to provide full information about their schemes.

As an alternative to occupational pension schemes or the state additional earnings-related pension, people are entitled to choose a personal pension available from a bank, building society, insurance company or other financial institution. Over 4·5 million people have taken out personal pensions.

A Pensions Ombudsman deals with complaints about maladministration of pension schemes and adjudicates on disputes of fact or law.

Mothers and Children

Most pregnant working women can receive their statutory maternity pay directly from their employer. Statutory maternity pay is normally paid for 18 weeks. There are two rates: where a woman has been working for the same employer for at least two years, she is entitled to 90 per cent of her average weekly earnings for the first six weeks and to the lower rate of £44·50 a week for the remaining 12 weeks; where a woman has been employed for between six months and two years, she is entitled to payments for the full 18 weeks at the lower rate.

Women who are ineligible for statutory maternity pay because, for example, they are self-employed, have recently changed jobs or given up their job, may qualify for a weekly maternity allowance of £40·60, which is payable for 18 weeks.

A payment of £100 from the social fund (see p 140), is available for each living child born or for a stillborn child if the pregnancy lasts for at least 28 weeks. It is also payable for an adopted baby if the mother or her partner are receiving income support or family credit.

Non-contributory child benefit of £8·25 for the eldest and £7·25 weekly for each other child is the main social security benefit for children. Tax-free and normally paid to the mother, it is payable for children up to the age of 16 and for those up to 19 if they continue in full-time non-advanced education. In addition, one-parent benefit of £5·60 a week is payable to certain people bringing up one or more children on their own, whether as their parents or not. A non-contributory guardian's allowance of £10·70 a week for an orphaned child is payable to a person who is entitled to child benefit for that child. In certain circumstances it can be paid on the death of only one parent.

As part of its wide-ranging review of family justice matters, the Government is to establish a Child Support Agency which will be responsible for assessing, collecting and enforcing child maintenance payments. Assessments will be made using a formula which will take into account the numbers and ages of children and the financial circumstances of all parties. The Agency is expected to operate from spring 1993.

Widows

Widows under the age of 60, or those over 60 whose husbands were not entitled to a state retirement pension when they died, receive a tax-free single payment of £1,000 following the death of their husbands, providing that their husbands had paid a minimum number of National Insurance contributions. Women whose husbands have died of an industrial injury or disease may also qualify, regardless of whether their husbands had paid National Insurance contributions. A widowed mother with a young family receives a widowed mother's allowance of £52 a week with a further £9·70 for the first child and £10·70 for each subsequent child. A widow's pension of £52 a week is payable to a widow who is 45 years or over when her husband dies or when her entitlement to widowed mother's allowance ends. Special rules apply for widows whose husbands died before 11 April 1988. Payment continues until the widow remarries or begins drawing retirement pension. Widows also benefit under the industrial injuries scheme.

A man whose wife dies when both are over pension age inherits his wife's pension rights just as a widow inherits her husband's rights.

Sick and Disabled People

Statutory Sick Pay and Sickness Benefit

There is a large variety of benefits for people unable to work because of sickness or disablement. Employers are responsible for paying statutory sick pay to employees for up to a maximum of 28 weeks. There are two weekly rates—£43·50 or £52·50—depending on average weekly earnings. Employees who are not entitled to statutory sick pay can claim weekly state sickness benefit of £39·60 instead, as can self-employed people. Sickness benefit is payable for up to 28 weeks.

Invalidity Pension and Allowance

A weekly invalidity pension of £52 with additions of £31·25 for a husband or wife or other adult dependant and £10·70 for each child is payable when statutory sick pay or sickness benefit ends, if the beneficiary is still incapable of work. For the period to count towards receiving invalidity pension, a claimant of statutory sick pay must have satisfied the contribution condition for sickness benefit. An invalidity allowance of up to £11·10 weekly may be paid with the pension to people who become sick more than five years before minimum retirement age.

Severe Disablement Allowance

A severe disablement allowance of £31·25 may be payable to people of working age who are unable to work and do not qualify for the National Insurance invalidity pension because they have not paid sufficient contributions.

Industrial Injuries Benefits

Various benefits are payable for disablement caused by an accident at work or a prescribed disease. Disablement benefit of up to £84·90 a week is usually paid after a qualifying period of 15 weeks if a person is physically or mentally disabled as a result of an industrial accident or a prescribed disease. During the qualifying period statutory sick pay or sickness benefit may be payable if the person is incapable of work. The degree of disablement is assessed by a medical authority and the amount paid depends on the extent of the disablement and how long it is expected to last. Disablement of 14 per cent or more attracts a weekly pension. Except for certain progressive respiratory diseases, disablement of less than 14 per cent does not attract basic benefit. In certain circumstances disablement benefits may be supplemented by a constant attendance allowance. An additional allowance may be payable in certain cases of exceptionally severe disablement.

Other Benefits

A non-contributory, tax-free attendance allowance of £27·80 or £41·65 a week may be payable to severely disabled people depending upon the amount of attention they require. People with a terminal illness receive the higher rate. A non-contributory invalid care allowance of £31·25 weekly may be payable to people between 16 and pensionable age who cannot take up a paid job because they are caring for a person receiving attendance allowance; an additional carer's premium may be paid if the recipient is also receiving income support, housing benefit or community charge benefit.

Physically disabled people unable to walk and those who are both deaf and blind may be entitled to a tax-free mobility allowance of £29·10 weekly to help with transport costs; there is automatic entitlement for people who are without both legs. People aged between 5 and 66 may claim, and payment can continue up to the age of 80. An independent organisation called Motability helps disabled drivers and passengers wanting to use their mobility allowance to obtain a vehicle.

In April 1992 the attendance and mobility allowances will be extended and replaced by the disability living allowance. Some 300,000 people who fail to qualify for mobility allowance and attendance allowance will receive a new lower rate for mobility and personal care needs. An independent

Disability Appeal Tribunal will settle appeals against non-award of disability living allowance.

A disability working allowance is also being introduced in 1992. It will for the first time provide help for disabled people in work. It will be an income-related benefit payable to people working as few as 16 hours a week. Awards will be for fixed periods of six months. People will have to be receiving disability living allowance or have recently received a long-term incapacity benefit or a disability premium with an income-related benefit as a condition for receiving the new benefit.

Unemployment Benefit

Unemployment benefit of £41·40 a week for a single person or £66·95 for a couple is payable for up to a year in any one period of unemployment. Periods covered by unemployment or sickness benefit, maternity allowance or some training allowances which are eight weeks or less apart, are linked to form a single period of interruption of work. Everyone claiming unemployment benefit has to be available for work, but unemployed people wishing to do voluntary work in the community may do so in some cases without losing entitlement to benefit. People seeking unemployment benefit are expected actively to look for work and must have good reasons for rejecting any job that is offered.

Income Support

Income support is payable to people who are not in work, or who work for less than 24 hours a week, and whose financial resources are below certain set levels. It consists of a personal allowance ranging (from October 1991) from £23·65 weekly for a single person or lone parent aged under 18 to £62·25 for a couple, at least one of whom is aged over 18. Additional sums are available to families, single parents, pensioners, long-term sick and disabled people, and those caring for them who qualify for the invalid care allowance.

Housing Benefit

The housing benefit scheme offers help with the cost of rents to people with low incomes, using general assessment rules and benefit levels similar to those for the income support scheme. People whose net income is below certain specified levels receive housing benefit equivalent to 100 per cent of their rent.

Both income support and housing benefit schemes set a limit to the amount of capital a person may have and still remain entitled, and any income is taken into account after income tax and National Insurance contributions.

Community Charge Benefit

The community charge benefit is a rebate scheme which offers help with the cost of the community charge (see p 342) to those claiming income support and others with low incomes. Subject to rules similar to those governing the provision of income support and housing benefit (see above), people can receive rebates of up to 80 per cent of their community charge. Under government plans for a new council tax, the rebate would be up to 100 per cent.

Family Credit

Family credit is payable to working families on modest incomes with children where one parent works for at least 24 hours a week. The amount payable depends on a family's net income (excluding child benefits) and the number and ages of the children in the family. A maximum award, consisting of an adult rate of £38·30 weekly, plus a rate for each child varying with age, is payable if the net income does not exceed £62·25 a week. The award is reduced by 70 pence for each pound by which net income exceeds this amount. Family credit is not payable if a family's capital exceeds £8,000.

Social Fund

Discretionary payments, in the form of loans or grants, may be available to people on low incomes for expenses which are difficult to meet from their regular income. There are three types: budgeting loans to help meet important occasional expenses, crisis loans for help in an emergency or a disaster, and community care grants to help people re-establish themselves or remain in the community and to ease exceptional pressure on families.

Payments are also made from the social fund to help with the costs of maternity or funerals or with heating during very cold weather. These payments are entitlements and are not subject to the same budgetary considerations as other social fund payments.

War Pensions and Related Services

Pensions are payable for disablement or death as a result of service in the armed forces or of certain injuries received in the merchant navy or civil defence during war-time, or to civilians injured by enemy action. The amount paid depends on the degree of disablement and rank held in service: the maximum disablement pension for a private soldier is £84·90 a week. An allowance is also paid for dependants.

There are a number of extra allowances. The main ones are for unemployability, restricted mobility, the need for constant attendance, the provision of extra comforts, and as maintenance for a lowered standard of occupation. An age allowance of between £6 and £18·50 is payable weekly to war pensioners aged 65 or over whose disablement is assessed at 40 per cent or more. Pensions are also paid to war widows and other dependants. (The pension for a private's widow is £67·60.)

The Department of Social Security maintains a welfare service for war pensioners, war widows and other dependants. It works closely with ex-Service organisations and other voluntary bodies which give financial aid and personal support to those disabled or bereaved as a result of war.

Taxation

Social security benefits are regarded as taxable income. Various income tax reliefs and exemptions are allowed on account of age or a need to support dependants. The following benefits are not taxable: income support (except when paid to the unemployed and to people involved in industrial disputes), family credit, attendance allowance, mobility allowance, severe disablement allowance, industrial injuries disablement benefit, reduced earnings allowance, and war pensions. The two new benefits, disability living allowance and disability working allowance, will both be tax-free.

Other Benefits

Other benefits for which unemployed people and those on low incomes may be eligible include exemption from health service charges (see p 115), grants towards the cost of spectacles, free school meals and free legal aid. Reduced charges are often made to the unemployed, for example, for adult education and exhibitions, and pensioners usually enjoy reduced transport fares.

Arrangements with Other Countries

As part of the European Community's efforts to promote the free movement of labour, regulations provide for equality of treatment and the protection of benefit rights for employed and self-employed people who move between member states. The regulations also cover retirement pensioners and other beneficiaries who have been employed, or self-employed, as well as dependants. Benefits covered include child benefit and those for sickness and maternity, unemployment, retirement, invalidity, accidents at work and occupational diseases.

Britain also has reciprocal social security agreements with a number of other countries. Their scope and the benefits they cover vary, but the majority cover most National Insurance benefits and family benefits.

7 Education

British education aims to develop fully the abilities of individuals, both young and old, for their own benefit and that of society as a whole. Compulsory schooling takes place between the ages of 4 or 5 and 16. Some provision is made for children under school age, and many pupils remain at school beyond the minimum leaving age. Post-school education, mainly at universities, polytechnics and colleges of further and higher education, is organised flexibly to provide a wide range of opportunities for academic and vocational education and continuing study throughout life. Educational provision in Britain meets the requirements laid down in the United Nations Convention on the Rights of the Child.

Major Reforms

During the last few years the education service has undergone the most far-reaching reforms since the second world war (1939–45). Two major Acts of Parliament covering education mainly in England and Wales, and separate legislation for Scotland and for Northern Ireland, have been introduced in order to implement the principal aims of the Government's education policies.

These are:

- to raise standards at all levels of ability;

- increase parental choice of schools and improve the partnership between parents and schools;

- make further and higher education[1] more widely accessible and more responsive to the needs of the economy; and

- to achieve the best possible return from the resources invested in the education service.

In schools, the Government has aimed to:

- improve school management;

- secure a broader and more balanced curriculum for all pupils so that they can develop the qualities and skills required for adult life and work in a technological age;

- see that examinations support curriculum objectives;

- implement schemes for the local management of schools; and

- improve the quality of teaching through better teacher training and appraisal.

Schools are also encouraged to be more responsive to the needs of a multi-ethnic society. Measures are being taken to widen the choice of schools available and to ensure that schools respond effectively to the demands of parents and the broader community. The Government is also acting to ensure that school governors are adequately trained in view of their increased responsibilities.

The Government's principal aims for the further education sector are:

- to enable local education authorities and colleges to meet more fully the requirements of students and employers through the provision of a wide range of vocational and academic courses;

- to contribute to an improvement in skill levels; and

- to increase participation in further education and training, particularly among 16- to 19-year-olds.

The Government is committed to maintaining a first class, cost-effective,

---

[1] Higher education is generally defined as higher courses in any institution—broadly, those of a standard higher than General Certificate of Education (GCE) Advanced (A) level or its equivalent—and further education as all other post-school courses.

higher education system which helps to satisfy the nation's economic and social needs and at the same time offers the necessary opportunities for the advancement of knowledge. It is promoting continuing growth in student numbers. The proportion of young people entering higher education rose from 1 in 8 in 1980 to 1 in 5 by 1990, and is expected to reach 1 in 3 by the year 2000. In order to spread the benefits of higher education more widely, the Government encourages educational institutions to recruit more students from ethnic minority and other under-represented groups.

In May 1991 the Government issued three White Papers designed to transform post-compulsory education and training. *Higher Education: A New Framework* covers England, Wales, Scotland and Northern Ireland; *Education and Training for the 21st Century* covers England and Wales; and *Access and Opportunity: a Strategy for Education and Training* relates to Scotland. The proposed reforms would mean the ending of the increasingly artificial distinction between universities and other higher education establishments. Also, barriers between academic and vocational education and training would be removed for 16- to 19-year-olds.

A single framework for higher education would be established, with higher education funding councils in England, Scotland and Wales allocating public funds for teaching and general research. New links would be created to continue the present close relationship with Northern Ireland's existing unitary structure. Degree-awarding powers would be extended to all major institutions and there would be new quality assurance arrangements. Polytechnics and other higher education colleges would have the right to call themselves 'universities'.

Further education and sixth-form colleges in England and Wales would become autonomous institutions outside local authority control, financed through further education councils from April 1993. New general vocational qualifications would be developed and Ordinary and Advanced Diplomas introduced for those reaching a required standard in either or both academic and vocational subjects, thereby ensuring equal recognition for academic and vocational qualifications of the same standard. By the mid-1990s every 16- and 17-year-old leaving full-time education would be encouraged to undertake vocational education or training by the offer of a training credit, enabling them to buy specific training from the establishment of their choice. Parallel reforms are proposed for further education and training in Scotland.

Parent's Charter

A parent's charter was published by the Government in September 1991, designed to enable parents to make more informed choices about their children's education. Approved inspections of all schools will take place at least every four years. Parents will receive five key documents:

- an annual report on their child's progress;
- performance tables with full information on all schools in their area;
- a summary of a recent inspection report on their child's school;
- an action plan for tackling weaknesses identified in the school inspection; and
- an annual report from the school governors with information about examination and test results for the school, truancy, school-leavers' destinations, the school budget, and election procedures for parent-governors.

Primary and Secondary Education

Measures to improve the quality and breadth of education and to extend parental choice and delegated decision-making in publicly-funded schools in England and Wales are embodied in two recent Acts. The Education (No 2) Act 1986 reformed the composition of school governing bodies (see p 149) and reallocated functions between school governors, local education authorities and head teachers. It also contained provisions to appraise the performance of teachers, and introduce more effective in-service training of teachers.

The Education Reform Act 1988, relating to both school and post-school education, provides for the establishment of a National Curriculum for children aged 5 to 16 in all English and Welsh maintained schools and for regular assessments of performance. Secondary schools are required to admit pupils up to the limit of their available physical capacity if there is sufficient demand on behalf of children eligible for admission. There are plans to extend this to primary schools from August 1992. This policy, known as 'more open enrolment', is designed to further increase parental choice of schools. The 1988 Act gives all schools responsibility for managing the major part of their budgets, including staffing costs, as well as the opportunity to withdraw from local authority control (see p 149). It also makes provision for the development of a network of city technology colleges (see p 146).

The School Boards (Scotland) Act 1988 requires Scottish education authorities to establish boards with the aim of increasing parental involvement in school management (see p 149). The Self-Governing Schools etc. (Scotland) Act 1989 enables parents to vote for local self-management of schools in place of control by education authorities. In addition, it provides for the establishment of technology academies outside education authority control (with a similar role to that of city technology colleges).

In Northern Ireland legislation which came into force in 1990 introduced reforms broadly in line with those being implemented in England and Wales under the Education Reform Act 1988. It also seeks to encourage further the development of integrated education (see p 150).

Post-school Education

Under the Education Reform Act 1988, changes were introduced in the structure and funding of further and higher education to help institutions improve their management and planning. The system of university funding was reformed in England, Wales and Scotland: the Universities Funding Council replaced the University Grants Committee and has executive powers to allocate finances to individual universities. Polytechnics and other major higher education colleges in England were removed from local authority control, and incorporated as higher education corporations with boards of governors, half of whose members are drawn from business and the professions. Their work is financed through the Polytechnics and Colleges Funding Council, with responsibilities parallel to those of the Universities Funding Council. Further education and higher education colleges remaining under local authority control have taken on greater responsibility for their annual budgets and are including more employers on their governing bodies.

The Government is altering the balance of public funding for full-time undergraduate higher education from institutional grant to tuition fees paid for individual students (see p 159). This is intended to create a more direct link between institutional income and recruitment, encouraging institutions to increase their efficiency by making full use of capacity.

Legislation was introduced in both Scotland and Northern Ireland in 1989 to allow further education colleges to assume increased financial powers and managerial responsibilities. The objectives are to improve their efficiency and responsiveness to local demand and to increase employment interests on governing bodies.

Education–Business Links

The Government considers that co-operation between the education system and business is essential to help people of all ages acquire the skills necessary to maintain Britain's position as a leading industrial and trading nation at a time of rapid technological change and intense international economic competition. Many organisations already work to strengthen such links, and further contacts are being encouraged.

Much is being done under the Government's Technical and Vocational Education Initiative (TVEI—see p 153), to which £900 million has been allotted from 1987 to 1997. As a result of this and other initiatives, industrial and commercial matters are being allocated a more prominent place in school, college and university curricula and examinations. The relevance of classroom activities to working life was central to the thinking behind the introduction of the General Certificate of Secondary Education and the National Curriculum. Businessmen and women are involved in curriculum development and enterprise activities for schoolchildren. They have been enabled to take a bigger part in the management of schools, colleges and polytechnics by joining their governing bodies in greater numbers and through membership of Training and Enterprise Councils, Local Enterprise Companies and local Education Business Partnerships (see p 147).

In line with the concern to maintain British expertise in science, engineering and technology, a shift in provision is occurring in post-school education away from the arts and social sciences towards these subjects and towards directly vocational courses. Business and higher education institutions are being encouraged to collaborate more closely for their mutual benefit. The latter may give enterprise training to students under the Government's Enterprise in Higher Education scheme to help students acquire the aptitudes and competence required by industry in the 1990s.

Secondary School Education

Government policy is to ensure that every year 10 per cent of teachers should be given the opportunity to gain some business experience; and that every trainee teacher should have an appreciation of the needs of employers. Some 30,000 teachers will spend time working in industry during 1991–92 under a scheme administered by the Confederation of British Industry.

The Government also wants all pupils to have at least two weeks' work experience before leaving school. Work experience involves pupils doing particular jobs much as would regular employees. More than 70 per cent of schoolchildren aged 15 to 16 undertook work experience placements in 1989.

City technology colleges, sponsored by industry and commerce, are being set up in urban areas in England to provide a broadly based secondary education for girls and boys of all abilities. The curriculum emphasises science, technology and business understanding within the framework of the National Curriculum. The colleges are state-aided but independent of local education authorities. They are managed by sponsors from universities and commerce, educational trusts, charities and other voluntary organisations. The first college opened in Solihull (West Midlands) in 1988, and by September 1991, 13 were in operation. The Government has announced plans to allow existing schools to transform themselves into grant-maintained technology colleges.

In 1988 the Government launched the Compacts initiative as part of the Action for Cities programme to regenerate inner city areas. Compacts are local agreements between employers, local education authorities and training providers. Young people, supported by their school or college, work to reach agreed targets, and employers undertake to provide a job with training or training leading to a job for those attaining the targets. By October 1991, 58 compacts were in operation (and three were being developed), with around 500 schools and colleges and over 92,000 young people participating. The Government is making available more than £28 million over four years from 1990 to support compacts. Under the White Paper proposals, the compact approach would be extended nationwide.

The Government's local Education Business Partnerships initiative, announced in 1990, is designed to foster the development of wide-ranging, formal local links between businesses, education and other community interests throughout Britain. It seeks to improve the coherence and co-ordination of government support and the integration of local and national education–business link organisations, programmes and activities.

Post-school Education

A network of employer-led Training and Enterprise Councils (TECs) is being built up by the Government in England and Wales. TECs are intended to make training and enterprise activities more relevant to the needs of employers and individuals locally. A total of 82 are expected to be fully operational by the end of 1991. In Scotland, 22 Local Enterprise Companies have been formed with a similar role to that of the TECs. A Training and Employment Agency was set up in 1990 in Northern Ireland with responsibilities for training and employment programmes and activities.

Some 11 TECs and Local Enterprise Companies, working in close co-operation with local education authorities and other education interests, have been running pilot schemes of Training Credits for young people. Training Credits schemes offer an entitlement to train to approved standards for young people leaving full-time education.

Over 40 science parks have been set up by higher education institutions in conjunction with industrial scientists and technologists to promote the development and commercial application of advanced technology. There are plans to establish more science parks. In addition, a network of regional technology centres links colleges, polytechnics and universities with local firms. The centres' incomes are derived from charges to companies which send their employees for training.

The Government's LINK scheme aims to encourage firms to work jointly with higher education institutions on government-funded research relevant to industrial needs.

Administration

One of the distinctive features of the education service is the degree to which responsibility for provision is decentralised. Overall responsibility for all aspects of education in England, and for the Government's relations with and support for polytechnics and other higher education colleges in England as well as universities throughout Britain, rests with the Secretary of State for Education and Science. The Secretaries of State for Wales and for Scotland have responsibility in their respective countries for non-university education, and are consulted about education in universities. The Secretary of State for Northern Ireland is responsible for both university and non-university education in the Province. Responsibility for sport and recreation in England was transferred to the Secretary of State for Education and Science in 1990.

The government departments responsible for education are the Department of Education and Science (DES) in England, the Welsh Office, the Scottish Office Education Department, and the Department of Education for Northern Ireland. Their chief concerns are formulating education policies, allocating resources and influencing the other partners in the education service— the local education authorities, governing bodies of educational institutions, the teaching profession, the churches and voluntary organisations. The departments are also responsible for the supply and training of teachers.

The Education Departments finance certain aspects of the education service directly (for instance, grant-maintained schools and city technology colleges) and also provide grants to local authorities. The DES's own expenditure is devoted mainly to higher education and science, which accounts for two-thirds of the total. The Department of Employment and Department of Trade and Industry also fund specific educational programmes; the former, for example, finances the Technical and Vocational Education Initiative (see p 153) and compacts (see p 146).

The provision of most maintained, that is, publicly financed, school and further education is the responsibility of local education authorities, which are funded by central government and, except in Northern Ireland, by local taxes. Local education authorities employ teachers and other staff, provide and maintain buildings, supply equipment and materials and, in England and Wales, award grants to students progressing to further and higher education. Universities and the English polytechnics are self-governing institutions receiving most of their income indirectly from central government grants.

In Scotland the higher education sector central institutions and colleges of education providing teacher training are administered by independent governing bodies. Northern Ireland colleges of education are controlled by the Department of Education (Northern Ireland) and by a voluntary agency.

Finance

Estimated spending on education and science in Britain in 1990–91 was £26,500 million. About 70 per cent was incurred by local education authorities, which are directly responsible for the funding of most maintained schools and colleges of further education. The authorities make their own expenditure decisions according to local needs and circumstances, such as the number of school-age children.

Primary, Secondary and Further Education

In England and Wales the grants for education support and training programmes enable the Government to support local education authority expenditure on educational activities of national priority. In 1991–92 the Government intends to make grants of £220 million supporting total spending of £364 million. Most spending will be deployed on the implementation of the Education Reform Act, including activities related to the National Curriculum (£170 million) and local management of schools and colleges (£77 million). A total of £10 million is to be devoted to teacher recruitment and £7 million to health education in schools. The balance of the programme is aimed at improving the general efficiency and effectiveness of the education service.

The Government funds directly the current and capital costs both of grant-maintained schools which have opted to leave the local authority sector (see p 149) and of city technology colleges (see p 146) in England and Wales and comparable institutions in Scotland and Northern Ireland.

Higher Education

The greater part of higher education institutions' income derives from public funds via the institutional grant and tuition fees paid for students through the awards system. Institutional funding for sectors within the responsibility of the DES will exceed £4,000 million in 1991–92.

Institutional grant for universities in Great Britain is distributed by the Universities Funding Council (UFC), a statutory body. Certain individual establishments, such as the Open University, are financed directly by the DES. In Northern Ireland grant is paid directly to the universities by the Northern Ireland Office with advice from the UFC. The private University of Buckingham receives no public grant.

For non-university higher education, the Polytechnics and Colleges Funding Council is responsible for financing higher courses in polytechnics and most colleges of higher education in England. Higher courses in Wales continue to be financed by local authorities. In Scotland all courses offered by the central institutions and colleges of education are funded by central government; advanced courses provided by local authority further education colleges are financed by the local authorities.

Universities, polytechnics and other higher education institutions undertake training, research or consultancy for commercial firms. The Government is encouraging them to secure a larger flow of funds from these sources. Many educational establishments have endowments or receive grants from foundations and benefactors.

SCHOOLS

Parents are required by law to see that their children receive efficient full-time education, at school or elsewhere, between the ages of 5 and 16 in Great Britain and 4 and 16 in Northern Ireland. Some 9·2 million children attend Britain's 35,000 state and private schools (of which about 25,600 are primary or nursery and 4,900 secondary schools in the state sector). Most pupils receive free education financed from public funds, but a small proportion attend schools wholly independent of direct public financial support.

Boys and girls are taught together in most primary schools, and more than 80 per cent of pupils in maintained secondary schools in England and Wales and over 60 per cent in Northern Ireland attend mixed schools. In Scotland nearly all secondary schools are mixed. Most independent schools for younger children are co-educational; the majority providing secondary education are single-sex, although the number of mixed schools is growing.

No fees are charged to parents of children at maintained schools, grant-maintained schools or city technology colleges, and books and equipment are free. In Northern Ireland at present a small proportion of grammar school pupils are fee-payers. Under legislation passed in 1989 Northern Ireland grammar schools will in the main have to discontinue the practice of admitting fee-paying pupils.

Parents throughout Britain have a statutory right to express a preference for a particular school for their children, and have an effective channel of appeal at local level. Schools are obliged to publish their admissions criteria and basic information about themselves and their public examination results.

Management

England and Wales

Schools supported from public funds are of two main kinds in England and Wales:

- County schools are owned and maintained by local education authorities wholly out of public funds; and

- Voluntary schools, mostly established by religious denominations, are also wholly maintained from public funds but the governors of some types of voluntary school contribute to capital costs. Around one-third of the 23,000 maintained primary and secondary schools are voluntary schools, most of them Anglican or Roman Catholic.

Each publicly maintained school has a governing body which includes governors appointed by the local education authority and teacher and parent representatives. Most maintained schools have equal numbers of parent and local authority governors so that no single interest predominates. Governing bodies are responsible for the main policies of their schools and for the preparation of a statement of their schools' curricular aims and objectives. They also have final responsibility for school discipline and a large say in the appointment and dismissal of staff.

The role of governing bodies in England and Wales has been further enlarged since 1990. Local education authorities have delegated responsibility for the management of school budgets to all secondary schools and primary schools with more than 200 pupils. Small primary schools will be able to apply to manage their own budgets from April 1992. This policy is known as 'local management of schools'. Local authorities allocate money to individual schools mainly on the basis of pupil numbers.

English and Welsh schools may seek to withdraw from local authority control, following a ballot of parents ('opting out'). They are then directly financed by central government as grant-maintained non-fee-paying schools.

Scotland

In Scotland most of the schools supported from public funds are provided by education authorities and are known as public schools; in England this term is used for a type of independent school (see p 151). Education authorities are required to establish school boards to play a significant part in the administration and management of schools. The boards consist of elected parent and staff members as well as co-opted members, thereby encouraging greater parental involvement and closer links between home, school and local community. Parents of children at public schools can opt for local self-management following a ballot; such schools receive funding directly from central government (see p 145).

Northern Ireland

In Northern Ireland there are three main categories of grant-aided school:

- controlled schools, owned and managed by the area education and library boards and having all their expenditure met from public funds;

- voluntary schools, mainly under Roman Catholic management and also maintained largely by public funds; and

- voluntary grammar schools, which may be under Roman Catholic or non-denominational management and receive grants from the Northern Ireland Department of Education.

All grant-aided schools include elected parents and teachers on their boards of governors.

While all Northern Ireland schools must be open to pupils of all religions, most Catholic pupils attend Catholic schools and most Protestant children are enrolled at local authority schools. The policy of successive governments has been to encourage integrated education, providing for both Protestant and Roman Catholic pupils, where there is a local desire for it. Local management of schools was introduced in Northern Ireland in April 1991. Under this, secondary school governors have taken on delegated responsibility for managing school budgets and staff numbers. At present primary and nursery school governors have delegated responsibility for managing non-staff costs only.

New integrated schools receive immediate government funding. Existing grant-aided schools can opt for grant-maintained integrated status after a ballot of parents. There are two categories of integrated schools. Grant-maintained integrated status can be applied for by new and independent schools as well as those already receiving public funds. Grant-maintained integrated schools are directly financed by the Northern Ireland Department of Education and are run by boards of governors. Controlled integrated status can be sought by voluntary and controlled schools; local education authorities can also apply to set up such schools. Local education authorities provide funding for and supervise controlled integrated schools.

Nursery and Primary Schools

Although there is no statutory requirement to educate under-fives, successive governments have enabled nursery education to expand. One-half of three- and four-year-olds receive education in nursery schools or classes or in infants' classes in primary schools. In addition, many children attend pre-school playgroups, most of which are organised by parents and affiliated to the Pre-School Playgroups Association.

Compulsory education begins at five in Great Britain and four in Northern Ireland, when children go to infant schools or departments; at seven many go on to junior schools or departments. The usual age for transfer from primary to secondary schools is 11 in England, Wales and Northern Ireland, but some local authorities in England have established 'first' schools for pupils aged 5 to 8, 9 or 10 and 'middle' schools for age-ranges between 8 and 14. In Scotland primary schools take children from 5 to 12.

Secondary Schools

The publicly maintained system of education aims to give all children an education suited to their particular abilities. Around nine-tenths of the maintained secondary school population in Great Britain attend comprehensive schools. These take pupils without reference to ability or aptitude and provide a wide range of secondary education for all or most of the children in a district. English and Welsh schools can be organised in a number of ways. They include:

- those that take the full secondary school age-range from 11 to 18;

- middle schools, whose pupils move on to senior comprehensive schools at 12, 13 or 14, leaving at 16 or 18; and

- schools with an age-range of 11 or 12 to 16, combined with a sixth-form or a tertiary college for pupils over 16.

Sixth-form colleges are schools which may provide non-academic in addition to academic courses. Tertiary colleges offer a range of full-time and part-time vocational courses for students over 16, as well as academic courses. Most other children attend 'grammar' or 'secondary modern' schools, to which they are allocated after selection procedures at the age of 11. By August 1991, over 100 schools had achieved grant-maintained status under the Education Reform Act's 'opting out' provisions (see p 149).

Scottish secondary education is almost completely non-selective; the majority of schools are six-year comprehensives. The Government, in partnership with private sponsors, is seeking to set up technology academies in Scotland with a role similar to that of the city technology colleges (see p 146).

In Northern Ireland secondary education is organised largely along selective lines, based on a system of testing. However, there are some secondary schools run on a non-selective basis.

Independent Schools

Independent schools are outside the publicly maintained sector, but they must register with the appropriate education department and are open to inspection. They can be required to remedy serious shortcomings in their accommodation or instruction, and to exclude anyone regarded as unsuitable to teach in or own a school. About 7 or 8 per cent of schoolchildren in Britain attend independent schools.

There are 2,500 independent schools educating 600,000 pupils of all ages. They charge fees varying from around £300 a term for day pupils at nursery age to £3,500 a term for senior boarding pupils. Many offer bursaries to help pupils from less well-off families. Such pupils may also be helped by local education authorities—particularly if the authorities' own schools cannot meet the needs of individual children—or by the Government's Assisted Places Scheme, under which assistance is given according to parental income. In 1990–91 over 33,000

places were offered at 295 schools in England and Wales, and around 3,000 at 59 schools in Scotland, under the scheme. The Government also gives income-related help with fees to pupils at certain specialist music and ballet schools.

Within the independent sector there is great variety of provision, ranging from small kindergarten to large day and boarding schools and from new and in some cases experimental schools to ancient foundations. The 600 boys', girls' and mixed preparatory schools are so called because they prepare children for the Common Entrance Examination to senior schools. The normal age-range is from seven-plus to 11, 12 or 13, but many of the schools now have pre-preparatory departments for younger children. A number of independent schools have been established by religious and ethnic minorities.

Independent schools for older pupils—from 11, 12 or 13 to 18 or 19—include about 550 which are sometimes referred to as 'public schools'. These are schools belonging to the Headmasters' Conference, the Governing Bodies Association, the Society of Headmasters and Headmistresses of Independent Schools, the Girls' Schools Association and the Governing Bodies of Girls' Schools Association. They should not be confused with the state-supported public schools in Scotland.

Special Educational Needs

Special educational needs comprise learning difficulties of all kinds, including mental and physical disabilities which hinder or prevent learning. In the case of children whose learning difficulties are severe or complex, local education authorities are required to assess the child's special educational needs and to provide a statement or record of these needs. Wherever possible, children with special educational needs are educated in ordinary schools, provided that the parents' wishes have been taken into account, and that this is compatible with meeting the needs of the child, with the provision of efficient education for the other children in the school, and with the efficient use of resources. In Scotland the choice of school is a matter for agreement between education authorities and parents.

There are 1,900 special schools (both day and boarding), including those run by voluntary organisations and those established in hospitals. They cater for a wide variety of pupils with special educational needs (about 120,000) who cannot be educated at ordinary schools. Developments in information technology (see p 156) are increasingly leading to better quality education for children with special needs.

Teachers

Teachers in publicly maintained schools are appointed by local education authorities or school governing bodies. A total of 528,000 teachers are employed in maintained and independent schools, and the average pupil–teacher ratio for all schools is 17 to 1. Teachers in maintained schools must hold qualifications approved by the appropriate education department (see p 162).

The Curriculum

England and Wales

The Government favours widening educational opportunities as much as possible through a broad and balanced curriculum differentiated to meet the individual needs of pupils and relevant to the modern world. In 1989 primary and secondary schools began the gradual introduction of the National Curriculum in England and Wales. The National Curriculum, which the Government believes should occupy not less than 70 per cent of teaching time, consists of the core subjects of English, mathematics and science, as well as the other foundation subjects of history, geography, technology, music, art, physical education and, for secondary level pupils, a modern foreign language. Economic and industrial awareness are important cross-curricular themes in the National Curriculum.

In Wales the Welsh language constitutes a core subject in Welsh-speaking schools and a foundation subject elsewhere under the National Curriculum. In the primary sector 80 per cent of schools either use Welsh as a teaching medium or teach it as a second language, while nearly 90 per cent of secondary schools teach Welsh as a first or second language.

Attainment targets are being devised to establish what children should normally be expected to know, understand and be able to do at the ages of 7, 11, 14, and 16, enabling the progress of each child to be measured against national standards. Pupils' performance in relation to attainment targets is assessed and reported on at the four key stages. Regulations have been introduced covering the manner and form in which assessments of individual pupils are to be made available to parents and others (see p 155).

Religious education is required for all pupils as part of the basic curriculum. However, parents have a right to withdraw their children from religious education classes (see p 154). The content of religious education courses is determined locally.

Scotland

The content and management of the curriculum in Scotland are the responsibility of education authorities and head teachers, though guidance is provided by the Secretary of State for Scotland and the Scottish Consultative Council on the Curriculum. The Council has recommended that secondary level pupils should follow a broad and balanced curriculum consisting of English, mathematics, science, a modern European language, social studies, technological activities, art, music or drama, religious and moral education, and physical education. A major programme of curricular review and development is in progress for the 5-to-14 age-range. The Government is in the process of issuing new guidelines on all aspects of the curriculum and assessment. Standardised tests in English and mathematics are being introduced for primary school pupils at stages 4 and 7, normally at ages 8 and 12.

A flexible system of vocational courses for 16- to 18-year-olds based on modules or short units of study has been introduced in schools and colleges in disciplines like business and administration and engineering and industrial production. Though designed primarily to improve the preparation of young people for working life, the courses are also intended to meet the needs of many adults entering training or returning to education. The courses lead to the award of a National Certificate.

A committee has been established to review courses and assessment arrangements in the final two years of secondary schooling. Provision is made for teaching in Gaelic in Gaelic-speaking areas.

Northern Ireland

A common curriculum is being introduced in all Northern Ireland grant-aided schools. It is based on six broad areas of study: English, mathematics, science and technology, the environment and society, creative and. expressive studies, and, for secondary schools, language studies. Religious education is obligatory at all stages.

Attainment targets, programmes of study and methods of assessment—at ages 8, 11, 14 and 16—are specified for all compulsory subjects. In addition, the school curriculum includes six compulsory cross-curricular themes: 'education for mutual understanding', cultural heritage, health education, information technology, and, in secondary schools, economic awareness and careers education.

Ethnic Minority Children

Most school-aged children from ethnic minorities were born in Britain and tend to share the interests and aspirations of children in the population at large. Nevertheless, a substantial number still have particular needs arising from cultural differences, including those of language, religion and custom.

The education authorities have done much to meet these needs. English language teaching continues to receive priority, but attention has been increasingly directed at supporting the use of mother tongues, especially in the early primary years.

Emphasis has been placed on the need for schools to take account of the ethnic and cultural backgrounds of pupils and curricula should reflect ethnic and cultural diversity. Measures are being taken to improve the achievement of ethnic minority pupils, and to prepare all children, not just those of ethnic minority origin, for living in a multi-ethnic society.

Curriculum Development

In England curriculum development is promoted by the National Curriculum Council and in Wales by the Curriculum Council for Wales. At some 480 teachers' centres, teachers meet for curriculum development work, discussion and in-service training. In Scotland such development work is undertaken by the Scottish Consultative Council on the Curriculum and in Northern Ireland by the Northern Ireland Curriculum Council.

Technical and Vocational Education Initiative

The Technical and Vocational Education Initiative (TVEI) applies in England, Scotland and Wales. It is financed and administered by the Department of Employment and the Scottish Office Industry Department working in close co-operation with local education authorities. It is intended that the education of 14- to 18-year-olds should equip them for working life by ensuring that the school curriculum relates to the working environment, and by improving skills and qualifications, particularly in science, technology and modern languages. The initiative aims to include all students aged 14 to 18 in maintained schools and colleges by 1992.

Religious Education and Collective Worship in Schools

In England and Wales maintained schools must provide religious education and a daily act of collective worship for all pupils except those withdrawn by their parents. The Education Reform Act 1988 requires that due recognition be given to the place of Christianity in teaching in county schools, but religious education also covers other faiths. In county schools collective worship must be wholly or mainly of a broadly Christian character. The law provides for the lifting of this requirement in appropriate circumstances. In county schools, and sometimes in voluntary schools, non-denominational religious education is given in accordance with a locally agreed syllabus which may include the comparative study of religions. Syllabuses have been revised in some areas to take account of the faiths of the local population. In all kinds of voluntary schools there is the opportunity for denominational religious education.

Scottish education authorities are required to see that schools practise religious observance and give pupils religious instruction; parents may withdraw their children if they wish. Certain schools provide for Roman Catholic children but in all schools there are safeguards for the individual conscience.

In Northern Ireland, too, schools are obliged to offer religious education and collective worship, although parents have the right to withdraw their children from both. In controlled schools clergy have a right of access which may be used for denominational instruction. In voluntary schools collective worship and religious education are controlled by the management authorities. It is intended that religious education will have an agreed core syllabus which grant-aided schools can expand according to their own needs and wishes.

Qualifications

England, Wales and Northern Ireland

The main examinations taken by secondary school pupils in England, Wales and Northern Ireland around the age of 16 are those leading to the General Certificate of Secondary Education (GCSE). GCSE examinations, which have a seven-point scale of grades, are usually taken after five years of secondary education and can lead on to more advanced education and training. The Government intends the GCSE to be the principal means for assessing attainment at stage 4 of the National Curriculum. Vocational qualifications may also be used to certify attainment in the whole or parts of National Curriculum foundation subjects.

The General Certificate of Education (GCE) Advanced (A) level is normally taken after a further two years of study. New examinations, Advanced Supplementary (AS) levels, were held for the first time in 1989 and enable sixth-form pupils to study a wider range of subjects than was possible before. Students specialising in the arts and humanities, for example, can continue to study mathematics and technological subjects at the new level. Requiring the same standard of work but with only half the content of A levels, an AS level occupies half the teaching and study time of an A level. A levels or a mixture of A and AS levels are the main standard for entrance to higher education and to many forms of professional training.

The Government wants more schools to offer vocational qualifications, which it considers should be seen as an equally valid route to further and higher education and training.

The Certificate of Pre-Vocational Education is for those at school or college wishing to continue in full-time education for a year after the age of 16 and to receive a broadly based preparation for work or vocational and other courses. Business & Technician Education Council (BTEC) qualifications can also serve as a preparation for work or a stepping-stone into higher education. The Certificate is being developed by the City and Guilds of London Institute. An improved version will be called the City and Guilds Diploma of Vocational Education. Schools are now allowed to offer BTEC First Diploma courses to 16- to 19-year-olds.

Scotland

The public examination system in Scotland is different from that in other parts of Britain. Scottish pupils take the Scottish Certificate of Education (SCE) at Standard grade at the end of their fourth year of secondary education (equivalent to the fifth year in England and Wales). Pupils in the fifth and sixth years sit the SCE Higher grade; passes at this grade are the basis for entry to higher education or professional training. However, entry is becoming more flexible as wider access to under-represented groups with non-standard qualifications is encouraged. For those who have completed their main studies at the Higher grade but wish to continue studies in particular subjects there is the Certificate of Sixth Year Studies (CSYS). Standard grade courses and examinations cater for the whole ability range. Higher and CSYS examinations are being revised to ensure compatibility with the Standard grade.

The National Certificate is for students over 16 who have successfully completed a programme of vocational courses based on study units known as modules (see p 153). These modules are used in schools for pupils in the 14-to-18 age-range, and other short courses specifically for use in schools are being devised.

A new system of Scottish Vocational Qualifications similar to that of the National Council for Vocational Qualifications (see p 161) is being introduced under the supervision of the Scottish Vocational Education Council.

Examinations and Assessment Councils

All GCSE and other qualifications offered to pupils of compulsory school age in maintained schools in England and Wales must be approved by the Government. Associated syllabuses and assessment procedures must comply with national guidelines and be approved by the School Examinations and Assessment Council. The aim is to secure a reasonably wide choice of qualifications and syllabuses which promote a broad and balanced curriculum and support the National Curriculum.

The Council keeps under review all aspects of examinations and assessment in England and Wales and carries out research and development. It co-operates with the National Curriculum Council (for England) and the Curriculum Council for Wales on work connected with the National Curriculum in schools.

The equivalent body in Scotland is the Scottish Examination Board, which liaises with the Scottish Consultative Council on the Curriculum. The Northern Ireland Schools Examinations and Assessment Council is responsible for keeping all aspects of examinations and assessment under review. It liaises with the Northern Ireland Curriculum Council.

Progress Reports

A system of school reporting of individual pupils' achievement was introduced in 1990, under which parents in England and Wales receive a yearly progress report on their child's National Curriculum achievements and results in public examinations. The National Record of Achievement, launched in February 1991, is designed to present a simple record of achievement in education and training throughout working life.

In Scotland the report card system is being reformed to give parents a clearer view of their children's progress. There is a commitment for all pupils in Northern Ireland to be issued with a record of their performance on leaving primary and secondary school.

Educational Standards

Her Majesty's Inspectors (HMI) report to the Government on the quality of education in schools and most further and higher education establishments outside the universities, and advise education authorities and schools as well as the Government. They also report on the youth service and education provision in hospitals, prisons and youth custody centres, and the armed services. Local education authorities employ inspectors or advisers to guide them on maintained schools.

Under the Parent's Charter, school governors would appoint independent HMI-approved inspection teams to inspect their schools. Some members of HMI would be drawn from outside education to bring a wider perspective to inspection.

The role of the Northern Ireland Education and Training Inspectorate is roughly comparable to that of Her Majesty's Inspectorate.

The Evaluation and Monitoring Unit, part of the School Examinations and Assessment Council (see p 155), is mainly concerned with evaluating the assessment arrangements for the National Curriculum. In England, Wales and Northern Ireland programmes of monitoring have been carried out in English language and mathematics at the ages of 11 and 15, in science at the ages of 11, 13 and 15, and in the first foreign language at the age of 13. In Scotland the Assessment of Achievement research programme has surveyed attainments of pupils in English and mathematics at ages 8, 12 and 14.

Information Technology

The National Curriculum places a strong emphasis on the use of information technology (IT). There have been government programmes for promoting curriculum use of IT since 1980. In 1987 the Government announced a major new strategy to encourage use of educational technology across the curriculum so that pupils become familiar with the new technologies and use them to enhance learning. In the three years since 1988 grant-supported expenditure of £75 million has been available to increase the number of microcomputers in schools and train teachers in the effective usage of IT. Most teachers have now received basic training in the use of IT. There are on average four computers for each primary school and 41 for every secondary school. From 1991 to 1993 grants will be available to increase the numbers of microcomputers in schools and for teacher training. In both years grants may be used to provide IT support for children with communication difficulties. In 1992–93 grants will be available to introduce CD-ROM (compact disc read only memory) technology in secondary schools.

In each of the three years 1991–92 to 1993–94 there will be grant-supported spending programmes of around £30 million to provide continuing support for IT in schools.

The Government is also making a grant of £5 million a year to support the National Council for Educational Technology (NCET). The NCET was set up by the Government in 1988 to evaluate the newest technologies in terms of their application to education. Its objectives are to support, encourage, develop and apply the use of learning systems and new technologies, including microcomputers, electronic systems and other aspects of IT, to education and training. The corresponding body in Scotland is the Scottish Council for Educational Technology.

Other specific government funding includes:

- £750,000 for the development of 19 new National Curriculum software packages. The programme is managed by the NCET and the developers are matching the Government's financial contribution. The software packages will be ready in 1992.

- £410,000 to install information relating to the National Curriculum on NERIS (National Educational Resources Information Service—an electronic database, see p 157).

- £1·3 million for the development of five mathematics interactive video discs. This programme is administered by the National Curriculum Council.

- £540,000 in 1991–92 to test the educational potential of CD-ROM prior to its introduction into the 1992–93 grants programme. This project is managed by the NCET.

Educational Aids

Teachers and pupils use a range of aids to assist the processes of teaching and learning. The government-funded National Educational Resources Information Service enables schools to find out about teaching aids. Most schools have audio-visual equipment such as slide projectors and overhead projectors, and educational broadcasting is of major importance. The BBC and the independent broadcasting companies transmit radio and television programmes designed for schools. Teachers' notes, pupils' pamphlets and computer software accompany many broadcast series. All primary and secondary schools use microcomputers (see p 156).

Careers Education and Guidance

Increasing importance is being attached by schools and colleges to careers education to raise awareness of further and higher education and careers opportunities, and help young people to prepare for working life. As a result, links between schools and the local authority careers service are being strengthened. The work of the careers service at local level is supported by careers information material produced by the Government's Careers and Occupational Information Centre. A computer-assisted careers guidance system known as PROSPECTS (HE) has been developed by the Government for students in higher education.

Under the White Paper proposals, local education authorities would be encouraged to co-operate with Training and Enterprise Councils and Local Enterprise Companies (see p 147) in overseeing the operation of the careers service locally.

Health and Welfare of Schoolchildren

Physical education, including organised games, is part of the curriculum of all maintained schools, and playing fields must be available for pupils over the age of eight. Most secondary schools have a gymnasium.

Government health departments are responsible for the medical inspection of schoolchildren and for advice on, and treatment of, specific medical and dental problems associated with children of school age. The Government believes that the education service has a role to play in preventing and dealing with juvenile drug misuse and in helping to prevent the spread of AIDS.

Local education authorities are largely free to decide what milk, meals or other refreshment to offer at their schools, and the charges to make. Provision has to be made free of charge, however, for pupils from families receiving certain social security benefits. Under certain conditions the authorities must supply free school transport, and they have discretionary powers to help with the cost of travel to school. In Northern Ireland school meals must be provided for primary school pupils.

Corporal punishment is prohibited by law in maintained schools in Britain.

POST-SCHOOL EDUCATION

Every 16- and 17-year-old is guaranteed a place in full-time education or training and all suitably qualified people are urged to go into higher education. About two-fifths of young people receive some form of post-school education, compared with a fifth in 1965. One in five of all young people enter higher education. The Government aims to have one in three young people in higher education by the year 2000.

The number of degrees awarded by age-group is comparable with that of other developed countries. The proportion of people in further and higher education also compares well, taking into account the high proportion of part-time students and the large group of students receiving professional training in firms.

Post-school education takes place at universities, polytechnics, the Scottish central institutions and colleges of education, further and higher education colleges, adult education centres, colleges of technology, tertiary colleges, colleges of art and design, and agricultural and horticultural colleges. There are also many independent specialist establishments, such as secretarial and correspondence colleges, and colleges for teaching English as a foreign language. Voluntary and public bodies offer cultural and general education, sometimes with assistance from local education authorities and central government. Many education and training schemes are run by public and private organisations.

The Credit Accumulation and Transfer Scheme, introduced in 1986, is used by many English and Welsh further and higher education establishments. In Scotland a credit accumulation scheme covers courses in all further and higher education. The Government aims to improve awareness of the opportunities for further and higher education and training through the development of national information services, such as the Educational Counselling and Credit Transfer Information Service funded by the Department of Education and Science.

The Further Education Unit, with funding from the Department of Education and Science, is an advisory and development body for further education. The Scottish Further Education Unit performs a parallel role.

Higher Education

Higher education is provided by universities, polytechnics, the Scottish central institutions and colleges of education and institutions of further and higher education, some concerned wholly with teacher training. The Government considers that access to higher education courses should be available to all those who can benefit from them and have the necessary intellectual competence, motivation and maturity.

Although GCE A levels and their equivalents in Scotland have traditionally been the standard for entry to higher education courses, other qualifications and courses are now considered equally appropriate. These are AS levels, BTEC and other vocational qualifications (see p 154) and access/foundation courses (see p 161). The Scottish Wider Access Programme (SWAP) is designed to promote wider participation in higher education, especially by more mature students and those without the normal entry requirements. Successful completion of a SWAP course guarantees a higher education place.

In 1989 there were 1 million students in higher education, about one-quarter more than in 1980. The Government aims to secure further increases in participation, and the number of students in full-time higher education is expected to rise by some 10 per cent between 1988–89 and 1992–93. One of its main aims in higher education is to bring about a change in the balance of provision in favour of scientific, technological and directly vocational courses.

In order to maintain British expertise in technology, recent government schemes have sought to expand higher education and research in electronics, engineering and computer science by making available extra student places, and additional staff and research fellowships in universities, polytechnics and Scottish central institutions. In 1988 the Department of Employment brought in a Graduate Enterprise Programme offering 450 places on management training courses for recently qualified graduates intending to start their own businesses.

Further Education

Further education comprises all provision outside schools to people aged over 16 of a standard up to and including GCE A level or equivalent. Courses are run by over 500 colleges of further education, many of which also offer higher education courses. Most of these colleges are controlled by local education authorities. In Scotland the new modular courses at the non-advanced level (see pp 152 and 155) can be taken in schools, further education colleges or as part of government training schemes. In Northern Ireland further education refers to full-time and part-time education for people over 16.

Much of the provision outside the universities is broadly vocational. It extends from lower-level technical and commercial courses to advanced courses for those aiming at higher-level posts in commerce, industry and administration, or taking up professions (for example, town planning or estate management). However, most colleges provide non-vocational courses, including GCSE and GCE A level courses. The system is flexible and enables the student to acquire whatever qualifications his or her capabilities and time allow.

Many students on further education courses attend part time, either by day release or block release from employment or during the evenings. A particular feature of the further education system is its strong ties with commerce and industry: much of the further education sector is devoted to work-related studies. Co-operation with the business world is encouraged by the Government and its agencies, and employers are normally involved in designing courses.

Further education colleges supply much of the education element in training programmes like Youth Training and Employment Training, both sponsored by the Department of Employment (see p 324). All young people on Youth Training will be offered training and vocational education leading to qualifications at or equivalent to a minimum of level two in the framework established by the National Council for Vocational Qualifications (see p 161) and the Scottish Vocational Education Council.

Local education authorities in England and Wales are obliged to prepare a scheme outlining procedures for planning further education provision, setting college budgets and delegating control over budgets to college governing bodies. They must also increase employer representation on governing bodies. There are similar requirements in Scotland and Northern Ireland.

Students

Around 1 million students take full-time courses, including sandwich courses where substantial periods of full-time study alternate with periods of supervised experience on a relevant job, at universities[2] and major establishments of further and

higher education in Britain. Of these over 330,000 are at universities, and another 310,000 are following higher courses at colleges of further and higher education, polytechnics and Scottish central institutions and other colleges. More than 400,000 are taking further education courses, the majority of which lead to recognised vocational or educational qualifications.

There are also 4 million part-time students, some of whom are released by their employers for further education during working hours. Many of the remainder take part in adult education classes.

Over 90 per cent of full-time students on higher courses are helped by grants from public funds, which are mandatory in England and Wales for eligible students taking first degree and other comparable courses. Grants for other courses are given at the discretion of a local education authority. They cover tuition fees and maintenance, with parents contributing to maintenance costs according to income. They are awarded by local education authorities in England and Wales up to first degree level. Equivalent schemes are administered in Scotland by the Scottish Office Education Department, and in Northern Ireland mainly by the education and library boards. Grants for postgraduate study and research are offered by the education departments and by the research councils. Some scholarships are available from endowments and also from particular industries or companies.

Student Loans Scheme

Under the Education (Student Loans) Act 1990 and corresponding Northern Ireland legislation, all home students in full-time higher education below postgraduate level are eligible for a top-up maintenance loan averaging at present over £400 a year, in addition to a maintenance grant. The standard repayment period will initially be five years. The scheme is designed to share the cost of student maintenance more equitably between students, parents and the

---

[2]Excluding the University of Buckingham.

taxpayer, as well as to promote a stronger sense of self-reliance among students. It is intended that loans will eventually provide about half of a student's maintenance entitlement.

Universities

There are 47 universities in Britain, including the Open University, compared with 17 in 1945. They are governed by royal charters or by Act of Parliament, enjoying complete academic freedom, appointing their own staff and deciding which students to admit, subjects and methods of teaching, and degrees to award. The universities of Oxford and Cambridge date from the twelfth and thirteenth centuries, and the Scottish universities of St Andrews, Glasgow, Aberdeen and Edinburgh from the fourteenth and fifteenth centuries. All the other universities in Britain were founded in the nineteenth and twentieth centuries. The 1960s saw considerable expansion in the university sector.

Admission to universities is by selection. Of the total number of 334,000 full-time home and overseas university students in 1989–90, excluding those at the University of Buckingham, 59,000 were postgraduate. There are just under 30,000 full-time university teachers paid wholly from university funds. The ratio of staff to full-time students is about 1 to 11.

Except at the Open University, first degree courses are mainly full time and usually last three years. However, there are some four-year courses, and medical and veterinary courses normally require five years. Degree titles vary according to the practice of each university. In England, Wales and Northern Ireland the most common titles for a first degree are Bachelor of Arts (BA) or Bachelor of Science (BSc) and for a second degree Master of Arts (MA), Master of Science (MSc), and Doctor of Philosophy (PhD). In the older Scottish universities Master is used for a first degree in arts subjects. Uniformity of standards between universities is promoted by employing

external examiners for all university examinations, and the general pattern of teaching is similar throughout Britain.

Research is an important feature of university work; most staff combine research with their teaching duties and about half of postgraduate students are engaged on research projects. The Government has been seeking greater accountability and selectivity in research. It is encouraging universities to co-operate closely with industry on research projects.

Open University

The Open University is a non-residential university offering degree and other courses for adult students of all ages in Britain and other parts of Europe. In the main it uses a combination of specially produced printed texts, correspondence tuition, television and radio broadcasts, audio and video cassettes, and residential schools. There is also a network of study centres for contact with part-time tutors and counsellors, and with fellow students. No formal academic qualifications are required to register for these courses, but the standards of the University's degrees are the same as those of other universities. Its first degree, for which courses began in 1971, is the BA (Open), a general degree awarded on a system of credits for each course completed. In 1991 there were 75,000 registered undergraduates, and in all 108,000 first degrees have been awarded since the University's inception.

By the year 2001 the Open University expects to have 100,000 undergraduate students on its rolls.

The University has a programme of higher degrees, Bachelor of Philosophy (BPhil), MPhil and PhD, available through research, and MA, MSc and Master of Business Administration (MBA) through taught courses. More than 5,700 students were registered on higher degree courses in 1991.

The University also has programmes for professionals in education and the health and social services, and for up-dating managers, scientists and technologists. Some of these are presented as multi-media courses in the same way as the undergraduate programme, and others are in the form of self-contained study packs. In 1990, 20,000 students were following courses in these areas and 62,000 study packs were sold.

Students must normally be resident in the European Community or in other countries where the University has agreed to register students. The University has also advised many other countries on setting up similar institutions. It has made a substantial contribution to the new Commonwealth of Learning project, which brings together distance-teaching establishments and students throughout the Commonwealth.

Polytechnics and Other Institutions

A major contribution to post-school education in England and Wales is made by the 34 polytechnics, most of which have been established since 1967. They offer mainly higher education courses in a wide range of subjects, including those leading to first and higher degrees and graduate-equivalent qualifications. They also run courses leading to the examinations of the chief professional bodies, and to qualifications such as those of the Business & Technician Education Council.

'Access' and foundation courses provide a preparation and an appropriate test before enrolment on a course of higher education for prospective students who possess non-standard entry qualifications. Many are from the ethnic minority communities. The growth of access courses has been very rapid in recent years; about 600 are now available nationwide.

Polytechnics have close links with commerce and industry, and many polytechnic students have jobs and attend on a part-time basis. Similar provision is made in Scotland in the 13 central institutions (which include polytechnics) and 50 further education colleges, and in Northern Ireland by the University of Ulster.

In England and Wales institutes and colleges of higher education, formed by the integration of teacher training with the rest of higher education, account for a significant proportion of higher education students. Some further education colleges run higher education courses, often of a specialised nature.

Council for National Academic Awards

Large numbers of students on higher education courses in Great Britain outside the universities take courses leading to the qualifications of the Council for National Academic Awards (CNAA). The Council awards degrees and other academic qualifications, ensuring that these are comparable in standard with those granted by the universities. The courses range from science and technology to the arts, social studies, business studies and law, but the proportion of technology, business or other broadly vocational courses is much higher than in universities.

Since 1987 institutions running CNAA-approved courses have been able to apply to have delegated responsibility for approving and reviewing their own courses. By August 1991 a total of 40 institutions had been accredited by the CNAA for taught degree courses.

The CNAA would be disbanded under the White Paper proposals announced in May 1991.

Vocational Qualifications

The National Council for Vocational Qualifications (NCVQ) was set up in 1986 to reform and rationalise the vocational qualifications system in England, Wales and Northern Ireland. The Council aims to make qualifications more relevant to the needs of employment by basing them on standards of competence set by industry. It is establishing a new framework of National Vocational Qualifications (NVQs) based on defined levels of achievement to which qualifications in all sectors can be assigned or accredited. By August 1991 about 300 qualifications drawn from 60 different employment sectors had been accredited. The immediate target is to complete by the end of 1992 the national framework up to level 4 for 80 per cent of the employed population and all the major occupational areas.

The competence-based system is being extended in Scotland, which already has its own modular system, through a new system of Scottish Vocational Qualifications (SVQs) along the lines of NVQs. SVQs are accredited by the Scottish Vocational Education Council (see p 155).

Under the White Paper proposals, more general job-related qualifications would be devised for those seeking a broad preparation for employment. The Government would promote equality of status for academic and vocational qualifications by developing new Ordinary and Advanced Diplomas. Students gaining an appropriate number of GCSE passes, equivalent vocational qualifications or a combination of these would receive the Ordinary Diploma. The Advanced Diploma would be awarded to those passing GCE A level and AS level examinations, students gaining vocational qualifications at the same level and those with passes in a mixture of the two.

Other Examining Bodies

The Business & Technician Education Council (BTEC) plans and administers a unified national system of courses at all levels for students in industry, commerce and public administration in England, Wales and Northern Ireland. Courses leading to BTEC awards are available at polytechnics, colleges of further and higher education, and in some schools.

The Scottish Vocational Education Council (SCOTVEC) is the principal examining and awarding body in the field of further education in Scotland. SCOTVEC administers and develops the non-advanced SCOTVEC National Certificate and the advanced level Higher National Certificate and Higher National Diploma.

Qualifications in a range of occupational areas are offered by the City and Guilds of London Institute, and qualifications in commercial and office practice are awarded by the Royal Society of Arts.

Teacher Training

Courses and Qualifications

Almost all entrants to teaching in maintained and special schools in England and Wales complete a recognised course of initial teacher training. Such courses are offered by university departments of education as well as by many polytechnics and colleges. Non-graduates usually qualify by taking a four-year Bachelor of Education (BEd) honours degree. There are also specially designed two-year BEd courses—mostly in subjects where there is a shortage of teachers at the secondary level—for suitably qualified people. Graduates normally take a one-year Postgraduate Certificate of Education (PGCE) course. Two-year PGCE courses are available in the secondary shortage subjects for those whose first degree in an associated subject included at least one year's study of the subject they intend to teach.

Articled teacher courses, offering school-based training for graduates, were introduced in 1990. Trainees, who receive a bursary, take on a progressively greater teaching load, and formal training is provided both in initial teacher-training institutions and in school by college tutors and school teachers.

In 1989 the Government introduced a licensed teacher scheme in England and Wales for people without formal teacher-training qualifications but with relevant qualifications and experience. Participants generally have to complete a period of two years of in-service training as a licensed teacher before achieving qualified teacher status. The Government has also made it easier for teachers trained abroad to take up posts in English and Welsh schools. Trained teachers from other European Community countries are automatically granted qualified teacher status, while non-Community teachers undergo a training and evaluation period of between three months and two years.

In Scotland all teachers in education authority schools must be registered with the General Teaching Council for Scotland. It is government policy that all entrants to the teaching profession in Scotland should be graduates. New primary teachers qualify either through a four-year BEd course or a one-year postgraduate course of teacher training at one of the five colleges of education. In addition, the University of Stirling offers courses which combine academic and professional training for intending primary and secondary teachers. Teachers of academic subjects at secondary schools must hold a degree containing two passes in the subjects which they wish to teach. Secondary teachers must undertake a one-year postgraduate training course. For music and technology, four-year BEd courses are also available, and for physical education all teachers take BEd courses.

Teacher training in Northern Ireland is provided by the two universities and two colleges of education. The principal courses are BEd Honours (four years), BA Honours (Education) and the one-year Postgraduate Certificate of Education.

Measures to Improve Standards

The Government is taking steps to improve the quality of teaching by revising selection, training and placement procedures for new teachers, and by increasing in-service training opportunities. Management training courses for head teachers are also being provided. The Government believes that more systematic planning is required by schools and local education authorities to match in-service training to both the career needs of teachers and to the curricular needs of schools. A major new in-service training programme to improve the quality of teaching in schools and institutions of further education was introduced under the Education (No 2) Act 1986 (see p 144).

Measures to strengthen initial teacher training in England, Wales and Northern Ireland have included the issuing of criteria which courses must meet and the establishment of the Council for the Accreditation of Teacher Education to review courses against the criteria. Formal teacher appraisal is being introduced in English and Welsh schools and the Government expects all teachers to have had their first appraisal by 1995.

In Scotland all courses have been revised following recommendations of working parties on teacher training. All new pre-service and major in-service courses provided by colleges of education must be approved by the Scottish Office Education Department and a validating body. Education authorities are to be asked to implement national guidelines for the introduction of systematic schemes of staff development and appraisal. The Government has taken reserve powers requiring authorities to operate schemes prescribed by it in the event of a breakdown of voluntary agreements.

Further Education for Adults

Further education for adults is provided by further education colleges, adult education colleges, local authority adult education services and in community schools and colleges. Provision is also made in six long-term residential colleges and by the Workers' Educational Association and other voluntary bodies.

More than 2·5 million people aged 19 or over enrol each year on further education courses.

In addition to cultural, physical and craft pursuits, students follow courses leading to academic and vocational qualifications, and courses which provide access to higher education. Adults' special educational needs for literacy and numeracy are also met, and there is provision for those seeking proficiency in English as a foreign language.

PICKUP

The Government has improved opportunities for both adult and continuing education. The Professional, Industrial and Commercial Updating Programme (PICKUP) is designed to help colleges, polytechnics and universities meet the need to up-date and broaden the skills of those in mid-career. Enrolments on PICKUP-type courses have been growing by about 20 per cent annually in recent years. Many courses are concerned with the single European market.

ALBSU

The Adult Literacy and Basic Skills Unit (ALBSU) is the central focus for adult literacy, numeracy and communications skills in England and Wales. A three-year literacy and numeracy initiative was launched in 1989 as a joint venture between the Government and the BBC. It involves the use of television and radio and specially printed material to improve the communications skills of an estimated 6 million adults. Basic Skills at Work is a programme for raising basic skill levels with government funding approaching £3 million. New nationally recognised qualifications in communication and numeracy are being developed, and a referral service is being created to put people in contact with 60 new open-learning centres and other local learning facilities.

In Scotland, responsibility for overseeing adult basic education rests with the Scottish Community Education Council.

Open College

Open learning opportunities have been extended with the formation in 1987 of the Open College, an independent company set up with government support. The College brings together broadcasters, educationists and sponsors, and provides vocational education and training courses below degree level. Up to £12 million is being allocated by the Government for the College's commercial activities as well as £6 million for broadcasting. The Open College of the Arts, also launched in 1987, offers an art foundation course to those wishing to study at home.

Other Institutions

Apart from provision for mature students at universities and polytechnics, courses are offered by the Open University, further education colleges, adult education centres, residential colleges, extra-mural departments of universities and bodies such as voluntary organisations. Most of the provision is made by the local education authorities in a variety of establishments, including schools used for adult evening classes and 'community schools' offering educational, social and cultural opportunities for the wider community. A majority of courses are part time. Local authorities also maintain or aid many of the short-term residential colleges or centres. Long-term residential colleges, grant-aided by central government departments, have courses of one or two years and aim to provide a liberal education for adults with few or no formal academic qualifications. Most students are entitled to full maintenance grants.

University extra-mural departments and the Workers' Educational Association, the largest recognised voluntary educational body in Britain, offer extended part-time courses of liberal studies. They also run short courses for special (including vocational) interests. Various kinds of education and training are provided by many other organisations, for example, the National Federation of Women's Institutes, the Young Men's Christian Association and the Pre-Retirement Association.

National Institute of Adult Continuing Education

The National Institute of Adult Continuing Education is a centre of information, research, development work and publication for adult and continuing education. It plays a central role in advising on and co-ordinating developments in policy and practice. Also, the Institute acts as a channel of co-operation and consultation for the many interested organisations which it represents in England and Wales. It administers with government funding the Unit for the Development of Adult Continuing Education, which undertakes research and development work. The Unit is to merge with the Further Education Unit in April 1992.

Scottish Community Education Council

The Scottish Community Education Council advises the Government and promotes all community education matters, including adult literacy and basic education, and the youth service in Scotland.

Teaching Methods

The general pattern of teaching and learning on full-time courses of higher education is a mixture of lectures; prescribed or suggested reading; seminars and tutorials; essays, exercises and tests; and practical work or work experience.

Radio and television programmes, both specifically educational and general, are important media for continuing education and are often linked to supplementary publications, courses and activities. The BBC, independent television and Channel 4 present programmes which range from basic education and progressive vocational training to domestic, social and craft skills. The BBC also works with the Open University (see p 160), producing and broadcasting radio and television programmes that form part of the University's courses. Channel 4 has a similar relationship with the Open College.

EDUCATIONAL RESEARCH

Research into the theory and practice of education and the organisation of educational services is supported financially by central and local government, the Economic and Social Research Council, philanthropic organisations, higher education institutions, teachers' associations and certain independent bodies.

The major research institution outside the universities is the autonomous National Foundation for Educational Research in England and Wales. The Scottish Council for Research in Education and the Northern Ireland Council for Educational Research have similar functions.

EDUCATIONAL LINKS OVERSEAS

Schoolchildren, students, teachers and others come to Britain from overseas to study, and British people work and train overseas. Many opportunities for such movement are the result of international co-operation at government level within the European Community and within the Commonwealth. Educational schemes, courses and professional contacts are organised in Britain by officially funded and voluntary organisations. The British aid programme encourages links between educational institutions in Britain and developing countries.

British membership of the European Community has created closer ties with other member countries. Member states are required to seek to incorporate a European perspective into their education systems. In schools, colleges and universities in Britain there has been an expansion of interest in European studies and languages, and exchanges of teachers, schoolchildren and students take place.

The European Community's European Action Scheme for Mobility of University Students (ERASMUS) promotes exchange of students throughout the Community. Some 30,000 students participated in the programme in 1990–91; 179 higher education institutions were involved. In 1991–92 British institutions are expected to be involved in more than 1,000 inter-university programmes. The Community's LINGUA programme seeks to promote an improvement in language competence.

Britain has adhered to the Statute of the European Schools (nine of which have been established throughout the Community, including one at Culham, Oxfordshire) to provide education for children of people employed in Community institutions. The European Community Action Programme for Education and Training for Technology (COMETT) aims to foster co-operation between higher education establishments and companies throughout the Community. The UK Centre for European Education, with government financing, promotes a European dimension in education.

Overseas Students in Britain

People come to Britain from all over the world to study. British universities, polytechnics and other further and higher education establishments have built up their reputation overseas by offering tuition of the highest standards, maintaining low student-to-staff ratios, and offering relevant courses and qualifications.

In the academic year 1989–90 there were about 52,000 overseas students at universities and 26,000 at polytechnics and other public sector establishments of further and higher education. In addition, many thousands of people from abroad were training for nursing, law, banking and accountancy, and service and other industries. About a third of all overseas students were from the Commonwealth and Britain's dependencies. There are now five times as many students from European Community states as in 1980. Many students come to Britain for advanced training: more than one-third of students enrolled for full-time postgraduate study or research in Britain in 1989–90 came from overseas. Several British colleges of further education have entered into arrangements with British universities to provide 'bridging' courses for overseas students before they enter university.

Most overseas students pay their own fees and expenses or hold awards from their own governments. Those following courses of higher or further education pay fees which cover the full cost of their courses. Nationals of other member countries of the European Community generally pay the lower level of fees that applies to British students.

Government Scholarship Schemes

The Government makes considerable provision for students and trainees from overseas under its overseas aid programme and other award and scholarship schemes. In 1990–91 nearly 25,000 overseas students were supported, including some studying overseas, at a cost of more than £140 million. The majority were from developing countries, mainly the Commonwealth, studying under the Technical Co-operation and Training Programme, which is financed from the aid programme. Under the Overseas Development Administration Shared Scholarship Scheme, 190 awards will be offered in 1991–92, primarily at postgraduate level, for students from the developing countries of the Commonwealth, with costs being shared between the British Government and the educational institutions.

The Foreign & Commonwealth Office Scholarships and Awards Scheme (FCOSAS), which operates in some 140 countries, is designed to bring to Britain present and future leaders, decision-makers and formers of opinion. A notable feature of the FCOSAS is the increasing number of awards jointly financed by the Foreign & Commonwealth Office in partnership with the private sector and academic institutions. The Department of Trade and Industry also finances a trade-related scholarship scheme in partnership with British industry. Outside the aid programme, the Overseas Research Students Awards Scheme, funded by the Department of Education and Science, provides assistance for overseas research students of high ability to attend British universities.

Other Schemes

Many public and private scholarships and fellowships are available to students from overseas and to British students who want to study overseas. Among the best known, and open to men and women in all walks of life, are the British Council Scholarships, the Commonwealth Scholarship and Fellowship Plan, the Fulbright Scholarship Scheme, the Marshall Scholarships, the Rhodes Scholarships, the Churchill Scholarships and the Confederation of British Industry Scholarships. Most British universities and colleges offer scholarships for which graduates of any nationality are eligible.

English as a Foreign Language

The continuing increase in interest in English as a foreign language is reflected in the growth of public sector English language courses and in the number of private language schools in Britain. Over 240 private schools are recognised by the British Council. The Council has expanded its own teaching of English overseas by opening centres and extending existing ones (155 in all by June 1991); it also runs a programme for teaching English related to specific jobs and skills. Other British language schools enable people to learn English in their own countries, while in Britain university language and linguistics departments are an important resource. The Government's aid programme supports the teaching of English in many developing countries by financing major projects in schools, universities and other institutions. Publications and other material relating to English language teaching have increased in number and are now a large component in many publishers' lists, constituting a major export.

BBC English, the English teaching arm of the BBC's World Service, offers a worldwide facility for the individual learner at home on radio and, with the advent of the new World Service Television operation, increasingly on television.

Educational Exchanges

British Council

The promotion of cultural and educational relations with other countries is a major concern of the British Council, which plays an important part in the management of the aid programme to education. It recruits teachers for work overseas, organises short overseas visits by British experts, and encourages cultural exchange visits. It also runs schemes to foster academic interchange between higher education institutions in Britain and other countries, and exchange schemes in other scientific, educational and cultural areas. Co-operation between higher education in Britain and developing countries is promoted with funding from the Overseas Development Administration. It is brought about through recruiting staff for overseas universities, the secondment of staff from British higher education establishments, interdepartmental faculty links, local staff development, short-term teaching and advisory visits, and general consultancy services.

Central Bureau for Educational Visits and Exchanges

The Central Bureau for Educational Visits and Exchanges is the national centre for information and advice on all forms of educational visits and exchanges. It develops and administers a variety of exchange schemes; links educational establishments and local education authorities with counterparts abroad; and organises meetings and conferences on professional international experience.

Among the schemes for professional exchange which the Bureau administers are teacher exchange in Europe, the Soviet Union and the United States; short courses for language teachers; and international study visits. Opportunities for young people include school and class links and English language summer camps. For the post-16 age group there are work placements and English language assistants' posts, as well as other exchange programmes.

Association of Commonwealth Universities

The Association of Commonwealth Universities promotes contact and co-operation between 376 member universities in 30 Commonwealth countries or regions. It assists student and staff mobility by administering award schemes, including, for Britain, the Commonwealth Scholarship and Fellowship Plan and the Overseas Development Administration Shared Scholarship Scheme, and by operating an academic appointments service. It publishes information about Commonwealth universities, courses and scholarships, and organises meetings in different parts of the world.

Other Organisations

The Commonwealth Education Liaison Committee supplements normal direct dealings on education between Commonwealth countries. The United Kingdom Council for Overseas Student Affairs is an independent body serving overseas students, and those concerned with student affairs.

The Youth Exchange Centre, managed by the British Council, gives advice, information, training and grants to British youth groups involved in international exchanges. The Centre is the national agency for the European Community-sponsored exchange scheme, Youth for Europe.

The Youth Service

The youth service forms part of the education system and is concerned with promoting the personal development and social education of young people by providing opportunities for them to participate in a broad range of leisure time and extra-curricular activities. Young people take part in the youth service on a voluntary basis. Extending the range of experiences open to young people and giving them opportunities to take part in the running of their organisations are seen as key elements in the provision.

The youth service is a partnership between central government, local authorities and voluntary youth organisations. At local level the youth service is provided by voluntary organisations and local education authorities. Government education departments formulate broad policy objectives and encourage their implementation through financial assistance and advice. Government funding for the national youth service bodies in England and Wales is channelled through the National Youth Agency, which is responsible for working with voluntary and local authority sectors to improve the quality, range and effectiveness of their work. The Agency's functions include curriculum development, youth worker training, support for managers of organisations within the youth service and support for international work. It is also responsible for collecting and publishing information on youth service matters.

In Scotland the youth service forms a part of adult education, which is integrated within community education. The Scottish Community Education Council has the role of promoting community education. The Youth Council for Northern Ireland, with executive and advisory powers, was set up in 1990.

At national level many voluntary organisations belong to the National Council for Voluntary Youth Services, a representative and consultative body which aims to develop the partnership between voluntary and statutory bodies in England. Similar councils exist in Wales, Scotland and Northern Ireland. The British Youth Council is a national forum for young people, youth organisations and youth councils, including the youth wings of the major political parties, and represents young people at an international level.

Voluntary Youth Organisations

National voluntary youth organisations undertake the major share of youth activities through local groups which raise most of their day-to-day expenses by their own efforts. Many receive financial and other help from local education authorities, which also make available facilities in many areas. The voluntary organisations vary greatly in character and include the uniformed and church organisations. Many local authorities and voluntary youth organisations have responded to new needs in society by making provision, for example, for the young unemployed, young people from the ethnic minorities, young people in inner cities or rural areas and those in trouble or especially vulnerable. Other areas of concern are homelessness and provision for handicapped young people.

Among the largest voluntary youth organisations are the Scout and Girl Guides Associations (with about 728,000 and 670,000 members), and the Young Men's Christian Association (1·5 million), all of which have worldwide affiliations; Youth Clubs UK (about 568,000); the National Association of Boys' Clubs (170,000); and clubs run by the churches. Organisations like the Outward Bound Trust provide opportunities for adventurous outdoor pursuits. The three pre-service organisations (the Sea Cadet Corps, Army Cadet Force and Air Training Corps), with a membership of 130,000, undertake activities related to the work of the armed forces.

Many authorities have youth committees on which official and voluntary bodies are represented, and employ youth officers to co-ordinate youth work and to arrange in-service training. There are also youth councils, which are representative bodies of young people from local youth organisations.

Youth Workers

In England and Wales a basic two-year training course at certain universities and higher education colleges leads to the status of qualified youth and community worker; several undergraduate part-time and postgraduate courses are also available. In Scotland one-, two- and three-year courses are provided at colleges of education and in Northern Ireland courses are run by the University of Ulster.

An estimated 5,500 full-time youth workers are supported by some 500,000 part-time workers, both qualified and unqualified, many of them unpaid. Short courses and conferences are held on youth and community work. There are also in-service courses for serving youth workers and officers. Initial and in-service courses are validated by the National Youth Agency. Youth counselling is supported by the National Association of Young People's Counselling and Advisory Services.

Other Organisations Concerned with Young People

A substantial sum of money is awarded by the many grant-giving foundations and trusts each year for activities involving young people. King George's Jubilee Trust, which distributed £879,000 in 1990–91, supports work involving young people aged 8 to 25. The Queen's Silver Jubilee Trust, which awarded £1·6 million in 1990–91, supports young people up to the age of 25 involved in voluntary community service work. In addition, The Prince's Trust, which was set up in 1976 to help disadvantaged young people aged 14 to 25, paid £2 million to individuals and small ad hoc groups in 1990–91.

The Duke of Edinburgh's Award Scheme operates through local authorities, schools, youth organisations and industrial firms. It enables young people from Britain and other Commonwealth countries to take part, with voluntary help from adults, in a variety of challenging activities in four areas: community service, expeditions, the development of personal interests and social and practical skills, and physical recreation.

Voluntary Service by Young People

Thousands of young people voluntarily undertake community service designed to help those in need, including elderly and disabled people, and many others work on environmental projects. Organisations providing opportunities for community service, such as Community Service Volunteers, International Voluntary Service and the British Trust for Conservation Volunteers, receive grants from the Government. Many schools also organise community service work as part of the curriculum, and voluntary work in the community is sponsored by a number of churches.

Young Volunteers in the Community is a national scheme which recruits young people aged 16 to 24 to work on a variety of community projects for 12 to 18 weeks. It is operated jointly by The Prince's Trust and the Commission on Citizenship.

8 Planning, Urban Regeneration and Housing

Britain seeks to reconcile the conflicting demands for land from business, housing, transport, farming and leisure, and to protect the environment by means of a comprehensive statutory system of land-use planning and development control. Most development requires 'planning permission'; applications are dealt with in the light of development plans, which set out land use strategies for each area on such matters as housing and industry. However, many minor developments do not need specific planning permission. The Government aims to remove unnecessary planning controls as part of its policy to promote enterprise. A comprehensive programme to revitalise the inner cities and other urban areas (such as peripheral housing estates) includes a number of initiatives designed to encourage enterprise, employment and educational opportunities, and to improve the quality of housing and the urban environment.

Planning

The system of land-use planning in Great Britain involves local authorities acting under the supervision of the Secretaries of State for the Environment, Wales and Scotland. The Department of the Environment brings together the major responsibilities in England for land-use planning, housing and construction, countryside policy and environmental protection. The Welsh Office and the Scottish Office have broadly equivalent responsibilities.

The Department of the Environment provides national and regional guidance on planning matters, while strategic planning at the county level is the responsibility of the county councils. District councils are responsible for local plans and development control. In the metropolitan areas and London, the borough and district councils are preparing new unitary development plans for each administrative area. In Scotland the planning context is set by the Scottish Office and planning functions are undertaken by regional and district councils, whose responsibilities are divided on a basis broadly similar to that in England and Wales. In the more rural regions and the islands, the regional and islands councils respectively have responsibility for planning. In Northern Ireland the Department of the Environment for Northern Ireland is responsible for planning matters through six divisional planning offices, which work closely with the district councils.

The Government's aim is for the maximum use to be made of urban land for new development, having regard to the need to retain green spaces within the urban environment and the need to ensure that the cumulative effects of development do not harm the character of established residential areas.

Development Plans

The present development plan system in England and Wales involves structure, local and unitary development plans:

- structure plans, prepared by county planning authorities and approved by the Secretary of State, set out broad policies for the development and other use of land;

- local plans provide detailed guidance for development expected to start within about ten years and are normally prepared by district councils in general conformity with the approved structure plan; and

- unitary development plans set out both strategic and detailed land use and development policies for metropolitan districts or boroughs.

Plans are kept under review and may be altered from time to time. Planning authorities must take account of any strategic or regional guidance issued by the Secretary of State when formulating the plans.

In Scotland structure plans are prepared by regional or islands authorities, and local plans by those districts with planning responsibilities, and by general planning and islands authorities. Under Northern Ireland's single-tier system, plans are prepared by the Department of the Environment for Northern Ireland.

The Planning and Compensation Act 1991 will reform the planning system in the non-metropolitan areas of England and Wales by introducing mandatory district-wide local plans and streamlining procedures for their adoption. The strategic role of the counties will continue under the new system but their planning policies will not be subject to the formal approval of the Secretary of State. They will, however, be required to ensure that their statements are consistent with any regional guidance issued by the Secretary of State.

Public Participation

Members of the public are given an opportunity to express their views on the planning of their area during the formative stages of plan preparation. Local planning authorities must ensure publicity for the proposed content of their plans; representations about them may be made to the authorities. There are also provisions for objecting to draft plans, and for hearing and resolving such objections.

Where specific proposals for development differ greatly from the intentions of a development plan, they must be publicised locally. Other schemes affecting a large number of people are usually advertised by the local planning authority, and applications seeking permission for certain types of development—for example, those affecting conservation areas—must also be advertised. In Scotland a neighbour notification system requires the applicant to notify the owners and occupiers of land and buildings adjoining the site of a proposed development at the same time as the application is submitted to the local planning authority.

The applicant has a right of appeal to the Secretary of State if the local authority refuses planning permission or grants it with conditions attached. Such appeals are decided either on the basis of written submissions or, generally in the case of important applications, after a public inquiry.

Similar provision is made in Northern Ireland for public participation in the planning process and for the hearing of representations at public inquiries. For planning applications which do not give rise to public inquiries the applicant has a right of appeal to the independent Planning Appeals Commission.

Major Schemes

The Secretaries of State can direct that a planning application be referred to them for decision. This power to 'call in' is generally exercised only for proposals which raise planning issues of national or regional importance. The applicant and the local planning authority have the right to be heard by a person appointed by the Secretary of State for that purpose and a public inquiry will normally be held. In Northern Ireland, major planning applications are dealt with under the Planning (NI) Order 1972, which allows for a public inquiry in certain circumstances.

For projects which are likely to have significant effects upon the environment, a planning application must be accompanied by an environmental statement. This should describe the likely significant effects and propose measures to avoid, reduce or remedy any significant adverse effects identified. Planning permission cannot be given without first taking into consideration environmental information—the environmental statement for the project and representations received in response to its publication. The public must be given the opportunity to comment on the statement, and copies will be sent to relevant public bodies, such as the Countryside Commission and English Nature, so that they can make representations to the local planning authority.

New Towns

The 32 new towns designated since 1946—21 in England, two in Wales, five in Scotland and four in Northern Ireland—have now largely achieved their aims of dispersal of industry and population from congested cities and the stimulation of regional economies.

The new towns have a total population of over 2 million; several have become regional centres for shopping and office accommodation.

The new town development corporations' priorities now are to maximise private investment in housing and employment, to achieve balanced communities able to generate their own growth, and to sell or transfer their assets before winding up.

With the completion of the new towns programme, the development corporations which administered the new towns are being dissolved. The remaining two corporations in England will be wound up by March 1992, and dissolution of the first two of the five Scottish development corporations is due to begin in late 1991. In Wales responsibility for Newtown rests with the Development Board for Rural Wales, while the corporation responsible for Cwmbran was dissolved in 1988.

Architectural Standards

High standards in new building are encouraged by the Government, although it advises local planning authorities not to impose their architectural tastes on developers. The Department of the Environment, in collaboration with the independent Royal Institute of British Architects (RIBA) and the National House-Building Council, sponsors the biennial Housing Design Awards Scheme for England and Northern Ireland, with categories for renovation as well as new building. Scotland and Wales have similar award schemes. Royal Fine Art Commissions for England and Wales and for Scotland advise government departments, planning authorities and other public bodies on questions of public amenity or artistic importance.

The RIBA, the principal professional body for architects, together with the Architects Registration Council of the United Kingdom, exercises control over standards in architectural education and encourages high architectural standards in the profession. The Royal Incorporation of Architects in Scotland is allied to it, as is the Royal Society of Ulster Architects.

Urban Regeneration

Despite much progress in urban regeneration, areas of deprivation still exist. These relatively small areas can have a blighting effect on a city's image. The Government is therefore continuing to tackle urban deprivation.

The 'Action for Cities' initiative, launched in 1988, contains a comprehensive package for revival in England and Wales, involving government departments in a co-ordinated effort. The Government spends some £4,000 million a year in the inner cities, spread across a range of programmes.

However, sustainable urban regeneration depends upon the commitment of all those with an interest in the well-being of an area. In May 1991 the Government announced a new initiative called 'City Challenge'. Under this programme, local authorities are invited to submit plans for regenerating their key neighbourhoods by tackling the problems of physical decay and poor quality of life. The best of these proposals will receive a commitment of government funding for up to five years. The local council will provide the leadership in developing and implementing the plan, but it will draw on the talent and expertise of local communities, the private sector, academic institutions, statutory agencies and the voluntary sector.

Pilot projects involving 11 councils will begin in 1992–93. The Government has set aside £82·5 million a year over a five-year period to help these areas. This will be combined with spending by the councils themselves, the private sector and other bodies. The Government intends to hold a further competition, open to all Urban Programme authorities, for 1993–94 and eventually to distribute more urban resources on a competitive basis.

Urban problems in Scotland, Wales and Northern Ireland are being tackled by Partnerships, the Programme for the Valleys and Belfast Action Teams respectively, as well as by many other government programmes.

Urban Programme

The Urban Programme is a special allocation to selected local authorities in addition to their normal resources. It is concentrated on target areas (see map, pp 176–7) where the problems are greatest and the levels of deprivation most severe, so as to achieve a greater impact with available funds. The local authorities concerned receive 75 per cent grant from central government to cover spending on approved projects. The programme supports some 9,000 projects at any one time and is directed at economic, social, environmental and housing problems.

In 1990–91 the Urban Programme supported some 471 new firms, helped to create or preserve 38,000 jobs and supported 80,000 inner city training places. It improved 6,000 buildings and around 1,600 hectares (3,950 acres) of unsightly land. It also supported environmental improvement schemes for 82,000 dwellings. The Government has allocated £269 million for spending on the Urban Programme in 1991–92.

City Action Teams

Eight 'City Action Teams' (CATs) have been established in England to co-ordinate and target government programmes to regenerate inner cities. These teams bring together the regional officials of the Department of Employment and its Employment Service, the Department of the Environment and the Department of Trade and Industry to ensure that their main programmes are working together effectively. They act as a central contact point with government for business and voluntary and community organisations. Each CAT has a sponsoring Minister to advise it and a small special budget for tackling local inner city problems which relate to unemployment, enterprise generation and environmental improvement.

Task Forces

A total of 16 'Task Forces' have been set up in England to bring together and focus the efforts of government departments, local government, the private sector and the local community to regenerate inner cities. They are small teams of five or six civil servants based in the most deprived parts of their inner city areas (see map, pp 176–7). Task Forces aim to help local people by increasing their chances of gaining employment and by building up local businesses. They also support schemes which improve the environment or reduce crime where these are linked directly to the creation of jobs. Since their inception they have committed some £80 million to over 3,000 projects. They are not permanent; an important part of their work is to build up local organisations to which they can hand over as they withdraw.

Urban Development Corporations

Eleven urban development corporations (UDCs) have been set up by the Government in order to reverse large-scale urban decline. The first two were established in London Docklands and Merseyside in 1981. By the end of March 1991 the London Docklands Development Corporation had received over £1,100 million in government grant and secured private investment commitments of about £8,400 million. It has reclaimed over 580 hectares (1,430 acres) of derelict land for housing, commercial and recreational use. Over 15,000 homes have been completed and 31,000 jobs have been attracted to the area. The Merseyside Development Corporation has reclaimed 312 hectares (770 acres) of derelict land, and 284,000 sq m (3·1 million sq ft) of commercial or industrial floorspace have been built or refurbished in its area.

Nine further UDCs have been set up: Trafford Park (Greater Manchester), Teesside, Tyne and Wear, Black Country (West Midlands) and Cardiff Bay in 1987 and Bristol, Leeds, central Manchester and Sheffield in 1988–89. UDCs cover about 16,000 hectares (about 40,000 acres), and public expenditure on the programme will be £470 million in 1991–92.

City Grant

City Grant was introduced in 1988 to simplify and replace the existing grants available for encouraging private sector developments in inner cities. It is paid direct to the private sector for projects which contribute to the regeneration of urban areas. By May 1991, 195 schemes in England had been approved, with £177 million of public money bringing in £770 million of private investment. Under these schemes, some 28,000 jobs and 4,500 homes were being provided and 384 hectares (950 acres) were being reclaimed.

Enterprise and Simplified Planning Zones

Since 1981 the Government has set up 27 'enterprise zones' (see map, pp 176–7); each zone runs for a period of ten years from designation. Benefits in the zones include:

- exemption from the uniform business rate (the local property tax payable by non-domestic property owners);
- 100 per cent allowances for corporation and income tax purposes for capital expenditure on industrial and commercial buildings;

- a much simplified planning system and
- a reduction in government requests for statistical information.

By December 1989, nearly 130,000 jobs in 5,200 establishments were located in enterprise zones. The Government does not propose to extend the scheme generally, although in exceptional circumstances a new zone might be created as the best way of tackling a particular local problem. The earliest zones have reached the end of their lives; research is being undertaken to identify the circumstances in which the benefits available in enterprise zones are most effective.

The Housing and Planning Act 1986 provided for the establishment of 'simplified planning zones', intended to stimulate regeneration by removing the uncertainty from the planning system. They use a simplified planning framework similar to that used in enterprise zones, under which advance planning permission is given for specified types of development within a zone. A simplified planning zone scheme lasts for ten years.

Land Reclamation and Use

The 1988 Derelict Land Survey found that there were just under 40,500 hectares (100,000 acres) of derelict land in England, 11 per cent less than in 1982. Although much land had been reclaimed, substantial areas had become derelict during this period. Derelict land is often concentrated in places associated with nineteenth-century industrial development, but the continuing restructuring of particular industries has added significantly to the problem in certain areas.

In England government grants are available to local authorities and to other public bodies, to the private sector and to nationalised industries for the reclamation of such land in order to bring it into beneficial use or to improve its appearance. In 1991–92 the funding available for derelict land reclamation in England will be about £72 million, of which some £21 million will be spent on derelict land reclamation in the

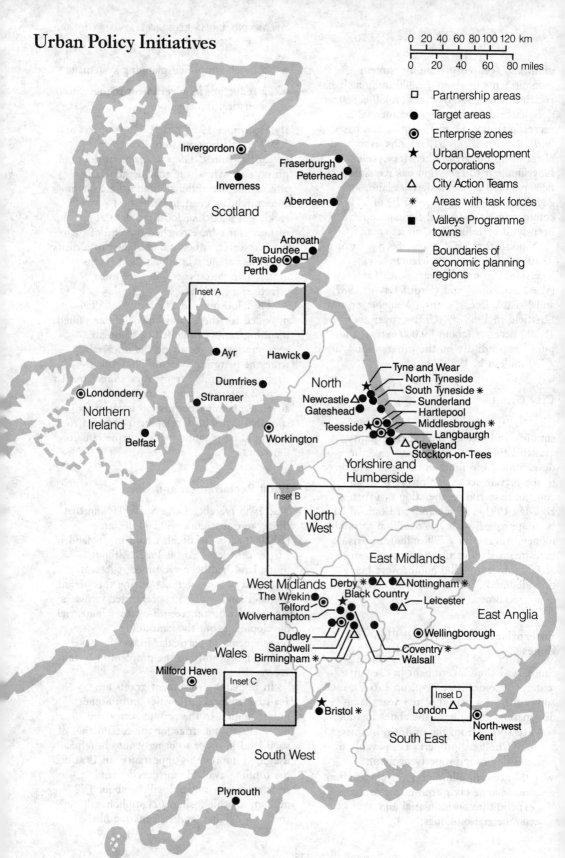

Urban Policy Initiatives

Scale:
0 20 40 60 80 100 120 km
0 20 40 60 80 miles

Legend:
- □ Partnership areas
- ● Target areas
- ◉ Enterprise zones
- ★ Urban Development Corporations
- △ City Action Teams
- ∗ Areas with task forces
- ■ Valleys Programme towns
- ▬ Boundaries of economic planning regions

Invergordon ◉
Fraserburgh
Peterhead
Inverness ●
Scotland
Aberdeen ●
Arbroath
Dundee
Tayside ◉ □
Perth ●

Inset A

Ayr ●   Hawick ●

Dumfries ●   North

◉ Londonderry   Newcastle △   Tyne and Wear ★
Northern   Gateshead   North Tyneside
Ireland   Stranraer ●   South Tyneside ∗
Workington ◉   Sunderland
Belfast ●   Teesside ★   Hartlepool
     Middlesbrough ∗
     Langbaurgh
     △ Cleveland
     Stockton-on-Tees

Yorkshire and
Humberside

Inset B

North
West

East Midlands

West Midlands   Derby ∗●△   △ Nottingham ∗
     Black Country
The Wrekin ●◉   Leicester
Telford ◉   △
Wolverhampton   East Anglia

Dudley ◉
Sandwell △   Wellingborough ◉
Birmingham ∗   Coventry ∗
Walsall

Wales

Milford Haven ◉

Inset C   Inset D
     London △
Bristol ★ ∗   North-west
     Kent ◉
South East

South West

Plymouth ●

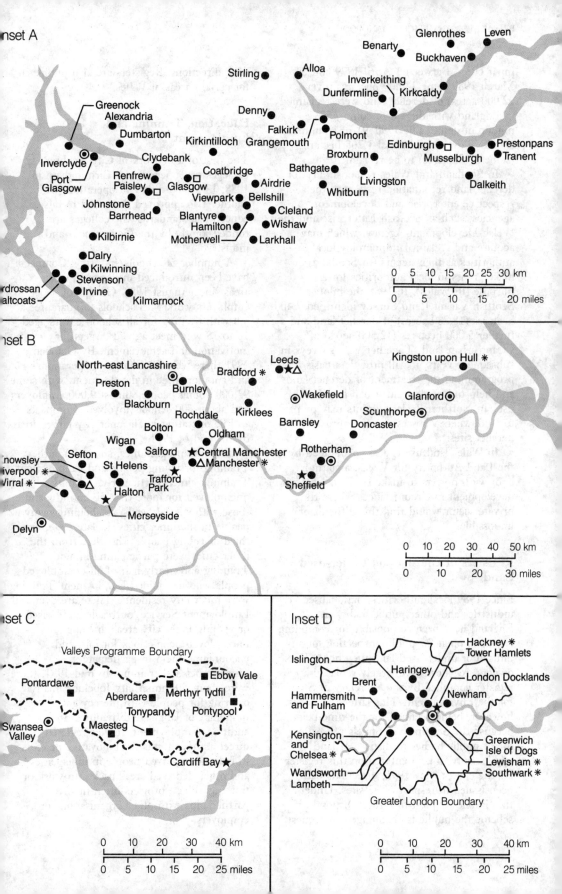

Inset A

Glenrothes
Leven
Benarty
Buckhaven
Stirling
Alloa
Inverkeithing
Dunfermline
Kirkcaldy
Greenock
Alexandria
Denny
Dumbarton
Falkirk
Polmont
Edinburgh
Prestonpans
Kirkintilloch
Grangemouth
Tranent
Clydebank
Broxburn
Musselburgh
Inverclyde
Bathgate
Port
Glasgow
Renfrew
Coatbridge
Airdrie
Livingston
Paisley
Glasgow
Dalkeith
Johnstone
Viewpark
Bellshill
Whitburn
Barrhead
Cleland
Blantyre
Wishaw
Hamilton
Motherwell
Larkhall
Kilbirnie
Dalry
Kilwinning
Stevenson
rdrossan
Irvine
altcoats
Kilmarnock

0 5 10 15 20 25 30 km
0 5 10 15 20 miles

Inset B

North-east Lancashire
Leeds
Bradford ✳
Kingston upon Hull ✳
Preston
Burnley
Blackburn
Wakefield
Glanford ◉
Rochdale
Kirklees
Scunthorpe ◉
Bolton
Oldham
Barnsley
Doncaster
Wigan
Salford
Central Manchester
Rotherham
nowsley
Sefton
St Helens
△ Manchester ✳
iverpool ✳
Trafford
Sheffield
Virral ✳
Park
Halton
Merseyside
Delyn ◉

0 10 20 30 40 50 km
0 10 20 30 miles

Inset C

Valleys Programme Boundary
Pontardawe
Ebbw Vale
Aberdare
Merthyr Tydfil
Tonypandy
Pontypool
Swansea
Valley
Maesteg
Cardiff Bay ★

0 10 20 30 40 km
0 5 10 15 20 25 miles

Inset D

Hackney ✳
Tower Hamlets
Islington
Haringey
London Docklands
Brent
Hammersmith
Newham
and Fulham
Kensington
Greenwich
and
Isle of Dogs
Chelsea ✳
Lewisham ✳
Wandsworth
Southwark ✳
Lambeth
Greater London Boundary

0 10 20 30 40 km
0 5 10 15 20 25 miles

inner cities. Between 1 April 1979 and 31 March 1989 some 13,000 hectares (over 32,000 acres) of derelict land were reclaimed in England with the aid of some £523 million of grant. The 1990–91 programme should allow an additional 1,265 hectares (some 3,125 acres) to be reclaimed.

In Scotland and Wales responsibility for derelict land reclamation rests with the respective enterprise and development agencies, such as Scottish Enterprise and the Welsh Development Agency, which may acquire and reclaim land, employ local authorities as their agents (in Scotland) or make grants to local authorities for the purpose (in Wales). In 1988 the pilot Scottish Vacant Land Survey identified 7,400 hectares (18,280 acres) of derelict land and a further 5,060 hectares (12,500 acres) of vacant urban land. Together with surveys in subsequent years, it will provide a basis for programming the treatment of derelict land and help to bring vacant urban land into use. In Northern Ireland grants may be paid to landowners who restore or improve derelict sites.

In Wales land use is also encouraged by the Land Authority for Wales, a statutory body with powers to make land available for development in circumstances where the private sector would find this difficult or impossible.

Registers of Unused and Under-used Land

Since 1989 local authorities, nationalised industries and other public bodies in England have been responsible for compiling registers, open for public inspection, of any unused or under-used land they hold. These owners' registers have largely replaced a register compiled by the Secretary of State for the Environment. This latter register is, however, being retained for the time being because the Secretary of State's power to direct public bodies to dispose of land applies only to land entered on this register. By the end of May 1991, directions had been issued in respect of 83 sites. Under the 'Public Request to Order Disposal' scheme the public is encouraged to request

such directions. Registers are also published for certain areas of Wales.

Education, Training and Employment

The first of a network of City Technology Colleges was opened near Birmingham in 1988; 13 are currently in operation, with another two approved. Intended to raise educational standards, the colleges are funded jointly by the Government and industry.

A number of schools/industry 'Compacts' have been introduced in deprived urban areas since August 1988. Groups of employers work with schools to guarantee a job with training for all school-leavers aged 16 to 18 who meet agreed targets for motivation and achievement. By October 1991 there were 58 Compacts operational and another three in development, with some 92,000 young people, almost 9,000 employers and about 500 schools involved. Compacts will be operating in all inner city target areas by the end of 1991.

Training programmes, such as Youth Training for young people and Employment Training, aimed particularly at adults unemployed for more than six months and those with special needs, are helping many people in the inner cities. In late 1990, one-third of young people who were from the inner cities were participating in Youth Training and nearly half of all unemployed people who had joined Employment Training were inner city residents. There are over 100 Employment Service 'outreach' staff based in or visiting inner city areas, helping unemployed people look for jobs and encouraging them to participate in programmes and training. In mid-1991, there were about 500 inner city Jobclubs, many catering for people with literacy and numeracy or language difficulties. In addition, Employment Service regional directors have funds for innovative projects to help unemployed people in inner cities and other deprived areas back into work or training. These projects often involve partnerships with other organisations or employers.

Other Measures

Higher than average crime rates, and the fear of crime, are particular problems in the inner cities. Safer Cities projects bring together all sections of the local community to tackle crime-related problems. The starting point for a project is the preparation of a detailed local crime profile, which a Home Office project team can then use to draw up an action plan. Examples of help include improving street lighting and fitting good quality locks to houses on estates with a high burglary rate.

A total of 16 Safer Cities projects are under way, supporting 1,330 local crime prevention initiatives with the help of grants worth £7 million. Four more projects are due to be established by the end of 1991.

The Government encourages tourism as a force for the improvement of inner city areas, and several major projects which create a cultural and artistic focus for inner city regeneration have been undertaken: for example, the Tate Gallery of the North at the Albert Dock in Liverpool and the Design Museum in London's Docklands. In 1990 the 'Vision for Cities' initiative was launched to help businesses in the inner cities to focus on the investment opportunities which tourism brings.

The Government's priorities for inner city housing are to secure a wide range of good quality housing available for rent or purchase, and to improve conditions and opportunities for residents, particularly on local authority estates (see p 184).

Research

The Government commissions research aimed at developing policies for regenerating inner cities and returning derelict land to productive use; 11 new research projects were launched in 1990–91, and the programme's budget totalled £800,000. Priority themes for research are:

- to assess the progress and achievements of policies and policy instruments;
- to examine the future for inner cities and the implications for policy; and
- to learn more about the capacity of the private and voluntary sectors, and of local communities, to undertake regeneration.

Wales

Spending on the Urban Programme in Wales is expected to be some £38 million in 1991–92, with priority being given to the ten most deprived urban areas. Urban Investment Grant was introduced in April 1989 to simplify the grants available to support private sector projects, replacing Urban Development Grant and Urban Regeneration Grant.

The Programme for the Valleys, launched in 1988, is the most extensive programme of economic and urban regeneration undertaken in Wales, and covers an area of some 2,200 sq km (860 sq miles) in the south Wales valleys (see map, p 177). It involves increased levels of factory building, land clearance and Urban Programme support, as well as action to stimulate private enterprise; improve health care and educational services; support private housing improvements; and strengthen tourism, the arts and voluntary organisations.

The Cardiff Bay Development Corporation was set up in 1987 to bring forward redevelopment in an area of south Cardiff, once its commercial centre. By the end of March 1991 the Corporation had received £92 million in government grant. Government support for the Corporation in 1991–92 will be £32 million. The Corporation's regeneration strategy includes proposals for the construction of a barrage across Cardiff harbour mouth, which would create a large freshwater lake and 12 km (7 miles) of waterside frontage. It is expected that over 30,000 new jobs will be created and that over £1,200 million of private investment will be attracted.

Scotland

In March 1988 the Government set out in the White Paper *New Life for Urban Scotland* its strategy for improving the quality of life for people living on peripheral estates in Scotland. Building on the experience gained from inner city regeneration schemes such as the Glasgow Eastern Area Renewal, the main aim of the strategy was to encourage residents to take more responsibility for the improvement and revitalisation of their own communities.

The focus of this effort was the establishment of four Partnerships led by the Scottish Office and involving other bodies and groups, including the Scottish Development Agency (SDA) and the Training Agency (now both part of Scottish Enterprise—see p 178), Scottish Homes, the local authorities, the private sector and the local communities. These four Partnerships have been set up in areas of Dundee, Edinburgh, Glasgow and Paisley. Their objectives include plans to:

● improve the type and tenure mix of housing available to local people;

● improve employment prospects by providing increased avenues to training and further education; and

● tackle social and environmental problems on the estates.

Other peripheral estates continue to receive substantial support through such sources as the Urban Programme, as do inner city areas in Scotland.

The Government and its agencies plan to spend about £450 million in urban Scotland in 1991–92. This includes the Urban Programme in Scotland, which has grown from £44 million in 1988–89 to £76 million in 1991–92. In addition to any new projects approved, these resources already support about 1,200 existing projects.

Scottish Enterprise operates a Local Enterprise Grants for Urban Project scheme, which aims to encourage private sector investment for projects in deprived areas. The scheme was reviewed by the Scottish Office Industry Department and the SDA and a new scheme was set up to run for five years from July 1989. The areas of need in which the scheme operates will include the four Partnership areas, as well as other areas showing similar characteristics of deprivation.

Local Enterprise Companies (see p 178), contracted to Scottish Enterprise, can support projects in their areas up to a limit of £250,000. Greater amounts can be spent with the approval of Scottish Enterprise.

The Compact scheme (see p 178) has been introduced in Scotland, with five Compacts in operation and four under development. Some 2,400 young people and 636 employers and training organisations are involved with the operational Compacts.

Northern Ireland

A comprehensive development programme aims to revitalise the commercial areas of Belfast. In 1990–91 regeneration programmes had a combined allocation of over £40 million. Nine Action Teams have been established to tackle the problems of particularly deprived areas of the city. The 'Making Belfast Work' initiative, launched in 1988, is designed to reinforce the efforts to alleviate the economic, educational, social and environmental problems in the most disadvantaged areas of Belfast. In addition to extensive funding already allocated to mainstream departmental programmes, Making Belfast Work has provided a further £124 million for the period 1988–89 to 1993–94. The Laganside Corporation was established in 1989 to regenerate Belfast's riverside area. Its government grant in 1991–92 is £7·5 million.

Housing

The pattern of housing tenure has changed considerably in recent years, with a substantial increase in owner-occupation and a decline in private renting.

Between the end of 1971 and 1990, the proportion of owner-occupied dwellings in Great Britain rose from about 50 per cent to nearly 70 per cent.

The promotion of home ownership and more choice in the rented sector are central to government housing policy. New house construction is undertaken by both public and private sectors, but the majority of dwellings are now built by the private sector for sale to owner-occupiers. Housing associations are becoming the main providers of new housing in the subsidised rented sector, while local authorities are being encouraged to see their housing role as more of an enabling one, working with housing associations and the private sector to increase the supply of low-cost housing for rent without necessarily providing it themselves and concentrating their resources on improving the management of their own stock. In order to stimulate the private rented sector, which has declined to less than 10 per cent of the total stock, the Housing Act 1988 deregulated rents on new private sector lettings.

Administration

The Secretary of State for the Environment in England and the Secretaries of State for Wales, Scotland and Northern Ireland are responsible for formulating housing policy and supervising the housing programme. Although the policies are broadly similar throughout Britain, provisions in Northern Ireland and Scotland differ somewhat from those in England and Wales.

The construction or structural alteration of housing is subject to building regulations laid down by the Government. In addition, most new houses are covered by warranty arrangements provided either by the National House-Building Council or the Housing Standards Company Ltd. Both organisations set standards and enforce them by inspection, and provide cover against major structural defects for not less than ten years.

Home Ownership

Over the last 40 years the proportion of people owning their own homes has risen from 29 per cent to 68 per cent, and the number of owner-occupied dwellings in Great Britain amounted to almost 15·5 million at the end of 1990, compared with some 4 million in 1950. Most public sector tenants have the right to buy the homes they occupy. Local authorities have been asked to

encourage low-cost home ownership in a variety of ways, for example, by selling land to builders to construct homes for first-time buyers, or to individuals or groups to build their own homes in partnership with private builders.

Changes in mobility have put pressure on rural housing in many areas. In 1989 the Department of the Environment announced that, where there was a need for low-cost housing in rural areas, sites which would not normally be released for housing development could exceptionally be released, provided arrangements were made to reserve the housing for local needs. Similar arrangements were introduced in Wales in 1991. Housing for Wales has a major role to play, alongside local authorities, in rural housing provision in Wales. In Scotland, Scottish Homes is developing a rural housing strategy. In Northern Ireland shared ownership has been developed by the Northern Ireland Co-ownership Housing Association.

Mortgage Loans

Most people buy their homes with a mortgage loan, with the property as security. Building societies are the largest source of such loans, although banks and other financial institutions also take a significant share of the mortgage market, while some companies also make loans for house purchase available to their own employees.

The amount that lenders are prepared to advance to a would-be house purchaser is generally calculated as a multiple of his or her annual income, typically up to three times earnings, and the term of the loan is commonly 25 years. The two major forms of mortgage are 'repayment' and 'endowment' mortgages. In the former, the borrower repays principal and interest on the sum outstanding. In the latter, he or she pays only interest to the lender but also puts money into an endowment policy, which on maturity provides a lump sum to repay the principal. Owner-occupiers get basic rate tax relief on interest payments on mortgages of up to £30,000 on their main home.

Public Sector Housing

Most of the public housing in Great Britain is provided by 460 local housing authorities. These are:

- the district councils in England and Wales, apart from in London;
- the London borough councils and the Common Council of the City of London; and
- in Scotland, the district and islands councils.

Public housing is also provided by the new town authorities, Scottish Homes (which has a stock of some 66,000 houses) and the Development Board for Rural Wales. The Northern Ireland Housing Executive is responsible for the provision and management of public housing in Northern Ireland. Public housing authorities in Great Britain own some 5·1 million houses and flats; the Northern Ireland Housing Executive owns over 165,000 homes. A number of local authorities have transferred all their housing stock to housing associations, and others are considering doing so.

Financial Regime

Local authorities meet the capital costs of new house construction and of modernisation of their existing stock by raising loans on the open market, by borrowing from the Public Works Loan Board (an independent statutory body set up to make loans to local authorities) or from part of the proceeds from the sale of local authority houses and housing land. The Northern Ireland Housing Executive is similarly financed.

From April 1990 a new financial regime for council housing was introduced. Councils must now have separate housing revenue accounts, 'ring-fenced' to keep them separate from other council funds. A Housing Revenue Account Subsidy, worth more than £3,500 million in 1991–92, replaced previous government subsidies to council housing. The aims of the new system are to:

- put councils' housing services on a more accountable and businesslike footing;

- encourage a more sensible pattern of rents reflecting the value of the accommodation being provided; and
- target government support for council housing more effectively.

Sheltered Housing

Sheltered housing, which comprises accommodation with an alarm system and a resident warden, is provided for elderly people who need support. 'Very sheltered' housing can be provided for the frail elderly, giving in addition a degree of care and enhanced communal facilities. Increasing emphasis is being placed on schemes to help elderly people to continue to live in their own homes, such as home improvement agency services and adaptations to existing housing to meet the needs of disabled people.

Homelessness

Under the homelessness legislation, local authorities have a duty to secure permanent accommodation for households which they accept as unintentionally homeless and in priority need. The latter category includes pregnant women, people with dependent children, and those who are vulnerable because of old age, mental or physical handicap or other special reasons. Following a homelessness review in 1989, which identified that the worst problems were concentrated in London and the South East, the Government made available an additional £300 million in 1989–90 and 1990–91 to move families out of bed-and-breakfast accommodation by bringing empty public sector dwellings back into use.

Tenants' Rights

Legislation gives public sector tenants in England and Wales statutory rights, including security of tenure. The Housing Act 1988 and the Housing (Scotland) Act 1988 (see p 183) enable public sector tenants to change their landlord where they are not satisfied with the service provided by their local authority ('Tenants' Choice'). With a few exceptions, secure tenants with at least two years' public sector standing are entitled to buy their house or flat at a discount which depends on the length of occupation (the 'right to buy'). Similar provisions are made for Scotland and Northern Ireland. By the end of 1990, 1·7 million council, housing association and new town homes had been sold in Great Britain, and 46,000 Housing Executive homes had been sold in Northern Ireland. In April 1991 Scottish Homes' Rents to Mortgages scheme, under which tenants can become homeowners for an initial payment which can be financed by a mortgage with payments similar to their rent, was extended to local authority tenants. Similar experimental schemes are at present available in England only to new town tenants of Basildon and Milton Keynes, and in Wales to tenants of the Development Board for Rural Wales. The Welsh scheme, called Flexi-Ownership, was introduced in 1989.

The Government is committed to encouraging mobility between all parts of the subsidised housing sector. Three former mobility bodies have been merged to form a single organisation, HOMES, to provide a more effective service. The aim is to enhance mobility between the local authority and housing association sectors, coupled with the efficient use of the national housing stock.

Privately Rented Housing

There has been a steady decline in the number of rented dwellings available from private landlords, from over 50 per cent of the housing stock in 1951 to 7 per cent in Great Britain in 1990. Many landlords are individuals owning a small amount of property, but some rented housing is provided by larger property companies.

The Government's policy is to increase the availability of privately rented accommodation by removing disincentives to letting. This is being implemented through the Housing Act 1988 for England and Wales and the Housing (Scotland) Act 1988, which provide for the deregulation of new private sector lettings.

The Housing Acts created two forms of

tenancy: the assured tenancy, which gives the tenant long-term security in return for a freely negotiated market rent; and the assured shorthold tenancy (short assured tenancy in Scotland), which is for a fixed term, again at a free market rent. Existing lettings were unaffected; they continue on the old basis. The Acts strengthen the law concerning harassment of tenants, which is a criminal offence, and provide for improved compensation for tenants driven out by harassment or illegally evicted. Tenants and most other residential occupiers may not be evicted without a court order.

In Northern Ireland only certain pre-1956 properties subject to rent restriction come under statutory control. Rent levels are linked to those of the Northern Ireland Housing Executive, and both landlords and tenants may apply to a rent assessment committee for rent determination in cases where the current rent is considered to be inappropriate. Rent increases are permitted only for properties which meet a prescribed standard. The only assured tenancies in Northern Ireland are those on properties made available under a Business Expansion Scheme; lettings under the shorthold concept are available.

Housing Associations

Housing associations, which are non-profit-making, are now the main providers of additional low-cost housing for rent and for sale to those on low incomes and in the greatest housing need.

The housing association sector is expanding rapidly; associations now own and manage over 600,000 homes and some 50,000 hostel bed-spaces in England alone.

Many associations specialise in providing accommodation to meet the special needs of the elderly, the disabled and the mentally disordered.

People in housing need with insufficient income to obtain a mortgage for outright purchase may be able to participate in a scheme in which a housing association buys the home and sells a share in it to them, allowing them to rent the remainder and to purchase it later if they wish. Housing associations can also purchase older properties to improve for sale.

In Great Britain housing schemes carried out by associations qualify for Housing Association Grant if the association concerned is one of about 2,800 registered with the Housing Corporation (in England), Scottish Homes or Housing for Wales. These three organisations are statutory bodies which supervise and pay grant to housing associations in their respective parts of Great Britain. Broadly similar assistance is available to associations in Northern Ireland. Scottish Homes has a wide range of general functions and powers, including giving financial assistance to housing associations.

The Government plans to increase the resources distributed to housing associations through the Housing Corporation from £938 million in 1989–90 to £2,005 million in 1993–94. The Government also aims to increase the amount of private finance being used by housing associations, allowing more homes to be built with the available public resources than would otherwise be the case. In 1991–92 Scottish Homes' total programme expenditure is expected to be about £312 million, of which over £200 million will go to housing associations. Housing for Wales is managing a programme of £150 million in 1991–92, providing 3,300 new homes in Wales. On current plans, it will have provided the housing association movement with nearly £500 million between 1989–90 and 1993–94.

In England and Wales the rights of housing association tenants are protected under the Tenants' Guarantee, which is issued by the Housing Corporation. It covers matters such as tenancy terms, principles for determining rent levels and the allocation of tenancies. Under this guarantee, tenants receive contractual rights in addition to their basic statutory rights, and associations are required to set and maintain rents at levels within the reach of people in low-paid employment. In Scotland, similar non-statutory guidance, in the form of a model tenancy agreement, has been implemented as proposed jointly by Scottish Homes and the Scottish Federation of Housing Associations.

Housing Benefit

Government support is being focused on tenants rather than on property, through the housing benefit system. Depending on their personal circumstances, occupiers may qualify for housing benefit to help them pay their rent (see Chapter 6, Social Welfare).

Improving Older Houses

In urban areas of Britain slum clearance and redevelopment used to be major features of housing policy, but there has been a trend in recent years towards the retention of existing communities, accompanied by the modernisation and conversion of sub-standard homes. Housing conditions have improved considerably, but problems remain in some areas where there are concentrations of dwellings lacking basic amenities or requiring substantial repairs; and there are still some pockets of unfit housing for which demolition is the best solution. The emphasis now is on area renewal, with an integrated approach to renewal and renovation.

In Scotland, Scottish Homes has been given a major role in tackling housing-related urban dereliction and providing rural housing opportunities, in co-operation with local communities, the private sector, local authorities and other statutory agencies. Some groups of tenants are joining together to form community-based housing associations and tenant ownership co-operatives.

Estate Action Programme

The Estate Action programme provides local authorities in England with additional resources to regenerate their run-down housing estates. Government support for the programme has increased considerably over the years; by March 1991 a total of £640 million had been made available to local authorities. Funds are provided to enable authorities to carry out an agreed package of measures on an estate, including physical refurbishment and improved management.

In 1991–92 funds have been increased significantly, to £270 million, to enable the larger and more run-down estates to be tackled. The Government is looking in particular for schemes in which local authorities can show:

- a strategic approach to promoting comprehensive regeneration;

- an effective partnership with tenants and the private sector; and

- that the investment in housing would complement and support training, enterprise and other urban policies.

Housing Action Trusts

The Housing Act 1988 provides for the establishment in England and Wales of Housing Action Trusts (HATs) to focus resources on some of the most run-down areas of predominantly local authority housing. Tenants vote on whether a HAT should be set up for their area. If the majority of tenants who vote support the proposal, the trust takes over responsibility for local authority housing in designated areas in order to renovate it, improve the environment, provide community facilities and stimulate local enterprise. When it has completed its work, the trust passes the housing on to other owners and managers, such as housing associations or tenants' co-operatives, or back to the local housing authority.

In April 1991 tenants on an estate in Hull (Humberside) were the first to vote for the establishment of a HAT.

Home Improvement Grants

Over 1·1 million home improvement grants, worth almost £3,750 million, were paid in respect of privately owned

dwellings in England alone between 1983 and 1990. A single system of renovation grants was introduced in England and Wales in 1990 to help private owners and some tenants with the costs of essential repair and improvement work. A mandatory grant enables dwellings to be brought up to a new and more effective fitness standard, with discretionary grant available for a wider range of works. Grants of up to 100 per cent may be available, subject to a test of the occupants' resources.

Grants are also available in certain circumstances for the provision of facilities for the disabled and for the repair of houses in multiple occupation and of the common parts of blocks of flats.

Minor works assistance is also available to help people in receipt of income-related benefits with small-scale jobs.

In Scotland, local authorities give grants for improvement and repair. Scottish Homes also has the power to provide grants to complement the role of local authorities in private house renewal.

In Northern Ireland, improvement and repair grants are available through the House Renovation Grants scheme, administered by the Northern Ireland Housing Executive.

Housing Renewal Areas

'Housing renewal areas' were introduced for England and Wales in 1990, replacing earlier powers. Renewal areas are intended to provide a sharper focus to area action, covering both renovation and selective redevelopment and taking account of a range of issues wider than just housing. Authorities are free to declare renewal areas without the specific consent of the Secretaries of State for the Environment and for Wales, provided they fulfil certain criteria. Authorities have additional powers to acquire land in renewal areas and to carry out improvement works for which additional government support is available.

In Scotland housing action area powers are available for the improvement of areas in which at least half the houses fail to meet a statutory tolerable standard. Since 1975, 1,815 housing action areas have been declared. Outside such areas in Scotland local authorities have powers to apply improvement orders to houses below the statutory tolerable standard or lacking certain basic amenities. Local authorities may also give grants towards improving the environment of predominantly residential areas.

Northern Ireland has a large number of houses which are either unfit or in serious disrepair. Since 1977, 53 housing action areas have been declared, involving a continuous programme of rehabilitation and associated environmental improvement schemes. In addition, the Northern Ireland Housing Executive undertakes a programme of improvement of its own stock.

9 Environmental Protection

For more than a century Britain has been evolving policies to protect the environment against pollution from industry and other sources. Laws were introduced at an early stage to control air and water pollution, to conserve wildlife, landscape, historic monuments and buildings, and to plan land use. They have been revised regularly to meet changing circumstances. Recently, with increasing scientific understanding of global pollution problems, the Government has been considering how its own policies and actions can be further guided by the principle of 'sustainable development'.

Britain supports international co-operation on matters of environmental protection. Increasingly, much of Britain's legislation on pollution control is being developed in co-operation with other member states of the European Community and organisations such as the Organisation for Economic Co-operation and Development and the United Nations and its agencies. The laws protecting the environment have been further strengthened by the Environmental Protection Act 1990, which provides added safeguards for the environment.

The Department of the Environment is responsible for countryside policy and environmental protection in England; the Welsh Office, the Scottish Office Environment Department and the Department of the Environment for Northern Ireland have broadly equivalent responsibilities. In addition, the local authorities and a wide range of voluntary organisations are actively involved in environmental conservation and protection.

This Common Inheritance

The environment White Paper *This Common Inheritance*, published in September 1990, was the first comprehensive statement by the Government of its policy on issues affecting the environment. It outlined action already taken by Government, and set out a strategy for preserving and protecting the environment both in Britain and the rest of the world. It summarised proposals for tackling such diverse issues as global warming, pollution control, the regulation of land use and planning, the rural economy (including action by the European Community), the countryside and wildlife. There was also coverage of action on heritage, air quality and pollution, noise, water, hazardous substances, waste and recycling, and separate sections on specific initiatives in Scotland, Wales and Northern Ireland. In September 1991 a first anniversary progress report was published, which reviewed progress and set out commitments to further action to protect the environment.

Conservation

Historic Buildings, Ancient Monuments and Conservation Areas

Lists of buildings of special architectural or historical interest are compiled by the Government. Some 440,000 buildings are listed in England, some 37,000 in Scotland and 14,000 in Wales. It is against the law to demolish, extend or alter the character of any 'listed' building without special consent from the local planning authority or the appropriate Secretary of State. The local planning authority can issue emergency 'building preservation notices' to protect buildings not yet listed. Ancient monuments are similarly protected through a system of scheduling. There are approximately 13,000 scheduled ancient monuments in England, about 5,000 in Scotland and 2,600 in Wales. English Heritage has embarked upon a programme to evaluate all known archaeological remains in England. This is expected to result in a significant increase in the number of scheduled monuments.

Many of the royal palaces and parks are open to the public; their maintenance is the responsibility of the Secretaries of State for the Environment and Scotland. English Heritage (the Historic Buildings and Monuments Commission for England) is charged with protecting and conserving England's architectural and archaeological heritage. It manages some 400 ancient monuments on behalf of the Secretary of State for the Environment, advises him on all applications for consent to alter scheduled monuments, and gives grants for the repair of ancient monuments, historic buildings and buildings in conservation areas in England. Most of its monuments are open to the public. In Scotland and Wales similar functions are performed by Historic Scotland, which cares for 330 monuments, and by Cadw: Welsh Historic Monuments, which manages 127, with advice from an ancient monuments board and a historic buildings council for each country. In April 1991, Historic Scotland and Cadw became executive agencies within the Scottish Office and Welsh Office respectively.

The National Heritage Memorial Fund helps towards the cost of acquiring, maintaining or preserving land, buildings, works of art and other items of outstanding interest which are also of importance to the national heritage. In 1990–91 the Fund assisted in the preservation of 49 heritage items.

Local planning authorities have designated over 7,000 'conservation areas' of special architectural or historic interest in England; there are over 350 in Wales and over 550 in Scotland. These areas receive special protection through the planning system. Grants and loans are available from the appropriate historic buildings and monuments body for works which make a significant contribution towards the preservation or improvement of a conservation area.

The Department of the Environment for Northern Ireland has 168 historic monuments in its care, and over 1,000 monuments are scheduled for protection. It is also responsible for designating conservation areas; there are about 7,800 listed buildings and 18 conservation areas. It may also provide grants and loans to help with the repair and maintenance of listed buildings and to preserve or enhance conservation areas. It is advised by a Historic Buildings Council and a Historic Monuments Council.

The Voluntary Sector

The Government supports the work of the voluntary sector in the protection of Britain's heritage. The Department of the Environment intends to make grants totalling £494,000 to 19 such organisations in 1991–92. Among the voluntary organisations which campaign for the preservation and appreciation of buildings are:

- the Society for the Protection of Ancient Buildings;
- the Ancient Monuments Society;
- the Georgian Group;
- the Architectural Heritage Society of Scotland;
- the Ulster Architectural Heritage Society;
- the Victorian Society; and
- the Council for British Archaeology.

The National Trust (for Places of Historic Interest or Natural Beauty), a charity with over 2 million members, owns and protects 319 properties open to the public, in addition to over 230,000 hectares (568,000 acres) of land in England, Wales and Northern Ireland. Scotland has its own National Trust.

The Civic Trust makes awards for development and restoration work which enhances its surroundings. It undertakes urban regeneration projects and acts as an 'umbrella' organisation for nearly 1,000 local amenity societies. There are associate trusts in Scotland, Wales and north-east England.

Tree Preservation and Planting

Tree preservation orders enable local authorities to protect trees and woodlands in the interests of amenity. Once a tree is protected, it is in general an offence to fell, damage or destroy it, and the courts can impose substantial fines for breaches, now increased by recent legislation. Where protected trees are felled in contravention of an order or are removed because they are dying, dead or dangerous, a replacement tree must be planted. The Government is undertaking a review of tree preservation policies and procedures, and has announced its intention to allow local authorities in England and Wales to safeguard key hedgerows by making hedgerow management orders. Tree planting is encouraged through grants. Recent initiatives include a proposal to create a major new forest in the Midlands and a series of 'community forests' near major towns and cities. These would be aimed at enhancing the environment and providing new opportunities for leisure and recreation.

Green Belts

'Green Belts' are areas intended to be left open and free from inappropriate development where people can seek recreation. They are intended to restrict the sprawl of large built-up areas, to prevent neighbouring towns merging, to preserve the special character of historic towns and to assist in urban regeneration. They have been established around major cities, including London, Edinburgh, Glasgow, Merseyside, Greater Manchester and the West Midlands. Some 1·5 million hectares (3·8 million acres) are designated as Green Belt in England, and 200,000 hectares (500,000 acres) in Scotland. The Government attaches great importance

to the protection of Green Belts and expects local planning authorities to do likewise when considering planning applications.

The Coast

Local planning authorities along the coastline are responsible for planning land use at the coast; they also attempt to safeguard and enhance the coast's natural attractions and preserve areas of scientific interest. The protection of the coastline against erosion is administered centrally by the Ministry of Agriculture, Fisheries and Food, the Welsh Office and the Scottish Office. Certain stretches of undeveloped coast of particular scenic beauty in England and Wales are treated as heritage coast; jointly with local authorities, the government countryside bodies have defined 44 coasts, protecting 1,508 km (937 miles).

The National Trust, through its Enterprise Neptune campaign, raises funds to acquire stretches of coastline of great natural beauty and recreational value. More than £16 million has been raised so far and the Trust now protects 840 km (522 miles) of coastline in England, Wales and Northern Ireland. The National Trust for Scotland also owns large parts of the Scottish coastline and protects others through conservation agreements.

Countryside Bodies

Three bodies are responsible for conserving and enhancing the natural beauty and amenity of the countryside:

- the Countryside Commission (which acts for England);
- the Countryside Council for Wales (CCW); and
- the Countryside Commission for Scotland (CCS).

These arrangements are in the course of reorganisation.

They encourage the provision and improvement of facilities for open-air recreation. Activities include the provision by local authorities (sometimes in association with other bodies) and private individuals of

Restructuring of Nature Conservation and Countryside Access

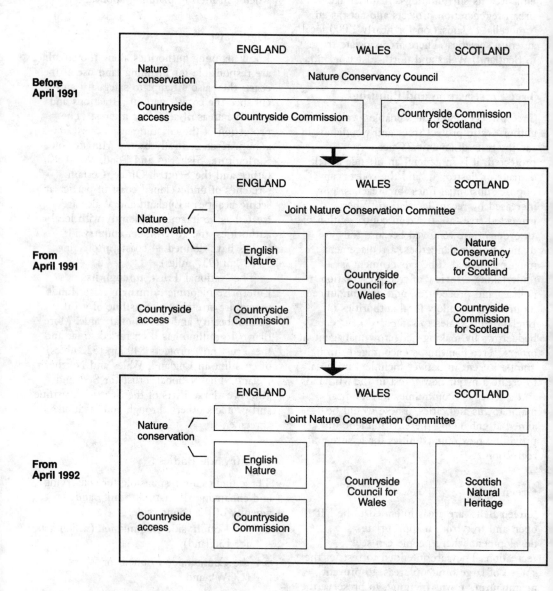

country parks and picnic sites often within easy reach of towns, the provision or improvement of recreational paths and the encouragement of amenity tree-planting schemes. The Countryside Commission recognises over 210 country parks and over 230 picnic sites in England. A further 24 country parks and about 40 picnic sites in Wales are recognised by the CCW. In Scotland 35 country parks are recognised by the CCS, and many local authority and private sector schemes for a variety of countryside facilities have been approved for grant aid. The countryside bodies undertake research projects and experimental schemes, often working in consultation with local authorities and groups such as the nature conservation bodies (see below) and the Sports Councils. They give financial assistance to public, private and voluntary organisations, and individuals carrying out countryside recreation and amenity projects and landscape conservation projects. Total funding in 1991–92 is over £30 million for the Countryside Commission, £14·5 million for the CCW and £6·9 million for the CCS.

Reorganisation of Countryside and Nature Conservation Bodies

Until April 1991, the main government body responsible for nature conservation was the Nature Conservancy Council (NCC). The Countryside Commission and the CCS were responsible for promoting access to the countryside for recreation, the former in England and Wales and the latter in Scotland.

New arrangements came into force in April 1991 under the Environmental Protection Act 1990. The NCC was split into separate bodies for England (English Nature), Scotland (the Nature Conservancy Council for Scotland—NCCS) and Wales (the Countryside Council for Wales—CCW). The CCW also took over the Countryside Commission's responsibilities in Wales, leaving the Commission responsible for countryside policy in England only. Another change will take effect in April 1992. The two Scottish bodies—the CCS and the NCCS—will merge to form a single body, to be called Scottish Natural Heritage (SNH). (See diagram on p 190.)

Nature Conservation

The official bodies responsible for nature conservation in Great Britain are English Nature, the CCW and the NCCS. Their role includes:

● establishing, maintaining and managing nature reserves;

● advising the Government;

● providing general information and advice;

● giving grants; and

● supporting research.

There is also a statutory Joint Nature Conservation Committee (JNCC) comprising representatives from the three bodies and from Northern Ireland, together with eminent scientists, to advise ministers and the bodies themselves on matters of national and international importance to nature conservation.

There are 245 national nature reserves covering some 168,000 hectares (415,000 acres). The first statutory Marine Nature Reserve, the island of Lundy, off the Devon coast, was designated in 1986; a second Marine Nature Reserve at Skomer, off the coast of Dyfed, in Wales, was declared in July 1990; and more are proposed. A total of 5,649 Sites of Special Scientific Interest (SSSIs) have been notified in Great Britain for their plants, animals or geological or physiographical features.

Local authorities have declared about 170 Local Nature Reserves. County nature conservation trusts and the Royal Society for the Protection of Birds play an important part in protecting wildlife, having established between them some 1,800 reserves. The county trusts are affiliated to a parent organisation, the Royal Society for Nature Conservation.

The Royal Society for the Protection of Birds is the largest voluntary wildlife conservation body in Europe.

In Northern Ireland the Council for Nature Conservation and the Countryside advises the Department of the Environment for Northern Ireland on nature conservation matters, including the establishment and management of land and marine nature reserves and the declaration of areas of special scientific interest. Some 44 national nature reserves have been established and 26 areas of special scientific interest declared.

Wildlife in Britain is protected largely by the Wildlife and Countryside Act 1981. This extended the list of protected species, restricted the introduction into the countryside of animals not normally found in the wild in Britain, and afforded greater protection for SSSIs and other important habitats. There is also provision for reviews of the list of protected species to be conducted by the three official nature conservation agencies, acting jointly through the JNCC, every five years and submitted to the Secretary of State for the Environment. In Northern Ireland two Orders, which came into force in 1985, have brought legislation into line with the rest of Britain on species and habitat protection.

Britain plays a full part in international action to conserve wildlife. Conservation measures promoted by the Government have included a ban (in conjunction with other European Community countries) on the import of whale products and harp and hooded seal pup skins, and stricter controls for the protection of wild birds. Britain continues to support the Convention on International Trade in Endangered Species of Wild Fauna and Flora.

National Parks, Areas of Outstanding Natural Beauty and National Scenic Areas

The Countryside Commission and the CCW can designate national parks and areas of outstanding natural beauty (AONBs), subject to confirmation by the Secretaries of State for the Environment and for Wales respectively, and define heritage coasts in conjunction with local authorities. They can also make proposals for the creation of long-distance footpaths and bridleways.

Ten National Parks cover 9,500 sq km (3,670 sq miles) of England and 4,200 sq km (1,580 sq miles) of Wales, in total some 9 per cent of total land area. Their aim is first to provide protection for the outstanding countryside they contain and secondly to provide opportunities for access and outdoor recreation. The parks are 'national' in the sense that they are of value to the nation as a whole. However, most of the land remains in private hands. Special national park authorities have been set up, one for each park. Among other things, they:
- act as the development control authority for their areas;
- negotiate public access and land management agreements and encourage farmers to manage their land in the traditional way;

- plant trees and look after footpaths; and
- set up information centres and employ rangers.

In 1989, a further special authority was set up to look after the Norfolk and Suffolk Broads.

A total of 39 AONBs have been designated, covering around 19,400 sq km (7,500 sq miles) in England and 832 sq km (321 sq miles) in Wales. They comprise parts of the countryside which lack extensive areas of open country suitable for recreation and hence national park status, but have an important landscape quality. Local authorities are encouraged to give attention to AONBs in their planning and countryside conservation work.

In Scotland there are four regional parks and 40 National Scenic Areas, covering more than 1 million hectares (2·5 million acres), where certain kinds of development are subject to consultation with the CCS, and in the event of a disagreement, with the Secretary of State for Scotland. In the wider countryside, the CCS provides grants for a range of countryside projects.

In Northern Ireland the Council for Nature Conservation and the Countryside advises the Department of the Environment for Northern Ireland on the preservation of amenities and the designation of areas of outstanding natural beauty. Nine such areas have been designated, covering 282,000 hectares (698,000 acres), and seven areas are being managed as country parks and one as a regional park.

There are 11 forest parks in Great Britain, covering some 244,000 hectares (603,000 acres) and administered by the Forestry Commission. There are nine in Northern Ireland, where they are administered by the Forest Service of the Department of Agriculture.

Many voluntary organisations are concerned to preserve the amenities of the countryside, including the Council for the Protection of Rural England, the Campaign for the Protection of Rural Wales, the Association for the Protection of Rural Scotland and the Ulster Society for the Preservation of the Countryside.

Public Rights of Way and Open Country

County and metropolitan district councils in England and Wales are responsible for keeping public rights of way signposted and free from obstruction. Public paths are usually maintained by these highway authorities, which also supervise landowners' duties to repair stiles and gates. In Scotland, planning authorities are responsible for asserting and protecting rights of way. Local authorities in Great Britain can create paths, close paths no longer needed for public use and divert paths to meet the needs of either the public or landowners. Recent legislation requires farmers in England and Wales rapidly to restore footpaths damaged by agricultural operations. In England and Wales there are some 225,000 km (140,000 miles) of rights of way. There are 15 approved national trails in England and Wales, covering over 3,000 km (1,870 miles), and three approved long-distance routes in Scotland, covering some 580 km (360 miles).

There is no automatic right of public access to open country, although many landowners allow it more or less freely. Local planning authorities can secure access by means of agreements with landowners. If agreements cannot be reached, authorities may acquire land or make orders for public access. Similar powers cover Scotland and Northern Ireland; in Northern Ireland the primary responsibility lies with district councils. In Scotland there is a long-standing tradition of freedom to roam, based on tolerance between landowners and those seeking reasonable recreational access to the hills.

Common land, much of which is open to the public, totals an estimated 600,000 hectares (1·5 million acres) in England and Wales (there is no common land in Scotland or Northern Ireland). This land is usually privately owned, but people other than the owner may have various rights over it, for example, as pasture land. Commons are protected by law and cannot be built on or enclosed without the consent of the Secretaries of State for the Environment or Wales.

Environmental Improvement Schemes

The Government assists local voluntary organisations to promote projects such as creating parks, footpaths and other areas of greenery in cities; conserving the industrial heritage and the natural environment; and recycling waste. The Department of the Environment makes grants through the Urban Programme (see p 174) and the Special Grants Programme to support projects with either direct or indirect environmental gains. Spending from the former on such projects was estimated at over £49 million in 1990–91; grants from the latter totalled £3·7 million. Welsh Office equivalents were £27 million and £87,000.

The Government's programme of Environmentally Sensitive Areas is a voluntary scheme, under which farmers are offered payments for agreeing to farm along environmentally beneficial lines. The Scottish Office Environment Department is making £275,000 available in 1991–92 to environmental organisations under its Special Grants (Environmental) Programme. A further £291,000 is being made available to UK 2000 Scotland, a partnership between central and local government, voluntary bodies and the private sector, which carries out practical environmental improvements. The Groundwork Foundation, a partnership of public bodies, the private sector, voluntary organisations and individuals, aims to tackle environmental problems arising from dereliction and vandalism and to increase public awareness of the opportunities to change and improve local environments.

World Heritage Sites

Britain is fully represented in the World Heritage List, which was established under the World Heritage Convention to identify and secure lasting protection for those parts of the world heritage of outstanding universal value. So far 13 sites in Britain have been listed:

- Canterbury Cathedral, with St Augustine's Abbey and St Martin's Church, in Kent;

- Durham Cathedral and Castle;
- Studley Royal Gardens and Fountains Abbey, in North Yorkshire;
- Ironbridge Gorge, with the world's first iron bridge and other early industrial sites, in Shropshire;
- the prehistoric stone circles at Stonehenge and Avebury, in Wiltshire;
- Blenheim Palace, in Oxfordshire;
- the city of Bath, in Avon;
- Hadrian's Wall;
- the Tower of London;
- the Palace of Westminster, Westminster Abbey and St Margaret's, Westminster, also in London;
- the islands of St Kilda, in Scotland;
- the castles and town walls of King Edward I, in north Wales; and
- the Giant's Causeway and Causeway Coast, in Northern Ireland.

Government support for these sites can be considerable. For example, in February 1991 a £4 million endowment for the Ironbridge Heritage Foundation was announced to ensure the future of these remains from the earliest days of the Industrial Revolution.

Control of Pollution

The Environmental Protection Act 1990, which applies to Great Britain, has strengthened the existing system of protection against pollution. British law sets out a wide range of powers and duties for central and local government, including controls over waste, air pollution, litter, noise, and emissions to water.

Administration

Executive responsibility for pollution control is divided between local authorities and central government agencies.

Central government makes policy, exercises general budgetary control, promotes legislation and advises pollution control authorities on policy implementation. The Secretary of State for the Environment has general responsibility for co-ordinating the work of the Government on environmental protection. In Scotland, Wales and Northern Ireland the respective Secretaries of State are responsible for pollution control co-ordination within their countries.

Local authorities also have important duties and powers. They are responsible for matters such as:

- collection and disposal of domestic wastes;
- keeping the streets clean from litter;
- control of air pollution from domestic and from many industrial premises; and
- noise abatement measures.

The National Rivers Authority (NRA) is responsible for the control of water pollution in England and Wales; in Scotland, the river purification authorities have statutory responsibility for water pollution control. In England and Wales Her Majesty's Inspectorate of Pollution (HMIP) has an important role in the control of emissions to land, air and water from certain industrial processes through the new mechanism of 'integrated pollution control' (see p 195). The Government has announced its intention to merge HMIP and the NRA into a single environmental agency.

An independent standing Royal Commission on Environmental Pollution advises the Government on national and international matters concerning the pollution of the environment, on the adequacy of research and on the future possibilities of danger to the environment. So far it has produced 15 reports.

Pollution Inspectorates

Her Majesty's Inspectorate of Pollution was formed in 1987 by the amalgamation of several existing inspectorates. It acts for England and Wales. Under the Environmental Protection Act, a system of 'integrated pollution control' (IPC) is being phased in to control certain categories of industrial pollution. The most harmful processes are specified for IPC, and require consent from HMIP. Less harmful air pollution is controlled under a system of local authority air pollution control. In granting a consent for discharges under IPC, the Inspectorate requires the use of the best available techniques not entailing excessive cost to prevent or minimise polluting emissions and to ensure that all substances released are made harmless.

Her Majesty's Industrial Pollution Inspectorate is the Scottish equivalent of HMIP, and administers IPC jointly with the river purification authorities. In Northern Ireland broadly similar controls are exercised by the Environmental Protection Division of the Department of the Environment for Northern Ireland, and the implications of introducing a system of IPC are being considered.

The Land

Under the Control of Pollution Act 1974, certain local authorities are designated as waste disposal authorities. They are responsible for regulating the disposal of controlled wastes. The Act requires them to draw up and revise periodically a waste disposal plan. It also establishes a licensing system for waste disposal sites, treatment plants and storage facilities receiving controlled wastes. It provides for a more intensive control system for certain especially difficult wastes. HMIP and the Hazardous Waste Inspectorate for Scotland advise local authorities on how to improve their control of waste management and on how to work towards environmentally acceptable standards for dealing with hazardous wastes.

Part II of the Environmental Protection Act, when implemented, will strengthen existing curbs on waste disposal. Responsibility for proper handling of waste will be imposed on everyone who has control of it from production to final disposal or reclamation. Authorities may refuse licences if the applicant is not a fit and proper person. Operators will be responsible for their sites until all risks of gas or pollution are eliminated. In England and Wales local authorities' waste disposal operations are to be transferred to 'arm's length' companies or private contractors so as to separate them from the authorities' other jobs of setting policies and standards, and enforcement. Waste regulation authorities will become both more locally accountable and more closely supervised by HMIP. In Scotland, the responsibility for collection, disposal and regulation remains with the district and islands councils, whose waste management function is examined by the Hazardous Waste Inspectorate. The Government has also taken powers to control international shipments of waste.

It is a criminal offence to leave litter in any public place in the open air or to dump rubbish except in designated places. The maximum penalty for this, previously set at £400, was increased under the Environmental Protection Act to £1,000. The Act also introduced new powers for the issue of litter abatement orders and new duties on local authorities to keep their public land as free of litter and refuse (including dog faeces) as practicable.

To help counteract the problem of litter, financial support is given to the Tidy Britain Group (£2·75 million in 1991–92), which provides a comprehensive litter abatement programme in collaboration with local authorities. The Group secures sponsorship from industry to undertake litter abatement promotions and programmes such as its Neighbourhood Litter Watch scheme.

Recycling and Materials Reclamation

The Government encourages the reclamation and recycling of waste materials wherever this is practicable; its target is for half of all recyclable household waste to be reused by 2000. There are over 5,000 'bottle banks' in Britain, where the public can deposit used glass containers for recycling. There are also similar 'can banks' and 'paper banks' and, in some cases, plastics or textiles banks to collect these materials for recycling. In addition, voluntary organisations arrange collections of waste material. Under the Environmental Protection Act 1990, local authorities have a duty to make plans for the recycling of waste. The Government is supporting pilot 'Recycling City' initiatives in places such as Sheffield, Cardiff and Dundee, which will include kerbside collections of recyclable waste.

Water

In general, it is against the law to allow any polluting matter to enter water in Britain except in accordance with a legal authorisation. In England and Wales the NRA is responsible for protecting water quality. Its principal method of controlling water pollution is through the regulation of all effluent discharges into rivers and other inland waters, except those controlled by HMIP through IPC. Discharge consents issued by the NRA specify what may be discharged and set limits on the volume and content of effluent, in order to achieve appropriate water quality standards. The NRA maintains public registers containing information about discharge consents and water quality. Similar arrangements apply in Scotland, where control is exercised by river purification authorities. The Department of the Environment for Northern Ireland is responsible for controlling water pollution in Northern Ireland.

Over the past 30 years, notable progress has been made in cleaning up the previously heavily polluted major estuaries of the east coast of England and Scotland—the Thames, Humber, Tees, Tyne and Forth—which now support varied populations of fish and other wildlife.

A 25-year scheme supported by the Government and the European Community aims to reduce river pollution and improve water quality throughout the Mersey river basin and estuary. Other major schemes in progress include programmes to improve water quality in the Clyde in Scotland and the Lagan in Northern Ireland.

More than 95 per cent of the population in Britain lives in properties connected to a sewer, and sewage treatment works serve over 80 per cent of the population. In England and Wales the water industry is planning to spend some £14,000 million at 1989 prices up to the year 2000 on improving sewage treatment and disposal. Progressively higher treatment standards for industrial waste effluents and new measures to combat pollution from agriculture are expected to bring further improvements in water quality. In Scotland, sewage treatment and disposal come within the water and sewerage programme, which will total more than £600 million in the three years to 1993–94.

The Government is committed to meeting the requirements of a number of European Community directives for the protection and improvement of water quality, for example, on the quality of surface water for abstraction for drinking water supply, the quality needed to support freshwater fisheries, the quality of water for bathing areas (see p 197) and the treatment of urban waste water.

Marine Environment

Britain is a leading participant in the series of North Sea Conferences. This international forum of the countries bordering the North Sea provides the prime focus for the development of Britain's policies on the marine environment. The Third North Sea Conference met in 1990 in The Hague, and the measures agreed are being applied by Britain to all its coastal waters, not just the North Sea.

Progress is being made in reducing the amount of toxic substances released into the sea. The Government's target is a reduction of the order of 50 per cent by 1995, and of 70 per cent in the most dangerous substances such as cadmium, mercury, dioxins and lead. Substantial reductions have already been achieved. For example, the discharge of mercury into Britain's coastal waters fell by 26 per cent between 1985 and 1988, and the discharge of cadmium fell by 18 per cent.

Prevention of marine pollution from ships is based largely on international conventions drawn up under the auspices of the International Maritime Organization, a United Nations agency with headquarters in London, and implemented for British ships by domestic legislation. British legislation requires ships to be fitted with specific pollution control equipment. It makes it an offence for ships of any nationality to discharge oil, oily mixtures or ships' garbage into British territorial waters. It is also an offence for British-registered ships to make similar discharges anywhere into the sea, except in accordance with the regulations. Enforcement of these regulations is undertaken by the Department of Transport.

Offshore oil operators must ensure that oil does not escape into the sea and are required to have contingency plans for dealing with oil spilled accidentally. Discharges containing oil are controlled under the Prevention of Oil Pollution Act 1971. It was agreed at the Third North Sea Conference to eliminate progressively discharges of oil-based drilling cuttings from offshore platforms.

The Department of Transport's Marine Pollution Control Unit is responsible for dealing with pollution at sea when oil or other dangerous substances from a shipping casualty threaten major coastal pollution. The Unit maintains a national contingency plan and dispersant spraying, cargo transfer, mechanical recovery and beach-cleaning resources. It also has two remote sensing aircraft capable of detecting possible illegal discharges and of quantifying oil pollution.

A licence has to be obtained for the permanent deposit of any substance or article into the sea and tidal waters below the high water mark. Dumping at sea is presently permitted where no harm to the marine environment can be shown and where there are no practicable alternatives on land. Nevertheless, a timetable for ending the dumping of industrial waste at sea was announced by the Government in 1990. The Government's intention is that no industrial waste should be dumped at sea beyond 1993. Britain has already stopped the dumping at sea of more than half the industrial wastes which were licensed in 1987. Powers to control dumping at sea are further strengthened by the Environmental Protection Act 1990. Waste is no longer being licensed for incineration at sea.

Bathing Waters

The Government has announced investment of around £2,160 million to provide increased sewage treatment, while a £1,400 million programme is intended to improve the quality of Britain's bathing waters. The Government has announced that sea dumping of sewage sludge will be terminated completely by the end of 1998.

In the 1990 tests of bathing water quality, it was found that 78 per cent of identified bathing waters (318 out of 407) in England and Wales met the mandatory coliform bacteria standards of the European Community Bathing Water directive. This compared with 76 per cent of the then identified beaches in 1989 and 66 per cent in 1988. In Scotland, 12 out of 23 bathing waters met the coliform standard in 1990. In Northern Ireland 15 out of the 16 identified bathing waters met the directive. The Government expects all but a handful of bathing waters to meet the directive's standards by the mid-1990s and to achieve full compliance soon thereafter.

Air Pollution

Responsibility for clean air rests primarily with local authorities. Under the Clean Air Acts 1956 and 1968 they may declare 'smoke control areas' within which the emission of smoke from chimneys is an offence. About two-thirds of the premises in conurbations are covered by smoke control orders—over 6,000 are in force. Emissions from most industrial processes are also subject to control by local authorities. Those processes with the greatest potential for harmful emissions are, however, controlled by HMIP. Under the Environmental Protection Act 1990, these are becoming subject to IPC. Processes with a significant but lesser potential for air pollution require approval from local authorities under the 1990 Act. Under the Clean Air Acts, emissions of dark smoke from any trade or industrial premises or from the chimney of any building are also prohibited, and new furnaces must be capable as far as is practicable of smokeless operation. The 1990 Act gave local authorities streamlined powers to deal with statutory nuisances, including smoke, dust and smells.

Considerable progress has been made towards the achievement of cleaner air and a better environment in the last 30 years or so.

Total emissions of smoke in the air have fallen by over 85 per cent since 1960.

The domestic smoke control programme has been particularly important in achieving this result. London no longer has the dense smoke-laden 'smogs' of the 1950s and in central London winter sunshine has increased by about 70 per cent since 1958. Similar improvement has been achieved in other cities.

Air pollution data from the Department of the Environment's monitoring network are released to the national press and television each day as Air Quality Bulletins. These give the concentrations of three main pollutants—ozone, nitrogen dioxide and sulphur dioxide—and grade air quality on a scale between 'very poor' and 'very good'. The data are also available to members of the public on a special telephone number.

Climate Change

The greenhouse effect is a natural phenomenon which keeps the earth at a temperature which can sustain life. But increasing man-made emissions of 'greenhouse gases' such as carbon dioxide, methane, chlorofluorocarbons (CFCs) and nitrous oxide are leading to greater concentrations of these gases in the atmosphere. In response to the concern about the effect this would have, the United Nations Environment Programme (UNEP) and the World Meteorological Organisation established the Intergovernmental Panel on Climate Change (IPCC) to study the issues. Britain chaired the working group which carried out an assessment of the available scientific evidence on climate change and published its report in August 1990. It concluded that man-made emissions of greenhouse gases would lead in general to additional warming of the earth, and could cause serious changes in the world's climate. In response, the international community agreed to draw up a convention to tackle the threat. Britain is contributing £750,000 to the continuing work of the IPCC, and is playing an active part in the Intergovernmental Negotiating Committee established by the United Nations to draw up a convention on climate change. The aim is to have a framework convention ready for signature during the United Nations Conference on Environment and Development in Brazil in 1992. This would provide the basis for international action to control greenhouse gases.

Britain is making a major research effort into global warming. The Hadley Centre for Climate Prediction and Research was opened in 1990 to build on the climate modelling programme of the Meteorological Office, at a cost of about £6 million a year to the Department of the Environment. The research councils (see p 202) allocated over £84 million in 1990–91 towards research into all aspects of global climate change. The value of the Government's total expenditure on research related to climate change will be about £150 million in 1991–92.

British measures to combat the problem include:

- a government pledge to achieve a 15 per cent improvement in the energy efficiency of its buildings over the next five years;

- a major three-year publicity campaign from November 1991, on the greenhouse effect and energy use in the home;

- tighter building regulations to promote the energy efficiency of new houses; and

- the non-fossil fuel obligation in the Electricity Act 1989, which requires that a proportion of Britain's electricity be generated in ways that will not produce greenhouse gases.

The environment White Paper reaffirmed Britain's willingness to return carbon dioxide emissions to 1990 levels by 2005, provided other countries take similar action.

Chlorofluorocarbons and the Ozone Layer

The Government is committed to the earliest possible phasing-out of all ozone-depleting substances, including CFCs—artificial gases used in the manufacture of foams, as solvents, in refrigeration and as aerosol propellants. Britain is closely involved in international action to protect the ozone layer. In 1990 Britain hosted the second meeting of the parties to the Montreal Protocol on Substances that Deplete the Ozone Layer. This meeting agreed to:

- phase out CFCs by the year 2000, with a 50 per cent reduction by 1995 and an 85 per cent reduction by 1997;

- phase out other ozone-depleting substances, including halons, carbon tetrachloride and methyl chloroform; and

- hold another meeting in 1992, with the objective of accelerating the phase-out schedules wherever possible.

The European Community has agreed to phase out CFCs by the end of 1997, with exemptions for any remaining essential uses until the end of 1999. The Government also announced in 1990 that Britain would contribute at least $9 million to help developing countries tackle the problem of ozone depletion. This will be increased to $15 million if other countries such as India and the People's Republic of China join the Protocol.

Emissions of Sulphur Dioxide and Oxides of Nitrogen and Acid Rain

National sulphur dioxide emissions have fallen by about 40 per cent since 1970. Under the European Community directive on the control of emissions from large combustion plants, the Government has announced a phased programme of reductions in emissions of sulphur dioxide and oxides of nitrogen from existing large combustion plants.
Britain is now implementing these reductions, which are greater than those stipulated in the directive.

The damaging effect of acid depositions

Table 9.1: Target Percentage Reductions from 1980 Baselines

By	1993	1998	2003
Sulphur dioxide	21	45	63
Oxides of nitrogen	21	35	–

Source: Department of the Environment.

from combustion processes on rivers, lakes and soils has been shown by scientific research. Britain is spending about £10 million a year on an extensive research programme into the causes and effects of acid rain, and the likely results of possible abatement technologies. Following lower emissions of sulphur dioxide over the past 20 years, the first signs of a decrease in acidification in some lochs in south-west Scotland have been found.

Vehicle Emissions

There are around 24 million vehicles on Britain's roads, contributing substantially to Britain's total emissions of carbon dioxide, carbon monoxide, hydrocarbons and oxides of nitrogen. Since 1970 a series of increasingly stringent regulations on cars and light vans has been implemented by the Government to bring carbon monoxide emissions from each new car down by 50 per cent and hydrocarbon and nitrogen oxide emissions by over 30 per cent. The European Community has agreed strict new standards for these vehicles, which will reduce all emissions from new cars by a further 75 per cent and in effect require virtually all new petrol-engined cars to be fitted with fully-controlled catalytic converters. The Community is committed to looking into possible controls on carbon dioxide emissions from cars. Britain has also pressed the Community to introduce very strict emission standards for heavy goods vehicles by the mid-1990s and a common position was agreed in March 1991. The Government intends to introduce checks on exhaust emissions into the annual test of vehicle roadworthiness, which will measure carbon monoxide and hydrocarbons from November 1991.

The amount of lead in the air in Britain has halved since the permitted lead content in petrol was reduced in 1986 from 0·4 to 0·15 grammes a litre. Britain had previously taken a leading role in negotiating a European Community directive which required unleaded petrol to be available throughout the Community by October 1989. Almost all petrol stations in Britain now sell unleaded petrol, and new cars must be able to run on it. A substantial tax differential has been created in favour of unleaded fuel, and demand for it has risen rapidly. By May 1991 unleaded petrol accounted for 41 per cent of petrol sales in Britain.

Internationally developed standards have also been introduced to control the emission from civil aircraft of smoke, vented fuel and unburned hydrocarbons. Current indications are that aircraft contribute only a small amount to overall pollution, although the Government is funding further research and taking a leading role in European studies on this issue.

Noise

Local authorities have a duty to inspect their areas for noise nuisance and to investigate complaints about it. They can serve a noise abatement notice on a person responsible for noise nuisance. They can also designate 'noise abatement zones' within which registered levels of noise from certain premises may not be increased without their permission. There are also specific provisions in law to:

- control noise from construction and demolition sites;

- control the use of loudspeakers in the streets; and

- enable individuals to take action through the courts against noise amounting to a nuisance.

Tougher measures against noise were proposed in the White Paper. These reflect much of the thinking of an independent working party set up by the Government to review noise control. Government spending on environmental noise research is expected to be about £750,000 in 1991–92.

Transport is a major source of noise, and control measures are aimed at reducing it at source, through requirements limiting the noise that aircraft and motor vehicles may make, and at protecting people from its effects. Regulations set out the permissible noise levels for various classes of new vehicle. Government research also looks at ways of reducing noise, and has demonstrated the feasibility of tougher noise limits for heavy goods vehicles.

Compensation is payable for loss in property values caused by physical factors, including noise from new or improved public works such as roads and airports. Regulations also enable highway authorities to carry out or make grants for insulation of homes that would be subject to specified levels of increased noise caused by new or improved roads. Noise insulation may be provided where construction work for new roads may seriously affect nearby homes.

Britain has played a leading role in negotiations aimed at the gradual phasing-out of older, noisier subsonic jet aircraft. Flying non-noise certificated aircraft has been banned in Britain, and since 1990 British operators have no longer been allowed to add to their fleets further 'Chapter 2' aircraft (noisier planes, as classified by international agreement). A complete ban on the operation of Chapter 2 aircraft will begin to be implemented in April 1995, and it is intended to phase out all these types by April 2002. Various operational restrictions have been introduced to reduce noise disturbance further at Heathrow, Gatwick and Stansted, where the Secretary of State for Transport has assumed responsibility for noise abatement. These measures include:

- restrictions on the type and number of aircraft operating at night;

- the routeing of departing aircraft on noise preferential routes; and

- quiet take-off and landing procedures.

The population affected by aircraft noise at Heathrow fell from nearly 1·5 million in 1978 to less than 550,000 in 1988, even though the number of air transport movements increased by about a quarter. This was largely because of the phasing out of older, noisier aircraft.

Radioactivity

Man-made radiation represents only a small fraction of that to which the population is exposed; most is naturally occurring. Nevertheless, that fraction is subject to stringent control. Users of radioactive materials must be registered by HMIP in England and Wales, and equivalents in Scotland and Northern Ireland, and authorisation is also required for the accumulation and disposal of radioactive waste. The Health and Safety Executive, through its Nuclear Installations Inspectorate, is the authority responsible for the granting of nuclear site licences for major nuclear installations. No installation may be constructed or operated without a licence granted by the Executive.

The National Radiological Protection Board (NRPB) provides an authoritative point of reference on radiological protection. Following the accident at the Chernobyl nuclear power station in the Soviet Union in 1986, the Government has set up a national radiation monitoring network and overseas nuclear accident response system (RIMNET). An interim version has been operating since 1988. This will be replaced during 1992 by a larger system with more than 90 monitoring stations across Britain. In 1987 the Government announced measures to deal with the problem of naturally occurring radon gas in houses, including a free survey by the NRPB for householders living in radon-affected areas. In 1990 the Government halved the level at which it is recommended that householders take action to reduce radon in their homes. The NRPB has designated Cornwall and Devon as a 'Radon Affected Area' (an area where more than 1 per cent of the houses exceed the action level).

Radioactive Waste Disposal

Radioactive wastes vary widely in nature and level of activity, and the methods of disposal reflect this. Some wastes can be disposed of safely in the same way as other industrial and household wastes. UK Nirex Ltd is responsible for developing a deep disposal facility for solid low-level and intermediate-level radioactive waste, and has been investigating sites. In July 1991 it announced that these investigations were being concentrated on Sellafield (Cumbria). The Department of the Environment is sponsoring research, in collaboration with other countries, into disposal of high-level or heat-generating waste. This waste will first be stored in vitrified form for at least 50 years to allow the heat and radioactivity to decay. The vitrification plant at Sellafield was opened in February 1991.

The Department of the Environment's 1991–92 budget for research into environmental radioactivity and radioactive waste is £10 million.

Genetically Modified Organisms

The Environmental Protection Act 1990 introduced stronger controls over genetically modified organisms (GMOs). Anyone who intends to import, acquire, keep, release or market GMOs first has to carry out an environmental risk assessment and in some cases, first notify the Government or obtain its consent. The Government has powers to prevent the import, acquisition, keeping or release of GMOs where this would involve a significant risk of damage to the environment, and inspectors have the power to destroy or render harmless organisms which are likely to cause damage to the environment. A unified system of administrative control for GMOs is being developed in parallel with these provisions, involving the Department of the Environment, the Health and Safety Executive and other interested departments.

Environmental Research

Research into environmental protection is generally co-ordinated by the Department of the Environment. It has been estimated that total government spending on environmental research and development in 1989–90 was about £200 million, excluding work in areas such as renewable energy. Government spending on research into marine protection was about £50 million, with a large additional effort by industry. The Department of the Environment expects to spend about £82 million in 1991–92 on research into subjects including:

- climate change;
- atmospheric pollution and its monitoring;
- toxic chemicals and GMOs;
- waste disposal; and
- water quality and health.

Other departments have substantial programmes, notably the Ministry of Agriculture, Fisheries and Food, the Department of Energy, the Scottish Office Agriculture and Fisheries Department and other official bodies such as the NRA and the Meteorological Office.

One of the initiatives launched under the White Paper was the Environmental Technology Innovation Scheme, which combines existing schemes to promote innovation and competitiveness in the environmental technology industry.

RESEARCH COUNCILS

Basic and strategic research is carried out by five government-funded research councils: agriculture and food; economic and social sciences; natural environment; medical; and science and engineering. All have a role in environmental protection research. Particularly important is the Natural Environment Research Council (NERC), which has a science budget allocation of £123 million in 1991–92, plus expected receipts of about £43 million from commissioned research and other income. The NERC, established in 1965, undertakes and supports research in the environmental sciences and funds postgraduate training. Its programmes encompass the marine, earth, terrestrial, freshwater, polar and atmospheric sciences. The NERC stresses international collaborative work on global environmental issues. For example, it is helping to develop global atmospheric climate models and strengthening atmospheric research in the Arctic. A major new research programme, the Terrestrial Initiative in Global Environmental Research, has been started, so that the impact of climate change on Britain and elsewhere can be foreseen.

10 Religion

Everyone in Britain has the right to religious freedom—in teaching, worship and observance—without interference from the community or the State. Religious organisations and groups may own property, run schools, and promote their beliefs in speech and writing. There is no religious bar to the holding of public office.

Religious Tolerance

Britain has a long tradition of religious tolerance, and the past 30 years have seen the acceptance of a wide variety of religious beliefs and traditions brought in by large numbers of immigrants of different nationalities. There are now large and growing communities of Muslims, Hindus and Sikhs, and arrangements are made at places of work to allow the members of non-Christian religions to follow their religious observances.

Freedom of conscience in religious matters in Britain was achieved gradually from the seventeenth century onwards. The laws discriminating against minority religious groups were gradually administered less harshly and then finally repealed. Heresy ceased to be a legal offence with the passing of the Ecclesiastical Jurisdiction Act 1677, and the Toleration Act 1688 granted freedom of worship to Protestant minority groups. In 1828 the repeal of the Test and Corporation Acts gave nonconformists full political rights, making it possible for them to be appointed to public office. Roman Catholics gained political rights under the Roman Catholic Relief Act 1829, and the Jewish Relief Act 1858 enabled Jews to become Members of Parliament. In addition, the religious tests imposed on prospective students and academic staff of the universities of Oxford, Cambridge and Durham were successively abolished by Acts of 1854, 1856 and 1871. Similar restrictions on the staff of Scottish universities were formally removed in 1932.

Relations with the State

There are two established churches in Britain, that is, churches legally recognised as official churches of the State: in England the (Anglican) Church of England, and in Scotland the (Presbyterian) Church of Scotland. Ministers of the established churches, as well as clergy belonging to other religious groups, work in services run by the State, such as the armed forces, national hospitals and prisons, and are paid a salary for such services by the State. Voluntary schools provided by religious denominations may be wholly or partly maintained from public funds.

The State makes no direct contribution to church expenses, although since 1977 limited state aid has been given for the repair of historic churches. In 1990 the Government announced that £11·5 million would be made available to assist with the cost of repairs to cathedrals and comparable buildings over the following three years. Such funding is not restricted to Church of England buildings. The Government also contributes towards the Redundant Churches Fund, a body which maintains some 270 redundant Church of England churches for which no alternative use can be found but which are of architectural or historic importance. The contribution for the period from 1989 to 1994 will be about £8·7 million.

Involvement in Social Issues

Religious involvement in broader social issues was highlighted in the Church of England report *Faith in the City: A Call for*

Action by Church and Nation, published in 1985. This made recommendations for improving conditions in the inner cities and other socially deprived areas, and led to the establishment in 1988 of the Church of England's Church Urban Fund, which aims to raise money for the Church's work in inner city and other priority areas. By July 1991 it had raised over £17 million and given grants to over 400 inner city projects. Two further reports, *Living Faith in the City* and *Faith in the Countryside*, were published in 1990.

Statistics on Religious Affiliation

There is no standard information about the number of members of religious groups since questions are not normally asked about religious beliefs in censuses or for other official purposes, except in Northern Ireland. Each group adopts its own way of counting its members, and membership figures are therefore approximate.

There has been a fall in recent years in both the number of full-time ministers and the number of adults recorded as members of most of the larger Christian churches. At the same time there has been significant growth in a range of independent and Pentecostal churches, and in new religious movements. However, the churches today share a desire to work together and the ecumenical movement is well supported.

Education

Religious education in publicly maintained schools is required by law throughout Britain. Under the Education Reform Act 1988 it forms part of the basic curriculum for all pupils in England and Wales. The Act requires due recognition to be given to the place of Christianity in teaching at county schools, but the subject also covers other faiths. Schools also have to provide a daily act of collective worship. In county schools collective worship must be largely Christian in character, although non-Christian worship may be allowed in certain circumstances. Parents may withdraw their children from religious education and collective worship if

they wish. The Education (Scotland) Act 1980 imposes slightly different requirements in Scotland.

Broadcasting

The Broadcasting Act 1990 allows Christian and other religious groups to compete for licences to have their own local radio stations. They can also seek licences for some cable and satellite television channels. The Act also requires those running television stations on the new Channel 3 service (which is to replace the Independent Television network) to show religious programmes at peak times.

The Church of England

The Church of England, founded by St Augustine in AD 597, became the established church of the land in the Reformation in the sixteenth century. Its form of worship was set out in the Book of Common Prayer, dating from 1549. The Church of England's relationship with the State is one of mutual obligation—the Church's privileges are balanced by certain duties it must fulfil. The Sovereign must always be a member of the Church, and promise to uphold it. Church of England archbishops, bishops and deans are appointed by the Sovereign on the advice of the Prime Minister, and all clergy swear their allegiance to the Crown. The Church can regulate its own worship. The two archbishops (of Canterbury and York), the bishops of London, Durham and Winchester, and 21 other senior bishops sit in the House of Lords. Clergy of the Church, together with those of the Church of Scotland, the Church of Ireland and the Roman Catholic Church, may not sit in the House of Commons.

The Archbishop of Canterbury is 'Primate of All England', and the Archbishop of York 'Primate of England'.

The Church has two provinces: Canterbury, comprising 30 dioceses, including the Diocese of Europe; and York, which has 14 dioceses.

The dioceses are divided into 13,150 parishes. In 1988 it was estimated that, in the two provinces (excluding the Diocese of Europe), some 233,000 people were baptised into the Church; of these, 189,200 were under one year old, representing 29 per cent of live births. In the same year there were 63,895 confirmations. Attendances at services on a normal Sunday are around 1·2 million. Many people who rarely, if ever, attend services still regard themselves as belonging to the Church of England.

The central governing body is the General Synod, to which belong bishops, clergy and lay members who are involved in decision-making. Lay people are also concerned with church government in the parishes. The Synod is the centre of an administrative system dealing with such matters as missionary work, inter-church relations, social questions, and recruitment and training for the ministry. It also covers other church work in Britain and overseas, the care of church buildings, church schools (which are maintained from public funds), colleges of education, and centres for training women in pastoral work. At present, only men may join the priesthood, but in 1987 the General Synod voted to proceed with legislation to enable women to become priests; final decisions on the matter, however, are not expected to be taken for some years. The Deacons (Ordination of Women) Measure 1986 has made it possible for women to become deacons.

Church finance is administered locally, with contributions to a central fund running central services. The Church's investment income is managed mainly by the Church Commissioners.

The Anglican Communion

The Anglican Communion comprises 28 autonomous provinces in Britain and abroad, and three regional councils overseas with a total membership of about 70 million. In the British Isles there are four provinces: the Church of England (established), the Church in Wales, the Scottish Episcopal Church in Scotland, and the Church of Ireland.

Every ten years the Lambeth Conference meets for consultation between all Anglican bishops. The last Conference was held in Canterbury in 1988. Presided over by the Archbishop of Canterbury, the Conference has no executive authority, but enjoys considerable influence. The Anglican Consultative Council, an assembly of lay people and clergy as well as of bishops, meets every two or three years and is intended to allow consultations within the Anglican Communion. The Council last met in Wales in 1990.

The Church of Scotland

The Church of Scotland has a presbyterian form of government, that is, government by ministers and elders, all of whom are ordained to office. It became the national church following the Scottish Reformation and legislation of the Scottish Parliament, consolidated in the Treaty of Union 1707 and the Church of Scotland Act 1921, the latter confirming its complete freedom in all spiritual matters. It appoints its own office bearers and its affairs are not subject to any civil authority.

The adult communicant membership of the Church of Scotland is over 785,000.

Both men and women may join the ministry and about 1,500 churches are governed locally by Kirk Sessions, consisting of ministers and elders. Above the Kirk Session is the Presbytery, then the Synod, and finally the General Assembly, consisting of elected ministers and elders. This meets annually under the presidency of an elected moderator, who serves for one year. The Sovereign is normally represented at the General Assembly by the Lord High Commissioner.

The Free Churches

The term 'Free Churches' is often used to describe those Protestant churches in Britain which, unlike the Church of England and the Church of Scotland, are not established churches. In the course of history they have developed their own traditions. All the major

Free Churches—Methodist, Baptist, United Reformed and Salvation Army—allow both men and women to become ministers.

The Methodist Church, the largest of the Free Churches, with over 430,000 adult full members and a community of more than 1·3 million, originated in the eighteenth century following the evangelical revival under John Wesley. The present church is based on a 1932 union of most of the separate Methodist Churches.

The Baptists are mainly organised in groups of churches, most of which belong to the Baptist Union of Great Britain (formed in 1812), with a membership of about 160,000. There are also separate Baptist Unions for Scotland, Wales and Ireland, and other independent Baptist Churches.

The United Reformed Church, with some 121,000 members, was formed in 1972, when the Congregational Church in England and Wales (the oldest Protestant minority in Britain) and the Presbyterian Church of England merged. This was the first union of two different churches in Britain since the Reformation in the sixteenth century.

Among the other Free Churches are the Presbyterian Church in Ireland; the Presbyterian (or Calvinistic Methodist) Church of Wales; and a number of independent Scottish Presbyterian churches.

Other Protestant Churches include the Unitarians, Free Christians, and the Pentecostalists, who are increasing in number. The two main organisations operating in Britain are the Assemblies of God and the Elim Pentecostal Church, many of whose members are of West Indian origin. There is also a growing number of black-led churches.

The Religious Society of Friends (Quakers), with about 18,000 adult members in Britain and 450 places of worship, came into being in the middle of the seventeenth century under the leadership of George Fox. Silent worship is central to its life as a religious organisation.

The Salvation Army was founded in Britain in 1865. Within Britain there are 55,000 members and nearly 1,000 centres of worship. The Salvation Army is well known for the work of its social service centres, which range from hostels for the homeless to homes for those in need, and for its prison chaplaincy service.

A recent development in Christian worship has been the house church movement, which began in the early 1970s and now has an estimated membership of 120,000. Services are held in private houses. House churches receive money from their members to enable them to support their leaders and carry out missionary and social work.

There are also several other religious organisations in Britain which were founded in the United States in the last century. These include the Jehovah's Witnesses, the Church of Jesus Christ of the Latter-Day Saints (the Mormon Church), the Christian Scientists and the Spiritualists.

The Roman Catholic Church

The formal structure of the Roman Catholic Church in England and Wales, which had ceased to exist after the Reformation in the sixteenth century, was restored in 1850. The Scottish Church's formal structure went out of existence in the early seventeenth century and was restored in 1878. However, throughout this period Catholicism never disappeared entirely. There are now seven Roman Catholic provinces in Great Britain, each under an archbishop, and 29 dioceses, each under a bishop (22 in England and Wales and seven in Scotland, independently responsible to the Pope). There are over 3,000 parishes. Northern Ireland has six dioceses, some with territory partly in the Irish Republic.

About one British citizen in ten claims to be a Roman Catholic.

Only men may become priests. In 1982 Pope John Paul II paid a pastoral visit to Britain, the first by a reigning pope.

The Roman Catholic Church attaches great importance to the education of its children and requires its members to try to bring up their children in the Catholic faith. Almost 5 per cent of the teachers in Catholic schools are members of religious orders. These orders also undertake other social work. The majority of Catholic schools are maintained out of public funds and new schools may be established with government grants.

Other Christian Communities

Christian communities of foreign origin, including the Orthodox, Lutheran and Reformed Churches of various European countries, together with the Armenian Church, have established their own centres of worship, particularly in London.

The Jewish Community

Jews first settled in England at the time of the Norman Conquest in the latter half of the eleventh century. The present community in Britain dates from 1656, having been founded by those of Spanish and Portuguese origin, known as Sephardim. Later more settlers came from Germany and Eastern Europe; they are known as Ashkenazim. The present community, numbering about 330,000, is the second largest in Europe.

The community is divided into two main groups. Some 70 per cent of the majority Ashkenazi Jews are Orthodox and most acknowledge the authority of the Chief Rabbi. The Sephardi Orthodox element follow their own spiritual head, the Haham. The recently established Masorti movement, the Reform movement, founded in 1840, and the Liberal and Progressive movement, established in 1901, account for most of the remaining 30 per cent.

Jewish congregations in Britain number about 300. About one in three Jewish children attend Jewish schools, some of which are supported by public funds. Several agencies care for elderly and handicapped people.

The officially recognised representative body is the Board of Deputies of British Jews.

The Muslim Community

The most recent estimates suggest that Britain's Muslim population is around 1 million. The largest number originate from Pakistan and Bangladesh, while sizeable groups have come from India, Cyprus, the Arab world, Malaysia and parts of Africa. A growing community of British-born Muslims, mainly the children of immigrant parents, includes an increasing number of converts to Islam. There are some 300 mosques and numerous prayer centres throughout Britain. Mosques are not only places of worship; they also offer instruction in the Muslim way of life and facilities for social and welfare activities. The first was established at Woking in Surrey in 1890. They now range from converted houses in many industrial towns to the Central Mosque in London and its associated Islamic Cultural Centre, one of the most important Muslim institutions in the Western world.

The Central Mosque has the largest congregation in Britain, and during festivals it may number over 60,000.

Important mosques and cultural centres are also to be found in Liverpool, Manchester, Leicester, Edinburgh and Glasgow.

Many of the mosques belong to various Muslim organisations, and both the Sunni and the Shia traditions within Islam are represented among the Muslim community in Britain. Members of some of the major Sufi traditions have also developed branches in British cities.

The Sikh Community

A large British Sikh community, comprising over 500,000, originates mainly from India. The largest groups of Sikhs are in Greater London, Manchester, Birmingham, Nottingham and Wolverhampton. Sikh temples or gurdwaras cater for the religious, educational, social, and cultural needs of their community. The oldest gurdwara in London was established in 1908 and the largest one is in Southall, Middlesex. There are over 170 gurdwaras in Britain.

The Hindu Community

The Hindu community in Britain comprises around 300,000 members and also originates largely from India. The largest groups of Hindus are to be found in Leicester, north and north-west London, Birmingham and Bradford. The first Hindu temple or mandir was opened in Leicester in 1969 and there are now over 150 mandirs in Britain.

Buddhism

There are also about 130 Buddhist groups in Britain and some 55 centres, with at least 13 monasteries and a number of temples. All the main schools of Buddhism are represented. The Buddhist Society, with its headquarters in London, promotes the principles of Buddhism; it does not belong to any particular school of Buddhism.

New Religious Movements

A large number of new religious movements or cults, mainly established since the second world war (1939–45) and often with overseas origins, are active in Britain. In response to public concern about the activities of some of these cults the Government has since 1987 provided funding for the Information Network Focus on Religious Movements (INFORM), which is also supported by the main churches. The aims of INFORM are to conduct research into new religious movements and to provide objective information about them.

Co-operation among the Churches

The Council of Churches for Britain and Ireland was established in 1990, replacing the former British Council of Churches and taking over its role as the main overall body for the Christian churches in Britain. The Council co-ordinates the work of the churches grouped in separate ecumenical bodies for England, Scotland, Wales, and Ireland.

The Free Church Federal Council includes most of the Free Churches of England and Wales. It promotes unity among the Free Churches and is a channel for communication with government.

Inter-church discussions about the search for unity now take place through international as well as national bodies. The Roman Catholic, Orthodox and Lutheran Churches are represented on some of these, as are the Anglican and some of the Free Churches.

The Anglican Church, the Church of Scotland and the main Free Churches are also members of the World Council of Churches. This links some 300 churches in over 100 countries.

The Sharing of Church Buildings Act 1969 enables agreements to be made by two or more churches for sharing church buildings.

Co-operation between Religions

A number of organisations exist which seek to develop relations between different religions in Britain. They include the Inter Faith Network, which has received support from Christian, Jewish, Muslim, Buddhist, Hindu and Sikh leaders. Other organisations include the Council of Christians and Jews, which works for better understanding among members of the two religions and deals with problems in the social field. Religious leaders belonging to different faiths have also officiated jointly at a number of important public occasions. Christians, Muslims, Sikhs, Hindus, Jews and Buddhists, for example, all took part in the annual religious observance to mark Commonwealth Day in March 1991, which was attended by the Queen.

11 National Economy

From 1981 to 1989 the British economy had eight years of sustained growth at an annual average rate of over 3 per cent. However, growth of gross domestic product (GDP) in 1990 was only 0·5 per cent, with output falling in the second half of the year. Investment underwent sustained growth from 1981 to 1989, to reach record levels, with particularly rapid growth between 1987 and 1989. It fell between 1989 and 1990. There has been a recent fall in the number of jobs, from the highest-ever levels of 1990, and a rise in unemployment since early 1990. The annual rate of retail price inflation in August 1991 was 4·7 per cent, down from 10·9 per cent in September and October 1990.

The current account of the balance of payments has been in deficit since 1986, following six successive years of surplus, but the deficit has been on a downward trend since 1989. Export volumes have continued to grow.

ECONOMIC BACKGROUND

Britain has an open economy, in which international trade is a vital part of economic performance. In 1990 exports of goods and services accounted for about a quarter of GDP—a comparatively high share among the major economies. The proportion has increased in recent decades, from about 20 per cent in the early 1960s. Similar rises have occurred in most other developed countries, reflecting the growing importance of international trade in an increasingly interdependent world economy.

The economy is primarily—and increasingly—based on private enterprise, and government policy is aimed at encouraging and expanding the private sector, which accounts for about three-quarters of GDP and over two-thirds of total employment.

While manufacturing, the traditional engine of economic growth in Britain, continues to play a vital role, recent decades have generally seen a faster growth in the services sector. An adjustment to the relative size of the manufacturing sector has also resulted from the growth of North Sea oil output. Services account for over three-fifths of GDP and for two-thirds of employment, compared with about half of both GDP and employment in 1950. Manufacturing accounts for less than a quarter of each, compared with over a third in 1950.

Around 2 per cent of Britain's workforce is engaged in agriculture—a lower proportion than in any other major industrialised country. However, because of a high level of productivity, Britain is able to produce over half of its own food.

With the exploitation of oil and natural gas from the Continental Shelf under the North Sea, the country is self-sufficient in energy in net terms and expects to remain so for some years. Together, the extraction of oil and gas accounted for some 2 per cent of GDP in 1990. Coal—traditionally the most important source of energy—still meets almost a third of Britain's energy needs.

One of the largest exporters of manufactures, Britain accounts for over 5 per cent of the world total. It is among the major exporters of aerospace products, electrical equipment, most types of machinery, chemicals and oil. It is also one of the world's largest importers of agricultural products, raw materials and semi-manufactures.

In about half the years since the end of the second world war in 1945, a deficit on Britain's visible trade has been offset by a surplus on transactions in invisibles. However, the surplus on invisibles declined sharply in 1989 and stayed at roughly the same level in 1990, mainly because of a fall in net investment income and an increase in net transfers to European Community institutions. The significant contribution made by invisibles to the current account is partly a reflection of Britain's position as a major financial centre. The banks, insurance underwriters and brokers, and other financial institutions of the City of London provide worldwide financial services, and the City contains one of the most comprehensive and advanced capital markets in the world.

Values for some of the main economic indicators in selected years since 1980 are shown in Table 11.1.

Economic Growth

The marked rise in living standards in recent years has been accompanied by the emergence of new industries and the renewal and improvement of much of the country's infrastructure. Britain had a higher rate of economic growth over the decade 1980–90 than either Germany or France. However, economic growth in 1990 was 0·5 per cent, and output fell between mid-1990 and mid-1991.

Inflation and Competitiveness

From the late 1960s until about 1980 Britain had generally high annual rates of inflation compared with other countries. Huge rises in the price of oil in 1973 and 1979 and substantial increases in the money supply and public spending were followed by upsurges in inflation in 1975 and 1980. Earnings also grew rapidly. Inflation fell in the early 1980s and stayed low for a number of years. However, it picked up towards the end of the decade, so that the annual rate was 10·9 per cent in September 1990. It then fell again, to 4·7 per cent in August 1991. In the year to July 1991 earnings rose at an underlying rate of some 7·5 per cent—down from about 10 per cent in the year to mid-1990.

Industrial Production

In the decade to 1973 output of the manufacturing industries grew at a faster rate than the economy as a whole. After the oil price rises of 1973–74, however, manufacturing output fell sharply. It later increased from this trough but, following another oil price rise and stagnation in the world economy, fell back in the late 1970s and early 1980s. This was followed by a period of steady growth until 1990, since when there has been a cyclical decline.

By 1985 output of the production industries as a whole (manufacturing, energy and water) had risen above its earlier peak of 1979. It experienced sustained growth between 1983 and 1989, but declined in 1990. In 1986 energy output was about twice the level of ten years earlier. With oil output having passed its peak of the mid-1980s and with the need to shut down fields in order to carry out safety work, it had fallen back by over 15 per cent by 1990.

Table 11.1: Economic Indicators

	1980	1985	1990
Gross domestic product (average estimate)[a]	323,419	356,083	416,888
Exports[a]	88,726	102,208	123,642
Imports[a]	80,781	98,866	139,123
Consumers' expenditure[a]	195,825	217,618	273,304
Gross domestic fixed capital formation[a]	53,416	60,353	79,893
Percentage increase in retail prices index	18·0	6·1	9·5
Workforce in employment (000s)	n.a.	24,530	28,510
Percentage of workforce unemployed	n.a.	10·9	5·8

Sources: *United Kingdom National Accounts 1991 Edition; Economic Trends; Employment Gazette.*
[a] £ million at 1985 market prices.
n.a.: not available.

Investment

From 1983 until 1989 fixed investment increased by about 7 per cent a year on average, with particularly rapid growth of nearly 10 per cent a year between 1986 and 1989. This was followed by a cyclical decline in 1990. Over the decade 1980–90 there was an increase in the private sector's share of fixed investment from 72 to 84 per cent (due in part to privatisation). Over the same period there was a rise in the share of investment undertaken by the services sector and a fall in that carried out by manufacturing. An improvement in the quality of investment contributed to the rise in the late 1980s in the net real rate of return on capital employed in non-North Sea industrial and commercial companies. However, there was a decline in 1990, when the rate fell to some 6 per cent.

Employment and Productivity

Britain's workforce in employment increased by 3·3 million in the seven years to June 1990. However, it has subsequently declined and in March 1991 amounted to 26·4 million. Since 1979 self-employment has risen every year, to reach 3·3 million by mid-1990. The number of women seeking work has also risen.

As in other industrialised countries, there is concern about unemployment. Even when the workforce was expanding, unemployment did not fall as quickly as employment rose. However, with the economy growing rapidly, unemployment fell by 1·6 million between July 1986 and March 1990. Subsequently unemployment has risen. In August 1991 it amounted to 2·4 million—equal to 8·5 per cent of the workforce.

Between 1980 and 1990 manufacturing productivity in Britain grew by an average of 4·7 per cent a year. This was higher than in any other major industrialised country and in contrast to the previous two decades, when Britain was at the bottom of the league. However, productivity in Britain's economy as a whole increased only slowly in 1990 as part of the normal reaction to a cyclical slowdown in activity.

As a result of demographic changes, the population of working age will grow more slowly during the 1990s than in recent years, with a fall in the number of young people. The increase in Great Britain between 1988 and 2001 is projected at 0·6 million, compared with a rise of 2·4 million in the previous 13 years. Accordingly, there will be a need for increased flexibility among those in work and for employers to tap new sources of recruitment. The Government has launched a new training framework, involving a greater role for employers.

Overseas Sector

Britain's overseas trade performance fluctuated during the 1970s. In general, imports of food, energy, raw materials and manufactured goods were greater than visible exports, around 80 per cent of which were manufactured goods. This deficit on visible trade was wholly or partly offset by a surplus on invisibles, which cover earnings from services, together with interest, profits and dividends, and transfers.

In the years 1980 to 1982 Britain ran surpluses on visible trade. Since then, however, imports—especially of manufactures—have tended to rise more sharply than exports (although the trend was reversed in 1990) and the deficit on visible trade has reappeared. After a long period of deterioration in the balance of trade in manufactures there was a deficit in 1983, which has continued in subsequent years. However, the deficit has declined and was virtually eliminated in the summer of 1991. Substantial net earnings on invisible transactions kept the current account in surplus up to 1985, but it has been in deficit since then.

Membership of the European Community has had a major impact on Britain's pattern of trade, increasing the proportion with other member countries. Between 1972 and 1990 the proportion of

Britain's exports of goods going to other members of the Community rose from 34 to 53 per cent. Imports followed a similar trend. Trade with Japan and with the newly industrialised countries, including Singapore, Korea, Taiwan and Malaysia, has risen substantially.

The invisibles account has had to adapt to new conditions, in particular, the abolition of exchange controls in 1979 and the growth in world markets of insurance, banking, tourism, construction, consultancy and other services. In 1990 exports of services were valued at around one-third of exports of goods.

The substantial cumulative surplus on current account in the first half of the 1980s contributed to a corresponding increase in Britain's net external assets. These are estimated to have risen from £18,000 million at the end of 1980 to £104,000 million at the end of 1986. They have since fallen, to £84,000 million at the end of 1989 and to £30,000 million at the end of 1990. The latter decline reflected mainly the effect of falling security prices on substantial portfolios held abroad. At the end of 1990 the book value of British direct investment holdings overseas was £127,000 million, reflecting the growth of multinational companies based in Britain, and that of British portfolio investment holdings overseas was £186,000 million. Direct and portfolio investment in Britain from overseas has also grown as overseas companies have become established in Britain, especially in recent years in preparation for the onset of the single European market by the end of 1992.

Oil

The development of North Sea oil and gas production has had a significant effect on the economy; in 1990 Britain was the world's ninth largest oil producer. The benefits to the balance of payments began to appear in the second half of the 1970s and in 1980 Britain had its first surplus on oil trade. In 1974 oil accounted for some 4 per cent of Britain's visible exports and 19 per cent of visible imports. In 1990 the proportions were 7 and 5 per cent respectively (the export

proportion having been as high as 21 per cent in the mid-1980s). The oil surplus reached its peak in 1985, at £8,100 million. With the fall in oil prices the surplus has fallen and amounted to some £1,500 million in 1990. Exports, mainly to other European Community countries, are equivalent to well over half of domestic oil production. They are partly offset in balance-of-payments terms by imports of other grades of crude oil from the Middle East and elsewhere.

North Sea oil helped to alleviate the fall in real national income which Britain, along with other industrialised countries, suffered following the oil price rises of the 1970s. In the early 1980s it helped to ease the task of controlling public sector borrowing, one component of the Government's counter-inflation strategy. Even as production falls from its mid-1980s peak, the stock of external assets that has been built up, largely during the period of oil surpluses, provides a flow of income.

ECONOMIC STRATEGY

The Government's economic policy is set in the context of a medium-term financial strategy, which is reviewed each year at the time of the Budget. Within this strategy, firm financial policies are designed to defeat inflation. This strategy was reaffirmed in the 1991 Budget. Short-term interest rates remain the essential instrument of monetary policy. The framework of monetary discipline has been reinforced by British membership of the exchange rate mechanism (ERM) of the European Monetary System (EMS). Fiscal policy is set over a medium-term horizon to support tight monetary policies.

Macroeconomic policy is directed towards bringing down the rate of inflation and ultimately achieving price stability. On top of this, microeconomic policies are aimed at improving the working of markets and encouraging enterprise, efficiency and flexibility. By means of policies such as deregulation and tax reform, these are designed to improve the supply-side performance of the economy (see p 213).

Monetary Policy

The central aim of monetary policy, which the Government sees as lying at the heart of macroeconomic policy, is the creation of conditions that will exert steady downward pressure on the rate of growth of money GDP, so bringing down the rate of inflation. Interest rates are the primary instrument for achieving this. Britain's membership of the ERM constitutes an added element of monetary discipline by making explicit the Government's commitment to a firm exchange rate and by linking sterling to the currencies of countries such as Germany, which have a record of low inflation.

Under the ERM the central exchange rate for sterling is £1 = 2·95 Deutsche Mark, with a permitted fluctuation of 6 per cent either side of the central rate.

In assessing the overall stance of monetary conditions, the Government pays attention to a range of indicators. In particular, narrow money, as measured by M0,[1] has had a stable relationship with money GDP over a number of years and has proved a reliable indicator of monetary conditions. A target range of 0 to 4 per cent has been set for M0 growth in 1991–92. This will help to underpin the Government's commitment to the ERM.

Changes in broad money, or liquidity, have become increasingly difficult to interpret; far-reaching changes in financial practices have meant that there is no simple relationship between the growth in broad money and in money GDP. Consequently, no explicit target range is set for broad money, though the assessment of monetary conditions continues to take broad money into account.

Fiscal Policy

The role of a tight monetary policy in reducing inflation is supported by a firm fiscal policy. Fiscal policy is set according to the medium-term objective of a balanced budget. This is consistent with cyclical variations in government spending and revenues—'automatic stabilisers'. The public sector therefore tends to run a surplus when the level of economic activity is high and a deficit when it is low. The Government does not attempt to 'fine-tune' the level of demand through changes in fiscal policy; it believes that the associated time lags generally mean that such changes will be destabilising. Frequent changes in taxation or spending policy may also produce an adverse supply-side response.

Within the overall policy of a balanced budget over the medium term, the Government aims to reduce taxes so as to leave people with more of their own money. In particular, the basic rate of income tax has already been cut from 33 to 25 per cent. The Government wishes to move towards 20 per cent when prudent to do so within the overall balanced budget constraint. Such tax cuts can only be achieved if public spending is kept under control. The Government therefore aims over the medium term to maintain general government expenditure, excluding privatisation proceeds (which count as negative expenditure), on a downward trend as a share of GDP. The ratio of general government expenditure, excluding privatisation proceeds, to GDP fell from 47·5 per cent in 1982–83 to some 40·5 per cent in 1990–91.

Supply-Side Policies

While macroeconomic policy is directed towards reducing inflation, the Government has sought to improve the supply response, and thus the efficiency, of the economy through microeconomic policies. Action has been taken to expose more of the economy to market forces. Direct controls (for example, on pay, prices, foreign exchange, dividend payments and commercial credit) have been abolished and competition in domestic markets strengthened. Labour market reforms have also been introduced,

---

[1] M0 is notes and coin in circulation with the public and banks' holdings of cash and their operational balances at the Bank of England.

Table 11.2: Gross Domestic Product, Gross National Product and National Income

£ million

	1980	1990
Total final expenditure	290,153	697,501
less imports of goods and services	−57,606	− 147,582
Gross domestic product at market prices[a]	231,772	550,597
plus net property income from abroad	− 182	4,029
Gross national product at market prices[a]	231,590	554,626
less factor cost adjustment (taxes less subsidies)	−30,755	− 72,850
Gross domestic product at factor cost[a]	201,017	477,747
Net property income from abroad	−182	4,029
Gross national product at factor cost[a]	200,835	481,776
less capital consumption	− 27,952	− 61,159
National income (net national product at factor cost)[a]	172,883	420,617

Source: *United Kingdom National Accounts 1991 Edition.*
[a] Average estimate.

measures taken to encourage saving and share ownership, and a substantial amount of activity transferred from the public to the private sector by privatisation and contracting work out. In addition, efforts have been made to improve value for money in the public sector by, for example, transferring many of the executive functions of government to new executive agencies, and to reduce regulatory burdens on business.

The Government has sought to improve work incentives by reducing personal income tax rates, raising tax thresholds and reforming the benefits system. It has also, through the tax system, encouraged the extension of share ownership among employees. A scheme of income tax relief has been introduced to encourage the spread of profit-related pay. The Government has taken steps to achieve a better-balanced legal framework for industrial relations and has expanded training opportunities. Obstacles to the mobility of labour have been reduced. For example, the rights of those leaving occupational pension schemes early have been improved and new arrangements for personal pensions introduced, both of which will reduce the pension disadvantage of changing jobs. Reforms in the housing market have been introduced to make it easier for people to move house. Policies

have been set in train to reduce the number of obstacles facing small firms and the self-employed.

Competition among financial institutions is being encouraged within a new statutory framework of investor protection. The Government has also taken steps to reduce the distorting effects of the tax system on investment and savings decisions by, among other things, reforming corporation tax (the burden of which has been eased) and the system of capital allowances. Planning restrictions on industrial investment have been eased, while government support to industry has become more selective and, where appropriate, more closely related to job creation. Particular efforts have been made to improve the flow of investment funds to small firms, to assist innovation in industry and to attract industry to the inner cities.

Economic Management

HM Treasury has prime responsibility for the formulation and conduct of economic policy, which it carries out in conjunction with the Bank of England (the central bank) and the Departments of Trade and Industry, Employment, Energy, the Environment and Transport, and the Ministry of Agriculture, Fisheries and Food.

Table 11.3: Total Final Expenditure in 1990 at Market Prices

	£ million	per cent
Consumers' expenditure	349,421	50·1
General government final consumption	109,495	15·7
Gross domestic fixed capital formation	105,195	15·1
Value of physical increase in stocks and work in progress	−718	−0·1
Total domestic expenditure	563,393	80·8
Exports of goods and services	134,108	19·2
Total final expenditure	697,501	100·0

Source: *United Kingdom National Accounts 1991 Edition.*

A number of other bodies deal with specific aspects of economic policy and the regulation of certain sectors of the economy. These include bodies such as the Office of Fair Trading and the Monopolies and Mergers Commission.

On major matters of public policy such as the broad economic strategy, and on the economic problems it faces, the Government makes known its policies and keeps in touch with developments throughout the economy by means of informal and continuous links with the chief industrial, financial, labour and other interests. Final responsibility for the broad lines of economic policy rests with the Cabinet.

NATIONAL INCOME AND EXPENDITURE

The value of all goods and services produced in the economy is measured by GDP. This can be expressed either in terms of market prices (the prices people pay for the goods and services they buy) or at factor cost (the cost of the goods and services before adding taxes and subtracting subsidies). It can also be expressed in current prices or in constant prices (that is, removing the effects of inflation in order to measure the underlying growth in the economy). In 1990 GDP at current factor cost totalled £487,000 million.

Estimation of GDP can be approached in three different ways as the sum total of expenditure, income or output. Each

method yields the same total in principle but in practice there are slight differences. The definitive measure of GDP is derived as an average of these approaches. In 1990 this index of the average estimate of GDP at constant factor cost was 116·2 (1985 = 100), compared with 90·7 in 1980, an increase of some 28 per cent.

Table 11.2 gives figures for the average estimate of GDP, at both current market prices and current factor cost, and also shows how two other main aggregates used in the national accounts, gross national product and national income, are derived.

Table 11.3 shows the categories of total final expenditure in 1990. Consumers' expenditure accounted for 50 per cent of total final expenditure, and exports of goods and services for 19 per cent.

Personal Incomes and Expenditure

Personal disposable income (that is, personal incomes after deductions—mainly taxation and social security contributions) rose rapidly and fairly steadily from £161,000 million in 1980 to £384,800 million in 1990, 3·3 per cent higher in real terms than in 1989. Consumers' expenditure amounted to 70·9 per cent of pre-tax personal income in 1990, compared with 74 per cent in 1989.

Table 11.4 shows the changing pattern of consumers' expenditure. Housing, food, alcoholic drink, clothing and footwear, and fuel and power together accounted for 42 per cent of the total. The changes in the

Table 11.4: Consumers' Expenditure in 1980 and 1990 at Market Prices

	1980 per cent	1990 per cent	1990 £ million
Food (household expenditure)	16·9	12·0	41,833
Alcoholic drink	7·1	6·2	21,730
Tobacco	3·5	2·5	8,835
Clothing and footwear	7·1	5·9	20,702
Housing	13·6	14·3	50,050
Fuel and power	4·6	3·5	12,214
Household goods and services	7·1	6·5	22,575
Transport and communications	16·8	17·7	62,016
Recreation, entertainment and education	9·2	9·4	32,677
Other goods and services	12·7	18·7	65,395
Other items[a]	1·4	3·3	11,394
Total	100·0	100·0	349,421

Source: *United Kingdom National Accounts 1991 Edition.*
[a]Household expenditure overseas plus final expenditure by private non-profit-making bodies, minus expenditure by foreign tourists in Britain.

pattern between 1980 and 1990 in Britain were paralleled in other industrialised countries, with declining proportions spent on food, tobacco, clothing and footwear, and fuel and power. Over the longer term, as incomes rise, people tend to spend increasing proportions on services. Consumers' expenditure increased by 1 per cent in real terms between 1989 and 1990.

Saving as a percentage of personal disposable income varied during the 1980s, but fell from 13·3 per cent in 1980 to 5·4 per cent in 1988. This reflected a number of factors, including lower inflation, higher property prices and the deregulation of the personal finance market, so making borrowing easier. However, the savings ratio increased in 1989 and 1990, reaching 9·2 per cent in the latter year.

Sources of Income

The proportion of total personal pre-tax income accounted for by income from employment was 64 per cent in 1990; average gross weekly earnings in April 1991 in Great Britain were £319 for full-time male workers and £222 for full-time female workers. The three other main sources of personal income were self-employment (12 per cent in 1990), rent, dividends and interest (11 per cent) and

social security benefits and other current grants from general government (13 per cent).

Current Government Expenditure

Final consumption by central government and local authorities amounted to £109,500 million in 1990; it rose by 12 per cent in real terms over the period 1980 to 1990. The main cause of this was the growth over the period in spending on the social services, health, and law and order.

In addition to their expenditure on goods and services, public authorities transfer large sums to other sectors, mainly the personal sector, by way of National Insurance and other social security benefits, grants, and interest and subsidies. Central government also makes grants to local authorities to finance about half of their current expenditure.

Gross Domestic Product by Industry

Table 11.5 shows GDP by industry in 1980 and 1990. Over a period of time agriculture and manufacturing have come to account for smaller proportions of national income, while services have grown relatively; services now account for 64 per cent of GDP.

Table 11.5: Gross Domestic Product by Industry[a]

	1980		1990	
	£ million	per cent	£ million	per cent
Agriculture, forestry and fishing	4,247	2·1	7,102	1·5
Energy and water supply	19,416	9·7	24,334	5·1
Manufacturing	53,588	26·8	106,995	22·4
Construction	12,269	6·1	36,085	7·6
Distribution, hotels and catering; repairs	25,929	12·9	70,151	14·7
Transport and communications	14,584	7·3	34,031	7·1
Banking, finance, insurance, business services and leasing	23,246	11·6	87,260	18·3
Ownership of dwellings	12,147	6·1	30,719	6·4
Public administration, defence and social security	14,547	7·3	31,524	6·6
Education and health services	18,023	9·0	45,143	9·5
Other services	10,710	5·3	30,983	6·5
Total	208,706	104·2	504,327	105·6
Adjustment for financial services	− 8,464	−4·2	− 26,740	−5·6
Gross domestic product at factor cost (income-based)	200,242	100·0	477,587	100·0

Source: *United Kingdom National Accounts 1991 Edition.*
[a]Before provision for depreciation but after deducting stock appreciation.
Note: Differences between totals and the sums of their component parts are due to rounding.

12 Industry and Commerce

Introduction

The most important industrial developments in the last 15 years have been the growth of the offshore oil and gas industries and the rapid development of electronic and microelectronic technologies and their wide application in industry and commerce generally. There has been a steady increase in the share of output and employment accounted for by private sector enterprises as privatisation has progressed. In addition, the proportion of jobs in the service industries has continued to rise.

The Government believes that economic decisions are best taken by those competing in the market place, and that government should encourage enterprise and create the right climate for markets to work better.

This chapter outlines some of the general features of industrial and commercial performance and organisation, and goes on to describe government policies and legislation, the functioning of markets, and research and innovation.

Performance

Between 1981 and 1989 Britain had eight successive years of growth, at an annual average rate of over 3 per cent. In the 1980s Britain grew faster than France and the then Federal Republic of Germany. This was in contrast to the experience of the previous two decades, when Britain had the lowest growth rate in Europe. Over the same period, productivity in manufacturing grew more rapidly than in all other major industrialised countries.

Following a very rapid rate of expansion in the late 1980s, however, the pace of activity began to falter in 1990; in common with other major industrialised countries, Britain entered recession.

Investment

Investment totalled £105,195 million in 1990 (see Table 12.3). In real terms investment was 32 per cent higher than in 1985. However, investment in 1990 was 2·4 per cent lower than in 1989, although in some sectors (such as energy) investment continued to rise. The figures for manufacturing industry do not include expenditure on leased assets since these are attributed to the service industries on the basis of ownership. Manufacturing industry is, however, a major user of leased assets.

Table 12.1: Gross Domestic Product[a] by Industry in 1990

Standard Industrial Classification Revised 1985		£ million	% of total	% Employment[b]
0	Agriculture, forestry and fishing	7,102	1·5	1·2
1	Energy and water supply	24,334	5·1	2·0
2–4	Manufacturing	106,995	22·4	22·5
5	Construction	36,085	7·6	4·6
6–9	Services	329,811	69·1	69·6
	Adjustment for financial services	−26,740	−5·6	–
GDP at factor cost (income-based)		477,587	100·0	100·0

Sources: *United Kingdom National Accounts 1991 Edition* and *Employment Gazette*.
[a]Before depreciation but after providing for stock appreciation.
[b]Statistics for employment relate to Great Britain.
Note: The difference between the totals and the sums of their component parts are due to rounding.

Table 12.2: Output and Employment (Indices: 1985 = 100)

	Output		Employment[a]	
	Index 1989	Index 1990	Index 1989	Index 1990
Agriculture, forestry and fishing	101·2	104·4	87·2	86·9
Production industries	109·9	109·2	94·9	94·1
of which: Energy and water supply	89·6	88·8	78·5	76·1
Manufacturing	118·9	118·3	96·7	96·0
Construction	130·4	131·8	106·2	106·7
Services	117·4	119·4	110·8	112·5
GDP (output-based)	115·3	116·4		
Employees in employment in all industries and services			105·8	106·7

Sources: *United Kingdom National Accounts 1991 Edition* and *Employment Gazette*.
[a]Employment figures relate to Great Britain and cover employees in employment at June.

Inward Investment

Britain is recognised as an attractive location for inward direct investment. This reflects its membership of the European Community and proximity to other European markets, stable labour relations and comparatively low corporate and personal taxation. Overseas-owned firms are offered the same facilities and incentives as British-owned ones.

The Invest in Britain Bureau of the Department of Trade and Industry (DTI) provides foreign companies with advice and assistance on locating and relocating businesses in Britain, and on expanding existing facilities. It reported 350 new inward investment projects in 1990–91. The promotion of England as a location for inward investment projects is handled by the English unit of the DTI. Similar advice and assistance is also available through Locate in Scotland, operated jointly by the Scottish Office Industry Department and Scottish Enterprise; Welsh Development International, the investment arm of the Welsh Development Agency; and the Industrial Development Board in Northern Ireland.

At the end of 1990 total United States investment in Britain was valued at $165,000 million, representing 42 per cent of United States investment in the European Community. Britain has for many years been the leading country for United States manufacturing investment in Europe. Britain also has about 39 per cent of Japanese investment in the European Community.

Table 12.3: Gross Domestic Fixed Capital Formation (Investment) by Sector 1990

	£ million at market prices	£ million at 1985 prices	Index at 1985 prices (1985 = 100)
Agriculture, forestry and fishing	1,475	1,133	95·9
Oil and gas extraction	3,527	2,683	95·2
Other energy and water supply	6,200	4,794	120·6
Manufacturing	14,809	12,142	120·0
Construction and services	56,556	44,341	161·6
Dwellings	18,449	12,460	105·1
Transfer costs of land and buildings	4,179	2,340	78·7
Whole economy	105,195	79,893	132·4

Source: *United Kingdom National Accounts 1991 Edition*.

Organisation and Ownership

The main categories of business and commercial organisation are:

- unincorporated businesses (sole traders and partnerships), of which there are more than 1 million;

- incorporated companies; and

- government-owned enterprises (see below).

In some sectors a small number of large companies and their subsidiaries are responsible for a large proportion of total production, notably in the vehicle, aerospace and transport equipment industries. Private enterprises generate about three-quarters of total domestic income. They account for the greater part of activity in the agricultural, manufacturing, construction, distributive, financial and miscellaneous service sectors. The private sector accounted for 77 per cent of total domestic final expenditure in 1990, general government for 22 per cent and public corporations for 1 per cent.

About 250 British industrial companies in the latest reporting period each had an annual turnover of more than £500 million. The annual turnover of the biggest, British Petroleum (BP), makes it the eleventh largest industrial grouping in the world and the second largest in Europe. Five British firms are among the top 25 European Community companies.

Nationalised Industries

The major nationalised industries are British Coal, British Rail, the Post Office and London Transport. The managing boards and staffs of the nationalised industries are not civil servants. The boards are appointed by ministers who have the power to give general directions but are not involved in day-to-day management.

The Government believes that nationalised industries should act as commercial enterprises and has set policies with which they are expected to conform.

These involve:

- clear government objectives for the industries;

- regular corporate plans and performance reviews;

- agreed principles relating to investment appraisal and pricing;

- financial targets and performance aims;

- external financing limits; and

- systematic monitoring.

The industries are expected to achieve a required rate of return, currently 8 per cent in real terms before tax. The financial target set by the Government is usually supported by a series of performance aims, covering costs and, where appropriate, standards of service. External financing limits, which control the amount of finance (grants and borrowing) that a nationalised industry can raise in any financial year, are an important operating control. They are set in the light of the industry's financial target and its expected performance and investment requirements. The proportion of investment financed from internally generated funds has risen in recent years.

External scrutiny of nationalised industry efficiency is conducted by the Monopolies and Mergers Commission (see p 231). Where appropriate, investigations may also be undertaken by management consultants. House of Commons Select Committees, such as the Treasury and Civil Service Committee and the Public Accounts Committee, also scrutinise the industries' performance.

Industrial Associations

The Confederation of British Industry (CBI) represents about 250,000 parent and subsidiary companies, as well as the members of some 150 trade associations and employers' organisations and the majority of public sector enterprises, together employing more than half the nation's workforce. The largest employers' organisation in the country, it provides members with a forum, a lobby and a range of advisory services. The CBI also conducts a series of surveys on manufacturing, distribution, financial services, regions, and pay and productivity.

British chambers of commerce represent business views and interests to the Government both at national and local levels. They promote local economic development, for example, through regeneration projects, tourism, inward investment promotion in certain areas of Britain and business services, including overseas trade missions, exhibitions and training conferences. The Association of British Chambers of Commerce represents over 90,000 businesses in over 100 chambers of commerce throughout Britain.

Trade associations consist of companies producing or selling a particular product or group of products. They exist to provide common services, regulate trading practices and represent their members to government departments.

Employers' organisations are usually concerned with the negotiation of wages and conditions of work in a particular industry, although sometimes one institution may combine this function with that of a trade association.

Industrial Financing

Over half of companies' funds for investment and other purposes are internally generated. Banks provide the chief external source of finance, but companies have increasingly turned to equity finance. The main forms of short-term finance available in the private sector are bank overdrafts, trade credit and factoring (making cash available to a company in exchange for debts owing to it).

Types of medium- and long-term finance include bank loans, the mortgaging of property and the issue of shares and other securities to the public through The London Stock Exchange. The leasing of equipment may also be regarded as a form of finance. Other sources of finance for industry include the Government, the European Community and specialist financial institutions.

There has been a growing number of schemes involving equity funds made available by financial institutions in support of innovative or other new and growing business ventures. This is known as venture capital. Since 1985 the members of the British Venture Capital Association have invested some £6,200 million and currently command an investment pool of £2,000 million.

There has also been a rise in the number of 'buy-outs', in which the staff or management of a company raise the finance to purchase it, and 'buy-ins', in which the staff or management of one firm purchase another. Since 1979 there have been over 3,000 buy-outs, with a total value of £17,040 million. The amount invested in management buy-outs and buy-ins in 1990 was £382 million.

Management Development and Industrial Training

Management education is provided by many polytechnics and colleges of higher and further education. Some regional management centres have been established in England and Wales by associations of these colleges, and there are several similar organisations in Scotland. Universities make an important contribution, especially through the full-time postgraduate programmes at business schools such as those of London, Manchester, Durham, Warwick and Strathclyde universities.

Training courses for managers are offered by several independent colleges, including the Management College (Henley-on-Thames), Ashridge College (Berkhamsted) and Cranfield School of Management (Bedford). Open and distance learning opportunities are becoming more widely available. The British Institute of Management encourages excellence in management. Other professional bodies are concerned with standards and training in specialised branches of management.

The Open University, which provides degree courses using distance learning techniques, notably television broadcasts, has its own Business School offering part-time courses leading to a diploma in management and to a Master's degree in Business Administration.

The employer-led Management Charter Initiative (MCI) is the operating arm of the

National Forum for Management Education and Development and the leading industrial body for management standards. Over 840 employers, representing 7 million employees, are members of MCI, which has 50 local networks working with local employers.

Government Management Initiatives

The DTI is working with other government departments and with industry to improve management education, and to spread awareness about best management practices. It strongly supports the MCI. The consultancy support offered by the DTI to businesses with fewer than 500 employees is designed to help businesses improve their management performance. Another programme, 'Managing into the 90s', is designed to encourage managers to integrate the role of design, quality, manufacturing management, and purchasing and supply, within an overall business strategy leading to improved competitiveness.

The DTI has also encouraged the growth of links between industry and higher education in recent years, primarily through collaborative research. One of the most successful ways has been the Teaching Company Scheme, under which young graduates undertake key projects in companies under the joint supervision of academic and company staff.

The Engineering Council

Established under Royal Charter in 1981, the Engineering Council promotes the science and practice of engineering and advances education in engineering. The Council maintains a register of 290,000 chartered engineers, incorporated engineers and engineering technicians. In co-operation with the various professional institutions and other organisations concerned with training in engineering, it has set standards for education, training and experience, and accredited courses by which people qualify for registration. The Council is advised by some 260 industrial affiliates on industrial requirements for engineers and technicians.

Government Policies and Legislation

The DTI is the main department responsible for the Government's relations with industry and commerce. Specific responsibilities include technology and innovation, overseas trade and export promotion, competition policy and consumer affairs, company legislation and the Patent Office. Through the Invest in Britain Bureau, it gives advice and assistance to foreign companies on locating in Britain. The Scottish, Welsh and Northern Ireland Offices are responsible for the range of industrial policies in their areas.

The Enterprise Initiative

The Enterprise Initiative brings together a wide range of the services that the DTI provides for industry and commerce. Its consultancy scheme encourages small and medium-sized businesses to use outside consultancy services as a regular part of their management strategy. It also offers consultancy support in design, marketing, manufacturing and service systems, quality, business planning, and financial and management information systems. In Scotland and Wales the scheme is operated by Scottish Enterprise and the Welsh Development Agency. Assistance is available to manufacturing and service businesses with fewer than 500 employees. In the Assisted Areas (see p 228) and Urban Programme Areas, two-thirds of the costs of a project are met; elsewhere the rate is 50 per cent. Some £46 million is being provided in 1991–92 to support the consultancy scheme.

Industrial Policy

In 1991 the DTI specified its objectives for industrial policy as:

- working for trade liberalisation worldwide and the completion of the single European market (see below);
- promoting British exports;
- stimulating innovation in industry;

- improving the flow of information to business;
- encouraging competition;
- aiming for a light but effective framework of market regulation;
- fostering a positive attitude towards wealth creation;
- reducing burdens on business;
- taking into account the concerns of business and consumers in the development of government policies; and
- responding to regional needs.

Single European Market

The Government is firmly committed to the completion of the single European market by the end of 1992. This will provide major benefits for business and consumers, and improve European competitiveness in world markets. The DTI runs campaigns to emphasise to businesses the importance of taking full advantage of the opportunities presented by the single market.

Small Firms

Small businesses make a major contribution to the economy by employing 36 per cent of the private sector workforce and producing 21 per cent of British turnover.

The Government runs schemes which provide either direct assistance or advice and guidance on a wide range of business problems affecting small firms. In addition to DTI schemes such as consultancy help under the Enterprise Initiative, the Government's Small Firms Service, available throughout Britain, provides information, advice, counselling and training services to prospective and established small businesses.

Other government help to small firms includes:
- guaranteed repayment of 70 per cent of medium-term loans made by financial institutions (rising to 85 per cent of loans in inner city Task Force areas);
- the Business Expansion Scheme, which improves the flow of equity finance to small firms by offering tax incentives to investors;

- the Enterprise Allowance Scheme, enabling unemployed people to claim an allowance while establishing a new business;
- the Manufacturing Planning and Implementation Studies Programme, set up to help companies exploit Advanced Manufacturing Technology (AMT) to the full, by offering grants towards the costs of hiring external advisors;
- the introduction of tax concessions and training for people setting up their own businesses;
- encouragement of new advisory services for small firms; and
- the Regional Enterprise Grants Scheme, designed to support small firms' investment and innovation projects.

Deregulation

In order to encourage enterprise, the Government is attempting to reduce the administrative and legislative burdens imposed on business, particularly small businesses, by central and local government. Under the Deregulation Initiative, all proposals for new regulation, whether of British or European Community origin, are examined for their impact on business. The costs to business are taken into account in deciding whether and how they should be imposed. Existing controls are also reviewed to identify any which may be unnecessary or outdated. There is a rolling review of existing regulation and an annual programme of work on deregulation, which covers all government departments and on which regular progress reports are published. The initiative is co-ordinated by the DTI's Deregulation Unit.

Privatisation

The Government believes that the best way to improve the performance of the nationalised industries in the long term is to expose them to market forces, through privatisation and the promotion of competition. Privatisation has also provided a major opportunity for the Government to widen and deepen share ownership by encouraging both employees and the general public to take a direct stake in British industry. Employees in privatised companies are normally given a preferential right to buy shares in the new companies.

Some 25 per cent of the adult population holds shares, compared with 7 per cent in 1979.

Since 1979 the Government has privatised 46 major businesses, with net proceeds of some £35,000 million. Planned privatisations include those of British Technology Group and the electricity supply industry in Northern Ireland. Work is also in hand on the planned privatisation of British Coal and on options for British Rail. The sale of part of the Government's residual shareholding in BT is planned for November 1991.

Taxation

The rates of corporate taxation have been progressively reduced. In the case of business plant and machinery, there is an annual allowance against profits for tax purposes of 25 per cent (on a reducing balance basis), beginning in the year in which expenditure occurs. There is an allowance for investment in industrial building of 4 per cent a year.

Special arrangements exist for short-life (often high-technology) assets. There are 100 per cent allowances for capital expenditure on scientific research, and, in designated Enterprise Zones, for expenditure on construction.

Business and Education

A well educated and well trained workforce is essential for economic growth, particularly at a time of intense international competition and rapid technological advance. The Government takes measures to ensure that education and training are broadly based and that people of all ages can acquire relevant knowledge and skills. It plans to introduce legislation to improve education and training for young people by, among other things, removing barriers between academic and vocational studies.

Industrial and commercial matters are being allotted a more prominent place in school and post-school curriculums. The introduction of the National Curriculum in England and Wales, with parallel developments in Scotland and Northern Ireland, is helping to achieve this in schools, and the Technical and Vocational Education Initiative contributes to this trend in schools and colleges. Businessmen and women contribute to curriculum development and

Table 12.4: Major Government Sales

	Year of sale	Net equity proceeds (£ million)
BAA	1987	1,181
British Gas	1986	5,293
British Petroleum	1979–87	6,648
British Steel	1988	2,425
British Telecom	1984	3,685
Britoil	1982–85	9,619
Cable and Wireless	1981–85	1,021
Rolls-Royce	1987	1,030
Water companies (England and Wales)	1989	3,454[a]
Regional electricity companies (England and Wales)	1990	5,182[ab]
Electricity generating companies (England and Wales)	1991	2,201[ab]
Scottish electricity companies	1991	2,918[ab]

Source: HM Treasury.
[a]Includes value of future instalment payments.
[b]Provisional estimates; the figures include the costs of the sales.

'enterprise activities' for schoolchildren and they have been enabled to take a larger part in the management of educational establishments.

The Government is setting up a network of 82 business-led Training and Enterprise Councils (TECs) in England and Wales and 22 Local Enterprise Companies (LECs) in Scotland (see p 230). Through their involvement in these bodies, employers will have a bigger role in the working of colleges and the careers service. Schoolchildren and teachers are given the opportunity to gain business experience. Colleges and universities co-operate with industry in joint ventures such as science parks and regional technology centres and in the provision of enterprise training to higher education students.

DESIGN, QUALITY, STANDARDS AND AWARDS

Design

The Design Council encourages industry and commerce to pay more attention to good design. It organises conferences to underline the importance of design and has encouraged design education at all levels, including business education.

As the DTI's main agent for design promotion, the Design Council has responsibility for linking design to innovation and technology to ensure that British products compete effectively in world markets, and for the design element of the Enterprise Initiative consultancy scheme. It is also responsible for the DTI's element of the 'Managing into the 90s' programme. Its activities include:

- offering advice on design matters and problems;

- organising conferences and seminars;

- providing help for design education; and

- producing publications and videos.

The Design Council operates the DTI's consultancy initiative on design, which offers firms employing up to 500 people 5 to 15 days of subsidised consultancy. The Council provides annual awards for consumer and

contract furniture, engineering products and components, computer software, medical equipment, and motor vehicles and accessories.

Quality and Standards

The Government is encouraging industry and commerce to pay attention to quality at all stages of design, production, marketing and delivery to customers.

Through its support for consultancy projects the Government is helping small and medium-sized firms to learn about and apply quality management techniques based on a national standard which meets international requirements. To increase customer confidence, companies are being encouraged to obtain assessment and registration to this standard. The competence and performance of organisations undertaking such certification are officially approved by the National Accreditation Council for Certification Bodies. Companies certified by accredited bodies are permitted to use the national 'crown and tick' accreditation mark.

The British Standards Institution (BSI), incorporated by Royal Charter, is the British member of the European and international standards organisations. It works with industry and government to produce standards which are of the required quality, relevant to the needs of the market, internationally respected, and suitable for public purchasing and regulatory purposes. Government support for BSI is directed particularly towards European and international standards work. Common standards will contribute to the aim of creating a single internal market in the European Community by the end of 1992. About 30 per cent of the 11,000 British Standards are now identical with European or international standards. The kitemark is BSI's registered certification trade mark. Resource, a joint venture between BSI and the Government, has been launched to promote collaboration with overseas countries in standards, quality assurance, metrology and testing.

Measurement Standards

The Department of Trade and Industry is responsible for policy relating to the National Measurement System. The National Physical Laboratory (NPL) is the main contractor for providing most of the physical measurement standards and associated calibration facilities necessary to ensure that measurements in Britain are made on a common basis and to the required accuracy. It maintains links with other national standards laboratories to ensure international compatibility in standards and measurement essential for overseas trade and technological co-operation. The NPL's National Measurement Accreditation Service (NAMAS) is the national accreditation service for calibration and testing laboratories. Its accredited laboratories offer calibration of scientific instruments and supply official certificates in many areas, primarily the physical, chemical and engineering fields.

The Laboratory of the Government Chemist (LGC) is the main contractor providing standards associated with chemical and analytical measurement. International agreement is based on the provision of appropriate standards and the utilisation of approved methods of analysis. These standards and approved methods also form the basis for NAMAS accreditation of laboratories carrying out analytical measurement.

The National Weights and Measures Laboratory administers legislation concerned with standards and measuring equipment for use in trade. New European Community directives on measuring instruments, which will replace national legislation by 1992, will ensure free circulation of approved equipment within the Community.

Industrial Awards

The Queen's Awards for Export and Technology recognise outstanding industrial performance in their respective fields. Awarded annually, they last for five years and are granted by the Queen on the advice of the Prime Minister, assisted by an Advisory Committee, which includes senior representatives from industry, commerce and the trade unions. Any self-contained 'industrial unit' in Britain is eligible to apply, regardless of size, if it meets the scheme's criteria.

Other awards include the Export Award for Smaller Businesses (for firms employing fewer than 200 people) and the MacRobert Award, the major award for engineering in Britain made by the Fellowship of Engineering for successful technological innovation.

REGIONAL INDUSTRIAL DEVELOPMENT

Regional industrial policy is designed to encourage enterprise and economic growth in all areas of Britain. In some areas, however, where additional help is needed, it is provided under the DTI's Enterprise Initiative. Help is focused on the Assisted Areas (Development Areas and Intermediate Areas), which cover 35 per cent of Britain's working population (see map).

The principal instruments are:

- regional selective assistance, available throughout the Assisted Areas, for investment projects undertaken by firms meeting certain criteria; and

- Regional Enterprise Grants, available in Development Areas and other areas covered by European Community schemes to support investment and innovation in firms with fewer than 25 employees.

England

The English Industrial Estates Corporation makes available industrial and commercial premises in certain parts of the Assisted Areas in England where private sector provision is insufficient.

The Rural Development Commission is responsible for advising the Government on issues affecting rural England and for promoting its economic and social development. It provides small factories and

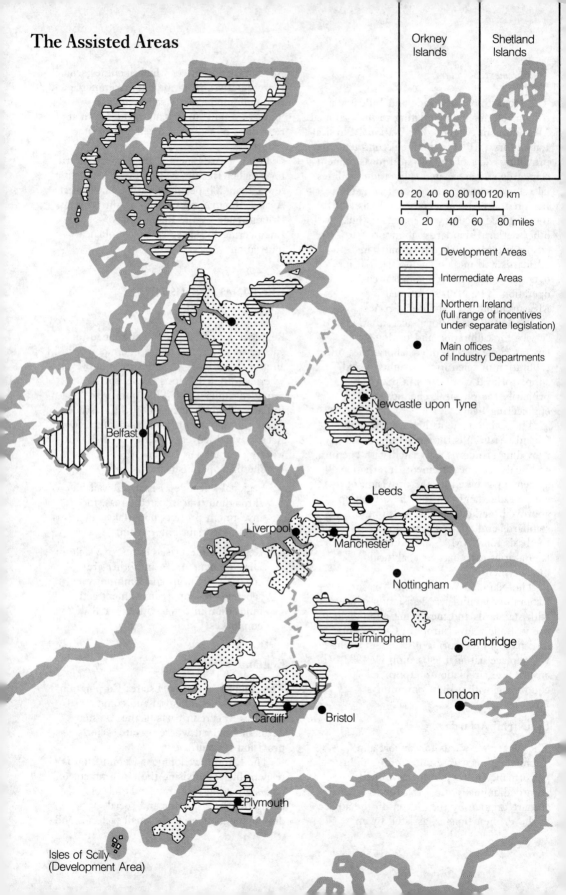

The Assisted Areas

Orkney Islands

Shetland Islands

0 20 40 60 80 100 120 km

0 20 40 60 80 miles

Development Areas

Intermediate Areas

Northern Ireland
(full range of incentives
under separate legislation)

● Main offices
of Industry Departments

Newcastle upon Tyne

Belfast

Leeds

Liverpool

Manchester

Nottingham

Birmingham

Cambridge

London

Cardiff

Bristol

Plymouth

Isles of Scilly
(Development Area)

workshops which are built and managed by English Estates, and administers a grant scheme for the conversion of redundant buildings to industrial or commercial premises. The Commission provides technical, management and financial advice; and training facilities and loans to small businesses. It also supports voluntary bodies in rural areas to encourage community activity and self-help and provides finance for small-scale rural housing and transport schemes. The Commission's resources are concentrated in the areas of greatest need, known as Rural Development Areas.

Scotland

Scottish Enterprise and Highlands and Islands Enterprise provide a wide range of support to industry and commerce, in lowland and highland Scotland respectively, operating mainly through a network of private-sector-led Local Enterprise Companies. They encourage investment in the development of skills throughout the workforce and invest directly in training, particularly for school-leavers and the long-term unemployed. Offering a range of advisory and training services to businesses to enhance the expertise of managers, the two bodies seek to ensure that the flow of sites, factories and investment funding for businesses in the private sector is adequate. Where necessary they contribute financially to such provision. They also remove obstacles to economic development through the treatment of derelict land and by contributing to tackling deficiencies in the physical environment and infrastructure of towns and cities. The development corporations of the five Scottish new towns contribute to the development of existing and new businesses and the attraction of companies to Scotland.

Wales

The Welsh Development Agency promotes industrial development in Wales by encouraging investment by overseas companies. It makes available equity and loan capital for industrial projects with maximum private sector participation. In addition, it provides government factories and has powers to assist small firms, promote new technology and undertake land reclamation and urban renewal.

The Development Board for Rural Wales provides factories, key worker housing and advice for small businesses. It has a general responsibility to promote the economic and social well-being of mid-Wales and a particular responsibility for the new town of Newtown, Powys.

Northern Ireland

The Industrial Development Board (IDB) offers incentives for the introduction and development of internationally competitive companies in the manufacturing and service sectors in Northern Ireland. IDB helps companies with marketing, exporting, product development and design, improved productivity and quality practices. Its full range of assistance is available to those companies with the greatest development potential and prospect of long-term competitive growth. Where appropriate, this assistance includes capital grants, revenue grants, loans and share capital investment. The IDB also offers stocks of land and industrial premises for purchase or lease.

Other forms of help include:

- training grants;
- exemption from local taxes for manufacturing premises; and
- grants to attract and retain good management.

Similar help is available to firms with fewer than 50 employees from the Local Enterprise Development Unit.

European Community Regional Policy and Aid

The European Community seeks to reduce disparities between its regions. The principal responsibility for helping less prosperous areas remains with national authorities, but the Community may complement schemes through aid from a number of sources.

European Regional Development Fund

The European Regional Development Fund, the largest of the European Community's structural funds, is intended to help redress the principal regional imbalances. Its budget for 1991–92 is £4,686 million, 10 per cent of which has been allocated to Britain.

European Investment Bank

European Community member states subscribe to the capital of the European Investment Bank, which aims to:

- facilitate development in less developed regions;
- modernise or convert undertakings; and
- help to create new economic activities.

The Bank also helps to finance projects of common interest to several member states. The Channel Tunnel is one such project currently being assisted in Britain.

Coal and Steel

The European Community makes loans and grants to encourage rational distribution of production and a high level of productivity in the coal and steel industries while safeguarding employment and avoiding unfair competition.

Schemes eligible for aid are coal industry projects, projects to create new activities in coal and steel areas, construction of housing for workers, allowances for redeployed workers, and research, including research of a social or medical nature.

Functioning and Regulation of Markets

While preferring to let markets operate as freely as possible, the Government recognises that action may be needed to ensure that markets are open and fair. The Government therefore seeks to control restrictive or anti-competitive practices.

Within the public sector the Government has taken a number of steps to increase competition, notably through privatisation (see p 225). The DTI's Deregulation Unit seeks to reduce regulations which inhibit competition, innovation or consumer choice (see p 225).

COMPETITION POLICY

The Government scrutinises and regulates monopolies, mergers, anti-competitive practices, restrictive trade practices, and resale price maintenance.

The Government is taking measures to increase competition in professional services by tackling restrictive practices. For instance, the opticians' monopoly on the dispensing of spectacles and the solicitors' monopoly on conveyancing have been ended. Certain professional groups (for example, accountants, solicitors, veterinary surgeons, stockbrokers, doctors, dentists and surveyors) have eased the restrictions on advertising by their members, and rules on fee scales have been made more liberal in a number of areas. Building societies are now allowed to offer a greater range of services. Legislation also provides greater competition in the provision of legal services (see p 110).

Monopolies

The Secretary of State for Trade and Industry and the Director General of Fair Trading can refer monopolies for investigation by the Monopolies and Mergers Commission, an independent body. Its members are drawn from a variety of backgrounds and include lawyers, economists, industrialists and trade unionists. The legislation defines a monopoly as a situation in which at least a quarter of a particular kind of product or service is supplied by a single person or a group of connected companies or by two or more people acting in a way which prevents, restricts, or distorts competition. The market definition of a monopoly can relate to all of Britain or part of it.

If the Commission finds that a monopoly operates against the public interest, the Secretary of State for Trade and Industry has powers to take action to remedy this. Alternatively the Director General may be

HOUSING

Derelict iron workers' cottages built in 1807 have been renovated at Cwmavon, Gwent, Wales.

Housing co-operatives are founded on the idea of tenant participation. Huyton Community Co-operative provided 34 bungalows for elderly people in Huyton, Knowsley, in Merseyside.

EDUCATION AND TRAINING

A sixth-form geography class at a London school for the physically handicapped. Britain is in the forefront of developments in the use of information technology in special education.

Trainee carpenters at a women's training workshop in London, funded jointly by the local authority and the European Social Fund.

Schoolchildren in the Coventry area take part in a pop group-in-residence scheme—their compositions will form part of their coursework.

A multi-cultural fashion design and garment manufacture course at Clarendon College, Nottingham.

RELIGION

The Right Reverend
George Carey at his
enthronement as
Archbishop of
Canterbury in April 1991.

The Central Mosque in
London's Regent's Park
is one of the largest
outside the Muslim
world.

asked to negotiate undertakings to remedy the adverse effects identified by the Commission.

Mergers

The Government believes that the market is, in most cases, the best judge of the advantages and disadvantages of mergers. The great majority of mergers which do not pose a threat to competition are therefore decided by the market. However, under the Fair Trading Act 1973, the Secretary of State for Trade and Industry can refer mergers for investigation by the Monopolies and Mergers Commission if they could lead to a significant reduction in competition or otherwise raise matters of public concern.

A merger is defined as occurring when two or more enterprises are brought under common ownership or control. A merger qualifies for investigation by the Commission where:

- an existing market share of 25 per cent or more is increased; or
- the total value of gross assets to be taken over exceeds £30 million.

After considering advice from the Director General of Fair Trading, the Secretary of State may refer a merger or proposed merger to the Commission. The primary criterion of the Government's reference policy is the possible effects on competition. To preserve competition in a free market, the Secretary of State takes account of the degree of state ownership of a prospective acquiring enterprise, whether British or foreign. If the Commission finds that a merger or proposed merger may be expected to operate against the public interest, the Secretary of State can prevent it by making a statutory order. Alternatively, the Director General may be asked to obtain suitable undertakings from the companies involved to remedy the adverse effects identified. If the merger has already taken place, the Secretary of State can take similar action to reverse it. There are special provisions for newspaper and water company mergers.

The Companies Act 1989 made changes to improve merger control procedure. This provided for:

- a voluntary procedure for pre-notification of proposed mergers which, for the majority of cases, permits prompt clearance;
- the acceptance of statutory undertakings by the parties concerned in order to obviate the need for a full investigation by the Monopolies and Mergers Commission in certain cases; and
- the temporary prohibition on reciprocal share dealing by the parties to a merger referred to the Commission.

The Secretary of State has powers to refer to the Commission any questions concerning the efficiency and costs of the service provided by, or the possible abuse of a monopoly situation by, certain bodies in the public sector. The results of inquiries are reported to Parliament.

Anti-competitive Practices

The Director General of Fair Trading can, with limited exceptions, investigate any business practice which appears anti-competitive. If the Director General concludes that a practice is anti-competitive, an undertaking may be sought from the business responsible for the practice; if this is not given, the matter may be referred to the Monopolies and Mergers Commission to establish whether it operates against the public interest. In the case of an adverse finding by the Commission, the Secretary of State has powers to take remedial action.

Restrictive Trade Practices

Certain kinds of commercial agreements containing restrictions on matters such as prices or conditions of sale have to be notified to the Director General of Fair Trading for registration. Failure to register an agreement within the required period means that the restrictions are void and unenforceable and the parties may be liable to legal proceedings.

Once an agreement has been registered, the Director General is under a general duty to refer it to the Restrictive Practices Court. In practice, however, the great majority of agreements never reach the Court because, for example, the parties elect to give up the restrictions rather than go to court, or the Secretary of State accepts the Director General's advice that the restrictions are not significant enough to warrant reference to the Court.

If an agreement goes to the Court, it must declare the restrictions contrary to the public interest unless the parties can satisfy the Court that this is not the case. Restrictions declared contrary to the public interest by the Court are void, the Court having the power to order the parties not to give effect to them.

In 1989 the Government published a White Paper which set out proposals to amend the existing legislation and make it more effective in the detection and investigation of restrictive agreements, particularly price-fixing and market-sharing cartels.

Retail Price Maintenance

It is now unlawful for suppliers to notify dealers of a minimum resale price for their goods or to make it a condition of supply that their goods must not be sold below a specified price. With some exceptions, it is also unlawful for suppliers to seek to impose minimum resale prices by withholding supplies of goods or discriminating in other ways. The Director General of Fair Trading, or anyone affected, can take proceedings against such actions in the civil courts.

Financial Services

Legislation has been passed to offer greater protection to investors. The Securities and Investments Board (see p 351) is empowered to set out general principles governing the conduct of investment business.

Under the Financial Services Act 1986, the Director General of Fair Trading is able to consider the effects on competition of the rules and practices of the various regulatory bodies operating under the Act. Where a significant or potentially significant effect has been identified, a report is made to the Secretary of State for Trade and Industry. If the Secretary of State agrees with this view and does not consider that the provisions are necessary for the protection of investors, he or she may refuse or revoke recognition of the organisation or require it to make alterations to its provisions.

European Community

European Community rules provide for free and fair competition in trade between member states. In most areas of economic activity the enforcement of these rules is primarily the responsibility of the European Commission, which has powers to investigate and terminate alleged infringements and to impose fines.

The Treaty of Rome prohibits agreements or concerted practices which affect trade between member states and which prevent, restrict or distort competition within the common market. Agreements meeting specified criteria may be exempted from this prohibition either individually or by category of agreement. The latter include certain agreements in exclusive distribution and exclusive purchasing, franchising, co-operative research and development, specialisation, patent licensing, and air services within the Community.

The Treaty also prohibits any abuse of a dominant position within the common market or a substantial part of it if this affects trade between member states.

In 1990 a Community regulation on the control of mergers came into force. Large mergers with a Community dimension, which are assessed by reference to turnover, are normally under the exclusive jurisdiction of the European Commission. The Commission can prohibit them if it considers that they create or strengthen a dominant position which would significantly impede effective competition within the common market.

Consumer Protection

The Government believes that consumers are best protected by open and competitive markets offering the widest range of choice in goods and services, backed by adequate information. There are, however, laws to ensure that consumers are adequately protected.

Legislation covers the sale of goods, the supply of goods and services, and the way that goods and services are described. The marking and accuracy of quantities are regulated by weights and measures legislation. The Food Safety Act 1990 contains measures to improve food safety and to protect consumers; these include tougher penalties and better enforcement powers. Another law provides for the control of medical products, and certain other substances and articles, through a system of licences and certificates. Under European Community legislation, it is a criminal offence to supply unsafe consumer products.

The Director General of Fair Trading can make recommendations to the Government for legislation to put a stop to trading practices that unfairly affect consumers' interests. He or she can also take action against persistent offenders of existing law. Under the Fair Trading Act 1973, the Director General has a duty to encourage trade associations to prepare and circulate to their members codes of practice aimed at raising trading standards.

The Director General is responsible for the operation of legislation regulating consumer credit and hire business and estate agency work. He or she also has certain responsibilities under legislation for controlling misleading advertisements.

The European Community's consumer programme covers a number of important activities, such as health and safety, protection of the consumer's economic interests, promotion of consumer education and strengthening the representation of consumers. The views of British consumer organisations are represented in Europe by the Consumers in the European Community Group (UK).

Consumer Advice and Information

Advice and information on consumer matters is provided by Citizens Advice Bureaux, the trading standards or consumer protection departments of local authorities, and, in some areas, by specialist Consumer Advice Centres.

The independent, non-statutory National Consumer Council (and the associated councils for Scotland and Wales), which receives government finance, presents the consumer's view to government, industry and others. The General Consumer Council for Northern Ireland has wide-ranging responsibilities in consumer protection and consumer affairs in general.

Consumer bodies for the rail and certain other nationalised industries and privatised industries investigate questions of concern to the consumer. Some trade associations in industry and commerce have established codes of practice. In addition, several private organisations work to further consumer interests. The largest is the Consumers' Association, funded by the subscriptions of around 900,000 members.

Company Law

All British companies are registered with the Registrar of Companies in Cardiff, Edinburgh or Belfast, depending on whether a company's registered office is in England or Wales, Scotland or Northern Ireland. Legislation deals with capital structure, the rights and duties of directors and members, and the preparation and filing of accounts. Most corporate businesses are 'limited liability' companies. The liability of members of a limited company is limited to contributing an amount related to their shareholding. In the case of unincorporated businesses, such as sole proprietorships or partnerships, individuals are personally liable for any business debts (except where a member of a partnership is a limited liability company).

Companies may be either public or private. A company must satisfy three conditions before it can be a public limited company (plc). It must:

- be limited by shares and have a share capital;
- state in its memorandum of association that it is to be a public limited company; and

- meet specified minimum capital requirements.

All other British companies are private companies and are generally prohibited from offering their shares to the public. Companies with a place of business in Britain, but which are incorporated overseas, are also required to register.

Laws relating to companies are designed to meet the need for proper regulation of business, secure open markets and create greater safeguards for those wishing to invest in companies or do business with them. They implement European Community directives dealing with company laws, and company and group accounts and their auditing. In addition, they permit the implementation of policy changes designed to reduce burdens on business, to strengthen rules on the disclosure of interest in shares, and to strengthen powers to investigate companies.

Insider dealing in shares is a criminal offence. Inspectors may be appointed to investigate possible insider dealing.

In England, Wales and Scotland there is a licensing procedure to ensure the professional competence, integrity and independence of people who act as trustees of bankrupt individuals, or as liquidators, receivers or administrators of insolvent companies.

The Serious Fraud Office investigates and prosecutes cases of fraud in England, Wales and Northern Ireland.

Industrial and Intellectual Property

Legislation exists to secure the rights of the originators of inventions, new industrial designs and trade marks. These matters are administered by the Patent Office, which includes the Design Registry and the Trade Marks Registry. The Patent Office is an executive agency of the DTI. Protection is also available under the European Patent Convention and the Patent Co-operation Treaty. Benefits may be claimed in other countries by virtue of the International Convention for the Protection of Industrial Property.

The Government supports innovation by protecting the ownership of ideas through patents, registered designs, trade marks and copyright. Recent measures include:

- a sharp increase in penalties for making and trading in pirate sound and film recordings (including video);
- the extension of copyright protection to owners of computer software;
- the widening of the law on trade marks to embrace services;
- the introduction of powers for customs authorities to prevent the entry of counterfeit goods;
- the introduction of a new form of protection for designs; and
- new laws to protect performers.

In 1990 the Government published a White Paper which proposed changes designed to modernise and simplify existing trade marks law, and to make trade mark registration and protection easier.

13 Manufacturing Industry

Manufacturing accounted for 22 per cent of gross domestic product (GDP) in 1990 and for about the same percentage of employment. Over 80 per cent of visible exports consisted of manufactured or semi-manufactured goods. Almost all manufacturing is carried out by private businesses.

Structure

The ten largest manufacturing concerns (by £million of turnover in the latest financial year) are BAT Industries (13,311), Imperial Chemical Industries (13,171), Grand Metropolitan (9,298), British Aerospace (9,085), Unilever (7,419), Hanson Trust (6,998), Ford Motor Company (6,732) General Electric Company (GEC) (5,878), British Steel (5,113) and Smithkline Beecham (4,897).

Growth

In 1990 manufacturing output was 18 per cent higher than in 1985 (see Table 13.2). Net manufacturing profitability, in terms of the rate of return on capital employed, rose steadily in the 1980s. Manufacturing employment in Great Britain fell from 7·1 million in 1979 to 5·8 million in 1982; in 1990 it was 4·9 million. Productivity rose until the late 1980s and has since stabilised.

Although there was a slight decline in manufacturing output in 1990, output in some industries, such as aerospace and other transport equipment, and paper, printing and publishing, continued to rise (see Table 13.2). In terms of constant (1985) prices, fixed investment in manufacturing reached £12,142 million in 1990. Total fixed capital expenditure in manufacturing at current prices was £14,800 million in 1990,

Table 13.1: Manufacturing—Size of Businesses by Turnover and Employment

Annual turnover (£'000)	Number of businesses[a] 1988–89	Employment size	Number of businesses[a] 1988–89	Employment[b]
23–50[c]	36,100	1–9	103,573	295,290
51–100	26,524	10–19	13,864	197,613
101–250	32,346	20–49	15,464	476,404
251–500	19,305	50–99	6,234	429,637
501–1,000	13,754	100–199	3,631	501,469
1,001–5,000	16,069	200–499	2,456	751,287
over 5,000	6,343	500–999	806	555,810
		1,000 and over	577	1,664,852
Total	150,441	Total	146,605	4,872,362

Source: *Size Analysis of United Kingdom Businesses 1990. Business Monitor PA 1003.*
[a] Defined as legal units, which includes companies, public corporations, partnerships, sole proprietors, general government and non-profit-making bodies.
[b] Employment figures are mainly derived from Central Statistical Office inquiries and from value added tax (VAT) sources and relate generally to 1988.
[c] The number of businesses analysed by turnover excludes 19,578 units with turnover up to £22,100, the threshold for filing compulsory VAT returns during the 12 months ended spring 1989.

Table 13.2: Indices of Manufacturing Output (1985 = 100)

	Share of output 1985 (weight per 1,000)	1984	1989	1990
Metal manufacturing	38	92·9	124·7	121·3
Other minerals and mineral products	50	100·4	120·1	113·4
Chemicals and man-made fibres	105	96·7	119·3	118·2
Other metal goods	55	104·4	113·5	110·9
Mechanical engineering	122	96·0	109·7	111·8
Electrical and instrument engineering	143	94·1	126·2	125·2
Motor vehicles and parts	55	93·5	125·3	121·0
Aerospace and other transport equipment	55	99·5	127·7	130·1
Food, drink and tobacco	130	100·4	105·6	106·1
Textiles	29	96·2	96·9	92·1
Clothing, footwear and leather	38	95·9	99·5	98·6
Paper, printing and publishing	101	97·8	132·0	133·8
Other manufacturing	80	99·1	132·6	132·4
Total	1,000	97·4	118·9	118·3

Source: Central Statistical Office.

comprising £11,699 million in plant and machinery, £2,233 million in new building work and £877 million in vehicles (investment by sector is shown in Table 13.3).

The underlying level of exports of manufactured goods has risen in volume terms. On the basis of overseas trade statistics, the index stood at 142·4 in 1990 (1985 = 100). Manufacturing exports rose to nearly £84,470 million in 1990.

Among the leading exports in 1990 were:

- machinery and other transport equipment (£42,200 million);

- chemicals (£13,200 million);

- consumer goods, including passenger cars (£12,900 million); and

- metal manufacturing and mineral products (£7,300 million).

Import volumes of manufactured goods rose strongly in the 1980s, with the index reaching 153·9 in 1990 (1985 = 100). Imports were valued at £98,190 million in 1990.

High-technology Industries

The high-technology manufacturing industries in Britain—electrical, electronic and instrument engineering, chemicals and aerospace—include industries with the highest levels of research and development spending in relation to their gross output. Most of the electrical and electronic industries—office machinery, electronic data-processing equipment, basic electrical equipment, telecommunications equipment, electric instruments and control systems, radio and electronic capital goods, and components—are included. Instrument engineering includes precision equipment for measuring and checking, plus medical, optical, photographic and filming equipment.

High-technology chemicals include specialised organics, plastics materials, synthetic resins, synthetic rubbers and pharmaceuticals. Aerospace production as a whole is defined as high-technology. All these industries have continued their growth, with levels of output, productivity and exports above the average for manufacturing.

Take-up of Advanced Technology

Computer technology is now commonplace in British production. Of 21,000 engineering sites, 55 per cent use computers for some aspect of manufacturing management. When sites with more than 50 employees are considered in isolation the proportion rises to over 80 per cent. Some 51 per cent of 12,300 design sites use computer aided design (CAD), while 25 per cent of 14,900 sites with machine tools use computer aided manufacturing (CAM). About 131,000 computers valued at £2,225 million were in use in the engineering sector in 1990 and firms reported that expenditure on computer hardware, software and services was planned to reach £935 million during 1991. Many British concerns are also making use of advanced materials, such as carbon fibre composites in the aerospace industry, new types of plastics in the automotive sector and high-fibre, cholesterol-free protein in food production.

In the traditional branches of heavy industry, further rationalisation continues to raise productivity. There has been a substantial increase in the use of robots in manufacturing industry since the mid-1980s; advanced robots function in conditions too hazardous for human operators, such as certain areas of mining, nuclear engineering and firefighting. The widespread adoption of Advanced Manufacturing Techniques (AMT) has also enabled the motor vehicle industry to become more efficient.

The Government provides financial assistance to companies and research organisations seeking to develop and improve the technologies needed by industry. It has, for example, made available resources to encourage and assist companies to take advantage of the emerging technologies of multi-vendor computer communications and exchange of data.

Sectors of Manufacturing

Relative sizes of the various branches of manufacturing are shown in the first columns of Tables 13.2 and 13.3. Table 13.3 also shows employment and investment levels in each sector. A more detailed description of the main branches is given below.

Table 13.3: Output, Employment and Investment in Manufacturing

	Net output (£ million) 1989	Employment[a] March 1991 ('000)	Gross domestic fixed capital formation (£ million) 1990
Metals, other minerals and mineral products	9,562	372	3,956
Chemicals and man-made fibres	10,869	318	
Other metal goods	5,512	300	
Mechanical engineering	11,774	717	
Electrical and instrument engineering	13,334	700	5,439
Motor vehicles and parts	6,198	233	
Other transport equipment and aerospace	5,739	244	
Food, drink and tobacco	12,224	511	
Textiles	2,805	468	
Clothing, footwear and leather	3,132		5,411
Paper, printing and publishing	10,860	467	
Other manufacturing	9,006	516	
Total	101,015	4,846	14,809

Sources: *United Kingdom National Accounts 1991 Edition; Employment Gazette.*
[a] Employees in employment in Great Britain.
Note: Differences between totals and the sums of their component parts are due to rounding.

Mineral and Metal Products

Iron and Steel Products

Britain is the world's tenth largest steel-producing nation. British producers delivered 16·1 million tonnes of finished steel in 1990, of which 60 per cent was sold on the home market and the remainder exported. The steel industry has operated a balance of payments surplus since 1983. The major areas of steel production are Wales, northern and eastern England, and Scotland, with substantial re-rolling and further processing in the Midlands.

British Steel plc is the fourth largest steel company in the Western world, producing 78 per cent of Britain's crude steel. British Steel's output is based on strip products, plate, heavy sections, tubes and stainless items. Its products are used principally in the packaging, construction, automotive, engineering, transport, metal goods and energy industries.

Forty other steel-producing firms, represented by the British Independent Steel Producers' Association, manufacture engineering and other special steels, wire rod, wire and wire products, reinforcements for use in the construction industry, and other more specialised goods. They are responsible for about 35 per cent by value of total British steel deliveries.

The industry has achieved significant advances in operational and cost efficiency over the past decade as a result of extensive rationalisation, investment in modern plant and continuous improvement of operating performance. Product ranges have been extended and product quality enhanced to meet home and export requirements. Exports have increased appreciably, particularly to the rest of the European Community.

Non-ferrous Metals

Output of non-ferrous metals and their alloys in 1990 included primary aluminium, of which nearly 300,000 tonnes were delivered, and secondary aluminium, of which over 120,000 tonnes were delivered. Britain produced over 120,000 tonnes of unwrought copper and over 450,000 tonnes of copper and copper alloy semi-manufactures. Primary metal production relies mainly on imported ores, concentrates and partially refined metal. Recycled metal plays an important part in raw material supply.

Britain is a major producer of specialised alloys for high-technology requirements in the aerospace, electronic, petrochemical, and nuclear and other fuel industries. Titanium and titanium alloys are used in aircraft production, power generation and North Sea oil production, and nickel alloys for aero-engines operating in high-temperature environments.

In recent years considerable progress has been made in the development of 'superplastic' alloys, which are more ductile and elastic than conventional alloys. Aluminium lithium, developed by British Alcan Aluminium, is ideal for use in aircraft, being lighter, stronger and stiffer than normal aluminium. Nearly half of the industry is situated in the Midlands and Wales.

Table 13.4: Mineral and Metal Products

	Exports (£ million) 1990	Imports (£ million) 1990
Metal manufacturing	5,589	6,145
of which: iron and steel products	2,980	2,591
non-ferrous metals	2,608	3,555
Non-metallic mineral products	1,510	1,602
of which: glass and glassware	394	654
ceramic and heat-resistant goods	555	366

Ceramics

The ceramics industry manufactures clay products, including domestic pottery, sanitaryware and tiles, and clay pipes for the building trade. Total sales of ceramic goods in 1990 were £1,189 million. Domestic pottery, which includes the manufacture of china, earthenware and stoneware, accounted for over 22 per cent of the industry's output. Tableware is produced in Stoke-on-Trent, and Britain is the world's leading manufacturer and major exporter of fine bone china.

Research is being conducted into ceramics for use in housebuilding and diesel and jet engines. Important industrial ceramics invented in Britain include silicon carbides developed by the United Kingdom Atomic Energy Authority and sialons developed at the University of Newcastle upon Tyne.

Other Mineral Products

Glass-reinforced cement composites for the construction industry were invented in Britain in the early 1970s and are manufactured under licence in over 40 countries.

Flat glass is manufactured through the float glass process, which was developed by Pilkington Brothers and licensed to glassmakers throughout the world. Pilkington has also produced an energy-saving window glass which reflects room heat without impairing visibility. Export sales of flat glass principal products amounted to £394 million in 1990.

Britain is the world's biggest exporter of china clay (kaolin). In 1990 some 2·5 million tonnes, valued at £183 million, were sold overseas. The main company involved is English China Clays.

Chemicals and Synthetic Fibres

Britain's chemicals industry is the third largest in Western Europe and the fifth largest in the Western world. Nearly half of its production of principal products is exported; in 1990 it had a trade surplus of more than £2,300 million. The most rapid growth in recent years has been in speciality chemicals, especially pharmaceuticals, pesticides and cosmetics. Imperial Chemical Industries (ICI) accounts for a substantial part of the industry's production and is the fourth largest chemicals company in the world. Traditionally Britain has been a major producer of basic industrial chemicals, such as inorganic and basic organic chemicals, plastics and fertilisers. Sales of principal fertiliser products reached £1,136 million in 1990.

Chemicals

Sales of the principal products of organic chemicals amounted to £6,439 million in 1990 and those of miscellaneous chemicals for industrial use were £2,782 million; the surplus on overseas trade in the latter sector was nearly £545 million.

A large proportion of world research and development in agrochemicals is conducted in Britain. Notable recent British discoveries include pyrethroid insecticides, ICI's diquat and paraquat herbicides, systemic fungicides and aphicides, genetically engineered microbial pesticides and methods of encouraging natural parasites against common pests in horticulture.

Exports of cosmetics, toiletries and perfumery in 1990 were £572 million, compared with imports of £355 million. Total sales amounted to £2,380 million.

Much of inorganic chemicals production consists of relatively simple bulk chemicals, such as sulphuric acid and metallic and non-metallic oxides, serving as basic materials for industry. The most important products sold in the organic chemicals range (by weight) are ethylene (1·1 million tonnes produced in 1990), benzene (489,000 tonnes) and propylene (464,000 tonnes). Exports of organic chemicals amounted to £715 million.

Plastics

About one-third of semi-manufactured plastics production is exported. Expansion in recent years has mainly been in thermoplastic materials, of which the most important are polyethylene, polyvinyl chloride, polystyrene

Table 13.5: Chemicals and Synthetic Fibres

	Exports (£ million) 1990	Imports (£ million) 1990
Chemicals and synthetic fibres	14,089	11,432
of which: basic industrial chemicals	6,481	6,448
specialised industrial products	2,275	1,384
pharmaceuticals	2,397	1,224
soap and toilet preparations	788	473

and polypropylene. Total sales of plastics packaging products, valued at £2,240 million in 1990, were largely accounted for by the home market. With up to three times the strength but only 20 per cent of the weight of steel, these plastics are used in aircraft and vehicle manufacture. ICI has produced the world's first biodegradable thermoplastic, Biopol, which is used as a slow release agent for drugs and herbicides and for making non-polluting bottles and films. Synthetic rubbers in large-scale production include butadiene-based neoprene for tyres, high-styrene for shoe soles and flooring, and oil-resistant nitrile rubbers. Plastics are fast replacing traditional packaging materials such as paper, tin and glass.

ICI is the world's largest paint manufacturer. Specialised products include new ranges of synthetic resins and pigments, powder coatings, non-drip and quick-drying paints and paints needing only one top coat. Two recent innovations have been solid emulsion paint and a temporary water-based finish which can be removed easily by chemical treatment, for vehicle bodies and road markings. Sales of principal paint and varnish products were £1,870 million in 1990.

Pharmaceuticals

The pharmaceutical industry in Britain includes some of the world's largest multinational research-intensive manufacturers, as well as middle-sized and smaller specialist companies, with a total gross output in 1990 of around £6,700 million. Pharmaceutical exports were valued

at £2,258 million; the industry's trade surplus of £955 million was the second largest of all manufacturing sectors. Employing over 70,000 people directly, it supports employment for 250,000 others in related activities.

The pharmaceutical industry invested more than £1,000 million in research and development in 1990. This sum amounts to more than 14 per cent of British manufacturing industry's research and development, representing about 8 per cent of total world expenditure on medicines research. Progress in pharmaceutical research has helped to reduce dramatically the impact of diseases such as polio, tuberculosis, diphtheria and measles.

British firms make four of the world's ten best-selling medicines.

Glaxo's ulcer treatment Zantac and ICI's beta-blocker Tenormin, for treating high blood pressure, are the first and sixth best-selling medicines in the world. The United States subsidiary of Britain's Wellcome Foundation developed Retrovir (also called Zidovudine), the first treatment for HIV infection to gain government approval, as well as Zovirax, the first routine treatment for the herpes group of viruses. Other recent major developments pioneered in Britain are semi-synthetic penicillins and cephalosporins, both powerful antibiotics, and new treatments for asthma, arthritis and coronary heart disease.

In biotechnology, Britain has made major advances in the development of human insulin, genetically-engineered vaccines and the production of antibiotics by fermentation. The British company Celltech was the first licensed by the United States Food and Drug Administration for the large-scale production of monoclonal antibodies, proteins which can seek out a particular substance. They are used to diagnose diseases, identify different blood types and can be used in the treatment of a range of conditions, including cancer.

Britain leads in the development of molecular graphics, which contribute to the rational design of new and improved medicines through a computer-aided technique for analysing the structures of complicated organic molecules on a visual display unit.

Fibres

The main types of synthetic fibre are still those first developed: regenerated cellulosic fibres such as viscose, and the major synthetic fibres such as nylon polyamide, polyester and acrylics. Extensive research continues to produce a wide variety of innovative products with characteristics designed to meet market needs, such as antistatic and flame-retardant fibres. More specialist products include the aramids (with very high thermal stability and strength), elastanes (giving very high stretch and recovery) and melded fabrics (produced without the need for knitting or weaving). Special acrylic fibre (SAF) is now being made for use in carbon fibre manufacturing.

Mechanical Engineering and Metal Goods

Exports of mechanical machinery amounted to about 14 per cent of all visible exports in 1990. Output includes pressure vessels, heat exchangers and storage tanks for chemical and oil-refining (process) plant, steam-raising boilers (including those of high capacity for power stations), nuclear reactors, water and sewage treatment plant, and fabricated steelwork for bridges, buildings and industrial installations.

Britain is among the Western world's largest producers of tractors, which make up over three-quarters of the country's total output of agricultural equipment. Sales of the principal products of the tractor industry were more than £1,300 million in 1990, of which about £1,057 million was accounted for by overseas sales. Recent technical innovations include computer-controlled tractors, a highly efficient pesticide sprayer and combined mower/conditioners that significantly reduce the drying time for grass. Much of the new machinery is designed for use in a variety of conditions to meet the needs of overseas farmers. The Royal International Agricultural Exhibition, held annually near Coventry, has a specialised tropical machinery centre, where demonstrations of such machinery are given.

With almost all of Britain's machine tools purchased by the engineering,

Table 13.6: Mechanical Engineering and Metal Goods

	Exports (£ million) 1990	Imports (£ million) 1990
Mechanical engineering	11,838	10,262
of which: industrial plant and steelwork	665	505
agricultural machinery and tractors	1,226	664
machine tools	951	1,107
machinery for process industries and non-metallic materials working	2,305	2,287
mining, construction and mechanical handling equipment	2,174	2,554
Other metal goods	2,909	2,414

vehicles and metal goods industries, the demand for computerised, numerically-controlled machine tools and flexible manufacturing systems has grown.

Britain is the world's seventh largest producer of machine tools. Total sales of metal-working machine tools reached £960 million in 1990, of which some 50 per cent were exports. British technology leads in probes, sensors, co-ordinate measuring devices, laser melting and the installation of flexible manufacturing systems. Computer numerical-controlled machines now account for 40 per cent of output.

In 1990 most sales of textile machinery were to export markets. Recent British innovations include computerised colour matching and weave simulation, friction spinning, high-speed computer-controlled knitting machines and electronic jacquard attachments for weaving looms.

Overseas sales of mining machinery and tunnelling equipment are substantial. J.C. Bamford is the world's leading manufacturer of backhoe loaders and telescopic handlers, of which 65 per cent are exported. Britain's mining equipment industry leads in the production of coal-cutting and road-heading (shearing) equipment, hydraulic roof supports, conveying equipment, flameproof transformers, switchgear, and subsurface transport equipment and control systems.

The mechanical handling equipment industry produces cranes and transporters, lifting devices, escalators, conveyors, powered industrial trucks and air bridges, as well as electronically controlled and automatic handling systems. Britain is also a major producer of industrial engines, pumps, valves and compressors, and of pneumatic and hydraulic equipment.

Despite an overall decline in the castings industry, some foundries have been investing in new melting, moulding and quality control equipment. Cosworth Engineering, for example, has developed a high-quality aluminium casting process to produce cylinder heads for Mercedes-Benz and Ford cars.

Electrical, Electronic and Instrument Engineering

Output by this group of industries continues to grow, with sales of the principal products of basic electrical equipment reaching £1,825 million in 1990. Sales of electronic data-processing equipment rose by more than half between 1985 and 1990, reaching £7,719 million.

Computers

This sector produces an extensive range of systems, central processors and peripheral equipment, from large computers for large-scale data-processing and scientific work to mini- and microcomputers for control and automation systems and for home, educational and office use. Total billings by companies for computer services rose by £500 million compared with 1989 to reach £3,560 million in 1990. The largest components of these billings were for software and related services, worth £1,468 million, and for bureau services, valued at £813 million. Total sales of home computers amounted to £245 million in 1990. Amstrad is Britain's largest personal computer manufacturer, whose products are aimed at the mass market.

Sales of microcomputers other than home computers reached £750 million in 1990, while total export sales of data-processing equipment amounted to £5,554 million. Several leading overseas manufacturers of data-processing equipment—for example, IBM, Unisys, Compaq and Seiko—have established manufacturing plants in Britain. Other companies have concentrated on developing new products for specialised markets. For example, the transputer, produced by Inmos, is effectively a computer on a single chip, which can be combined with hundreds of others in parallel to form a machine as powerful as existing 'supercomputers' but at less than a quarter of their price. British firms and research organisations, with government support, are also heavily involved in the development and application of the new family of 'three-five' semiconductor materials, such as gallium

Table 13.7: Electrical and Electronic Engineering

	Exports (£ million) 1990	Imports (£ million) 1990
Data-processing equipment	5,554	6,877
Basic electrical equipment	1,807	1,593
Communications equipment	478	643
Radio and electronic capital goods	1,695	1,462
Electronic components	2,801	3,687
Consumer electrical and electronic goods	1,550	2,527

arsenide, which are already used in a number of microwave devices and which will ultimately enable much faster computers to be produced.

Communications Equipment

Britain's main communications products are switching and transmission equipment, telephones and terminals, with BT (formerly British Telecom) the main customer for communications network equipment. Mercury Communications is licensed to compete with BT in the provision of network services, while the market for terminals and telephones has been fully liberalised. Innovative work is being stimulated by the expansion of cable television and the growth in value added network services. There was rapid expansion in the market for cellular telephones in the second half of the 1980s, with sales peaking in 1989 at £144 million, although they declined in 1990 to £127 million.

Transmission equipment and cables for telecommunications and information networks include submarine and high-specification data-carrying cables. Supported by a technically advanced cable industry, BT has led in the development of optical fibre communications systems and has paved the way for simpler and cheaper optical cables by laying the first non-repeatered cable over 100 km (62 miles) long, and by developing the first all-optical repeater. More than half of the world's undersea communications cables have been made and laid by STC Submarine Systems, which, with its United States and French partners, completed the laying of the

first transatlantic optical fibre cable, TAT 8, in 1988. Britain also has a world lead in the transmission of computerised data along telephone lines for reproduction on television screens. Export sales of telegraph and telephone apparatus and equipment by British firms almost doubled between 1985 (£242 million) and 1990 (£478 million).

Another expanding sector of the industry manufactures radio communications equipment, radar, radio and sonar navigational aids for ships and aircraft, thermal imaging systems, alarms and signalling equipment, public broadcasting equipment and other capital goods. Radar was invented in Britain and British firms are still in the forefront of technical advances. Racal Avionics' X-band radar can distinguish different types of aircraft flying at very low altitude and is in use at airports in several countries. Cable and Wireless's submarine cable-laying robot 'CIRRUS' can work at depths of up to 1 km (3,280 ft) controlled entirely by a computer on its mother ship.

Other Electronic Equipment

A range of electronic measurement and test equipment is made in Britain, as well as analytical instruments. Production of process control equipment is expanding, as is the manufacture of numerical control and indication equipment for use in machine tools. British companies lead in several types of advanced electronic medical equipment, such as magnetic resonance imaging (MRI), a technique which enables internal examination of large body areas without recourse to surgery or potentially harmful radiation.

British companies such as GEC and Oxford Instruments also produce other advanced electronic medical equipment, including ultrasound scanners, electromyography systems and patient monitoring systems for intensive and coronary care and other uses.

The indigenous electronics components industry is supplemented by subsidiaries of several large overseas companies. An area of very rapid change in which Britain is particularly strong is the manufacture of advanced components, such as integrated circuits.

Electrical Engineering and Appliances

Making extensive use of advanced technologies, the electrical engineering industry manufactures products for the electricity supply sector, including power plant, cable transformers and switchgear, as well as lighting, plugs and sockets. The domestic electrical appliance sector is dominated by a few large firms. The major electronic consumer goods produced are radio and television sets, and high-fidelity audio and video equipment. In the audio field British manufacturers have a reputation for high-quality goods but are less strong in the mass market.

The instrument engineering industry produces measuring, photographic, cinematographic and reprographic equipment; watches, clocks and other timing devices; and medical and surgical instruments. Its precision instrument and medical branches both earn significant and growing export surpluses, but the sector as a whole is contracting.

Motor Vehicles and Other Transport Equipment (excluding Aerospace)

A total of 2,302,400 new cars and commercial vehicles were sold in 1990. Car output is dominated by five groups, accounting for 99 per cent of the total: Rover, Ford (including Jaguar), Vauxhall, Peugeot-Talbot and Nissan. The remainder is in the hands of smaller, specialist producers such as Rolls-Royce, whose cars are renowned for their quality and durability.

Despite falling domestic demand, British car manufacturers have been able to maintain production levels due to substantial exports over the past year. Recent inward investment projects by Nissan, Honda and Toyota will lead to increased production and employment in the sector by the mid-1990s.

Ranked as one of the most important industries in Britain, the motor components industry consists of over 2,000 companies employing 120,000 people. A period of major change has accompanied the arrival of the three major Japanese assemblers. The established motor manufacturers are undergoing restructuring to respond to this new situation. The production of motor cycles is set to rise with the return of Triumph to the market. Sales of pedal cycles came to £2·25 million in 1990.

Shipbuilding and Marine Engineering

Britain has a long tradition of shipbuilding and remains active in the construction, conversion and repair of merchant vessels, warships and offshore structures. The

Table 13.8: Motor Vehicles and Other Transport Equipment

	Exports (£ million) 1990	Imports (£ million) 1990
Motor vehicles (including bodies, trailers, caravans and engines)	4,940	8,895
Motor vehicle parts	3,105	4,077
Other transport equipment	7,872	6,373

largest sector is the building of warships. As well as meeting all the needs of the Royal Navy, the warship yards build and convert ships for overseas governments.

British yards build some of the most sophisticated merchant vessels in the world, including gas carriers, cross-Channel superferries and offshore support and research vessels, as well as more traditional ships and craft for the leisure market. The Shipbuilders and Ship Repairers Association estimates that orders taken by British merchant shipbuilders for the construction of vessels were around £120 million in 1990.

The shipbuilding industry is supplemented by ship-repairers which modernise and convert vessels. The British marine equipment industry offers a complete range of products, from engines to sophisticated navigational systems.

More than two decades of oil exploitation in the North Sea have generated a major offshore industry. Shipbuilders and fabricators build fixed platforms and semi-submersible units for drilling, production and emergency/maintenance support, drill ships, jack-up rigs, modules and offshore loading systems. Several thousand manufacturing and service industry firms supply goods and services, including consultancy, design, project management, and research and development to the offshore industry.

Aerospace

Britain's aerospace industry is the third largest in the world, after those of the United States and the Soviet Union. With more than 300 companies involved, it had a turnover in 1990 of around £11,000 million. Exports totalled £8,167 million and contributed £1,664 million in net terms to the balance of payments.

As the largest British exporter of manufactured goods, British Aerospace (BAe) produces both civil and military aircraft. Civil aircraft include the 146 family of regional quiet-jet airliners, the 64-seat ATP (advanced turboprop) airliner, the 19/29-seat Jetstream 31 and 41 commuterliners, and the 125 (the world's best-selling middle-sized

business jet). BAe owns a 20 per cent share of the European consortium Airbus Industrie, which has sold over 1,400 aircraft. BAe designs and supplies the wings for all Airbus airliners. Together with other international aerospace organisations, BAe is studying the feasibility of developing a successor to the Concorde supersonic airliner. Steady growth in demand for air travel is expected in the 1990s following further consolidation of the commercial aerospace industry, with British parts-makers increasing business with the commercial sector to offset reductions in defence orders.

The military production of BAe includes the Harrier, a unique vertical/short take-off and landing (V/STOL) military combat aircraft. Sea Harriers are being supplied to the Royal Navy and, in association with McDonnell Douglas in the United States, BAe is building the improved Harrier II. BAe also produces the Hawk fast-jet trainer and, with McDonnell Douglas, the Goshawk carrier jet trainer. BAe has a 33 per cent share in the development of the next-generation European Fighter Aircraft (EFA)—a co-operative venture between Britain, Germany, Italy and Spain. BAe is a major supplier of tactical guided weapon systems.

Short Brothers of Belfast produces a range of aerospace products, including the Shorts 330 and 360 commuter airliners and the military freighter version of the 330 known as the Sherpa. It also produces the Tucano, a turboprop basic military trainer which is in use with the Royal Air Force. The company, which was privatised in 1989, also produces guided missiles and airframe components for overseas aerospace manufacturers.

In addition to its production of aerospace equipment, Westland manufactures the Sea King and Lynx military helicopters. In collaboration with Agusta of Italy, Westland is developing the multi-role EH101 three-engine helicopter, which will be delivered to the Royal Navy and the Italian Navy by the mid-1990s. The company is also a leading manufacturer of composite helicopter blades.

Rolls-Royce is one of the three major manufacturers of aero-engines in the

Western world, with a turnover in 1990 of some £3,670 million and an order book at the end of 1990 of £5,700 million. The company's civil engine group produces engines for airliners and executive and corporate jets. Rolls-Royce RB211-535 engines have been selected by 75 per cent of airlines using Boeing 757 airliners. The RB211-524G and H engines, which were launched in 1986 with orders from Cathay Pacific and British Airways to power Boeing 747-400 airliners, entered service in 1989. The company's new Tay turbofan engines are in service with the Gulfstream IV and Fokker 100 airliners, and are available as replacement engines for older aircraft.

Rolls-Royce's latest and most powerful engine, the Trent, is being built for the new generation of wide-body airliners.

Rolls-Royce is a partner in the five-nation International Aero Engine consortium which produces the V2500 aero-engine, now in service on some versions of the Airbus Industrie A320 airliner.

The military engine group of Rolls-Royce produces engines for military aircraft and helicopters. Rolls-Royce is a partner in Eurojet, a consortium from four countries formed to develop the EJ200 for the Eurofighter's EFA. It also produces gas turbines for power generation and for oil and gas pumping, gas turbine power for 25 of the world's navies, and propulsion systems for the Royal Navy's nuclear-powered submarines.

Aviation equipment manufacturers provide essential systems for engines and aircraft, including engine and flight controls, electrical generation, mechanical and hydraulic power systems, cabin furnishings, flight-deck control and information displays.

British firms have made important advances in developing ejector seats, firefighting equipment and flight simulators, as well as fly-by-wire and fly-by-light technology, where control surfaces are moved by means of automatic electronic signalling and fibreoptics respectively, rather than by mechanical means. Britain's aerospace companies provide radar and air traffic control equipment and ground power supplies to airports and airlines worldwide.

Satellite Equipment

Over 400 companies in Britain are involved in space activities. The British industry's major strength is in the manufacture of satellites. British Aerospace Space Communications Systems is Europe's largest—and the world's third largest—producer of communications satellites. It was prime contractor for all such satellites built for the European Space Agency (ESA), as well as the Marecs and Inmarsat-2 series of maritime communications satellites, and the Skynet and NATO IV military communications satellites. BAe was also prime contractor for Giotto, the scientific satellite that intercepted Halley's Comet. BAe built 18 payload pallets for the United States Space Shuttle and supplies SPELDA, a structure that enables the ESA's Ariane 4 launcher to carry two spacecraft on the same mission. BAe has set up the National Remote Sensing Centre to process and supply commercial data derived from Earth observation satellites.

Marconi Space Systems has acted as principal contractor on many telecommunications satellite payloads, including those for the ESA's Olympus satellite. GEC Ferranti Defence Systems produces the inertial guidance system for the

Table 13.9: Aerospace

	Exports (£ million) 1990	Imports (£ million) 1990
Aircraft and parts	5,010	4,140
Aero-engines and parts	2,490	1,650
Aerospace equipment	800	750

European Ariane launcher and Pilkington Space Technology is the world's leading producer of solar cell coverglasses for satellites.

The trade association for the industry is the Society of British Aerospace Companies, which organises the Farnborough international air show every two years.

Food, Drink and Tobacco

Britain has a large and sophisticated food processing industry, which has accounted for a growing proportion of total domestic food supply in recent decades. The industry's interests are advanced by Food From Britain, a body with a wide remit to improve the marketing of British food and agricultural produce both domestically and overseas.

Convenience foods (particularly frozen foods, annual sales of which now stand at approximately £2,500 million), yoghurts, other dairy desserts and instant snacks have formed the fastest-growing sector of the food market in recent years. The market in health and slimming foods continues to grow.

Production of milk was 14,766 million litres in 1990, of which 6,954 million litres was sold as liquid milk. Nearly seven out of ten households in Britain receive milk through a doorstep delivery system employing about 35,000 people driving electric vehicles. Domestic milk consumption per head—1·9 litres (3·42 pints) per week in 1990—is among the highest in the world. Consumption of skimmed and semi-skimmed milk is rising as people seek to reduce the fat content in their diet.

The main milk products are butter (138,000 tonnes produced in 1990), cheese (312,000 tonnes), condensed milk (204,000 tonnes) and dried whole and skimmed milk (236,000 tonnes). The British dairy industry accounted for 65 per cent of new butter supplies to the domestic market in 1990 and 66 per cent of new cheese supplies. Butter exports in 1990 came to 38,423 tonnes and cheese exports 40,447 tonnes. The other main exports are skimmed and whole milk powder (103,656 and 54,655 tonnes).

About 80 per cent of bread is manufactured in large mechanised bakeries using the British 'Chorleywood' process, which is also used in other countries. After years of decline, overall consumption of bread stabilised in the 1980s. This reflected increased demand for wholemeal varieties at the expense of the standard sliced white loaf, although this has slowed down with the introduction of soft-grained white bread. Biscuit exports were valued at £110 million in 1990.

Of prime importance among the alcoholic drinks produced in Britain is Scotch whisky. There are 110 distilleries in Scotland, where the best known brands of blended Scotch whisky are made from the products of malt and grain whisky distilleries. Some 84 per

Table 13.10: Food, Drink and Tobacco

	Exports (£ million) 1990	Imports (£ million) 1990
Food manufacturing	3,073	7,782
of which: meat products	620	1,959
milk and milk products	428	769
flour-based products	224	165
sugar and confectionery	96	515
cocoa and chocolate goods	386	436
animal feedstuffs	213	180
Drinks	2,232	1,736
of which: brewing and malting	166	229
distilling and compounding	1,938	274
soft drinks	83	399
Tobacco	640	126

cent of all Scotch whisky produced is exported. The value of whisky exports was over £1,700 million in 1990, Europe taking 30 per cent and the United States taking nearly 20 per cent by volume.

The brewing and malting industry has five major brewery groups whose products are sold nationally. One of the main raw materials in beer is malt. British malt, which is made almost entirely from home-grown barley, is used by brewers throughout the world. Demand for traditional cask-conditioned ales, which had been falling, has now stabilised, while lager now accounts for just over half of all beer sales. In 1990 purchases of beer in Britain were £11,743 million, nearly 3·5 per cent of total consumers' expenditure.

Several companies produce up to 20 brands of soft drinks, which are marketed on a national scale. Purchases of soft drink products reached £3,300 million in 1990, an increase of 95 per cent compared with 1985.

The British tobacco industry manufactures 99 per cent of cigarettes and tobacco goods sold in Britain. Almost all of domestic output is provided by three major manufacturers (Imperial Tobacco, Gallaher and Carreras Rothmans). The industry specialises in the production of high-quality cigarettes made from flue-cured tobacco and achieves significant exports, with the participation of BAT Industries. Countries in Europe, the Middle East and Africa are important markets.

Textiles, Footwear, Clothing and Leather

These products make a substantial contribution to the British economy in terms of employment, exports and turnover. Together, they employ some 480,000 people, equal to around 10 per cent of manufacturing employment. For textiles, there is a high degree of regional concentration. Particularly important areas are the North West, West Yorkshire (mainly wool), the East Midlands (knitwear), Scotland and Northern Ireland. Most of the clothing industry is widely scattered throughout the country and does not represent a large proportion of employment in any region, although there are significant concentrations in inner city areas of cities such as Manchester, Leicester, Leeds and London. The industries' main products are yarn, woven and knitted fabrics, apparel, industrial and household textiles, and carpets based mainly on wool, cotton and synthetic fibres.

The textile and clothing industry has around 15,000 firms, comprising a few large multi-process companies and including two of the world's largest—Coats Viyella and Courtaulds Textiles—as well as a large number of small and medium-sized firms. Increased investment in new machinery and enhanced attention to design, training and marketing have helped the industry to raise its competitiveness. A new export record for textiles and clothing of £4,500 million was

Table 13.11: Textiles, Footwear, Clothing and Leather

	Exports (£ million) 1990	Imports (£ million) 1990
Textile industry	2,483	4,516
of which: woollen and worsted industry	578	379
cotton and silk industry	658	1,957
hosiery and other knitwear	620	1,215
carpets, rugs and matting	221	472
Footwear	268	1,166
Clothing, hats and gloves	1,154	2,775
Made-up textiles	156	256
Leather and leather goods	394	578

achieved in 1990. The Multi-Fibre Arrangement (MFA) of the General Agreement on Tariffs and Trade (GATT) allows a measure of restraint on imports of textiles and clothing from low-cost countries into the European Community.

Britain's wool textile industry is one of the largest in the world, with two main branches making woollen and worsted. In the past few years the industry's export earnings have been consistently high. Synthetic fibre is sometimes blended with wool. West Yorkshire is the main producing area, but Scotland is also famous as a specialised producer of high-quality yarn and cloth. Large quantities of raw wool are scoured and cleaned in Britain in preparation for spinning. British mills also process the bulk of rare fibres such as cashmere. Sales of the principal products of the woollen and worsted industry amounted to £1,600 million in 1990, with exports amounting to £589 million of this total.

Low-cost competition has cut progressively into British markets for cotton and allied products, but output in 1990 still exceeded £1,000 million. Production includes yarn and fabrics of cotton, spun synthetic fibres and cotton-synthetic mixes, with large-scale dyeing and printing of cotton and synthetic fibre fabric. The linen industry is centred in Northern Ireland.

Over half the value of carpet and rug output is made up of tufted carpets. Woven carpets, mainly Axminster, account for most of the remaining sales. There is a higher wool content in woven types, although in these, too, considerable use is being made of synthetic fibres. The high quality and variety of design make Britain one of the world's leading producers of woven carpets. Industrial textiles account for an increasing proportion of the industry's output, covering products such as conveyor belting and geotextiles used in civil engineering projects. Many of these are non-woven, made of fibres assembled using advanced techniques.

Synthetic polypropylene yarn is used in the manufacture of carpet backing and ropes, and woven into fabrics for a wide range of applications in the packaging, upholstery, building and motor vehicle industries.

The clothing industry is labour intensive, involving about 9,000 companies. While a wide range of clothing is imported from the rest of Europe and Asia, British industry supplies almost two-thirds of domestic demand. Exports have risen since the British fashion designer industry became prominent during the 1980s and traditional British tailoring enables clothing companies such as Burberry's to compete overseas. The hosiery and knitwear industry comprises about 1,600 small to medium-sized companies, mainly in the East Midlands and Scotland. The footwear manufacturing industry is made up predominantly of small companies, increasingly under pressure from imports, which accounted for about 87 per cent of total sales in 1990.

Other Manufacturing

Nearly 400 companies in the wooden furniture industry supply domestic, contract and institutional markets. Domestic production of wood for industrial use has been steadily increasing and deliveries in 1990 amounted to 6·6 million cubic metres (233 million cubic feet). There were 112 paper and board mills employing 131,000 people in 1990. Among the largest British groups are Wiggins Teape, St Regis and Davidsons. Overseas paper and board groups with manufacturing investments in Britain include Georgia Pacific, Kimberly Clark, Consolidated Bathurst, the Scott Corporation and United Paper Mills of Finland.

There has been a significant trend towards waste-based packaging grades in order to reduce the industry's reliance on imported woodpulp supplies. The use of recycled waste paper is increasing and research is helping to extend it. Waste paper provides about half of the industry's fibre needs. Domestically produced wood pulp represents only a small percentage of raw material supplies.

Mergers have led to the formation of large groups in newspaper, magazine and book publishing. Printing, engraving, bookbinding and specialist publishing activities still involve many small firms using new technology such as computer typesetting and desktop publishing. The book–publishing industry is a major exporter, selling one-third of production in overseas markets. Security printers (of, for example, banknotes and postage stamps) are important exporters, the major company being De La Rue. Total employment in the paper, printing and publishing industries in 1990 was 467,000. Most of the printing and publishing industry's employment and output is concentrated in firms based in the South East.

Rubber tyres and tubes sold by British manufacturers in 1990 were valued at £1,349 million, about £560 million of which went overseas. Other important rubber goods include vehicle components and accessories, conveyor belting, cables, hoses, latex foam products, and footwear, gloves and clothing. Tyre manufacturers include subsidiaries of United States and other overseas companies. The industry's consumption of rubber includes natural, synthetic and recycled rubber.

Toys, games and sports equipment are established in export markets, while jewellery, gold and silverware and the refining of precious metals are industries maintaining a strong craft tradition.

Table 13.12: Other Manufacturing

	Exports (£ million) 1990	Imports (£ million) 1990
Timber and wooden furniture	520	3,211
Paper and paper products	1,621	4,789
Printing and publishing	1,226	938
Processing of rubber and plastics	2,603	3,319
Toys and sports goods	381	792

14 Construction and Service Industries

Introduction

Services contribute about 64 per cent of gross domestic product and some 70 per cent of employment. Overseas earnings from services amounted to nearly 40 per cent of the value of exports of manufactures in 1990.

The number of employees in services in Great Britain rose from just over 13 million in 1982 to nearly 15·5 million by the end of 1990. Much of this was accounted for by growth in part-time (principally female) employment. In the past decade employment has grown more rapidly in the private sector than in the public sector, partly reflecting the Government's policy of restricting employment in public sector services.

With the rise in real incomes, consumers have spent more on personal, financial and leisure services. While consumers have to some extent exchanged services such as public transport, laundries and cinemas for goods such as cars, washing-machines and television sets, this has generated demand for distribution, maintenance and repair of these goods.

Demand for British air travel, hotel and catering services has also resulted from the increase in real incomes in other countries. By the same token, the substantial rise in real disposable incomes in Britain has resulted in more holidays being taken by Britons both within Britain and overseas.

Other factors include the increased use of a wide variety of banking services and the spread of home ownership, which has increased demand for legal and estate agency services. Demographic changes, such as the increasing proportion of elderly people in the population, help to explain the growth of medical services.

Changes in technology have also played a part in the growth of services. Examples range from the computer services industry to the provision of cash and credit by means of cards, and the growth of information systems such as viewdata and teletext.

A notable trend is the growth in franchising, an operation in which a company owning the rights to a particular form of trading licenses them to franchisees, usually by means of an initial payment with continuing royalties. The main areas include cleaning services, film processing, print shops, hairdressing and cosmetics, fitness centres, courier delivery, car rental, engine tuning and servicing, and fast food retailing. It is estimated that franchising's share of total retail sales is about 10 per cent, a figure which is likely to increase.

Construction

The construction industry accounts for 7·6 per cent of gross domestic product and employs just under 1 million people; there are also more than 700,000 self-employed in the industry. It accounts for just under 5 per cent of employment.

Efficiency and productivity are benefiting from new computerised techniques such as electronic load safety measures for cranes, distance measuring equipment, computerised stock ordering and job costing, and computer-aided design. Increasingly, major contractors are managing projects (particularly higher value ones) and using subcontractors to do the actual work.

The Department of the Environment's building regulations prescribe minimum standards of construction in England and Wales. Administered and enforced by local government authorities, the regulations apply to new building, the installation or replacement of fittings, and alterations and extensions to existing buildings. There are similar controls in Scotland and Northern Ireland.

An alternative to local authority building control was introduced in 1984; under this there is a system of private certification of compliance with building regulations.

The British Board of Agrément, sponsored by the Department, assesses and issues reports and certificates relating to products and systems for use in the construction industry. The British Standards Institution is providing Britain's contribution to the drafting of European standards, which are increasingly replacing national construction standards.

Structure

Construction work is carried out by private contractors and by public authorities which employ their own labour. In 1990 some 92 per cent of the work was done by private firms, 98 per cent of which employ fewer than 25 people. Some of the large firms own quarries and workshops, mechanised plant and standard builders' equipment. Some undertake responsibility for all stages of projects from initial design to finished building.

All but the smallest projects are generally carried out under professional direction by architects or, in the case of the more complicated civil engineering projects, by consulting engineers. The latter, acting on behalf of a client, may advise on the feasibility of projects, draw up plans and supervise the construction work.

The financial aspects and control of project costs are undertaken by quantity surveyors and construction surveyors. The inspection and maintenance of buildings are carried out by building surveyors. In addition, town planning and municipal surveyors deal with local planning issues. Independent estates and valuation surveyors manage privately-owned property.

Two organisations have special responsibilities for construction work undertaken by the Government. Property Holdings acts as landlord for its Common User Estate. The functions of the second

body, PSA Services (formerly Property Services Agency), are to:

● offer management and design services for major projects;

● provide services in maintenance and estates surveying;

● manage and design locally designed projects;

● provide specialist professional services; and

● organise support services overseas for the Ministry of Defence.

Departments are no longer required to use PSA Services, as the Government has announced its intention to privatise the organisation.

Housing

During 1990 a total of 158,300 dwellings were started in Great Britain. Starts in the public sector were 25,300 and those for private owners 133,000. Some 184,100 dwellings were completed: 31,000 in the public sector and 153,100 in the private sector.

Major Construction Projects

Among important construction projects in hand or recently completed are the Channel Tunnel, the M25 motorway widening scheme, the Dartford Bridge, the A55 Conwy Tunnel, the extensive development in London's Docklands (including the Limehouse link road), the new British Library, the Glasgow Concert Hall and Birmingham's Symphony Hall.

Consultancy

In 1990 members of the Association of Consulting Engineers were involved in new work overseas valued at £15,935 million, a 10·3 per cent increase over the figure for 1989. The capital value of projects underway at the end of 1990 or completed during the year was £44,685 million. The three largest categories of work covered railways; roads, bridges and tunnels; and water supply. The largest markets were the Middle East, the Far East and Africa. Projects include:

- the Channel Tunnel (£5,500 million);
- a thermal power station in Sabriyah, Kuwait (£3,000 million);
- a river project in Libya (£2,600 million); and
- the Hong Kong International Airport (£2,400 million).

British consulting engineers, process engineers and chartered surveyors had estimated net earnings in 1990 of £480 million from overseas commissions.

Contracting

Overseas construction contracts awarded to British companies in 1990 included:

- a concrete gravity platform off Newfoundland, with a French partnership, worth £500 million;
- expansion of Kuentan Airport in Malaysia;
- a wastewater treatment plant in Canada;
- the design, construction and equipping of eight district hospitals in Malaysia, with a Malaysian partnership, worth £112 million; and

- a joint venture to build a major section of the Lesotho Highlands Water Development Project.

Research and Advisory Services

The Government's research and advisory body on construction is the Building Research Establishment, part of the Department of the Environment. It has four laboratories, including a fire research station, and is the site of a building energy management systems centre. The major construction and materials firms, universities, colleges of technology and research associations carry out research and provide advisory services.

The Building Centre, run by its own trust, provides exhibition and information services on materials, products, techniques and building services.

Service Industries

DISTRIBUTION

There were some 3·5 million employees in the distributive and allied trades in Great Britain in early 1990, together with a large number of owners of businesses. The distributive and allied trades accounted for about 15 per cent of national income in 1990.

Table 14.1: Wholesale Trade in Great Britain 1988[a]

	Number of businesses	Turnover[b] (£ million)
Food and drink	16,530	41,673
Petroleum products	976	20,267
Clothing, furs, textiles and footware	9,986	8,898
Coal and oil merchants	3,436	1,846
Builders' merchants	4,364	8,490
Agricultural supplies and livestock dealing	3,175	7,821
Industrial materials	5,690	30,041
Scrap and waste products	3,867	2,919
Industrial and agricultural machinery	8,282	12,980
Operational leasing	2,783	3,181
Other goods	55,874	66,783
Total wholesaling and dealing	114,963	204,899

Source: *Business Monitor SDA26. Wholesaling, 1988.*
[a]Figures cover businesses registered for value added tax with an annual turnover of £149,000 or more and are grossed up to include those not surveyed.
[b]Excludes value added tax.

WHOLESALE TRADES

According to the most recently published Census of Production, there were 115,000 businesses, with a turnover valued at nearly £205,000 million (see Table 14.1), engaged in wholesaling and dealing in Great Britain in 1988. This represented a growth in stock of businesses of 26 per cent and of turnover at current prices of 94 per cent since 1980.

The co-operative movement has its own wholesale organisation, the Co-operative Wholesale Society (CWS). Retail co-operative societies are encouraged to buy from the CWS, which is their main supplier. The CWS is also a major retailer in Scotland, Northern Ireland and south-east England.

In the food and drink trade almost all large retailers have their own buying and central distribution operations. Elsewhere in the trade voluntary groups have been formed by wholesalers with small independent retailers, in which the retailers are encouraged by discounts and other incentives to buy as much as possible from the wholesaler. This has helped to preserve many smaller retail outlets for the wholesaler, including the traditional 'corner shops' and village stores, and has given small retailers the advantages of bulk buying and co-ordinated distribution.

London's wholesale markets play a significant part in the distribution of foodstuffs. New Covent Garden is the main market for fruit and vegetables, Smithfield for meat and Billingsgate for fish.

RETAIL TRADES

Of the 25 largest retailers in Western Europe by sales reported in either financial or calendar years embracing 1988 to 1990, ten were British firms. The Census of Production 1988 found 237,832 retail businesses, with 338,248 outlets, in Great Britain (see Table 14.2). In recent years, the large multiple retailers have grown in size, decreasing their store numbers but increasing outlet size and diversifying their product ranges. Decline has been particularly evident among small independent businesses and retail co-operative societies. Food retailers

Table 14.2: Retail Trade in Great Britain 1988[a]

	Number of businesses	Number of outlets	Number of people engaged ('000s)	Turnover[b] (£ million)
Single-outlet retailers	212,711	212,711	754	31,642
Small multiple retailers	24,286	61,637	298	13,326
Large multiple retailers (ten or more retail outlets)	835	63,900	1,294	69,737
Food retailers	67,755	87,758	809	39,890
Drink, confectionery and tobacco retailers	48,893	60,877	259	11,398
Clothing, footwear and leather goods retailers	30,170	57,768	298	11,314
Household goods retailers	45,678	63,795	319	19,239
Other non-food retailers	39,604	52,944	237	10,310
Mixed retail businesses	3,528	9,402	387	21,248
Hire and repair businesses	2,204	5,703	38	2,305
Total retail trade	237,832	338,248	2,347	114,705

Source: *Business Monitor SDA25 Retailing. 1988.*
[a]Figures cover businesses registered for value added tax; it is estimated that the total number of retail businesses too small to register for value added tax is about 30,000, but these businesses account for no more than 0·5 per cent of total retail turnover.
[b]Includes value added tax.
Note: Differences between totals and the sums of their component parts are due to rounding.

have experienced the fastest growth in turnover, while hire and repair businesses and shops selling durable household goods have recorded the slowest growth.

The largest multiple retailers in the grocery market are Sainsbury, Tesco, Safeway, Asda and Gateway. These five groups are responsible for around £25,000 million of grocery sales a year.

Retail co-operative societies are voluntary organisations controlled by their members, membership being open to anyone paying a small deposit on a minimum share. Retail co-operatives and the Co-operative Wholesale Society (see p 254) are members of the Co-operative Union, as are a number of other co-operative bodies such as the Co-operative Bank. There are 4,671 retail co-operative outlets, 62 per cent of which sell food and groceries.

The leading mixed retail businesses are Marks and Spencer, Boots, Kingfisher, Storehouse, W.H. Smith, Argos, Littlewoods, Savacentre, John Menzies, Sears, Burton Group and House of Fraser.

About 20 million people regularly purchase goods through mail order catalogues. In 1990 sales by general mail order totalled some £3,700 million, representing nearly 3 per cent of all retail sales and 4·5 per cent of non-food retail sales. Leading items sold by the mail order companies include clothing, footwear, furniture, household textiles, televisions, radios and electrical goods.

Trends

Although one of the most significant trends in retailing has been the decline of the specialist sector and the development of the large supermarket and superstore, the nine largest multiple retailers have only 27 per cent of retail turnover. Other trends include:

- more very large self-service stores selling a wide variety of products;

- the slowing down of recent diversification by food multiples into selling a wider range of goods; and

- the creation of specially designed shopping precincts.

Large Shopping Centres

Britain has a wide range of complementary shopping facilities inside and outside town and city centres. There continues to be a demand for the services provided by small, specialised shops, but the trend is towards larger shops in order to increase efficiency and the range of goods available. The main multiple grocery companies have been steadily increasing the size of their stores both in towns and cities and on suburban and out-of-town sites. Also, retailers of goods such as do-it-yourself products, furniture and electrical appliances have built retail warehouses outside town and city centres, particularly to attract shoppers with cars. More recently, there has been a trend towards the grouping of retail warehouses into retail warehouse parks. Many towns and cities have purpose-built shopping centres.

Proposals have also been made recently for a number of regional out-of-town shopping centres, on sites which offer good access to large numbers of customers with cars and ample space for car parking, and which benefit from low acquisition and operating costs. One of the first centres was the Metro Centre at Gateshead, Tyne and Wear, which includes over 93,000 sq m (1 million sq ft) of floorspace. The Meadowhall shopping centre in Sheffield was opened in September 1990 and the Lakeside centre at Thurrock in Essex in October 1990.

All new retail development requires planning permission from the local government planning authority. These authorities must consult the appropriate central government department before granting permission for developments of 23,325 sq m (250,000 sq ft) or more. The Government's policy is to encourage the provision of a wide range of shopping facilities to the public, while ensuring that the effects of major new retail development do not undermine the viability and vitality of existing town centres.

Diversification

Many of the large multiple groups offer a much bigger range of goods and services than previously. However, extensive diversification has proved unprofitable and large food retailers are increasing their range of foods instead. More emphasis is also being placed on selling own-label goods and environmentally friendly products. Many superstores and large supermarkets offer fresh as well as packaged food, often with special counters or areas for fresh meat, fish, vegetables and bread baked on the premises. Some large retailers have in recent years begun to provide financial and estate agency services.

Promotions

Retailers are placing greater emphasis on price competition and quality as a means of promoting sales. Some large retailers have issued their own credit cards for regular customers in an attempt to increase sales, particularly of high-value goods.

Use of Technology

Laser-scanning electronic check-outs are already having a major impact on British retailing. Substantial savings are being made from improved stock control and a reduction of individual price marking in stores. Some large multiple retailers are using electronic order and invoice systems in dealing with their suppliers, following a legal change permitting tax invoices in forms other than paper. Small independent retailers are also using electronic ordering, pricing and delivery systems. High-speed labelling techniques are being adopted, including the use of electronic printers which can overprint labels, the use of pressure-sensitive glues and printing in foil instead of ink.

'EFTPOS' (electronic funds transfer at point of sale) is a system which enables shoppers to pay for goods using a debit or credit card to transfer funds electronically via terminals in retail premises. Several major EFTPOS schemes are well established, with altogether more than 190,000 terminals, a number that is growing quickly. In many cases the terminals are integrated with the retailers' in-house computer systems.

Vehicle and Petrol Retailing

In 1990 there were 460,000 people employed in the retail distribution of motor vehicles and parts, in petrol stations and in the repair and recovery of vehicles. Many of the businesses selling new vehicles are franchised by the motor manufacturers.

One-third of the 19,500 petrol stations are owned by oil companies. The three companies with the largest number of outlets in 1990 were Shell (2,653), Esso (2,520) and BP/National (1,992). Unleaded petrol is sold at more than 94 per cent of outlets, its sales accounting for about 41 per cent of petrol sold. The majority of petrol stations are self-service. About 15,500 outlets sell diesel fuel.

Hotels and Catering

The hotel and catering trades employed some 1·2 million people in Great Britain at the end of 1990 as follows:

- hotels and other residential establishments, 266,000;
- public houses and bars, 333,000;
- restaurants, cafés and snack bars, 301,000;
- clubs, 150,000; and
- canteens, 148,000.

A large number of self-employed people are also engaged in hotels and catering.

There were about 29,000 hotels in Great Britain in 1989–90, with a turnover of £7,000 million in 1989. Many licensed hotels as well as most of the numerous guest houses have fewer than 20 rooms. Of the major hotel business groups, the biggest is Trusthouse Forte plc, which runs 800 hotels, including some 240 in Britain, and has catering and leisure interests. Among the largest firms running holiday centres (including holiday camps with full board, self-catering centres and caravan parks) are Butlins, Warner Holidays and Pontin's. Britain has a very wide range of restaurants, of which a substantial number specialise in Chinese, Italian, Indian and Greek foods. The Food Safety Act 1990 has contributed to a raising of food safety standards.

In 1990 there were about 20,000 public houses (pubs), which mainly sell beer, wines, soft drinks and spirits for consumption on the premises. Many pubs are owned by the large brewing companies, which either provide managers to run them or offer tenancy agreements; others, called free houses, are independently owned and managed. The Government has acted to strengthen competition in the sale of beer and other drinks in pubs.

BUSINESS SERVICES

Business services include advertising, market research, management consultancy, exhibition and conference facilities, computing services and auction houses.

Advertising

Advertising expenditure in 1990 amounted to £7,900 million. The press accounted for 64 per cent of the total, television for 30 per cent, posters for nearly 4 per cent, and commercial radio and cinema for the rest. The largest advertising expenditure is on food, retail and mail order services, financial services, motor cars, drink, household goods and leisure equipment. Campaigns are planned mainly by several hundred advertising agencies which, in some cases, provide marketing, consumer research and other services.

Computing Services

The computing services industry comprises software houses; production of packaged software; consultancy; facilities management; processing services; and the provision of complete computer systems. It also includes companies providing information technology education and training, independent maintenance, contingency planning and recruitment, and contract staff. The industry is one of the fastest growing sectors of the British economy.

The turnover of companies in the Computing Services Association totalled over £3,500 million in 1990. Members of the Association provide employment for over 60,000 people, representing about 75 per cent of the industry in Britain. Developments include the adoption of advanced software engineering techniques, the design of systems kernels, systems integration and facilities management.

Management Consultancy

There are about 15,000 management consultants, of whom 3,800 are individual practising members of the Institute of Management Consultants. Among the largest management consultancy companies are the 32 members of the Management Consultancies Association, with revenue earned within Britain comprising £706 million, and overseas revenue amounting to almost £104 million in 1990. The Association reports a growing demand for the application of information technology to all aspects of business. The Association's members account for some 45 to 55 per cent of Britain's fee-paying management consultancy market.

Market Research

Market research is a well-established sector of the marketing services industry in Britain. Britain accounts for about 10 per cent of worldwide expenditure, and spends more on market research, per head, than any other European country.

The Association of Market Survey Organisations (AMSO) is the main trade organisation. AMSO's member companies account for over 70 per cent of all commercial market research. In 1990 they accounted for total research revenues of £265 million—a growth in revenues of 11·4 per cent over 1989. Research revenues come from a wide range of clients and industries.

Exhibition and Conference Centres

Britain is one of the world's three leading countries for international conferences (the others being the United States and France).

With the steady increase in new and renovated facilities, some 80 towns and cities have facilities for conferences and exhibitions.

Among the most modern purpose-built conference and exhibition centres are the International Conference Centre and the National Exhibition Centre at Birmingham, the Wembley Conference Centre, the Queen Elizabeth II Conference Centre and the Barbican Centre for Arts and Conferences in London. Others are situated in Brighton (East Sussex), Harrogate (North Yorkshire), Bournemouth (Dorset), Manchester, Nottingham and Torquay. Wales has a conference centre in Cardiff and in Scotland Glasgow and Aberdeen both have exhibition and conference centres.

Other large exhibition facilities are the Earls Court, Olympia, Alexandra Palace and Wembley Arena sites in London. New centres are being constructed in Glasgow and Cardiff.

Auction Houses

Britain's chief auction houses are active in the international auction markets for works of art, trading on the acknowledged expertise of British valuers and dealers. The two largest houses, Sotheby's and Christie's, are established worldwide. Sotheby's handled sales valued at £727 million in 1990, while Christie's handled sales valued at £650 million.

TOURISM AND TRAVEL

Tourism is one of Britain's most important industries and is a major and growing source of employment. It is estimated that about 1·4 million jobs in Great Britain were supported by tourism spending in 1990.

In 1990 over 18 million overseas visitors came to Britain and spent nearly £7,800 million. British residents made 31 million trips abroad and spent £9,900 million, giving a deficit on the travel account of £2,100 million. Fifty-nine per cent of overseas visitors to Britain came from Western Europe and 21 per cent from North America. Eighty-three per cent of trips

abroad by British visitors were to Western Europe.

Some 90 per cent of travel agencies belong to the Association of British Travel Agents (ABTA). Although most travel agents are small businesses, there are a few large firms—for example, Lunn Poly and Thomas Cook, each of which has hundreds of branches. Computerised information and booking systems are used extensively in travel agencies. There are also 700 tour operator members of ABTA; about half are both retail agents and tour operators.

ABTA operates financial protection schemes to safeguard its members' customers, maintains codes of conduct drawn up with the Office of Fair Trading, and offers a free consumer affairs service to help to resolve complaints against members and an independent arbitration scheme for tour operators' customers.

Tourist Authorities

Official support for tourism is provided by the British Tourist Authority (BTA) and the tourist boards for England, Scotland, Wales and Northern Ireland. The BTA promotes overseas tourism to Britain and is represented in 32 countries. The tourist boards improve and promote facilities for tourism in each area. The English Tourist Board (ETB) works closely with 12 regional tourist boards, which are responsible for the planning, development and marketing of tourism in their areas. Each board is a partnership between the ETB, local government and trade interests in their region.

Some 17,000 hotels and other serviced accommodation are inspected and classified by the tourist boards. The various classifications—'listed' and one to five crowns—indicate the range of facilities and services provided. A similar arrangement applies to self-catering holiday homes. There is also a 'Q' quality grading scheme for caravans, chalets and camping parks.

Information on tourist facilities and accommodation is available from official tourist information centres, most of which are administered by local government.

15 Energy and Natural Resources

Energy and non-fuel minerals make an important contribution to the British economy. The approximate value of minerals produced in 1989 was £15,880 million (representing nearly 3·9 per cent of gross domestic product—GDP), of which crude oil accounted for 45 per cent, coal 26 per cent and natural gas 16 per cent.

All minerals in Great Britain are mainly privately owned, with the exception of gold, silver, oil and natural gas (which are owned by the Crown), and coal and some minerals associated with coal. In Northern Ireland gold and silver are owned by the Crown, while rights to exploit petroleum and other minerals are vested in the Department of Economic Development.

On the United Kingdom Continental Shelf the right to exploit all minerals except coal is vested in the Crown.

The exclusive right to extract coal, or license others to do so, both on land in Great Britain and under the sea, is vested in the British Coal Corporation. Normally, ownership of minerals belongs to the owner of the land surface, but in some areas, particularly those with a long history of mining, these rights have become separated. Mining and quarrying, apart from coalmining, are usually carried out by privately owned companies.

Energy

Britain has the largest energy resources of any country in the European Community and is a major world producer of oil, natural gas and coal—called primary sources. The other main primary sources are nuclear power and some water power; secondary sources (derived from primary sources) are electricity, coke and smokeless fuels, and petroleum products. In 1990 Britain was a small net importer of energy, amounting to 9·6 million tonnes of oil equivalent. In financial terms, however, the higher value of its exports meant that it was a net exporter of energy, to the value of £471 million. There are large reserves of coal, which is expected to continue to supply a significant proportion of the country's energy needs. Nuclear power provided about 19 per cent of electricity available from the British electricity companies in 1990.

Private sector companies carry out offshore oil and gas production and oil refining, while a publicly owned body is at present responsible for most coal production. The electricity supply industry in Great Britain, apart from nuclear power, has been privatised. Plans to privatise the electricity supply industry in Northern Ireland have been announced. The Secretary of State for Energy is responsible for energy matters in Great Britain, except for electricity in Scotland, which is under the Secretary of State for Scotland. The Secretary of State for Northern Ireland is responsible for all energy matters there.

Energy Policy

Energy policy is designed to ensure the secure, adequate and economic provision of energy to meet Britain's requirements. The Government encourages the exploitation of Britain's diverse energy sources. It seeks to ensure that all economic forms of energy are produced, supplied and used as efficiently as possible, having regard also to the international application and environmental implications of the technologies involved. Central government spending on energy is planned to decline by about 10 per cent over

Table 15.1: Inland Energy Consumption (in terms of primary sources)

million tonnes oil equivalent

	1980	1985	1988	1989	1990
Oil	71·4	67·7	68·3	69·5	71·3
Coal	71·1	62·0	65·9	63·6	63·7
Natural gas	41·8	48·4	47·9	47·4	49·0
Nuclear energy	7·9	13·0	13·5	15·2	14·2
Hydro-electric power	1·1	1·2	1·4	1·4	1·5
Net imports of electricity	–	–	3·1	3·0	2·9
Total	193·3	192·3	200·1	200·1	202·5

Source: Department of Energy.
Note: Differences between totals and the sums of their component parts are due to rounding.

the next three years, with an increasing share of expenditure directed at non-nuclear items and at energy efficiency.

The Government stresses the importance of the continued profitable development of Britain's oil and gas resources, the development of a competitive coal industry, the safe and economic development of nuclear power, and the most cost-effective use of energy through the adoption of energy efficiency measures. It also funds an extensive research and development programme into renewable sources of energy.

Privatisation has already had an impact in the energy field, with the transfer of British Gas, Britoil, Enterprise Oil, and the non-nuclear electricity supply industry in Great Britain to the private sector. The Government wishes to privatise the coal industry during the next Parliament. It considers that these industries will thus improve their competitiveness and efficiency, free of government pressures, and attract new investment to provide cheaper and cleaner energy.

Britain is actively engaged in international collaboration on energy questions, notably through its membership of the European Community and of the International Energy Agency (a body with 23 member countries attached to the Organisation for Economic Co-operation and Development). In 1990 the European Community introduced the THERMIE scheme for the promotion of energy technology, including support for demonstration projects in the hydrocarbons sector.

ENERGY CONSUMPTION

During 1979–90, when Britain's GDP rose by 24 per cent, energy consumption on a 'heat supplied' basis declined by 3·8 per cent. Energy consumption by final users in 1990 amounted to 59,381 million therms[1] on a 'heat supplied' basis, of which transport consumed 32·5 per cent, industrial users 27 per cent, domestic users 27 per cent, and commerce, agriculture and public services 13 per cent.

ENERGY EFFICIENCY

The Energy Efficiency Office (EEO), established in 1983, provides a wide range of services and programmes designed to encourage cost-effective energy efficiency improvements. Its work focuses on major energy users in industry, commerce and the public sector, and on low-income households. Since 1983, EEO programmes have cost some £150 million and have led to savings now worth over £500 million a year. The EEO's budget for 1991–92 is £42 million. It promotes its programmes through 11 regional energy efficiency officers.

Consumers in Britain spent £42,000 million (including taxes) on energy in 1989—8·3 per cent of GDP. The EEO estimates that about 20 per cent of this could have been saved if consumers had invested in cost-effective energy efficiency measures, which pay for themselves through reductions

---

[1] 1 therm = 105,506 kilojoules.

in energy consumption within three years. The Government stresses that improved energy efficiency not only saves valuable energy resources, but also helps to stabilise carbon dioxide (CO_2) emissions and reduces acid rain pollution.

An interdepartmental ministerial group, chaired by the Secretary of State for Energy, aims to ensure that energy efficiency objectives are incorporated into publicity, policy and management of government departments, and of public and private sector organisations. It promotes the environmental benefits of improved energy efficiency as well as the savings in fuel bills, and highlights concern for efficient energy use as part of a modern lifestyle. It also leads the Government's public sector energy efficiency campaign. The major government departments and English health authorities have been set a target to reduce their energy consumption by 15 per cent over five years.

The EEO's main programme, Best Practice, provides information and advice on energy use and efficiency in industry, commerce, the public sector and housing. This includes extensive guidance on energy efficiency technologies and management techniques. Best Practice's current target is to encourage recurrent energy savings worth a further £500 million a year by the year 2000.

The EEO's Home Energy Efficiency Scheme provides advice and grants to low-income households for insulation and draughtproofing. Householders are eligible if they receive income support, housing benefit, family credit or community charge support.

The EEO promotes Combined Heat and Power (CHP) technology under the Best Practice programme. CHP plant produces usable heat as well as electricity. It also has an overall efficiency of fuel utilisation as high as 80 to 90 per cent, compared with 30 per cent for conventional power plant. By using less fuel for a similar output of energy, CHP significantly reduces the emissions which damage the environment. CHP is already cutting energy costs on about 500 sites in Britain. It has a total installed capacity of some 2,000 megawatts (MW). This accounts for about 3 per cent of electricity generated.

In 1991 the EEO and the Department of the Environment started a three-year campaign to promote energy efficiency in the home and explain the impact of energy use on the environment. The EEO also runs a promotional campaign aimed at senior management of top energy users in Britain.

Britain is also carrying out work with European Community partners on the development of effective legislative measures on appliance labelling. Energy labels for refrigerators and freezers initially should be produced before the end of 1992. The Government is also exploring with retailers and manufacturers the possibilities for an interim voluntary scheme in Britain.

OIL AND GAS

Britain's energy position is strengthened by substantial oil and gas reserves offshore on the United Kingdom Continental Shelf (UKCS). The Government has granted exploration and production licences as a result of 12 offshore licensing rounds since 1964. In 1991, it awarded licences for 74 blocks in the twelfth round after receiving the highest number of applications for ten years. It also awarded licences for six of the 11 groups of blocks on offer in the first separate round of offshore licensing for frontier areas. Expenditure on offshore and onshore exploration and development amounted to some £3,500 million in 1990. By the end of 1990, 4,516 wells had been or were being drilled in the UKCS: 2,054 development wells, 1,553 exploration wells and 909 appraisal wells.

Offshore Supplies

Britain's offshore supplies industry is the second largest in the world and has headed considerable technological advance. It is estimated that British suppliers are winning orders worth between £7,000 million and £8,000 million a year worldwide.

The Offshore Supplies Office (OSO) of the Department of Energy is responsible for promoting a fair commercial opportunity for

British suppliers in the UKCS and throughout the world. The OSO provides the secretariat for the Offshore Industry Advisory Board. The Board, chaired by an energy minister, is the principal source of high-level co-ordinated advice on the development of strategy for Britain's offshore supplies industry.

Offshore Safety

In November 1990, the Cullen report into the destruction by fire of the Piper Alpha fixed oil production platform in July 1988 resulted in 106 recommendations for a new regulatory system of offshore safety. The Government accepted them and is acting to implement them. Offshore safety responsibilities have been transferred from the Department of Energy to the Health and Safety Executive.

OIL

Before the 1970s Britain was almost wholly dependent for its oil supplies on imports, the only indigenous supplies coming from a small number of land-based oilfields. However, the first notable offshore discovery of oil in the UKCS was made in 1969 and the first oil was brought ashore in 1975. Output of crude oil in Britain in 1990 averaged over 1·83 million barrels (about 241,000 tonnes) a day, making Britain the world's ninth largest producer.

North Sea Fields

There were 48 offshore fields producing crude oil at the end of 1990, and the Secretary of State for Energy approved ten new offshore development projects during the year.

The fields with the largest cumulative production totals are Forties and Brent. Ninian, Piper, Beryl, Fulmar, Thistle and Claymore are other high-producing fields. Production from most large fields is controlled from production platforms of either steel or concrete which have been built to withstand severe weather, including gusts of wind of up to 260 km/h (160 mph) and waves of 30 m (100 ft). The Petroleum Act 1987 lays down measures to be taken in connection with the abandonment of offshore installations and pipelines.

Output is forecast to decline slowly, but Britain should remain self-sufficient in oil well into the 1990s and a significant producer into the twenty-first century. The

Table 15.2: Oil Statistics

					million tonnes
	1980	1985	1988	1989	1990
Oil production[a]					
land	0·2	0·4	0·8	0·7	1·8
offshore	80·3	127·2	113·7	91·1	89·9
Refinery output	79·2	72·9	79·8	81·4	82·3
Deliveries of petroleum products for inland consumption	71·2	69·8	72·3	73·0	74·0
Exports (including re-exports)					
crude petroleum	38·5	79·6	70·5	49·2	54·3
refined petroleum products and process oils	16·1	18·9	18·9	20·1	20·7
Imports:					
crude petroleum	44·8	26·9	32·8	36·3	43·5
refined petroleum products and process oils	14·1	25·0	21·4	21·7	24·5

Sources: Department of Energy and HM Customs and Excise.
[a]Crude oil plus condensates and petroleum gases derived at onshore treatment plants.

Oil

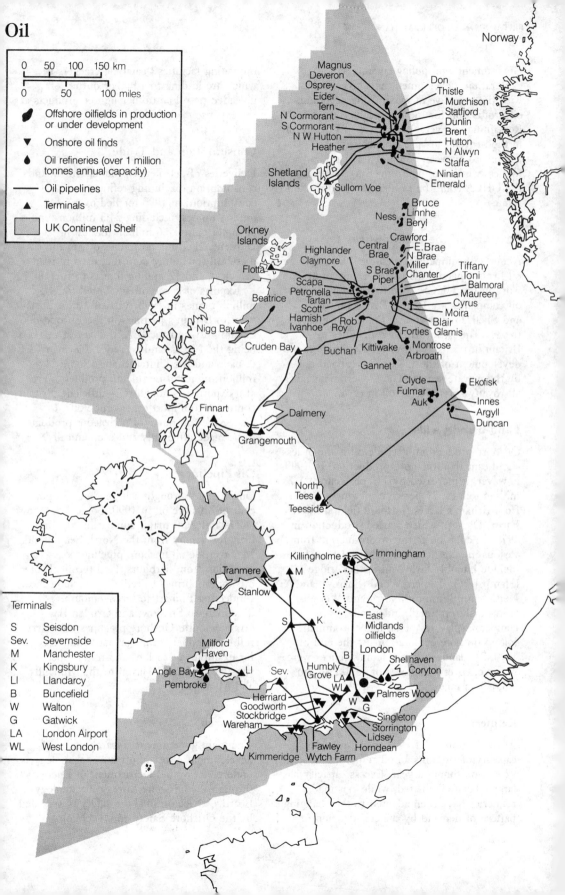

Norway

Scale:
0 50 100 150 km
0 50 100 miles

- Offshore oilfields in production or under development
- ▼ Onshore oil finds
- Oil refineries (over 1 million tonnes annual capacity)
- Oil pipelines
- ▲ Terminals
- UK Continental Shelf

Magnus
Deveron
Osprey
Eider
Tern
N Cormorant
S Cormorant
N W Hutton
Heather

Don
Thistle
Murchison
Statfjord
Dunlin
Brent
Hutton
N Alwyn
Staffa
Ninian
Emerald

Shetland Islands
Sullom Voe

Bruce
Ness
Linnhe
Beryl

Orkney Islands

Highlander
Claymore
Flotta

Crawford
Central Brae
E. Brae
N Brae
Miller
Chanter
S Brae
Piper

Tiffany
Toni
Balmoral
Maureen
Cyrus
Moira
Blair
Glamis

Scapa
Petronella
Tartan
Scott
Hamish
Ivanhoe
Rob Roy
Beatrice

Nigg Bay
Cruden Bay
Buchan
Kittiwake
Forties
Montrose
Arbroath
Gannet

Clyde
Fulmar
Auk

Ekofisk
Innes
Argyll
Duncan

Finnart
Dalmeny
Grangemouth

North Tees
Teesside

Killingholme
Immingham

Tranmere
Stanlow
M

S
K

East Midlands oilfields

Milford Haven
Angle Bay
Pembroke
LI
Sev.

Humbly Grove
B
London
LA
WL
W
G

Shellhaven
Coryton
Palmers Wood

Herriard
Goodworth
Stockbridge
Wareham
Kimmeridge
Fawley
Wytch Farm
Singleton
Storrington
Lidsey
Horndean

Terminals

S	Seisdon
Sev.	Severnside
M	Manchester
K	Kingsbury
LI	Llandarcy
B	Buncefield
W	Walton
G	Gatwick
LA	London Airport
WL	West London

Government's oil policy encourages exploration, development and investment, with the objective of maximising economic oil production for the foreseeable future. Remaining recoverable reserves of UKCS oil in the proven plus probable categories amount to between 535 and 1,195 million tonnes, while the total remaining reserves of the UKCS could be as high as 5,300 million tonnes.

Structure of the Oil Industry

About 250 companies, including several large oil firms, operate in Britain or engage in work in the UKCS. The two leading British oil companies are British Petroleum (BP) and Shell Transport and Trading, which are the two largest industrial companies in Britain in terms of turnover. Exploration and development of the UKCS are carried out by the private sector. The Government takes all royalty from UKCS oil in cash.

Land-based Fields

Onshore production of crude oil is much less significant than offshore production. In 1990, however, it increased by 142 per cent to 1·75 million tonnes, 77 per cent of which came from Britain's largest onshore field at Wytch Farm (Dorset), which started production in 1979. In addition to minor production from various mining licensees, other onshore fields include Humbly Grove and Stockbridge (Hampshire), Palmers Wood (Surrey), and Nettleham, Scampton North and Welton (Lincolnshire). Small, independent companies play an increasingly prominent role in onshore exploration. At the end of 1990, 215 landward petroleum licences were in force, covering an area of 35,522 sq km (13,850 sq miles).

Refineries

At the beginning of 1991 the distillation capacity of Britain's 13 oil refineries stood at 92 million tonnes a year. Excess capacity has largely been eliminated, while existing refineries have been adapted to the changing pattern of demand by the construction of upgrading facilities ('catalytic crackers'), which are leading to a higher output of unleaded petrol and other lighter products at the expense of fuel oil.

Consumption and Trade

Deliveries of petroleum products for inland consumption (excluding refinery consumption) in 1990 totalled over 74 million tonnes, including 24·3 million tonnes of motor spirit, 8·6 million tonnes of kerosene, 18·7 million tonnes of gas and diesel oil (including derv fuel used in road vehicles), and 12 million tonnes of fuel oil.

Exports of crude oil amounted to 54·3 million tonnes in 1990. Virtually all exports went to Britain's partners in the European Community and the IEA, the largest markets being the Netherlands, France, Germany, Canada and the United States. Some 21 million tonnes of petroleum products were also exported. Though self-sufficient, Britain continues to import other crude oils, to enable the full range of petroleum products to be made efficiently and economically.

Oil Pipelines

Oil pipelines brought ashore about 73 per cent of offshore oil in 1990. Some 1,878 km (1,174 miles) of major submarine pipeline bring oil ashore from the North Sea oilfields. Major crude oil onshore pipelines in operation from harbours, land terminals or offshore moorings to refineries include those connecting Finnart to Grangemouth, Tranmere to Stanlow, and Cruden Bay to Grangemouth. Onshore pipelines also carry refined products to major marketing areas; for example, a 423-km (263-mile) pipeline runs from Milford Haven to the Midlands and Manchester.

Research

The main government research and development effort in offshore technology is undertaken by the Department of Energy through the Offshore Energy Technology Board. Advice on offshore safety is provided by the Offshore Safety and Technology

Board. The Petroleum Science and Technology Institute, set up in Edinburgh in 1989, works in conjunction with Heriot-Watt and Edinburgh universities, and is funded by 35 oil companies and the OSO. Its activities are concentrated on exploration, appraisal, development and production. The Offshore Technology Park in Aberdeen comprises several projects and is part-funded by Scottish Enterprise.

GAS

Public supply of manufactured gas in Britain began in the early nineteenth century in central London. For many years gas was produced from coal, but during the 1960s growing imports of oil brought about production of town gas from oil-based feedstocks. Following the first commercial natural gas discovery in the UKCS in 1965 and the start of offshore gas production in 1967, supplies of offshore natural gas grew rapidly and by 1977 natural gas had replaced town gas in the public supply system in Great Britain. Some £12,000 million has been spent on developing natural gas resources on the UKCS and over 785,250 million cubic metres have been produced.

Structure

The gas industry in Great Britain, in state ownership since 1949, was privatised in 1986. British Gas plc is the main public gas supplier, but has an obligation to act as a common carrier for other companies, and five now supply gas, in competition with British Gas, through the company's transport network. Its activities are monitored by the Office of Gas Supply, and the Gas Consumers Council looks after the interests of consumers.

British Gas has about 2·3 million private and institutional shareholders. In 1990–91 the turnover of British Gas and its subsidiary companies amounted to £9,491 million, of which gas supply in Britain accounted for £7,930 million. Current cost operating profit was £1,655 million. British Gas has nearly 80,000 employees in Britain.

Production

Total production of natural gas from the 33 fields in the UKCS in 1990 amounted to 49,549 million cubic metres. This includes gas used for drilling, production and pumping operations. Gas produced and used on North Sea production platforms and at terminals accounted for 3,273 million cubic metres, leaving 46,276 million for general supply. Total sales of UKCS gas to gas suppliers amounted to 46,000 million cubic metres—11·3 per cent higher than in 1989. In addition, 7,000 million cubic metres of gas were imported from Norway. UKCS production comes mainly from eight major gasfields: Leman, Indefatigable, North Alwyn, Audrey, Hewett and Della, Vulcan, Frigg (UK) and Viking. Gas from the South Morecambe field in the Irish Sea and from the twin North Sean and South Sean fields is used to augment supplies to meet peak demand in winter. In 1990 two new developments were approved, Anglia and Pickerill.

Remaining recoverable gas reserves, including possible gas from existing discoveries and potential future discoveries, are estimated to be in the range of 963,000 million to 3·35 million million cubic metres. Indigenous offshore natural gas reserves are likely to meet most of the British demand well into the next century.

Transmission and Storage

The British Gas national and regional high-pressure pipeline system of some 17,600 km (11,100 miles) transports natural gas around Great Britain. It is supplied from four North Sea shore terminals, and from a terminal in Barrow-in-Furness (Cumbria). The high-pressure transmission system is inspected regularly.

Various methods of storage of natural gas to meet peak demand are used, including salt cavities and storage facilities for liquefied natural gas. British Gas has also developed the partially depleted Rough field as a major gas store. This, the first such use of an offshore field, involves the injection into the Rough reservoir in

Gas

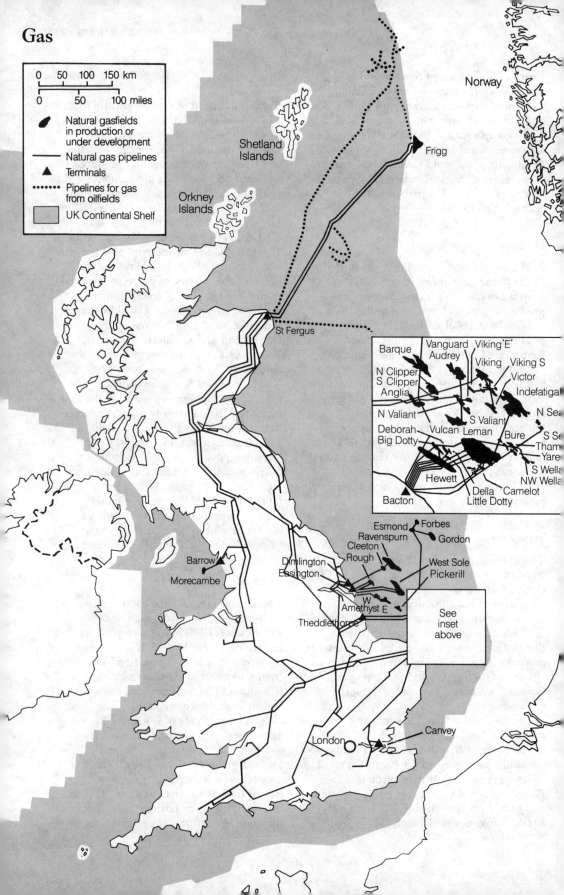

Legend:
- Natural gasfields in production or under development
- Natural gas pipelines
- ▲ Terminals
- ••• Pipelines for gas from oilfields
- UK Continental Shelf

Scale:
0 50 100 150 km
0 50 100 miles

Norway

Shetland Islands

Orkney Islands

Frigg

St Fergus

Inset (See inset above):
Barque
Vanguard
Viking 'E'
Audrey
Viking
Viking S
N Clipper
S Clipper
Anglia
Victor
Indefatiga
N Valiant
S Valiant
N Sea
Deborah
Big Dotty
Vulcan
Leman
Bure
S Se
Tham
Yare
S Wella
NW Wella
Hewett
Della
Little Dotty
Camelot
Bacton

Esmond
Forbes
Ravenspurn
Gordon
Cleeton
Rough
West Sole
Pickerill
Dimlington
Easington
W
Amethyst E
Theddlethorpe

Barrow
Morecambe

London

Canvey

See inset above

summer of gas drawn from the national transmission system for recovery at high rates during periods of peak winter demand.

Consumption

Sales of gas by the supply industry in Britain totalled 19,626 million therms in 1990–91. About 45 per cent of all gas sold by British Gas to its almost 18 million consumers is for industrial and commercial purposes, the remainder being for household use.

Gas is used extensively in industries requiring the control of temperatures to a fine degree of accuracy, such as the pottery industry, and in certain processes for making iron and steel products.

In 1990–91, 5,598 million therms of gas were sold to industry in Britain, and 3,188 million therms to commercial and other non-domestic users. An increasingly large part of domestic demand is for gas for central heating. In 1990–91, 10,840 million therms were sold to domestic users.

Research

British Gas has a worldwide reputation for gas technology, with a research programme costing £85 million in 1990–91. It is involved in joint research with overseas gas companies. Its technology transfer group is assisting utilities in over 20 countries in transmission, distribution and other areas. British Gas is today exploring for and producing gas and oil in some 20 countries.

COAL

Coalmining in Britain can be traced back to Roman times. It played a crucial part in the industrial revolution of the eighteenth and nineteenth centuries. In its peak year, 1913, the industry produced 292 million tonnes of coal, exported 74·2 million tonnes and employed over 1 million workers. In 1947 the coalmines passed into public ownership, and the National Coal Board (now the British

Coal Corporation) was set up. The Government has announced that it will introduce legislation to privatise the coal industry during the next Parliament. It has also reduced the debt under which the industry was operating and eliminated accumulated liabilities incurred by British Coal.

British Coal Corporation

British Coal has, with limited exceptions, exclusive rights over the extraction of coal in Great Britain. It is empowered to license private operators to work mines with an employee limit of 150 and opencast sites with a production limit of 250,000 tonnes, so that underground and opencast deposits too small for British Coal to work can be usefully exploited. It also has powers to work other minerals, where discoveries are made in the course of searching for, or working, coal; and to engage in certain petrochemicals activities beneficial to the future of the coal industry.

Production

In 1990–91 total output of 91·6 million tonnes comprised 72·3 million tonnes of deep-mined coal, 17 million tonnes from opencast mines and 2·3 million tonnes from licensed mines. At the end of March 1991 there were 65 British Coal collieries in operation. At the same date its workforce was 74,300, of whom 57,300 were miners. British Coal Opencast also had 61 sites in operation at the end of March 1991. Since 1984 British Coal, through its job creation activity, British Coal Enterprise, has helped create job opportunities for 71,000 people in areas where mining was previously the main source of employment.

Development

Britain's coal industry is the largest hard-coal industry in Western Europe, and one of the world's most technologically advanced. British Coal has a substantial investment programme, which amounted to £368 million in 1990–91. Technical progress has been concentrated on equipment capable of obtaining higher output from fewer faces. By

Coal

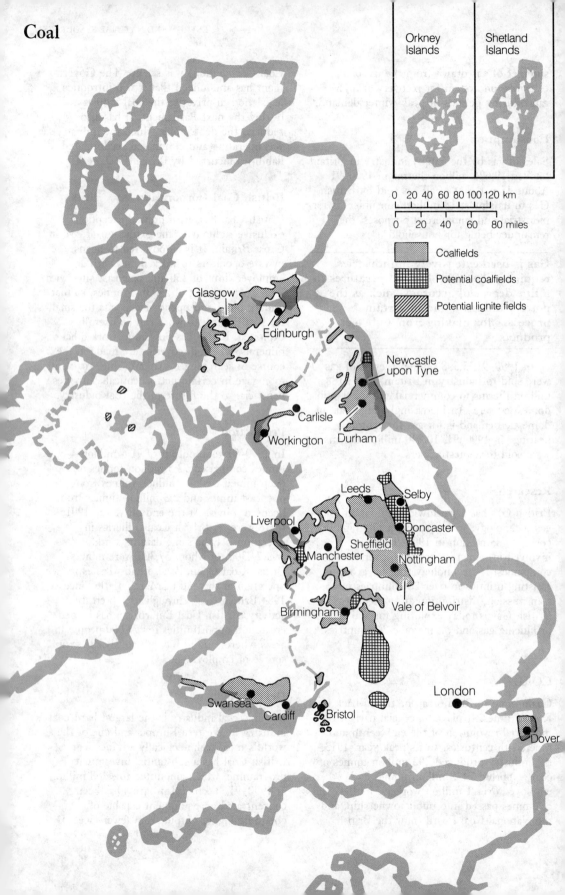

Orkney Islands

Shetland Islands

0 20 40 60 80 100 120 km	
0 20 40 60 80 miles	

Coalfields

Potential coalfields

Potential lignite fields

Glasgow

Edinburgh

Newcastle upon Tyne

Carlisle

Workington

Durham

Leeds

Selby

Liverpool

Doncaster

Sheffield

Manchester

Nottingham

Birmingham

Vale of Belvoir

Swansea

Cardiff

Bristol

London

Dover

early 1991 some 75 per cent of all coal faces were equipped with heavy duty supports available in all seam sections. The new mining complex at Selby in North Yorkshire (one of the world's most advanced deep mines) is planned to produce up to 10 million tonnes a year. The development of a new mine at Asfordby within the Vale of Belvoir (Leicestershire) is in progress.

Significant reserves of lignite (brown coal) have been discovered in Northern Ireland in the clay basins around Lough Neagh and at Ballymoney. Companies under government licence are prospecting to determine their extent, possibly over 1,000 million tonnes.

Consumption

In 1990–91 inland consumption of coal was 108·7 million tonnes, of which 75·3 per cent was by power stations, 9·8 per cent by coke ovens and 5·2 per cent by domestic users. With a substantial proportion of coal being used by power stations for electricity generation, British Coal sales of coal to them totalled 74·3 million tonnes in 1990–91. Exports of coal in 1990–91 were 2·1 million tonnes, while imports amounted to 16·9 million tonnes.

Research

The Government's and British Coal's principal research objective is to make the burning of coal more environmentally acceptable. It aims to reduce emissions of sulphur dioxide, nitrogen oxides (NOx), CO_2 and other gases associated with the greenhouse effect. Key projects are the British Coal topping cycle development programme, designed to improve the efficiency of combined cycle power generation to 45 per cent. It offers a 20 per cent reduction in CO_2 emissions from coal-fired power stations. Further studies into combined cycle power plant worked by coal gasification have been possible through the British Coal gasification development programme. A number of projects aimed at reducing NOx emissions in pulverised coal combustion have government support, some in collaboration with the IEA.

The coal liquefaction plant at Point of Ayr (Clwyd), opened in 1990 and costing £40 million, converts 2·5 tonnes of coal a day into petrol, diesel and other transport fuels. The Government has also established a coal task force, to review clean coal technologies and technologies aimed at maximising economically recoverable coal from Great Britain's coal reserves.

ELECTRICITY

In 1990–91 certain parts of the electricity supply industry were restructured and offered for sale. The sales took place between November 1990 and June 1991. Electricity from the supply system is available to all premises in Britain except for some very remote households.

Restructuring after Privatisation

The privatised electricity supply industry in England and Wales consists of three main generating companies, the National Grid Company (NGC) and 12 regional electricity companies (RECs). The two main non-nuclear generators, National Power and PowerGen, the publicly owned nuclear generator, Nuclear Electric plc, and other generators and importers sell electricity to suppliers through a market known as the pool. The NGC operates the transmission system—the bulk transfer of electricity across the national grid—and owns the pumped storage stations at Dinorwig and Ffestiniog. It is owned by the RECs through a holding company. Distribution and supply of electricity are the business of the RECs. Distribution involves transfer of electricity from the national grid and its delivery, across local systems, to consumers. Supply is the sale of electricity to customers. Each REC is authorised to supply any premises within its area. Other companies may obtain a second-tier licence to supply, although initially competition is limited to premises with a maximum consumption of 1 MW.

The Government retains approximately 40 per cent of the issued ordinary share capital of each of National Power and

PowerGen, and will not sell, or otherwise dispose of, this holding before 1 April 1993.

Restructuring in Scotland has created three companies. Two vertically integrated companies, ScottishPower plc and Scottish Hydro-Electric plc, generate, transmit, distribute and supply electricity. They also buy it from Scottish Nuclear Ltd, a government-owned company which operates the nuclear power stations at Hunterston (Strathclyde) and Torness (Lothian), and, under long-term contracts, from each other. Opportunities exist to export and import electricity to and from the pool (see above). The boundary separating the ScottishPower and Scottish Hydro-Electric supply areas runs from Loch Long on the Firth of Clyde to Newburgh on the Firth of Tay.

Certain service and co-ordinating functions for the industry are carried on by the Electricity Association, jointly owned by the electricity companies of Great Britain. Regulation of the industry is the responsibility of the Office of Electricity Regulation, headed by the Director General of Electricity Supply, whose duties include the promotion of competition and the protection of consumer interests.

Details of government proposals to privatise the electricity supply industry in Northern Ireland have been published. Generation, transmission and distribution are at present carried out by Northern Ireland Electricity, a public corporation.

Consumption

In 1990 sales of electricity through the distribution system in Britain amounted to 271,940 gigawatt hours (GWh). Domestic users took 34 per cent of the total, industry 33 per cent and commercial and other users the remainder. About 24 per cent of domestic sales is for space heating, 13 per cent for water heating and 8 per cent for cooking. Electricity is used in industry mainly for motive power, melting, heating and lighting.

Generation

National Power owns 35 operational fossil-fuelled power stations which generate approximately 46 per cent of the electricity supplied to the transmission and distribution networks in England and Wales. PowerGen owns 19 fossil-fuelled power stations which generate approximately 30 per cent of this electricity. The 12 nuclear stations of Nuclear Electric generate approximately 17 per cent. In 1990–91, about 38 per cent of electricity supplied in Scotland was produced by Scottish Nuclear's two stations. The power stations operated by ScottishPower

Table 15.3: Generation by and Capacity of Power Stations owned by the Major Generating Companies in Britain

	Electricity generated (GWh)			Output Per cent capacity[a]	
	1980	1985	1990	1990	(MW)
Nuclear plant	33,462	56,354	61,306	21	10,733
Other steam plant	227,973	216,255	230,376	77	51,365
Gas turbines and oil engines	451	1,084	437[b]	–	3,136[b]
Pumped-storage plant	1,188	2,831	1,982	1	2,787
Natural flow hydro-electric plant	3,309	3,447	4,393	1	1,302
Total	266,383	279,972	298,495	100	69,323
Electricity supplied (net)[c]	247,667	258,242	277,978		

Source: Department of Energy.

[a] At 31 March 1991.

[b] These figures include generation by and capacity of wind power stations.

[c] Electricity generated less electricity used at power stations (both electricity used on works and that used for pumping at pumped-storage stations).

Note: Differences between totals and the sums of their component parts are due to rounding.

Electricity

Orkney Islands

Shetland Islands

0 20 40 60 80 100 120 km

0 20 40 60 80 miles

■ Conventional power stations (1,000 MW and over)

● Nuclear power stations

○ Under construction

◆ Power-producing reactors of the UKAEA or BNFL

★ Hydro-electric power stations (over 45-MW capacity)

▲ Pumped storage schemes

⋯⋯ Boundary of ScottishPower and Scottish Hydro-Electric

Dounreay

Fasnakyle
Foyers
Peterhead

Errochty
Rannoch
Cruachan
Clunie
Lochay
Sloy
Longannet
Torness
Inverkip
Cockenzie
Hunterston B Hunterston A

Chapelcross
Blyth B

Hartlepool

Calder Hall

Heysham I Heysham II
Ferrybridge C Drax
Eggborough

Wylfa
Fiddler's Ferry
West Burton
Cottam
Dinorwig Ince
High Marnham
Ffestiniog
Trawsfynydd
Ratcliffe-on-Soar
Rugeley B
Rheidol
Drakelow B and C

Sizewell A
Sizewell B

Tilbury
W. Thurrock Bradwell
Pembroke
Aberthaw B
Didcot
Oldbury
Littlebrook Grain
Kingsnorth
Hinkley Pt. A Hinkley Pt. B
Dungeness B
Fawley
Winfrith
Dungeness A

rated by
tishPower

and Hydro-Electric provided most of the balance. ScottishPower has 15 power stations and in 1990–91 its three coal-fired stations produced 52 per cent of the electricity supplied in its area, with nuclear power contributing 39 per cent. Hydro-Electric has 59 stations (mostly hydro, but one major oil/gas station), and in 1990–91 they produced 65·5 per cent of the electricity supplied in its area, with nuclear power contributing 26 per cent. All of Scottish Nuclear's production is sold to ScottishPower and Hydro-Electric in the proportions 74·9 per cent and 25·1 per cent respectively.

Power stations owned by Britain's major generating companies consumed 69·8 million tonnes of oil equivalent in 1990, of which coal accounted for 70 per cent and oil 9·6 per cent. The declared net capacity of these stations at the end of March 1991 totalled 69,323 MW.

Independent generators are allowed to compete on equal terms with the major generators and have equal access to the grid transmission and local distribution systems.

To control acid emissions the Government expects National Power and PowerGen each to fit flue gas desulphurisation (FGD) equipment to 4 GW of their existing coal-fired power stations. Work is in progress towards fitting FGD equipment to National Power's Drax station (North Yorkshire). For its part, ScottishPower expects to fit FGD as necessary at the Longannet station. In addition, a ten-year programme to control NOx emissions through the installation of low-NOx burners at the 12 largest power stations in England and Wales, at a cost of approximately £185 million, is also in progress. Both Scottish companies are expected to fit low-NOx burners at their main stations.

For new stations the trend is towards the construction of combined cycle gas turbines (CCGT). They are less costly to build than other types of station, and have shorter construction times. Their use of natural gas, low in sulphur, also helps to reduce acid and CO_2 emissions. The installation of the more efficient CCGT plant should also help to stabilise CO_2 emissions from the electricity supply industry. In England and Wales, nine stations over 50 MW have been given planning consent under the Electricity Act 1989.

The pumped-storage station at Dinorwig (Gwynedd), the largest of its type in Europe, has an average generated output of 1,728 MW. (In pumped-storage schemes electricity generated in off-peak periods is used to pump water to high-level reservoirs, from which it descends to drive turbines, rapidly providing a large supply of electricity at peak periods or to meet sudden increases in demand.)

The National Grid Company, together with Electricité de France, runs a 2,000-MW cross-Channel cable link, providing the capacity for the transmission of electricity between the two countries. Transmission lines linking the Scottish and English grid systems enable cross-border trading. This interconnector is run jointly by the NGC and ScottishPower. Its capacity is planned to be increased from 850 MW to 1,600 MW by 1994–95. Electrical interconnection, from the mid-1990s, between Northern Ireland and Great Britain has been agreed.

Nuclear Power

In 1956, the world's first industrial-scale nuclear power station, at Calder Hall (Cumbria), began to supply electricity to the national grid. There are 16 commercial nuclear power stations in Britain: nine Magnox stations (with capacities ranging from 200 to 840 MW) and seven Advanced Gas-cooled Reactor stations (AGRs; ranging from 1,200 MW to 1,320 MW). Construction of a pressurised water reactor (PWR) of 1,182 MW at Sizewell (Suffolk) is expected to be completed in 1994. Two of the smaller Magnox stations are now shut down and undergoing decommissioning.

The Government wishes to maintain the role of nuclear power, to increase the diversity of supply, and thus to help to maintain security of supply. Nuclear power can also play an important part in curbing acid rain and ameliorating global warming, as nuclear power stations emit almost no sulphur dioxide, NOx or CO_2. The Government intends to review the prospects for nuclear power in 1994, when the PWR at Sizewell will be nearing completion. The Magnox stations, AGRs and PWR in England and Wales, owned by Nuclear Electric, provide between 15 and 20 per cent of electricity in England and Wales. The two AGRs in Scotland, owned by Scottish Nuclear, supplied 37 per cent of the electricity generated in Scotland in 1990–91.

In England and Wales the RECs are statutorily required, under the non-fossil fuel obligation, to buy a minimum amount of non-fossil-fuelled generating capacity, including nuclear. Since the price of nuclear electricity is somewhat higher than that of fossil-fuelled electricity, a levy may be raised on all sales from sources which could be environmentally damaging, including fossil fuels, so that the additional cost is shared by all electricity suppliers. The Government has no plans at present to introduce such an obligation in Scotland, which already has a high level of non-fossil-fuel generating capacity.

British Nuclear Fuels

British Nuclear Fuels plc provides services covering the whole nuclear fuel cycle. All of its shares are held by the Government. The company, with headquarters at Risley (Cheshire), conducts operations at four further sites: Springfields (Lancashire), where fuel is manufactured; Capenhurst (Cheshire), where uranium is enriched to provide fuel for nuclear reactors; Sellafield (Cumbria), where Calder Hall is located and where spent fuel is reprocessed; and Chapelcross Magnox power station (Dumfries and Galloway).

A substantial investment programme, mainly at Sellafield, includes the thermal oxide reprocessing plant (THORP), expected to be completed in 1992, which will take spent fuel from British and overseas oxide reactors, and a vitrification treatment plant, completed in 1991, to turn the high-level

liquid waste left after reprocessing spent nuclear fuel into stable glass blocks for storage before eventual disposal.

Nuclear Research

The nuclear research and development funded by the Department of Energy is carried out by the UKAEA—nine semi-autonomous businesses operating as AEA Technology. The work is carried out at six sites: Harwell and Culham (Oxfordshire), Risley, Winfrith (Dorset), Windscale (Cumbria) and Dounreay (Highland). In addition, safety research is carried out by AEA Safety and Reliability at Culcheth (Cheshire).

Co-operation on nuclear energy between Britain and other countries takes place within a framework of intergovernmental agreements and membership of bodies such as the International Atomic Energy Agency and the Nuclear Energy Agency, as well as through direct links on research between AEA Technology and equivalent organisations overseas.

Britain takes part in the co-operative research programmes of the European Atomic Energy Community (Euratom). A major component of this programme is the Joint European Torus (JET) project at Culham, which started operating in 1983. AEA Technology has an agreement with its French and German counterparts to set out the terms for European fast reactor research and development collaboration. The fast reactor project, sponsored by nuclear utilities in Britain, France and Germany, is due to complete the initial design phase of a commercial demonstration reactor in 1993.

Nuclear Safety

Britain has a rigorous system of nuclear safety regulation, enforced by the Health and Safety Executive's Nuclear Installations Inspectorate, which ensures that high standards of safety are incorporated into the design, construction, operation, maintenance and eventual decommissioning of all nuclear plant. While the safety of such plant in Britain is the ultimate responsibility of the nuclear operator, the Inspectorate has extensive powers and an operator must satisfy it before a licence is granted. Operators must protect their workers and the public by complying with the Health and Safety at Work etc. Act 1974, as well as with the conditions of their nuclear site licences under the Nuclear Installations Act 1965. The Inspectorate has the power to shut down a plant if it is believed to be unsafe and may also require improvements to an installation if it thinks the appropriate safety standards are not being met.

Discharges have to be kept within the limits and conditions set by authorisations granted under the Radioactive Substances Act 1960. In England and Wales authorisations are granted jointly by the Secretary of State for the Environment and the Minister of Agriculture, Fisheries and Food, and in Scotland by the Secretary of State for Scotland. Within maximum dose limits, operators of nuclear facilities are required to keep discharges as low as reasonably achievable and failure to do so makes them liable to prosecution. Compliance with the legislation is overseen by Her Majesty's Inspectorate of Pollution in England and Wales, and by Her Majesty's Industrial Pollution Inspectorate in Scotland.

On nuclear safety, Britain has a number of bilateral agreements and arrangements, with, for example, France, the Soviet Union and the United States, covering the exchange of information relating to all matters affecting nuclear safety. International conventions have been established on the early notification of a nuclear accident with possible transboundary effects, and on the mutual provision of assistance in the event of a nuclear accident or radiological emergency.

Emergency Plans

The precautions taken in the design and construction of nuclear installations in Britain, and the high safety standards in their operation and maintenance, reduce the chance of accidents which might affect the public to an extremely low level. However, all operators are required to prepare emergency plans, including those for dealing with an accidental release of radioactivity, which are regularly tested in exercises under the supervision of the Nuclear Installations Inspectorate.

Research on Electricity

Research and development are a matter for the individual companies, but some research is carried out jointly. National Power and PowerGen maintain a joint environmental programme. Technological research on generation and main transmission is undertaken primarily by the generating companies and by the NGC. The research establishments comprise: Berkeley Nuclear Laboratories (Gloucestershire; Nuclear Electric); the Technology and Environment Centre at Leatherhead (Surrey; National Power); the Marchwood Engineering Laboratories at Southampton Water (PowerGen); the Ratcliffe Technology Centre at Ratcliffe-on-Soar (Nottingham; PowerGen); and the Research and Development Centre at Leatherhead.

RENEWABLE SOURCES OF ENERGY

The Department of Energy supports research, development and demonstration in the renewable energy technologies. It aims to exploit alternative sources of energy which have the potential to be economically viable and environmentally acceptable. It also encourages industry to develop both internal and export markets. Its current programme includes some 300 projects with a financial commitment of £60 million. Work is at present concentrated on the most promising technologies.

The Government is aiming at a figure of 1,000 MW of electricity generation capacity from renewable energy by the year 2000. In 1990, the first Order under the non-fossil fuel obligation identified 75 projects qualifying as non-fossil fuel electricity capacity, which will increase the renewable capacity in England and Wales to 250 MW.

Wind Power

Wind power remains one of the most promising technologies. The Department of Energy's research programme for 1991–92 is estimated to cost £7·7 million, with an aim of 25 new projects initiated and 100 projects managed. Among the projects supported by the Department are:

- two vertical-axis wind turbines, inaugurated in 1986 and 1990 at Carmarthen Bay (Dyfed);
- a 300-kW turbine also at Carmarthen Bay;
- a 3-MW, 60-m (200-ft) turbine, in collaboration with Scottish Hydro-Electric, on Orkney, inaugurated in 1987;
- a 1-MW, 55-m (180-ft) diameter turbine at Richborough (Kent), inaugurated in 1990; and
- two 300-kW turbines at the National Wind Turbine Centre (East Kilbride), opened in 1991.

Plans for experimental wind farms are progressing. National Wind Power Limited, formed in 1991, plans to install complete wind farm packages on suitable sites.

Geothermal Energy

Under its geothermal hot dry rock programme, during 1976–91, the Government investigated, through work carried out in Cornwall by the Camborne School of Mines, the economic possibilities of extracting heat from rocks at a depth of 2 to 6 km (1·25 to 4 miles). It has concluded that further funding should go largely towards participating in a joint programme with France, Germany and the European Community, which could resolve some of the technical uncertainties.

Tidal Power

Tidal power is one of the most promising of the renewable technologies for large-scale electricity generation. Its exceptionally high tidal range makes the Severn estuary one of the best potential sites in the world, and the Department of Energy has funded, with the Severn Tidal Power Group and the electricity supply industry, a £4·2 million study into the viability of a Severn tidal barrage, of which a general report has been published. The Government has contributed some £5 million to three phases of studies on an energy barrage on the Mersey estuary.

Passive Solar Design

The Government continues support for a solar programme. Passive solar design is considered the best way to utilise solar energy in Britain and has already proved cost-effective in both domestic and non-domestic buildings, using their form and fabric to admit, store and distribute solar energy for heating and improving daylight. The Best Practice programme of the EEO encourages the technology. Recent advances in photovoltaics—in which treated glass plates convert sunlight directly into electricity—have suggested that photovoltaic materials incorporated into the cladding and roofing of buildings could provide competitive electricity generation.

Biofuels

Biofuels offer possibly the largest contribution from the renewable energy resources in the medium term. The main work of the Department's programme is on the combustion of wastes, anaerobic digestion (particularly as applied to the production and use of landfill gas) and energy forestry. Britain is the largest user of landfill gas as an energy source in the European Community, and is second only to the United States in its exploitation. Each year about 30 million tonnes of waste are produced in Britain. Over 90 per cent is landfilled.

Wave Energy

The Department of Energy also has a research and development programme into wave energy, based on a project on the island of Islay. The small-scale shoreline

Some Minerals Produced in Britain

Orkney Islands

Shetland Islands

talc

talc

0 20 40 60 80 100 120 km

0 20 40 60 80 miles

● Major metallic and industrial mineral workings

▲ Major mineral deposits (unworked)

silica sand

barytes, lead, zinc

▲ gold

gold

barytes

silica sand

silica sand

gold ▲ ▲ salt

diatomite

fluorspar, lead

NORTHERN PENNINE OREFIELD

gypsum

barytes

salt

potash

salt

silica sand

SOUTHERN PENNINE OREFIELD

zinc, copper, lead, silver ▲

silica sand

salt

salt

fluorspar, barytes, lead

gypsum

gold ▲

CHESHIRE SALTFIELD

gypsum

gypsum

silica sand

silica sand

fuller's earth

fuller's earth

silica sand

fuller's earth

celestite ▲

fuller's earth

silica sand

fuller's earth

gypsum

ball clay

china clay

ball clay

ball clay

china clay ▲

china clay

tungsten, tin

tin ▲

device has been constructed by the Queen's University of Belfast, which is carrying out a complementary study to assess the potential for shoreline devices in Britain. A review of wave energy is expected to be completed by the end of 1991.

Non-fuel Minerals

Although much of Britain's requirements for industrial raw materials is met by imports, non-fuel minerals produced in Britain make an important contribution to the economy. Output of non-fuel minerals in 1989 totalled over 394 million tonnes, valued at £2,018 million. The total number of employees in the extraction industry was some 43,500 in 1989.

Exploration

Exploration for, and exploitation of, indigenous mineral resources to meet the needs of industry are encouraged by the Government. The British Geological Survey is carrying out a long-term programme for the Department of Trade and Industry aimed at identifying areas with the potential for the economic extraction of minerals.

Production

In terms of value, production of sand and gravel was estimated at £583 million in 1989, limestone and dolomite £574 million, clays £284 million, igneous rock £223 million, sandstone £78 million, potash £60 million, silica sands £46 million, chalk £46 million, salt £33 million, gypsum and anhydrite £24 million, tin £19 million, fuller's earth £15 million and fluorspar £12 million. In 1989 the production of metals in non-ferrous ores totalled 12,300 tonnes, mainly tin and zinc from Cornwall. The Cornish mines, one of the very few sources of tin in the European Community, produced some 3,800 tonnes in 1989, satisfying about half of Britain's demand. Small amounts of copper and silver were produced in association with tin and zinc, and some lead and zinc with barytes and fluorspar. A little gold came from a mine in north Wales.

Water

Britain's water supplies are obtained partly from surface sources such as mountain lakes, streams impounded in upland gathering grounds and lowland river intakes, and partly

Table 15·4: Production of Some of the Main Non-fuel Minerals

			million tonnes
	1979	1984	1989
Sand and gravel	111·5	106·0	138·4
Silica sand	5·8	4·3	4·4
Igneous rock	36·2	36·9	54·5
Limestone and dolomite	92·2	93·5	132·7
Chalk[a]	16·3	12·0	13·9
Sandstone	13·5	15·1	19·6
Gypsum	3·5	3·1	4·0
Salt including salt in brine	7·8	7·1	n.a.
Common clay and shale	21·6[a]	17·8[a]	19·4
China clay and ball clay	4·4	3·6	3·9
Fireclay	1·7	0·8	1·1
Iron ore	4·3	0·4	–
Potash	0·4	0·5	0·8
Fluorspar	0·1	0·1	0·1
Fuller's earth	0·2	0·2	0·2

Source: *United Kingdom Minerals Yearbook 1990.*
[a] Great Britain only.
n.a. = not available.

from underground sources by means of wells, springs, adits and boreholes. About 99 per cent of the population in Great Britain and 97 per cent in Northern Ireland are connected to the public water supply system. Water for public supply in England and Wales amounted to about 16,600 megalitres (Ml) a day in 1989–90 and average daily domestic consumption per head was 136 litres.

Supplies

Some 33,333 Ml a day were abstracted in England and Wales in 1989, of which public water supplies accounted for 17,884 Ml a day. The electricity generating companies and other industry took some 15,050 Ml a day. Agriculture took 398 Ml a day.

England and Wales

The Water Act 1989 privatised the utility functions of the ten former water authorities in England and Wales. It provided for the Secretaries of State for the Environment and for Wales, the Director General of Water Services and the National Rivers Authority (NRA) to be the principal regulators of the industry. The Minister of Agriculture, Fisheries and Food and the Secretary of State for Wales are responsible for policy relating to land drainage, flood protection, sea defence, and the protection and development of fisheries. The Drinking Water Inspectorate was set up to regulate drinking water quality.

Water Companies

The ten water service companies are the principal operating subsidiaries of the ten water holding companies. They have statutory responsibilities for water supply, sewerage and sewage treatment, and for ensuring adequate supplies. The 29 supply only companies, which in 1989 were already in the private sector, operate as water undertakers in certain areas. Those which convert to plc status may also become sewerage undertakers by agreement with the relevant water service company or on sites

where no service exists.

The Water Act 1989 allows the water companies to determine their own methods of charging. At present most charges are based on the former rateable value system, although customers may choose to pay to have a water meter installed. In general, companies require new properties to have metered supplies. An alternative to the system based on rateable values, however, must be found by the year 2000. Wide-scale water metering is one of the choices being considered.

A system of economic regulation and guaranteed standards of service is overseen by the Director General of Water Services. The Water Supply (Water Quality) Regulations 1989 define wholesomeness and incorporate the requirements of the European Community's drinking water directive. They impose physical, chemical and microbiological standards for water intended for domestic and food production purposes. The task of the Drinking Water Inspectorate is to ensure that drinking water is wholesome and that companies comply with the Regulations.

National Rivers Authority

The NRA is the environmental regulatory arm of the water industry. The Authority is a non-departmental public body with statutory duties and powers in relation to water resources, pollution control, flood defence, fisheries, recreation, conservation and navigation in England and Wales. The water environment for which it has responsibility includes all rivers, lakes, reservoirs, estuaries, coastal waters and water stored naturally underground. The NRA's consent is needed for the abstraction of water and for discharges to water.

Development Projects

The water industry in England and Wales is committed to a ten-year investment programme costing over £26,000 million. Thames Water is constructing an 80-km (50-mile) distribution system to meet the growing demand for water in London. This is due to be completed in 1996. North West Water has a major 25-year programme of investment to clean up the polluted rivers of the Mersey Basin.

Water is seen as an increasingly scarce resource, but more in demand. The industry, through contingency planning and publicity campaigns, aims to encourage the wise use of water, especially when supplies run low because of prolonged warm, dry weather. The NRA has published a survey of the prospects for public water supplies to the year 2011 in England and Wales. It is investigating the strategic development of water resources, including major new transfer schemes, and is reviewing the possibilities of a national grid and desalination.

Scotland

In Scotland responsibility for public water supply, sewerage and sewage disposal rests with the nine regional and three islands councils. In addition, the Central Scotland Water Development Board is responsible for developing new sources of water supply to provide water in bulk to the regional councils in an area of 25,900 sq km (10,000 sq miles) in central Scotland. Water is charged for according to type of consumer: domestic consumers pay community water charges; non-domestic consumers pay by means of non-domestic water rates, or through metered charges. Charges and rates are decided by each authority.

Scotland has a relative abundance of unpolluted water from upland sources. An average of 2,248 Ml a day was supplied in Scotland in 1989–90. The Secretary of State for Scotland is responsible for the promotion of the conservation of water resources and

the provision by water authorities of adequate water supplies, and has a duty to promote the cleanliness of rivers and other inland waters, and the tidal waters of Scotland. River purification authorities have a statutory responsibility for water pollution control.

Northern Ireland

The Department of the Environment for Northern Ireland is responsible for public water supply and sewerage throughout Northern Ireland. It is also responsible for the conservation and cleanliness of water resources and, with the Department of Agriculture for Northern Ireland, may prepare a water management programme with respect to water resources in any area. There is a domestic water charge which is contained in the regional rate, while agriculture, commerce and industry pay metered charges. There are abundant potential supplies of water for both domestic and industrial use. An average of 666 Ml of water a day was supplied in 1989–90.

Research

Several organisations and centres of expertise provide water research services to government, the NRA, water companies and the Scottish river purification boards. The Water Research Centre has main laboratories at Medmenham (Buckinghamshire) and at Swindon (Wiltshire). Research undertaken includes environmental issues. Other organisations conducting research include Hydraulics Research Limited, universities, the Meteorological Office, the Ministry of Agriculture, Fisheries and Food, and several institutes of the Natural Environment Research Council.

16 Agriculture, Fisheries and Forestry

Agriculture

British agriculture is noted for its high level of efficiency and productivity. In 1990 it employed 2·1 per cent of the total workforce and Britain was self-sufficient in 56 per cent of all types of food and animal feed. It was self-sufficient in about 73 per cent of indigenous-type food and feed. Food, feed and beverages accounted for just over 10 per cent of Britain's imports by value in 1990, compared with about a quarter in the 1960s. The agricultural contribution to gross domestic product was £6,378 million in 1990, about 1·4 per cent of the total. Britain is also a major exporter of agricultural produce and food products, agrochemicals and agricultural machinery.

The Government aims to foster an efficient and competitive agriculture industry through the provision and sponsorship of research, development and advisory services, the provision of financial support where appropriate, measures to control disease, pests and pollution, and improved marketing arrangements for food and food products. It also insists on high standards of animal welfare. Agriculture ministers must balance the needs of an efficient agricultural industry with other interests in the countryside. These include conservation of its natural beauty and promotion of its enjoyment by the public.

Land Use

The area of agricultural land has been declining, although there has been a reduction in the net rate of loss in recent years. In 1990 there were just under 12 million hectares (29·4 million acres) under crops and grass. Just under 6 million hectares (14·3 million acres) were used for rough grazing, most of it in hilly areas. Soils vary from the thin poor ones of highland Britain to the rich fertile soils of low-lying areas such as the fenlands of eastern England. The temperate climate and the relatively even distribution of rainfall over the year ensure a long growing season; streams rarely dry up and grassland normally remains green throughout the year.

Farming

In 1990 there were some 237,400 farm holdings in Britain (excluding minor holdings), of which about 63 per cent in England, Scotland and Wales were wholly or mainly owner-occupied. Virtually all the farms in Northern Ireland are owner-occupied. The average farm size (including rough grazing) is 100·7 hectares (249 acres), again excluding minor holdings. It is estimated that just under 13 per cent of holdings are in the largest-size group, which accounted for 57 per cent of activity, while the smallest-size group (41 per cent of farms)

Land Use in Britain

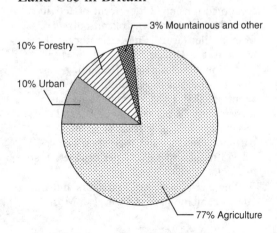

3% Mountainous and other
10% Forestry
10% Urban
77% Agriculture

Agricultural Land Use 1990

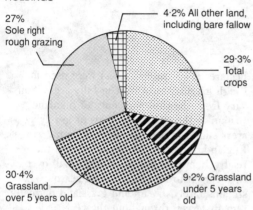

TOTAL AREA ON AGRICULTURAL HOLDINGS

- 27% Sole right rough grazing
- 4·2% All other land, including bare fallow
- 29·3% Total crops
- 9·2% Grassland under 5 years old
- 30·4% Grassland over 5 years old

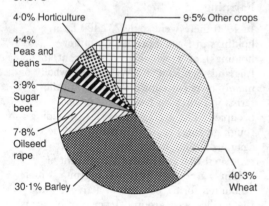

CROPS

- 4·0% Horticulture
- 9·5% Other crops
- 4·4% Peas and beans
- 3·9% Sugar beet
- 7·8% Oilseed rape
- 30·1% Barley
- 40·3% Wheat

accounted for only 2·5 per cent of activity. In Wales and Northern Ireland output from smaller farms is more significant than in the rest of Britain.

The number of people (excluding spouses) engaged in agriculture in 1990 was about 566,000. Labour productivity has increased by 72 per cent since 1979. Total income from farming (that of farmers, partners, directors and their spouses) was £2,113 million in 1990, 7 per cent less than in 1989.

There are over 500,000 tractors and over 60,000 combine harvesters in use. Most

farms have a direct electricity supply, the remainder having their own generators. Horticultural crops such as blackcurrants and brussels sprouts are frequently harvested by machine, and milking machines are used on the vast majority of dairy farms.

Most farms in Britain produce a range of commodities. In choosing both their products and their inputs, farmers may be assisted by computer models.

PRODUCTION

Home production of the principal foods is shown in Table 16.1 as a percentage by weight of total supplies (that is, production plus imports minus exports).

Livestock

Over half of full-time farms are devoted mainly to dairying or beef cattle and sheep. The majority of sheep and cattle are reared in the hill and moorland areas of Scotland, Wales, Northern Ireland and northern and south-western England. Beef fattening occurs partly in better grassland areas, as does dairying, and partly on arable farms. British livestock breeders have developed many of the cattle, sheep and pig breeds with worldwide reputations, for example, the Hereford and Aberdeen Angus beef breeds, the Jersey, Guernsey and Ayrshire dairy breeds, Large White pigs and a number of sheep breeds. Because of developments in artificial insemination and embryo transfer, Britain is able to export semen and embryos from high-quality donor animals.

Cattle and Sheep

Most dairy cattle in England and Wales and a significant proportion in Scotland and Northern Ireland are bred by artificial insemination. In 1990 the average size of dairy herds in Britain was 63, while the average yield of milk per dairy cow was 5,137 litres (1,130 gallons). Average household consumption of liquid

Table 16.1: British Production as a Percentage of Total New Supplies

Food Product	1979–81 average	1990 (provisional)
Beef and veal	90	93
Eggs	100	93
Milk for human consumption (as liquid)	100	100
Cheese	68	64
Butter	53	65
Sugar (as refined)	48	55
Wheat	116	127
Potatoes	94	89

Source: Ministry of Agriculture, Fisheries and Food.

(including low-fat) milk per head in 1990 was 1·3 litres (2·2 pints) a week.

About two-thirds of home-fed beef production derives from the national dairy herd, in which the Friesian breed is predominant. The remainder is derived from suckler herds producing high-quality beef calves in the hills and uplands, where the traditional British beef breeds, such as Hereford and Aberdeen Angus, continue to be important. Imported breeds which have established themselves include the Charolais, Limousin, Simmental and Belgian Blue. In 1990 the size of the beef-breeding herd continued to expand and reached its highest level since 1977.

Britain has a long tradition of sheep production, with more than 40 breeds and many crosses between them. Research has provided vaccine and serum protection against nearly all the epidemic diseases. Although lamb production is the main source of income for sheep farmers, wool is also important.

Grass supplies 60 to 80 per cent of the feed for cattle and sheep. Grass production has been enhanced by the increased use of fertilisers, irrigation and methods of grazing control, and improved herbage conservation for winter feed. Rough grazings are used for extensively grazed sheep and cattle, producing young animals for fattening elsewhere.

16.2: Livestock and Livestock Products

	1979–81 average	1988	1989	1990 (provisional)
Cattle and calves ('000 head)	13,384	11,872	11,977	12,057
Sheep and lambs ('000 head)	31,163	40,942	42,967	43,788
Pigs ('000 head)	7,836	7,980	7,509	7,447
Poultry ('000 head)[a]	125,712	130,809	120,198	124,384
Milk (million litres)	15,286	14,445	14,225	14,583
Eggs (million dozen)[b]	1,134	1,037	932	947
Beef and veal ('000 tonnes)	1,076	945	972	991
Mutton and lamb ('000 tonnes)	268	342	385	391
Pork ('000 tonnes)	700	801	731	756
Bacon and ham ('000 tonnes)	207	196	191	179
Poultry and meat ('000 tonnes)	751	1,050	997	1,029

Source: Ministry of Agriculture, Fisheries and Food.

[a]Excluding ducks, geese, turkeys and guinea fowls. Data for 1988–90 cannot be compared with data for earlier years owing to changes in coverage of poultry holdings.

[b]Gross commercial production, including production for breeding and for human consumption.

Pigs and Poultry

Pig production occurs in most areas but is particularly important in eastern and northern England. There is an increasing concentration into specialist units and larger herds.

Output of poultry meat has continued to benefit from better husbandry and genetic improvements. Since 1979 British production has increased by just over a third to over 1 million tonnes in 1990. Production of broilers from holdings of over 100,000 birds accounts for over a half of total production. In 1990 British egg production continued to recover following stringent government measures to deal with salmonella. Over two-thirds of laying birds are on holdings with 20,000 or more birds. Britain remains broadly self-sufficient in poultry meat and eggs.

Animal Welfare

The welfare of farm animals is protected by legislation and it is an offence to cause unnecessary pain or distress to commercially reared livestock. For example, there are regulations requiring owners of intensive units to arrange for the daily inspection of their stock and the equipment on which it depends. There is increased protection for all livestock, poultry, rabbits and horses at markets, and specific controls on the marketing of foals and calves. There are laws which ban close confinement crates for keeping veal calves, phase out tether and close confinement systems for keeping pigs and protect animals

Table 16.3: Main Crops

	1979-81 average	1988	1989	1990 (provisional)
Wheat				
Area ('000 hectares)	1,435	1,886	2,083	2,013
Production ('000 tonnes)	8,116	11,750	14,032	14,035
Yield (tonnes per hectare)	5·66	6·23	6·74	6·97
Barley				
Area ('000 hectares)	2,335	1,878	1,652	1,517
Production ('000 tonnes)	10,059	8,771	8,070	7,894
Yield (tonnes per hectare)	4·31	4·67	4·88	5·20
Oats				
Area ('000 hectares)	142	120	119	107
Production ('000 tonnes)	587	547	528	529
Yield (tonnes per hectare)	4·12	4·55	4·45	4·94
Potatoes				
Area ('000 hectares)	200	181	175	178
Production ('000 tonnes)	6,524	6,899	6,198	6,390
Yield (tonnes per hectare)	32·57	38·07	35·40	35·84
Oilseed rape				
Area ('000 hectares)	97	347	321	390
Production ('000 tonnes)	279	1,040	976	1,209
Yield (tonnes per hectare)	2·88	3·00	3·04	3·10
Sugar beet				
Area ('000 hectares)	210	198	194	194
Production ('000 tonnes)	7,478	8,152	8,113	8,000
Yield (tonnes per hectare)	35·56	41·30	41·80	41·24

Sources: *Agriculture in the United Kingdom: 1990* and *Agricultural Census June 1990*.

at slaughter from unnecessary pain or distress. The Farm Animal Welfare Council, an independent body set up by the Government, advises on any legislative or other changes it considers necessary. The Government's proposed charter on animal welfare in the European Community aims to raise welfare standards in Europe.

Crops

The farms devoted primarily to arable crops are found mainly in eastern and central- southern England and eastern Scotland. In Britain in 1990 cereals were grown on 3·7 million hectares (9·1 million acres). Production of cereals, at 22·6 million tonnes, was similar to that in 1989. Between 40 and 50 per cent of available wheat supplies (allowing for imports and exports) are normally used for flour milling, and about half for animal feed. About a quarter of barley supplies are used for malting and distilling, and the remainder for animal feed. There was an increase of 24 per cent in 1990 in the production of oilseed rape, the increase in area reflecting the relatively high price paid for the 1989 crop.

Large-scale potato and vegetable production is undertaken in the fens (in Cambridgeshire and south Lincolnshire), the alluvial areas around the rivers Thames and Humber and the peaty lands in south Lancashire. Early potatoes are an important crop in Pembrokeshire (Dyfed), Kent and Cornwall. High-grade seed potatoes are grown in Scotland and Northern Ireland.

Sugar from home-grown sugar beet provides just under 50 per cent of requirements, most of the remainder being refined from raw cane sugar imported levy-free from developing countries under the Lomé Convention.

Horticulture

In 1990 the land utilised for horticulture was about 208,000 hectares (514,000 acres). Vegetables grown in the open (excluding potatoes) accounted for 68 per cent, orchards for 16·6 per cent, soft fruit for 7·4 per cent and ornamentals (including hardy nursery stock, bulbs and flowers grown in the open) for 6·6 per cent. More than one vegetable crop is, in some cases, taken from the same area of land in a year, so that the estimated area actually cropped in 1990 was 259,000 hectares (639,000 acres).

Field vegetables account for about one-third of the value of horticultural output and are widely grown throughout the country. Most horticultural enterprises are increasing productivity with the help of improved planting material, new techniques and the widespread use of machinery. Some field vegetables, for example, are raised in blocks of compressed peat or loose-filled cells, a technique which reduces root damage and allows plants to establish themselves more reliably and evenly.

Glasshouses are used for growing tomatoes, cucumbers, sweet peppers, lettuces, flowers, pot plants and nursery stock. Widespread use is made of automatic control of heating and ventilation, and semi-automatic control of watering. Energy-efficient glasshouses use thermal screens, while low-cost plastic tunnels extend the season for certain crops previously grown in the open. Government grants are available for replacing heated glass and heating systems.

The Government also provides grants for replanting apple and pear trees.

Under the European Community's Common Agricultural Policy (see p 287), a wide range of horticultural produce is subject to common quality standards.

Under Community rules, Britain has a production limit of 2·5 million litres of wine a year. It is produced in southern England and south Wales.

Organic Farming

The Government aims to establish a framework in which organic farming in Britain can respond to consumer demand. The organic sector is eligible for the support given to all farmers under a number of general schemes. Other support includes a significant commitment to research and development.

The United Kingdom Register of Organic Food Standards is an independent body set up in 1987 with government support. It has established national voluntary standards for organic food production tied to a certification and inspection scheme. It will also be responsible for enforcing the Community regulation on organic foodstuffs, adopted in June 1991.

FOOD SAFETY

The Food Safety Directorate within the Ministry of Agriculture, Fisheries and Food focuses ministry resources on ensuring adequate supplies of the right kinds of food, and its safety, wholesomeness and proper labelling, through regulations and guidelines. Food safety responsibilities are separated from food production and agriculture responsibilities within the Ministry. The Government's commitment to food safety was emphasised by the Food Safety Act 1990, which ensures food safety and consumer protection throughout the food chain. It combines basic provisions with wide enabling powers, so that detailed regulations made under the Act can adapt to technological change and innovation. It also introduces more effective enforcement powers and greatly increased penalties for offenders. A number of independent advisory committees consisting of recognised experts advise the Government.

The Food Advisory Committee advises ministers on the exercise of powers under the Food Safety Act relating to the labelling, composition and chemical safety of food. The Advisory Committee on Novel Foods and Processes advises on any matter relating to the irradiation of food or to the manufacture of novel foods or foods produced by novel processes. The Steering Group on the Chemical Aspects of Food Surveillance is charged with keeping under review possible chemical contamination of the national food supply and monitoring the intakes of food additives and nutrients. It is assisted by 11 working parties covering detailed aspects of

its work. The Advisory Committee on the Microbiological Safety of Food advises on matters relating to this topic and there is also a Steering Group on the Microbiological Safety of Food.

In addition, a consumer panel—nine consumer members nominated by the main consumer organisations, but appointed to serve as individuals—gives consumers a direct means of conveying their views on food safety and consumer protection issues to the Government.

EXPORTS

The Government encourages the growth of exports related to agriculture. The volume of these exports rose in 1990, when their value amounted to £6,334 million, the main markets being Western Europe, North America and the Middle East.

Exports include speciality products such as fresh salmon, Scotch whisky, biscuits, jams and conserves, as well as beef and lamb carcases and cheese.

Food From Britain is a national organisation which promotes the marketing of food and agricultural produce in the domestic and overseas markets. Food From Britain and its export arm, the British Food Export Council, receive support for their export activity jointly from the Government and from the food and drink industry, while the British Agricultural Export Committee of the London Chamber of Commerce represents exporters of technology, expertise and equipment. The Agricultural Engineers' Association represents exporters of agricultural and horticultural machinery. In 1990 Britain exported £1,011 million of farm machinery and spares.

One of the world's largest agricultural events, the annual Royal International Agricultural Exhibition, held at Stoneleigh in Warwickshire, provides an opportunity for visitors to see the latest techniques and improvements in British agriculture. Over 201,000 visitors attended in 1991, of whom 26,500 were from overseas. Virtually every British agricultural machinery manufacturer is represented at the exhibition, which is also the most important pedigree livestock event in the country. Other major agricultural displays include the annual Royal Smithfield Show, held in London, which exhibits agricultural machinery, livestock and carcases; the Royal Highland Show; the Royal Welsh Show; and the Royal Ulster Agricultural Show. There are also important regional shows.

MARKETING

Agricultural products are marketed by private traders, producers' co-operatives and marketing boards. The latter are producers' organisations (each including a minority of independent members appointed by agriculture ministers) with certain statutory powers to regulate the marketing of milk, wool and potatoes. For the most part the boards buy from producers or control contracts between producers and first-hand buyers; the Potato Marketing Board, however, maintains only a broad control over marketing conditions, leaving producers free to deal individually with buyers. For home-grown cereals, meat and livestock, apples and pears, there are marketing organisations representing producer, distributor and independent interests.

Food From Britain is responsible for improving the marketing of food and agricultural products, both in the domestic market and abroad. Its quality assurance schemes guarantee a repeatable quality in a number of product sectors.

Co-operatives

A substantial amount of agricultural and horticultural produce, such as grain, fruit and vegetables, is handled by marketing co-operatives, whose turnover exceeds £1,600 million a year. They have been formed to meet the demand from retailers for a continuous supply of fresh, quality produce. Food From Britain provides a range of advisory services for co-operatives.

ROLE OF THE GOVERNMENT

Four government departments have joint responsibility—the Ministry of Agriculture, Fisheries and Food; the Scottish Office Agriculture and Fisheries Department; the Welsh Office; and the Department of Agriculture for Northern Ireland.

Common Agricultural Policy

The European Community's Common Agricultural Policy (CAP) accounts for about two-thirds of the Community's budget and aims to ensure stable agricultural markets and a fair standard of living for agricultural producers, and to guarantee regular supplies of food at reasonable prices. For many commodities minimum prices are set annually at which agencies of the member states will purchase products, and there are levies on imports to maintain internal support prices. Surpluses are bought by intervention boards (the Intervention Board executive agency in Britain) to be stored and sold when appropriate. Intervention stocks can be disposed of within the Community where this can be done without disrupting internal markets. Exports are facilitated by the provision of export refunds to bridge any gap between Community prices and world prices. In some cases, in particular in the beef and sheep sectors, there are also direct payments to producers—the suckler cow premium and the annual premium on ewes.

The support prices, as well as rates of levy, export refunds and other aids, are set in European Currency Units and are converted into the currencies of the member states at fixed rates of exchange— 'green rates'—which can be out of line with the market rate of exchange between each currency and the European Currency Unit. Monetary compensatory amounts, based on the percentage difference between the green and market rates of each currency, are applied to prevent distortions in trade. They operate as import subsidies and export levies for countries whose currencies' market rates are below the green rates, and as import levies and export subsidies for countries whose currencies' market rates are above the green rates.

Nearly all the Community's agricultural expenditure (£20,622 million in 1990) is channelled through the European Agricultural Guidance and Guarantee Fund. The Fund's guarantee section finances market support arrangements, while the guidance section provides funds for structural reform—for example, farm modernisation and investment—and payments to assist certain farmers to change to alternative enterprises.

Agricultural production under the CAP has increased considerably in recent years, partly in response to rapid technical progress and farming efficiency, but also reflecting the high level of price support under the CAP. As consumption has remained relatively stable, this has resulted in the emergence of surpluses.

Britain has consistently pressed for CAP reform, to bring supply and demand into better balance, to increase the role of market forces in agriculture and to make environmental considerations an integral part of the CAP. Britain has therefore welcomed the Community's recognition of the urgent need for radical reform, resulting in the publication in July 1991 of detailed proposals for consideration by

member states. Considerable progress has already been made. Average effective Community support levels have been reduced in real terms each year since 1984. Since 1988 there has been a legally binding limit on CAP market support expenditure. Stabilisers have been brought in or extended for most CAP commodities. Stabilisers ensure that CAP support is automatically cut if production exceeds specified quantities. Significant price cuts of up to 20 per cent have already been made in a number of sectors.

Each annual price-fixing settlement since 1988 has consolidated this reform process, the cost being within the guidelines established by the Council of Ministers, and the stabiliser mechanisms have remained intact. The settlements have also helped to improve the competitive position of British farmers. Green pound devaluations have been agreed which represent a significant step in the process of meeting the Community's commitment to phasing out the differences between 'green' and market rates of exchange by the end of 1992.

GATT Uruguay Round

Agriculture was identified as a major issue for the GATT round of multilateral trade negotiations launched in 1986 (see p 370). These aimed to achieve a freer and more market-oriented agricultural trading system, and to agree cuts in production—and exemptions from them. The Community proposed reform on an aggregate measure of support, which would be reduced by 30 per cent between 1986 and 1996, with credit for reforms already made. Tariffs would replace other restrictions on market access, and be reduced over the next five years, with a corrective mechanism reflecting changes in world markets. Britain hopes the round can be completed before the end of 1991.

Public Expenditure under the CAP by the Intervention Board and the Agricultural Departments

FORECAST 1990/1

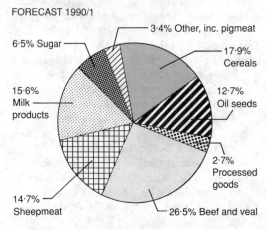

3·4% Other, inc. pigmeat
6·5% Sugar
17·9% Cereals
15·6% Milk products
12·7% Oil seeds
2·7% Processed goods
14·7% Sheepmeat
26·5% Beef and veal

Price Guarantees, Grants and Subsidies

Expenditure in Britain in 1990–91 on price guarantees, grants and subsidies and on CAP market regulations was estimated to be £293 million and £1,665 million respectively. About £1,615 million is to be reimbursed from the Community budget.

Potatoes and wool are not covered by the CAP; potato market support measures are operated through the Potato Marketing Board and the Department of Agriculture for Northern Ireland, and a price stabilisation fund for wool is administered by the British Wool Marketing Board. The Government intends to end the guarantee arrangements when parliamentary time permits.

Farmers are eligible for grants aimed at environmental enhancement of their farms and pollution control. Hill and upland farmers can also benefit from headage payments on cattle and sheep, known as compensatory allowances. Launching aid is available to production and marketing groups in the horticultural sector.

In 1990 a further 36,000 hectares (88,950 acres) in Britain were designated Less Favoured Areas by the Community. In these districts, where land quality is poor, farmers benefit from enhanced rates of grant and special payments on livestock.

Smallholdings and Crofts

Local authorities provide some 5,650 statutory smallholdings in England and 920 in Wales. They make loans of up to 75 per cent of required working capital to their tenants. Land settlement in Scotland has been carried out by the Government, which, while now seeking to dispose of holdings to its sitting tenants, still owns and maintains 121,461 hectares (300,000 acres) of land settlement estates, comprising 1,479 crofts and holdings.

In the crofting areas of Scotland (in Strathclyde, Highland, Western Isles, Orkney and Shetland) much of the land is held by tenants known as 'crofters'. Crofting is administered by the Crofters Commission, and benefits from government grants for land improvements and some other agricultural work.

Tenancy Legislation

Approximately 36 per cent of agricultural land in England and Wales is tenanted. The agricultural holdings legislation protects the interests and rights of landlords and tenants, with provision for arbitration in the event of a dispute. Most agricultural tenants have the right to contest a notice to quit, which is then ineffective unless the landlord obtains consent to its operation from an independent body (in England and Wales, the Agricultural Land Tribunal and in Scotland, the Scottish Land Court). On termination of tenancy, the tenant is entitled to compensation in accordance with a special code. Practically all farms in Northern Ireland are owner-occupied, but, under a practice known as 'conacre', occupiers not wishing to farm all their land let it annually to others. About one-fifth of agricultural land is let under this practice and is used mainly for grazing.

Agriculture and Protection of the Countryside

Agriculture ministers have a general duty, under the Agriculture Act 1986, to seek to achieve a reasonable balance between the needs of an efficient and stable agriculture industry and other interests in the countryside, including the conservation of its natural beauty and amenity and the promotion of its enjoyment by the public. In addition, they are required to further conservation of the countryside in the administration of farm capital grant schemes both in National Parks and in Sites of Special Scientific Interest designated by the nature conservancy bodies.

Environmentally Sensitive Areas

Under the Environmentally Sensitive Areas (ESA) Scheme, a British idea which other European Community members are following, 19 areas in Britain—ten in England, five in Scotland, two in Wales

289

and two in Northern Ireland—have been designated. They are notable for the quality of their landscape, the wealth of their flora and fauna, and their vulnerability to change in farming practices.

The areas are diverse in character and include low-lying wetland grazing marshes, chalk downs and upland tracts of heather—for example, the Somerset Levels in England; Loch Lomond in Scotland; the Cambrian Mountains in Wales; and Mourne in Northern Ireland. The scheme is voluntary and farmers in ESAs are offered agreements under which they receive payments (partly funded by the European Community) for farming along environmentally beneficial lines intended to conserve the special character of the area. Monitoring and evaluation of those areas in operation since 1987 have confirmed the achievements of the scheme.

A ministerial review of ESA policy concluded that ESAs should continue, with the aim of securing further environmental protection and enhancement. Some 115,960 hectares (286,500 acres) in the English ESAs were covered by the agreements in summer 1991—92 per cent of the target area or 47 per cent of the potentially available agricultural land. In the Scottish ESAs, 104,725 hectares (258,785 acres) were covered—60 per cent of eligible land.

Agricultural Buildings

The Government also intends to allow the extension to all areas of England and Wales of arrangements similar to those which apply in National Parks. These arrangements give local planning authorities discretion to examine and approve the siting, design and external appearance of new agricultural and forestry buildings. Authorities will also have to consider the desirability of preserving ancient monuments and their settings, known archaeological sites, the settings of listed buildings, and sites of recognised nature conservation. Full development control is to be extended to all farm holdings of less than 5 hectares (12 acres).

Other Schemes

Farmers are encouraged to develop new sources of income as an alternative to surplus production through grants to diversify into tourism and other non-agricultural activities on the farm. The Farm Woodland Scheme assists the planting of woodlands on agricultural land, with incentives for broadleaved trees and a planting limit of 36,000 hectares (88,950 acres) over three years. The European Community set-aside scheme, introduced in Britain in 1988, offers annual payments to farmers to take at least 20 per cent of their arable land out of agricultural production for five years. Another, temporary (one-year), set-aside scheme is available to producers who set aside at least 15 per cent of the 1991 arable area for 1991–92 and also reduce their cereals area by 15 per cent in the same period. Additional payments for managing five-year set-aside land for the benefit of wildlife, landscape and the local community are available under the Countryside Premium Scheme (at present limited to eastern England). Under pilot Beef and Sheep Extensification Schemes, farmers receive annual compensation payments to reduce output by at least 20 per cent and to maintain this reduction over a five-year period. The Government has also designated ten nitrate-sensitive areas in England, where payments are being made to farmers who voluntarily undertake to restrict their agricultural practices and thus prevent unacceptable levels of nitrate leaching from farmland into water sources. Applications covering 87 per cent of the eligible agricultural land had been received by the scheme's closing date of 31 May 1991.

In the Highlands and Islands of Scotland, considered vulnerable to changes in the CAP, the Rural Enterprise Programme offers special funding, with Community support, to encourage farmers and crofters to develop new businesses.

Agricultural Training

The Agricultural Training Board receives government grant to arrange training for the agricultural industry. A recent report, which envisaged the Board evolving a more strategic role, as a broker for training provision rather than as a direct course provider, has led to considerable change. A network of employer-led local boards has been set up, to identify and arrange local training needs in co-operation with existing training providers (primarily agricultural colleges) and in liaison with Training and Enterprise Councils. Training provision is arranged through some 600 autonomous training groups throughout Great Britain.

Professional, Scientific and Technical Services

In England and Wales the Government's Agricultural Development and Advisory Service (ADAS) provides a wide range of professional, scientific and technical services for agriculture and its ancillary industries. Most types of advice and servicing are on a fee-paying basis, although initial advice to farmers on conservation, rural diversification (including use of land for woodlands) and animal welfare is available free. Similar services are provided in Scotland by the Scottish Office Agriculture and Fisheries Department and the Scottish Agricultural College. In Northern Ireland these services are available from the Department of Agriculture's advisory and scientific services.

These organisations also advise the Government on the scientific, technical and business implications of policy proposals and assist in implementing policies concerning disease and pest eradication, food hygiene, animal welfare, land drainage and other capital grant schemes, and safeguarding agricultural land in relation to other land uses.

ADAS carries out research and development work under commission from the Ministry of Agriculture, Fisheries and Food, and works under contract directly for others and for levy-funded bodies. These undertakings are carried out at a range of experimental husbandry farms

across England and Wales, and through regional centres or on clients' premises. The Central Science Laboratory also carries out research and development work commissioned by the Ministry.

CONTROL OF DISEASES AND PESTS

Farm Animals

Britain is free from many serious animal diseases. If they were to occur, diseases such as foot-and-mouth disease and classical swine fever would be combated by a slaughter policy applied to all animals infected or exposed to infection, and by control over animal movements during the outbreaks.

The Government has taken comprehensive measures to tackle the cattle disease bovine spongiform encephalopathy and to ensure that consumers are protected from any remote risk. It has:

- banned the feeding of ruminant protein to ruminants;
- ordered the destruction of the milk and carcases of affected animals;
- banned from human or animal use those offals from other cattle which might be harbouring the agent; and
- committed significant funding for research.

It has also established an expert committee to advise on matters relating to spongiform encephalopathies.

The Government has also ordered restrictions on the movement of pigs to prevent the spread of blue-eared pig disease.

Strict controls are exercised on the import of animals, birds, meat, and meat products so as to prevent the introduction of animal or avian diseases. Special measures apply to prevent the introduction of rabies, and dogs, cats and certain other mammals are subject to import licence and six months' quarantine. There are severe penalties for breaking the law. There have been no cases of rabies outside quarantine in Britain since 1970.

It is the responsibility of the livestock sector to dispose of its waste, including the carcases of dead animals, within the framework of health and environmental restrictions. Research is in progress to find ways of minimising the cost of waste disposal.

Professional advice and action on the control of animal disease and the welfare of farm livestock are the responsibility of the government State Veterinary Service. Its laboratory facilities and investigation centres perform specialist research work and advise private practitioners responsible for treating animals on the farm.

Fish

The fisheries departments operate statutory controls to prevent the introduction and spread of serious diseases of fish and shellfish. These controls include the licensing of live fish imports, the licensing of deposits of shellfish on the seabed, and movement restrictions on sites where outbreaks of notifiable diseases have been confirmed.

Plants

The agriculture departments are responsible for limiting the spread of plant pests and diseases and for preventing the introduction of new ones. They also issue the health certificates required by other countries to accompany plant material exported from Britain. Certification schemes encourage the development of healthy and true-to-type planting stocks.

Pesticides

There are strict controls on the supply and use of pesticides, and their maximum residue levels. All pesticides supplied in Britain must be approved for their safety and efficacy in use. Controls on pesticides are the joint responsibility of six government departments on the basis of advice from the independent Advisory Committee on Pesticides. The Government is currently reviewing pesticides approved before 1981.

Veterinary Medicinal Products

The manufacture, sale and supply of veterinary medicinal products are prohibited except under licence. Licences are issued by the agriculture ministers, who are advised on safety, quality and efficacy by the Veterinary Products Committee, which comprises independent experts.

Fisheries

Britain, one of the European Community's leading fishing nations, plays an active role in the implementation and development of the Community's Common Fisheries Policy (CFP) agreed in 1983. The CFP covers access to coastal waters, the conservation and management of fish stocks, fisheries arrangements with third countries, the allocation of catch quotas among member states, the trade in and marketing of fish and fish products, and financial aid to promote the adaptation and development of the Community's fishing fleet.

The fishing industry provides 59 per cent by quantity of British fish supplies, and is an important source of employment and income in a number of ports.

Cod, haddock, whiting, herring, plaice and sole are found in the North Sea off the east coasts of Scotland and England; mackerel, together with cod and other demersal fish, off the west coast of Scotland; sole, plaice, cod, herring and whiting in the Irish Sea; and mackerel, sole and plaice off the south-west coast of England. Nephrops, crabs, lobsters and other shellfish are found in the inshore waters all around the coast. At the end of 1989 there were 17,825 fishermen in regular employment and 5,137 occasionally employed. The Government aims to encourage the development of a viable, efficient and market-oriented fisheries industry within the CFP framework.

Fishing Catches

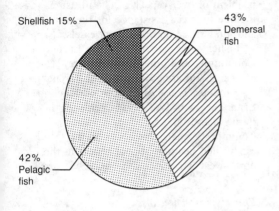

Shellfish 15%

43% Demersal fish

42% Pelagic fish

Fish Caught

In 1990 demersal fish (caught on or near the bottom of the sea) accounted for 43 per cent by weight of total British landings, pelagic fish (caught near the surface) for 42 per cent and shellfish for 15 per cent. Landings of all types of fish (excluding salmon and trout) by British fishing vessels totalled 621,010 tonnes. Cod and haddock represented 23 and 18 per cent respectively of the total value of demersal and pelagic fish landed, while anglerfish (8 per cent), whiting (8 per cent), plaice (7 per cent), mackerel (5 per cent), and sole (4 per cent) were the other most important sources of earnings to the industry. Landings of nephrops represented 11 per cent of the total value of all British landings of fish and shellfish in 1990.

Imports of fresh, frozen, cured and canned salt-water fish and shellfish in 1990 totalled 439,720 tonnes, those of freshwater fish 43,328 tonnes, those of fish meal 274,358 tonnes and those of fish oils 164,186 tonnes. Exports and re-exports of salt-water fish and fish products amounted to 343,663 tonnes and those of freshwater fish to 17,722 tonnes.

The Fishing Fleet

At the end of 1989 the active British fishing fleet consisted of 8,079 inshore vessels under 24·4 m (80 ft) in length and 204 deep-sea vessels longer than 24·4 m. Among the main ports from which the fishing fleet operates are Aberdeen, Peterhead, Fraserburgh (Grampian), Lerwick (Shetland), Kinlochbervie, Ullapool (Highland), North Shields (Tyne and Wear), Grimsby (Humberside), Lowestoft (Suffolk), Brixham (Devon), Newlyn (Cornwall), and Kilkeel, Ardglass and Portavogie (Northern Ireland). With the extension of fishery limits to 200 miles, Britain's distant water fleet was considerably reduced. A much smaller fleet has, however, continued to maintain its activities in distant waters.

Fish Farming

Fish farming production is centred on Atlantic salmon and rainbow trout, which are particularly suited to Britain's climate and waters. Production of salmon and trout has grown from less than 1,000 tonnes in the early 1970s to some 32,400 tonnes of salmon and 15,000 tonnes of trout in 1990. Scotland produces the largest amount of farmed salmon (32,000 tonnes in 1990—with a first-sale value of £120 million) in the European Community. Shellfish farming concentrates on molluscs such as oysters, mussels, clams and scallops, producing an estimated 5,000 tonnes a year.

The fish and shellfish farming industries make an important contribution to rural infrastructure, especially in remote areas such as the Highlands and Islands of Scotland. In 1990 the industries were estimated to have a combined wholesale turnover of some £140 million. Production is based on almost 1,200 businesses operating from some 1,800 sites and employing more than 5,000 people.

Administration

The fisheries departments are responsible for the administration of legislation concerning the fishing industry and for fisheries research. The safety and welfare of crews of fishing vessels and other matters common to shipping generally are provided for under legislation administered by the Department of Transport.

The Sea Fish Industry Authority is concerned with all aspects of the industry, including consumer interests. It undertakes research and development, provides training, and encourages quality awareness. It also administers a government grant scheme for fishing vessels, to promote a safe, efficient and modern fleet.

Fishery Limits

Only British vessels may fish within 6 miles of the coast; certain other Community member states have traditional fishing rights between 6 and 12 miles, as British vessels have in other member states' coastal waters. Outside 12 miles the only non-Community countries whose vessels may fish in Community waters are those (for example, Norway) with which the Community has reciprocal fisheries agreements.

Common Fisheries Policy

The CFP's system for the conservation and management of the Community's fishing resources means that total allowable catches—with these decisions based partly on independent scientific advice—are set each year in order to conserve stocks. These catch levels are then allocated between member states on a fixed percentage basis, taking account of traditional fishing patterns. Activity is also regulated by a number of technical conservation measures, including minimum mesh sizes, minimum landing sizes and closed areas designated mainly to protect young fish. Each member state is responsible for ensuring that its fishermen abide by the various fisheries regulations and their performances are monitored by the Community's inspectors.

The 1983 settlement also covered the common organisation of the market in fish and fish products, and a policy for restructuring the Community fleet during 1987–97, designed to address the current problem of over-capacity. The measures include financial assistance for the building and modernisation of fishing vessels.

Fishery relations between the European Community and other countries are extensive and are governed by different agreements. Those of most importance to Britain are with Norway, Greenland, the Faroe Islands and Sweden. Annual Community quotas have also been established in international waters in the north-west Atlantic and around Svalbard.

Fish Hygiene Directive

The single European market aims to facilitate trade among Community members and to protect public health by harmonising measures for the handling and treatment of all fish and shellfish (including aquaculture products) at all stages up to, but excluding, retail level. It will take effect from 1 January 1993, and lays down rules to ensure the safe and hygienic handling of fish and fish products. This includes the conditions on board factory vessels; requirements during and after landing, including auction markets on shore; and establishments on land, primarily processors. The single market provisions also lay down the conditions for processed products, as well as hygiene rules for those who come into contact with fish and fish products.

Salmon and Freshwater Fisheries

Salmon and sea-trout are fished commercially in inshore waters around the British coast. Eels and elvers are also taken commercially in both estuaries and freshwater. Angling for salmon and sea-trout (game fishing) and for other freshwater species (coarse fishing) is popular throughout Britain. In England and Wales fishing is licensed by the National Rivers Authority; in Scotland salmon fishing is administered by salmon district fishery boards. In Northern Ireland fishing is licensed by the Fisheries Conservancy Board for Northern Ireland

SCIENCE AND TECHNOLOGY

At the Natural History Museum's Ecology Exhibition, visitors 'shrink' into the heart of a leaf, where they are taken on a tour explaining the process of photosynthesis.

Helen Sharman, Britain's first astronaut, during training for the May 1991 mission of the Soviet Mir space station.

EMERGENCY SERVICES

Ambulancemen using a portable defibrillator, developed in Belfast, Northern Ireland, which can automatically analyse the heart for the presence of life-threatening rhythms and advise operators what action needs to be taken.

Firemen training at the Civil Aviation Authority Fire Training School at Teesside Airport. They are wearing new safety helmets which combine integrated breathing and communications apparatus and offer protection for hearing and against impact and flash fires.

Police assisting at the scene of damage caused by a storm.

The Royal National Lifeboat Institution is a voluntary organisation which operates a fleet around the coast of Great Britain and Ireland. In 1989 lifeboats were launched 4,525 times and saved 1,517 lives.

ENERGY

The Shell/Esso Eider oil production
platform in the North Sea, north-east
of the Shetlands.

A wind turbine supplies
electricity to energy-efficient houses at
Milton Keynes, Buckinghamshire.

and the Foyle Fisheries Commission in their respective areas, and 65 public angling waters, including salmon, trout and coarse fisheries, are accessible to Department of Agriculture permit holders.

Agriculture, Fisheries and Research

The total government-funded programme of research and development in agriculture, fisheries and food in 1991–92 amounts to some £250 million, including funding by the Ministry of Agriculture, Fisheries and Food, the Scottish Office Agriculture and Fisheries Department, the Department of Agriculture for Northern Ireland and the Department of Education and Science science budget.

The agriculture departments, the Agricultural and Food Research Council (AFRC) and private industry share responsibility for research, which is carried out in a network of research institutes, specialist laboratories and experimental husbandry farms, and with Horticulture Research International (HRI; established in 1990) and in higher education institutions.

Agriculture and Food Research

The research aims to maintain an efficient and competitive industry in Britain consistent with high standards of animal welfare and care for the environment. The work of the AFRC and the agriculture departments is co-ordinated into national programmes, primarily on the recommendations of the Priorities Board for Research and Development in Agriculture and Food. The Board advises on the research needs and on the allocation of available resources between and within areas of research.

The AFRC (see p383), a non-departmental public body, receives funds from the science budget through the Department of Education and Science, and income from work commissioned by the Ministry of Agriculture, Fisheries and Food, by industry and by other bodies. The Council is responsible for research

carried out in its seven institutes and in British higher education institutions through its research grants scheme. In addition to commissioning research with the AFRC and other organisations, such as HRI, the Ministry commissions research and development at its Food Science Laboratories, at the Central Veterinary Laboratory and at the Central Science Laboratory, and with ADAS.

The five Scottish Agricultural Research Institutes, funded by the Scottish Office Agriculture and Fisheries Department, cover areas of research complementary to those of the AFRC institutes, while including work relevant to the soils, crops and livestock of northern Britain. Development work in Scotland is carried out by the Scottish Agricultural College, which operates from three centres.

In Northern Ireland research is carried out by the Department of Agriculture in a number of research divisions and at the three agricultural colleges. Links with the Queen's University of Belfast and the Agricultural Research Institute of Northern Ireland include basic and strategic research.

Agricultural research is also conducted or sponsored by private industry, in particular by related industries such as agrochemicals and agricultural machinery.

In addition, the food industry funds or undertakes relevant research. The Government funds strategic research essential for the public good, for example, into food safety, human health, animal welfare and flood protection, but has withdrawn funding from research which promises commercial application or exploitation within a reasonable timescale—for which it looks to industry to take on a greater degree of funding.

The Ministry spends £50 million of its £120 million annual research budget on research relevant to the environment. This includes the protection of the countryside, water supplies and rivers; ensuring that straw and other crop residues are disposed of other than by burning—a practice to be banned after the 1992 harvest; reducing the use of pesticides to the minimum compatible with efficient production; flood and coastal defences; and care of the marine environment. By the end of 1992–93 the Ministry will have spent £12 million on research into bovine spongiform encephalopathy.

Fisheries and Aquatic Environment Research

The Ministry of Agriculture, Fisheries and Food laboratories deal with marine and freshwater fisheries, shellfish, marine pollution, fish farming and disease. Research work is also commissioned by the Ministry with the Natural Environment Research Council, with the Sea Fish Industry Authority and with a number of universities and polytechnics. The Ministry has two seagoing research vessels. In Scotland, the Scottish Office Agriculture and Fisheries Department undertakes a similar, and complementary, range of research and also has two seagoing vessels. The Department of Agriculture laboratories in Northern Ireland undertake research on marine and freshwater fisheries, and also have a seagoing research vessel.

Forestry

Woodland covers an estimated 2·38 million hectares (5·88 million acres) in Britain: about 7 per cent of England, 13 per cent of Scotland, 12 per cent of Wales and 5 per cent of Northern Ireland. The Government supports the continued expansion of forestry in order to reduce dependence on imports of timber and to provide employment in forestry and related industries.

The area of productive forest in Great Britain is 2·13 million hectares (5·26 million acres), 40·6 per cent of which is managed by the Forestry Commission and the rest by private owners. The rate of new planting in 1989–90 was 4,081 hectares (10,084 acres) by the Commission and 18,892 hectares (46,682 acres) by private woodland owners, with the help of grants from the Commission, mainly in Scotland. Most planting is of conifers in upland areas, though the planting of broadleaved

trees is encouraged on suitable sites. An increasing proportion of new planting is by private owners.

The Commission's expanded Woodland Grant Scheme pays establishment grants to help in the creation of new woodlands and forests and for the regeneration of existing ones. It highlights such features as native tree species, woody shrubs, short-rotation coppice and agroforestry. Management grants under the scheme contribute to the cost of managing woodlands to provide silvicultural, environmental and social benefits.

Total employment in state and private forests in Great Britain was estimated at 40,245 in 1989–90, including about 10,000 people engaged in processing home-grown timber.

British woodlands meet 12·7 per cent of the nation's consumption of wood and wood products. The volume of timber harvested on Commission lands in 1989–90 totalled 3·55 million cubic metres (125·37 million cubic feet).

The Forestry Commission and Forestry Policy

The Forestry Commission is the national forestry authority in Great Britain. The Commissioners give advice on forestry matters and are responsible to the Secretary of State for Scotland, the Minister of Agriculture, Fisheries and Food and the Secretary of State for Wales. Timber production, landscape amenity, environmental protection and employment are all forestry policy objectives. The Commission's activities also include wildlife and flora conservation, plant health, research, and the provision of facilities for recreation. The Commission has sold 76,737 hectares (189,624 acres) of plantation and plantable land since 1981 and has been asked by the Government to dispose of a further 100,000 hectares (247,000 acres) by the end of the century. The Commission is financed partly by the Government and partly by receipts from sales of timber and other produce and from rents.

Forestry Initiatives

The Countryside Commissions and the Forestry Commission plan the creation of 12 community forests (covering between 10,000 and 20,000 hectares each—40 to 80 sq miles) on the outskirts of major cities in England and Wales. These include the Great North Forest (Tyne and Wear), the Forest of Mercia (Staffordshire) and Thames Chase, east of London. As part of its rural initiative for Wales, the Government plans to give local communities greater involvement in the development of 35,000 hectares (135 sq miles) of forest in the coalfield valleys of south Wales—about 20 per cent of the land area—owned by the Forestry Commission.

Forestry Research

The Forestry Commission maintains two principal research stations, at Alice Holt Lodge near Farnham (Surrey) and at Bush Estate near Edinburgh, for basic and applied research into all aspects of forestry.

Aid is also given for research work in universities and other institutions.

The Commission conducts an annual forest health survey which monitors the effects of air pollution and other stress factors on a growing range of broadleaves and conifers. It has increased research into wildlife conservation and farm forestry, including an evaluation of agroforestry systems combining wide-spaced conifers and broadleaves with sheep grazing. The Government has set up an expert scientific review group on tree health in Britain.

Forestry in Northern Ireland

The Department of Agriculture may acquire land for afforestation and give financial and technical assistance for private planting. The state forest area has grown steadily since 1945. By 1991, 60,000 hectares (150,000 acres) of plantable land had been acquired, of which 59,000 hectares (147,500 acres) were planted. There were 15,500 hectares (38,750 acres) of privately owned forest. Some 500 professional and industrial staff work in state forests.

17 Transport and Communications

Major improvements in transport have resulted from the construction of a network of motorways, the extension of fast inter-city rail services and expansion schemes at many airports. Transport policy rests on the fundamental aims of:

- promoting economic growth and higher national prosperity;

- ensuring a reasonable level of personal mobility;

- improving safety;

- conserving and enhancing the environment; and

- using energy economically.

Britain is taking an active part in the European Community's development of a common transport policy.

Users' expenditure on transport, including taxation, in Britain totalled an estimated £86,600 million in 1988, of which £71,500 million represented expenditure on road transport (including buses).

Inland Transport

There has been a considerable increase in passenger travel in recent years. Travel in Great Britain rose by 39 per cent between 1979 and 1989. Travel by car and taxi rose by 42 per cent and air travel expanded rapidly. However, recently, travel by motor cycle has been declining, and travel by bus and coach and by pedal cycle has changed little.

Car and taxi travel accounts for 85 per cent of passenger mileage within Great Britain, buses and coaches for about 6 per cent, rail for 6 per cent and air less than 1 per cent.

Car ownership has also risen substantially, and 66 per cent of households in Great Britain have the regular use of one or more cars, with 22 per cent having the use of two or more cars in 1989. At the end of 1990 there were 24·7 million vehicles licensed for use on the roads of Great Britain, of which 20·2 million were

Table 17.1: Road Length (as at April 1990)

km

	Public roads	All-purpose trunk roads and trunk motorways	Trunk motorways[a]
England	273,136	10,823	2,638
Scotland	51,601	3,145	234
Wales	33,297	1,699	120
Northern Ireland	24,081	2,306[b]	112
Britain	382,115	17,973	3,104

Sources: Department of Transport, Northern Ireland Department of the Environment, Scottish Office and Welsh Office.
[a] In addition, there were 68 km (42 miles) of local authority motorway in England and 24 km (15 miles) in Scotland. In April 1990, 108 km (67 miles) of trunk motorway were under construction in England and 11 km (7 miles) in Scotland.
[b] Motorway and Class A roads.

cars (including over 2·5 million cars registered in the name of a company); 2·2 million light goods vehicles; 482,000 other goods vehicles; 833,000 motor cycles, scooters and mopeds; and 115,000 public transport vehicles (including taxis).

ROADS

Total traffic for 1990 was 404,000 million vehicle–km. The total road network in Great Britain in 1990 was 358,000 km (222,000 miles). Trunk motorways accounted for 2,993 km (1,860 miles) of this length, less than 1 per cent, and trunk roads for 12,700 km (7,900 miles), or about 3·5 per cent. However, motorways carry over 15 per cent of all traffic and trunk roads over 17 per cent. Combined, they carry over half of all heavy goods vehicle traffic in Great Britain.

Administration

Responsibility for trunk roads, including most motorways, in Great Britain rests in England with the Secretary of State for Transport, in Scotland with the Secretary of State for Scotland and in Wales with the Secretary of State for Wales. The costs of construction and maintenance are paid for by central government. The highway authorities for non-trunk roads are:

- in England, the county councils, the metropolitan district councils, the London borough councils and the Common Council of the City of London;
- in Wales, the county councils; and
- in Scotland, the regional or islands councils.

In Northern Ireland the Northern Ireland Department of the Environment is responsible for the construction, improvement and maintenance of all public roads.

Research into all aspects of road transport is carried out by the Transport and Road Research Laboratory, which is part of the Department of Transport. It provides the technical help and advice which enables the Government to set standards for highway and vehicle design and to formulate transport, environmental and road safety policies.

Through the Overseas Development Administration, the Laboratory also helps developing countries with research to help solve their particular road transport problems.

Private Finance

The Government encourages greater private sector involvement in the design, construction, operation and funding of roads. A framework for encouraging privately funded schemes is provided in the New Roads and Street Works Act 1991. Privately funded schemes being undertaken include:

- a crossing of the River Thames at Dartford, which will open to traffic in autumn 1991 and link into the M25 London orbital motorway;
- a second crossing of the River Severn, which is expected to be completed by late 1995;
- a relief road north of Birmingham, which will be the first overland toll route in Britain; and
- a bridge between the mainland of Scotland and Skye, for which a tenderer has been chosen.

The Government is considering how the private sector can help provide longer term additional motorway capacity between Birmingham and Manchester. It also proposes to hold a competition for an orbital route to complete the motorway box around the West Midlands conurbation. A new crossing of the Tamar estuary at Plymouth and a link between the M25 and Chelmsford (Essex) have also been identified as suitable for private finance.

Other Developments

The Government has a major programme to improve motorways and other trunk roads. In mid-1991, some 80 trunk road and motorway schemes were under construction in England, costing nearly £1,300 million, while over 400 schemes were in preparation. Bypasses and relief roads account for nearly one-third of the programme, which also includes projects intended to increase the traffic capacity of major through routes and to improve junctions on heavily used roads. In 1991–92 the Department of Transport is supporting 306 major local authority road schemes, the majority of which are bypasses or relief roads.

Road communications in Wales are expected to benefit from the second Severn crossing and improvements to the M4 motorway. Other priorities in Wales are improvements to the coast road in north Wales (including the construction under the Conwy estuary of the first immersed tube road tunnel to be built in Britain, due to be opened in October 1991) and the upgrading of roads which are important for industrial redevelopment.

The key priorities within the programme in Scotland include the upgrading of the A74 to three-lane motorway standard and completion of the central Scotland motorway network. These routes provide links for commerce and industry to the south and Europe. The programme also includes completion of the dual-carriageway improvement between Stirling and Aberdeen. Other planned improvements include a series of 'route action plans' designed to improve substantially safety and journey times on specific major routes.

In Northern Ireland the emphasis is on improving arterial routes, constructing more bypasses, and improving roads in the Belfast area, including the construction of a new cross-harbour link planned for the mid-1990s.

Licensing and Standards

Official records of drivers and vehicles are maintained by the Driver and Vehicle Licensing Agency. It holds records on 33 million drivers and 24.2 million licensed vehicles in Great Britain. In April 1990 the Agency began to issue a new harmonised European Community driving licence. New drivers of motor vehicles are required to pass a driving test before being granted a full licence to drive. The Driving Standards Agency is the national driver testing authority. It also supervises professional driving instructors and is responsible for the compulsory basic training scheme for motorcyclists. Minimum ages for driving are:

- 16 for riders of mopeds and disabled drivers of specially adapted vehicles;
- 17 for drivers of cars and other passenger vehicles with nine or fewer seats (including that of the driver), motor cycles and goods vehicles not over 3·5 tonnes permissible maximum weight;
- 18 for goods vehicles over 3·5 but not over 7·5 tonnes; and
- 21 for passenger vehicles with over nine seats and goods vehicles over 7·5 tonnes.

Before most new cars and goods vehicles are allowed on the roads, they are required to meet a number of safety and environmental requirements, based primarily on standards drawn up by the European Community. This form of control, known as type approval, is operated by the Vehicle Certification Agency.

The Secretary of State for Transport has a statutory responsibility for ensuring the roadworthiness of vehicles in use on the roads. The Vehicle Inspectorate is the national testing authority. It meets this responsibility mainly through:

- annual testing and certification of heavy goods vehicles, buses and coaches;
- administration of the car and motor cycle testing scheme, under which vehicles are tested at private garages authorised as test stations; and
- means such as vehicle 'spot checks' and inspection of operators' premises.

In Northern Ireland private cars five or more years old are tested at official vehicle inspection centres.

Road Safety

Although Great Britain has one of the highest densities of road traffic in the world, it has a good record on road safety, with one of the lowest road accident death rates in the European Community. In 1990 some 5,100 people were killed on the roads, 60,400 seriously injured and 274,600 slightly injured. This compares with over 8,000 deaths a year in the mid-1960s. A number of factors, such as developments in vehicle safety standards and improvements in roads, the introduction of legislation on seat belt wearing and drinking and driving, plus developments in road safety training, education and publicity, have contributed to the long-term decline in casualty rates.

The Government's aim is to reduce road casualties by one-third by the end of the century, compared with the 1981–85 average. To achieve this, resources are being concentrated on measures which are demonstrably cost-effective in terms of casualty reduction. Priority is given to reducing casualties among vulnerable road-users (pedestrians, cyclists and motor cyclists), particularly in urban areas, where some 70 per cent of road accidents occur. Other areas for achieving lower casualties are improvements in highway design, better protection for vehicle occupants and measures to combat drinking and driving.

Road Traffic Act

The Road Traffic Act 1991 introduces several additional measures to improve road safety, including:

- a new offence of dangerous driving;
- mandatory retesting of drivers convicted of the most serious driving offences;
- a new offence, in England and Wales, of endangerment, to deal with vandals who put lives at risk by damaging road signs or dropping objects onto roads;
- tougher measures to deal with drink-drive offenders;
- the use of new technology, such as remote-operated cameras and radar speed-detectors, to improve the detection of speeding and traffic-light offences;
- new powers to prohibit dangerous vehicles; and
- measures to reduce the impact of congestion through the introduction of better facilities for cyclists and pedestrians and traffic calming measures near busy routes.

Traffic in Towns

Traffic management schemes are used in many urban areas to reduce congestion, create a better environment and improve road safety. Such schemes include, for example, one-way streets, bus lanes, facilities for pedestrians and cyclists, and traffic calming measures such as road humps to slow traffic in residential areas. Many towns have shopping precincts which are designed for the convenience of pedestrians and from which motor vehicles are excluded for all or part of the day. Controls over on-street parking are enforced through excess charges and fixed penalties, supported where appropriate by powers to remove vehicles. In parts of London wheel clamping to immobilise illegally parked vehicles is also used.

In London the Road Traffic Act 1991 authorises a network of 'red routes', on which special parking controls and other traffic management measures, rigidly enforced, will improve traffic movement. Monitoring of a pilot scheme introduced in north and east London in January 1991 has so far shown significant falls in journey time and greater reliability, especially for buses. The Act also allows for more effective parking enforcement shared between the police and local authorities, with London-wide powers to clamp or remove offenders' vehicles.

A pilot electronic driver information system called 'Autoguide' will be introduced in the London area in 1992. It uses roadside beacons to transmit route information to vehicles equipped to receive it; data can be updated continuously to take account of changing traffic conditions.

ROAD HAULAGE

Road haulage traffic by heavy goods vehicles amounted to 130,600 million tonne–km in 1990, 1 per cent more than in 1989. There has been a move towards larger and more efficient vehicles carrying heavier loads—about 78 per cent of the traffic, in terms of tonne–km, is carried in vehicles of over 25 tonnes gross laden weight. Much of the traffic is moved over short distances, with 75 per cent of the tonnage being carried on hauls of 100 km (62 miles) or less. Public haulage (private road hauliers carrying other firms' goods) accounts for 72 per cent of freight carried in Great Britain in terms of tonne–km. In 1990 the main commodities handled by heavy goods vehicles were:

- crude minerals (354 million tonnes);
- food, drink and tobacco (299 million tonnes); and
- building materials (178 million tonnes).

Road haulage is predominantly an industry of small, privately owned businesses. There were some 132,000 holders of an operator's licence in 1990. About half the heavy goods vehicles are in fleets of ten or fewer vehicles. The biggest operators in Great Britain are NFC plc, Transport Development Group plc, TNT Express (UK) Ltd and United Carriers International Ltd.

Licensing and Other Controls

In general, those operating goods vehicles over 3·5 tonnes gross weight require an operator's licence. Licences are divided into restricted licences for firms carrying their own goods, and standard licences for hauliers operating for hire or payment. Proof of professional competence, financial standing and good repute is needed to obtain a standard licence. Regulations lay down limits on the hours worked by drivers of goods vehicles, as well as minimum rest periods. Tachographs (which automatically record speed, distance covered, driving time and stopping periods) must be fitted and used in most goods vehicles over 3·5 tonnes gross weight in Great Britain. In Northern Ireland operators carrying their own goods do not require a licence. The Government has announced a proposal to fit speed limiters to heavy lorries, preventing them from travelling above 60 mph (97 km/h).

International Road Haulage

International road haulage has grown rapidly and in 1990 over 1·3 million road goods vehicles were ferried to the continent or the Irish Republic. Of these, 347,000 were powered vehicles registered in Britain; they carried over 9 million tonnes to and from continental Europe. The average length of haul by these vehicles was 1,167 km (725 miles) outwards and 1,097 km (683 miles)

inwards, compared with 79 km (49 miles) for national road haulage. In addition, much traffic crossed the Irish land boundary.

International road haulage has been constrained by the need for permits issued under bilateral agreements with the 26 countries concerned. Many countries place no restriction on the number of British lorries entering the country concerned, but some agreements specify an annual quota of permits. Quotas of European Community permits are also available which allow international haulage or cabotage anywhere within the Community. Full liberalisation of international road haulage within the Community without permits will apply from January 1993.

PASSENGER SERVICES

Major changes in the structure of the passenger transport industry have occurred in recent years. Privatisation of the National Bus Company (which was the largest single bus and coach operator in Britain, operating through 72 subsidiaries in England and Wales) was completed in 1988. Each subsidiary was sold separately, and encouragement was given for a buy-out by the local management or employees. Under the Transport (Scotland) Act 1989 the Scottish Bus Group, the largest operator of bus services in Scotland, is being privatised as ten separate companies. It had some 3,000 buses. Legislation also facilitated the privatisation of bus services run by municipal authorities.

London Transport (LT) is a statutory corporation, with its board members appointed by the Secretary of State for Transport. Within LT the main wholly owned operating subsidiaries are London Underground Ltd, London Buses Ltd and Docklands Light Railway Ltd. Financial support—almost entirely for capital projects —is provided by central government. LT is required to involve the private sector in the provision of services where this is more efficient, and has been set objectives on safety, the quality of services and on its financial performance. Many London bus routes are now run by private firms operating under contract to LT.

In Northern Ireland almost all road passenger services are provided by subsidiaries of the publicly owned Northern Ireland Transport Holding Company. Citybus Ltd operates services in the city of Belfast and Ulsterbus Ltd operates most of the services in the rest of Northern Ireland. These companies have some 300 and 1,000 vehicles respectively.

As well as the major bus operators, there are also a large number of small, privately owned undertakings, often operating fewer than five vehicles. Double-deck buses are the main type of vehicle used for urban road passenger transport in Britain, with some 23,000 in operation. However, there has been a substantial increase in the number of minibuses and midibuses in recent years, with some 19,000 now in use. In addition, there are some 31,000 other single-deck buses and coaches. Blackpool and Llandudno have Britain's only remaining tramway systems.

Deregulation

Local bus services in Great Britain (except in London) were deregulated in 1986. Bus operators are now able to run routes without needing a special licence. Local authorities can subsidise the provision of socially necessary services after competitive tendering. Six weeks' notice of the introduction, variation or cancellation of a service has to be given to the appropriate traffic commissioner (one for each of the nine traffic areas of Great Britain).

Deregulation led to an increase of 19 per cent in local bus mileage outside London between 1985–86 and 1989–90, with some 83 per cent of services operated without subsidy. Over the same period the number of passengers has fallen by 14 per cent outside London, in line with long-term trends. Deregulation also had a noticeable effect during the 1980s on long-distance express coach services, bringing about reductions in fares, the provision of more services and an increase in passengers. The Government is proposing the deregulation of bus services in London.

Taxis

There are about 51,000 licensed taxis in Great Britain, mainly in urban areas; London has some 16,000. In London and a number of other cities taxis must be purpose-built to conform to very strict requirements and drivers must have passed a test of their knowledge of the area. Private hire vehicles with drivers may be booked only through the operator and not hired on the street; in most areas outside London private hire vehicles are licensed.

A local authority can refuse to grant a taxi licence only if it is satisfied that there is no unfulfilled demand for taxis in its area. Taxi operators are able to run regular local services and can tender in competition with bus operators for services subsidised by local authorities. To do this, they may apply for a special 'restricted' bus operator's licence, allowing them to run local services without having to obtain a full bus operator's licence. Taxis and licensed private hire vehicles may also offer shared rides to passengers paying separate fares.

In Northern Ireland there are some 4,000 licensed taxis. Licences are issued by the Department of the Environment for Northern Ireland on a basis broadly similar to that in Great Britain.

RAILWAYS

Railways were pioneered in Britain: the Stockton and Darlington Railway, opened in 1825, was the first public passenger railway in the world to be worked by steam power. The main railway companies in Great Britain were nationalised in 1948. In Northern Ireland the Northern Ireland Railways Company Ltd, a subsidiary of the Northern Ireland Transport Holding Company, operates the railway service on some 320 km (200 miles) of track.

Organisation

The British Railways Board, set up in 1962, controls most of the railway network in Great Britain. Of its five business sectors, InterCity, Network SouthEast and Regional Railways services are responsible for the passenger services. The other two sectors are Railfreight Distribution and Trainload Freight. A subsidiary company, European Passenger Services Ltd, has been set up to operate international rail services through the Channel Tunnel. Other subsidiary businesses are British Rail Maintenance Ltd, which is responsible for maintenance and light repair of British Rail rolling stock; Transmark, which provides consultancy services overseas on railway and associated operations; and BR Telecommunications, a new company marketing communications services.

British Rail is currently developing its sector structure further to devolve decision-making from the Board's headquarters. The aim is to make the sectors more responsive to customer requirements.

The Government has decided to privatise British Rail and is considering how best this can be achieved.

Operations

In 1990–91 the Board's turnover, including financial support and income from other activities but excluding internal transactions, was £3,777 million, of which £2,825 million was derived from rail passenger services and £682 million from freight services. It received grants of £602 million as compensation for the public service obligation to operate sections of the passenger network in the Regional sector and Network SouthEast which would not otherwise cover their cost.

New objectives for British Rail were announced in December 1989. Safety remains a high priority, including the implementation of the safety recommendations of the inquiry into a major railway accident at Clapham Junction (south London) in December 1988.

British Rail has a substantial investment programme. Investment totalled £858 million in 1990–91 and is expected to rise to over £1,000 million in each of the three years from 1991–92.

Major areas of expenditure in British Rail's investment programme include:

- rolling stock and facilities for Channel Tunnel traffic from 1993 (see p 308);

- new rolling stock and infrastructure improvements in Network SouthEast; and

- investment in new diesel multiple-unit trains in the Regional Railways sector.

Passenger Services

The passenger network (see map, p 307) comprises a fast inter-city network, linking the main centres of Great Britain; local stopping services; and commuter services in and around the large conurbations, especially London and south-east England. British Rail runs over 700 InterCity expresses each weekday, serving about 90 business and leisure centres. InterCity 125 trains, travelling at maximum

Table 17.2: Railway Operations

	1985–86	1987–88	1988–89	1989–90	1990–91
Passenger journeys (million)	686	727	764	758	763
Passenger-km (million)	30,233	33,141	34,322	33,648	33,191
Freight traffic (million tonnes)	139	144	150	143	138
Trainload and wagonload traffic (million net tonne–km)	16,047	17,466	18,103	16,742	15,986
Assets (at end of period):					
Locomotives	2,581	2,270	2,180	2,095	2,030
High Speed Train power units	197	197	197	197	197
Other coaching vehicles	16,164	14,648	14,258	13,833	13,631
Freight vehicles [a]	39,007	28,884	24,922	21,970	20,763
Stations (including freight and parcels)	2,526	2,554	2,596	2,598	2,615
Route open for traffic (km)	16,729	16,633	16,598	16,588	16,584

Source: British Railways Board.
[a] In addition, a number of privately owned wagons and locomotives are operated on the railway network for customers of British Rail. Some 13,640 freight vehicles and 15 diesel locomotives were authorised for working on the network at the end of March 1991.

sustained speeds of 125 mph (201 km/h), provide over 40 per cent of InterCity train mileage and are the world's fastest diesel trains. They operate from London:

- to the west of England and south Wales;

- to the East Midlands; and

- on cross-country services through the West Midlands, linking south-west England or south Wales with north-west England or north-east England and Edinburgh.

About 28 per cent of route-mileage is electrified, including British Rail's busiest InterCity route, linking London, the West Midlands, the North West and Glasgow. The most recent major electrification scheme is that for the east-coast main line between London and Edinburgh (including the line from Doncaster to Leeds). This scheme, covering some 644 km (400 miles) and costing £450 million at 1990–91 prices, commenced full passenger services between London King's Cross and Edinburgh in July 1991, using InterCity 225 electric trains.

A new generation of diesel multiple-unit trains is being introduced on regional services, while many of the older electric multiple units used for commuting services in London and south-east England are being replaced by more efficient rolling stock. The first of a new generation of 'Networker' trains is due to enter service in Kent early in 1992. Some 400 coaches will be progressively introduced, with a further 274 on order. A diesel version is being brought into service on lines to the west of London, with 180 vehicles due to be delivered between 1992 and 1994. Three major new rail links to airports have been built or are planned:

- a new link between Stansted airport and London Liverpool Street, which was opened in January 1991;

- a joint venture with BAA plc for a £235 million project (to be financed largely by BAA) between Heathrow airport and London Paddington; and

- a link to connect Manchester airport to the Manchester to Wilmslow (Cheshire) line, currently under construction.

Freight

Over 90 per cent of rail freight traffic is of bulk commodities, mainly coal, coke, iron and steel, building materials and petroleum.

The opening of the Channel Tunnel (see p 308) will present an important opportunity for non-bulk freight movement. Freight routes in Kent and Sussex are being upgraded in preparation for the traffic, and new locomotives are being purchased. Container traffic to the continent of Europe and further afield is being developed and new container-carrying wagons have been ordered. Intermodal services are being developed to give easy transfer of loads between road and rail vehicles.

Railways in London

London Underground Ltd operates services on 408 km (254 miles) of railway, of which about 169 km (105 miles) are underground. The system has 272 stations, with 478 trains operating in the peak period. Some 770 million passenger journeys were made on London Underground trains in 1990–91. Major investment in the Underground is planned, including:

- an extension of the Jubilee Line to Stratford (east London) via Docklands and the north Greenwich peninsula;

- the East-West Crossrail linking Paddington with Liverpool Street, the tunnel of which would be used by British Rail as well as Underground trains; and

- a new line running through central London from Chelsea in the west to Hackney in the north-east.

The Docklands Light Railway, a 12-km (7·5-mile) route with 15 stations, is being upgraded. An extension westward to the City of London was opened in July 1991, and another eastward to Beckton is under construction. Engineering studies are in progress for a new light railway network planned by London Transport and the London Borough of Croydon for the Croydon area of south London.

Main Railway Passenger Routes

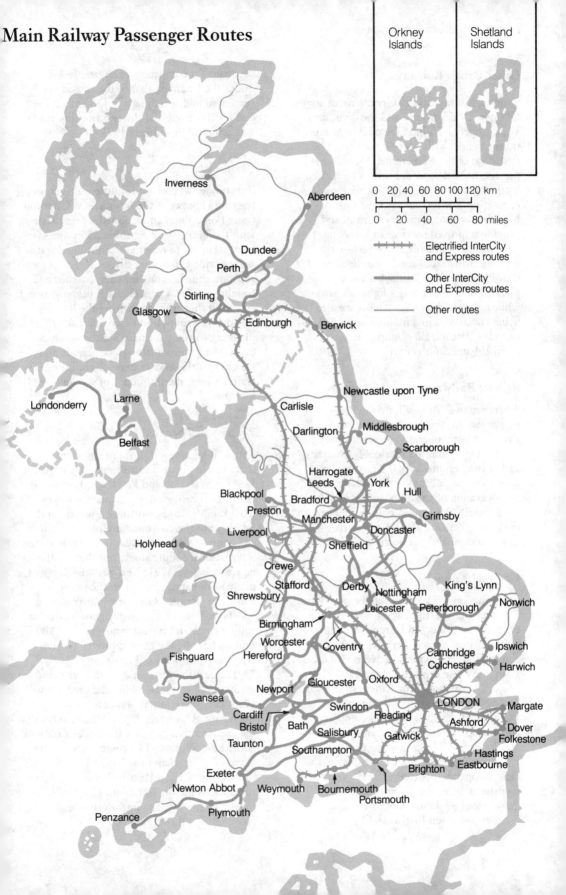

Orkney Islands

Shetland Islands

0 20 40 60 80 100 120 km
0   20   40   60   80 miles

┼┼┼┼ Electrified InterCity and Express routes

━━━ Other InterCity and Express routes

─── Other routes

Inverness
Aberdeen
Dundee
Perth
Stirling
Glasgow
Edinburgh
Berwick
Londonderry
Larne
Belfast
Newcastle upon Tyne
Carlisle
Darlington
Middlesbrough
Scarborough
Harrogate
Leeds
York
Hull
Blackpool
Bradford
Preston
Manchester
Grimsby
Liverpool
Doncaster
Holyhead
Sheffield
Crewe
Stafford
Derby
Nottingham
King's Lynn
Shrewsbury
Leicester
Peterborough
Norwich
Birmingham
Worcester
Coventry
Hereford
Cambridge
Ipswich
Fishguard
Colchester
Harwich
Gloucester
Oxford
Swansea
Newport
Swindon
LONDON
Margate
Cardiff
Reading
Ashford
Bristol
Bath
Salisbury
Gatwick
Dover
Taunton
Folkestone
Southampton
Hastings
Brighton
Eastbourne
Exeter
Weymouth
Bournemouth
Newton Abbot
Portsmouth
Penzance
Plymouth

Other Urban Railways

Other urban railways in Great Britain are the Glasgow Underground and the Tyne and Wear Metro, a 56-km (35-mile) light rapid transit system with over 40 stations. The first stage of the Manchester Metrolink project, to be designed, built and operated by the GMA Group (a private sector consortium), will from 1991–92 link Manchester's main railway termini and provide improved services to Bury and Altrincham as a result of conversion of existing British Rail services to light rapid transit. In the West Midlands work is planned on another major light rail project, while light rapid transit systems are also being considered in a number of other areas, including Bristol, Edinburgh, Glasgow, Sheffield and Southampton.

Private Railways

There are over 70 small, privately owned passenger-carrying railways in Great Britain, mostly operated on a voluntary basis and providing limited services for tourists and railway enthusiasts. The main aim of most of these railways is the preservation and operation of steam locomotives. They are generally run on old British Rail branch lines, but there are also several narrow-gauge lines, mainly in north Wales.

Channel Tunnel

Construction work is well under way on the Channel Tunnel, the largest civil engineering project in Europe to be financed by the private sector. Services in the twin single-track rail tunnels between Britain and France are due to start in June 1993. The project, with a total financing requirement of £8,500 million, is being undertaken by Eurotunnel, a British-French company. A concession agreement between the British and French governments and the Eurotunnel partners gives Eurotunnel the right to operate the tunnel for 55 years. Construction is being carried out for Eurotunnel by Transmanche Link, a consortium of ten British and French construction companies. The first link-up under the Channel, that of the subsidiary service tunnel, took place in December 1990, and break-through of the two running tunnels was achieved in summer 1991.

Eurotunnel Services

Eurotunnel will operate shuttle trains through the tunnel between the terminals at Cheriton (near Folkestone) and Coquelles (near Calais), with the journey taking about 35 minutes from terminal to terminal. Eurotunnel trains will provide a drive-on, drive-off service, with separate shuttle trains for cars, coaches and freight vehicles. Car and coach passengers will stay with their vehicles during the journey through the tunnel. Initially Eurotunnel is planning to run passenger shuttle services every 15 minutes during peak periods and freight shuttle services every 20 minutes. As traffic grows, the frequency of services will be increased.

Through Rail Services

Some 30 high-speed through passenger services are planned to run each day between London Waterloo and Paris, and London and Brussels. Through day passenger services from the Midlands, northern England and Scotland to the continent are planned; these will require a specially adapted version of the international rolling stock, but these will not be ready before 1994. New regional depots are planned to handle freight traffic to the continent. British Rail plans to invest some £1,400 million in new passenger and freight rolling stock and infrastructure; over £800 million has already been approved by the Secretary of State for Transport.

To meet the forecast growth in demand for through rail services, additional capacity will eventually be required between London and the Channel Tunnel. British Rail believes that the construction of a new high-speed rail link is the best solution. The route between the Channel Tunnel and the North Downs is broadly agreed and British Rail is reviewing the options for the route into London to maximise the benefits for international passengers and commuters.

INLAND WATERWAYS

The inland waterways of Great Britain are popular for recreation, make a valuable contribution to the quality of the environment, play an important part in land drainage and water supply, and are used to a limited extent for freight-carrying. An official survey of inland waterway freight traffic reported that in 1989, 68 million tonnes of freight were carried on inland waterways and estuaries, amounting to some 2,400 million tonne–km moved. The publicly owned British Waterways Board is responsible for some 3,200 km (2,000 miles) of waterways in Great Britain. The majority of waterways are primarily for leisure use, but about 620 km (385 miles) are maintained as commercial waterways. The Board is taking steps to develop its business more commercially with greater responsiveness to market needs and waterway users. In 1990–91 the Board's turnover amounted to £27·1 million and it received a government grant of £49·7 million to maintain its waterways to statutory standards.

Ports

There are about 100 ports of commercial significance in Great Britain, but in addition there are many small harbours which handle small amounts of cargo or mainly serve fishing or recreational interests. Port authorities are of three broad types—trusts, local authorities and companies—and most operate with statutory powers under private Acts of Parliament. Major ports controlled by trusts include Clyde, Dover, Forth, London, Medway, Milford Haven, and Tees and Hartlepool. Local authorities own many small ports and the much larger ports of Bristol and Portsmouth, and the oil ports in Orkney and Shetland.

Associated British Ports Holdings PLC (a private sector company) operates 22 ports, including Southampton, Grimsby and Immingham, Hull, Newport, Cardiff and Swansea. Other major ports owned by companies include Felixstowe, Liverpool and Manchester, and a group of ferry ports, including Harwich (Parkeston Quay) and Stranraer.

The Government has suggested that ports not already owned by companies may wish to consider whether company status would be advantageous. The Ports Act 1991 will facilitate the transfer of trust ports to the private sector; before its passage any trust port which wanted a transfer required a private Act of Parliament.

Port Traffic

In 1990 traffic through the ports of Great Britain amounted to 473 million tonnes, comprising 136 million tonnes of exports, 181 million tonnes of imports and 156 million tonnes of domestic traffic (which included offshore traffic and landings of sea-dredged aggregates). About 53 per cent of the traffic was in fuels, mainly petroleum and petroleum products. Traffic through Northern Ireland ports totalled 17 million tonnes.

Britain's main ports, in terms of total tonnage handled, are given in Table 17.3. Sullom Voe (Shetland), Milford Haven and Forth mostly handle oil, while the main ports for non-fuel traffic are London, Tees and Hartlepool, Grimsby and Immingham, Felixstowe and Dover. Ports on the south and east coasts have increasingly gained traffic at the expense of those on the west coast as the emphasis of Britain's trade has switched towards the continent of Europe, and with the worldwide switch from conventional handling methods to container and roll-on, roll-off traffic.

Container and roll-on, roll-off traffic in Great Britain has almost trebled since 1975 to 80 million tonnes in 1990 and now accounts for about 71 per cent of non-bulk traffic. The leading ports for container traffic are Felixstowe, London and Southampton. Those for roll-on, roll-off traffic are Dover (Britain's leading seaport in terms of the value of trade handled), Felixstowe, Portsmouth, Grimsby and Immingham, and Harwich.

Development

Most recent major port developments have been at east- and south-coast ports. For example, at Felixstowe a £50 million extension to the terminal was completed in

Table 17.3: Traffic through the Principal Ports of Great Britain [a]

million tonnes

	1975	1985	1986	1987	1988	1989	1990
London	50·3	51·6	53·6	48·9	53·7	54·0	54·5
Tees and Hartlepool	20·2	30·6	30·7	33·9	37·4	39·3	40·2
Grimsby and Immingham	22·0	29·1	32·0	32·2	35·0	38·1	38·9
Milford Haven	44·9	32·4	30·0	32·7	33·3	33·0	32·2
Sullom Voe	—	59·0	57·2	50·0	50·6	40·7	30·6
Southampton	25·3	25·2	25·7	27·2	31·4	26·1	28·8
Forth	8·4	29·1	28·8	30·0	29·0	22·9	25·4
Liverpool	23·4	10·4	10·7	10·2	19·6	20·2	23·2
Felixstowe	4·1	10·1	10·8	13·3	15·6	16·5	16·4
Medway	21·7	10·4	10·4	11·6	12·7	14·0	15·9
Dover	3·7	9·3	9·9	10·6	10·4	13·5	13·0

Source: Department of Transport.

[a] Belfast and Larne are the main ports in Northern Ireland and handled 8 million tonnes and 4 million tonnes respectively in 1990.

1990. New facilities are being developed for bulk and containerised cargoes on the Medway, and there are plans for bulk and roll-on, roll-off cargoes on the Humber.

Purpose-built terminals for oil from the British sector of the North Sea have been built at Hound Point on the Forth, on the Tees, at Flotta and at Sullom Voe (one of the largest oil terminals in the world). Supply bases for offshore oil and gas installations have been built at a number of ports, notably Aberdeen, Great Yarmouth and Heysham.

Shipping

In April 1991 British companies owned 787 trading vessels of 15·4 million deadweight tonnes.

Among the ships owned by British companies were 205 vessels totalling 9·5 million deadweight tonnes used as oil, chemical or gas carriers and 554 vessels totalling 5·7 million deadweight tonnes employed as dry bulk carriers, container ships or other types of cargo ships.

Some 80 per cent of British-owned vessels are registered in Britain or British dependent territories such as Bermuda.

The tonnage of the British-registered trading fleet has been declining in recent years. To help address this, in September 1990 a joint working party of the Government and the General Council of British Shipping produced a report on the merchant shipping industry which contained an agreed analysis and made a number of recommendations. These are being taken forward; some have already been completed.

Cargo Services

About 94 per cent by weight (76 per cent by value) of Britain's overseas trade is carried by sea. In 1990 British seaborne trade amounted to 300 million tonnes (valued at £173,000 million) or 1,153 million tonne–km (716,500 million tonne–miles). British-registered ships carried 18 per cent by weight and 34 per cent by value. Tanker cargo accounted for 45 per cent of this trade by weight, but only 8 per cent by value; foodstuffs and manufactured goods accounted for 83 per cent by value.

Virtually all the scheduled cargo liner services from Britain are containerised. The British tonnage serving these trades is dominated by a relatively small number of private sector companies and, in deep sea trades, they usually operate in conjunction with other companies on the same routes in organisations known as 'conferences'. The object of these groupings is to ensure regular and efficient services with stable freight rates, to the benefit of both shipper and shipowner. In addition to the carriage of freight by liner and bulk services between Britain and Europe, there are many roll-on, roll-off services to carry cars, passengers and commercial vehicles.

Passenger Services

In 1990 there were 30 million international sea passenger movements between Britain and the rest of the world, compared with some 78 million international air movements. Almost all the passengers who arrived at or departed from British ports in 1990 travelled to or from the continent of Europe or the Irish Republic. In 1990 some 79,000 embarked on pleasure cruises from British ports. Traffic from the southern and south-eastern ports accounts for a substantial proportion of traffic to the continent of Europe. The main British operators are Sealink Stena Line, P & O and Hoverspeed, although not all of their vessels are under the British flag. Services are provided by roll-on, roll-off ferries, hovercraft, hydrofoils and high-speed catamarans. Passenger and freight ferry services also run to many of the offshore islands, such as the Isle of Wight, the Orkney and Shetland islands, and the islands off the west coast of Scotland. It is estimated that in 1989 there were some 45 million passengers on such internal services.

Merchant Shipping Legislation and Policy

The Government's policy is one of minimum intervention and the encouragement of free and fair competition. However, regulations, administered by the Department of Transport, provide for marine safety and welfare, the investigation of accidents and the prevention and cleaning up of pollution from ships. The Government also has certain reserve powers for protecting shipping and trading interests from measures adopted or proposed by overseas governments.

The first stage of a European Community shipping policy involved agreement in 1986 on regulations designed to:

- liberalise the Community's international trade;

- establish a competitive regime for shipping; and

- enable the Community to take action to combat protectionism from other countries and to counter unfair pricing practices.

Under the second stage, now under consideration, a range of measures have been proposed to harmonise operating conditions and strengthen the competitiveness of Community members' merchant fleets. One such measure, facilitating the transfer of ships between member states' registers, has already been agreed.

The Government has made funds available for Merchant Navy officer training, the repatriation of crews in the deep-sea trades and a Reserve of ex-seafarers willing to serve in the Merchant Navy in an emergency.

Safety at Sea

HM Coastguard Service, part of the Department of Transport, is responsible for co-ordinating civil maritime search and rescue operations around the coastline of Britain. In a maritime emergency the Coastguard calls on and co-ordinates facilities such as lifeboats of the Royal National Lifeboat Institution (a voluntary body), and Ministry of Defence aircraft, helicopters and ships, as well as merchant shipping, commercial aircraft, its own aircraft and rescue companies. In 1990 the Coastguard Service co-ordinated action in some 7,100 incidents (including cliff rescues), in which 13,500 people were assisted.

The lighthouse authorities, which between them control about 370 lighthouses and many minor lights and buoys, are:

- the Corporation of Trinity House, which covers England and Wales;

- the Northern Lighthouse Board, for Scotland; and

- the Commissioners of Irish Lights for Ireland.

Responsibility for pilotage rests with harbour authorities under the Pilotage Act 1987.

Compliance with rules of behaviour when navigating in traffic separation schemes around the shores of Britain is mandatory for all vessels of countries party to the Convention on the International Regulations for Preventing Collisions at Sea 1972. The most important scheme affecting British waters is in the Dover Strait, the world's busiest seaway. Britain and France jointly operate the Channel Navigation Information Service, which provides navigational information and also monitors the movement of vessels in the strait.

Among measures to improve the safety of roll-on, roll-off ferries introduced following the sinking of the *Herald of Free Enterprise* in 1987 is a duty on shipowners to ensure the safe operation of their vessels. Most measures introduced by Britain have been incorporated in the relevant international maritime safety convention.

Civil Aviation

The demands of passengers, both domestic and international, are responded to by an innovative British air transport industry. Airlines are seeking opportunities for modernisation, and this is complemented by the work of the aviation authorities in negotiating new international rights and improving facilities such as air traffic control. British airlines are entirely in the private sector.

Role of the Government

The Secretary of State for Transport is responsible for aviation matters, including:

- negotiation of air service agreements with more than 100 other countries;
- control of air services into Britain by overseas airlines;
- British participation in the activities of international aviation bodies;
- aviation security policy;
- amenity matters, such as aircraft noise and other environmental matters;
- investigation of accidents; and
- airports policy.

The Government's civil aviation policy aims to maintain high standards of safety and security and to achieve environmental improvements through reduced noise and other emissions from aircraft. It is concerned to promote the interests of travellers by encouraging a competitive British industry. The Government has taken the lead in the European Community and with bilateral partners in negotiating freer arrangements within which airline competition can flourish. New arrangements with an increasing number of countries are resulting in better provision of services at more competitive fares.

Civil Aviation Authority

The Civil Aviation Authority (CAA) is an independent statutory body, responsible for the economic and safety regulation of the industry and, jointly with the Ministry of Defence, for the provision of air navigation services. The CAA's primary objectives are to ensure that British airlines provide air services to satisfy all substantial categories of public demand at the lowest charges consistent with a high standard of safety and to further the reasonable interests of air transport users.

Air Traffic

Total capacity offered on all services by British airlines amounted to 20,377 million available tonne–km in 1990: 15,274 million tonne–km on scheduled services and 5,103 million tonne-km on non-scheduled services. The airlines carried 38·4 million passengers on scheduled services and 21·6 million on charter flights; some 77·6 million passengers travelled by air (international terminal passengers) to or from Britain, a 3 per cent increase on 1989.

The value of Britain's overseas trade carried by air in 1990 was some £21,957 million—20 per cent of the value of exports and 18 per cent of imports. Air freight is important for the carriage of goods with a high value-to-weight ratio, especially where speed of movement is essential.

British Airways

British Airways plc is one of the world's leading airlines. In terms of international scheduled services it is the largest in the world. During 1990–91 British Airways' turnover was £4,937 million (including £4,834 million from airline operations), and the British Airways group carried 25·6 million passengers on scheduled and charter flights.

The British Airways scheduled route network serves over 160 destinations in some 75 countries. Its main operating base is London's Heathrow airport, but services from Gatwick and regional centres such as Manchester and Birmingham have been expanding. Scheduled Concorde supersonic services are operated from London (Heathrow) to New York, Washington and, in the summer, Toronto, crossing the Atlantic in about half the time taken by subsonic aircraft. In March 1991 British Airways had a fleet of 230 aircraft, the largest fleet in Western Europe, comprising 7 Concordes, 50 Boeing 747s, 8 McDonnell-Douglas DC10s, 13 Lockheed TriStars, 37 Boeing 757s, 10 Airbus A320s, 48 Boeing 737s, 9 Boeing 767s, 31 BAC One-Elevens, 8 British Aerospace Advanced Turboprops and 9 British Aerospace 748s. A further 68 aircraft were on order.

Other Airlines

About 570 aircraft are operated by other airlines. Dan-Air Services is a major operator of both scheduled and charter services, and had a fleet of 51 aircraft in May 1991. British Midland and Air UK are both major domestic airlines and also operate a number of international and charter services. Virgin Atlantic began scheduled services between Gatwick and New York (Newark) in 1984 and is also continuing to extend its services to other long-haul routes. It has eight aircraft.

Britannia Airways carried over 6 million passengers in 1989 and is one of the largest charter operators in the world. It has charter flights from 20 British airports to more than 100 destinations in Europe and elsewhere, mostly operated for its associated company, Thomson Holidays. It has 39 aircraft.

Helicopters and Other Aerial Work

Helicopters are engaged on a variety of work, especially operations connected with Britain's offshore oil and gas industry. The three main operators in Britain are Bristow Helicopters, Bond Helicopters and British International Helicopters, with 76, 48 and 26 helicopters respectively. Light aircraft and helicopters are also involved in other activities, such as charter operations, search and rescue services, medical evacuation, crop-spraying, aerial survey and photography, and police operations.

Air Safety

The CAA is responsible for both technical and operational air safety. Its Safety Regulation Group deals with the development and application of safety requirements for all civil aviation operations. It licenses flight crew, ground engineers and air traffic control officers, as well as aerodromes and fire and rescue services. Training of air traffic controllers is also provided by the CAA.

Every company operating aircraft used for commercial purposes must possess an Air Operator's Certificate, which is granted by the CAA when it is satisfied that the operator is competent to secure the safe operation of its aircraft. The CAA's flight operations inspectors, all of whom are experienced airline pilots, and airworthiness surveyors check that satisfactory standards are maintained.

Each member of the flight crew of a British-registered aircraft and every licensed ground engineer must hold the appropriate official licence issued by the CAA. Except for those with acceptable military or other qualifying experience, all applicants for a first professional licence must have undertaken a full-time course of instruction which has been approved by the CAA.

Air Traffic Control and Navigation Services

Responsibility for civil and military air traffic control over Britain and the surrounding seas rests with the National Air Traffic Services (NATS), jointly operated by the CAA and the

Ministry of Defence. At 13 civil aerodromes, including most of the major British airports, the NATS provides the navigation services necessary for aircraft taking off and landing, and integrates them into the flow of traffic within British airspace.

Britain is one of 13 members of Eurocontrol, a European air traffic control body. In recent years Britain has put forward a number of initiatives, including the Central Flow Management Unit, which will be fully operational in 1993, and an initiative agreed in 1990 to increase airspace capacity by integrating air traffic control systems and optimising the air traffic route network. For Britain the CAA has a substantial annual investment programme of about £80 million, which includes the construction of a new air traffic control centre for England and Wales.

Aircraft and the Environment

The replacement of older aircraft with new quieter types has done much to reduce the problem of noise near airports, as have noise abatement measures such as noise-preferential routes, night restrictions and house insulation. Research is in hand on the effect of aircraft emissions on the upper atmosphere, and in the mean time consideration is being given internationally to tightening the emission standards for aircraft.

Airports

Of the 141 licensed civil aerodromes in Britain, about one-fifth handle more than 100,000 passengers a year each. Twelve handle over 1 million passengers a year each (see Table 17.4).

In 1990 Britain's civil airports handled a total of 104·1 million passengers (102·4 million terminal passengers and 1·7 million in transit), and 1·2 million tonnes of freight.

Heathrow airport is the world's busiest airport for international travel and is Britain's most important airport for passengers and air freight, handling 43·0 million passengers (including transit passengers) and 695,300 tonnes of freight in 1990. Gatwick is one of the world's busiest international airports.

Ownership and Control

Eight airports—Heathrow, Gatwick, Stansted and Southampton in south-east England, and Glasgow, Edinburgh, Prestwick and Aberdeen in Scotland—are owned and operated by BAA plc. Together they handle about 70 per cent of air passengers and 85 per cent of air cargo traffic in Britain.

Many of the other public airports are controlled by local authorities. A total of 15 major local authority airports now operate as Companies Act companies. The Government is encouraging the introduction of private capital into these new companies.

The CAA has responsibility for the economic regulation of major airport companies. It has powers to take action to remedy practices considered to be against the public interest, in particular any abuse of an airport's monopoly position. All airports used for public transport and training flights must be licensed by the CAA. Stringent requirements, such as the provision of adequate fire-fighting, medical and rescue services, must be satisfied before a licence is granted. Strict security measures are in force, and the Aviation and Maritime Security Act 1990 provides for greater powers to enforce such requirements.

Development

The Government's policy is to promote a strong and competitive British airline industry by providing airport capacity where it is needed and by making effective use of existing capacity, including regional airports.

Major expansion is under way at Stansted. A new terminal was opened in March 1991, with an initial capacity of 8 million passengers a year. After further expansion it will cater for 15 million passengers a year. Under major expansion plans at Manchester, the first phase of a second terminal is under construction and is expected to open in 1993, increasing capacity by one-half to 18 million passengers a year. A second terminal at Birmingham was

Table 17.4: Passenger Traffic at Britain's Main Airports

million passengers

	1985	1987	1988	1989	1990
London (Heathrow)	31·3	34·7	37·5	39·6	43·0
London (Gatwick)	14·9	19·4	20·7	21·1	21·2
Manchester	6·0	8·6	9·5	10·1	10·5
Glasgow	2·7	3·4	3·6	3·9	4·4
Birmingham	1·6	2·6	2·8	3·3	3·6
Luton	1·5	2·6	2·8	2·8	2·7
Edinburgh	1·6	1·8	2·1	2·4	2·6
Belfast (Aldergrove)	1·6	2·1	2·2	2·2	2·3
Aberdeen	1·7	1·5	1·6	1·7	2·0
Newcastle upon Tyne	1·0	1·3	1·4	1·5	1·6
East Midlands	0·9	1·3	1·3	1·5	1·3
London (Stansted)	0·5	0·7	1·0	1·3	1·2

Source: Civil Aviation Authority.

Note: Statistics relate to terminal passengers only and exclude those in transit.

officially opened in 1991, increasing capacity to 6 million passengers a year. Construction of a new airport at Sheffield is planned to start in 1992. Facilities are also being improved at other regional airports.

Communications

The telecommunications services sector is one of the most rapidly growing in the economy. Major changes occurred in the 1980s with the privatisation of British Telecommunications plc (BT) and the abolition of its monopoly on the provision of basic telecommunications over fixed links. A second major telecommunications carrier, Mercury Communications, started services in 1986, while, following a government review of policy announced in March 1991, others will be able to apply for licences to run services.

Licensing

Those running telecommunications systems, including BT and Mercury, need to be licensed by the Secretary of State for Trade and Industry. The Government has hitherto licensed only BT and Mercury to provide fixed services—the so-called 'duopoly' policy. This was reviewed in a White Paper published in March 1991. Important proposals include:

- the right for other companies to apply for licences to run new telecommunications networks within Britain;

- the introduction of 'number portability', so that people can move from one network to another without changing their number, subject to a cost-benefit study;

- the introduction of telecommunications 'retailers', who would deal with the public to arrange, but not themselves provide, telecommunications services;

- greater freedom for existing mobile telecommunications companies and cable operators to provide telecommunications services in their own right;

- the early introduction of 'equal access', by which customers can exercise a choice over the trunk operator that carries their calls; and

- the introduction of class licences to allow companies to provide telecommunications circuits for their own use, and for the development of a wide range of new satellite services catering for specialist markets.

The Government concluded that it would be unlikely to license any new international operators in the short term, but would keep this under review.

Office of Telecommunications

The Office of Telecommunications (OFTEL), a non-ministerial government department, is the independent regulatory body for the telecommunications industry. It is headed by the Director General of Telecommunications, among whose functions are:

- to ensure that licensees comply with the conditions of their licences;

- to promote effective competition in the telecommunications industry;

- to provide advice to the Secretary of State for Trade and Industry on telecommunications matters; and

- to investigate complaints.

The Director General also has a duty to promote the interests of consumers in respect of prices, quality and variety in telecommunications services.

BT

In 1984 BT was reconstituted as a public limited company and a majority of the ordinary voting shares were sold to private investors. It has about 1 million registered shareholders. Some 90 per cent of its 230,000 employees own shares and nearly 44 per cent are members of the Employee Share Save Scheme. The Government intends to sell its remaining shares.

BT runs one of the world's largest public telecommunications networks, including:

- 19·6 million residential lines;

- 6·4 million business lines;

- 78,200 telex connections;

- 98,200 public payphones; and

- a wide range of specialised voice, data, text and visual services.

The inland telephone and telex networks are fully automatic. International direct dialling is available from Britain to 201 countries, representing 99 per cent of the world's telephones. Automatic telex service is available to more than 200 countries.

Network Modernisation

BT is investing some £11 million per working day in the modernisation and expansion of its network to meet the increasing demand for basic telephone services and for more specialised services. The company has more than 1·4 million km (870,000 miles) of optical fibre laid in its network in Britain, a higher proportion than any other world operator. There are more than 3,650 digital exchanges serving some 73 per cent of telephone lines. The combination of digital exchange switching and digital transmission techniques, using optical fibre cable and microwave radio links, is substantially improving the quality of telephone services for residential and business customers, as well as making possible a wider range of services through the company's main network.

General Services

BT's services include:

- a free facility for emergency calls to the police, fire, ambulance, coastguard, lifeboat and air-sea rescue services;

- directory enquiries;

- various chargeable operator-connected services, such as reversed-charge calls and alarm calls;

- an operator-handled Freefone service and automatic 'LinkLine' facilities that enable callers to contact organisations anywhere in Britain, either free or at local call rates;

- a number of Callstream services, which allow callers to obtain information by paying a premium call rate; and

- network services such as three-way calling, call waiting and call diversion, which are available to customers on digital exchanges.

Other premium-rate services are offered by independent service providers using the BT network. In 1988 the company opened a £70 million optical fibre flexible access system, for intensive voice and data traffic, to serve the financial organisations of the City of London.

Under a public payphone service modernisation programme, a total of £165 million is being spent on modernisation and additional provision on sites convenient for travellers, such as railway stations and motorway service areas. A number of cashless call developments are being carried out, including the Phonecard service, using prepaid encoded cards; Phonecard payphones account for 19,000 of the total of 98,200 payphones. There are about 280,000 private rented payphones on premises to which the public has access and these are also being upgraded with push-button equipment.

Prestel, BT's videotex service, and Telecom Gold (an electronic mail and information service) form part of the company's data services division, BT Tymnet Europe. Prestel was the first service of its kind to enable a wide variety of computer-stored information to be called up via the telephone on a computer, a terminal or an adapted television. Some 100,000 terminals are attached to Prestel, primarily in businesses. Through its 'gateway' links with other databases, a wide range of other services, such as home shopping and banking services, holiday booking and reservation facilities, and insurance and financial markets information, is available.

International Services

BT has much experience as an international network and service provider. It is the second largest shareholder in the International Telecommunications Satellite Organisation (of which 120 countries are members) and in the European Telecommunications Satellite Organisation. It is also a leading shareholder in the International Maritime Satellite Organisation, with interests in a number of other consortia.

A substantial proportion of the intercontinental telephone traffic to or from Britain is carried by satellite. BT operates satellite earth stations at Goonhilly Downs (Cornwall), Madley (near Hereford), London Docklands and Aberdeen. Its range of digital transmission services includes a number available overseas, including 'Satstream' private circuit digital links covering North America and Western Europe using small-dish aerials, and an 'International Kilostream' private circuit service available to the United States, Australia and most major business centres in Asia and the rest of Europe. Extensive direct-dial maritime satellite services are available for vessels worldwide. In-flight operator-controlled telephone call facilities are available via Portishead radio station near Bristol. Digital transmission techniques have been introduced for services to the United States, Japan, Hong Kong and Australia via the Madley and Goonhilly stations. The London-Tokyo link, which was set up in 1986, includes the first all-digital telephone link between two continents.

Recent improvements in submarine cable design (including the use of optical fibre technology) have helped to increase capacity and reduce pressure on satellite systems. A second high-capacity transatlantic optical fibre cable (TAT 9), which will cost about £250 million and be able to carry about 75,000 telephone calls simultaneously, is scheduled to be in operation by the end of 1991 to supplement an earlier link.

British Telecom's overseas consultancy service, Telconsult, has so far completed 270 projects in more than 60 countries.

Mercury Communications

Mercury Communications Ltd, a wholly owned subsidiary of Cable and Wireless plc, is licensed as a public telecommunications operator in Britain. Mercury has constructed its own long-distance network comprising optical fibre cables and digital microwave links. The network runs from the north of Scotland to the south coast, serving some 85 cities and towns across Britain. Coverage is enhanced through Mercury's own city cable networks as well as partnerships with local cable television operators.

Mercury offers a full range of long-distance and international telecommunications services for both business and residential customers. In addition to voice and data transmission, the company supplies sophisticated messaging systems, mobile telecommunications and a range of equipment for customers' premises. Major customers can have a direct digital link between their premises and the Mercury network. A number of routeing devices have also been developed to enable customers to use Mercury indirectly via their existing exchange lines. Residential customers can buy a Mercury-compatible phone and access the network at the touch of a button.

International services are provided by satellite communications centres in London's docklands and in Oxfordshire, as well as by submarine cable links to Europe and the United States.

Mobile Communications

The Government encourages the expansion of mobile radio telecommunications services. It has licensed Vodafone Ltd and Telecom Securicor Cellular Radio Ltd (a joint venture between BT and Securicor) to run competing national cellular radio telephone systems. Considerable investment has been made in establishing their networks to provide increased capacity for the growing number of cellular radio telephone users, estimated at over 1 million in mid-1990.

In 1989 the Government announced an increase in the number of channels available for cellular radio and the issue of licences for 'Telepoint' systems, which allow subscribers to make outgoing telephone calls from Telepoint base stations in public places using their own portable digital cordless handsets.

Britain will be the first country to offer personal communications network (PCN) services, which would allow the same telephone to be used at home, at work and in a mobile capacity. In 1989 the Government allocated licences to three operators—Mercury PCN Ltd, Microtel Communications Ltd and Unitel Ltd—to run PCNs in the frequency range 1·7 to 1·9 gigahertz. The first service is expected to start in late 1992.

Two national operators (GEC National One and Band 3 Radio Ltd) have been licensed to offer a nationwide trunked mobile radio service, while a number of licences have been awarded for London and regional services.

Other Services

The Department of Trade and Industry has licensed 116 companies which have been awarded franchises by the Cable Authority to run local broadband cable telecommunications systems. At present they mainly provide television programmes, but some are already offering interactive services, including local voice telephony. The duopoly review (see p 315) will encourage them to provide a wider range of services. Home banking services, accessed by multi-frequency telephone, are being developed by a number of banks.

Cable & Wireless

Cable and Wireless plc provides a wide range of telecommunications in some 50 countries worldwide. Its main business is the provision and operation of public telecommunications services in 37 countries and territories, including the United States, Japan and Hong Kong, under franchises and licences granted by the governments concerned. It also provides and manages telecommunications services and facilities for public and private sector customers, and undertakes consultancy work. It operates a fleet of ten ships and three submersible vehicle systems for laying and maintaining submarine telecommunications cables. The company's strategy is the construction and operation of a broadband digital network linking major world economic and financial centres in Europe, north America and the Pacific rim. The first leg of this 'Global Digital Highway', the private transatlantic optical fibre cable linking Britain, the Irish Republic, the United States and Bermuda, entered service in 1989, and the North Pacific Cable, the first direct cable between the United States and Japan, entered service in 1991, connecting to other optical fibre cables in the Pacific rim region.

Postal Services

The Post Office, founded in 1635, pioneered postal services and was the first to issue adhesive postage stamps as proof of advance payment for mail.

The Post Office has a monopoly on the conveyance of letters, but the Secretary of State for Trade and Industry has the power to suspend the monopoly in certain areas or for certain categories of mail and to license others to provide competing services. The Secretary of State has suspended the monopoly on letters subject to a minimum fee of £1, and has issued general licences enabling mail to be transferred between document exchanges and allowing charitable organisations to carry Christmas and New Year cards. As part of the Government's Citizen's Charter proposals, it is intended to reduce the monopoly from the £1 level to one much nearer the present cost of a first-class stamp (24p).

The Royal Mail provides deliveries to 24 million addresses and handles over 60 million letters and parcels each working day (over 14,000 million items a year). Mail is collected from over 100,000 posting boxes, as well as from post offices and large postal users.

Mail sorting was traditionally done by hand at some 600 offices of varying size and capacity. During the past 20 years, however, much of the process has been mechanised and concentrated into larger offices. Some 80 such mechanised letter offices are now in operation. The British postcode system is the most sophisticated in the world, allowing mechanised sorting down to part of a street on a postman's round and, in some cases, to an individual address. The Post Office's parcels operation, Royal Mail Parcelforce, has a programme of modernisation including the establishment of 150 local collection and delivery depots throughout Britain.

Post Office Counters Ltd handles a wide range of transactions; it acts as an agent for the letters and parcels businesses, government departments, local authorities and Girobank, which was transferred to the private sector in July 1990. There are 20,900 post offices, of which some 1,300 are operated directly by the Post Office. The remainder are operated on an agency basis by sub-postmasters.

Post Office Specialist Services

The Post Office provides a range of specialist services. 'Datapost', a door-to-door delivery service, has overnight links throughout Britain and provides an international service to over 160 countries. 'Datapost Sameday' provides a rapid delivery within or between more than 100 cities and towns in Britain and between London and Amsterdam, Paris and Dublin. The Philatelic Bureau in Edinburgh handles about one-third of the Post Office's philatelic business, much of it involving sales to overseas collectors or dealers. The British Postal Consultancy Service offers advice and assistance on all aspects of postal business to overseas postal administrations, and nearly 40 countries have used its services since 1965.

Private Courier and Express Service Operators

Private sector couriers and express operators are able to handle time-sensitive door-to-door deliveries, subject to a minimum fee of £1. The courier/express service industry has grown rapidly, by about 20 per cent a year, and the revenue created by the carriage of these items is estimated at over £1,500 million a year. Britain is one of the main providers of monitored express deliveries in Europe, with London an important centre for air courier/express traffic.

18 Employment

Employment in Britain has risen substantially since the mid-1980s, and remains at a high level. There was also a considerable decline in unemployment during the late 1980s. This represented the longest period of falling unemployment since the second world war, although in common with many other industrialised countries unemployment has recently been rising again.

The Government has taken a number of steps to improve the labour market, with the aim of creating an economic climate in which business can flourish and create more jobs. These include:

- increasing the flexibility of the labour market;

- removing burdens on employers, including regulatory barriers which hinder recruitment; and

- encouraging better training, especially by setting up Training and Enterprise Councils and, in Scotland, Local Enterprise Companies (see pp 323–4).

However, Britain has expressed concern about the operation of the European Community's draft Social Charter, covering various aspects of employment. The Government has indicated its willingness to accept some of the proposed regulations, such as on health and safety, but opposes a number of other proposals which it believes would add to labour costs and discourage employment.

TRENDS IN THE LABOUR MARKET

The total workforce in June 1990 was 28·5 million, of whom 22·9 million (12·1 million men and 10·8 million women) were classed as employees in employment. Major trends have included the growth in the proportion of the workforce accounted for by women, as more married women have sought work, especially in part-time employment; and a substantial increase in self-employment. By June 1990, the number of self-employed people is estimated to have risen to 3·3 million, representing 12·3 per cent of the employed workforce.

Table 18.1: Manpower in Britain 1980–90

						Thousands (as at June), seasonally adjusted	
	1980	1985	1986	1987	1988	1989	1990
Employees in employment[a]	22,965	21,414	21,379	21,586	22,266	22,670	22,864
Self-employed	2,013	2,614	2,633	2,869	2,988	3,253	3,298
Unemployed[b]	1,274	3,019	3,121	2,839	2,299	1,791	1,618
Armed forces	323	326	322	319	316	308	303
Work-related government training programmes[c]	–	176	226	311	343	462	424
Workforce[d]	26,759	27,743	27,877	28,077	28,347	28,486	28,509

Sources: Department of Employment and Northern Ireland Department of Economic Development.
[a] Part-time workers are counted as full units.
[b] Figures are adjusted for discontinuities and exclude school-leavers.
[c] Not seasonally adjusted.
[d] Comprises employees in employment, the self-employed, the armed forces, participants in work-related government training programmes and the unemployed (including school-leavers).

Patterns of Employment

As in other industrialised countries, there has been a marked shift in jobs from manufacturing to service industries.

Between 1955 and 1990 the proportion of employees in employment engaged in service industries rose from 36 per cent to 69 per cent as higher living standards and technological developments stimulated the growth of many service industries.

During the period 1980 to 1990 the number of employees in service industries in Great Britain rose by 2·1 million (16 per cent) to 15·5 million. Employment in most service industries, with some exceptions such as transport, has grown considerably. The largest rise in this period was in the banking, finance and insurance sector (by 62 per cent to 2·7 million), while there was also a substantial increase in hotels and catering (31 per cent). Manufacturing industry accounted for 43 per cent of employees in employment in 1955, but by 1990 the proportion had fallen to 23 per cent. Nearly all manufacturing industries experienced a decline in employment as markets for manufactured goods changed and as new technology brought greater efficiency.

Unemployment

Unemployment reached a peak in July 1986 when, on a seasonally adjusted basis (excluding school-leavers), it totalled over 3·1 million, 11·2 per cent of the workforce. Subsequently it declined significantly, and in

Table 18.2: Employees in Employment[a]

Industry or service (1980 Standard Industrial Classification)	Thousands (as at June)				Per cent
	1980	1985	1989	1990	1990
Primary sector	**1,099**	**932**	**765**	**749**	**3·3**
Agriculture, forestry and fishing	373	341	300	298	1·3
Energy and water supply	727	591	465	451	2·0
Manufacturing[b]	**6,937**	**5,362**	**5,187**	**5,151**	**22·5**
Construction	**1,243**	**1,021**	**1,082**	**1,087**	**4·8**
Services	**13,712**	**14,108**	**15,627**	**15,868**	**69·4**
Wholesale distribution and repairs	1,173	1,173	1,231	1,253	5·5
Retail distribution	2,177	2,080	2,283	2,299	10·1
Hotels and catering	972	1,042	1,217	1,272	5·6
Transport	1,049	900	915	940	4·1
Postal services and communications	437	427	447	434	1·9
Banking, finance and insurance	1,695	2,068	2,627	2,734	12·0
Public administration	1,980	1,921	1,931	1,949	8·5
Education	1,642	1,616	1,778	1,802	7·9
Health	1,258	1,347	1,465	1,466	6·4
Other services	1,327	1,533	1,734	1,718	7·5
Total	**22,991**	**21,423**	**22,661**	**22,855**	**100·0**

Sources: Department of Employment and Northern Ireland Department of Economic Development.

[a] Figures are not seasonally adjusted.

[b] In June 1990 employment in the main sectors of manufacturing industry included 752,000 in mechanical engineering; 645,000 in office machinery, electrical engineering and instruments; 540,000 in food, drink and tobacco; 518,000 in textiles, leather, footwear and clothing; 476,000 in paper products, printing and publishing; 475,000 in timber, wooden furniture, rubber and plastics; 330,000 in chemicals and man-made fibres; and 248,000 in motor vehicles and parts.

Note: Differences between totals and the sums of their component parts are due to rounding.

the first seven months of 1990 it was about 1·6 million (5·7 per cent of the workforce), one of the lowest rates in the European Community. Unemployment fell in all regions, with reductions being greatest in some of the regions with above-average unemployment. Unemployment began to rise again in April 1990, but still remains below 1986 levels. In August 1991 it totalled 2·4 million, 8·5 per cent of the workforce. The Government believes that an increase on the scale of the early 1980s is avoidable, depending in part upon the moderation of pay settlements.

Extra help for unemployed people to find work was announced in March 1991, including up to 100,000 extra Jobclub places (see p 327) and a guaranteed offer of an interview for all those who do not find work within 13 weeks to help them consider their options for getting back to work. Further help was announced in June 1991, including a new £180 million programme, Employment Action, which will offer unemployed people the chance to keep their skills up to date by work experience on local projects.

TRAINING

Employers in Britain spend over £20,000 million a year on employee training and development. A wide-ranging survey of training in 1986–87 found that the health sector provided most training in terms of the number of days per employee. Overall, the 1990 Labour Force Survey found that the number of employees who had received recent training was 85 per cent higher than it had been six years previously. Individuals are also being encouraged to train by means of tax reliefs and loan schemes.

Government Policy

The Government's major aims for the 1990s are that:

- employers should invest more effectively in the skills their businesses need;
- young people should have the motivation to achieve their full potential and to develop skills the economy needs;

- individuals should be persuaded that training is worthwhile and that they should take more responsibility for their own development;
- people who are unemployed or at a disadvantage in the job market should be helped to get back to work and to develop their abilities to the full;
- those who give education and training should offer flexible provision which meets the needs of individuals and employers; and
- enterprise should be encouraged throughout the economy, particularly through the continued growth of small business and self-employment.

Training and Enterprise Councils

A network of 82 Training and Enterprise Councils (TECs) has been set up throughout England and Wales. Of these, 77 are now operational, a little over two years since TECs were first announced. Their main functions are:

- to promote more effective training by employers and individuals;
- to provide practical help to employers through Business Enterprise Training;
- to deliver and develop Youth Training and Employment Training (see p 324); and
- to stimulate enterprise and economic growth by providing support to new and existing small firms.

In November 1990 the Government announced changes in the funding arrangements for TECs to allow them greater discretion in adapting their programmes to meet local needs. TECs now have one single budget to cover all their enterprise activities, and so have considerable flexibility in deciding how to use it. It is also planned to give TECs a wider role in education, especially in the development of the Technical and Vocational Education Initiative (see p 153). TECs have also taken charge of the money that the Department of

Employment previously spent on work-related further education; this amounts to some £105 million in 1991–92. They have thus become able to work directly with further education colleges and local education authorities. Total government funding to TECs in 1991–92 will be some £1,600 million.

A separate network of 22 Local Enterprise Companies (LECs) exists in Scotland. These have wider-ranging responsibilities than the TECs, covering economic development and environmental improvement. LECs operate the same programmes as TECs, but, unlike them, have no responsibility for work-related further education. They run in conjunction with two new enterprise bodies, Scottish Enterprise and Highlands and Islands Enterprise (see p 326).

National Training Task Force

The National Training Task Force was established in 1989. Its members are drawn from a wide spectrum, including employers, trade unions, local authorities and education. Its most important job is to assist in the establishment and development of TECs.
In addition, it is helping to promote to employers the importance of investing in the skills of their workforce.

Industry Training Organisations

Industry Training Organisations (ITOs) have a major role in developing occupational standards and reviewing future skill requirements for their sectors in Great Britain. The Government's preference is for them to be independent employer-led bodies. Accordingly, most statutory training boards are being phased out.

There are over 100 independent ITOs, many of which superseded former statutory boards, covering sectors employing about 80 per cent of the civilian workforce. The National Council of Industry Training Organisations, a voluntary body set up to represent the interests of ITOs, aims to improve the effectiveness of these bodies, for example, by encouraging good practice.

Employment Training

Employment Training provides a flexible and individually adapted training programme for the longer-term unemployed. An individual's training needs are identified and an agreed action plan is drawn up. Training is carried out by training managers under contract with the local TEC or LEC. For 1991–92 Employment Training has a budget of £900 million to provide training opportunities for up to 250,000 trainees.

Entry to the programme can be through a variety of routes, including a Restart interview (see p 327) or by application at a jobcentre. Trainees receive a training allowance of £10 a week more than their benefit entitlement, and they may also receive help towards fares and other expenses.

Youth Training

Youth Training gives all eligible young people the opportunity of a broad-based vocational education and to achieve a vocational qualification or a credit towards one. It puts an emphasis on raising the level of qualifications of new entrants to the workforce and on results, such as vocational qualifications, rather than on time spent in training. It offers the chance to gain specific skills of relevance to work and to improve the employment prospects of young people.

The new Training Credits scheme gives young people who have left full-time education to join the labour market an entitlement to train to approved standards. Ten TECs and one LEC started pilot projects in April 1991. Some 45,000 young people now enjoy the greater opportunity that the scheme brings. The Government has announced the expansion of the credits pilot to a further 10 per cent of eligible young people in 1993. The eventual aim is to offer Training Credits to all young people by 1996.

Enterprise Development

TECs and LECs are taking over the running and development of business and enterprise training to meet the needs of local employers. They now have a combined budget covering all their enterprise development activities which includes training and financial support to new entrepreneurs.

The TECs offer a range of flexible programmes designed to help small- to medium-sized businesses to improve their planning, and to develop the business skills of owner-managers. Training advice, information and financial support are also available for people wishing to set up in business.

Education Initiatives

In May 1991 the Government published a White Paper containing its proposals for education and training. The main aims are to:

- ensure that high-quality further education or training becomes the norm for all 16- and 17-year-olds who can benefit from it;
- increase the all-round levels of attainment by young people; and
- increase the proportion acquiring higher levels of skill and expertise.

The White Paper sets out proposals to achieve a fully-integrated system of education and training; to fulfil the potential of more young people who would otherwise miss out on education and training after 16; to equip everyone with stronger basic skills and more with higher-level skills; to bridge the traditional academic–vocational divide; and to build up a partnership between employers and the education system.

Specific government initiatives to make education more relevant to the needs of working life include:
- the Technical and Vocational Education Initiative, which aims to equip all 14- to 18-year-olds in full-time education for the demands of working life;
- Work-Related Further Education, which aims to link vocational education to the needs of employers;
- the Enterprise in Higher Education Initiative, which aims to make higher education more relevant to the world of work;
- Compacts, where employers guarantee jobs with training, or further education followed by a job, to young people in inner-city areas, provided they reach agreed targets; and
- Education Business Partnerships, which aim to encourage a range of activities to help young people reach their highest potential and prepare them better for work.

Vocational Qualifications

The National Council for Vocational Qualifications (NCVQ) was set up in 1986 to reform and rationalise the vocational qualifications system in England, Wales and Northern Ireland. It aims to make qualifications more accessible and more relevant by basing them on standards of competence set by industry, and to establish a coherent framework—the National Vocational Qualification (NVQ)—based on defined levels of achievement to which qualifications in all sectors can be assigned or accredited. The immediate aim is to have the framework for levels I to IV (from the most basic level to the management supervisory level) in place and available by the end of 1992. Eventually it is expected to cover all occupational levels up to and including the professions. Work is under way to develop broader-based NVQs to allow young people to keep their career options open and assist older adults wishing to make a career change.

Scotland has not been covered by the NCVQ as it already had its own modular system, but in 1989 the Government announced that a system of Scottish Vocational Qualifications would be introduced, which would be compatible with the framework elsewhere in Britain.

Other Training Measures

Open learning opportunities have been increased by the creation of the Open College, an independent company which promotes the acquisition of skills through the method of open learning. Over 165,000 people have taken its courses since 1987. Further funds were announced in 1989: a maximum of £12 million for its commercial activities over the three years to 1992, and a further £6 million for its broadcasting activities. The Government's aim is for the College to be self-financing by March 1992.

In 1988 the Government, in partnership with three major banks, made Career Development Loans available throughout Great Britain. Loans of £300 to £5,000 can help to pay for vocational training courses between a week and a year in length. Loans may cover up to 80 per cent of course fees, plus the cost of books and materials. A contribution towards living expenses may be available for full-time courses. The Government pays the interest on the loan during training and for up to three months thereafter. The individual then begins repaying the loan, and any further interest due, over a period that has been agreed with the bank.

Scotland

Two new bodies have been set up under recent legislation—Scottish Enterprise for the lowlands of Scotland, and Highlands and Islands Enterprise for the highlands and islands area. They assumed responsibility for the functions of economic development and training previously exercised by the Scottish Development Agency, the Highlands and Islands Development Board and the Training Agency in Scotland. Their main duties are to:

- stimulate self-sustaining economic development;

- maintain and safeguard employment;

- enhance employment skills; and

- promote industrial efficiency and international competitiveness.

The new bodies contract out much of their work to a network of Local Enterprise Companies led by the private sector (see p 324). This network is complete, with 22 companies now fully operational throughout Scotland.

Northern Ireland

The Training and Employment Agency, an executive agency within the Department of Economic Development for Northern Ireland, has primary responsibility for training and employment services. Its overall aim is to assist economic growth by ensuring the provision and operation of training and employment services that contribute to Northern Ireland firms becoming more competitive and individuals obtaining the skills required. The Agency works closely with employers and is encouraging each of the key sectors of industry to form a Sector Representative Body to represent the opinions of employers, and others, on individual sectoral training needs. It has also established Sectoral Working Groups to develop training strategies for individual sectors.

Northern Ireland has its own training and work experience schemes, including:

- the Action for Community Employment programme, which provides training and jobs for long-term unemployed people;

- the Job Training programme, which parallels Employment Training in Great Britain; and

- the Youth Training programme.

Management training and development is an important area for the Training and Employment Agency, which provides a range of schemes designed to improve and develop management skills both for existing managers and for graduates seeking to follow managerial careers. The Agency's Consultancy and Advisory Service promotes the benefits of training and offers advice suited to the needs of individual companies and industrial sectors. The Manpower Training Scheme offers financial support to companies seeking to introduce comprehensive training programmes and aims to improve the overall competitiveness of Northern Ireland industry.

EMPLOYMENT SERVICES

The main priorities of the Employment Service, an executive agency within the Department of Employment, are to help unemployed people back to work and to maintain the accurate and prompt payment of benefit to unemployed people, while ensuring that payment is made only to those entitled to it.

The Employment Service has a number of ways of helping the unemployed to find work:

- by placing people directly into jobs;
- by offering advice and guidance, so that people can find the best route to return to employment, for example, by training; and
- through special programmes such as Jobclubs and the Job Interview Guarantee.

The jobcentre network handles about one-third of vacancies in the economy, and 81 per cent of the 1·85 million people whom
it placed in jobs in 1989–90 were unemployed.

Advisory Services

As part of the Employment Service programme of individual interviews, advisers provide unemployed people with information on employment and training opportunities available to them locally. New client advisers interview newly unemployed people to check their eligibility for benefit. Together with the unemployed person, they agree a 'Back to Work Plan' which shows them the best course of action to follow to get back to work. These plans are reviewed at every advisory interview.

Under the Restart programme, everyone who has been unemployed six months or more is asked to attend a Restart interview with a claimant adviser. The adviser and unemployed person discuss that person's

circumstances, with the aim of helping him or her back into work as soon as possible. This could include:

- advice on job vacancies;
- enrolment on a training programme;
- a place in a jobclub, where participants are given training and advice in job-hunting skills and have access to facilities to help an intensive job search;
- help through the Job Interview Guarantee programme, whereby employers guarantee interviews to everyone submitted for their vacancies through the programme;
- a Restart course, usually over five days, designed to rebuild self-confidence and motivation and including help with job-hunting skills; or
- the chance of self-employment with direct financial help through the Enterprise Allowance Scheme, which gives financial support to unemployed people to enable them to start their own business.

Other Functions

The Employment Service also aims to help people with disabilities to find work. All Employment Service programmes make provision for people with disabilities. Disablement Resettlement Officers offer practical help and counselling, and a wide range of programmes, such as one offering sheltered employment opportunities, is available for people with disabilities who need specialist help.

Incentives to Work

The Government has taken action to improve incentives to work, such as raising personal tax allowances and reducing the standard rate of income tax to 25 per cent, while improving benefits for people in work. These measures, together with reforms in the social security system in 1988, have helped to ensure that most people are better off in work than remaining unemployed.

The Employment Service's claimant advisers are able to give individual calculations which take account of the benefits people in work are entitled to, to show the extent to which someone is better off in work.

Careers Service

Local education authorities provide a careers service for people attending educational institutions (apart from universities, which normally have their own careers service) and an employment service for those leaving them. The careers services in Wales and Scotland are the responsibility of the respective Secretaries of State, while in Northern Ireland responsibility rests with the Training and Employment Agency.

INDUSTRIAL RELATIONS

The structure of industrial relations in Britain has been established mainly on a voluntary basis. The system is based chiefly on the organisation of employees and employers into trade unions and employers' associations, and on freely conducted negotiations at all levels.

Collective Bargaining and Joint Consultation

In many industries terms and conditions of employment and procedures for the conduct of industrial relations have traditionally been settled by negotiation between employers and trade unions. Trade unions are widely recognised by employers, especially in the public sector and in large firms and establishments. Agreements may be industry-wide, as has generally been the case in the public sector, but they are often supplemented by local agreements in companies or factories (plant bargaining). Individual companies may have their own agreements, either for the whole company or for each plant.

In some industries or companies, negotiations are conducted by meetings held when necessary. In others, joint consultative committees have been established on a permanent basis. Joint committees are fairly widespread, especially in large firms. The scope of the various bodies (from national joint industrial councils for whole industries to works committees in individual workplaces) varies widely. It can cover matters other than pay and conditions, such as:

● production plans;

● training;

● welfare; and

● safety.

Such committees often also act as a forum for more general consultation between workers and employers. Day-to-day negotiations on various aspects of pay (such as bonuses or performance pay) are normally handled at plant level. Arrangements for collective bargaining usually suffice to settle all questions which are raised, but there is often provision for matters which cannot be settled in this way to be referred to independent conciliation or arbitration. The law provides for information needed for collective bargaining purposes to be disclosed by employers to trade unions, subject to certain safeguards.

Developments

In recent years there have been a number of developments which have affected Britain's industrial relations system. There has been a continuing shift towards part-time, temporary and sub-contracting employment. Together with the growth of self-employment, this has encouraged greater labour market flexibility. Many employers have sought greater flexibility through a closer relationship between pay and performance, particularly through performance-related pay schemes. In many sectors job demarcation (for example, between manual, technical and clerical skills) has been relaxed. Other developments have included the introduction of new technology and related organisational changes.

There has been a trend away from national bargaining machinery towards negotiation at a more local level; the proportion of the workforce covered by multi-employer national agreements declined from 60 per cent in 1978 to 35 per cent in 1989. The Government has favoured moves away from national pay bargaining towards systems where pay increases are dependent primarily on performance, merit, company profitability, and local labour market conditions. Areas in which national industry-wide pay bargaining has recently been ended include merchant shipping, the printing of national newspapers, commercial broadcasting and the London clearing banks. Where industry-wide bargaining remains important, employers often seek a degree of flexibility to permit modifications to national agreements.

Another recent feature has been the development of 'new style' agreements, often associated with overseas-owned companies, although they are also found in British-owned firms. These agreements often involve:

- the recognition of a single union for all of a company's employees (particularly for companies recognising unions for the first time);
- 'single status', involving the elimination of the traditional distinction between managers, supervisors and other employees;
- a greater emphasis on employee participation; and
- flexibility in working practices.

Employee Involvement

Employers practise a wide variety of methods of informing and consulting their employees, not only through committees but also through direct communication between management and employees. These methods include:

- employee bulletins and reports;
- briefing systems;

- quality circles; and
- financial participation schemes.

Arrangements of this sort, voluntarily introduced by employers and employees according to their own priorities, needs and circumstances, are seen by the Government as a key factor in increasing employee commitment and improving business productivity and performance.

Trade Unions

Trade unions have members in nearly all occupations. As well as negotiating pay and other terms and conditions of employment with employers, they provide benefits and services such as educational facilities, financial services, legal advice and aid in work-related cases. In recent years several unions have extended considerably the range of services they offer to members. Trade unions vary widely in the composition of their membership, and may be organised either by occupation (for example, they may recruit clerical staff or managers wherever employed) or by industry, while some are based on a combination of both. Staff associations represent the employees of a particular company.

There has been a decline in trade union membership, and by the end of 1989 total union membership was about 10 million, of whom 81 per cent were in the 23 largest unions. The decline reflects the moves away from manufacturing and public services, both of which have a relatively high level of membership.

The number of unions has also fallen, reflecting a number of mergers and the absorption by larger unions of small unions and of long-established craft unions. For example, in 1990 the National Union of Railwaymen merged with the National Union of Seamen to form the National Union of Rail, Maritime and Transport Workers. Several other unions are discussing possible mergers. At the end of 1990 there were 323 trade unions on the list maintained by the Certification Officer. To be eligible for entry on the list a trade union must show that it consists wholly or mainly of workers and that its principal purposes include the regulation of relations between workers and employers or between workers and employers' associations.

Six unions had over 500,000 members at the end of 1989:

- **the Transport and General Workers' Union (1·3 million);**
- **the GMB (823,000);**
- **the National and Local Government Officers' Association (751,000);**
- **the Amalgamated Engineering Union (742,000);**
- **the Manufacturing, Science and Finance Union (653,000); and**
- **the National Union of Public Employees (605,000).**

Trade union organisation varies widely, but the central governing body usually consists of a national executive council or committee, elected by a secret ballot of the individual members and responsible to the conference of delegates from local branches, normally held annually. Many unions also have regional and district organisations. At the level of the individual member there are local branches, covering one or more workplaces. The organising of members in individual places of work and the negotiation of local pay agreements with management at the workplace may be done by full-time district officials of the union or, in many cases, by elected workplace representatives, often called 'shop stewards'. Where two or more unions have members in the same workplace, shop stewards' committees may discuss matters of common concern.

Trades Union Congress

In Britain the national centre of the trade union movement is the Trades Union Congress (TUC), founded in 1868. Its affiliated membership comprises 74 trade unions which together represent some 8·2 million people, or about 85 per cent of all trade unionists in Britain. It has more members than any other trade union centre in Western Europe. The TUC's objectives

are to promote the interests of its affiliated organisations and to improve the economic and social conditions of working people. The TUC deals with all general questions which concern trade unions, both nationally and internationally, and provides a forum in which affiliated unions can collectively determine policy. There are eight TUC regional councils for England and a Wales Trades Union Council.

The annual Congress meets in September to discuss matters of concern to trade unionists. A General Council represents the TUC between annual meetings by:

- carrying out Congress decisions;
- watching economic and social developments;
- providing educational and advisory services to unions; and
- presenting in national debate the trade union viewpoint on economic, social and industrial issues.

The TUC organises extensive education services relating to many aspects of trade unionism and other subjects, such as health and safety.

The TUC plays an active part in international trade union activity, through its affiliation to the International Confederation of Free Trade Unions and the European Trade Union Confederation. It also nominates the British workers' delegation to the annual International Labour Conference.

Scotland and Northern Ireland

Trade unions in Scotland also have their own national central body, the Scottish Trades Union Congress, which in many respects is similar in constitution and function to the TUC. Trade unions in Northern Ireland are represented by the Northern Ireland Committee of the Irish Congress of Trade Unions (ICTU). Most trade unionists in Northern Ireland are members of organisations affiliated to the ICTU, while the majority also belong to unions based in Great Britain which are also affiliated to the TUC. The Northern Ireland

Committee of the ICTU enjoys a high degree of autonomy.

Legal Framework

The Government's reforms of employment and trade union law have helped obtain a better balance of power between trade unions and employers, and between trade unions and their own members. This has played a key role in transforming Britain's industrial relations. The Government believes that the Employment Acts of 1980, 1982, 1988 and 1990, and the Trade Union Act of 1984 have helped to make union leaders more accountable to their members and to promote an acceptance of the role of the law in industrial relations. In 1990 industrial disputes reached their lowest recorded level since 1935.

Trade Union Recognition and Responsibilities

The previous statutory recognition procedure was repealed in 1980. Employers are now free to decide whether or not they wish to recognise a particular union, or unions, for collective bargaining purposes.

The law now makes a trade union responsible if industrial action is called for or organised by any of its officials. This means that if a trade union acts unlawfully, for example, by calling for industrial action without a proper secret ballot, legal proceedings can be taken against the union itself.

The law also means that if a union defies a court order, for example, an order to withdraw an unlawful call for industrial action, it can be held to be in contempt of court. In such circumstances severe penalties can be imposed, including sequestration of the union's assets.

Industrial Action

Under common law, it is unlawful to induce workers to break a contract or to threaten to do so. Thus, without special protection, trade unions would face the possibility of legal action for inducing breaches of contract every time they called a strike or other form of industrial action. To prevent this, 'statutory immunities' were introduced, which provide that trade unions and individuals can, in certain circumstances, organise industrial action without fear of being sued in the courts. These immunities only protect those who call for or organise industrial action. They do not protect individuals who choose to take industrial action from being dismissed, or from legal action by their employer.

Prior to the 1980s, the circumstances in which these immunities applied were very wide, so that the organisation of almost any industrial action was protected. The legislative reforms of the past decade have restricted the scope of these immunities in a number of ways. To have the benefit of statutory immunity, the organisation of industrial action must now:

- be in contemplation or furtherance of a trade dispute between workers and their own employer;
- not involve workers who have no dispute with their own employer (so-called 'secondary' action);
- not involve unlawful picketing;
- not be done to establish or maintain a union–only labour agreement (the 'closed shop'); and
- not be done in support of any employee dismissed while taking unofficial industrial action.

Before calling for industrial action, a trade union must first obtain the support of its members in a properly-conducted secret ballot. Moreover, any trade union member has the right to restrain his union from calling on him, and other members, to take action unless a ballot has supported the action.

Trade Union Elections

The law requires a trade union to elect every member of its governing body, its general secretary and its president. Elections must be held at least once every five years and be carried out by secret postal ballot of the union's members. The election must be held under independent scrutiny. Any union member who believes that the union has not complied with the statutory requirements may complain to the courts or to the Certification Officer.

Members' Rights

All individuals have the right under the law not to be dismissed or refused employment because they are not or will not become trade union members. They also have the right not to be refused any of the services of an employment agency because they are, or are not, members of a union. Individuals who believe that they have been dismissed or refused employment on grounds related to their union membership or non-membership may complain to an industrial tribunal. Other rights include:

- a statutory remedy for workers who have been unjustifiably disciplined by their union;
- inspection of their union's accounting records; and
- the right to have automatic deduction of their union subscription from their pay stopped if they leave the union.

The Government has established a Commissioner for the Rights of Trade Union Members to help ensure that members need not be disadvantaged in bringing legal proceedings against their union to enforce certain rights and duties.

Political Funds

A trade union may establish a political fund if it wishes to use its money for what the law defines as 'political objects'—the support of party political activities. If a union wishes to set up a political fund, its members must first agree in a secret ballot a resolution adopting those political objectives as an aim of the union. The union must also ballot its members every ten years to maintain the fund. Where a political levy from union members is deducted from pay, the law provides that an individual member may choose to opt out of paying.

Government Proposals

Further proposals were included in a Green Paper, *Industrial Relations in the 1990s*, published in July 1991. These include:

- provision that seven days' notice should be given before strikes and other industrial action;
- a right for members of the public to seek injunctions to halt unlawful industrial action affecting public services;
- the right for employees to join the union of their choice;
- the right to a postal ballot on union mergers;
- a proposal that collective agreements should have the status of contracts binding upon both parties unless they include specific provisions making them unenforceable; and
- new powers for the Certification Officer to investigate mismanagement of union finances.

Employers' Organisations

Many employers in Britain are members of employers' organisations, some of which are wholly concerned with labour matters, although others are also concerned with commercial matters or trade associations. The primary aims of such organisations are:

- to help to establish suitable terms and conditions of employment;
- to promote good relations with employees and the efficient use of manpower; and
- to provide means of settling any disputes which may arise.

Combined employers' organisations and trade associations may also represent members' points of view as manufacturers or traders on commercial matters.

Employers' organisations are usually established on an industry basis rather than a product basis, for example, the Engineering Employers' Federation. A few are purely local in character or deal with a section of an industry or, for example, with small businesses; most are national and are concerned with the whole of an industry. In some of the main industries there are local or regional organisations combined into national federations. In others, within which different firms are engaged in making different principal products, there is a complex structure with national and regional federations for parts of an industry as well as for the industry as a whole. At the end of 1990, 135 listed and 162 unlisted employers' associations were known to the Certification Officer. Those which are national organisations negotiate the national collective agreements for their industry with the trade unions concerned; most of these national organisations belong to the Confederation of British Industry.

Confederation of British Industry

The Confederation of British Industry (CBI) is the largest central employers' organisation in Britain, representing directly or indirectly some 250,000 businesses which together employ about half the working population. It aims primarily to ensure that government, national and international institutions and the public understand the needs, intentions and problems of business. Membership ranges from the smallest to the largest companies, private sector and nationalised, and covers a broad spectrum, including manufacturing, agriculture, construction, distribution, mining, finance, retailing and insurance. Most national employers' organisations, trade associations and some chambers of commerce are members. Policy is determined by a council of 400 members, and there is a permanent staff of 295; there are 13 regional offices and an office in Brussels. The CBI is the British member of the Union of Industries of the European Community.

Terms and Conditions of Employment

Basic rates of pay vary widely, and in private industry rates are frequently determined locally, with less importance attached to national agreements. Higher rates are usually paid for overtime and shift work, and weekly earnings may be further increased by incentive bonus schemes or other performance-related arrangements.

Earnings

According to the Department of Employment's New Earnings Survey, the average weekly earnings, unaffected by absence and including overtime payments, in April 1990 of full-time employees on adult rates were £263. Earnings were higher for non-manual employees (£291) than for manual employees (£221). Some 51 per cent of manual employees and 19 per cent of non-manual employees received overtime payments. In the year to April 1991 the underlying average increase in earnings was about 8·8 per cent.

Remuneration in commercial, technical and professional careers is normally by annual salary paid monthly, often on a scale carrying annual increments. Many of the top posts in leading commercial and industrial companies carry salaries which are performance-related, and the majority are between £100,000 and £300,000 a year before tax, reflecting increasing competition for top management. Senior management salaries are generally in the range of £40,000 to £100,000 a year, while middle management salaries typically fall between £20,000 and £40,000 a year.

There has been a move towards performance-related pay, which has been encouraged by the Government. Since 1987 income tax relief has been available for employees receiving profit-related pay under schemes registered by the Inland Revenue. The 1991 Budget doubled this tax relief to cover all profit-related pay within certain existing limits. By the end of June 1991, there were 1,329 live schemes covering over 350,000 employees.

Employee Share Schemes

The Government has taken a number of steps to encourage direct ownership by employees of shares in the businesses for which they work. The number of profit-sharing and savings-related share option schemes, which must be open to all eligible employees in a company, has risen from 78 in 1979 to over 1,898 in 1990, benefiting over 2 million employees.

Other Benefits

Additional benefits exist in varying degrees. About half of employees in employment are covered by pension schemes provided by their employers. Many employees are also covered by occupational sick-pay schemes which are additional or complementary to the state schemes, and by schemes to provide private medical treatment. Such benefits are more usual among clerical and professional employees than among manual workers. The provision of low-priced meals at the place of employment is usual in large undertakings and quite common in smaller ones. Many offices and shops which are unable to provide çanteen facilities for their staff have adopted luncheon voucher schemes. Company cars are provided for directors and employees in a wide variety of circumstances. Other fringe benefits available include life assurance and low-interest loans.

Hours of Work

The basic working week in Great Britain is in the range 37·5 to 40 hours for manual work and 35 to 38 for non-manual work; a five-day week is usually worked. While the basic working week has been gradually shortening, the general trend in total hours worked has been rising since 1981. In spring 1990 total hours a week actually worked (including overtime) for full-time employees were 45·6 for men, compared with 40·1 for women. Men and women in non-manual occupations generally work less overtime than manual employees.

In general, there are no limits on hours worked by adults except in a few occupations (such as for drivers of goods vehicles and public service vehicles). Restrictions on working hours for women and for school-leavers aged under 18 were repealed by the Sex Discrimination Act 1986 and the Employment Act 1989.

Holidays with Pay

There are no general statutory entitlements to holidays, and holiday entitlements are frequently determined by collective agreements. These generally provide for at least four weeks' paid holiday a year, and nearly all manual employees covered by national collective agreements have entitlements of four weeks or more, with nearly 25 per cent having five weeks or more. Non-manual workers tend to have longer holidays than manual workers. Holiday entitlements may also be dependent upon length of service.

Office of Manpower Economics

The Office of Manpower Economics is an independent non-statutory organisation responsible for servicing independent review bodies which advise on the pay of various public-sector groups. These are:

- the Top Salaries Review Body;
- the Armed Forces' Pay Review Body;
- the Doctors' and Dentists' Review Body; and
- the Review Body for Nurses and other National Health Service professions.

The Office also provides services for the Pharmacists' Review Panel, the Police Negotiating Board and the Civil Service Arbitration Tribunal. It is responsible for research into pay and associated matters as requested by the Government. A review body for teachers' salaries was established in 1991.

Wages Councils

Wages councils fix statutory minimum pay for 2·5 million workers aged 21 and over, primarily in service industries such as retailing, catering and hairdressing. There are 26 such councils in Great Britain, each consisting of equal numbers of representatives of employers and employees in the industry concerned, and up to five independent members. Councils are empowered to fix a minimum hourly rate, an overtime rate and a limit on the amount an employer can charge for accommodation provided. However, the Government is concerned about the continued relevance of the system, and is keeping it under review. In Northern Ireland there are nine wages councils, which fix statutory minimum pay for some 36,000 workers.

Employment Protection

Employment protection legislation provides a number of safeguards for employees. For example, most employees are entitled to receive from their employers written information on their main terms and conditions of employment, while minimum periods of notice when employment is to be terminated are laid down for both employers and employees. Employees with the necessary period of continuous employment with their employer (currently two years for those working 16 hours a week or more) are entitled to lump-sum redundancy payments if their jobs cease to exist (for example, because of technological improvements or a fall in demand) and their employers cannot offer suitable alternative work. Where employers are insolvent, the cost is partly met from the National Insurance fund, and direct payments are made by the Department of Employment. Most employees who believe they have been unfairly dismissed have the right to complain to an industrial tribunal, provided they have the necessary qualifying period of employment. If the complaint is upheld, the tribunal may make an order for reinstatement or award compensation. Most pregnant women who have the necessary qualifying period of continuous employment have the right to return to their former job, or a suitable alternative, after maternity absence. Legislation forbids any employment of children under 13 years of age, and employment in any industrial undertaking of children who have not reached the statutory minimum school-leaving age, with some exceptions for family undertakings.

The Government is keeping under review the legislation affecting terms and conditions of employment. Its aim is to ensure that the obligations placed on employers do not involve significant costs which discourage recruitment. The Employment Act 1989 contained a number of provisions designed to reduce burdens on employers. For example, employers with fewer than 20 employees have become exempt from the requirement to provide employees with a separate note of disciplinary rules in the written statement of their main terms and conditions of employment. In addition, the Act extended the qualifying period for the right to receive a written statement of reasons for dismissal from six months to two years, to bring it into line with the qualifying period for unfair dismissal.

Equal Opportunities

The Race Relations Act 1976 makes it unlawful to discriminate on grounds of colour, race, nationality (including citizenship) or ethnic or national origin, in employment, training and related matters. The Department of Employment operates a nationwide Race Relations Employment Advisory Service. Its objective is to promote the Government's policies aimed at eliminating racial discrimination in employment and promoting fair treatment and equality of opportunity in employment. Advisers provide employers with advice and practical help in developing and implementing equal opportunity strategies.

The Sex Discrimination Act 1975, as amended, makes it generally unlawful in Great Britain to discriminate on grounds of sex or being married when it comes to recruiting, training, promoting, dismissing or retiring staff. It also provides redress against victimisation and may also, in certain circumstances, do so against sexual harassment. The Equal Pay Act 1970 makes it generally unlawful to discriminate between men and women in pay and other terms and conditions of employment. The Act was significantly extended in 1984 to meet European Community requirements by providing for equal pay for work of equal value. There is equivalent legislation in Northern Ireland.

Practical advice to employers and others on the best arrangements for implementing equal opportunities policies in Great Britain is given in codes of practice from the Commission for Racial Equality and from the Equal Opportunities Commission (see pp 24 and 25).

Northern Ireland

Similar legislation to that in Great Britain on equal pay and sex discrimination applies in Northern Ireland, but there is no legislation on race relations. Discrimination, both direct and indirect, in employment on grounds of religious belief or political opinion is unlawful. The Fair Employment Commission has the task of promoting equality of opportunity and investigating employment practices, with powers to issue legally enforceable directions. The Fair Employment Tribunal adjudicates on individual complaints of religious or political discrimination and enforces the Commission's directions. All but the smallest employers are required to monitor the religious composition of their workforce and periodically to review their employment practices. Where fair participation is not being enjoyed by both Protestants and Roman Catholics, the introduction of 'affirmative action' measures must be considered.

Advisory, Conciliation and Arbitration Service

The Advisory, Conciliation and Arbitration Service (ACAS) is an independent statutory body with the general duty of promoting the improvement of industrial relations. ACAS is directed by a council consisting of a full-time chairman and employer, trade union and independent members experienced in industrial relations. The Service conciliates in industrial disputes in both the public and private sectors. ACAS assistance was sought in nearly 1,260 disputes in 1990. In addition, there were 200 further requests for ACAS to provide arbitration. It may do this either by appointing single arbitrators or boards of arbitration, or by referring cases to the Central Arbitration Committee (see below). Although ACAS has prime responsibility

for helping to resolve disputes, and has also set up major committees of inquiry, the Secretary of State for Employment retains powers to appoint a court of inquiry or committee of investigation into a dispute. However, these are rarely used.

ACAS gives advice on all aspects of industrial relations and employment policies to employers, managers, trade unions, employee representatives and individuals. It handled over 418,000 enquiries in 1990. Specialist staff made nearly 7,000 advisory visits. ACAS also carries particular responsibility for attempting conciliation on complaints of infringement of individual employee rights. These include individual complaints of unfair dismissal; complaints under the equal pay legislation; and complaints on employment matters under the sex discrimination and race relations legislation. There were over 52,000 individual conciliation cases in 1990. Its Work Research Unit aims to encourage industry and commerce to adopt measures that can lead to improvements in the quality of working life and so to improvements in economic performance.

In Northern Ireland the Labour Relations Agency, an independent statutory body, provides services similar to those provided by ACAS in Great Britain.

Central Arbitration Committee

The Central Arbitration Committee is an independent standing arbitration body. It provides boards of arbitration for the settlement of trade disputes referred to it with the consent of the parties concerned. It also adjudicates on claims made under the disclosure of information provisions of the Employment Protection Act 1975.

HEALTH AND SAFETY AT WORK

Recent statistics indicate a reduction in the rate of major and other reported injuries to employees, although a high rate of injuries remains in certain industries, such as construction and agriculture. Employers have a duty in law to take reasonable care of their staff, as well as others affected by their work activities. Employees have a duty to take care of their own safety and that of their fellow workers. The principal legislation is the Health and Safety at Work etc. Act 1974. It places general duties on everyone concerned with work activities, including employers, the self-employed, employees, and manufacturers and suppliers of materials for use at work. Supporting Acts and regulations deal with particular hazards and types of work. Employers with five or more staff must prepare a written statement of health and safety policy and inform their staff of it.

The Act requires the Health and Safety Commission to develop workable proposals to update earlier legislation, much of which was not adaptable to technical innovation. Reforms have since been completed in many areas. Much of the old law has been replaced by modern provisions, supported by codes of practice and other guidance material.

The Control of Substances Hazardous to Health Regulations 1988 are some of the most important regulations made under the 1974 Act. They replaced a range of inflexible and outdated legislation by a comprehensive and systematic approach to the control of exposure to virtually all substances hazardous to health. These include chemicals, fumes, dust and micro-organisms.

Health and Safety Commission

The Health and Safety Commission (HSC), which is accountable to Parliament through the Secretary of State for Employment, has responsibility for developing policies, including guidance, codes of practice, or proposals for regulations. In the case of proposals for changes in legislation, the HSC consults those who would be affected and makes recommendations to the Secretary of State concerned.

The HSC has seven advisory committees covering subjects such as toxic substances, genetic manipulation and the safety of nuclear installations. There are also 12 industry advisory committees, each of which deals with a specific industry.

Health and Safety Executive

The Health and Safety Executive (HSE) is the primary instrument for carrying out the HSC's policies and has day-to-day responsibility for enforcing health and safety law, except where other bodies, such as local authorities, are responsible. The HSE's field services and inspections over the country as a whole are carried out by the Field Operations Division. This incorporates the Factory, Agricultural and Quarries inspectorates; the regional staff of the Employment Medical Advisory Service (which advises on medical aspects of employment problems), and the Field Consulting Groups, which provide technical support to the inspectorates. The HSE also includes:

- the Health Policy Division;
- the Technology Division, which provides technical advice on industrial health and safety matters; and
- the Research and Laboratory Services Division, which provides scientific and medical support and testing services, and carries out research.

In premises such as offices, shops, warehouses, restaurants and hotels, health and safety legislation is enforced by inspectors appointed by local authorities, working under guidance from the HSC. Some other official bodies work under agency agreement with the HSC.

Northern Ireland

In Northern Ireland the Health and Safety Agency, roughly corresponding to the HSC, and an Employment Medical Advisory Service were set up by the Health and Safety at Work (NI) Order 1978. The general requirements of the Northern Ireland health and safety legislation, similar to those for Great Britain, are enforced mainly by the Department of Economic Development through its Health and Safety Inspectorate.

19 Public Finance

Public finance is concerned with taxation, expenditure and borrowing (or debt repayment) by central and local government, management of the public sector's assets and liabilities and the financing of public corporations. Central government raises money from individuals and companies by direct and indirect taxation and from National Insurance contributions. It spends money on goods and services, such as health and defence, and in payments to people, such as social security and pensions. Local government receives substantial grants from central government and raises revenue mainly through the community charge and rates (local property taxes, which may be levied òn domestic and business properties). Domestic rates have been abolished in Great Britain but not in Northern Ireland. Business rates apply throughout Britain. Local government provides services such as education, police and fire services, and refuse collection. The diagram (see p 346) shows the relative importance of the various items of receipts (including borrowing) and expenditure for general government.

The government department responsible for broad control of public finance and expenditure is HM Treasury. The Bank of England (the central bank) advises the Government on financial matters, executes monetary policy and acts as banker to the Government.

PUBLIC EXPENDITURE

The three main definitions of public expenditure are general government expenditure, the planning total and Supply expenditure.

General government expenditure is the spending of central and local government, excluding transfers between them such as central government grants to local authorities. It is the key public spending aggregate and is used in the medium-term financial strategy (see below), where public spending is set in the context of macroeconomic policy. It is more appropriate than the other measures for making international comparisons as it is usually less affected by institutional differences.

The planning total is used by the Government for the purposes of planning and control. The Government seeks to achieve its wider medium-term objective (expressed in terms of general government expenditure) by controlling spending within this total. The planning total covers:

- expenditure for which central government is itself responsible;
- the support it provides or approves for local authority expenditure;
- the financing requirements of public corporations (including nationalised industries);
- privatisation proceeds; and
- a reserve to cover unanticipated expenditure.

Supply expenditure is financed out of money voted by Parliament in the Supply Estimates (see below). Practically all of Supply expenditure counts in the planning total, and accounts for about three-quarters of it. The main element of the planning total not funded through Supply Estimates is expenditure financed from the National Insurance Fund.

The background to the present Government's planning of public expenditure is the medium-term financial strategy, introduced in 1980. The Government's aim is to preserve a firm financial framework in order to defeat inflation and to ensure the continuation of the conditions for sustainable growth. With commitments also to reduce taxation and curb the role of the State, the Government therefore seeks to reduce public expenditure as a proportion of national income as well. For 1991–92 taxes and social security contributions are forecast to amount to 37 per cent of gross domestic product (GDP).

General government expenditure (excluding privatisation proceeds) as a proportion of gross domestic product fell from over 47 per cent in the early 1980s to some 40·5 per cent in 1990–91.

The Government expects small variations on a public expenditure level of 40·5 per cent of GDP in the next few years.

Table 19.1 gives projections for government expenditure and receipts and the borrowing requirement for the years up to 1994–95.

The Planning Cycle

Each year the Government conducts a review of its expenditure plans for the forthcoming three years (the 'public expenditure survey') and publishes the resulting totals, together with any changes in National Insurance, in the Autumn Statement in November. Details of these plans are published early in the following year in a series of departmental reports. Detailed summary analyses are published in a statistical supplement to the Autumn Statement.

The Government's updating of the medium-term financial strategy and consequent plans for the public finances over the following year, including any tax changes, are set out in the Financial Statement and Budget Report, published with the Budget around the end of the financial year (31 March). Details of the tax changes are included in the Finance Bill, which is presented to Parliament shortly after the Budget and becomes law during the summer.

Public Expenditure Totals

Public expenditure totals are analysed in Table 19.2. The largest departmental programmes are those of the Department of Social Security (37 per cent of central government expenditure in 1990–91), the Department of Health and the Office of Population Censuses and Surveys, and the Ministry of Defence (both 16 per cent).

About half of local authority spending is financed by grants from central government. The rest is met from the community charge and rates, surpluses on trading, rents and borrowing. Education accounts for over one-third of local authority spending; law and order,

---

Table 19.1: Projected Public Expenditure, Receipts and Borrowing Requirement

£ thousand million

	1991–92	1992–93	1993–94	1994–95
General government expenditure	235	252	266	279
of which: public expenditure planning total	*205*	*221*	*232*	*243*
General government receipts	226	240	260	281
of which: taxes	*177*	*188*	*204*	*219*
social security contributions	*37*	*40*	*44*	*48*
Fiscal adjustments[a]	—	0	1	2
Public sector borrowing requirement (PSBR)	8	12	7	0
PSBR as percentage of GDP	1.25	2	1	0

Source: *Financial Statement and Budget Report 1991–92.*
[a]These imply lower taxes or higher expenditure than assumed in the figures for general government expenditure and receipts.

Table 19.2: Planned Public Expenditure Totals

£ thousand million

	1991–92	1992–93	1993–94
Central government expenditure	152·1	161·6	167·9
Central government support for local authorities	52·5	55·7	56·6
Financing requirements of nationalised industries	2·3	2·1	2·0
Privatisation proceeds	-5·5	-5·5	-5·5
Reserve	3·5	7·0	10·5
Planning total	205·0	221·0	231·5
Local authority self-financed expenditure	9·1	9·5	11·5
Central government debt interest	16·7	17·0	17·5
Other adjustments	3·9	5·0	5·5
Central government expenditure	234·8	252·0	266·0

Source: *Financial Statement and Budget Report 1991-92.*
Differences between totals and the sums of their component parts are due to rounding.

housing and other environmental services, personal social services and transport account for most of the remainder.

Reserve

Planned expenditure includes an unallocated reserve for each year of the plans to cover additions to departmental spending, whether arising from policy changes, new initiatives or revisions to the estimated costs of demand-led programmes. For the current year the reserve is used as a control mechanism. The reserve has been set at higher levels for each of the next two years but some will normally be allocated to departments as spending forecasts are made firmer within the public expenditure planning total. The balance will be retained for contingencies which might arise during the current year.

The Estimates

The annual public expenditure survey conducted by HM Treasury provides the basis for the Estimates which each government department submits to HM Treasury in December, giving details of its cash requirements for the financial year beginning in the following April. After Treasury approval, these Supply Estimates are presented to Parliament in March, usually about the same time as the Budget (see p 342). Parliament approves them in July as part of the Annual Appropriation Act; expenditure between 1 April and this date is covered by Votes on Account approved before the start of the financial year. Supplementary Estimates may also be presented to Parliament during the course of the year.

If any Supply Estimate is overspent, the Public Accounts Committee (see p 342) may investigate fully before Parliament is asked to approve any Excess Vote to balance the account. In each parliamentary session, up to three 'Estimates days' are available for debates on the Supply Estimates, following scrutiny by select committees of the House of Commons.

Cash Limits

The Government sets cash limits on about 60 per cent of Supply expenditure. The imposition of cash limits indicates that the Government intends to avoid extra provision for programmes even in the event of unexpected increases in costs. It is government policy to extend the coverage of cash limits wherever possible. They cover the major part of grants to local authorities, which are financed out of Supply expenditure. Cash limits also apply to some expenditure not voted in the Estimates.

Running cost limits are imposed on the administrative costs of central government, which are separately identified in the Estimates.

There is a limited facility for carrying forward underspending on the capital components of cash limits and on running cost limits. Any overspending of cash or running cost limits leads to an investigation into the causes and, where appropriate, a reduction in the limits in the following year.

Those Estimates that are not subject to cash limits mainly finance demand-led services such as income support. In such cases, once policy and rates of payment are determined, expenditure depends on factors beyond the direct control of government, such as the number of eligible recipients.

Examination and Audit of Public Expenditure

Examination of public expenditure is carried out by select committees of the House of Commons, which study in detail the activities of particular government departments and require the attendance of ministers and officials for cross-examination. The audit of the Government's spending which follows up the control inherent in parliamentary approval of the Estimates is exercised through the functions of the Comptroller and Auditor General and the Public Accounts Committee.

Comptroller and Auditor General

The Comptroller and Auditor General, an officer of the House of Commons appointed by the Crown, has two distinct functions. The duty of Comptroller General is to ensure that all revenue and other public money payable to the Consolidated Fund and the National Loans Fund (see below) is duly paid and that all payments out of these funds are authorised by statute. The duty of the Auditor General is to certify the accounts of all government departments and those of a wide range of other public sector bodies; to examine revenue accounts and inventories; and to report the results of these examinations to Parliament.

Public Accounts Committee

The Public Accounts Committee considers the accounts of government departments and the Comptroller and Auditor General's reports on them and on departments' use of their resources. The Committee takes evidence from the official heads of departments and relevant public sector bodies and submits to Parliament reports which carry considerable weight; its recommendations are taken very seriously by the departments and organisations that it examines. The Government's formal replies to the reports are presented to Parliament by HM Treasury in the form of Treasury minutes, and the reports and minutes are usually debated annually in the Commons.

Central Government Funds

The Government's sterling expenditure is largely met out of the Consolidated Fund, an account at the Bank of England into which tax receipts and other revenues are paid. Any excess of expenditure over receipts is met by the National Loans Fund, which is another official sterling account at the Bank of England and is the repository for funds borrowed by the Government. The National Insurance Fund, into which contributions are paid by employers and employed people, is used mainly to pay for social security benefits; a small proportion of National Insurance contributions is paid direct to the Consolidated Fund in order to help finance the National Health Service.

THE BUDGET

The Budget, which usually takes place in March, sets out the Government's proposals for changes in taxation and is the main occasion for an annual review of economic policy. The proposals are announced to the House of Commons by the Chancellor of the Exchequer in the Budget statement and are published in the Financial Statement and Budget Report. This report also contains a review of recent developments in the economy, together with an economic forecast, and sets out the fiscal and monetary framework within which economic policy operates. This is the medium-term financial strategy (see p 339).

The Budget statement is followed by the moving of a set of Budget resolutions in which the proposals are embodied. These resolutions are the foundation of the Finance Bill, in which the proposals are set out for detailed consideration by Parliament. Some of the resolutions give temporary effect, under the Provisional Collection of Taxes Act 1968, to certain of the tax proposals in the Budget. This enables the Government to collect certain taxes provisionally, at the levels provided by the Budget proposals, pending enactment of the Finance Bill.

For two taxes—income tax and corporation tax—annual Ways and Means resolutions followed by Finance Bill clauses are required to maintain their existence, since they are annual rather than permanent taxes. Thus, a Budget and a Finance Bill are necessary at or about the beginning of each financial year. Following completion of its parliamentary stages, the Finance Bill becomes an Act, usually around the end of July. Tax changes can be made at other times, however, either by specific legislation or by the use of the regulator, which permits limited changes between Budgets in value added tax (by up to 25 per cent) and the main excise duties (by up to 10 per cent).

MAIN SOURCES OF REVENUE

The main sources of revenue are:
- taxes on income (including profits), which include personal income tax, corporation tax and petroleum revenue tax;
- taxes on capital, which comprise inheritance tax and capital gains tax; and
- taxes on expenditure, which include value added tax (VAT) and customs and excise duties.

Other sources of revenue are National Insurance contributions, which give entitlement to a range of benefits, and the community charge and business rates.

Thresholds and rate bands for income tax, inheritance tax and capital gains tax are raised automatically each year in line with the rise in retail prices over the previous calendar year unless Parliament decides otherwise. The Inland Revenue assesses and collects the taxes on income, profits and capital, and also stamp duty. Taxes on individual incomes are progressive in that larger incomes bear a proportionately greater amount of tax. HM Customs and Excise collects the most important taxes on expenditure (VAT, most duties and car tax). Vehicle excise duty is the responsibility of the Department of Transport and National Insurance contributions that of the Department of Social Security (although the latter are generally collected by the Inland Revenue). The community charge and business rates are collected by local authorities.

A new taxpayer's charter was launched in 1991. It sets out the standard of service that people can expect from the Inland revenue and HM Customs and Excise.

Taxes on Income

Income Tax

Income tax is imposed for the year of assessment beginning on 6 April. For 1991–92 the basic rate of 25 per cent applies to the first £23,700 of taxable income. A rate of 40 per cent applies to income above this level. These rates apply to total income, including both earned and investment income.

A number of personal allowances and reliefs reduce the amount of a person's taxable income compared with gross income. All taxpayers, irrespective of sex or marital status, are entitled to a personal allowance against income from all sources. Married women pay their own tax on the basis of their own income. In addition, there is a married couple's allowance, which goes to the husband in the first instance. However, if his income is not high enough to use it in full, he can transfer the unused portion to his wife, to set against her income. The current values of the main allowances are £3,295 for the personal allowance and £1,720 for the married couple's allowance.

Assuming only the basic personal allowances, a single person or married woman with an income of £14,000 in 1991–92 pays £2,676 in income tax, while a married man with the same income pays £2,246. The amount of tax payable by a single person or married woman varies from, for example, £1,176 on an annual income of £8,000 to £27,127 on one of £80,000. Among the most important of the reliefs is that for mortgage interest payments on borrowing for house purchase up to the statutory limit of £30,000. Relief is restricted to the basic rate and is usually given 'at source' (that is, repayments which the borrower makes to the lender are reduced to take account of tax at the basic rate and the tax refund is then passed directly by the tax authorities to the building society or bank making the loan rather than to the individual taxpayer). Another relief is that under the Business Expansion Scheme, whereby certain investors in trading companies without a stock market quotation (usually small companies) are able to obtain relief on up to £40,000 invested in any one year.

Most wage and salary earners pay their income tax under a Pay-As-You-Earn (PAYE) system whereby tax is deducted (and accounted for to the Inland Revenue) by the employer, thus enabling employees to keep as up to date as possible with their tax payments.

In general, income tax is charged on all income which originates in Britain (although some forms of income—such as certain social security benefits—are exempt) and on all income arising abroad of people resident in Britain. Interest on certain British government securities belonging to people not ordinarily resident in Britain is exempt. Britain has entered into agreements with many countries to provide relief from double taxation; where such agreements are not in force unilateral relief is often allowed. British residents working abroad for the whole year benefit from 100 per cent tax relief.

Corporation Tax

The rates of company tax in Britain are lower than in most other industrialised countries. Companies pay corporation tax on their income after deduction of certain allowances and any capital gains. A company which distributes profits to its shareholders is required to make an advance payment of corporation tax to the Inland Revenue. In general, this payment is set against a company's liability to corporation tax on its income and capital gains. The recipient of the distribution (if resident in Britain) is entitled to a tax credit, which satisfies his or her liability to income tax at the basic rate.

The main rate of corporation tax is 33 per cent for 1991–92, with a reduced rate of 25 per cent for small companies (those with profits below £250,000 in a year). Marginal relief between the main rate and the small companies' rate is allowed for companies with profits between £250,000 and £1·25 million. Expenditure on plant and machinery, on scientific research and on industrial and certain other buildings qualifies for annual allowances.

Petroleum Revenue Tax

Petroleum revenue tax (deductible in computing profits for corporation tax) is charged on profits from the production, as opposed to the refining or other forms of processing, of oil and gas under licence in Britain and on its Continental Shelf. The rate of tax is 75 per cent. Each licensee of an oilfield is charged on the profits from that field after deduction of certain allowances and reliefs which, among other things, encourage exploration, appraisal and future field development. The tax is computed at half-yearly intervals and the bulk of it is collected in monthly instalments.

Taxes on Capital

Inheritance Tax

Inheritance tax applies to transfers of property made on, or up to seven years before, the donor's death. It is also immediately chargeable on certain lifetime transfers. Subject to certain exemptions and reliefs, the first £140,000 of the cumulative total of chargeable transfers is not liable to tax; higher amounts are taxed at a single rate of 40 per cent. A tapered system of relief reduces the tax on transfers made between three and seven years before the donor's death. Relief ranges from 20 per cent of the tax payable on transfers made between three and four years prior to death to 80 per cent on those made between six and seven years prior to death.

There are several exemptions. All transfers to a spouse living in Britain are exempt while gifts and bequests to charities, political parties and heritage bodies are also normally exempt. Business property qualifies for relief of up to 50 per cent.

Capital Gains Tax

Capital gains realised on the disposal of assets are liable to capital gains tax or, in the case of companies, to corporation tax. Individuals are exempt from tax in respect of total net gains of up to £5,500 in any one year and most trusts on gains of up to £2,750. Gains are treated as the taxpayer's top slice of income, being charged at the individual's higher income tax rate or the company's higher corporation tax rate.

Only gains arising since March 1982 are subject to tax and the effects of inflation are allowed for when measuring gains. The tax on certain types of gift and certain deemed disposals of assets may be deferred until the assets are sold. Some assets, including the principal private residence, movable possessions worth less than £6,000 (and any movable possessions with a predictable life of less than 50 years except those on which the expenditure qualifies for a capital allowance), private motor cars, and National Savings Certificates and Bonds are normally exempt. Gains on government securities and certain corporate bonds are exempt from the tax, as are gains on shares owned under the Personal Equity Plan (designed to encourage wider share ownership).

Taxes on Expenditure

Value Added Tax

Value added tax (VAT) is a broadly based tax, chargeable at 17·5 per cent. It is collected at each stage in the production and distribution of goods and services by taxable persons (generally those whose business has a turnover of more than £35,000 a year). The final tax is borne by the consumer. When a taxable person purchases taxable goods or services, the supplier charges VAT (the taxable person's input tax). When the taxable person supplies taxable goods or services to customers, then they in turn are charged VAT (the taxable person's output tax). The difference between the output tax and the input tax is paid to, or repaid by, HM Customs and Excise.

Certain goods and services are relieved from VAT, either by charging at a zero rate (a taxable person does not charge tax to a customer but reclaims any input tax paid to suppliers) or by exemption (a taxable person does not charge a customer any output tax and is not entitled to deduct or reclaim the input tax). Zero-rating applies to exports and to most food; books, newspapers and periodicals; fuel (except for petrol and other fuels for road use) and power for domestic users; construction of new residential buildings; certain international services; public transport fares; caravans and houseboats; young children's clothing and footwear; drugs and medicines supplied on prescription; specified aids for handicapped people; and certain supplies by or to charities. Exemption applies to land (including rents), insurance, postal services, betting, gaming (other than by gaming machines and lotteries), finance, education, health, burial and cremation, and supplies by trade unions and professional bodies to their members.

Customs Duties

Customs duties are chargeable in accordance with the Common Customs Tariff of the European Community (no such duties are chargeable on goods which qualify as Community goods). Special customs import and export procedures are operated under the Common Agricultural Policy, and Community levies are chargeable on a wide range of agricultural products from non-Community countries. Under the single

Planned Receipts and Expenditure of General Government 1991-92

Pence in every pound

Receipts

Receipt	Pence
Income tax	25
Corporation tax	8
Capital gains tax	1
Inheritance tax	1
Value added tax	15
Community charge and local authority rates	9
Duties on petrol, alcoholic drinks and tobacco	9
Social security receipts	16
Interest and dividends	3
Gross trading surpluses and rent	1
Other duties, taxes, levies and royalties	6
Other receipts	2
General government borrowing	4
Total	**100**

Expenditure

Pence	Expenditure
10	Defence
1	Foreign and Commonwealth Office
1	Agriculture, Fisheries and Food
1	Trade and Industry
1	Employment
2	Transport
3	Environment – housing
1	Environment – other environmental services
10	Environment – local government
3	Home Office and legal departments
3	Education and Science
11	Health
27	Social Security
5	Scotland
2	Wales
3	Northern Ireland
2	Chancellor of the Exchequer's departments
1	Other departments and European Community
4	Local authority self-financed expenditure
1	Reserve
7	Central government debt interest
2	Accounting adjustments
−2	Privatisation proceeds
100	**Total**

Cash totals £234,800 million

Sources: *Financial Statement and Budget Report 1991–92*
and *Public Expenditure Analyses to 1993–94*.

Note: Differences between totals and the sum of their component parts are due to rounding.

European market programme, all remaining barriers to the free movement within the European Community of goods, services, capital and people will be abolished by the end of 1992.

Excise Duties

Hydrocarbon oils used as road fuel bear higher rates of duty than those used for other purposes. Kerosene, most lubricating oils and other oils used for certain industrial processes are free of duty. There are duties on spirits, beer, wine, made-wine, cider and perry, based on alcoholic strength and volume. Spirits used for scientific, medical, research and industrial processes are generally free of duty. The cigarette duty is based partly on a charge per 1,000 cigarettes and partly on a percentage of retail price. Duty on other tobacco products is based on weight. Duties are charged on off-course betting, pool betting, gaming in casinos, bingo and gaming machines. The rates vary with the particular form of gambling. Duty is charged either as a percentage of gross or net stakes or, in the case of gaming machines, as a fixed amount per machine according to the cost of playing it and its prize level.

Vehicle excise duty on a private motor car or light van is £100 a year; for motor cycles it is £10, £20 or £40 a year according to engine capacity. The duty on goods vehicles is levied on the basis of gross weight and, if over 12 tonnes, according to the number of axles; the duty is designed to ensure that such vehicles cover at least their road costs through the tax paid (licence duty and fuel duty). The duty on taxis and buses varies according to seating capacity.

Car Tax

Cars, motor cycles, scooters, mopeds and some motor caravans, whether British made or imported, are chargeable with car tax at 10 per cent of the wholesale value (motor caravans are charged at 10 per cent of 60 per cent of the wholesale value).

VAT is charged on the price including car tax.

Stamp Duty

Certain kinds of transfer are subject to stamp duty. These include purchases of houses (1 per cent on the total price if this exceeds £30,000) and instruments such as declarations of trust (usually 50p). Stamp duty is also charged on transfers of stocks and shares other than government stocks (broadly 0·5 per cent of the value of the transaction). However, this is to be abolished in late 1991–92. Transfers by gift and transfers to charities are exempt.

OTHER REVENUE

National Insurance Contributions

There are four classes of National Insurance contribution:

- Class 1—paid by employees and their employers;
- Class 2—paid by the self-employed;
- Class 3—paid voluntarily for pension purposes; and
- Class 4—paid by the self-employed on their taxable profits over a set lower limit, currently £5,900 a year, and up to a set upper limit, currently £20,280 a year (in addition to their Class 2 contribution).

Employees with earnings below £52 a week do not pay Class 1 contributions. Contributions on earnings of £52 a week and over are at the rate of 2 per cent of the first £52 of total earnings and 9 per cent of the balance, up to the upper earnings limit of £390 a week. Employers' contributions are subject to the same threshold. On earnings above the threshold, contributions rise in stages from 4·6 per cent of total earnings up to a maximum of 10·4 per cent when earnings are £185 or more a week; there is no upper earnings limit.

Class 2 and Class 3 contributions are at a flat rate—£5·15 and £5·05 a week respectively. The self-employed may claim exemption from payment of Class 2 contributions if their profits are expected to be below £2,900 for the 1991–92 tax year.

Class 4 contributions are payable at the rate of 6·3 per cent.

Local Authority Revenue

A major source of local authority revenue in Great Britain (but not Northern Ireland) is the community charge. This is set at a level reflecting spending decisions reached by a council, for which it has to account to its electors. However, following a review of local government, the Government has announced that the community charge is to be replaced by a new council tax.

Under the council tax, each household would receive a single bill. For households consisting of two or more adults, the full bill would normally be payable; single-adult households would receive a 25 per cent discount.

Properties would be allocated to one of eight broad tax bands in accordance with their value in relation to the national average in England, Scotland or Wales as appropriate. The Government is aiming for the council tax to be in place in 1993–94.

In England and Wales the national non-domestic rate is set by central government (although collected by local authorities). It is paid into a national pool and then redistributed to local authorities. In Scotland non-domestic rates are levied by local authorities.

FINANCIAL CONTROL

Control of public sector finances is a central part of the Government's medium-term financial strategy. Between 1987–88 and 1990–91 the public sector was in surplus, so that the Government repaid debt. From 1991–92 to 1993–94 the public sector is expected to be in deficit, reflecting the cyclical downswing in the economy. However, as output revives, the public sector finances are expected to return to their underlying balance. Balanced public sector finances over the medium term remain the Government's objective. It sees them as a firm buttress for monetary policy in the

defeat of inflation. They also ensure that public debt and debt interest fall steadily in relation to GDP.

The major government debt instrument is known as gilt-edged stock as there is no risk of default. Gilt-edged stock is marketable and is widely traded. Individuals may also make transactions through post offices in stocks included on the National Savings Stock Register. Pension funds and life insurance companies have the largest holdings. The Bank of England on behalf of the Government issues both conventional and indexed stock (on which principal and interest are linked to the movement in the retail prices index).

An important additional source of government finance is the range of National Savings products, which are non-marketable and are designed to attract personal savings. The chief products are Income Bonds, National Savings Certificates (which may be index-linked), the Investment Account, Capital Bonds and a Children's Bonus Bond.

Other central government debt instruments are Treasury bills and certificates of tax deposit. Sterling Treasury bills are sold at a weekly tender; the majority have a maturity of three months. The Government has also issued bills denominated and payable in European Currency Units (ECUs) since 1988. The proceeds have been added to the official foreign exchange reserves as opposed to being used to finance public expenditure. Certificates of tax deposit may be purchased by individuals or corporate bodies to be tendered in settlement of a range of taxes and are non-marketable.

The bulk of public corporations' borrowing is met by central government, although their temporary borrowing needs are met largely from the market, usually under Treasury guarantee. That part of local authority borrowing met by central government is supplied by authorisation of Parliament through the Public Works Loan Board from the National Loans Fund. (The Board remains an independent body even though it is merged for administrative purposes with the former National Debt

Office, forming the National Investment and Loans Office.) Local authorities may also borrow directly from the market, both short-term and long-term, through a range of instruments. Some public corporations and local authorities also borrow on occasion, under special statutory power and with Treasury consent, in foreign currencies.

Net Public Sector Debt

Public sector borrowing (or debt repayment) each year represents an addition to (or subtraction from) the net debt of the public sector. This debt is the consolidated debt of the public sector less its holdings of liquid assets. At the end of March 1990 consolidated debt amounted to £190,000 million. Central government accounted for nearly 97 per cent, local authorities for almost 3 per cent and public corporations for under 1 per cent. With consolidated liquid assets amounting to £39,000 million, net public sector debt was £151,000 million. Central government accounted for nearly 73 per cent of consolidated liquid assets, local authorities for almost 22 per cent and public corporations for under 6 per cent.

20 Banking and Financial Institutions

Britain is a major financial centre providing a wide range of specialised services.

Historically the industry was located in the famous 'Square Mile' in the City of London. This remains broadly the case even though the markets for financial and related services have grown and diversified greatly. 'The City' refers to a collection of markets and institutions in and around the Square Mile. This area is remarkable for having:

- the greatest concentration of banks in the world (responsible for about a fifth of total international bank lending);

- the world's biggest insurance industry (with about one-fifth of the international market);

- one of the world's largest stock exchanges; and

- the role of principal international centre for transactions in a large number of commodities.

Banking, finance, insurance, business services and leasing accounted for 18 per cent of Britain's total output in 1990, a share which has risen sharply over the past decade. Banking, finance and insurance accounted for 11·9 per cent of all employment at the end of 1990. The net identified overseas receipts of British financial institutions in 1990 were £14,100 million.

Development of Financial Services

The increase in the rate of international movements of capital in the 1960s and 1970s mainly took the form of increased bank lending and foreign exchange trading. London became the international centre of this activity, particularly in the eurocurrency markets (see p 362), and the number of overseas banks represented in London is larger than in any other financial centre. In the last decade, with increasing international competition in financial services and with developments in technology, there has been rapid growth in the international markets for securities. London has again played an important role, especially in the market for eurobonds, in a variety of currencies (see p 362).

Supervision

Three Acts have helped Britain's financial services industry to respond to the new competitive climate, while at the same time maintaining adequate safeguards for the investing public:

- the Financial Services Act 1986;

- the Building Societies Act 1986 (see p 356); and

- the Banking Act 1987 (see p 353).

They have also assisted the implementation in Britain of certain European Community (EC) directives on banking and building societies, investment services and securities transactions.

Under the Financial Services Act a new supervisory framework has been built up. Investment businesses (those effecting transactions in, managing or giving advice on investments) require authorisation and have to obey rules of conduct based on principles set out in the legislation. Supervision is in the hands of the Securities and Investments Board (SIB), which is empowered to recognise self-regulating organisations (SROs), provided that they offer investors protection equivalent to that provided by the SIB. The SROs are practitioner-based bodies. Most investment businesses have opted to achieve authorisation by obtaining membership of an SRO. The SROs are:

- the Financial Intermediaries, Managers and Brokers Regulatory Association (FIMBRA), which covers firms such as financial advisers and insurance brokers;
- the Investment Management Regulatory Organisation (IMRO), for concerns such as merchant banks and pension fund managers with mainly corporate clients;
- the Life Assurance and Unit Trust Regulatory Organisation (LAUTRO); and
- the Securities and Futures Authority (SFA), whose members include the member firms of The London Stock Exchange, as well as futures brokers and dealers.

In each Act there is provision for improved co-operation and information-sharing between supervisors in different financial sectors. The Bank of England, the Building Societies Commission (see p 356), the Department of Trade and Industry, the SIB and the SROs have statutory responsibility for financial supervision in the sectors to which these Acts apply. There are strengthened government powers to investigate insider dealing (dealing carried out on the basis of privileged access to relevant information), and a separate department, the Serious Fraud Office, to deal with cases of serious or complex fraud. The Government is helping to extend international co-operation in investigating suspected breaches of rules or requirements in the field of investment business—agreements about exchange of information are in place with the United States and Japan.

Changes within financial services have been eroding traditional distinctions between financial institutions, with single firms providing a broader range of services, both in domestic and international markets.

THE BANK OF ENGLAND

The Bank of England was established in 1694 by Act of Parliament and Royal Charter as a corporate body; the entire capital stock was acquired by the Government in 1946. The Bank's main functions are:

- to execute monetary policy;
- to act as banker to the Government;
- to act as a note-issuing authority; and
- to exercise prudential supervision over, and to provide banking facilities for, the banking system.

As agent for the Government, the Bank is responsible for arranging government borrowing or repayment of debt and for managing the National Debt. It also manages the Exchange Equalisation Account (see p 353) and maintains the register of holdings of government securities on behalf of the Treasury. More generally, the Bank has a responsibility for overseeing the soundness of the financial system as a whole and for promoting the efficiency and competitiveness of financial markets. For this reason the Bank took part on 5 July 1991 in a worldwide operation by financial authorities to seize the assets of the Bank of Credit and Commerce International (BCCI), after an auditor's report revealed evidence of large-scale fraud in the supervision of that bank. Subsequently the Bank and the Treasury jointly sponsored an inquiry into the supervision of BCCI.

The Bank of England has the sole right in England and Wales to issue banknotes. The note issue is no longer backed by gold but by government and other securities. The Scottish and Northern Ireland banks have limited rights to issue notes. These issues, apart from a small amount specified by legislation for each bank, must be fully covered by holdings of Bank of England notes. Responsibility for the provision of coin lies with the Royal Mint, a government trading fund which became an executive agency in April 1990.

The Bank is able to influence money-market conditions through its dealings with the discount houses (see p 357), which developed in the nineteenth century as bill brokers for industrialists. The discount houses hold mainly Treasury, local authority and commercial bills, and negotiable certificates of deposit financed by short-term loans from the banks. If on a particular day there is a shortage of cash in the banking system as a result, for example, of large tax payments, the Bank relieves the shortage either by buying bills from the discount houses or by lending directly to them. This permits the banks to replenish their cash balances at the Bank by recalling some of their short-term loans to the discount houses. The terms on which the Bank's dealings with the discount houses take place allow the authorities to set and maintain interest rates at the level they consider appropriate.

On behalf of the Treasury, the Bank manages the Exchange Equalisation Account (EEA), which holds Britain's official reserves of gold, foreign exchange, Special Drawing Rights (SDRs, which are claims on the International Monetary Fund) and European Currency Units (ECUs). Using the resources of the EEA, the Bank may intervene in the foreign exchange markets to check undue fluctuations in the exchange value of sterling.

Under the Financial Services Act, the Bank is responsible for the supervision of the main wholesale markets in London for money, foreign exchange and gold bullion. (The markets are wholesale in the sense that the participants are professional operators dealing in substantial amounts of money.)

Under the Banking Act 1987, deposit-taking organisations require authorisation from the Bank of England (unless they are specifically exempted) and are subject to the Bank's supervision. The Act created a Board of Banking Supervision and increased the Bank's powers to modify the conduct of banking institutions, to investigate cases of illegal deposit-taking, to block bank mergers and takeovers on prudential grounds and to require information from banks. The Act also enables information to be shared, in strictly controlled ways, among supervisors in different financial services, and permits auditors to make reports to the Bank of England about a bank if the circumstances justify it.

The Bank has an interest in the financial sector which extends beyond its main functions. It is closely involved in the proper functioning of payment and settlement systems and ensuring that providers of financial services are efficient and competitive.

BANKS AND BUILDING SOCIETIES

In addition to banks, which are authorised under the Banking Act 1987 and are supervised by the Bank of England, the chief institutions which offer banking services are the building societies and the National Savings Bank.

Banks and building societies are broadly covered by the definition of 'credit institutions' used in EC banking legislation. The First Banking Directive, adopted in 1977, established the principle of non-discrimination for credit institutions in one member state wishing to operate elsewhere in the Community. The Second Banking Directive, which will come into operation at the beginning of 1993, will complete the single European market in banking by establishing mutual recognition of home country authorisation for credit institutions.

A useful distinction is that between 'retail' banking and 'wholesale' banking. Retail banking is primarily for personal customers and small businesses. Its main services are cash deposit and withdrawal facilities, and systems for transferring funds, notably by cheque. Competition between the banks and the building societies in the provision of money transmission services to individuals has increased during the last two decades and is expected to increase further (see p 356). Building societies can now also offer money transmission services to companies. Wholesale business involves the taking of large deposits at higher rates of interest, the deployment of funds in money-market instruments (see p 361) and the making of large loans and investments. Nearly all the banks in Britain engage in some wholesale activities and some, such as the merchant and overseas banks, centre their business on them. Many such wholesale dealings are conducted on the inter-bank market, that is, between banks themselves.

In June 1991 there were 525 institutions authorised under the Banking Act 1987, including retail banks, merchant banks, branches of overseas banks, discount houses and banking subsidiaries of both banking and non-banking institutions from Britain and overseas. Of these, 325 were members of the

British Bankers' Association, which is the main representative body for British banks.

Retail Banks

The major retail banks are those with a significant branch network, offering a full range of financial services to both individuals and companies. They provide current accounts including, generally, interest-bearing current accounts; deposit accounts; and various kinds of loan arrangements, together with a full range of money transmission facilities increasingly featuring plastic card technology.

The major banks in England and Wales are Barclays, Lloyds, Midland, National Westminster, the TSB Group and Abbey National; and in Scotland the Bank of Scotland and The Royal Bank of Scotland. Other important retail banks are the Clydesdale Bank, the Co-operative Bank, the Yorkshire Bank and Girobank, which was previously a subsidiary of the Post Office but which was offered for sale to the private sector and in 1990 became a subsidiary of the Alliance and Leicester Building Society. Northern Ireland is served by branch networks of five banks.

With the growth of financial services since the 1970s, and a relaxation of restrictions on competition among financial institutions, the major banks have diversified their services. They have lent more money for house purchases, and have established or acquired substantial interests in finance houses, leasing and factoring companies, merchant banking, securities dealers, insurance companies, unit trust companies and estate agencies.

The banks provide loan facilities to industrial companies and, since the 1970s, have provided more medium- and long-term loans than they did formerly. They have also become important providers of finance for small firms. They have supported a loan guarantee scheme under which 70 per cent of the value of loans to small companies is guaranteed by the Government, and some banks have set up special subsidiaries to provide venture capital for companies (see p 360).

Most retail banks also conduct international operations, which account for a substantial proportion of their business. In addition to maintaining overseas subsidiaries, they are active in eurocurrency markets (see p 362).

Deposits and Assets

The total liabilities/assets of the retail banks amounted to £436,000 million at the end of June 1991. Of the liabilities, 69 per cent was sterling deposits, 16 per cent other currency deposits, and the remainder items in suspense or transmission, and capital and other funds. Of the £300,000 million of sterling deposits, sight deposits withdrawable on demand constituted about 48 per cent and time deposits requiring notice of withdrawal some 45 per cent. Certificates of deposit and other short-term instruments accounted for the remaining 7 per cent. The banks' main liquid assets consist of money at call (mainly short-term loans to discount houses), their holdings of Treasury and some other bills, short-dated British government securities and balances at the Bank of England. They also hold a proportion of their assets as portfolio investments (mainly longer-dated British government securities) or trade investments.

Branches and Accounts

At the beginning of 1991 the retail banks in Britain operated through some 13,900 branches and sub-branches. National Westminster had the largest number (2,898), followed by Barclays (2,606), Lloyds (2,100), Midland (2,036) TSB (1,538), The Royal Bank of Scotland (841) and Abbey National (681). Some 85 per cent of adults in Britain have a current account and over one-third a deposit account.

Payment Systems and Services

The main payment systems are run by three separate companies operating under an umbrella organisation, the Association for Payment Clearing Services (APACS). One covers bulk paper clearings (cheques and credit transfers). A second covers high-value clearings for same-day settlement, namely the nationwide electronic transfer service Clearing House Automated Payment System (CHAPS) and the cheque-based Town Clearing (which operates only in the City of London). A third covers the bulk electronic clearing which handles standing orders and direct debits. Membership of each of these clearing companies is open to any bank, building society or other financial institution that meets the criteria for appropriate supervision and volume of transactions.

All the major retail banks and building societies have substantial networks of automated teller machines or cash dispensers with, in all, almost 17,000 machines at the beginning of 1991.

Automated teller machines give customers access to cash and other services for up to 24 hours a day. Many banks and building societies offer home banking services whereby customers can use telephone or screen-based access devices to obtain account information, make transfers and pay bills.

The banks and major building societies also offer their customers cheque guarantee cards which entitle holders to reciprocal cheque-cashing facilities up to, in most cases, £50 a day, although some cards now have higher limits. The cards will also guarantee transactions with retailers up to the same amount. Uniform eurocheques supported by a eurocheque card are available from all major banks. These standard-format cheques may be used to obtain cash or make payments in Britain, elsewhere in Europe and in a few other overseas countries. The cheques are made out in the currency of the country in which they are being used, with a guarantee limit of approximately £100 per cheque.

Credit cards issued by major retail banks and building societies are also a popular means of payment and are very widely accepted throughout Britain. Most cards are affiliated to one of the two major international credit card organisations, Visa and MasterCard. Some of the major retail stores issue their own cards, which operate like credit cards. A charge card, like a credit card, enables the holder to make retail payments, but there is either no credit limit or a very high limit, and the balance must be settled in full on receipt of a monthly statement.

Debit cards, which allow payments to be deducted directly from the purchaser's bank account, are becoming increasingly popular. Most cards are affiliated either to Visa or to the Switch organisation, which is based in Britain.

As well as the traditional paper-based systems for making retail payments by credit or debit cards, many stores and garages now provide electronic funds transfer at point of sale (EFTPOS) facilities for transferring funds electronically.

Building Societies

Building societies are mutual institutions, owned by their savers and borrowers. They raise short-term deposits from savers, who are generally able to withdraw their money on demand or at short notice. The societies provide long-term loans, mostly at variable rates of interest, against the security of property—usually private dwellings purchased for owner-occupation.

Building societies are the major lenders for house purchase in Britain and are the principal repository for the personal sector's liquid assets (although banks' shares have increased in both areas since 1985). Some 60 per cent of adults have building society savings accounts. Competition among the building societies and between building societies and other financial institutions has increased in the last decade. A variety of savings schemes have been established, and a growing number of societies provide current account facilities such as cheque books and automated teller machines. In 1991 there were some 2,900 building society automated teller machines, about 17 per cent of the total. About ten building societies issue credit cards.

At the end of April 1991 there were 116 registered societies, of which 98 were members of The Building Societies' Association. Building societies' assets totalled £217,000 million at the end of May 1991;

about £43,000 million was advanced in new mortgages in the course of 1990. The three largest societies (the Halifax, Nationwide Anglia and Woolwich) account for nearly 50 per cent of the total assets of all societies and the 20 largest for some 90 per cent.

The Building Societies Act 1986 allows the societies to provide a wider range of services. Up to 17·5 per cent of a society's commercial assets may be used for purposes other than loans on first mortgage of owner-occupied houses, including up to 7·5 per cent in other types of asset such as unsecured loans. These limits will increase to 25 per cent and 15 per cent respectively in 1993. Directly or through subsidiaries, societies may now offer services within the general areas of banking, investment, insurance, trusteeship, executorship and estate agency. Societies may also operate throughout the European Community. However, their main business will continue to be the provision of financial and housing-related services.

The 1986 Act established the Building Societies Commission to carry out the prudential supervision of building societies. It also made provision for a society to seek the approval of its members to convert into a public limited company. In this event the society becomes an authorised institution under the Banking Act 1987 (see p 353) and is then supervised by the Bank of England. Abbey National pursued this course and no longer contributes to building society statistics.

The Council of Mortgage Lenders is a trade body established in 1989 for all mortgage lending institutions, including building societies, insurance companies, finance houses and banks.

National Savings Bank

The National Savings Bank is run by the Department for National Savings, based in Glasgow, and provides a system for depositing and withdrawing savings at 21,000 post offices around the country, or by post.

There are about 20 million accounts. Ordinary Accounts earn interest at a rate which depends on the balance maintained; the first £70 of annual interest is tax free. Investment Accounts earn a higher, variable rate of interest, which is taxable. At the end of May 1991 the sum of the two accounts totalled just over £10,000 million. Other National Savings instruments include:

- tax-free Savings Certificates, which either pay a fixed rate of interest alone or a (lower) fixed rate of interest combined with index-linking;

- Premium Bonds, where interest is paid in the form of prizes chosen by lottery;

- taxable Income and Capital Bonds; and

- Children's Bonus Bonds.

All National Savings interest is paid without deduction of tax at source and some instruments encourage savers to leave their savings untouched for five years. The National Savings Bank does not offer lending facilities. At the end of May 1991 the total amount of money invested in National Savings was £37,000 million, and this forms a part of government borrowing.

Merchant Banks

Merchant banks have traditionally been concerned primarily with the accepting (or guaranteeing) of commercial bills and with the sponsoring of capital issues on behalf of their customers. Today they have a widely diversified and complex range of activities, with important roles in equity and debt markets; the provision of expert advice and financial services to industrial companies, especially where mergers, takeovers and other forms of corporate reorganisation are involved; and in the management of investment holdings, including trusts, pensions and other funds. The sector is split between independent houses and those which are part of larger banking groups.

Overseas Banks

A total of 256 banks incorporated overseas were represented in Britain in June 1991. Of these, 28 were from the United States and

24 from Japan. They provide a comprehensive banking service in many parts of the world and engage in the financing of trade not only between Britain and other countries but also between third-party countries.

British Overseas Banks

A small number of banks have their head offices in Britain, but operate mainly abroad, specialising in particular regions such as Africa and South East Asia. One example of a bank in this sector is Standard Chartered.

The Discount Houses

The discount houses, of which there are eight, are specialised institutions unique in their function and central position in the British monetary system. They act as financial intermediaries between the Bank of England and the rest of the banking sector, promoting an orderly flow of short-term funds between the authorities and the banks, and lending to the Government by guaranteeing to tender for the whole of the weekly offer of Treasury bills (which are instruments to raise funds over a period of up to six months). In return for acting as intermediaries, the discount houses have privileged daily access to the Bank of England, which acts as 'lender of last resort'. Assets of the discount houses consist mainly of Treasury and commercial bills, negotiable certificates of deposit and short-term loans. Their liabilities consist mainly of short-term deposits.

INSURANCE

The British insurance industry provides a comprehensive and competitive service domestically and internationally. It falls broadly into two parts: long-term life insurance, where contracts may be for periods of many years; and general insurance, including accident and short-term life insurance, where contracts are for a year or less. The London market is the world's leading centre for insurance and for the placement of international reinsurance. It has been estimated that it handles some 20 per cent of general insurance business placed on the international market.

In addition to the British companies and Lloyd's, a large number of overseas companies are represented, with which many British companies have formed close relationships. Some British companies confine their activities to domestic business but most large companies undertaking general business transact a substantial amount overseas through branches and agencies or affiliated local companies.

Insurance companies carrying on business in Britain are supervised by the Department of Trade and Industry under the Insurance Companies Act 1982. Marketing of life insurance is regulated by the Securities and Investments Board (see p 351). EC directives cover reinsurance, compulsory motor insurance, freedom of establishment for life and non-life insurers, Community co-insurance and insurance intermediaries. A directive regulating cross-frontier trade in non-life insurance services came into force in June 1990, and agreement has been reached on a directive on cross-frontier trade in life insurance services.

Some 840 companies are authorised to carry on one or more classes of insurance business in Britain, of which 7 per cent are European Community companies with their head office outside Britain, and a further 10 per cent are companies established outside the Community. The total invested assets of these companies amounted to £311,000 million at the beginning of 1991. Some 450 companies belong to the Association of British Insurers (ABI). Some companies are mutual institutions, owned by their policy holders. Insurance is also available from some friendly societies—mutual institutions administered by trustees.

Long-term Insurance

Long-term insurance is handled by some 270 companies. As well as providing life cover, long-term insurance is a vehicle for saving and investment by individuals, premiums being invested in securities and other assets. The net long-term insurance premium income of ABI member companies in 1990 was some £32,000 million.

General Insurance

General insurance business is undertaken by insurance companies and by Lloyd's. It covers fire, accident, general liability, short-term life, motor, marine, aviation and transport. Total ABI member company premiums in Britain in 1990 were some £15,400 million, of which £4,900 million was for motor insurance and £1,100 million for marine, aviation and transport insurance. The bulk of business by ABI companies in the latter categories was written through the Institute of London Underwriters (see below).

Lloyd's

Lloyd's, the origins of which go back to the seventeenth century, is an incorporated society of private insurers in London. Although its activities were originally confined to the conduct of marine insurance, a very considerable worldwide market for the transaction of other classes of insurance business (such as aviation and motor) has been built up.

Lloyd's is not a company but a market for insurance administered by the Council of Lloyd's. Business is carried out for individual elected underwriting members, or 'names', who must show sufficient available wealth and lodge a deposit. Insurance is transacted for them with unlimited liability, in competition with each other and with insurance companies. In June 1991 there were 26,500 members, grouped into 354 syndicates. Each syndicate is managed by an underwriting agent responsible for appointing a professional underwriter to accept insurance risks and settle claims on the syndicate members' behalf. Insurance may only be placed through accredited Lloyd's brokers, who negotiate with Lloyd's syndicates on behalf of the insured.

The net premium income of Lloyd's in 1989, the most recent year for which figures are available, was some £4,200 million, of which around £500 million was for motor insurance and around £1,500 million for marine, aviation and transport insurance.

Institute of London Underwriters

The Institute of London Underwriters was formed in 1884, originally as a trade association for marine underwriters. It now provides a market where insurance companies transact marine, commercial transport and aviation business. The Institute issues combined policies in its own name which are underwritten by the companies which form its membership. The premium income processed by the Institute in 1990 was some £1,400 million. About half of its 114 member companies are branches or subsidiaries of overseas companies.

Insurance Brokers

Insurance brokers, acting on behalf of the insured, are a valuable part of the company market and an essential part of the Lloyd's market. Many brokers specialise in reinsurance business, acting as intermediaries in the exchange of contracts between companies, both British and overseas, and often acting as London representatives of the latter. The Insurance Brokers (Registration) Act 1977 provides for the voluntary registration and regulation of insurance brokers by the Insurance Brokers Registration Council. Only those registered with the Council can use the title 'insurance broker'. In July 1991 some 16,000 individuals were registered with the Council, through 1,427 partnerships or sole traderships and 3,112 limited companies.

INVESTMENT FUNDS

Pension Funds

Virtually all occupational pension schemes are based on trust funds managed so as to protect the interests of the members. Pension contributions are invested either directly in the securities and other investment markets or through intermediaries such as insurance companies. The funds are a dominant force

AGRICULTURE

A tomato glasshouse, using energy-efficient thermal screens, in Essex.

A heavy-duty press roll unit, working behind British-made disc harrows, mixes chopped straw and soil, thus helping to solve the problem of surplus straw, the burning of which is to be banned in Britain.

MUSIC

Craftsman Zachary Taylor makes and plays copies of ancient instruments such as lyres, dulcimers, lutes and this two-man organistrum, and sells them to collectors and players worldwide.

Lisa Stansfield, one of Britain's best-known pop singers.

A rehearsal at the new Symphony Hall, Birmingham, officially opened by the Queen in June 1991. It is designed in the traditional style of great nineteenth-century halls, but is equipped with the most advanced acoustic technology in the world.

Percussionist Evelyn Glennie, currently enjoying worldwide acclaim.

CHANNEL TUNNEL

A tunnel-boring machine passes through an underground cavern. The largest machines are 8·72 m high and, including their service trains, some 260 m long.

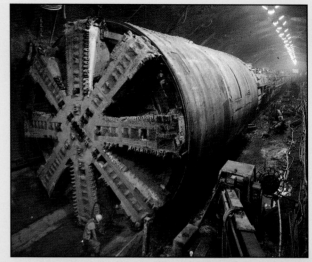

British and French Channel Tunnel teams meet under the sea after completing one of the two 50-km rail tunnels between Folkestone and Calais.

in securities markets. The Government has introduced legislation to allow people more choice in opting out of occupational pension schemes and setting up personal pension arrangements. Over 11 million people belong to occupational pension schemes and over 4·5 million people belong to personal pension schemes. The market value of assets held directly by pension funds rose from £2,000 million in 1957 to some £300,000 million at the beginning of 1990.

Investment and Unit Trusts

An investment trust is a collective investment fund which is structured as a company and quoted on The London Stock Exchange. It invests in securities, which are purchased mainly out of the capital subscribed by shareholders. The investments are carried out for the benefit of these shareholders. The shares of an investment trust are available only to the extent that existing shareholders are prepared to sell some or all of their holdings. The total assets of the 206 members of the Association of Investment Trusts were £22,500 million in July 1991.

A unit trust is a fund made up of the cash contributions of many individual investors, who pool their resources in order to be able to invest a sufficient amount to obtain professional management and the spread of risk that they could not afford individually.

Unit trusts operate a dual pricing system. This means that two prices are always quoted: the bid price, at which the manager will buy units back from the unitholder; and the offer price, at which the manager will sell units.

Unit trusts may invest in British shares in general or in certain sectors or in the securities of other countries. Unit trusts are subject to the provisions of the Financial Services Act 1986. The power to make regulations governing authorised unit trusts lies with the Securities and Investments Board. Only an authorised unit trust may be promoted to the general public.

There were 1,400 authorised unit trusts in June 1991, with total holdings of some £56,500 million.

COMPANY FINANCING INSTITUTIONS

There are many specialised financial institutions meeting the needs of specific groups of borrowers which are not adequately covered by other institutions. They are to be found in both the public and the private sectors. Some of the latter were set up with official support, but with financing from banks and other financial institutions. They may offer loan finance or equity capital.

The main private sector institutions are described below. Among public sector agencies are Scottish Enterprise, the Welsh Development Agency, the Industrial Development Board for Northern Ireland, the Co-operative Development Agency and ECGD (Export Credits Guarantee Department), Britain's official export credit insurer. The Insurance Services Group of ECGD, which handles the export of capital goods sold on short-term credit, is to be privatised.

Finance Houses

Finance houses are major providers of instalment credit facilities for the personal sector and of both loan and leasing finance (see below) to the corporate sector. Forty-two firms constitute the Finance Houses Association (FHA); at the beginning of 1991 loan and leasing credit outstanding to the members of the FHA was some £36,500 million. Many of the finance houses are owned by banks, and most are institutions authorised under the Banking Act 1987.

Leasing Companies

Leasing companies buy and own plant or equipment required and chosen by businesses and lease it at an agreed rental. This form of finance grew quickly in importance in the 1970s, partly because the leasing companies were able to take advantage of investment incentives to the benefit of customers whose tax position would otherwise have made this impossible. In 1990 the 72 members of the Equipment

Leasing Association acquired assets in Britain valued at some £14,300 million, which represented 36 per cent of all investment in plant and machinery.

Factoring Companies

Factoring comprises a range of financial services which provide growing companies with a flexible source of finance in exchange for the outstanding invoices due to them. Since the early 1960s factoring has developed as a major financial service, covering international activities as well as domestic trade. In 1990 member companies of the Association of British Factors and Discounters handled business of £13,800 million (representing about 90 per cent of all factoring business in Britain) and some 8,800 companies made use of the Association's services. Just over two-thirds of the companies had a turnover of less than £1 million.

Venture Capital Companies

Venture capital companies meet the need for medium- and long-term capital when such funds are not easily or directly available from traditional sources such as the stock market or the banks.

There are over 120 British venture capital companies, which take equity stakes in small and medium-sized firms. Many of these companies are subsidiaries of other financial institutions, including banks, insurance companies and pension funds. The 120 full members of the British Venture Capital Association invested almost £1,394 million in Britain, elsewhere in Europe, and in the United States in 1990.

Formerly Investors in Industry, 3i supports investment programmes over a whole range of industries. During the year ended 31 March 1991 the corporation invested £382 million. Within the last few years it has become increasingly prominent in financing management 'buy-outs', which involve the purchase of businesses from their owners by the management and other staff. The shares in 3i are currently owned by the Bank of England (15 per cent) and six of the major retail banks.

FINANCIAL MARKETS

The City of London has a wide range of financial markets. They include The London Stock Exchange, the foreign exchange market, the financial futures and options market, the eurobond and eurocurrency markets, the Lloyd's insurance market (see p 358), and the bullion and commodity markets.

The London Stock Exchange

The London Stock Exchange has its main administrative centre in London, as well as centres in Belfast, Birmingham, Dublin, Glasgow and Manchester.

As a result of a set of reforms known popularly as 'Big Bang', the Exchange has changed radically in recent years. The main reforms were as follows:

- the Exchange's rules on membership were altered to allow corporate ownership of member firms;

- the system under which dealers charged fixed minimum scales of commission to investors was abolished in favour of negotiated commissions;

- dealers were permitted to trade in securities both on their own behalf, as principals, and on behalf of clients, as agents, these two roles formerly having been kept distinct; and

- a screen-based dealing system came into operation, which has been so successful that the trading floor has been closed (except for dealing in traded options).

The London Stock Exchange is one of the largest in the world in terms of the number and variety of securities listed. Its turnover of equities in 1990 accounted for some 10 per cent of equity trading worldwide. Some 7,200 securities are quoted; at the end of June 1991 these had a market value of £2,200,000 million. Nearly 5,000 company securities are quoted, including those of a growing number of leading overseas companies, with a value of some £1,900,000 million. The remainder is made up of

British and overseas government and corporation stocks as well as eurobonds (see p 362).

In recent years the largest market for new issues has been that for companies' securities, including issues of shares resulting from the Government's privatisation programme. Trading in British government securities ('gilt-edged stocks') in the first six months of 1991 accounted for about 47 per cent of transactions by value (excluding traded options). New issues are made on the Government's behalf by the Bank of England when required.

The Exchange's London Traded Options Market enables investors not only to buy options to purchase or sell shares in the future at pre-fixed prices, but also to trade in the options themselves. There is trading in around 70 equity options of prominent British and overseas companies and in stock index options. The Market is due to merge with the London International Financial Futures Exchange (see p 362) by the end of 1991.

Listing Changes

The London Stock Exchange altered its rules in 1990 to conform to EC directives on listing particulars, prospectuses and mutual recognition. The major effect of the EC directive on Mutual Recognition of Listing Particulars is that, subject to certain limitations, each member state is required to recognise listing particulars accepted in another member state. In order to put British companies on an equal footing with those in other EC countries, the Exchange reduced the minimum trading record requirement for full listing from five years to three. At the same time the corresponding requirement for the Unlisted Securities Market, on which the securities of smaller companies are quoted, was reduced from three years to two. The Third Market, which previously provided a structure for dealing in the securities of companies which did not qualify for the Unlisted Securities Market, was phased out at the end of 1990. A majority of Third Market companies joined the Unlisted Securities Market.

The Money Markets

The London money markets channel wholesale funds (mainly short-term) from lenders to borrowers. They consist of a series of integrated groups of financial institutions conducting negotiations primarily by telephone, telex and automated dealing systems, there being no physical market-place. Under the Financial Services Act 1986 (see p 351), the Bank of England is responsible for regulating some market participants and has developed a code of conduct which is observed by all market participants. The discount houses (see p 357) play an important role. The main financial instruments dealt in are bills (issued by the Treasury, local authorities or companies), certificates of deposit (CDs, large-denomination transferable deposits) and short-term deposits. The bill markets and the markets in which the discount houses borrow from the rest of the banking system are often referred to as the 'traditional' markets. Newer markets, known as 'parallel' markets, emerged in the 1960s, and include the inter-bank market and the market in CDs. Since a large proportion of the latter is held by banks, the CD market is effectively an extension of the inter-bank market.

Capital markets have been undergoing continuous transformation since the 1960s (see p 351). In the 1980s a trend towards the 'securitisation of debt' developed—major borrowers increasingly raised funds by issuing securities instead of seeking bank loans. In 1986 large companies were permitted to develop a sterling commercial paper market: this consisted initially of issues of short-term debt denominated in sterling with a maturity of up to one year. Since 1989 the sterling commercial paper and the short-term corporate bond markets have been consolidated. The range of issuers has been broadened since 1986 to include, for example, banks and building societies, certain unquoted companies and overseas public sector bodies. The market now provides a way for such bodies to issue short-term debt of up to five years' maturity and to borrow directly from the money market by issuing short-term debt of up to five years' maturity.

The Euromarkets

The eurocurrency market enables banks to deal in deposits and loans denominated in a currency other than that of the country in which the bank is situated. Transactions can thus be carried out in eurodollars, eurodeutschmarks, euroyen and so on. London and Tokyo are the main world centres for this business.

The eurobond market performs a similar service in transferring funds from lenders to borrowers but over a longer period by means of bonds issued in currencies other than that of the issuing country. Transactions in both markets tend to be in large denominations.

The euromarkets developed in the late 1950s following the restoration of convertibility between the major currencies, partly in order to avoid incurring the costs of exchange control and other regulations.

The participants in the markets include multinational corporations, non-bank financial institutions, and governments, as well as the international banking community.

In the 1980s there was considerable growth in the euro-commercial paper market. As with the establishment of the sterling commercial paper market (see above), this represents a further movement towards the securitisation of debt.

The Foreign Exchange Market

The foreign exchange market has no physical centre, but consists of telephone links between the participants, which include banks, other financial institutions and several firms of foreign exchange brokers which act as intermediaries between the banks. It provides those engaged in international trade and investment with foreign currencies for their transactions. The banks are in close contact with financial centres abroad and are able to quote buying and selling rates for both immediate and forward delivery in a wide range of currencies and maturities. The forward market enables traders and dealers who, at a given date in the future, wish to receive or make a specific foreign currency payment, to contract in advance to sell or buy the foreign currency involved for sterling at a fixed exchange rate. The most recent Bank of England survey (in April 1989) showed that average daily turnover on London's foreign exchange market was about £110,000 million, making it the largest such market in the world.

Financial Futures

The London International Financial Futures Exchange (LIFFE) trades on the floor of the Royal Exchange building, although it is due to move to new premises at the Cannon Bridge development in January 1992. Over 200 banks, other financial institutions, brokers and individual traders are members of the market. Futures markets allow parties that could be affected by movements in prices, interest rates or exchange rates to reduce their vulnerability or to speculate on the possibility of making a gain. Financial futures contracts are legally binding documents for the purchase or sale of a fixed amount of a financial commodity, at a price agreed in the present, on a specified future date. They facilitate the transfer of risk from those who do not wish to bear it to those who are prepared to bear it. LIFFE has the widest range of financial futures and options products of any exchange in the world. Turnover in the first half of 1991 was some £35,000 million, representing average daily trading of about 180,000 futures and futures options contracts. LIFFE is due to merge with the London Traded Options Market (see p 361) by the end of 1991.

The London Bullion Market

Over 60 banks, securities and trading companies comprise the London gold and silver markets which, like the foreign exchange market, trade by telephone and telex links. Five of the members meet twice daily to establish a London fixing price for gold which provides a reference point for worldwide dealings. The silver fixing is held once a day and has three participants. Although much interest centres upon the fixings, active dealing takes place throughout the day. London and Zurich are the main world centres for gold dealings.

Commodity, Shipping and Freight Markets

Britain remains the principal international centre for transactions in a large number of commodities, although most of the sales negotiated in London relate to consignments which never pass through the ports of Britain. The need for close links with sources of finance and with shipping and insurance services often determined the location of these markets in the City of London. There are also futures markets in cocoa, coffee, grains (wheat, barley and rice), soya bean meal, sugar, pigmeat, non-ferrous metals (aluminium, copper, lead, nickel, silver and zinc), potatoes, gas oil (heating oil) and crude petroleum oil. The markets are collaborating in the development of new arrangements to safeguard participants.

In ship brokerage, London's Baltic Exchange is responsible for a substantial proportion of the world's tramp fixtures. A freight futures market is in operation at London Fox, the Futures and Options Exchange, where all Britain's agricultural futures markets are operated; commodity futures trading is also carried out there.

21 Overseas Trade

Overseas trade has been of vital importance to the British economy for hundreds of years, and especially since the mid-nineteenth century, when the rapid growth of industry, commerce and shipping was accompanied by Britain's development as an international trading centre. Today, although small in area and accounting for only about 1 per cent of the world's population, Britain is the fifth largest trading nation in the world, and, as a member of the European Community, part of the world's largest trading bloc, accounting for about a third of all trade.

Exports of goods and services in 1990 were equivalent to over a quarter of gross domestic product (GDP). Britain is a major supplier of machinery, vehicles, aerospace products, electrical and electronic equipment and chemicals, and a significant oil exporter. It relies upon imports for about a third of total consumption of foodstuffs, and for many of the basic materials needed for its industries.

Trade in invisibles is of great significance to the economy: in 1990 overseas earnings from services were equivalent to nearly a third of those from total visible exports.

VISIBLE TRADE

In 1990 Britain's exports of goods were valued at about £102,700 million and its imports of goods at some £120,700 million on a balance-of-payments basis (see Table 21.1). Between 1989 and 1990 exports rose by 6·8 per cent in terms of volume and by 5·5 per cent in terms of unit value, leading to an increase in the total value of exports of almost 11 per cent. Import volume rose by 1·3 per cent, unit value rose by 3·8 per cent and total value rose by just over 3 per cent.

Table 21.1: Exports and Imports 1987–90 (balance-of-payments basis)

	1987	1988	1989	1990
Value (£ million)				
Exports f.o.b.[a]	79,446	80,776	92,831	102,746
Imports f.o.b.[a]	90,670	101,853	116,829	120,657
Volume index (1985 = 100)				
Exports	109·7	111·8	117·3	125·3
Imports	115·3	131·0	141·5	143·4
Unit value index (1985 = 100)				
Exports	93·8	93·9	101·2	106·8
Imports	97·8	96·7	103·4	107·3
Terms of trade (1985 = 100)[b]	95·9	97·2	97·9	99·5

Source: *Monthly Review of External Trade Statistics.*
[a] f.o.b. = free on board, that is, all costs accruing up to the time of placing the goods on board the exporting vessel having been paid by the seller.
[b] Export unit value index as a percentage of import unit value index.

Commodity Composition

Although Britain has traditionally been an exporter of manufactured goods and an importer of food and basic materials, it has not had a surplus on manufactures since 1983. In 1970 manufactures accounted for 85 per cent of exports. The proportion fell sharply in the early 1980s—to around 67 per cent by the middle of the decade—as fuels increased their share; it has since risen, to 81 per cent in 1990. The share of finished manufactures in total imports rose from 25 per cent in 1970 to 52 per cent in 1990. Machinery and transport equipment account for over a third of exports and a similar proportion of imports. Export sectors that have declined in relative importance include textiles and vehicles. Textiles accounted for 5 per cent of total exports in 1970 but only 2 per cent in 1990; the corresponding figures for vehicles were 11 per cent and 7 per cent. Over the same period, the share of food, beverages and tobacco in total imports fell from 22 per cent to 10 per cent and that of basic materials from 15 per cent to 5 per cent.

Since the mid-1970s North Sea oil has made a significant contribution to Britain's overseas trade both in terms of exports and in terms of import substitution. In 1990 exports of fuels in volume terms were over four times their 1975 level; imports were less than three-quarters of their 1975 level. Over this period the share of fuels in exports changed from 4 per cent to 7·5 per cent and

Table 21.2: Commodity Composition of Trade 1990[a]

	Exports (f.o.b.)		Imports (c.i.f.)[b]	
	£ million	per cent	£ million	per cent
Non-manufactures	**17,120**	**16·5**	**26,222**	**20·8**
Food, beverages and tobacco	7,094	6·8	12,316	9·8
Basic materials	2,251	2·2	6,098	4·8
Fuels	7,774	7·5	7,809	6·2
Manufactures	**84,469**	**81·3**	**98,191**	**77·8**
Semi-manufactures	29,002	27·9	32,734	26·0
of which: Chemicals	13,182	12·7	10,834	8·6
Textiles	2,447	2·4	3,937	3·1
Iron and steel	3,036	2·9	2,686	2·1
Non-ferrous metals	2,194	2·1	3,003	2·4
Metal manufactures	2,118	2·0	2,595	2·1
Other	6,025	5·8	9,679	7·7
Finished manufactures	55,465	53·4	65,460	51·9
of which: Machinery	29,619	28·5	30,519	24·2
Road vehicles	7,299	7·0	12,588	10·0
Clothing and footwear	1,975	2·1	5,075	4·0
Scientific instruments and photographic apparatus	4,108	4·0	4,071	5·1
Other	12,464	12·0	13,207	10·5
Miscellaneous	**2,296**	**2·2**	**1,718**	**1·4**
Total	**103,882**	**100·0**	**126,135**	**100·0**

Source: *Monthly Review of External Trade Statistics.*
[a]On an overseas trade statistics basis. (This differs from a balance-of-payments basis because, for imports, it includes the cost of insurance and freight and, for both exports and imports, includes returned goods.)
[b]c.i.f. = cost, insurance and freight, that is, including shipping, insurance and other expenses incurred in the delivery of goods as far as their place of importation in Britain. Some of these expenses represent earnings by companies resident in Britain and are more appropriate to the invisibles account.
Note: Differences between totals and the sums of their component parts are due to rounding.

in imports from 18 per cent to 6 per cent. North Sea oil production has now passed its peak of the mid-1980s, when exports of fuels had accounted for over 20 per cent of total exports. In 1990 the surplus on trade in oil amounted to about £1,500 million.

Since the early 1960s Britain's imports of semi-manufactures have exceeded those of basic materials; they are now more than five times as high. This reflects the increasing tendency for producing countries to carry out the processing of primary products up to the semi-finished and, on occasions, the finished stage. The fall in the share of food in total imports (from around 35 per cent of total imports in the 1950s to 8 per cent in 1990) is a result both of the increasing extent to which food demand has been met from domestic agriculture and the decline in the proportion of total expenditure on food.

Geographical Distribution

Britain's overseas trade is mainly—and increasingly—with other developed countries. In 1970 these accounted for 73 per cent of exports and a similar proportion of imports;

by 1990 the shares were 81 per cent and 85 per cent respectively. In 1970 non-oil developing countries accounted for 17 per cent of Britain's exports and 15 per cent of Britain's imports; by 1990 they accounted for 13 per cent of Britain's exports and 12 per cent of Britain's imports. In 1972 (the year before Britain joined the European Community) around a third of Britain's trade was with the other 11 countries which now make up the Community. The proportion is now about a half, and is expected to increase with the completion of the single European market in 1992 (see p 368). Trade with other Commonwealth countries has declined in importance.

European Community countries accounted for seven of the top ten export markets and for six of the ten leading suppliers of goods to Britain in 1990 (see Table 21.3). From 1981 to 1989 the United States was Britain's largest single market but it was overtaken in 1990 by Germany. Germany is also Britain's largest single supplier. In 1990 Germany accounted for almost 13 per cent of Britain's exports and supplied almost 16 per cent of Britain's imports.

Geographical Distribution of Trade 1990

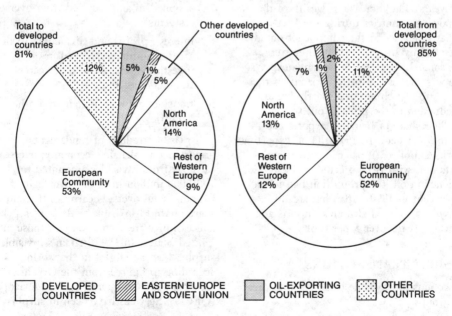

Differences between totals and the sums of their component parts are due to rounding.

Source: *Monthly Review of External Trade Statistics.*

Table 21.3: Britain's Main Markets and Suppliers 1990[a]

	Value (£ million)	Share (per cent)
Main markets		
Germany	13,216	12·7
United States	12,998	12·5
France	10,886	10·5
Netherlands	7,517	7·2
Belgium/Luxembourg	5,651	5·4
Italy	5,613	5·4
Irish Republic	5,311	5·1
Spain	3,749	3·6
Sweden	2,713	2·6
Japan	2,632	2·5
Main suppliers		
Germany	20,006	15·9
United States	14,358	11·4
France	11,756	9·3
Netherlands	10,485	8·3
Japan	6,762	5·4
Italy	6,735	5·3
Belgium/Luxembourg	5,731	4·5
Irish Republic	4,499	3·6
Switzerland	4,254	3·4
Norway	4,236	3·4

Source: *Monthly Review of External Trade Statistics.*
[a]On an overseas trade statistics basis. Exports are f.o.b.; imports c.i.f.

There have been a number of changes in the trends of Britain's overseas trade in recent years. The increase in wealth of the oil-exporting countries during the 1970s led to a sharp increase in their imports from all sources and by the early 1980s they were taking some 12 per cent of Britain's exports. There was then a fall in the capacity of these countries to absorb imports (partly because of a reduction in the price of oil) so that, by 1990, their share of Britain's exports had fallen to 5 per cent. In 1973 the oil-exporting countries supplied 10 per cent of Britain's imports but, with Britain achieving self-sufficiency in oil, the proportion had fallen to 2 per cent in 1990. Japan has steadily increased its share of Britain's imports and now accounts for over 5 per cent.

INVISIBLE TRANSACTIONS

Transactions on invisible trade fall into three main groups:

- services (receipts and payments arising from services, as distinct from goods, supplied to and received from overseas residents);

- interest, profits and dividends (income arising from outward and inward investment, loans and other capital transactions); and

- transfers between Britain and other countries.

Invisible trade is of fundamental importance to Britain's economy; overseas earnings from invisibles amounted to £117,000 million in 1990—over half of Britain's total overseas earnings. Britain's share of world invisible trade is 14·5 per cent and earnings are second only to those of the United States. In 1990 Britain's invisibles surplus was the largest in the world, according to figures from the Organisation for Economic Co-operation and Development (OECD). Services have been in surplus for

Table 21.4: Britain's Invisible Transactions 1990

£ million

	Credits	Debits	Balance
Private sector and public corporations	112,915	101,074	11,841
Services	31,638	24,116	7,522
of which: Sea transport	3,847	3,591	256
Civil aviation	4,358	4,674	-316
Travel	7,784	9,916	-2,132
Financial and other services	15,649	5,935	9,714
Interest, profits and dividends	79,477	74,858	4,619
Transfers	1,800	2,100	-300
General government	4,435	11,981	-7,547
Services	432	2,753	-2,321
Interest, profits and dividends	1,810	2,400	-591
Transfers	2,193	6,828	-4,635
Total invisible transactions	117,350	113,055	4,295

Source: *United Kingdom Balance of Payments 1991 Edition.*
Note: Differences between totals and the sums of their component parts are due to rounding.

over 200 years (excluding war periods), while interest, profits and dividends have rarely been in deficit; transfers, however, have almost always been in deficit. For invisible trade as a whole, the deficit of general government is more than offset by the substantial surplus of the private sector (including public corporations), to give an overall surplus. General government transactions are relatively unimportant in either the services or the interest, profits and dividends accounts but they form the greater part of the transfers account. In 1990 the private sector had a surplus of almost £12,000 million on invisible trade while government had a deficit of about £7,500 million. British Invisibles, which is financed almost entirely by contributions from the private sector, especially City institutions, promotes measures to encourage invisible trade.

Earnings from private sector services rose in value by 6 per cent in 1990 to £31,600 million; debits, at £24,100 million, were 5 per cent higher than a year previously.

The surplus on private sector interest, profits and dividends was £4,600 million in 1990—about the same as in 1989. Earnings on portfolio investment (investment in overseas securities) and on direct investment overseas remained high—at £8,100 million and £17,800 million respectively— reflecting in part the substantial volume of overseas investment following the abolition of exchange controls in 1979 and changes in the method of foreign currency lending by banks located in Britain.

The deficit on private sector transfers in 1990 was £300 million, while that on government transfers was £4,600 million, mainly as a result of contributions and subscriptions to the European Community and other international organisations, and bilateral aid.

COMMERCIAL POLICY

Britain remains committed to the open multilateral trading system and to the further liberalisation of world trade. To this end it has taken a leading part in the activities of such organisations as the General Agreement on Tariffs and Trade (GATT), the International Monetary Fund (IMF) and the Organisation for Economic Co-operation and Development (OECD) and has given full support to the current round of multilateral trade negotiations. Since 1973, when Britain

Britain joined it, the European Community has acted for Britain in international trade negotiations. The Community's common customs tariff is, at a trade-weighted average of 2·5 per cent, at a low level, similar to the tariffs of most major industrialised countries.

Single European Market

Britain strongly supports the drive to complete the single European market by the end of 1992. The single market programme is designed to eliminate the remaining trade barriers within the Community and is expected to provide substantial opportunities for business and benefits for consumers.

The single European market programme was launched in 1985 and, by August 1991, 197 out of a proposed 282 measures had been adopted or agreed in principle.

By May 1991 Britain was the third most successful member state in turning single market measures into national legislation.

General Agreement on Tariffs and Trade

Tariffs and non-tariff barriers to trade have been considerably reduced in the seven rounds of multilateral trade negotiations completed since 1947 under the auspices of GATT, the most recent one completed being the Tokyo Round (1973–79). Britain participates in these negotiations as a member of the European Community.

The eighth round of GATT multilateral trade negotiations (the Uruguay Round) was launched in September 1986. It is the most ambitious and wide-ranging round of trade negotiations ever. It was due to be completed in December 1990 but this was not possible. However, negotiations were resumed in February 1991. The Uruguay Round's main concerns are:

- to bring trade in agriculture and textiles fully within the GATT system;
- to achieve further reductions in tariff and non-tariff barriers;

- to extend GATT disciplines to the new areas of intellectual property, investment and services; and
- to strengthen the GATT system, so that it can deal more effectively with trade distortions and disputes.

The British Government remains committed to a successful conclusion to the Round and is working to bring this about as soon as possible.

European Community Agreements

Britain applies the common customs tariff to all countries neither belonging to, nor having any special arrangement with, the European Community. There is duty-free trade between those member states that joined before 1986. Portugal and Spain joined at the beginning of that year. Their trade with the rest of the Community is in a transitional stage: tariffs on industrial products are due to be phased out by the start of 1993, but those on certain agricultural products will be dismantled over a longer period.

The Community has reciprocal agreements with the European Free Trade Association (EFTA) countries (Austria, Finland, Iceland, Norway, Sweden and Switzerland) and Liechtenstein, which allow for industrial products to be traded free of duty. Following the Luxembourg Declaration of 1984, the Community and EFTA are working towards closer economic co-operation. In 1989 Community and EFTA ministers agreed on further action to this end and to remove remaining non-tariff barriers to trade. Negotiations are continuing, with the aim of extending the single market to the EFTA countries.

The Community also has reciprocal preferential trading agreements with Cyprus, Israel, Malta and Turkey and non-reciprocal agreements with Algeria, Morocco, Tunisia, Egypt, Jordan, the Occupied Territories, Lebanon, Syria and Yugoslavia and, under the Lomé Convention, with a group of 69 African, Caribbean and Pacific developing countries. The Lomé Convention gives these countries tariff-free access (subject to certain safeguards) to the Community for industrial goods and most agricultural products.

Tariff preference is also given to developing countries (under the Generalised System of Preferences), the Faroe Islands, and the overseas dependencies and territories of member states.

The Community also has economic co-operation agreements with a number of Latin American countries, with the People's Republic of China and with the six members of the Association of South East Asian Nations.

An economic co-operation agreement is in force with the six members of the Gulf Co-operation Council. Negotiations are in progress which may lead to the establishment of a free trade area embracing the Community and the Council.

Following the establishment of diplomatic relations between the Central and Eastern European countries and the Community, the Community negotiated trade, commercial and economic co-operation agreements with Bulgaria, Czechoslovakia, Hungary, Poland, Romania and the Soviet Union. These agreements cover trade concessions and co-operation in areas such as energy, agriculture, transport and the environment. 'Association agreements' are currently being negotiated with Czechoslovakia, Hungary and Poland. Their aim is to develop closer association, leading to reciprocal free trade. The next stage, as economic and political reform is consolidated, will be the development of closer association agreements with individual Eastern and Central European countries.

CONTROLS ON TRADE

Britain maintains few restrictions on its international trade. Most goods may be imported freely and only a narrow range of goods is subject to any sort of export control.

Import Controls

In accordance with its international obligations under GATT and to the European Community, Britain has progressively removed almost all quantitative import restrictions imposed on economic grounds. The few remaining quantitative restrictions mainly affect textile goods (in view of the rapid contraction of the domestic textile industry). They stem primarily from the Multi-Fibre Arrangement (MFA), under which there exists a series of bilateral agreements covering international trade in textiles, designed to balance the interests of both exporting and importing countries. The present MFA expired in July 1991 but has been extended to the end of 1992, pending its phasing out as part of the Uruguay Round.

A small number of quantitative restrictions are also maintained against non-GATT countries. Britain, in accordance with European Community directives, operates a ban on the import from North Korea and South Africa of certain iron and steel products. Quantitative restrictions have been removed from imports of goods of Community origin. However, there are exceptions: Britain continues to apply internationally recognised restrictions on non-economic grounds on imports from all countries of products such as firearms, ammunition and nuclear materials. Other government departments apply similar non-economic restrictions on goods such as meat and poultry; animals, birds, bees, fish and plants and some of their derivatives; controlled drugs; explosives; fireworks; certain offensive weapons; certain citizens' band radios; indecent or obscene articles and products derived from endangered species.

Export Controls

The great majority of British exports are not subject to any government control or direction except for presentation and declaration to HM Customs and Excise on export for the purpose of collecting the overseas trade statistics. However, there are controls governing the export of goods associated with biological, chemical and nuclear weapons and missiles. Controls also exist on the export of military equipment and of advanced industrial goods of strategic significance as well as on steel sales to the United States.

Other controls include those for health

certification purposes on certain animals, meat and fish exported to another member of the European Community; on endangered animal and plant species; on photographic and artistic material over a certain age and value; and on documents, manuscripts and archaeological items.

The Co-ordinating Committee for Multilateral Export Controls (COCOM),[1] of which Britain is a member, announced major changes in 1990 to the control of exports on certain goods and technologies that are enforced by its members. Many items have been removed from control, and significant relaxations have been achieved on the controls on telecommunications equipment, computers and machine tools. COCOM is continuing to seek to remove and relax its controls on other industrial goods and technologies in order that the burden placed upon exporters by these controls is reduced as much as possible. The Government wishes to assist in creating more favourable export conditions while maintaining an embargo on the most strategically sensitive equipment and technologies.

GOVERNMENT SERVICES

The Government assists exporters by creating conditions favourable to the export trade and by providing practical help, advice and support. This includes a wide range of services.

Export Promotion Services

The major government departments involved in export promotion collaborate to provide Overseas Trade Services. The departments are: the Department of Trade and Industry (DTI), the Foreign & Commonwealth Office, the Industry Departments of the Scottish and Welsh Offices and the Industrial Development Board of Northern Ireland. The operation is conducted from the DTI's

London headquarters, from 11 regional offices throughout Britain and from nearly 200 diplomatic posts overseas.

The range of services available includes the dissemination of export intelligence, assistance in researching potential markets, help at trade fairs and support for firms participating in trade missions. In 1990–91 some £166 million was spent on support for exporters.

Overseas Trade Services also uses the advice of the British Overseas Trade Board—part of the DTI—and its 17 area advisory groups. The Board has been involved in identifying priorities for export promotion. Priority markets are Western Europe, North America and the Asia/Pacific Rim.

ECGD

ECGD is a government department, responsible to the Secretary of State for Trade and Industry. Since 1919 it has been helping British exporters overcome many of the risks in selling overseas.

ECGD underwrites credit contracts for projects running into the medium term and longer periods. Exporters are helped to break into new markets through guarantees of credit. In 1991 arrangements were made for the sale to the private sector of its Insurance Services Group, which dealt with exports sold on short-term credit. ECGD assists companies by providing insurance for new investments overseas—mainly in developing countries—against the political risks of nationalisation, war and restrictions on remittances.

BALANCE OF PAYMENTS

The balance-of-payments statistics record transactions between residents of Britain and non-residents. The transactions are classified into two groups: current account (visibles and invisibles) and transactions in assets and liabilities. The balance on current account shows whether Britain has had a surplus of income over expenditure.

Since 1983 Britain has had a deficit on visible trade. It has traditionally run a

---

[1] COCOM is an informal body of countries of the North Atlantic Treaty Organisation except Iceland, plus Australia and Japan. It was established in 1950 to co-ordinate controls on East–West trade and on the export of strategic equipment, including atomic energy material, munitions and industrial goods of potential military use.

Table 21.5: Britain's Balance of Payments 1986–90

£ million

	1986	1987	1988	1989	1990
Current account					
Visible trade balance	−9,559	−11,582	−21,624	−24,598	−18,675
Invisible transactions balance	9,747	7,423	6,103	4,195	4,295
Current balance	187	−4,159	−15,520	−20,404	−14,380
Financial account					
Transactions in assets and liabilities					
British external assets	−92,663	−79,627	−55,426	−83,199	−72,301
British external liabilities	85,430	85,438	65,071	96,115	84,381
Balancing item	7,047	−1,651	5,875	7,488	2,299

Source: *United Kingdom Balance of Payments 1991 Edition.*
Note: Differences between totals and the sums of their component parts are due to rounding.

surplus on trade in invisibles. Between 1989 and 1990 the surplus on invisibles rose slightly from £4,200 million to £4,300 million. The surplus on services increased by £500 million; that on interest, profits and dividends declined by £59 million; and the deficit on transfers grew by £357 million.

Capital Flows

Britain has no exchange controls; residents are free to acquire foreign currency for any purpose, including direct and portfolio investment overseas. There are also no controls on the lending of sterling abroad and non-residents may freely acquire sterling for any purpose. Gold may be freely bought and sold. The abolition of exchange controls in 1979 means that Britain meets its full obligations on capital movements under the OECD code on capital movements and under European Community directives.

The Government welcomes both outward and inward investment. Outward investment helps to develop markets for British exports, while providing earnings in the form of interest, profits and dividends. Inward investment creates employment directly; introduces new technology, products, management styles and attitudes; and provides an opportunity to increase exports or substitute imports. Inward investment is particularly encouraged by the DTI's Invest in Britain Bureau.

Inward direct investment in 1990 was £19,000 million, compared with £17,100 million in 1989. In 1990 direct investment overseas by British residents was £11,700 million, just over half the 1989 level. Outward portfolio investment was £12,600 million. The inflow of direct and portfolio investment into Britain amounted to £24,100 million. An analysis of transactions in Britain's external assets and liabilities is given in Table 21.6.

External Assets and Liabilities

At the end of 1990 Britain's identified external assets exceeded identified external liabilities by £30,000 million; this compares with £84,000 million a year earlier and reflects significant falls in securities prices in 1990. Net assets of the private sector and public corporations amounted to over £19,000 million and those of general government to £10,000 million.

Direct investment assets overseas of British residents (investment in branches, subsidiaries and associated companies) totalled £127,000 million at the end of 1990 and portfolio investment £186,000 million. At the end of 1987 (the latest year for which data are available) over 84 per cent of direct investment was in developed countries, with over 35 per cent in the United States and nearly 28 per cent in the European Community. In terms of industries, manufacturing accounted for 35 per cent of

Table 21.6: Summary of Transactions in External Assets[a] and Liabilities[b] 1988–90

£ million

	1988	1989	1990
Overseas direct investment in Britain	10,236	17,145	18,997
Overseas portfolio investment in Britain	14,387	13,239	5,070
British direct investment overseas	-20,880	-21,521	-11,702
British portfolio investment overseas	-8,600	-31,283	-12,587
Borrowing from overseas	39,618	63,546	59,617
Deposits and lending overseas	-22,294	-34,894	-46,708
Official reserves[a]	-2,761	5,440	-77
Other external liabilities of general government	831	2,186	697
Other external assets of central government	-891	-942	-1,227
Total	9,645	12,916	12,081

Source: *United Kingdom Balance of Payments 1991 Edition.*
[a]Increase −/decrease +
[b]Increase +/decrease −
Note: Differences between totals and the sums of their component parts are due to rounding.

direct investment holdings. By type of company, oil companies were responsible for 26 per cent, insurance companies for 7 per cent and banks for 4 per cent.

The significance of any inventory of Britain's aggregate external assets and liabilities is limited because a variety of claims and obligations are included that are very dissimilar in kind, in degree of liquidity and in method of valuation. For example, while portfolio investment is valued at market prices, direct investment is stated at book value, which is likely to understate its current market value.

Direct investment in Britain by overseas residents amounted to £107,000 million at the end of 1990 and portfolio investment to £103,000 million. At the end of 1987 investment from developed countries accounted for 95 per cent of overseas direct investment in Britain: 46 per cent originated

in the United States and 26 per cent in the European Community. A total of 36 per cent was in manufacturing. Oil companies were responsible for 29 per cent, insurance companies for 4 per cent and banks for 10 per cent.

Another type of overseas transaction is company cross-border acquisitions and mergers. In 1990 overseas acquisitions and mergers less disposals carried out by British companies were valued at £6,300 million, while the corresponding figure for operations in Britain by overseas companies was £10,000 million. The United States accounted for 55 per cent of the value of acquisitions and mergers by British companies and the European Community for 31 per cent. The European Community also accounted for 31 per cent of the value of acquisitions and mergers by overseas companies.

22 Promotion of Science and Technology

Britain's tradition for innovation in science and technology is upheld by contemporary British scientists, who continue to conduct pioneering work in a wide range of areas. During the 1980s Professor Michael Green helped to develop the superstring theories, which shed new light on the composition of matter. In 1985 Professor Alec Jeffreys invented genetic fingerprinting, while the first combined heart, lungs and liver transplant was carried out at Papworth Hospital, Cambridge, in 1986. Agricultural research in Britain has produced the first microbial pesticides not to harm the environment. A recent landmark in genetic research has been the identification of the gene in the Y chromosome responsible for determining sex.

Nobel prizes for science have been won by 70 British citizens. Table 22.1 lists British prizewinners (excluding those in economic sciences) since 1980.

Research and Development Expenditure

International comparisons of expenditure on research and development (R & D) are based on definitions agreed by the Organisation for Economic Co-operation and Development. According to these, total expenditure in Britain on scientific research and development in 1989 was about £11,532 million, 2·3 per cent of gross domestic product. Some 50 per cent of this was provided by industry and 37 per cent by government. Significant contributions were also made by overseas sources, private endowments, trusts and charities.

Government finance for R & D goes to research establishments, including its own, to institutions of higher education and to private industry, as well as to support collaborative research programmes. In many cases nationalised and private-sector industries finance their own research and run

Table 22.1: Recent British Winners of Nobel Prizes for Science

	Year of Award	Category	Subject
Dr Frederick Sanger	1980	Chemistry (jointly)	Determination of base sequences in nucleic acids
Sir Aaron Klug	1982	Chemistry	Work on the structure of viruses and genetic material in cells
Sir John Vane	1982	Physiology or Medicine (jointly)	Clarification of the pathways of prostaglandin metabolism in the body
Dr César Milstein	1984	Physiology or Medicine (jointly)	Production of monoclonal antibodies
Sir James Black	1988	Physiology or Medicine (jointly)	Discovery of therapeutic drugs, especially for heart disease and stomach ulcers

their own laboratories. Industry also funds university research and spends money on contracts to government establishments. Charities may have their own laboratories as well as offering grants for outside research.

Expenditure in Industry

According to a survey, R & D expenditure in industry in 1989 amounted to £7,600 million, of which £1,249 million came from government, £1,023 million from overseas and the remaining £5,328 million chiefly from industry's own funds. The main areas of expenditure were electronics (£2,259 million), chemicals (£1,692 million) and aerospace (£1,070 million).

Expenditure by Government

Government figures for its R & D expenditure differ somewhat from those used in international comparisons and those resulting from industrial surveys because they include expenditure on social science and the humanities, and also expenditure overseas. Survey methods, too, tend to produce an understatement of government funding of research in industry. Total government R & D expenditure (both civil and defence) in 1990–91 was some £5,153 million. Among departments, the Ministry of Defence has the largest research budget. The main civil departments involved are the Department of Education and Science (see p 378); the Department of Trade and Industry (see below); the Department of Energy (see p 380); and the Ministry of Agriculture, Fisheries and Food (see p 380).

Government and Scientific Research

The main objectives of the Government's science programme are to advance scientific knowledge and technological capability in Britain, and provide training for scientists, in order to achieve economic, social and cultural benefits for Britain. The Government considers that public funding should support the pursuit of basic scientific knowledge, while industry should bear the chief responsibility for the commercial

development of scientific advances.

Science and technology policy is decided collectively by ministers under the leadership of the Prime Minister. The Government is advised by the Chief Scientific Adviser and by an independent Advisory Council on Science and Technology (ACOST). Members of ACOST are industrialists and scientists appointed by the Prime Minister for their personal eminence in their field. There are also two ex officio members: the chairman of the Advisory Board for the Research Councils (ABRC) and the chairman of the Universities Funding Council and the Innovation Advisory Board. The remit of ACOST covers defence as well as civil research, and both academic science and industrial R & D. It advises on national priorities in science and technology, on the application of science and technology, on the co-ordination of science and technology activities and on Britain's participation in international science and technology collaboration.

Responsibility for basic civil science rests with the Secretary of State for Education and Science, who is advised by the ABRC. Responsibility for technology rests mainly with the Secretary of State for Trade and Industry. Other departments with a substantial involvement in science and technology have a departmental advisory body; these bodies work closely with ACOST. A committee of Departmental Chief Scientists, under the chairmanship of the Chief Scientific Adviser, is responsible for co-ordination among departments.

The Centre for Exploitation of Science and Technology (CEST) was set up in 1988. By studying the evolution of markets, it aims to identify the science and technologies needed to improve competitive performance in particular industries. CEST is supported by industry and by the Government.

The Department of Trade and Industry

Although most industrial research and development is financed by industry itself, the Department of Trade and Industry (DTI) provides support where there is a sound case for doing so. Following a review in 1988, the Department moved away from general support for research with a strong commercial emphasis towards collaborative programmes of pre-competitive research, with greater emphasis on encouraging links between industry and the science base, and on technology transfer.

In 1989–90 the DTI spent £310 million on R & D, covering general industrial innovation, aeronautics, space (see p 388) and support for statutory, regulatory and policy responsibilities. A further £90 million was allocated to technology transfer and related activities.

General Industrial Innovation

There are four main schemes of collaborative R & D: LINK, EUREKA (see p 387), Advanced Technology Programmes and Club R & D. They complement the European Community R & D programmes (see p 387).

The LINK scheme encourages collaboration on pre-competitive research between industry and the higher education institutions and research councils. The aim of this is to bridge the gap between scientific research and its resulting commercial applications. Under the scheme the DTI funds up to 50 per cent of the costs. Government funding of £190 million has been committed to 30 LINK programmes, mainly in the areas of biotechnology, advanced materials, advanced manufacturing and electronics.

Advanced Technology Programmes encourage and support pre-competitive research in new technologies. Twelve programmes had been approved by July 1991, in high-temperature superconductivity, marine exploitation and several aspects of electronics and information technology.

Club R & D enables companies, particularly of small and medium size, to benefit from collaborative research in a major research organisation at a subsidised rate. The research is conducted in a host organisation, such as a higher education institution or a research and technology organisation. To encourage research work and innovation in small companies, the DTI runs a competitive scheme called the Small

Firms Merit Award for Research and Technology (SMART). In the 1990 competition 180 awards were announced. Since February 1991 support for small and medium-sized companies has been available under the SPUR (Support for Products under Research) scheme, which encourages development of new products and processes.

Aeronautics

Funding from the DTI supports research and innovation in Britain's aircraft and aeroengine industry, helping it to compete effectively in world markets. Over half of the work supported is conducted in industry and universities, and the remainder in Ministry of Defence establishments. The Civil Aircraft and Aeroengine Research and Demonstration Programme (CARAD) is part of a national aircraft research effort conducted by industry, the Government, research establishments and higher education institutes. In 1989–90 this programme was supported by government funding of £28 million. The DTI is also supporting the European Wind Tunnel project in Cologne, due to be completed by the end of 1992.

Launch Aid is a scheme providing government assistance for specific development projects in the aerospace industry. British Aerospace is currently receiving aid for its participation in the European Airbus Industrie consortium for the A330/340 airliner project.

Research Establishments

The DTI has four research establishments, which accounted for £35 million of the Department's R & D expenditure in 1989–90. Their primary role is to provide the Government with an effective source of scientific and technological expertise. They provide technological services to industry and also undertake research commissioned by industry. The laboratories are also involved in a variety of international activities.

1. The Laboratory of the Government Chemist provides government with a comprehensive service in analytical chemistry

and serves to underpin sound chemical measurement in Britain as part of the National Measurement System (see below). Its Biotechnology Unit takes the lead within government for promoting the industrial development of biotechnology.

2. NEL, the National Engineering Laboratory, carries out R & D in a wide range of engineering and related disciplines and maintains the British standards of flow measurement, of special importance in the oil and gas industries.

3. The National Physical Laboratory is Britain's national standards laboratory and the focus of the National Measurement System. As well as developing and disseminating standards of measurement, it undertakes research on materials standards and information technology.

4. The Warren Spring Laboratory is devoted to research into environmental technology dealing with pollution of air, land and water.

All four laboratories are now executive agencies and the Government has long-term plans to privatise the NEL, as the majority of its work is for the benefit of industry.

Technology Transfer

The DTI has introduced several programmes specifically to encourage technology transfer. They promote the use of best-practice techniques and modern technology as well as exploiting the most recent research. Examples are the Open Systems information technology standards programme and the Materials Matter programme, concerned with modern materials and associated manufacturing methods. Each programme comprises an integrated package of activities which may include seminars, conferences and demonstration activities, as well as the production of case study material and other practical literature.

There are also general technology transfer programmes not related to specific technology areas. For example, in association with the Departments of Education and Science and Employment, the DTI supports 13 Regional Technology Centres. These

assist small and medium-sized enterprises and help to promote the expertise of higher education institutions.

Two new schemes were launched in February 1991 to further support small and medium-sized companies. The Manufacturing Planning and Implementation Studies Programme and the Technical Action Line help companies to plan their use of advanced manufacturing technology and gain access to technical advice.

The Department of Education and Science

The Department of Education and Science discharges its responsibilities for basic and applied civil science mainly through the five research councils (see p 380), to which it allocates funds from its science budget. For 1991–92 this is over £927 million (see Table 22.2).

The allocations provide support for research in the following ways:

● grants and contracts to universities, polytechnics, research units and other research council establishments;

● support for postgraduate study; and

● subscriptions to international scientific organisations.

Table 22.2: Recommended Allocations for Science Budget 1991-92

	£ million
Agricultural and Food Research Council	93·6
Economic and Social Research Council	35·6
Medical Research Council	201·9
Natural Environment Research Council	123·7
Science and Engineering Research Council	454·9
Royal Society	15·7
Fellowship of Engineering	1·4
Advisory Board for the Research Councils	0·4
Centre for Exploitation of Science and Technology	0·1
Total	**927·3**

Source: Department of Education and Science.

The Department is responsible for some aspects of international scientific relations and helps to co-ordinate and implement government policy on scientific and technical information. Together with the Scottish and Welsh education departments, the DTI and the Department of Employment, the DES funds a number of schemes for training full-time students and those working in industry in the latest technology. For example, under the Professional, Industrial and Commercial Updating (PICKUP) initiative, scientists from higher education institutions spend some of their time at 13 Regional Technology Centres (see p 378), training employees of private sector companies in recent developments in their fields.

The Department is also the main source of funding for the universities, whose individual allocations are determined by the Universities Funding Council (see p 383). Until 1990 each university decided on the division of its resources between teaching and research. The overall proportion committed to research was thought to be about 40 per cent. Research funding is now identified separately by the Council.

The Advisory Board for the Research Councils

The Advisory Board for the Research Councils (ABRC) advises the Secretary of State on matters relating to civil science, particularly with regard to the operation of the research council system. The ABRC assesses the resource needs of the research councils and other bodies, and advises on the allocation of the science budget between them. It also advises on the proper balance between national and international scientific activities.

The ABRC promotes effective collaboration between the five research councils, for example, in cases where there is an overlap of scientific subject responsibilities. It also fosters close liaison between the councils and those using their research, including industry and government departments. The Board's membership includes the heads of the research councils and senior scientists from industry and the academic world.

The Ministry of Defence

The expenditure of the Ministry of Defence (MoD) on research and development in 1989–90 was some £2,427 million. About £932 million of this was medium- and long-term applied research relevant to known military needs, much of it carried out in the MoD's defence research establishments. Some £172 million of this research was carried out under contract in industry and the academic sector. The Government is committed to achieving a gradual reduction in real terms in spending on defence research and development in future years. An increasing emphasis is placed on research funded jointly with industry, and initiatives have also been taken to encourage 'spin-off' from defence technology to the civil market.

Examples of technological innovations at research establishments include:

- Royal Aerospace Establishment: reduction in jet engine exhaust noise, which has led to changes in Rolls-Royce's new civil engines.

- Royal Signals and Radar Establishment: pioneering work on liquid crystal displays, now widely used in the civil sector. Development of infra-red detectors now adopted by fire services.

- Admiralty Research Establishment: development of a Multi-function Electronically Scanned Adaptive Radar (MESAR), which can perform the functions of several different radars in one system. This was a joint project with Plessey, now part of GEC.

In 1991 these three non-nuclear research establishments, together with the Royal Armament Research and Development Establishment, merged to become the Defence Research Agency. Its role is to provide scientific and technical services to the MoD and other government departments.

The major part of the Ministry's R & D expenditure (more than £1,298 million in 1989–90) is on the development of individual items of equipment. Most of this takes place in industry, and represents the bulk of government expenditure on R & D in industry.

Other Government Departments

The Department of Energy funds research in support of offshore oil and gas technology, energy efficiency and the development and demonstration of British renewable energy sources. The major part of its R & D is on nuclear energy (£132 million in 1989–90), most of which is carried out by the United Kingdom Atomic Energy Authority.

The Ministry of Agriculture, Fisheries and Food co-ordinates its research programme with the Scottish Office Agriculture and Fisheries Department, the Department of Agriculture for Northern Ireland and the Agricultural and Food Research Council (see p 383). Overall, the Ministry's research has three main objectives: to protect the consumer and the environment; to assist in the formulation and assessment of policy; and to underpin the applied R & D done by the agricultural industry.

The Ministry's wide-ranging responsibilities are reflected in its research activities, which cover land use and conservation, animal welfare, food safety and quality, and conservation of fish stocks. Expenditure in 1989–90 was £112 million, about half of which was in the Ministry's own laboratories and agencies. Most of the rest was in contracts to the Agricultural and Food Research Council.

The Department of the Environment funds research in seven policy areas: environmental protection, including radioactive substances; water; countryside; planning and inner cities; local government; housing; and building and construction. The largest individual sub-programme is on the safe disposal of radioactive waste. An area of research of increasing importance is that of pollution-related climate change. Total research expenditure in 1990–91 was £74 million.

The Department of Health is introducing the first comprehensive R & D strategy for the National Health Service, which will focus on improving methods of health care and achieving a cost-effective use of resources. The Department also manages a Health and Personal Social Services research programme, which is concerned with the needs of ministers and policy-makers, with emphasis on improving efficiency. The Department's Director of Research and Development advises the Secretary of State as required on the research undertaken by non-departmental public bodies for which he is responsible.

The National Computing Centre promotes best practice in software engineering in industry, while the Central Computer and Telecommunications Agency, part of HM Treasury, encourages the establishment of standards of computer compatibility and the best use of information technology in the public sector.

THE RESEARCH COUNCILS

Each of the four research councils engaged in scientific research is an autonomous body established under Royal Charter, with membership drawn from the universities, professions, industry and the Government. They conduct research through their own establishments and by supporting selected research, study and training in universities and other higher education establishments. In addition to funding from the Department of Education and Science (see p 378), they also receive income for research commissioned by departments under the customer–contractor principle and from the private sector. Income from commissioned research is particularly important for the Agricultural and Food Research Council and the Natural Environment Research Council.

Institutions undertaking research with the support of research council grants have the rights and responsibility for the commercial exploitation of that research, subject to prior agreement with the sponsoring research council. Universities and research institutes may make use of the expertise of the British Technology Group (see p 385) to patent and license their inventions, but are not obliged to do so.

Science and Engineering Research Council

The Science and Engineering Research Council (SERC) is responsible for the support of research and postgraduate training in pure and applied science (including engineering) outside the areas of agriculture, medicine and the environment. SERC is the most highly funded of the research councils. Its expenditure in 1989–90 was allocated as follows:

- research grants, chiefly to higher education institutions (£150 million);
- contributions to international organisations (£90 million, see p 387);
- the Council's own establishments (£82 million); and
- funding of postgraduate training (£64 million).

The Council has funded Interdisciplinary Research Centres in fields such as high-temperature superconductivity, engineering design, molecular sciences, high performance materials, and optical and laser-related science and technology. It encourages collaboration between higher education and industry, partly by sponsoring co-ordinated research programmes in areas of special industrial concern.

The SERC maintains four research establishments: the Rutherford Appleton Laboratory at Chilton (Oxfordshire), the Daresbury Laboratory at Warrington (Cheshire), the Royal Greenwich Observatory at Cambridge, and the Royal Observatory, Edinburgh. They are centres of specialised research, providing experimental facilities beyond the resources of individual academic institutions; they also undertake contract research.

SERC research support is organised under four boards, covering science (£123 million in 1989–90); engineering (£111 million); nuclear physics (£76 million); and astronomy and planetary science (£69 million). In recent years the SERC's policy has been to transfer funds from the astronomy and nuclear physics boards, representing largely 'big' science and basic research, to the more general areas of science and engineering, representing largely strategic research on a smaller scale.

Science

The Science Board supports academic research in chemistry, physics, mathematics, the biological sciences and science-based archaeology. Its main priority is the provision of research grants to universities and polytechnics. About 50 per cent of grants are awarded as part of co-ordinated programmes of interdisciplinary strategic research falling within the areas of materials; molecular sciences; and mathematics, computational and cognitive science. They may be part of a LINK programme (see p 377) or associated with an Interdisciplinary Research Centre.

Engineering

The Engineering Board, whose funding has increased greatly in recent years, supports strategic research into the development of advanced technology. It aims to identify promising areas of national importance and initiates co-ordinated programmes of research which will benefit British industry. Some of the areas identified for priority action are training, computer software research, materials research, supercomputing in engineering and biotechnology (where a special directorate funded jointly with the Science Board is in operation).

The Teaching Company Scheme is jointly sponsored by the SERC and the DTI, with contributions from the Northern Ireland Department of Economic Development and the Economic and Social Research Council. The scheme supports some 380 collaborative ventures between academic engineering departments and industrial companies, to improve their manufacturing and management methods.

Nuclear Physics

The Nuclear Physics Board supports particle physics and nuclear structure physics. The Rutherford Appleton Laboratory co-ordinates

Britain's experimental particle physics research programme and links university researchers with overseas centres such as CERN (see p 387). The laboratory's spallation neutron source (called 'ISIS') is the world's leading pulsed neutron facility. The nuclear structure physics programme is concentrated largely at the Daresbury laboratory, which has a 20-million volt tandem accelerator. The laboratory operates a synchrotron radiation facility which provides high-intensity X-ray and ultraviolet radiation used in a wide range of experiments in protein crystallography, surface physics, chemical structure and materials science.

Astronomy and Planetary Science

The Astronomy and Planetary Science Board supports space science, including contributions to international programmes (see p 000), ground-based astronomy and geophysics. In optical astronomy the SERC is a principal partner in the international observatory on the island of La Palma in the Canary Islands. The observatory's four telescopes include the 4·2-m William Herschel. Opened in 1987, it is the third largest single-mirror optical telescope in the world. On Mauna Kea, Hawaii, the SERC has a 3·8-m infra-red telescope, the largest telescope in the world designed specifically for infra-red observations, and the 15-m James Clerk Maxwell radio telescope (built in collaboration with the Netherlands and Canada). Such telescopes have proved invaluable to scientists researching into the creation of the universe.

Medical Research Council

The Medical Research Council (MRC) is the main government agency for the support of biomedical research. Some three-quarters of its budget is used to fund research projects at its own centres and units; it also allocates grants to research workers at higher education institutions and hospitals. The MRC's major research establishments are the National Institute for Medical Research at Mill Hill, London; the Clinical Research Centre at Northwick Park Hospital, London;

and the Laboratory of Molecular Biology at Cambridge. The Council has more than 50 other research units, located in universities and medical schools throughout Britain.

Four Interdisciplinary Research Centres are being set up, in toxicology, molecular medicine, protein engineering and cell biology. Two more are planned, in brain and behaviour and brain repair.

The MRC's scientists and doctors have pioneered developments in molecular biology, therapeutic clinical trials, applied psychology, and methods of imaging the body such as magnetic resonance and ultrasound. The Council's larger research programmes include psychiatric and neurological (including Alzheimer's) disease, heart and respiratory ailments, infectious diseases, tropical medicine, and antenatal screening for cystic fibrosis and muscular dystrophy.

Major new projects are:

- specially funded work on AIDS;
- research on vaccines against meningitis and whooping cough; and
- the mapping of the human genome, the complete sequence of genes in a human cell.

Research is also continuing into the use of monoclonal antibodies in transplant operations.

The Council's policy is to foster collaboration between its establishments and industry in order to promote the transfer of skills and technologies, the exploitation of Council discoveries, and the development of new health care products.

Natural Environment Research Council

The Natural Environment Research Council (NERC) seeks to advance understanding of the biological, physical and chemical processes of the planet, and how the natural environment is changing, either by natural causes or through human activities.

In 1991–92 about 75 per cent of NERC's funds are from the science budget, and about 25 per cent from commissioned work for public authorities and industry in Britain and overseas.

The Council supports research and training in over 14 NERC Institutes and research units and in universities and polytechnics. NERC Institutes include the British Geological Survey, the Institute of Terrestrial Ecology, the Institute of Oceanographic Sciences Deacon Laboratory, and the British Antarctic Survey.

NERC conducts local and regional research in Britain and in other countries, while also participating in major international environmental projects. Examples of NERC research and new developments include:

- a comprehensive geological survey of Britain's inner continental shelf completed by the British Geological Survey. Britain is the first country in the world to complete such a survey;

- the NERC Biogeochemical Ocean Flux Study, which examines how carbon dioxide is absorbed by the oceans and buried in the sea floor sediments, helping to balance the 'greenhouse effect'; and

- participation by scientists at the Institute of Terrestrial Ecology in a major new Countryside Survey of Britain, using satellite and field information.

Applied projects in progress overseas include initiatives in biological pest control; regeneration of tropical hardwoods; drip irrigation techniques for tropical crops; and surveys of potential resources.

In 1991 NERC opened the James Rennell Centre in Southampton to act as a focus for Britain's contributions to the World Ocean Circulation Experiment, which investigates the vital role of the oceans in controlling climate.

In the same year NERC also opened an Interdisciplinary Research Centre for population biology at Imperial College, Silwood Park, Berkshire. The centre includes a series of 16 computer-controlled environmental chambers which provide suitable living conditions for small communities of plants and animals. This will aid research into ecology and population interactions.

Several computer-based environmental data centres have been established at NERC sites, providing an information and advisory service for a wide range of users.

Agricultural and Food Research Council

The Agricultural and Food Research Council (AFRC) supports research underpinning agriculture, food and the biologically based industries. The Council's main research areas include animal health, animal physiology and genetics, food safety and quality, diet and health, agricultural engineering, grassland and the environmental aspects of agriculture. Work is carried out at seven AFRC institutes, at Horticulture Research International and in higher education institutions. The AFRC also offers scientific advice to the Scottish Agricultural Research Institutes, funded by the Scottish Office Agriculture and Fisheries Department. The Council plans to increase its support for higher education institutions over the next five years to about 30 per cent of its science budget funding.

The AFRC at present draws almost two-thirds of its funding from the science budget, about a quarter from the Ministry of Agriculture, Fisheries and Food for commissioned research, and an increasing proportion from industry. The Council aims to raise 25 per cent of its institute funding from commercial and other sources by 1994–95.

Recent research conducted by the AFRC has demonstrated the link between bovine spongiform encephalopathy and the disease scrapie in sheep. New, rapid methods have been designed to detect food poisoning organisms. Promising research is being conducted into 'anti-sense' genes in plants, which can block unwanted genetic changes. The anti-sense genes could stop leaf-drop in crop plants, or delay the ripening process in fruit, prolonging the storage period.

UNIVERSITY RESEARCH

About half the research carried out in universities is financed from resources allocated by the Universities Funding

Council. These funds contribute to the cost of academic staff—who teach as well as carry out research—and provide for support staff, administration, equipment and accommodation. The research councils also support scientific research in the universities and other institutions of higher education, in two ways. First, they allocate maintenance awards to over a quarter of postgraduate students in science and technology. Secondly, they give grants and contracts to the universities and other institutions for specified projects, particularly in new or developing areas of research.

From August 1992 the research councils will be responsible for meeting in full the research costs of the projects they support in universities and polytechnics. The higher education institutions will, however, continue to provide the salaries of academic staff and meet other costs, such as the upkeep of premises.

The other main channels of support for scientific research in the universities are various government departments, the Royal Society, industry and the independent foundations. Universities are encouraged to recover the full cost of research from these foundations. They are also encouraged to direct their resources into those areas where they have existing research strength, or where they may contribute to new and promising spheres of science and technology.

Increasingly, close relationships are being fostered between the universities, industry and the Government in numerous joint projects. British universities' earnings from industry and other outside agencies are rising rapidly and amounted to some £915 million in 1989–90. The money comes from a range of sources, including research grants and contracts and services to industry. Many universities now operate industrial liaison service units.

The universities sector has produced a number of recent technological breakthroughs. At Heriot-Watt University in Edinburgh, researchers have developed optoelectronic devices for future super-fast optical computers. A further innovation announced in 1991 has been the production of an electronic video camera on a single silicon chip less than 10 mm square. This could lead to the development of video telephones, allowing people to see the caller at the end of the line. At the universities of Cambridge and Essex, scientists are pioneering techniques for the active cancellation of unwanted sound and other vibrations. Important research on optical fibres is being carried out at Southampton, Exeter and Essex universities, and on pharmaceutical products and biotechnology at Strathclyde.

Science Parks

Science parks were designed to promote closer links between industry and university research departments. By mid-1991 there were 39 such parks in operation, at or near universities, providing accommodation for around 1,000 companies. Most of these companies are involved in computing, electronics, instrumentation, robotics, electrical engineering, chemicals and biotechnology. Research, development and training activities are emphasised, rather than large-scale manufacturing.

OTHER ORGANISATIONS

Charitable Foundations

Charitable foundations sponsoring research in Britain include the Cancer Research Campaign, the Imperial Cancer Research Fund, the Wellcome Trust and the Nuffield Foundation. In 1990 the largest spenders on medical research were the Imperial Cancer Research Fund at £50·4 million and the Wellcome Trust at £47·2 million.

Industrial Research Organisations

In Britain there are over 40 independent companies which undertake research contracts and provide consultancy and training services for a wide range of industrial companies. Between them they employ over 9,000 people and had a turnover in 1990 of £300 million. The companies are linked by the Cambridge-based Association of Independent Research and Technology Organisations.

British Technology Group

British Technology Group (BTG) promotes the development of new technology into commercial products, particularly where the technology originates from public sector sources, such as universities, polytechnics, research councils and government research establishments. It offers to take responsibility for protecting and licensing inventions from these sources, provides funds for development, seeks licensees and negotiates licence agreements with industry.

BTG provides finance to British industry to encourage innovation, most commonly through equity or project finance. The latter offers companies up to 50 per cent of their development costs. The Group also helps companies to negotiate licences overseas for their inventions. BTG expects to recover its investment by means of a percentage levy on sales of the resulting product or process.

At present, BTG is involved with 1,672 inventions, some 700 of which are at universities and other public sector institutions. In 1990–91 the Group's income exceeded £30 million. Legislation to privatise BTG is before Parliament.

Professional Institutions and Learned Societies

There are numerous technical institutions and professional associations in Britain, many of which promote their own disciplines or are interested in the education and professional well-being of their members.

More than 300 learned societies play an important part in the promotion of science and technology through meetings, publications and sponsorship.

The Council of Science and Technology Institutes has seven member institutes representing biology, chemical engineering, chemistry, food science and technology, geology, hospital physics and physics.

The Engineering Council, established in 1981, promotes the study of all types of engineering in schools and other organisations, in co-operation with its 260 industrial affiliates. These include large private sector companies and government departments. Together with 47 professional engineering institutions, the Council accredits courses in higher education institutions. It also advises the Government on a range of academic, industrial and professional issues.

The national academy of engineering in Britain is the Fellowship of Engineering, set up in 1976. It promotes the discipline and advises the Government on related policy issues. Its membership consists of distinguished engineers.

The Royal Society

The most prestigious learned society is The Royal Society, or, more fully, The Royal Society of London for Improving Natural Knowledge, founded in 1660. The Society has over 1,000 Fellows, many of whom serve on the governmental advisory councils and committees concerned with research. It administers a grant-in-aid from the Department of Education and Science (£15·7 million in 1991–92) which represents some 75 per cent of its annual expenditure. The remainder is derived from private funds.

The Royal Society encourages scientific research and its application through a programme of meetings and lectures, its publications, and through the award of grants, fellowships and other funding. It recognises scientific and technological achievements through election to the Fellowship and the award of medals and endowed lectureships. As the national academy of sciences, it represents Britain in a number of international non-governmental organisations and is involved in a variety of international scientific programmes. It also facilitates collaborative projects and the exchange of scientists through bilateral agreements with academies and research councils throughout the world. It provides independent advice on scientific matters, notably to government, and represents and supports the scientific community as a whole. The Society is increasingly active in promoting science understanding and awareness in the public, and also science education. It also supports research into the history of scientific endeavour.

Other Societies

In Scotland the Royal Society of Edinburgh, established in 1783, promotes science through scholarships, the organisation of meetings and symposia, the publication of journals and the award of prizes. The Society also administers various fellowship schemes for post-doctoral research workers.

Three other major institutions publicise scientific developments through lectures and publications for specialists and for schoolchildren. Of these, the British Association for the Advancement of Science, founded in 1831, is mainly concerned with science, while the Royal Society of Arts, dating from 1754, deals with the arts and commerce as well as science. The Royal Institution, founded in 1799, also performs these functions and runs its own research laboratories.

Zoological Gardens

The Zoological Society of London, an independent scientific body, runs the world-famous London Zoo, which occupies some 15 hectares (36 acres) of Regent's Park, London. The zoo has successfully operated a captive breeding programme to conserve some of the world's most endangered animals, such as Brazilian golden lion tamarins. The Society is responsible for the Institute of Zoology, which carries out research in conservation and comparative medicine. It also organises scientific meetings and symposia, and publishes scientific journals.

Whipsnade Wild Animal Park near Dunstable (Bedfordshire) is also run by the Society. Other well-known zoos include those at Edinburgh, Bristol, Chester, Dudley and Marwell (near Winchester).

Botanical Gardens

The Royal Botanic Gardens, founded in 1759, cover 121 hectares (300 acres) at Kew in west London and a 187-hectare (462-acre) estate at Wakehurst Place, Ardingly, in West Sussex. They contain the largest collections of living and dried plants in the world. Research is conducted into all aspects of plant life, including physiology, biochemistry, genetics, economic botany and the conservation of habitats and species. Kew also has the world's largest seed bank for wild origin species and is active in programmes to return endangered plant species to the wild. It participates in joint research programmes in 52 countries.

The Royal Botanic Garden in Edinburgh, founded in 1670, is a centre for research into taxonomy, for the conservation and study of living plants and for horticultural education.

Scientific Museums

The Natural History Museum, which now includes the Geological Museum, has some 60 million specimens ranging in size from a blue whale skeleton to minute insects. It is one of the world's principal centres for research into natural history, offering an advisory service to institutions all over the world. The museum is keen to promote public appreciation of nature conservation and in 1991 opened a major exhibition on ecology, illustrating the diversity of living species.

The Science Museum promotes understanding of the history of science, technology, industry and medicine. Its extensive collection of scientific instruments and machinery is complemented by interactive computer games and audio-visual equipment for visitors to use. In this way the museum explains scientific principles to the public and documents the history of science, from early discoveries to space age technology.

These two museums are in South Kensington, London. Other important collections include the Museum of Science and Industry in Birmingham, the Museum of the History of Science at Oxford, and the Royal Scottish Museum, Edinburgh.

INTERNATIONAL SCIENTIFIC RELATIONS

European Community

Since 1984 the European Community has run a series of R & D Framework Programmes in a number of strategic sectors, with the aim of strengthening the international competitiveness of European industry. The Third Framework Programme runs from 1990–94, with a European Community budget of £4,200 million. It overlaps with the Second Framework Programme (1987–91) and covers the following broad categories:

- information and communication technologies;
- industrial and material technologies;
- the environment;
- life sciences and technologies;
- energy; and
- human capital and mobility.

Overall, British organisations—research organisations, companies and higher education institutions—have performed well, securing some 20 per cent of the total funding available. This is broadly equal to Britain's contribution to the R & D budget of the European Community.

Britain hosts the Joint European Torus nuclear fusion project (JET), which is based at Culham, Oxfordshire.

Non-EC Activities

EUREKA is a scheme to encourage European co-operation in the development and production of high-technology products with worldwide sales potential. There are currently 385 approved EUREKA projects, involving an estimated total investment of £5,000 million. British companies are participating in 100 of these, 28 of which are British-led. The members of EUREKA are the 12 countries of the European Community, the six countries of the European Free Trade Association, Turkey and the European Commission.

COST (European Co-operation in the Field of Scientific and Technical Research) encourages the co-operation of national research activities. There are currently 19 member states: the 12 countries of the European Community, Austria, Finland, Norway, Sweden, Switzerland, Turkey and Yugoslavia. British organisations are involved in 35 out of 46 projects.

Britain is a member of the European Organisation for Nuclear Research (CERN) in Geneva. Britain's contributions to CERN, to the high-flux neutron source at the Institut Laue-Langevin and to the European Synchrotron Radiation Facility, both at Grenoble, are paid through the SERC. The SERC is also a partner in the European Incoherent Scatter radar facilities in northern Scandinavia, which are used for atmospheric research. Through the NERC, Britain is a member of the Ocean Drilling Program led by the United States, and of the World Ocean Circulation Experiment, which aims to discover how the oceans help to control the Earth's climate. Through the MRC, Britain participates in the European Molecular Biology Organisation.

Britain is also a member of the science and technology committees of international organisations such as the Organisation for Economic Co-operation and Development and the North Atlantic Treaty Organisation, and various specialised agencies of the United Nations.

Britain has concluded a number of inter-governmental and inter-agency agreements with other countries for co-operation in science and technology. Among non-governmental organisations, the five research councils, the Royal Society and the British Academy were founder members of the European Science Foundation in 1974. The research councils also maintain a joint office in Brussels to further European co-operation in research.

Staff in British Embassies and High Commissions promote contacts in science and technology between Britain and the countries in which they are accredited. The British Council promotes better understanding and knowledge of Britain and its scientific and technological achievements. It encourages exchanges of specialists, provides specialised information, and fosters co-operation in research, training and education. The Council also identifies and manages technological, scientific and educational projects in the developing countries. Many British companies are involved in commercial co-operative research projects with overseas manufacturers.

Space Activities

Britain's involvement in civil space research is co-ordinated by the British National Space Centre (BNSC), which is a partnership between various government departments and research councils. Through BNSC, Britain spent some £150 million on space activities in 1990–91, financed mainly by the DTI and the SERC. Of this over 60 per cent was devoted to programmes shared with the European Space Agency (ESA). The remainder supported a programme of research and development in government establishments, universities and industry.

A major part of Britain's space programme is concerned with earth observation, or remote sensing. Britain has committed around £70 million to the ESA's satellite ERS-1, launched in July 1991, which is designed to provide all-weather, 24-hour coverage of the Earth. Britain has provided the main active microwave instrument for ERS-1, along with a precision instrument to measure thermal infra-red emissions from the sea surface. A £30 million Earth Observation Data Centre was opened in 1991 at Farnborough, Hampshire, to process the data output from ERS satellites and distribute it to scientists and commercial users.

Britain is also contributing some £250 million to the Columbus programme, Europe's contribution to the United States-led International Space Station project. Britain is playing a major role in developing the polar-orbiting platform and key instruments for the Columbus project.

In space science, British groups have been involved with almost all of the ESA's missions, including the investigation of Halley's Comet by the British-built Giotto spacecraft, the International Ultraviolet Explorer, the Hipparcos star-mapping mission and the Ulysses solar polar probe. Britain is contributing substantially to the Cluster and SOHO missions to be launched in 1995 to study the Sun, the Earth's magnetosphere and the solar wind. It is also expected that Britain will participate in the ESA's X-ray spectroscopy mission due for launch in 1998.

Britain has bilateral arrangements for space research with other countries, notably the United States through its National Aeronautics and Space Administration (NASA), the Soviet Union and the People's Republic of China. British groups have participated in several NASA space science missions, and have developed instruments for NASA's Hubble Space Telescope. Other collaborations include the development of the wide-field camera for Germany's X-ray satellite ROSAT and the X-ray sensor for the Japanese-built Ginga satellite.

In satellite communications Britain has collaborated with the ESA in such programmes as Olympus, DRTM and ASTP-4, with the aim of encouraging the use and development of new services and research concepts.

In May 1991 Britain's first astronaut, Helen Sharman, participated in a mission of the Soviet Mir space station (a private sector venture), during which she performed a number of scientific experiments in orbit.

23 Promotion of the Arts

Artistic and cultural activity in Britain ranges from the highest professional standards to the enthusiastic support and participation of amateurs. London is one of the leading world centres for drama, music, opera and dance, and festivals held in towns and cities throughout the country attract much interest. Many British playwrights, composers, film-makers, sculptors, painters, writers, actors, singers, choreographers and dancers enjoy international reputations. Television and radio bring a wide range of artistic events to a large audience. Arts activities introduced and developed by the ethnic minorities are also thriving. At an amateur level, numerous choral, orchestral, operatic, dramatic and other societies for the arts make use of local talent and resources.

Policies

The Government's policies for the arts aim to develop a high standard of artistic and cultural activity throughout Britain; to encourage innovation and scholarship; and to promote public access to, and appreciation of, the arts and the cultural heritage. This is achieved through providing funds and advice, and expanding total resources by encouraging partnership with the private sector, including business sponsorship. National museums and galleries are encouraged and given an incentive to increase their resources, for example, through trading and other activities which, in 1991–92, will provide an estimated £46 million. An important concept in funding policy is the 'arm's length' principle, by which government funds are distributed to arts organisations indirectly, through bodies such as the Arts Councils and the British Film Institute; this helps safeguard against political interference in the arts.

Administration

Promotion and patronage of the arts are the concern of both official and unofficial bodies. The Government and local authorities play an active part, and a substantial amount of help comes from private sources, including trusts and commercial concerns.

The Minister for the Arts is responsible for general arts policy and heads the Office of Arts and Libraries, which administers government expenditure on national museums and art galleries in England, the Arts Council, the British Library and other national arts and heritage bodies. English Heritage (the Historic Buildings and Monuments Commission for England) manages some 400 ancient monuments and historic buildings on behalf of the Department of the Environment. The regulation of the film industry and of broadcasting is conducted by the Department of Trade and Industry and the Home Office respectively. The Secretaries of State for Wales, Scotland and Northern Ireland are responsible for the national museums, galleries and libraries in their countries, and for other cultural matters.

Local authorities maintain more than 1,000 local museums and art galleries and some 4,000 public libraries in England. They also support many arts organisations and artistic events in their areas, providing grant aid for professional and voluntary organisations, including orchestras and theatre, opera and dance companies. They undertake direct promotions through local arts councils and contribute to the cost of new or converted buildings for the arts. In England this support is estimated to be over £100 million a year. Arts education in schools, colleges, polytechnics, evening institutes and community centres is the responsibility of central government education departments, in partnership with local education authorities and voluntary bodies.

Finance

Since 1988 the Government has set the arts budget for a three-year period in order to give recipient arts bodies a firm basis on which to plan future activities and to encourage greater self-reliance and diversification in their sources of funding. It considers that this strategy has proved successful in encouraging arts bodies to match their plans to a realistic view of the total resources likely to be available. The three-year settlement applies to the larger part of the central government arts programme. Planned central government expenditure through the Office of Arts and Libraries amounts to £559 million in 1991–92. About 35 per cent is spent on 11 national galleries and museums in England, with 40 per cent channelled through the Arts Council to support the performing and visual arts throughout England, Scotland and Wales; about 11 per cent goes to the British Library. Grants are also made to the British Film Institute, the Crafts Council, certain other museums and arts bodies, and to the National Heritage Memorial Fund. The Fund helps organisations wishing to acquire, for the public benefit, land, buildings, works of art and other objects associated with the national heritage.

Industrial and commercial concerns offer vital sponsorship and patronage to a wide range of arts, including exhibitions, concerts and opera seasons. The Business Sponsorship Incentive Scheme was launched by the Office of Arts and Libraries in co-operation with the Association for Business Sponsorship of the Arts (ABSA) in Great Britain in 1984, with the aim of raising the overall level of business sponsorship. (A similar scheme was set up in Northern Ireland in 1987.) Since its inception the Scheme has attracted nearly £40 million of new money and over 1,700 sponsors into the arts. An estimated 70 per cent of the awards have been made to arts organisations outside London. ABSA is also participating in UK Charity Lotteries, a venture launched in February 1991 designed to benefit 200 charities, among them many arts organisations.

In 1990–91 the Scheme made available £3·5 million to match new sponsorships. Further support is encouraged by tax concessions which allow companies and individuals to obtain tax relief on donations to arts charities. For example, under the Gift Aid scheme, announced in 1990, single gifts of between £600 and £5 million in any one year qualify for tax relief.

In 1991–92 the Arts Council is creating an Enhancement Fund, with the aim of strengthening leading arts organisations and enhancing standards. It is setting aside £22·5 million for schemes in England, Scotland and Wales in the period 1991–92 to 1993–94, and is seeking matching contributions.

The Foundation for Sport and the Arts was set up in 1991 by the Pool Promoters Association, with grants expected to total £60 million a year. About two-thirds of the revenue will be used to benefit sport and the remainder will benefit the arts.

Arts Councils

The independent Arts Council of Great Britain, established in 1946, is the main channel for government aid to the performing and visual arts. Its chief aims are to improve the knowledge, understanding and practice of the performing and visual arts, increase their accessibility to the public, and advise and co-operate with government departments, local authorities and other organisations. The Council gives financial help and advice to organisations ranging from the major opera, dance and drama companies; orchestras and festivals; to small touring theatres and experimental groups.

It also trains arts administrators and helps arts organisations to develop other sources of income. It encourages contemporary dance, mime, jazz, literature, photography and art films, and helps professional creative writers, choreographers, composers, artists and photographers through a variety of schemes. It also promotes art exhibitions and tours and makes funds available for some specialist training courses in the arts. The Council has allocated £2 million a year from 1988–89 to 1991–92 for increased touring to help widen access to the arts. Emphasis is being placed on obtaining funds through partnership arrangements with local authorities and other agencies, and from commercial sources.

Organisations in Scotland and Wales receive their subsidies through the Scottish and Welsh Arts Councils, which are committees of the Arts Council of Great Britain with a large measure of autonomy. Northern Ireland has an independent Arts Council with aims and functions similar to those of the Arts Council of Great Britain.

Developments

Government plans to change the structure of arts funding in England will take effect from April 1993. These changes will strengthen the policy-making role of the Arts Council and involve a major shift in direct funding responsibilities from the Council to ten regional arts boards (see below). The Council will retain the funding of the four national companies—the Royal Opera House, the English National Opera, the Royal Shakespeare Company and the Royal National Theatre—and a number of other national centres of excellence, and will retain responsibility for touring, broadcasting, research, education and training. The Council is preparing a national arts strategy, due for completion in mid-1992.

Local Arts Councils

Local arts councils in towns and communities throughout Britain, some of them founded and supported by local authorities, aim to develop and co-ordinate arts activities in their localities. Industrial and commercial interests also give financial help.

Regional Arts Boards

Regional development of the arts is currently promoted by 12 regional arts associations in England and three in Wales. They bring together all those in a region, from local authorities and private sector companies to local artists, with an interest in improving the artistic life of their area. The associations offer financial assistance to artists and arts organisations, and advise on, and in some cases promote, activities. They are financed mainly by the Arts Council, with smaller sums from the British Film Institute, the Crafts Council and local authorities, and these interests are represented on their governing bodies. Business sponsorship is also an increasingly important source of regional funds.

From October 1991 these associations will become incorporated as ten regional arts boards, each with its own chair. The boards will be subject to a greater financial accountability through a system of forward planning and budgeting, under the direction of the Arts Council.

Arts of Minority Communities

A wide range of arts activities is undertaken by Britain's diverse communities, embracing both the traditional and new forms of artistic expression. In its support for cultural equity the Arts Council has, over the last five years, devoted particular attention to black and Asian dance and drama. It has expanded its training schemes to include arts administration and technical skills. The Commonwealth Institute arranges a varied programme of artistic events, and the Minorities Arts Advisory Service is an independent organisation which provides advice and information on, and training in, the arts of these communities.

Arts Centres

More than 250 arts centres in Britain provide opportunities for enjoyment of and participation in a range of activities in both the performing and visual arts, with educational projects becoming increasingly important. Nearly all are professionally managed and most are supported by volunteer groups. About 70 per cent of all arts centres are converted buildings, including former churches, warehouses,

391

schools, town halls and private houses. Nearly 90 per cent arrange holiday programmes for young people. The centres are assisted mainly by regional arts boards and local authorities, while the Arts Council funds two large centres in London—the South Bank Centre and the Institute of Contemporary Arts. Many theatres and art galleries also provide a focal point for the community by making available facilities for other arts.

British Council

The British Council promotes a knowledge of British culture overseas and maintains libraries in many of the 90 countries in which it is represented. The Council initiates or supports overseas tours by British theatre companies, orchestras, choirs, opera and dance companies, and jazz, rock and folk groups, as well as by individual actors, musicians and artists. It also arranges for directors, designers, choreographers and conductors to work with overseas companies, orchestras and choirs. The Council organises and supports fine arts and other exhibitions overseas as well as British participation in international exhibitions and film festivals. It also maintains film libraries in many of the countries in which it works, and encourages professional interchange between Britain and other countries in all cultural fields.

Visiting Arts Office

The Visiting Arts Office, an autonomous body administered by the British Council, promotes foreign arts in Britain. It provides a clearing house for British and overseas arts organisations, advises on touring matters and makes awards for projects.

Broadcasting Organisations

Both BBC radio and television and the independent companies broadcast a wide variety of drama (including adaptations of novels and stage plays), opera, ballet, and music; and general arts magazine programmes and documentaries. These have won many international awards at festivals such as the Prix Italia and Montreux International Television Festivals. Independent television companies also make grants for arts promotion in their regions.

The BBC has six orchestras which employ many of Britain's full-time professional musicians. Each week it broadcasts about 100 hours of classical and other music (both live and recorded) on its Radio 3 channel. A large part of the output of Radios 1 and 2 and of many independent local radio stations is popular and light music. The BBC regularly commissions new music, particularly by British composers, and sponsors concerts, competitions and festivals. Each summer it presents and broadcasts the BBC Promenade Concerts at the Royal Albert Hall.

Festivals

Some 650 professional arts festivals take place in Britain each year. The Edinburgh International Festival, featuring a wide range of arts, is the largest of its kind in the world. Other annual festivals held in the Scottish capital include International Folk and Jazz Festivals and the Film and Television Festival, while the Mayfest, the second largest festival in Britain, takes place in Glasgow. Some well-known festivals concentrating on music are the Three Choirs Festival, which has taken place annually for 260 years in Gloucester, Worcester or Hereford; the Cheltenham Festival, largely devoted to contemporary British music; and the Aldeburgh and Bath festivals. Among others catering for a number of art forms are the Royal National Eisteddfod of Wales, the Llangollen International Musical Eisteddfod, the National Gaelic Mod in Scotland, and the festivals in Belfast, Brighton, Buxton, Chichester, Harrogate, Malvern, Pitlochry, Salisbury, Windsor and York.

DRAMA

Professional Theatre

Britain is one of the world's major centres for theatre, and has a long and rich dramatic tradition. There are many companies based in London and other major cities and towns, as well as numerous touring companies which visit theatres, festivals and other venues throughout Britain, including arts and sports centres and social clubs. There are 64 companies in receipt of subsidies from the Arts Council; 27 of these are touring companies. Contemporary British playwrights who have received international recognition include Harold Pinter, Tom Stoppard, Alan Ayckbourn, Caryl Churchill, Alan Bennett, Peter Shaffer and David Hare. The musicals of Andrew Lloyd Webber have been highly successful both in Britain and overseas. Among the best-known directors are Sir Peter Hall, Trevor Nunn, Adrian Noble, Richard Eyre, Jonathan Miller, Terry Hands and Deborah Warner, while the many British performers who enjoy international reputations include Sir John Gielgud, Sir Alec Guinness, Vanessa Redgrave, Sir Ian McKellen, Derek Jacobi, Jeremy Irons, Albert Finney, Dame Judi Dench, Glenda Jackson and Diana Rigg. British stage designers such as John Bury, Ralph Koltai and Carl Toms are internationally recognised.

'West End' theatre attendances exceeded 11 million in 1990.

Britain has about 300 theatres intended for professional use which can seat between 200 and 2,300 people. Some are privately owned, but most are owned either municipally or by non-profit-distributing organisations. Over 30 of these house resident theatre companies receiving subsidies from the Arts Council. London is the main focus, with about 100 West End and suburban theatres, 15 of them permanently occupied by subsidised companies. These include the Royal National Theatre, which stages a wide range of modern and classical plays in its three auditoriums in the South Bank Centre; the Royal Shakespeare Company, which presents plays mainly by Shakespeare and his contemporaries, as well as modern work, both in Stratford-upon-Avon and in its two auditoriums in the City's Barbican Centre; and the English Stage Company at the Royal Court Theatre, which stages the work of

many talented new playwrights.

In 1989 the partial remains of the Globe Theatre, where Shakespeare acted, were excavated on the south bank of the Thames in central London; it has since been listed as an ancient monument. A modern reconstruction of the Globe Theatre, on its original site, is in progress. This is planned to open in 1992, at the cost of £18 million.

Regional Theatres

Outside London most cities and many large towns have at least one theatre; some, like the Theatre Royal, Newcastle upon Tyne, date from the eighteenth century and have been handsomely restored. Others, like the West Yorkshire Playhouse, Leeds, and the Theatre Royal, Plymouth, have been built to the latest designs. Several universities have theatres which house professional companies playing to the general public. Most regional repertory companies mount about eight to ten productions a year; several have studio theatres in addition to the main auditorium, where they present new or experimental drama and plays of specialist interest. Repertory theatres also often function as a social centre by offering concerts, poetry readings and exhibitions, and by providing restaurants, bars and theatre shops. Successful productions from regional theatre companies often transfer to London's West End, while the largest regional theatres receive visits from the Royal National Theatre or the Royal Shakespeare Company. The English Shakespeare Company, a recently formed classical company, tours worldwide.

Theatre for Young People

A number of companies provide theatre for young audiences. Unicorn Theatre for Children and Polka Children's Theatre, both in London, present plays specially written for young people; and the Whirligig Theatre tours throughout Britain. The Young Vic Company in London and Contact Theatre Company in Manchester stage plays for young people. Numerous Theatre-in-Education companies perform in schools for all age ranges and abilities. Some of these companies operate independently—Theatre Centre, for example, plays in London and tours further afield. Others are attached to regional repertory theatres such as the Belgrade in Coventry and the West Yorkshire Playhouse in Leeds. Most regional repertory theatres also mount occasional productions for younger audiences, and concessionary ticket prices are generally available for those at school, college or university. There are also a number of puppet companies.

There has been a marked growth in youth theatres, which number more than 500 in England alone; both the National Youth Theatre in London and the Scottish Youth Theatre in Glasgow offer early acting opportunities to young people.

Dramatic Training

Training for actors, directors, lighting and sound technicians, and stage managers is provided mainly in drama schools. Among the best known are the Royal Academy of Dramatic Art, the Central School of Speech and Drama, the London Academy of Music and Dramatic Art, and the Drama Centre (all in London); the Bristol Old Vic School, the Royal Scottish Academy of Music and Drama (Glasgow) and the Manchester Polytechnic School of Drama. Theatre design courses, often based in art schools, are available for people wanting to train as stage designers. A number of universities, polytechnics and other colleges offer degree courses in drama.

Amateur Theatre

There are several thousand amateur dramatic societies throughout Britain. Their work is encouraged by a number of organisations, such as the Central Council for Amateur Theatre, the National Drama Conference, the Scottish Community Drama Association and the Association of Ulster Drama Festivals. Amateur companies sometimes receive financial support from local government, regional arts boards and other bodies.

MUSIC, OPERA AND DANCE

A wide range of musical interests is catered for in Britain, ranging from classical music to rock and pop music, the latter being extremely popular, especially among younger people. Folk music, jazz, light music and brass band music also have substantial followings.

Music

Orchestral and Choral

Seasons of orchestral and choral concerts are promoted every year in many large towns and cities. The principal concert-halls in central London are the Royal Festival Hall in the South Bank Centre, next to which are the Queen Elizabeth Hall and the Purcell Room, which accommodate smaller-scale performances; the Barbican Hall (part of the Barbican Centre for Arts and Conferences); the Royal Albert Hall; the Wigmore Hall, a recital centre; and St John's, Smith Square. A major new concert venue, the Symphony Hall, opened in Birmingham in April 1991.

The leading symphony orchestras are the London Philharmonic, the London Symphony, the Philharmonia, the Royal Philharmonic, the BBC Symphony, the Royal Liverpool Philharmonic, the Hallé (Manchester), the City of Birmingham Symphony, the Bournemouth Symphony, and the Ulster and the Royal Scottish Orchestras. The BBC's six orchestras provide broadcast concerts which are often open to the public. There are also chamber orchestras such as the English Chamber Orchestra, the Academy of St Martin-in-the-Fields, the Bournemouth Sinfonietta, the Northern Sinfonia (Newcastle upon Tyne), and the Scottish Chamber Orchestra. Specialised ensembles include the Orchestra of the Age of Enlightenment, the English Baroque Soloists and the English Concert. The London Sinfonietta and the Birmingham Contemporary Music Group specialise in performing contemporary music.

British conductors such as Sir Colin Davis, Sir Neville Marriner, Simon Rattle, Andrew Davis, Jane Glover and Jeffrey Tate reach a wide audience through their recordings as well as by their performances. The works of living composers such as Sir Michael Tippett, Sir Peter Maxwell Davies and Sir Harrison Birtwistle enjoy international acclaim. Younger composers include George Benjamin, Oliver Knussen, Colin Matthews, Nigel Osborne and Robert Saxton. The Master of the Queen's Music, Malcolm Williamson, holds an office within the Royal Household with responsibility for organising and writing music for state occasions. Percussionist Evelyn Glennie and violinist Nigel Kennedy are among solo performers currently enjoying great acclaim.

The principal choral societies include the Bach Choir, the Brighton Festival Chorus, the Royal Choral Society, the Huddersfield Choral Society, the Cardiff Polyphonic Choir, the Edinburgh International Festival Chorus and the Belfast Philharmonic Society. Almost all the leading orchestras maintain their own choral societies. The English tradition of church singing is represented by choirs such as those of King's College Chapel, Cambridge, and Christ Church Cathedral, Oxford. There are many male-voice choirs in Wales and in certain parts of England.

Pop and Rock Music

Among the characteristics of modern pop and rock music are the diversity of styles, the frequency with which new styles and stars emerge, and the short lifespan of many groups. Electric guitars and drums usually provide the instrumental basis, but there has been an increasing use of synthesisers, while modern production techniques have widened the range of music being released. In the 1960s and 1970s groups such as the Beatles, the Rolling Stones, the Who, Led Zeppelin and Pink Floyd achieved international success. British groups continue to be popular throughout the world and are often at the forefront of new developments in music. Some of the more recent groups include the Cure, Iron Maiden, Fine Young Cannibals, the Pet Shop Boys and Simple Minds. Well-known performers include George Michael, Phil Collins, Sting and Lisa Stansfield. In recent years young black

musicians have further strengthened the development of popular music.

The pop and rock music industry continues to contribute significantly to Britain's overseas earnings.

Jazz

Jazz has an enthusiastic following in Britain and is played in numerous clubs and pubs. British musicians such as Barbara Thompson, Stan Tracey, John Surman, Andy Sheppard and Courtney Pine have established strong reputations throughout Europe. Festivals of jazz music are held annually in Soho (London), Edinburgh, Glasgow, Crawley (West Sussex) and at a number of other places. Jazz Services provides a national touring network.

Jazz FM, Britain's first radio station devoted exclusively to jazz, was launched in 1990. It broadcasts both live and recorded music 24 hours a day to listeners in the London area.

Opera and Dance

Regular seasons of opera and ballet are held at the Royal Opera House, Covent Garden, London. The Royal Opera and Royal Ballet, which rank among the world's leading companies, are supported by a permanent orchestra. Seasons of opera in English are given by the English National Opera at the London Coliseum. Scottish Opera has regular seasons at the Theatre Royal in Glasgow, and tours mainly in Scotland and northern England. Welsh National Opera presents seasons in Cardiff and other cities. Opera North, based in Leeds, tours primarily in the north of England and Opera Factory stages experimental work in opera and music theatre. Opera 80 takes opera to towns throughout England, playing in a wide range of venues. Opera in Northern Ireland is promoted by Opera Northern Ireland.

An opera season for which international casts are specially assembled is held every summer at Glyndebourne in East Sussex. This is followed by an autumn tour by Glynde-bourne Touring Opera, often using casts drawn from the chorus of the festival season.

Subsidised Dance Companies

Subsidised dance companies include: the Birmingham (formerly Sadler's Wells) Royal Ballet, which tours widely in Britain and overseas; English National Ballet, which divides its performances between London and the regions; Northern Ballet Theatre, which is based in Halifax and also tours, particularly in the north of England; and Scottish Ballet, based in Glasgow. Also included are Rambert Dance (Britain's oldest ballet company, which re-formed in 1966 as a leading contemporary dance company); London Contemporary Dance Theatre, which provides regular seasons in London besides touring extensively; Adzido Pan African Dance Ensemble; and the KOSH, which combines dance, theatre and acrobatics. The Arts Council also supports Dance Umbrella, an organisation which promotes an annual festival of contemporary dance. In addition, the three Arts Councils and the regional arts boards support individual artists and offer project grants to several small groups.

Sir Kenneth Macmillan, David Bintley, and Siobhan Davies are among the foremost British choreographers, and Michael Clark and Darcey Bussell among the leading dancers.

Training

Professional training in music is given mainly at colleges of music. The leading London colleges are the Royal Academy of Music, the Royal College of Music, the Guildhall School of Music and Drama, and Trinity College of Music. Outside London the main centres are the Royal Scottish Academy of Music and Drama in Glasgow, the Royal Northern College of Music in Manchester, the Welsh College of Music and Drama, Cardiff, and the Birmingham Conservatoire. The National Opera Studio provides advanced training courses.

Leading dance schools include the Royal Ballet School, the Ballet Rambert School and the London School of Contemporary Dance which, with many private schools, have helped in raising British dance to its present standard. Dance is a subject for degree studies at the Laban Centre (University of London), the University of Surrey and Dartington College of the Arts. Courses for students intending to work with community groups are available at three institutions. In June 1991 the Royal Ballet announced a scheme to widen access to dance training for children from ethnic minorities.

A city technology college offering studies in drama, music and dance to pupils aged from 13 to 18, with the emphasis on the application of technology to the performing arts, opened in Croydon, Surrey, in September 1991. The capital cost of £5·9 million is being shared between the Government (60 per cent) and the British phonographic industry (40 per cent).

Youth and Music, an organisation affiliated to the international Jeunesses Musicales, encourages attendance by young people at opera, dance and concert performances. Special performances of orchestral music for children include the Robert Mayer Concerts, held in London on Saturday mornings. Ludus Dance-in-Education Company and Outreach (in the north of England) work mainly with young people. Scottish Ballet Steps Out works in schools throughout Scotland.

Many children learn to play musical instruments at school, and some take the examinations of the Associated Board of the Royal Schools of Music. Music is one of the foundation subjects in the National Curriculum in publicly maintained schools in England and Wales. The National Youth Orchestras of Great Britain, of Scotland and of Wales and other youth orchestras have established high standards. Nearly a third of the players in the European Community Youth Orchestra come from Britain. There is also a National Youth Jazz Orchestra.

National Youth Music Theatre, which is based in London, gives young people between 11 and 18 the opportunity to perform music theatre under the guidance of professional directors and choreographers. All the work takes place in the school holidays.

FILMS

British films, actors, and the creative and technical services supporting them are widely acclaimed in international film festivals and other events. Besides feature films, including co-productions with other countries, the industry produces films for television as well as promotional, advertising, industrial, scientific, educational and training films.

There are approximately 1,424 cinema screens in Britain and estimated attendances are currently running at about 2 million a week.

Cinema admissions in 1990 totalled 98 million—85 per cent more than in 1984.

The present resurgence in attendance figures can be attributed partly to the rapid growth in the rental of video films, which has stimulated not only an interest in films generally but also a wish to see popular action films in their original medium. There has been a growth in recent years in the number of grant-aided regional film theatres and film societies offering alternative programmes to those of the commercial cinema chains.

Government Support for the Film Industry

An annual government grant (£14 million for 1991–92) is made to the British Film Institute and one of over £706,000 to the Scottish Film Council and the Scottish Film Production Fund. In 1990 the Government agreed to provide £5 million over three years to help British film producers wishing to enter European co-production.

In May 1991 the UK Film Commission was launched, with government funding of £3·5 million over four years. The Commission aims to attract film productions from overseas by offering a service to assist film-makers.

British Screen Finance, a private sector company with shareholders from the film and television industries, provides a source of finance for new film-makers with commercially viable productions who have difficulty in attracting funding. The

company, investing its own money together with contributions from the Government, part-finances the production of low- and medium-budget films involving largely British talent. With further government funding of £2·5 million over five years from 1991, the company manages schemes to encourage the early stages of film project development and the production of short films.

British Film Institute

The development of film, video and television as art forms is promoted by the British Film Institute (BFI), founded in 1933, and in Scotland by the Scottish Film Council. The Institute offers direct financial and technical help through its Film Production Board to new and experienced film-makers who cannot find support elsewhere, and helps to fund film and video workshops in liaison with the Channel Four Television Company.

It administers the National Film Theatre in London and the National Film Archive, and has a library from which films and video-cassettes may be hired. The Institute holds extensive international collections of books, periodicals, scripts, stills and posters. Its Education Department aims to enable as many people as possible to discover new ways of producing and enjoying film, video and television.

The National Film Archive contains over 175,000 films and television programmes, including newsreels and other miscellaneous items. BFI South Bank comprises the Museum of the Moving Image, which traces the history of film and television, and the National Film Theatre. The latter has two cinemas showing films of historical, artistic or technical interest, and is unique in offering regular programmes unrestricted by commercial considerations. In November each year it mounts the London Film Festival, at which some 160 new films from all over the world are screened.

The British Film Institute has promoted, and helps to fund, the development of some 32 regional film theatres, with 44 screens; and is involved in establishing film and television centres with a range of activities and facilities in a number of major cities. It also co-operates with the regional arts boards and grant-aids their film activities. The Institute received £500,000 in incentive funding in 1989–90, which it is using to generate a further £1 million from other sources. It has raised some £15 million from private sources for capital development.

The Welsh Arts Council acts as the Institute's agent in Wales. In Scotland the Scottish Film Council supports regional film theatres, administers the Scottish Film Archive, and promotes and provides material for media education. Together with the Scottish Arts Council, it has set up the Scottish Film Production Fund, which makes grants towards film production in Scotland. The BFI is working with the newly established Northern Ireland Film Institute. Grants in Northern Ireland are made by the Arts Council of Northern Ireland. An annual festival of film and television in the Celtic countries is held in rotation in Scotland, Wales, Ireland and France.

Children's Film

The Children's Film and Television Foundation produces and distributes entertainment films specially designed for children. These are shown largely through video and television.

Training in Film Production

The National Film and Television School, which is financed jointly by the Government and the film and television industry, offers postgraduate and short course training for directors, editors, camera operators, animators and other specialists. Training in film production is also given at the London International Film School, the Royal College of Art, and at some polytechnics and other institutions.

Cinema Licensing and Film Classification

Cinemas showing films to the public must be licensed by local authorities, which have a legal duty to prohibit the admission of children under 16 to unsuitable films, and may prevent the showing of any film. In assessing the suitability of films the authorities normally rely on the judgment of an independent non-statutory body, the British Board of Film Classification, to which films offered to the public must be submitted. The Board was set up on the initiative of the cinema industry to ensure a proper standard in films shown to the public. It does not use any written code of censorship, but can require cuts to be made before granting a certificate; on rare occasions, it refuses a certificate.

Films passed by the Board are put into one of the following categories:

- U, meaning universal—suitable for all;
- PG, meaning parental guidance, in which some scenes may be unsuitable for young children;
- 12, 15 and 18, for people of not less than 12, 15 and 18 years of age respectively; and
- Restricted 18, for restricted showing only at segregated premises to which no one under 18 is admitted—for example, licensed cinema clubs.

Videos

The British Board of Film Classification is also legally responsible for classifying videos. The system of classification is similar to that for films. It is an offence to supply commercially a video which has not been classified or to supply it in contravention of its classification—for example, to sell or hire a video classified 18 to a person under the age of 18.

VISUAL ARTS

State support for the visual arts consists largely of maintenance and purchase grants for the national museums and galleries, purchase grants for municipal museums and galleries, and funding through local authorities, the Museums and Galleries Commission and the area museum councils (see p 399). It also includes funding for living artists channelled through the Arts Councils, the Crafts Council and the regional arts boards, and grants towards the cost of art education. The Government encourages high standards of industrial design and craftsmanship through grants to the Design Council.

All national museums and galleries are financed chiefly from government funds. They may levy entrance charges to their permanent collections, special exhibitions and outstations at their discretion. Government policy is to give priority to the conservation of the buildings and collections of the national institutions rather than to increase purchase grants for acquisitions. All the national collections are managed by independent trustees.

Museums and art galleries maintained by local authorities, universities and private benefactions may receive help in building up their collections through annual government grants administered by the Museums and Galleries Commission (for England and Wales) and the Scottish Museums Council. Financial and practical assistance to both national and local museums and galleries is also given by the Arts Council and by trusts and voluntary bodies, including the Calouste Gulbenkian Foundation, the National Art-Collections Fund and the Contemporary Art Society.

Pre-eminent works of art accepted by the Government in place of inheritance tax are allocated to public galleries. Financial help may be available from the National Heritage Memorial Fund, which was allocated £3 million by the Government in 1990–91. In recent years the Fund has made important contributions towards pictures bought by the Birmingham, Leeds and Manchester City Art Galleries, and by the national galleries and museums.

In co-operation with regional arts boards, the Arts Council makes grants towards the public display of the visual arts, especially contemporary and experimental works, and the publication of books and magazines. It also encourages the commissioning of works of art in public places. The South Bank Board maintains a collection of contemporary British art and organises touring exhibitions throughout the country on behalf of the Arts Council. The Council supports a number of art and photography galleries in London, including the Hayward Gallery, Serpentine Gallery, Photographers' Gallery and Whitechapel Art Gallery; and in the regions, the Arnolfini in Bristol and the Museum of Modern Art in Oxford. It also provides support for artists and photographers through purchasing and commissioning fellowships and residencies. Similar support is given by the Scottish Arts Council to galleries in Scotland such as the Fruitmarket Gallery in Edinburgh. The Welsh and Northern Ireland Arts Councils have galleries in Cardiff and Belfast respectively.

A number of modern British sculptors and painters have international reputations, and have received international prizes and commissions for major works in foreign cities. Among the best known are Francis Bacon, David Hockney, Lucian Freud, Eduardo Paolozzi and Elizabeth Frink.

Museums and Art Galleries

A major expansion in the number of museums is taking place and many are introducing new display techniques that attract increasing numbers of visitors. About 100 million people a year attend some 2,500 museums and galleries open to the public, which include the major national collections and a wide variety of municipally and independently or privately owned institutions. Government provision for museums and galleries is £248 million in 1991–92. The Museums and Galleries Improvement Fund, which is jointly financed by the Government and the Wolfson Charities, is providing an annual budget of £4 million over the three years from 1991–92 for renovating and improving galleries, focusing on priority work which museums are unable to fund fully from their own resources. The British Museum, the Royal Museum of Scotland, the Manchester Museum of Science, the Walker Art Gallery in Liverpool and the Science Museum have all received refurbishment awards.

The Government takes advice on policy matters from the Museums and Galleries

Commission. The Commission also promotes co-operation between national and provincial institutions. Nine area museum councils supply technical services and advice on conservation, display, documentation and publicity.

The Government encourages the loan of objects from national and provincial museums and gallery collections so that works of art can be seen by as wide a public as possible. It provides funds for promoting the touring of exhibitions and for facilitating the loan of items between institutions.

The Museum Training Institute is responsible for developing training standards and programmes.

Museums Association

The independent Museums Association, to which many museums and art galleries and their staffs belong, and which has many overseas members, facilitates exchange of information and discussion of matters relating to museums and galleries. It provides training, seminar, research and publishing programmes. Its subsidiary, Museum Enterprises, provides consultancy services to museums and galleries in planning, trading and recruitment.

National Collections

The national museums and art galleries, most of which are located in London, contain some of the world's most comprehensive collections of objects of artistic, archaeological, scientific, historical and general interest. They are the British Museum (including the Museum of Mankind), the Natural History Museum, the Victoria and Albert Museum (V&A), the Science Museum, the National Gallery, the Tate Gallery, the National Portrait Gallery, the Imperial War Museum, the National Army Museum, the Royal Air Force Museum, the National Maritime Museum, the Wallace Collection, the Geological Museum and a group of museums and galleries on Merseyside. An extension to the National Gallery, the Sainsbury Wing, opened in July 1991. A gift from the

Sainsbury family, it provides a venue for major international touring exhibitions and other events.

Some of the museums in London have branches in the regions, examples being the National Railway Museum (York) and the National Museum of Photography, Film and Television (Bradford), which are part of the Science Museum. The V&A plans to open a branch in Bradford. The Tate Gallery opened a branch in Liverpool in 1988, and is planning to open another in St Ives, Cornwall.

Some of the national museums' and galleries' recent acquisitions include:

- **five nineteenth-century French paintings by Monet, Corot, Jongkind, Boudin and Renoir—National Gallery;**

- **collection of foreign artillery equipment and medals—Imperial War Museum;**

- **Egyptian red granite sarcophagus—British Museum; and**

- ***Standing by the Rags* by Lucian Freud—Tate Gallery.**

In Scotland the national collections are held by the National Museums of Scotland and the National Galleries of Scotland. The National Museums of Scotland include the Royal Museum of Scotland and the Scottish United Services Museum, both in Edinburgh; the Museum of Flight, near North Berwick; the Scottish Agricultural Museum, at Ingliston; and the Shambellie House Museum of Costume, near Dumfries. A new Museum of Scotland is to be built next to the Royal Museum to house the National Museums' Scottish collection. The National Galleries of Scotland comprise the National Gallery of Scotland, the Scottish National Portrait Gallery and the Scottish National Gallery of Modern Art.

The National Museum of Wales (where a major expansion scheme is in progress), in Cardiff, has a branch at St Fagan's Castle, where the Welsh Folk Museum is housed; an Industrial and Maritime Museum in Cardiff's dockland; the Museum of the Woollen Industry at Drefach Felindre; and the Slate Museum at Llanberis. Northern Ireland has two national museums: the Ulster Museum in Belfast and the Ulster Folk and Transport Museum in County Down.

Other Collections

Other important collections in London include the Royal Armouries in the Tower of London, the Museum of London, Sir John Soane's Museum, the Courtauld collection and the London Transport Museum. The Queen's Gallery in Buckingham Palace has exhibitions of pictures from the extensive royal collections.

Most cities and towns have museums devoted to art, archaeology and natural history, usually administered by the local authorities but sometimes by local learned societies or by individuals or trustees. Both Oxford and Cambridge are rich in museums. Many are associated with their universities, such as the Ashmolean Museum in Oxford (founded in 1683—the oldest in the world), and the Fitzwilliam Museum in Cambridge. Many private art collections in historic family mansions, including those owned by the National Trusts, are open to the public, while an increasing number of open air museums depict the regional life of an area or preserve early industrial remains. These include the Weald and Downland Museum in West Sussex, the North of England Open Air Museum in Durham, and the Ironbridge Gorge Museum in Shropshire. Skills of the past are revived in a number of 'living' museums like the Gladstone Pottery Museum near Stoke-on-Trent and the Quarry Bank Mill at Styal in Cheshire.

Among the newest museums are the National Horseracing Museum at Newmarket; the Jorvik Viking Centre, a reconstruction of the Viking settlement in York; a new maritime museum in Portsmouth, housing the restored wreck of the *Mary Rose*, the flagship of Henry VIII, which sank in 1545 and was raised in 1982; and Catalyst: Museum of the Chemical Industry, at Widnes, Cheshire. The Burrell Collection in Glasgow houses world-famous tapestries, paintings and *objets d'art*. The

Design Museum opened in London's Docklands in 1990. It houses exhibits charting changes in design and technology.

Apart from their permanent collections, most museums and galleries stage temporary exhibitions on particular themes. There are also a number of national art exhibiting societies, the most famous being the Royal Academy of Arts at Burlington House. The Academy holds an annual Summer Exhibition, where the works of hundreds of professional and amateur artists can be seen, and important exhibitions during the rest of the year. The Royal Scottish Academy holds annual exhibitions in Edinburgh. There are also children's exhibitions, including the National Exhibition of Children's Art.

Crafts

Government aid for the crafts, amounting to just over £2·5 million in 1991–92, is administered in England and Wales by the Crafts Council. The Council supports craftsmen and women by promoting interest in their work, making it accessible to the public and encouraging the creation and appreciation of articles of contemporary craftsmanship. Grants are available to help with setting up workshops and acquiring equipment. The Council arranges exhibitions, crafts fairs and seminars, and circulates information. It also runs a gallery in London and a crafts shop at the Victoria and Albert Museum. Funding is given to the Welsh Arts Council and the regional arts boards in England for the support of crafts, and to Contemporary Applied Art, a membership organisation that holds exhibitions and sells work through its London gallery.

New arrangements for the support of crafts in Scotland came into effect in April 1991. A wide range of commercial services is now provided by a company, Made in Scotland, while training and business development support is provided by two new government-funded bodies, Scottish Enterprise and Highlands and Islands Enterprise, each with a network of local enterprise companies led by the private sector.

Training in Art and Design

Most practical education in art and design is provided in colleges of art (among the best known of which are the Slade School and the Royal College of Art, both in London), further education colleges and private art schools. Degrees at postgraduate level are awarded by the Royal College of Art. Art is also taught at an advanced level at the four Scottish Central (Art) Institutions.

Courses at universities and polytechnics concentrate largely on academic disciplines such as the history of art. The leading institutions include the Courtauld and Warburg Institutes of the University of London and the Department of Classical Art and Archaeology at University College, London. Art is one of the foundation subjects in the National Curriculum in publicly maintained schools in England and Wales; and the Society for Education through Art encourages, among other activities, the purchase by schools of original works of art by organising an annual Pictures for Schools exhibition.

The Open College of the Arts offers correspondence courses in art and design, painting, sculpture, textiles, photography and creative writing to people wishing to study at home.

The Art Market

London is a major centre for the international art market, and sales of works of art take place in the main auction houses (two of the longest established being Sotheby's and Christie's), and through private dealers. Certain items are covered by export control. These are as follows:

- works of art and collectors' items over 50 years old and worth £20,000 or more (£5,000 or more in the case of British historical portraits);

- photographic material over 50 years old and valued at £500 or more an item; and

- documents, manuscripts and archives over 50 years old, irrespective of value.

A licence from the Department of Trade and Industry is required before such items can be exported. If the Department's advisers recommend withholding a licence, the matter is referred to the Reviewing Committee on the Export of Works of Art. If the Committee considers a work to be of national importance it can advise the Government to withhold the export licence for a specified time to give a public museum, art gallery, or private collector an opportunity to buy at a fair price.

LITERATURE AND LIBRARIES

A number of literary activities receive public subsidy through the Arts Council of Great Britain. In 1990, for example, the Council sponsored its first writer's tour, and contributed to an innovative television series on modern poetry. It continued to foster an interest in writing from diverse cultures through its support for translations and the black sound archive.

There are free public libraries throughout Britain, private libraries and several private literary societies. Book reviews are featured in the press and on television and radio, and numerous periodicals concerned with literature are published. Recognition of outstanding literary merit is provided by a number of awards, some of the most valuable being the Booker, National Cash Register and Whitbread prizes. Awards to encourage young writers include those of the Somerset Maugham Trust Fund and the E. C. Gregory Trust Fund. Many British writers are internationally recognised and in 1983 the Nobel prize for literature was awarded to the novelist Sir William Golding. Other well-known living authors include Sir Kingsley Amis, Anthony Burgess, Penelope Lively and Fay Weldon. Distinguished British poets include Ted Hughes, the Poet Laureate, who writes verse to mark royal occasions; Geoffrey Hill; Tony Harrison; James Berry; Gavin Ewart; and Elizabeth Jennings.

Authors' Copyright and Performers' Protection

Original literary, dramatic, musical or artistic works, films, sound recordings and broadcasts are automatically protected in

Britain. This protection is given to foreign works under the terms of international conventions.[1] The copyright owner has rights against unauthorised reproduction, public performance, broadcasting and issue to the public of his or her work; and against dealing in unauthorised copies. In most cases the author is the first owner of the copyright, and the term of copyright is the life of the author and a period of 50 years after death (50 years from the year of release for films and sound recordings and 50 years from the year of broadcast for broadcasts).

The Copyright, Designs and Patents Act 1988 reformed and restated copyright law and introduced the concept of moral rights, whereby authors have the right to be identified on their works and to object to derogatory treatment of them. The Act introduced a statutory framework of civil rights to protect performers against making and trading in unauthorised recordings of live performance, the term of protection for these rights being 50 years from the year in which the performance is given.

Literary and Philological Societies

Societies to promote literature include the English Association and the Royal Society of Literature. The leading society for studies in the humanities is the British Academy for the Promotion of Historical, Philosophical and Philological Studies (the British Academy).

Other specialist societies are the Early English Text Society, the Bibliographical Society and several societies devoted to particular authors, the largest of which is the Dickens Fellowship. Various societies, such as the Poetry Society, sponsor poetry readings and recitals.

Libraries

The British Library

The British Library, the national library of Britain, is one of the world's greatest

libraries. Its collections comprise over 18 million items—monographs, manuscripts, maps, newspapers, patents, stamps and recorded sound. Publishers must deposit there a copy of most items published or available in Britain.

The National Bibliographic Service processes material legally deposited at the Library for inclusion in catalogues and maintains a machine-readable database of bibliographical records from which is derived the *British National Bibliography* (a list of new and forthcoming British books) and a range of automated bibliographical services.

The Research and Development Department is a major source of funding for research and development in library and information services.

The Library's Document Supply Centre at Boston Spa (West Yorkshire) is the national centre for inter-library lending within Britain and between Britain and countries overseas. It supplies 3·5 million requests a year, mostly from its own stock of 7 million documents.

In 1990 the Library set up the self-supporting Centre for the Book, to promote awareness of books and their role in British life, past and present.

The Library's new London headquarters at St Pancras is being built at a cost of £450 million, and will be open to the public from 1993. It will provide reading rooms for most of the Library's London-based collections—humanities, science, technology and industry—and also specialist reading areas. The new Library aims to offer greatly improved services, including exhibition galleries, a bookshop, a lecture theatre and a conference centre.

Other Libraries

The National Libraries of Scotland and Wales, the Bodleian Library of Oxford University and the Cambridge University Library can also claim copies of all new British publications under legal deposit. The first phase of a new building for the National Library of Scotland was opened in 1989. Costing £11·5 million, it provides 49 km (30 miles) of storage shelving and accommodates

---

[1] All countries which are members of the Berne Copyright Convention, the Universal Copyright Convention and the Rome Convention are obliged to protect works of British origin.

a map library, lending services and the Scottish Science Library. Work on the second stage began in late 1990, for completion in 1994.

Some of the national museums and government departments have important libraries. The Public Record Office in London and in Kew, Surrey, contains the records of the superior courts of law and of most government departments, as well as famous historical documents. The Scottish Record Office in Edinburgh serves the same purpose.

Besides a number of great private collections, such as that of the London Library, there are the rich resources of the learned societies and institutions. Examples are the libraries of the Royal Institute of International Affairs, the Commonwealth Trust, the Royal Geographical Society, the Royal Academy of Music, the National Library for the Blind and the Book Trust. The Poetry Library, owned by the Arts Council, is a national collection of twentieth century poetry written in or translated into English.

University Libraries

The university libraries of Oxford and Cambridge are unmatched by those of the more recent foundations. However, the combined library resources of the colleges and institutions of the University of London total 9 million volumes, the John Rylands University Library in Manchester contains 3·4 million volumes, Edinburgh 2 million, Leeds 1·8 million, and Birmingham, Glasgow, Liverpool and Aberdeen each have over 1 million volumes. Many universities have important research collections in special subjects; examples include the Barnes Medical Library at Birmingham and the British Library of Political and Economic Science at the London School of Economics.

Special Libraries

Numerous associations and commercial and industrial organisations run library and information services. Although most are primarily intended for use within the organisation, many special libraries can be used, by arrangement, by people interested in the area covered, and the specialist publications held are often available for inter-library lending.

Public Libraries

Local authorities have a duty to provide a free lending and reference library service in their areas, and Britain's network of libraries has a total stock of about 156·7 million books. Over half of the total population are members of public libraries. Some areas are served by mobile libraries, and domiciliary services cater for people unable to visit a library. Many libraries have collections of records, audio- and video-cassettes, and musical scores for loan to the public, while a number also lend from collections of works of art, which may be originals or reproductions. Most libraries hold documents on local history, and nearly all provide children's departments, while reference and information sections and art, music, commercial and technical departments meet the growing and more specific demands in these fields. The information role is one of increasing importance for many libraries, and greater use is being made of information technology, including microcomputers and reference databases.

The Government remains committed to providing a free basic library service—the borrowing and consultation of books and other printed materials—but believes there is scope for greater private sector involvement. Since 1988 it has made available £250,000 a year through an incentive funding scheme to encourage new developments and increase efficiency in public library services in England. Priority is given to projects involving collaboration with other libraries and the private sector.

Public library authorities charge for some services, such as research services and the lending of non-printed materials, including cassettes and records.

The Public Lending Right Scheme gives registered authors the right to receive payment from a central fund (totalling £4·75 million in 1991–92) for the use of their books borrowed from public libraries. Payment is made in proportion to the number of times the authors' books are lent out.

The Government is advised on library and information matters by four library and information services councils or committees, representing England, Wales, Scotland and Northern Ireland.

The Library Association

The Library Association is the principal professional organisation for those engaged in library and information services. Founded in 1877, the Association has 24,000 members working in all kinds of libraries and information units. It maintains a Register of Chartered Librarians and publishes books, pamphlets and an official journal.

The Library Association is the designated authority for the recognition of qualifications gained in other member states of the European Community.

Historical Manuscripts

The Royal Commission on Historical Manuscripts is the central investigatory and advisory body on manuscripts, records and archives other than the public records. It maintains the National Register of Archives and advises owners, custodians and government, assists researchers and co-ordinates the activities of bodies working in the field. It also publishes a series of *Guides to Sources for British History*.

The National Manuscripts Conservation Trust was established in 1989 with government assistance of £300,000. It provides grants to record offices, libraries and other owners of manuscripts and archives accessible to the public.

Books

In 1990 British publishers issued nearly 64,000 separate titles, of which about 48,000 were new titles and the remainder reprints and new editions. The British publishing industry devotes much effort to developing overseas markets, and in 1990 the value of exports of British books amounted to £700 million. The industry is also noted for its interest in new technological developments, including electronic publishing and the development of software for educational and other purposes.

Among the leading organisations representing publishing and distribution interests are the Publishers Association, which has 170 members, representing over 450 separate publishing companies; and the Booksellers' Association, with 3,300 members. The Publishers Association, through its associated body the Book Development Council, promotes the export of British books worldwide.

The British Council (see p 392) publicises British books through its 116 libraries overseas, participation in international book fairs and a programme of travelling exhibitions. The Council also publishes a monthly periodical, *British Book News*.

The Book Trust, whose membership includes authors, publishers, booksellers, librarians and readers, encourages an interest in books and arranges exhibitions throughout Britain.

24 The Press

More daily newspapers, national and regional, are sold per person in Britain than in most other developed countries.

Three out of four adults regularly read a paid-for regional or local newspaper as well as a free local paper. National papers have a total circulation of 13·9 million on weekdays and 16·6 million on Sundays, though the total readership is considerably greater. There are about 160 daily (Monday to Saturday) and Sunday newspapers, over 2,000 weekly paid-for and free newspapers (including business, sporting and religious newspapers) and 6,700 periodical publications.

On an average day two out of three people over the age of 15 read a national morning newspaper; about three out of four read a Sunday newspaper.

There is no state control or censorship of the press, but it is subject to the general laws on publication (see p 416). Following the 'Calcutt Report' on privacy and the press (see p 415), the Press Complaints Commission was set up by the newspaper industry in what is seen as a final attempt to make self-regulation of the press work properly. The report also proposed that in certain circumstances physical intrusion into privacy by journalists should be unlawful (see p 415). These measures were prompted by growing criticism of press standards, with allegations of unjustified invasion of privacy and inaccurate and biased reporting, among other abuses, resulting in calls for increased government regulation of the press.

The press caters for a variety of political views, interests and levels of education. Newspapers are almost always financially independent of any political party. Where they express pronounced views and show obvious political leanings in their editorial comments, these derive from proprietorial and other non-party influences. Nevertheless, during general election campaigns many newspapers recommend their readers to vote for a particular political party. Even newspapers which adopt strong political views in their editorial columns include feature and other types of articles by authors of a variety of political persuasions. In order to preserve their character and traditions, some newspapers and periodicals are governed by trustee-type arrangements. Others have management arrangements to ensure their editors' authority and independence.

In recent years working practices throughout the newspaper industry have undergone profound changes in response to the challenges posed by computer-based technology and the need to contain costs. Newsprint, about three-quarters of which is imported, forms about a quarter of average national newspaper costs; labour represents over half. In addition to sales, many newspapers and periodicals derive considerable earnings from their advertising. Total yearly spending of around £2,900 million on newspaper advertising makes newspapers by far the largest advertising medium in Britain. Unlike most of its European counterparts the British press receives no subsidies and relatively few tax and postal concessions.

In discussions on a 'new world information and communication order' Britain has opposed measures designed to increase governmental regulation of the media or limit the free flow of information. At the same time, it has reaffirmed its willingness to support efforts to improve communications systems in the developing world.

Table 24.1: National Newspapers

Title and foundation date	Controlled by	Circulation[a] average January–June 1991
National dailies		
'Populars'		
Daily Express (1900)	United Newspapers	1,564,596
Daily Mail (1896)	Associated Newspapers Group	1,719,819
Daily Mirror (1903)	Mirror Group Newspapers (1986)	2,956,627
Daily Star (1978)	United Newspapers	878,891
Morning Star (1966)	Morning Star Co-operative Society	9,000
The Sun (1964)	News International	3,692,788
Today (1986)	News International	490,049
'Qualities'		
Financial Times (1888)	Pearson	291,531[b]
The Daily Telegraph (1855)	The Daily Telegraph	1,074,580
The Guardian (1821)	The Guardian and Manchester Evening News	431,423
The Independent (1986)	Newspaper Publishing	394,438
The Times (1785)	News International	406,123
National Sundays		
'Populars'		
News of the World (1843)	News International	4,807,646
Sunday Express (1918)	United Newspapers	1,622,846
Sunday Mirror (1963)	Mirror Group Newspapers (1986)	2,805,904
Sunday Sport (1986)	Apollo	371,287
The Mail on Sunday (1982)	Associated Newspapers Group	1,940,401
The People (1881)	Mirror Group Newspapers (1986)	2,338,014
'Qualities'		
Sunday Telegraph (1961)	The Daily Telegraph	576,438
The Independent on Sunday (1990)	Newspaper Publishing	385,045
The Observer (1791)	Lonrho International	579,045
The Sunday Times (1822)	News International	1,176,616

[a] Circulation figures are those of the Audit Bureau of Circulations (consisting of publishers, advertisers and advertising agencies) and are certified average daily or weekly net sales for the period. The circulation figure of the *Morning Star* is otherwise audited.
[b] January to June 1990.

Newspaper Ownership

Ownership of the national, London and regional daily newspapers is concentrated in the hands of a number of large press publishing groups. The groups controlling the national press are listed in Table 24.1. There are, in addition, some 350 independent regional and local newspaper publishers.

Although most enterprises are organised as limited liability companies, individual and partner proprietorship survives. The large national newspaper and periodical publishers are major corporations with interests ranging over the whole field of publishing and communications. Some have shares in independent television and radio companies, while others are involved in industrial and commercial activities.

The law provides safeguards against the risks inherent in undue concentration of the means of communication. It is unlawful to transfer a newspaper or newspaper assets to a proprietor whose newspapers have an average daily circulation amounting, with that of the newspaper to be taken over, to 500,000 or more copies without government consent. Except in certain limited cases, consent may be given only after the Secretary of State for Trade and Industry has referred the matter to the Monopolies and Mergers Commission and received its report.

If it appears that newspaper shareholdings in independent television or independent local radio companies have led or are leading to results contrary to the public interest, the Independent Television Commission and the Radio Authority (which regulate commercial television and radio) can, with the consent of the Home Secretary, notify the companies that their programmes may cease to be transmitted. There are additional controls over newspaper interests in cable television services.

The Broadcasting Act 1990 (see p 420) introduced further ownership rules to curtail cross-media ownership. Under the Act, national newspapers are only allowed a 20 per cent stake in direct broadcasting by satellite channels, television Channels 3 and 5, and national and local radio.

The National Press

Twelve morning daily papers and ten Sunday papers (see Table 24.1) circulate throughout most parts of Britain, and are known as national newspapers. Formerly they were produced in or near Fleet Street in London with, in some cases, northern editions being printed in Manchester. All of the national papers have now moved their editorial and printing facilities to other parts of London (including the Docklands) or away from the capital altogether; some use contract printing. *Today* is printed at Poyle (Middlesex) and Manchester. The *Independent* uses printing presses in Bradford, Northampton and Portsmouth. Scottish editions of *The Sun*, *The Times*, *News of the World* and *The Sunday Times* are printed in Glasgow.

In order to improve distribution and sales overseas, editions of the *Financial Times* are printed in Frankfurt, Roubaix (northern France), New Jersey and Tokyo, while *The Guardian* prints an international edition in Frankfurt. In 1990 Mirror Group Newspapers began publishing *The European*, a weekly English-language international newspaper. It is printed in Britain, France, Germany and Hungary.

Several newspapers have had very long and distinguished histories. For example, *The Observer*, first published in 1791, is the oldest national Sunday newspaper in the world, and *The Times*, one of the most influential newspapers and Britain's oldest daily national newspaper, began publication in 1785.

National newspapers are often thought of as either 'quality' or 'popular' papers on the basis of differences in style and content. Five dailies and four Sundays are usually described as quality newspapers. Quality papers are directed at readers who want full information on a wide range of public matters and are prepared to spend a considerable amount of time reading them. Popular newspapers appeal to people wanting news of a more entertaining character, presented in a more concise form and with ample illustrations. At present, all quality papers are broadsheet in format and all popular papers, with the exception of the *Sunday Express*, tabloid.

Many newspapers are printed in colour and a number produce colour magazines as part of the Saturday or Sunday paper. Several of the Sunday newspapers, and some of the dailies on Saturday, publish supplements with articles on travel, food and wine, and other leisure topics. The leading Scottish papers, *The Scotsman* and the *Glasgow Herald*, have considerable circulations outside Scotland.

There is a growing market for news and information in the electronic media, and quality papers like the *Financial Times* provide material for use on databases and videotext services such as Prestel. *The Times* supplies a news service to British Sky Broadcasting, a direct broadcasting by satellite (DBS) company under the same ownership.

The total circulation of national newspapers amounted to 32 million in 1990, compared with 33·5 million in 1980. Sales of quality papers have risen by 10 per cent since 1986, while the popular press has experienced a fall of 8 per cent.

Regional Newspapers

England

Outside London around 70 morning or evening dailies and Sundays and several hundred newspapers appearing once or twice a week provide mainly regional and local news. The daily newspapers also cover national and international affairs. Generally, regional evening newspapers are non-political, while the morning newspapers adopt a more positive political stance and tend to be independent or conservative in outlook.

Of the morning papers the *Yorkshire Post* (Leeds), the *Northern Echo* (Darlington) and the *Eastern Daily Press* (Norwich) each have a circulation of over 85,000, and two provincial Sunday papers—the *Sunday Sun* (Newcastle upon Tyne) and the *Sunday Mercury* (Birmingham)—sell 117,000 and 151,000 copies respectively. Circulation figures of evening papers start at about

10,000 and most are in the 20,000 to 100,000 range. Those with much larger sales include the *Manchester Evening News* (255,000), the *Birmingham Evening Mail* (220,000), Wolverhampton's *Express and Star* (236,000) and the *Liverpool Echo* (194,000). Paid weekly papers are of mainly local appeal and are a valuable medium for local advertising. Most have circulations in the 5,000 to 60,000 range.

London has one evening newspaper, the *Evening Standard*, with a circulation of 502,000. It contains national and international news as well as coverage of local affairs. A number of evening newspapers are published in the outer metropolitan area. Local weeklies include papers for every district in Greater London, often in the form of local editions of an individual paper.

Wales

Wales has one daily morning newspaper, the *Western Mail*, published in Cardiff, with a circulation of 74,000 throughout Wales. In north Wales the *Daily Post*, published in Liverpool, gives wide coverage to events in the area. A new Sunday newspaper—*Wales on Sunday*—also published in Cardiff, was launched in 1989. It has a circulation of 46,000. Evening papers published in Wales are the *South Wales Echo*, Cardiff; the *South Wales Argus*, Newport; the *South Wales Evening Post*, Swansea; and the *Evening Leader*, Wrexham. Their circulation range is between 30,000 and 83,000. North Wales is also served by the *Liverpool Echo*, and the *Shropshire Star* covers parts of north and mid-Wales. There is also coverage to a smaller extent by the *Manchester Evening News*.

The weekly press (82 publications) includes English-language papers, some of which carry articles in Welsh; bilingual papers; and Welsh-language papers. Welsh community newspapers receive an annual grant as part of the Government's wider financial support for the Welsh language.

Scotland

Scotland has six morning, six evening and four Sunday newspapers. Local weekly newspapers number 110 and there are 59 free local papers. The daily morning papers, with circulations of between 85,000 and 778,000, are *The Scotsman* (published in Edinburgh); the *Glasgow Herald*; the *Daily Record* (sister paper of the *Daily Mirror*); the *Dundee Courier and Advertiser*; the *Aberdeen Press and Journal*; and the *Scottish Daily Express* (printed in Manchester). The daily evening papers have circulations in the range of 11,000 to 167,000 and are the *Evening News* of Edinburgh, Glasgow's *Evening Times*, Dundee's *Evening Telegraph*, Aberdeen's *Evening Express*, the *Paisley Daily Express* and the *Greenock Telegraph*.

The Sunday papers are the *Sunday Mail*, the *Sunday Post*, the *Scottish Sunday Express* (printed in Manchester); and a quality broadsheet paper, *Scotland on Sunday*, launched in 1988. The national Sunday newspapers *The Observer* and *The Sunday Times* carry Scottish supplements.

Northern Ireland

Northern Ireland has two morning newspapers, one evening and three Sunday papers, all published in Belfast, with circulations ranging from 22,000 to 133,000. They are the *News Letter* (unionist), the *Irish News* (nationalist), the evening *Belfast Telegraph*, the *Sunday News*, *Sunday Life* and *Sunday World* (Northern Ireland edition).

The *News Letter*, established in 1737, is the oldest English-language newspaper in the world.

There are about 45 weeklies. Newspapers from the Irish Republic, as well as the British national press, are widely read in Northern Ireland.

Free Distribution Newspapers

More than 1,150 free distribution newspapers, mostly weekly and financed by advertising, are published in Britain; over half of them are produced by established newspaper publishers. They have enjoyed rapid growth in recent years and now have an estimated total weekly circulation of about 42 million.

Ethnic Minority Publications

Some 100 newspapers and magazines are produced in Britain by members of the ethnic minorities. They are mainly published weekly, fortnightly or monthly. Two Chinese newspapers, *Sing Tao* and *Wen Wei Po*, the Urdu *Daily Jang* (see below) and the Arabic *Al-Arab* are dailies.

The *Asian Times* and *Indiamail* are English language titles for people of Asian descent, published weekly; the *Sikh Messenger* and *Sikh Courier* are both produced quarterly. Afro-Caribbean newspapers include *The Weekly Gleaner*, a local edition of the long-established *Jamaican Gleaner*, and *West Indian Digest*. The *Voice* and *Caribbean Times*, both weeklies, are aimed at the black population in general, as is the monthly magazine *Root*.

Leading ethnic language newspapers in Britain include the Urdu *Daily Jang*, an offshoot of the largest circulation paper in Pakistan, and the weekly *Gujarat Samachar*, a Gujarati tabloid. Publications also appear in Bengali (such as the weeklies *Jagoran* and *Janomot*); in Hindi (the weeklies *Amar Deep*, *Hind Samachar* and *Navin Weekly*); and in Punjabi (such as the weeklies *Des Perdes* and *Punjab Darpan* and the monthlies *Rachna* and *Perdesan*).

British provincial newspaper groups are examining the possibility of printing special editions for their local populations. In 1989 the *Leicester Mercury* started publishing a daily Asian edition, incorporating news from the South Asian sub-continent.

The Periodical Press

The 6,700 periodical publications are classified as 'consumer general interest', 'special interest' and 'business-to-business'. There are also several hundred 'house magazines' produced by industrial undertakings, business houses or public services for the benefit of their employees and/or clients. Directories and similar publications number more than 2,200. The 'alternative' press comprises a large number of titles, many of them devoted to radical politics, community matters, religion, the occult, science or ecology.

Consumer general and specialist periodicals comprise magazines for a wide range of interests. These include women's magazines; publications for children; religious periodicals; fiction magazines; magazines dealing with sport, motoring, gardening, teenage interests and pop music; hobbies, humour and retirement; and computer magazines. Also included are the publications of learned societies, trade unions, regiments, universities and other organisations.

The weekly periodicals with the highest sales have traditionally been *Radio Times* and *TV Times*, which carry full details of all the coming week's television and radio programmes, including the satellite schedules. The *Radio Times/TV Times* listings duopoly came to an end in March 1991, and the advent of competition has led to a reduction in the circulation figures of both magazines. Rival publications include *TV Quick* and *What's on TV*. Of monthly magazines *Reader's Digest* has the highest circulation (1·5 million).

Woman's Weekly, *Woman's Own*, *Woman*, *Weekly News* (which sells mainly in Scotland), *Woman's Realm* and *My Weekly* have circulations in the 450,000 to 1 million range. A new magazine aimed at young women, *Me*, first appeared in 1989 and has a circulation of 715,000. In recent years several women's magazines from overseas have achieved large circulations: *Prima* and *Best*, for instance, each sell over 650,000 copies, while *Bella* and *Hello!* are also widely read. *Smash Hits*, with a circulation of 443,000, is a fortnightly magazine dealing with pop music and teenage life styles. *Viz*, a cartoon comic aimed at young adults, sells 1·1 million copies.

The leading journals of opinion include *The Economist*, an independent conservative publication covering a wider range of topics than its title implies. The *New Statesman and Society* reviews social issues, politics, literature and the arts from an independent socialist point of view, and the *Spectator* covers similar subjects from an independent conservative standpoint. *Tribune* represents certain left-wing views within the Labour Party.

New Scientist reports on science and technology in terms that the non-specialist can understand. *Punch*, traditionally the leading humorous periodical, and *Private Eye*, a satirical fortnightly, also cover public affairs. Weekly 'listings' magazines, including *Time Out* and *City Limits*, provide details of cultural and other events in London and other large cities.

Literary and political journals, and those specialising in international and Commonwealth affairs, appear monthly or quarterly, and generally appeal to the more academically-oriented reader. Business, scientific and professional journals, publication of which ranges from twice weekly to quarterly, are an important aspect of British publishing and business communication, many having a considerable circulation overseas. There are about 4,500 publications covering business and industrial affairs.

New Printing Technology

The heavy production costs of newspapers and periodicals continue to encourage publishers to look for ways of reducing these costs, often by using advanced computer systems to control editing and production processes. The 'front end' or 'single stroking' system, for example, allows journalists or advertising staff to input 'copy' directly into a video terminal, and then to transform it automatically into computer-set columns of type. Although it is possible for these columns to be assembled electronically on a page-sized screen, turned into a full page, and made automatically into a plate ready for transfer to the printing press, at present very few such systems are in operation. Most involve the production of bromides from the computer setting, which are pasted up into columns before being placed in a plate-making machine.

The most advanced systems present opportunities for reorganisation which have implications throughout a newspaper office and may give rise to industrial relations problems. Generally, and most recently in the case of national newspapers, the introduction of computerised systems has led to substantial reductions in workforces, particularly, but not solely, among print workers.

All the national newspapers utilise computer technology, and its use in the provincial press, which has generally led the way in adopting new techniques, is widespread. Journalists type articles directly into, and edit them on, computer terminals; colour pictures and graphics are entered into the same system electronically. Where printing plants are some distance from editorial offices, pages for printing are sent by facsimile machine from typesetter to print plant. Other technological developments include the use of full-colour printing, and a switch from traditional letterpress printing to the web-offset litho or plastic-plate processes.

News International, publisher of three daily and two Sunday papers, has at its London Docklands headquarters more than 500 computer terminals, one of the largest systems installed at one time anywhere in the world. The *Financial Times* opened a new printing plant in the Docklands in 1988 with about 200 production workers, compared with the 650 employed at its former printing facility in the City of London. The new Docklands plant of the Associated Newspapers Group uses flexography, a rubber-plate process. Other national papers have also moved into new computer-based printing plants outside Fleet Street.

News Agencies

The principal news agencies in Britain are Reuters, an international news organisation registered in London, the Press Association and Extel Financial.

Reuters

Reuters is a publicly owned company, employing 10,800 full-time staff in 78 countries. It has 1,170 staff journalists and photographers. The company serves subscribers in 128 countries, including financial institutions; commodities houses; traders in currencies, equities and bonds; major corporations; government agencies; news agencies; newspapers; and radio and television stations.

Reuters has developed the world's most extensive private leased communications network to transmit its services. It provides the media with general, political, economic, financial and sports news, news pictures and graphics, and television news. Services for business clients comprise constantly updated price information and news, historical information, facilities for computerised trading; and the supply of communications and other equipment for financial dealing rooms. Information is distributed through video terminals and teleprinters. Reuters is the major shareholder in Visnews, a television news agency whose service is estimated to reach 1,500 million viewers every day.

Press Association

The Press Association, the British and Irish national news agency, is co-operatively owned by the principal daily newspapers of Britain outside London, and of the Irish Republic. It offers national and regional newspapers and broadcasters a comprehensive range of home news—general and parliamentary news, legal reports, and all types of financial, commercial and sports news. It also includes in its services to regional papers the world news from Reuters and Associated Press (see p 414).

News is sent by satellite from London by the Press Association, certain items being available in Dataformat, as camera-ready copy. Its 'Newsfile' operation provides general news, sports and foreign news on screen to non-media as well as media clients by means of telephone and view data terminals. The photographic department offers newspapers and broadcasters a daily service of pictures. The NewsFeatures service supplies reports of local or special interest and grants exclusive rights to syndicated features. In addition, it offers a dial-in graphics facility, as well as extensive cuttings and photograph libraries.

Extel Financial

Extel Financial supplies information and services to financial and business communities throughout the world. Based in London, it has a network of offices in Europe and the United States and direct representation in Japan and South-East Asia. Data is collected from all the world's major stock exchanges, companies and the international press. The agency is a major source of reference material on companies and securities. It supplies a full range of data products on international financial matters, and undertakes investment accounting for banks, insurance companies and other institutions. Up-to-the-minute business and company news is made available by the agency's specialist financial news operation.

Other Agencies

The British press and broadcasting organisations are also catered for by Associated Press and United Press International, which are British subsidiaries of United States news agencies. A number of other British, Commonwealth and foreign agencies and news services have offices in London, and there are minor agencies in other cities. Syndication of features is not as common in Britain as in some countries, but a few agencies specialise in this type of work.

Training for Journalism

The National Council for the Training of Journalists (NCTJ), which represents the principal regional press organisations, sets and conducts examinations, and organises short training courses for journalists.

The two main methods of entry into newspaper journalism are selection for a one-year NCTJ pre-entry course at a college of further education or direct recruitment by a regional or local newspaper. Both categories of entrant take part in an apprenticeship scheme consisting of 'on-the-job' training. Block-release courses, preceded by a period of distance learning, are provided for those who have not attended a pre-entry course. There are similar courses for press photographers. Postgraduate diploma courses in journalism are available at the University of Wales College of Cardiff; City University, London; Lancashire Polytechnic, Preston; and Strathclyde University/Glasgow Polytechnic (jointly).

Courses for regional newspapers in such subjects as newspaper sales, advertising, industrial relations and management are provided by the Newspaper Society Training Service. Some newspaper publishers carry out journalist training independently of the NCTJ, awarding their own diplomas. New vocational qualifications based on workplace performance are being developed in regional newspaper journalism.

Specialist training courses for journalists and editorial managers from developing countries are offered by the Thomson Foundation in Cardiff. The Foundation also conducts training courses in developing countries and provides consultants to assist newspapers and magazines in advertising, management, circulation and the introduction and operation of new technology. It runs an international journalism training centre in collaboration with Xinhua News Agency in Peking.

Reuters offers assistance to overseas journalists to study and train in Britain, as well as in other parts of Europe and the United States. The Reuter Foundation awards fellowships to journalists from developing nations to spend a year at Oxford University. The company has also started to run practical training courses in London for journalists from Eastern Europe; these cover international news writing and business news skills.

The Periodicals Training Council is the official training organisation in periodical publishing. It offers a range of short courses covering management, editorial work, advertisement sales and circulation sales. It has special responsibility for editorial training and administers an industry-wide editorial training scheme for those already in employment. The postgraduate courses in journalism at the University of Wales College of Cardiff and City University, London, contain periodical journalism options, and the London College of Printing provides postgraduate courses and General

Certificate of Education Advanced level courses in periodical journalism. Reed Business Publishing, one of the largest publishing companies, has a company training course for suitable candidates from the general public on a fee-paying basis.

Press Institutions

Employers' organisations include the Newspaper Publishers Association, whose members publish national newspapers, and the Newspaper Society, which represents 1,500 regional, local and London suburban papers. The Scottish Daily Newspaper Society represents the interests of daily and Sunday newspapers in Scotland; the Scottish Newspaper Proprietors' Association acts on behalf of the owners of weekly newspapers in Scotland; and Associated Northern Ireland Newspapers is made up of proprietors of weekly newspapers in Northern Ireland. The membership of the Periodical Publishers' Association embraces most independent publishers of business, professional and consumer journals.

Organisations representing journalists are the National Union of Journalists, with over 30,000 members, and the Institute of Journalists, with about 2,000 members. The main printing union is the Graphical, Paper and Media Union, the result of a merger in 1991 between the Society of Graphical and Allied Trades (SOGAT) '82 and the National Graphical Association (NGA) 1982, with a membership of around 300,000.

The Guild of British Newspaper Editors is the officially recognised professional body for newspaper editors. It has approximately 350 members and aims to maintain the professional status and independence of editors, defend the freedom of the press, and improve the education and training of journalists. The British Association of Industrial Editors is the professional organisation for editors of house journals. The Association of British Editors represents the whole range of media, including radio, television, newspapers and magazines.

The main aim of the Foreign Press Association, formed in 1888, is to help the correspondents of overseas newspapers in their work by arranging press conferences, tours, briefings, and other services and facilities.

Press Conduct

Readers' representatives have been appointed by most national papers to handle complaints. They also help to guarantee standards of accuracy, fairness and good behaviour on the part of journalists.

In 1990 a report on privacy and the press by a government-appointed independent committee, under the chairmanship of Mr David Calcutt, QC, recommended the formation of a non-statutory Press Complaints Commission by the newspaper industry in place of the Press Council. The Council was a voluntary non-statutory body set up by the newspaper industry in 1953 to safeguard press freedom and ensure that the press conducted itself responsibly.

The 'Calcutt Report' also proposed creating three new criminal offences of physical intrusion to obtain personal information for publication and extending reporting restrictions on criminal cases so that the anonymity granted to rape victims would apply also to victims of other sexual offences. These proposals are under consideration by the Government.

Press Complaints Commission

The new Press Complaints Commission took over from the Press Council on 1 January 1991. The membership of the Commission is drawn from newspaper and magazine editors as well as from people from outside the industry. The Commission operates a comprehensive code of practice agreed by editors governing respect for privacy, opportunity to reply, corrections, journalists' behaviour, references to race, colour and religion, payments to criminals for articles and protection of confidential sources.

The Government will review the Commission's performance in 1992 to determine whether it has been sufficiently effective in maintaining high press standards or whether a statutory underpinning is needed.

Advertising Practice

Advertising practice in the press is regulated and controlled by the Advertising Standards Authority, an independent body. It aims to promote and enforce the highest standards of advertising in the interests of the public and the industry, in particular through the British Code of Advertising Practice. The objects of the code are to ensure

- that advertisements are legal, decent, honest and truthful;
- that they are prepared with a sense of responsibility to the consumer;
- that they conform to the principles of fair competition as generally accepted in business; and
- that no advertisement brings advertising into disrepute or reduces confidence in advertising as a service to industry and the public.

The Authority's chief activities are monitoring advertisements for their compliance with the code and dealing with complaints received directly from members of the public. Its main sanction is the recommendation to media that advertisements considered to be in breach of the code should not be published. It also publishes regular reports on the results of its investigations, naming the companies involved. The Director General of Fair Trading has the power to seek a court injunction to prevent the publication of a misleading advertisement.

The Press and the Law

The press generally has the same freedom as the individual to comment on matters of public interest. No specific press laws are in operation, but certain statutes include sections which apply to the press.

There are laws governing:

- the extent of newspaper ownership in television and radio companies (see p 409);
- the transfer of newspaper assets (see p 409);
- restrictions on reporting certain types of court proceedings and on publishing material likely to stir up racial hatred; and
- the right of press representatives to be admitted to meetings of local authorities.

Publication of advertisement and investment circulars is governed by laws dealing with the publication of false or misleading descriptions of goods and services and with fraud. Advertisements for remedies for certain diseases are covered by public health legislation. Legal restrictions are imposed on certain types of prize competition; copyrights come under various copyright laws.

Of particular relevance to the press are laws on contempt of court, official secrets, libel and defamation. A newspaper may not publish comments on the conduct of judicial proceedings which are likely to prejudice the courts' reputation for fairness before or during the actual proceedings, nor may it publish before or during a trial anything which might tend to influence the result. The unauthorised acquisition and publication of official information in such areas as defence and international relations are offences under the Official Secrets Acts 1911 to 1989 where unauthorised disclosure would be harmful (see below).

Most legal proceedings against the press are libel actions brought by private individuals. In such cases, the editor, proprietor, publishers, printer and distributor of the newspaper, as well as the author, may all be held responsible.

There is a legal requirement to reproduce 'the printer's imprint' (the printer's name and place of publication) on all publications, including newspapers. Publishers are legally obliged to deposit copies of newspapers and other publications at the British Library.

Defence Notices

Government officials and representatives of the media form the Defence, Press and Broadcasting Committee, which has agreed that in some circumstances the publication of certain categories of information might endanger national security. Details of these categories are contained in Defence Notices (D Notices) circulated to the media, members of which are asked to seek advice from the Secretary of the Committee, a retired senior military officer, before publishing information in these areas. Compliance with any advice offered by the Secretary is expected but there is no legal force behind it and the final decision on whether to publish rests with the editor, producer or publisher concerned.

25 Television and Radio

Broadcasting in Britain has traditionally been based on the principle that it is a public service accountable to the people through Parliament. While retaining the essential public service element, it is now also embracing the principles of competition and choice.

Three public bodies—the British Broadcasting Corporation (BBC), the Independent Television Commission (ITC) and the Radio Authority—are responsible for television and radio services throughout Britain. The BBC broadcasts television and radio programmes, and the ITC and the Radio Authority license and regulate independent television and radio. In Wales, Sianel Pedwar Cymru (S4C) broadcasts programmes on Wales's fourth channel. These authorities work to broad requirements and objectives defined by Parliament, but are otherwise independent in their day-to-day conduct of business.

The government department responsible for overseeing the broadcasting system is the Home Office. The Home Secretary may issue directions on technical and other matters. Since 1988, for example, the BBC and the independent sector have been prohibited from broadcasting direct statements made by representatives of Northern Ireland terrorist groups and their supporters.

Television

Television viewing is by far the most popular leisure pastime: nearly everyone watches television, average viewing time per person being over 24 hours a week.

There are four terrestrial television channels, offering a mixture of drama, light entertainment, films, sport, news and current affairs, documentaries and educational programmes. BBC 1 and BBC 2, which are complementary national networks, are operated by the BBC and financed principally by licence fees. Independent Television (ITV) is controlled by, and at present Channel 4 is a subsidiary of, the ITC. ITV and Channel 4 are expected to complement each other and are largely funded by advertising. All four channels broadcast on 625 lines UHF (ultra-high frequency). Over 99 per cent of the population live within range of transmission.

Over nine-tenths of households have more than one television receiver and one-half have a video recorder.

British television productions continue to win many international awards, and in 1989 television companies received £194 million in export earnings.

Radio

Practically every home has a radio set, and the widespread ownership of portable sets and car radios means that people can listen to radio throughout the day. BBC Radio has five national networks, which transmit all types of music, news, current affairs, drama, education, sport and a broad range of feature programmes. At present there are no national commercial radio stations, but three new national independent stations are planned.

A total of 37 BBC local radio stations serve England and the Channel Islands, and regional and community radio services are operated in Scotland, Wales and Northern Ireland. Some 79 independent local radio (ILR) stations are also available to local communities throughout Britain and further commercial local stations are in the planning stage. About 90 per cent of the population is within range of BBC or ILR stations.

Stations supply a comprehensive service of local news and information, music and other entertainment, education, consumer advice and coverage of local events. 'Phone-in' programmes allow listeners to express their views on air.

Government Approach to Broadcasting

During the last few years broadcasting in Britain has seen considerable changes. The availability of more radio frequencies, together with satellite, cable and microwave transmissions[1] is making more services possible—locally, nationally and internationally. Furthermore, the technical quality of sound and pictures is improving. With rapidly developing technology and rising public demand for a wider choice of programmes and services, the Government introduced legislation in November 1990 to make the regulatory framework for broadcasting more flexible and efficient and to give viewers and listeners access to a broader range of services. At the same time it aims to promote increased competition and maintain high standards of taste and decency. The new law is the Broadcasting Act 1990.

The Act takes full account of the need to guarantee programme quality and diversity, regional links, widespread ownership of broadcasting companies and proper geographical coverage. Provision is made for 'sharply focused statutory safeguards' backed by enforcement sanctions, including financial penalties.

Provisions of the Broadcasting Act 1990

The Broadcasting Act 1990 overhauls the regulation of independent television and radio and permits the introduction of additional services. The Independent Broadcasting Authority (IBA) and the Cable Authority were replaced on 1 January 1991 by the Independent Television Commission and the Radio Authority. The ITC and the Radio Authority are initially being financed

by government loans, but are obliged to repay these and to support themselves from licence fees within three years. There is provision for the privatisation of the IBA's transmission system (see p 422).

The ITC and the Radio Authority are implementing new licensing arrangements for all commercial broadcasters. The ITC is to award major broadcasting licences by competitive tender to the highest bidders satisfying stipulated quality tests. The Radio Authority awards national radio licences by competitive tender to the highest cash bidders. Local radio licences will not be allocated by competitive tender; the success of licence applications will in part be determined by audience demand and the extent to which prospective stations would increase variety. Although regulation will be light, rules will be enforced so that ownership remains widely spread and undue concentrations and cross-media ownership are kept in check.

A new national independent television station and as many as three national commercial radio stations will be established. There will be opportunities for launching hundreds of independent local radio and television channels.

Programming Obligations

The Government does not wish to reduce the role of public service broadcasting. Hence, it has made no change to the BBC's 'cornerstone' public service role of providing high quality programming throughout the full range of public tastes and interests. The programming remits of BBC 1 and BBC 2; BBC Radios 1, 2, 3, 4 and 5; and BBC local radio remain unchanged under the Broadcasting Act 1990. Channel 4—in addition to retaining public service obligations—is, as before, required to be innovative and distinctive, and to cater for tastes and interests not adequately met by ITV/Channel 3. Three of the four current terrestrial television channels have, therefore, the same programming obligations as before the passing of the Act.

Licence-holders of the new independent television Channels 3 and 5 will need to pass

---

[1] Microwave transmission (MVDS) is a form of terrestrial broadcasting using frequencies higher up the spectrum than those normally used for television.

demanding quality tests. A 'proper proportion' of programme material will have to come from Britain and other European countries. Between them, Channels 3, 4 and 5 will need to cater adequately for schools programmes.

By 1993 both the BBC and commercial television licensees will be required to ensure that a minimum of 25 per cent of their original programming comes from independent producers. The system whereby major sporting occasions ('listed events'), such as the Grand National horse race and the Olympic Games, are made generally available to television audiences on the main terrestrial channels is retained.

Programme Standards

Recognising that television and radio are powerful media with the potential to offend, exploit and cause harm, the Act contains guarantees on programme standards which are extended to all British-based broadcasters. These guarantees cover taste, decency, accuracy and balance. The Act removes broadcasters' exemptions from the law of obscenity and incitement to racial hatred. It also makes provision for effective sanctions against those supporting unacceptable foreign satellite services receivable in Britain, and it gives the Broadcasting Standards Council a key role (see p 428).

The ITC and the Radio Authority have already approved programme codes and guidelines dealing with standards and impartiality (see p 427). National television and radio are subject to a 'due impartiality' test, while local radio must comply with a less demanding test for 'undue prominence'.

Ownership Rules

In order to enjoy high standards and diversity, the Government believes that it is necessary to have ownership rules. The Act includes clearer and more extensive rules than existed previously. Non-European-Community controlling ownership is largely prohibited and national newspapers are permitted relatively small stakes in direct

broadcasting by satellite (DBS) channels (see p 426), Channels 3 and 5, and national and local radio.

British Broadcasting Corporation

The constitution and finances of the BBC are governed by a Royal Charter, which expires in December 1996, and by a Licence and Agreement. The Corporation's board of 12 governors, including the chairman, vice-chairman and national governors for Scotland, Wales and Northern Ireland, is appointed by the Queen on the advice of the Government. It has final responsibility for all aspects of broadcasting on the BBC. The governors appoint the Director-General, the Corporation's chief executive officer, who heads the board of management, which is in charge of the daily running of the services.

The BBC has a strong regional structure. The four English regions and the Scottish, Welsh and Northern Ireland national regions make programmes for their local audiences as well as contributing to the national network. The National Broadcasting Councils for Scotland, Wales and Northern Ireland give advice on the policy and content of television and radio programmes intended primarily for reception in their areas. Local radio councils, representative of the local community, advise on the development and operation of the BBC's local radio stations.

Finance

The domestic services of the BBC are financed principally from the sale of television licences. Households with television must buy an annual licence costing £25·50 for black and white and £77 for colour. Over 19 million licences were current in April 1991; of these about 18 million were for colour. More than two-thirds of expenditure on domestic services relates to television.

Licence income is supplemented by profits from trading activities, such as television programme exports, sale of recordings and publications connected with BBC programmes, hire and sale of educational films, film library sales, and exhibitions based on programmes. The BBC meets the cost of its local radio stations, and local education authorities help with the funding and preparation of educational programmes. BBC World Service radio is financed by a grant-in-aid from the Foreign & Commonwealth Office.

In early 1992 the BBC plans to set up a range of specialist subscription services, including one for the legal profession, which will be transmitted during the night. The services will be 'down-loaded' onto video recorders fitted with decoders.

On 1 April 1991, licence fee collection became the responsibility of the BBC. Previously, the Post Office had undertaken this task. With the object of improving efficiency and encouraging the BBC to continue developing alternative sources of revenue, the Government has decided that annual rises in the licence fees should be lower than the rate of inflation. The financing of the BBC will be considered during the next Charter review.

BBC Television

Apart from a break during the second world war (1939–45) the BBC has made regular television broadcasts since 1936.

BBC 1 transmits an average of 124 hours of programmes a week and BBC 2 114 hours; the majority are broadcast on the national network.

More than 70 per cent of the BBC's home-produced network programmes for 1989–90 were produced in London. Both the BBC and the commercial television companies enter into agreements with overseas television corporations in order to make new programmes economically.

Through co-ordinated planning of its two services the BBC caters simultaneously for people of different interests. Although both services cover the whole range of television output, BBC 1 presents more programmes of general interest, such as light entertainment, sport, current affairs, children's programmes and outside broadcasts. BBC 2 places greater emphasis on minority interests, but also

shows documentaries, travel programmes, serious drama, music, programmes on pastimes and international films. On BBC 1 the daytime schedule consists of an early morning service of news and information (from Monday to Friday), followed during the rest of the day by documentaries, children's programmes, films and other programmes catering for many interests.

BBC National Radio

BBC Radio 1 broadcasts rock and pop music 24 hours a day, while Radio 2 (on VHF/FM only) transmits popular music and light entertainment also for 24 hours a day. Although Radio 3 broadcasts mainly classical music, it presents drama, poetry, and short stories and talks too. Radio 4 is the main speech network, providing the principal news and current affairs service, together with drama, comedy, documentaries and panel games. It also carries parliamentary coverage and live relays of major public events. In 1990 the BBC launched Radio 5 (on medium wave only), which is devoted chiefly to sport and education.

Independent Broadcasting

Independent Television Commission

Like the Radio Authority and S4C, the Independent Television Commission's constitution and finances are governed by the Broadcasting Act 1990. The ITC is responsible for licensing and regulating all non-BBC television services, including:

- ITV and its successor, Channel 3;
- Channel 4;
- the proposed Channel 5;
- cable and other local delivery services;
- independent teletext services; and
- domestic and non-domestic satellite services available to viewers in Britain.

The former Independent Broadcasting Authority's television and radio transmission networks and other facilities were transferred to a new state company—National Transcommunications Limited—on 1 January 1991. The company will be sold to

GALLERIES

The Nehru Gallery of Indian Art at the Victoria and Albert Museum aims to encourage the study and appreciation of the Indian heritage. It features a floor of Indian stone and a seventeenth-century Ajmer colonnade.

The new Sainsbury Wing of the National Gallery, which opened in July 1991. A gift from the Sainsbury family, it will provide a venue for major international touring exhibitions and other events.

SPORT

Martine Le Moignan, one of Britain's leading women's squash players, was world champion between March 1989 and October 1990.

Britain's top Formula One racing driver Nigel Mansell won three Grand Prix races in a row in 1991 in the British-French Williams Renault.

Kriss Akabusi, one of Britain's gold-medal-winning 4×400 metres relay team, gains a bronze medal in the 400 metres hurdles at the World Athletics Championships in Tokyo in September 1991.

Don Valley stadium, Sheffield, was the athletics venue for the 1991 World Student Games. The games attracted 6,000 competitors from 120 countries.

BRITISH COUNCIL

The British Council is helping to develop the
Science Faculty at Yarmouk University, Jordan.
Here a student learns to produce laboratory
equipment in the glass-blowing workshop.

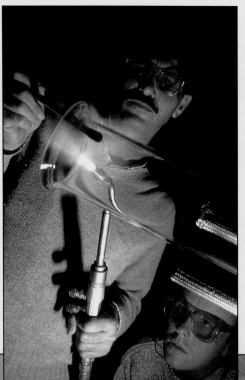

Foreign students in the UK attend an English
language course run by the British Council.

the private sector before the end of 1991.

The ITC is advised by committees on educational broadcasting, religious broadcasting, charitable appeals and advertising. Viewer consultative councils also comment on the commercial services' programmes.

Until December 1992, when the present ITV franchises (see below) end, the ITC will continue to fulfil the IBA's obligations towards the ITV contracts. It will be legally responsible for broadcasting programmes shown on ITV, Channel 4 and by direct broadcasting by satellite (DBS) services. Channel 4 will be a subsidiary company of the ITC till the end of 1992, after which it will be set up as a corporation in its own right.

From 1993, when the new Channel 3 licences begin, the ITC will not broadcast or 'publish' programmes. These responsibilities will pass to the new licensees. The ITC will supervise with a 'light touch' in that it will not be involved in detailed scheduling of programmes. It has wider powers than the IBA to enforce licence conditions and rules designed to limit cross-media ownership and excessive concentration of ownership (see p 420).

ITV Programme Companies

At present 15 independent (ITV) companies hold contracts to supply programmes in the 14 independent television geographical regions. Two companies share the contract for London, one providing programmes during weekdays and the other at the weekend. A contract for a national early morning service, transmitted on the ITV network, is held by an additional company.

The companies operate on a commercial basis, deriving most of their revenue from the sale of advertising time. The financial resources, advertising revenue and programme production of the companies vary considerably, depending largely on the size of population in the areas in which they operate. Although newspapers may acquire an interest in programme companies, there are safeguards to ensure against concentration of media ownership and thereby protect the public interest.

Each programme company plans the content of the programmes to be broadcast in its area. These are produced by the company itself, or by other programme companies or bought from elsewhere. The five largest companies—two serving London and three serving north-west England, the Midlands and Yorkshire—supply more programmes for broadcast elsewhere on the national network than do the smaller ones.

A common news service is provided 24 hours a day by Independent Television News (ITN), a non-profit-making company in which all the programme companies are shareholders.

ITV Programmes

The first regular ITV programmes began in London in 1955. ITV programmes are broadcast 24 hours a day in all parts of the country. About one-third of the output comprises informative programmes—news, documentaries, and programmes on current affairs, education and religion. The remainder cover sport, comedy, drama, game shows, films, and a range of other programmes with popular appeal. Over a half of programmes are produced by the programme companies and ITN.

Channel 3

Under the Broadcasting Act 1990 the present independent television system (ITV) will be replaced by Channel 3 in January 1993. The new channel will be made up of 15 regionally based licensees of the Independent Television Commission (see p 422), which decides the areas to be covered, and an additional ITC licensee providing a national breakfast-time programme. A total of 40 applications for licences have been received by the ITC, which intends to award the licences by 31 October 1991.

Licences are to be awarded for a ten-year period by competitive tender to the highest bidder who has passed a quality threshold; in exceptional cases a lower bid can be selected. Such circumstances might include those where an applicant was able to offer a quality of service significantly better than that offered by the highest bidder.

There will be substantial safeguards for quality programming. Licensees will be required to offer a diverse programme service and a proportion of good quality programmes, as well as high quality regional and national news and current affairs programmes and children's and religious programmes. There is to be, for the first time, a statutory duty to present programmes made in and about the region. Distinct regional programming aimed at different areas within regions will also be required.

Channel 3 licensees will be obliged to operate a national programme network. Networking arrangements are to be subject to government approval so that anti-competitive practices are avoided.

ITN has been appointed to supply a service of national and international news to Channel 3 for a ten-year period starting in January 1993.

Channel 4 and S4C

Channel 4, which began broadcasting in 1982, provides a national television service throughout Britain, except in Wales, which has a corresponding service—Sianel Pedwar Cymru (S4C). It is required to present programmes that are complementary to those of ITV, appealing to tastes and interests not normally catered for by the original independent service.

Channel 4 must present a suitable proportion of educational programmes and encourage innovation and experiment. Its schedules include a substantial proportion of programmes from independent producers. Channel 4 broadcasts for approximately 140 hours a week, about half of which are devoted to informative programmes. The service, both nationally and in Wales, is financed by subscriptions from the ITV programme companies in return for advertising time in fourth channel programmes broadcast in their own regions.

In Wales programmes on the fourth channel are run and controlled by S4C,

formerly the Welsh Fourth Channel Authority. Its members are appointed by the Government. S4C is required to see that a significant proportion of programming, in practice 23 hours a week, is in the Welsh language and that programmes broadcast between 18.30 and 22.00 hours are mainly in Welsh. At other times S4C transmits national Channel 4 programmes.

Channel 4 and S4C's distinctive remit to screen diverse programmes has been strengthened under the Broadcasting Act 1990 and the services are guaranteed by special arrangements to protect revenue levels. Channel 4 is to become a public corporation from 1993, selling its own advertising time and retaining the proceeds. S4C will be government-funded.

Channel 5

A new national terrestrial television channel—Channel 5—is to be established by the beginning of 1994. Owing to limited frequency availability it will cover only about 70 per cent of households.

The ten-year franchise will be awarded by competitive tender subject to a quality threshold. The new channel will have similar programming obligations to Channel 3. However, there is to be no requirement to provide either regional or local programmes. The ITC expects the franchise-holder to be based outside the south of England. The new channel will be financed through advertising, subscription or sponsorship, or a combination of all three.

Local Television

The Broadcasting Act 1990 makes provision for the further development of local television services. Local delivery franchises will be awarded by competitive tender and there will be no quality threshold. ITC franchise-holders will be able to supply national and local television channels using both cable and microwave transmission systems. Services delivered could include DBS channels or Channel 5 in parts of the country where it was not available on UHF. Other services could be aimed at communities such as ethnic minorities and Gaelic speakers.

Independent Radio

The underlying principles of independent local radio (ILR) are similar to those of ITV (see p 423). The programme companies operate under licence to the Radio Authority and are financed mainly by advertising revenue. News coverage is supplied by Independent Radio News. Licences for existing operators will expire by 31 December 1996.

The Radio Authority took over responsibility for independent radio from the IBA on 1 January 1991. Like the Independent Television Commission, it supervises with a light touch. The new authority will allocate licences by competitive tender for up to three national commercial radio services. One of these must be speech-based and another has to include a large proportion of music that is not pop music. The first national radio franchise was awarded to Classic FM in August 1991, which will play mainly popular classical music.

The Radio Authority is required to encourage the provision of licensed services which, taken as a whole, are of a high quality and offer a broad range of programmes calculated to appeal to a variety of tastes and interests. Powers to deter 'pirate' or illegal broadcasters have been strengthened.

In the course of the 1990s, 200 to 300 new stations could come on the air, some of which could be neighbourhood and community-of-interest stations. Areas to be covered will initially be those which are presently unserved or only marginally served or which form distinctive communities within existing ILR areas. Local audience demand and the extent to which the service could broaden the variety of local programmes will affect local licence allocation.

In 1988 the Government approved the issue of contracts for 23 new community-of-interest and ethnic minority radio stations. The first to go on the air, in 1989, was Sunset Radio, aimed at Manchester's multi-cultural population. Jazz FM became the first of the new London music stations, starting up in 1990.

Teletext

The BBC and independent television each operate a teletext service, offering constantly updated information on a variety of subjects, including news, sport, travel, local weather conditions and entertainment. The teletext system allows the television signal to carry additional information which can be selected and displayed as 'pages' of text and graphics on receivers equipped with the necessary decoders. Both Ceefax, the BBC's service, and independent television's Oracle service have a subtitling facility for certain programmes for people with hearing difficulties.

The Broadcasting Act 1990 introduced a new regulatory system for the licensing of spare capacity within the television signal. This allows more varied use of spare capacity—data transfer, for instance—but the position of teletext on commercial television is safeguarded. Channels 3 and 5 will be obliged to offer a subtitling service for at least 50 per cent of their programmes by 1998, with further increases after that.

Cable Services

Cable services are delivered to consumers by means of underground cables and are normally paid for by subscription. The Cable Authority was established in 1984 to issue licences, supervise programme services and promote cable development. By the time it handed over its responsibilities to the Cable Division of the ITC—on 1 January 1991—it had awarded 135 new broadband (multi-channel) cable franchises. These cover two-thirds of all homes and nearly all urban areas, around 14·5 million households in total. Some 37 broadband franchises are now in operation and over 900,000 homes have access to broadband cable. The ITC is continuing the Cable Authority's practice of awarding only one broadband cable franchise in any given area so that the new franchisee is protected from direct competition in the early stages.

Since the formation of the ITC 53

channel licences have been issued. Licences are granted, on a non-competitive basis, to programme services which are likely to meet consumer protection standards and are run by suitably qualified people.

The new broadband cable systems carry up to 30 television channels, including terrestrial broadcasts, satellite television, channels delivered by videotape and local services. Some are also able to offer telephone services, home shopping and other interactive services. Since January 1991 new operators, and some established ones, have had the choice of using microwave transmissions to extend their coverage beyond viewers who already have cable.

Cable investment must be privately financed. Although all cable channels require a licence from the ITC, regulation is as light as possible to encourage the development of a wide range of services and facilities, and flexible enough to adapt to changing technology. Safeguards protect the viability of existing broadcasting services.

Broadcasting by Satellite

Several British-based satellite television channels have been set up to supply programmes to cable operators in Britain and, in many cases, throughout Europe. While some offer general entertainment, others concentrate on specific areas of interest, such as sport, music and children's programmes.

Direct broadcasting by satellite (DBS), by which television pictures are transmitted directly by satellite into people's homes, has been available throughout Britain since 1989. The signals from satellite broadcasting are receivable using specially designed aerials or 'dishes' and associated reception equipment. A European Community directive requires the use of the MAC/packet family of standards for all DBS services (see p 431).

British Sky Broadcasting (BSkyB) carries channels devoted to light entertainment, news, feature films and sport transmitted from the Astra and Marcopolo satellites. The Astra satellites can transmit 32 channels in all, nine of which are in English and are available to cable subscribers. Other channels broadcast sport, general entertainment for women, and a service for children. MTV is a pop video channel. BSkyB plans to introduce additional channels using the recently launched second Astra satellite.

The Marcopolo satellite carries BSkyB broadcasts made under contract to the ITC on the five DBS channels allocated to Britain under international agreement. The company has agreed to surrender any of these channels on six months' notice from the ITC, which would then license a new user.

Educational Broadcasting

Both the BBC and independent television broadcast educational programmes for children and adults in educational institutions and at home. Broadcasts to schools deal with most subjects of the curriculum, while education programmes for adults cover many fields of learning, vocational training and recreation. Supporting material, in the form of books, pamphlets, filmstrips, computer software, and audio and video cassettes, is available to supplement the programmes.

The BBC broadcasts television and radio programmes made specially for students of the Open University. The BBC Open University Centre also produces educational and training audio-visual materials in collaboration with external agencies such as the Department of Trade and Industry and the Department of Education and Science. The Open College, set up in 1987 with government support, transmits courses on Channel 4 ranging from basic literacy and numeracy to high-level technological studies.

The Independent Television Commission has a duty to ensure that schools programmes are presented on independent television.

Advertising and Sponsorship

The BBC does not give publicity to any outside firm or organised interest except when it is necessary in order to make effective and informative programmes. It must not broadcast any commercial advertisement or any sponsored programme;

it may, however, cover sponsored events.

After considering a report commissioned by the Department of Trade and Industry on cross-media promotion, the Government has decided to refer the way the BBC promotes its own publications to the Monopolies and Mergers Commission. It has also asked the newspaper industry to draw up a code of practice on cross-media promotion.

Advertising and sponsorship are allowed on independent television and radio subject to controls. Codes of advertising standards and programme sponsorship covering commercial television and radio are operated by the ITC and the Radio Authority.

Advertising

Advertisements are broadcast on independent television in between programmes as well as in breaks during programmes. Advertisers are not allowed directly to influence programme content or editorial control. Food manufacturers and retailers are the largest category of advertisers.

Advertisements must be clearly distinguishable and separate from programmes. The time given to them must not be so great as to detract from the value of the programmes as a medium of information, education or entertainment. Television advertising between 18.00 and 23.00 hours is limited to seven and a half minutes an hour. The overall amount of advertising throughout the day is normally restricted to seven minutes an hour. Independent television's Oracle teletext service (see p 425) carries paginated advertisements.

The ITC and the Radio Authority operate codes governing standards and practice in advertising, and giving guidance on the types and methods of advertisement which are prohibited; these include political advertising and advertisements for cigarettes or betting. Television advertising for cigar and pipe tobacco will be banned from October 1991. At present religious advertising is not allowed on ITV and Channel 4, and while permitted on radio must comply with the Radio Authority's code on religious advertising. From 1993 Channels 3 and 4

will be allowed to screen religious advertisements.

Advertisements may not be inserted in certain types of programme, such as broadcasts to schools. Both the ITC and the Radio Authority have the power to prevent transmission of advertisements which they consider misleading. The Broadcasting Standards Council's code of practice (see p 428) covers advertisements.

Sponsorship

Sponsorship of certain programmes shown by independent television is permitted, provided that it conforms with ITC guidelines and relevant national and international laws.

The ITC's sponsorship code takes as its guiding principle the safeguarding of programme integrity. News and current affairs programmes may not be sponsored. In the case of other programmes, sponsorship is not allowed where there might be a clash of interests. References to sponsors or their products have to be confined to the beginning and end of a programme and around commercial breaks; they must not appear in the programme itself. All commercial radio programmes other than news bulletins can be sponsored.

Government Publicity

The Government has no general privileged access to radio or television but government publicity material to support non-political campaigns may be broadcast on independent radio and television. This is paid for on a normal commercial basis. Short public service items, concerning health, safety and welfare, are also produced by the Central Office of Information for free transmission by the BBC and independent television and radio.

Broadcasting Standards

The independence enjoyed by the broadcasting authorities carries with it certain obligations towards programmes and programme content. Programmes must display, as far as possible, a proper balance and wide range of subject matter, impartiality in matters of controversy and accuracy in news coverage, and they must not offend against good taste. In addition, broadcasters must now comply with legislation relating to obscenity and incitement to racial hatred.

Codes providing guidance on violence and standards of taste and decency in television programmes, particularly during hours when large numbers of children are likely to be viewing, are applied by the BBC and the other regulatory authorities.

Under the 1990 Act the Government can prohibit unacceptable foreign satellite services receivable in Britain. Anyone in Britain supporting such a service can be prosecuted for a criminal offence.

Broadcasting Standards Council

The Broadcasting Standards Council was set up by the Government to act as a focus for public concern about the portrayal of violence and sex, and about standards of taste and decency. Its remit covers television and radio programmes and broadcast advertisements. A code of practice has been drawn up by the Council on these matters. It monitors programmes, examines complaints from the public and undertakes research. The Council has already published the results of several public attitude surveys.

Under the Broadcasting Act 1990 the Council has been granted statutory powers under which the BBC and other broadcasting regulatory bodies' codes of practice are required to reflect the Council's own code. Broadcasters are obliged to publish the Council's findings on complaints in whatever form it considers appropriate.

Programmes broadcast to Britain from abroad are monitored by the Council.

Broadcasting Complaints Commission

The Broadcasting Complaints Commission is financed by contributions from the BBC, ITC, Radio Authority and S4C. It deals with allegations of unfair treatment in broadcast programmes and of unwarranted infringement of privacy in programmes or in their preparation. In 1989–90 it received 550 complaints.

Parliamentary and Political Broadcasting

The proceedings of both Houses of Parliament may be broadcast on television and radio, either live, or more usually in recorded and edited form on news and current affairs programmes.

The proceedings of the House of Commons have been televised since 1989. They are produced by an independent company appointed by the House of Commons, which makes television pictures available to the BBC, Independent Television News and other approved broadcasters for use in news and current affairs programmes. House of Lords proceedings have been televised since 1985.

The BBC and the commercial services provide time on radio and television for an annual series of party political broadcasts. Party election broadcasts are arranged following the announcement of a general election. In addition, the Government may make ministerial broadcasts on radio and television, with opposition parties also being allotted broadcast time.

Audience Research

Both the BBC and the independent sector are required to keep themselves informed on the state of public opinion about the programmes and advertising which they broadcast. This is done through the continuous measurement of the size and composition of audiences and their opinions of programmes. For television, this work is undertaken through the Broadcasters' Audience Research Board, which is owned jointly by the BBC and the Independent Television Association, the trade association for the ITV companies.

Regular surveys are conducted by both the BBC and the independent sector to gauge audience opinion on television and radio services. Public opinion is further assessed by the BBC and ITC through the work of their advisory committees, councils and panels. Regular public meetings are also held to debate services, and careful consideration is given to correspondence and telephone calls from listeners and viewers.

BBC World Service Radio

The BBC World Service broadcasts by radio worldwide, using English and 35 other languages, for 780 hours a week. The main objectives are to give unbiased news, reflect British opinion and project British life, culture and developments in science and industry. News bulletins, current affairs programmes, political commentaries and topical magazine programmes form the main part of the output. These are supplemented by a sports service, music, drama and general entertainment. Regular listeners are estimated to number 120 million.

The languages in which the World Service broadcasts and the length of time each is on the air are prescribed by the Government. Otherwise the BBC has full responsibility and is completely independent in determining the content of news and other programmes.

There are broadcasts by radio for 24 hours a day in English, which are supplemented at peak listening times by programmes of special interest to Africa, South Asia and the Falkland Islands.

BBC World Service news bulletins and other programmes are re-broadcast by more than 250 stations in over 60 countries, which receive the programmes by satellite. Two World Service departments also specialise in supplying radio material for re-broadcast. One sells recordings to more than 100 countries, and the other mails some 260 tapes of original programmes to over 50 countries each week.

BBC English is the most extensive language-teaching undertaking in the world. English lessons are broadcast daily by radio with explanations in over 25 languages, including English, and re-broadcast by many radio stations. BBC English television programmes are also shown in more than 100 countries. A range of printed and audio material accompanies these programmes.

Another part of the World Service, BBC Monitoring, listens to and reports on foreign broadcasts, providing a daily flow of significant news and comment from overseas to the BBC and the Government. This information is also sold to the press, private sector companies, academic staff and public bodies.

BBC World Service Television

In April 1991 the BBC launched a new television service along the lines of BBC World Service radio. It replaces BBC TV Europe, a service based on BBC 1 and 2 transmissions. The new service comprises a World Service Television News programme, a selection of BBC 1 and 2 programmes and English language teaching programmes produced by BBC English.

World Service Television News is being sold in English and different language versions for re-broadcasting throughout the world. It incorporates pictures from NBC (National Broadcasting Company of the United States) and Visnews (see below) and draws on the resources of BBC Monitoring. In addition to existing BBC television news coverage, it includes specially recorded material. The programme combines the editorial priorities and global news agenda established by BBC World Service radio news with the facilities offered by the BBC television news and current affairs service.

The BBC generates its own funding for the new service; no licence fee or taxpayers' money is involved.

COI Overseas Radio and Television Services

The Central Office of Information (COI), which provides publicity material and other information services on behalf of government departments and other public agencies, produces radio programmes for overseas. A wide range of recorded material is sent to radio stations all over the world. COI television services make available material such as documentary and magazine programmes for distribution to overseas stations.

News Agencies

Visnews is the largest television news agency in the world, supplying world newsfilm to over 400 broadcasters in 84 countries and running bureaux in 31 major cities throughout the world. The BBC and Reuters are shareholders in the company. Worldwide Television News, owned by Independent Television News, the American Broadcasting Company and Channel 9 in Australia, supplies news services to around 1,000 broadcasters in 75 countries. Both agencies provide services through the Eurovision network (see below) and by satellite.

International Relations

European Agreements

The Government will implement two important European agreements on cross-border broadcasting in October 1991: the European Community Directive on Broadcasting and the Council of Europe Convention on Transfrontier Television. These contain rules about programme standards, advertising, sponsorship and other matters. Programmes must not be indecent, contain pornography, give undue prominence to violence or be likely to incite racial hatred. Nor should programmes unsuitable for children be broadcast at a time when they are likely to be watching.

European Broadcasting Union

The BBC, ITC and Radio Authority are members of the European Broadcasting Union, which manages Eurovision, the international network of television news and programme exchange. The Union is responsible for the technical and administrative arrangements for co-ordinating the exchange of programmes and news over the Eurovision network and intercontinental satellite links. It also maintains a technical monitoring station where frequency measurements and other observations on broadcasting stations are carried out. The Union provides a forum linking the major public services and national broadcasters of Western Europe and other parts of the world, and co-ordinates joint operations in radio and television.

International Telecommunications Union

The BBC, ITC and Radio Authority participate in the work of the International Telecommunications Union, the United Nations agency responsible for regulating and controlling all international telecommunications services, including radio and television. It also allocates and registers all radio frequencies, and promotes and co-ordinates the international study of technical problems in broadcasting.

Other International Bodies

The BBC, ITC and Radio Authority are associate members of the Asia-Pacific Broadcasting Union, and the BBC also belongs to the Commonwealth Broadcasting Association, whose members meet every two years to discuss public service broadcasting issues.

Training

The BBC provides non-financial technical assistance, particularly in training the staff of overseas broadcasting organisations. The Government finances overseas students on broadcasting training courses at the BBC, British Council[2] and the Thomson Foundation Television College in Glasgow, which sends lecturers, and arranges courses, overseas.

Technological Developments

One of the most important recent developments in television has been in news coverage, where compact electronic cameras have replaced film cameras, eliminating the 'need for film processing and enabling pictures to be transmitted directly to a studio or recorded on video tape on location.

---

[2] This aims to promote a wider knowledge of Britain and the English language abroad and to develop closer cultural relations between Britain and other countries.

Other recent advances in television broadcasting include:

- adoption of digital video tape recorders;
- increasing use of computer-aided equipment for picture generation and manipulation;
- use of portable satellite links to transmit pictures from remote locations to studios; and
- the introduction of stereo sound on the NICAM 728 digital system, developed jointly by the BBC, IBA and the British Radio and Electronic Manufacturers' Association.

The independent television networks are being adapted for digital stereo sound. The independent sector is also engaged in the further development of digital techniques for studio applications and inter-city links. In satellite broadcasting, the MAC transmission format was developed by IBA engineers, who went on to devise refinements for the MAC system compatible with widescreen television. The 1,250-line high definition television (HDTV) is being developed by the EUREKA 95 group of British and other European manufacturers. The BBC and IBA co-operated in the development of teletext, and teletext sets in 30 countries are based on the British system. British Telecom's public viewdata service, 'Prestel', offers a broad range of information transmitted by telephone and viewed on the television screen.

26 Sport and Recreation

The British invented and codified the rules of many of the sports and games now played all over the world, and today there is widespread participation in and watching of sport in Britain. British sportsmen and women compete internationally in some 70 different sports and among their number are around 70 world champions in 27 sports. Large crowds attend occasions such as the football and rugby league Challenge Cup Finals at Wembley Stadium, international rugby union matches at Twickenham (near London), Murrayfield (Edinburgh) and Cardiff Arms Park; the Wimbledon lawn tennis championships; the classic horse races; the Open Golf Championship; Grand Prix motor racing; and international cricket matches.

Sport is a major industry in Britain: in addition to the professional sportsmen and women, some 370,000 people are employed in the provision of sports clothing, publicity, ground and club maintenance and other activities connected with sport. In total an estimated £3,500 million is spent on sport annually in Britain.

Participation

Levels of participation in sport have been rising, due mainly to an increase in leisure time and facilities, greater mobility and improvements in living standards. A growing awareness of the importance of regular exercise for good health has also contributed to this trend and is reflected in the upsurge of interest in jogging, keep fit and dance-related forms of exercise.

It has been estimated that 25 million people over the age of 13 regularly take part in sport or exercise, with men outnumbering women. Walking, including rambling and hiking, is by far the most popular recreation, followed by swimming, football, golf, keep fit and yoga, athletics, angling, squash, badminton and cycling. Other widely practised spare-time physical activities include gardening and 'do-it-yourself' repair and improvement work.

Women and Sport

A major priority in official development plans for sport is to narrow the gap between men's and women's participation in active sport and recreation. A more positive attitude towards physical fitness has led to growing participation by women in athletics. Women also take part more in 'physical contact' sports such as football and rugby, which were previously regarded as 'unfeminine'. Sports from which they had been excluded by tradition, rather than on the grounds of physical differences, are similarly increasing in popularity among women: for instance, larger numbers now play snooker and billiards.

Many sports have separate governing bodies for women and competitive events are normally organised in divisions for men and women. One notable exception is equestrianism, where women riders compete on equal terms with men. Mixed events in which men and women take part together are traditional in sports such as tennis, badminton and ice-skating, and have been growing in popularity in golf.

Lacrosse and netball are played predominantly by women; these, together with tennis, badminton, athletics, hockey, swimming and gymnastics, are the sports most usually played by girls at school. Pressure from schools is leading to the inclusion of girls in formerly all-boy sports teams, particularly soccer teams at junior level. Men's and women's governing bodies are amalgamating increasingly, and women are encouraged to adopt leadership positions in coaching and administration.

Televised Sport

Extensive coverage on television (2,700 hours on the four terrestrial channels in 1990) has helped to generate interest in a growing number of sports and recreations. Sports attracting the larger television audiences include association football, cricket, athletics and snooker. The advent of direct broadcasting by satellite and the greater availability of cable are increasing televised coverage of sport substantially. At present three satellite channels are devoted to sport.

Important sporting occasions ('listed events'), such as the Grand National horse race, Olympic Games and cricket Test matches involving England, have to be made generally available to television audiences; they may not be shown exclusively on 'pay-per-view' television.

GOVERNMENT POLICIES

The Government has long recognised the importance of physical recreation for the health and general welfare of the community. The social role that sport can play has become more important at a time of rapid change in work and leisure patterns. Success in sport is also thought to strengthen Britain's international status and prestige.

Increased emphasis is being placed on the need to provide new and improved sports facilities in areas of urban deprivation. A range of sports and recreational projects in urban areas have been supported under the Government's Urban Programme. The Derelict Land Grant scheme offers funding towards sports and recreational facilities on reclaimed sites. Water companies are required to ensure that water and land under their control are put to the best use for sport and recreation.

In 1987 the Government initiated a public debate on the future direction of official sports policy. It asked whether a correct balance was being achieved between funding sporting excellence and encouraging wider participation, and whether enough was being done to promote private sector investment in sport, especially through corporate sponsorship (see p 441). A major review of sport and recreation provision in inner cities was undertaken in 1988 by a government-appointed group of business people, athletes and sports administrators. The main conclusions were that there was a need for more small, local facilities and for ways of enabling inner city communities to run their own facilities.

A government statement of its policies on sport and active recreation is expected to be published late in 1991.

Organisation and Administration

Government policy on sport, active recreation and children's play is co-ordinated in England by the Minister for Sport, a Parliamentary Under-Secretary of State at the Department of Education and Science (DES). The Government transferred responsibility for sport from the Department of the Environment to the DES in 1990 in order to give a greater emphasis to school sport, which it considers to be the foundation for continuing sporting activity in adulthood. The Secretaries of State for Wales, Scotland and Northern Ireland are responsible for sport in their countries.

Responsibility for the organisation and promotion of sport is largely decentralised, and many sports and recreation facilities are provided by local authorities. The Government gives financial and other assistance through a number of official bodies and schemes. This 'arm's length' principle of funding safeguards the long-established independence of sports organisations in Britain. Some of these bodies, such as the Sports Councils (see p 437) and the Countryside Commission, have specific responsibilities for sport and/or recreation, and help other public and private bodies to make facilities available. Others, like the Forestry Commission, provide recreational amenities in addition to their main functions.

Government support for the development of sport in Britain is channelled through four independent bodies—the Sports Council (for England and for general matters affecting Britain as a whole), the Sports Council for Wales, the Scottish Sports Council and the Sports Council for Northern Ireland. In Northern Ireland the Department of Education makes direct grants towards the capital cost of facilities to local authorities and voluntary sports bodies.

The Minister for Sport co-ordinates policy on children's play in England. The Sports Council is responsible for the National Children's Play and Recreation Unit. This advises the Government on policy and practice regarding children's play and play-providers and other bodies on such issues as playground safety.

Sports in Education

Publicly maintained schools must provide for the physical education of their pupils. Physical education is one of the ten foundation subjects of the National Curriculum, which are compulsory for all schoolchildren in England and Wales between the ages of 5 and 16. Formal programmes of study, attainment targets and tests for physical education will be introduced from 1992. In Northern Ireland, physical education is one of the compulsory subjects for 4- to 16-year-olds, and programmes of study and attainment targets are to be phased in from September 1991. Physical education also features in the recommended curriculum for Scottish schools. As part of the Government's review of sport and active recreation (see p 434), consideration is being given to ways of increasing participation by schoolchildren in sport both during and after school hours.

All schools (except those solely for infants) are expected to have a playing field or the use of one, and most secondary schools have a gymnasium. Some have other amenities such as swimming pools, sports halls and halls designed for dance and movement. The School Sports Forum was established by the Sports Council in 1987 to consider all aspects of the provision of sport in schools.

Sports and recreation facilities are available at institutions of higher and further education, some of which have departments of physical education. There are also 'centres of sporting excellence', often at universities and colleges, which enable selected young athletes to develop their talents and which cater, where appropriate, for their educational needs.

To achieve the maximum use of sports facilities, the Government and the Sports Councils are encouraging greater community use of sports halls and other facilities owned by schools, colleges and institutions such as football clubs. Stronger links are being developed between schools and the wider community to ensure that children have access to sports amenities which clubs and associations can make available outside school hours.

Competitive Tendering

The Government is instituting competitive tendering for the management of local authority sports and leisure facilities to make them more cost-effective and responsive to consumer demand. School and college facilities are exempted from competition, and councils will retain controls over pricing, admission and opening hours.

Safety at Sports Grounds

Safety at sports grounds is governed by legislation. The main instrument of control is a safety certificate which is issued by the relevant local authority. When determining the conditions of a safety certificate the local authority is expected to comply with the Home Office guide, *Safety at Sports Grounds*. This was revised in 1990 to include recommendations of the 'Taylor Report' on the Hillsborough stadium disaster in Sheffield in 1989, when 95 spectators were crushed to death. The Government has accepted all of the report's safety recommendations, including:

● reducing density on terraces;

● better training of and greater vigilance by all those responsible for controlling and stewarding spectators; and

- painting of all emergency exit gates in perimeter fences in distinctive colours and keeping them unlocked while spectators are present.

In compliance with another of the report's recommendations, by 1994 spectators will only be admitted to seated accommodation at grounds in the First and Second Divisions of the Football League and the Premier Division in Scotland. The requirement for seated accommodation will apply at Third and Fourth Division League grounds by 1999. By reducing the pool betting duty (see p 452), the Government is making available £100 million over five years to assist clubs in making the necessary ground improvements.

The Football Licensing Authority, established under the Football Spectators Act 1989, will be responsible for issuing licences for designated matches. A condition of a licence is likely to be that the deadlines for becoming all-seated are met. The authority will also monitor the way in which local authorities carry out the safety functions.

Spectator Violence

Spectator violence associated with football both in Britain and overseas has been a subject of widespread concern, and the Government has worked closely with the football authorities and the governments of other European countries to implement measures to combat the problem. The British Government has also continued to press for the closest co-operation with the football authorities and the police and their counterparts throughout Europe. Within the Council of Europe, Britain contributes to the work of the Standing Committee on the European Convention on Spectator Violence, which it chaired until 1990. Britain was the first country to sign and ratify the Convention. It has welcomed the Committee's recommendation urging tough action against hooliganism, including prosecution where appropriate.

Recognising the link between excessive alcohol consumption and crowd disorder, the Government introduced legislation in Scotland in 1980 and in the rest of Britain in 1985 to establish firm controls on the sale and possession of alcohol at football grounds and on transport to and from grounds. The Public Order Act 1986 gave courts in England and Wales the power to prohibit convicted football hooligans from attending football matches. It also introduced a new offence of disorderly conduct and banned possession of fireworks and smoke bombs at matches. Closed-circuit television at all Football League grounds has greatly assisted the police controlling crowds and is an important evidence-gathering tool. The National Football Intelligence Unit, formed in 1989, co-ordinates police intelligence about football hooligans and strengthens liaison with overseas police forces. Courts in England and Wales have powers to impose restriction orders on convicted football hooligans to prevent them travelling abroad to attend specified matches.

New legislation makes it an offence to:

- throw objects at football matches;
- run onto the pitch without good reason; and
- chant indecent or racist slogans.

Drug Misuse

The problem of drug-taking in sport in order to improve performance unfairly has been a cause of concern to the Government, Sports Councils and governing bodies of sport. A campaign to tackle the problem, launched by the Sports Council, led to the introduction of a new drug testing regime in 1988. This provides for random testing of competitors in and out of competition by independent sampling officers, and the publication of adverse findings. The Sports Council provides financial support for the British drug testing programme. It also funds the International Olympic Committee (IOC)-accredited laboratory at London University, which carries out analysis and research into methods of detection for new drugs that unfairly aid performance.

International Co-operation

The Government and the Sports Council have taken action against drug misuse at international level. For example, they supported the adoption of a Council of Europe Anti-Doping Charter in 1984 and chaired an international working party to examine ways of promoting effective anti-doping measures.

In 1990 a new Council of Europe Anti-Doping Convention came into force to tackle the problem of drug abuse in sport. This was a British initiative, whose main aims are to reinforce the ban on the use of drugs and doping methods specified by the IOC and to require signatory states to restrict the availability of prohibited drugs. The convention seeks to ensure that grants are given only to those sports bodies with anti-doping regulations. Signatory states are encouraged to set up doping-control laboratories meeting IOC standards, and sports governing bodies are urged to harmonise out-of-competition testing and other anti-doping regulations with those of the IOC. Testing at international events and out-of-competition testing by international sports bodies are also promoted under the new agreement. Britain has already implemented many provisions of this agreement.

Gleneagles Agreement

In accordance with the statement on apartheid in sport, agreed by the Commonwealth heads of Government at Gleneagles in Scotland in 1977, the Government has sought to discourage sporting contacts with any country where sports are organised on the basis of race, colour or ethnic origin. However, it has been for individuals and organisations concerned to decide whether to heed this advice.

SPORTS COUNCILS

The Sports Councils are allocating government funds amounting to about £70 million in 1991–92. They make grants for sports development, coaching and administration to the governing bodies of sports and other national organisations, and administer the national sports centres (see p 438). Grants and loans are also made to voluntary organisations, local authorities and commercial organisations, to help them provide sports facilities. British representatives at international sports meetings are assisted by the Sports Council, which encourages links with international and overseas organisations. The Councils are also concerned with preserving and extending recreational and sporting access to the countryside.

Facilities receiving support include sports halls, indoor swimming pools, intensive-use pitches, indoor tennis halls and school facilities. The Indoor Tennis Initiative is a major building programme to increase the availability of indoor tennis courts. It is sponsored by the Sports Council and the tennis authorities.

Ten regional councils for sport and recreation in England, on each of which sporting, recreational, educational, and local authority interests are represented, advise on investment in, and the planning of, sporting and recreational facilities and the promotion of sport.

The Sports Council is exploring ways of attracting greater private sector investment in sport, including the use of incentive funding schemes whereby public money is used to generate revenue from private sources.

Campaigns

The ten-year strategy for the development of sport in England was drawn up by the Sports Council in 1982, and reviewed in 1988. It aims:

- to encourage further participation, particularly among women and young people;
- to provide adequate facilities for the whole community, especially in the inner cities and in deprived rural areas; and
- to continue to encourage high standards of performance.

Similar strategies are being followed by the Sports Councils for Scotland, Wales and Northern Ireland. The Sports Councils have designated 1991 the 'year of sport'.

Much of the Sports Council's budget is directed at increasing participation by the general public.

The Council is also concentrating on raising participation rates among inner city dwellers, people with disabilities (see p 440) and other groups experiencing difficulties in gaining access to sporting opportunities. It works towards improving coaching, sports science and sports medicine as part of the drive to increase standards of performance.

One of the Sports Council's objectives is to encourage 1·25 million more women and 750,000 more men to take part in sport by 1993–94.

The Sports Council's 'Action Sport' programme, designed principally to encourage socially disadvantaged people to take up sport and recreation, has been managed in partnership with local authorities; around 60 schemes are still running with the aid of Sports Council funding. Many local authorities have gone on to provide their own schemes without Sports Council financial support. The Council has also supported initiatives aimed at strengthening links between football clubs and their local communities. 'What's Your Sport?', a campaign to increase participation in sports, was launched by the four Sports Councils in 1987.

'Team Sport Scotland', administered by the Scottish Sports Council, aims to encourage team sports by promoting links between schools, sports clubs and other interested organisations.

Sports Centres

Five national sports centres, four in England and one in Wales, are run by the Sports Council, and offer a range of competition and training facilities. As well as running residential courses for national teams, coaches and enthusiasts from all over Britain, the centres are used extensively by local sports clubs and the local community. Combined facilities for a number of sports are available at three of the centres: Crystal Palace, in London; Bisham Abbey, in Buckinghamshire; and Lilleshall, in Shropshire. Crystal Palace has major competition venues for athletics, swimming and a variety of indoor sports; Lilleshall

houses the training school of the Football Association. The other two are specialist centres: the National Water Sports Centre at Holme Pierrepont, Nottinghamshire, which caters for rowing, canoeing and water-skiing; and the Plas-y-Brenin National Centre for Mountain Activities in north Wales.

The Sports Council for Wales runs the National Sports Centre for Wales in Cardiff and the National Outdoor Pursuits Centre at Plas Menai in north Wales. The Scottish Sports Council operates three national sports training centres: Glenmore Lodge, near Aviemore, for outdoor pursuits; Inverclyde, at Largs, for general sports; and a national water sports training centre on the island of Great Cumbrae, in the Firth of Clyde. The Sports Council for Northern Ireland runs one national facility, the Northern Ireland Mountain Centre at Tollymore, in County Down.

OTHER ORGANISATIONS CONCERNED WITH SPORT AND RECREATION

Countryside Commissions

The Countryside Commission (for England), the Countryside Council for Wales and the Countryside Commission for Scotland are responsible for conserving and improving the natural beauty and amenity of the countryside, and for encouraging the provision and improvement of facilities for open-air recreation. The Countryside Commission has launched a series of policy initiatives aimed at increasing people's enjoyment of the countryside. These focus on the maintenance and sign-posting of public footpaths and other 'rights of way' and the development of national routes for long-distance walking and riding. Rural communities are encouraged to build up local facilities which promote public enjoyment of the countryside. These initiatives operate alongside established policies for helping local authorities and private bodies to provide country parks, picnic sites and informal recreation facilities.

In Northern Ireland the Ulster Countryside Committee advises the

Department of the Environment on the preservation of amenities and the designation of 'areas of outstanding natural beauty'.

British Waterways Board

The British Waterways Board is a publicly owned body responsible for managing and developing much of Great Britain's inland waterways, which are preserved primarily for leisure use. Many leisure and recreational pursuits are practised on waterways and reservoirs and in waterside buildings; these include angling and numerous types of sailing and boating.

Local Authorities

Local authorities are major providers of land and large-scale facilities for community recreation: their estimated annual expenditure on sport and recreation amounts to about £1,000 million. Provision of facilities was substantially increased in the 1970s to meet growing demand and to encourage expansion of participation. The facilities include parks, lakes, playing fields, sports halls, tennis courts, golf courses, swimming pools, gymnasiums and sports centres catering for a wide range of activities. Local authorities manage 1,700 indoor centres, largely built in the last 20 years, as well as numerous outdoor amenities for sport and recreation (including 150 golf courses).

There has been a rapid growth in the provision of artificial pitches, largely for hockey use. The number of leisure pools is also rising quickly: these often have wave machines, waterfalls, jacuzzis and other leisure equipment.

World Student Games

Sheffield city council hosted the World Student Games in July 1991, which attracted some 6,000 competitors and officials from nearly 120 countries. A new athletics stadium and swimming complex were constructed for use during and after the Games. The Sports Council contributed £3 million to help cover costs and some £26 million was provided by the Government for games-

related projects under various programmes designed to promote urban renewal.

Sports Governing Bodies

Individual sports are run by 395 independent governing bodies, whose functions usually include drawing up rules, holding events, regulating membership, selecting and training national teams and promoting international links. There are also organisations representing people who take part in more informal physical recreation, such as walking and cycling.

Central Council of Physical Recreation

The Central Council of Physical Recreation provides a forum for 280 national governing and representative bodies of sport and physical recreation in England. The equivalent bodies in Scotland, Wales and Northern Ireland are the Scottish and Welsh Sports Associations and the Northern Ireland Council of Physical Recreation.

The Central Council discusses policy issues with the Sports Council, the main provider of its funding. A Community Sports Leadership Award designed to increase the numbers of people with community sport development skills is administered by the British Sports Trust on behalf of the Central Council.

National Coaching Foundation

The National Coaching Foundation was established in 1983 to provide educational and advisory services for coaches in all sports. Its work complements coaching development carried out by national sporting governing bodies. There are 16 national coaching centres delivering the Foundation's services to coaches.

British Olympic Association

The British Olympic Association, founded in 1905, is the national Olympic committee for Britain and its primary function is to organise the participation of British teams in the Olympic Games. The Association comprises representatives of the 29 governing bodies of those sports in the programme of the Olympic Games (summer and winter). It determines the size of British teams, raises funds, makes all arrangements and provides a headquarters staff for the management of the teams. It also makes important contributions in the fields of coaching, drug testing and control, and sports medicine. The Association's British Olympic Medical Centre supplies a medical back-up service for competitors before and during the Olympic Games.

In 1988 the British Olympic Association, the Sports Council and the Central Council of Physical Recreation agreed to form the British International Sports Committee to co-ordinate and promote British interests at international sporting forums.

National Playing Fields Association

The National Playing Fields Association is a charity with a Royal Charter, whose purpose is to promote the provision of recreation and play facilities for all age groups. It aims to preserve, improve and acquire playing fields, playgrounds and playspace, and to specialise in the play and recreation needs of children and young people, in particular those with special needs. There are affiliated associations in the English and Welsh counties and branches in Scotland and Northern Ireland.

The Government has awarded a grant of £500,000 to the Association, in conjunction with the Sports Council and the Central Council of Physical Recreation, to compile a register of recreational land as part of a strategy to safeguard playing fields.

Sports Clubs

Recreational facilities are provided by local sports clubs. Some cater for indoor recreation, but more common are those providing sports grounds, particularly for cricket, football, rugby, hockey, tennis and golf. Many clubs linked to business firms cater for sporting activities. Commercial facilities include tenpin bowling centres, ice and roller-skating rinks, squash courts, golf

courses and driving ranges, curling rinks, riding stables, marinas and, increasingly, fitness centres. The Civil Service Sports Council, with a membership of 200,000, has extensive facilities at its disposal for a large number of sports. In all the private sector owns and runs some 500 major sports facilities.

SPORT FOR PEOPLE WITH DISABILITIES

Opportunities exist for people with disabilities to take part in a variety of physical and sporting activities. The structure of sport for disabled people is undergoing change. There are national disability sports organisations representing the seven main disability groups, but the trend is towards sports-specific governing bodies. For example, the Riding for the Disabled Association caters for some 24,000 riders and the British Disabled Water Ski Association offers training and competition to a growing number of skiers.

The governing bodies of sport are increasingly taking responsibility for both able-bodied and disabled participants. The British Paralympic Association, which liaises closely with the British Olympic Association, looks after the preparation and training of paralympic and other international teams.

In 1989 the Government published a major report calling for the reorganisation of the structure of sport for people with disabilities. Under this, disabled sportsmen and women would be integrated into able-bodied sport and the governing bodies would assume responsibility for all participants in their sport, whether able-bodied or disabled. Disabled athletes would also be encouraged to participate in sporting events either in direct competition with able-bodied athletes or in parallel events. In 1991 the Government awarded a special grant to the Sports Council to help promote the integration of sport.

The British Sports Association for the Disabled aims to encourage and enable people with disabilities to take part in all forms of sport and physical recreation. Sports clubs for disabled people throughout

Britain are affiliated to the Association, which helps to organise sporting and physical activities at all levels. As well as offering advice to local clubs and groups, the Association arranges conferences, seminars and coaching courses. The Scottish Sports Association for the Disabled, the Federation of Sports Associations for the Disabled (Wales) and the Northern Ireland Sports Association for the Disabled have similar co-ordinating roles.

In the last few years greater emphasis has been placed on making provision for people with a mental handicap, this work being co-ordinated by the United Kingdom Sports Association for People with a Mental Handicap. Non-competitive activities, including outdoor pursuits, are also receiving closer attention, evidence of which is seen in the growing number of specialist centres, such as those run by the Calvert Trust. More community facilities are becoming available, and disabled awareness courses are being offered to professional and voluntary staff.

Britain has continued to play an active part at international level since Sir Ludwig Guttmann began sport for paraplegics and established the first sports stadium in the world designed for people with disabilities at Stoke Mandeville in Buckinghamshire in 1969. At the Paralympic Games in Seoul, Korea, held in 1988, the British team gained 62 gold, 67 silver and 53 bronze medals, finishing third in the overall medals table. More than 2,000 athletes with a mental handicap took part in the European Summer Special Olympic Games held in Glasgow in 1990. The 40th annual World Wheelchair Games were staged at Stoke Mandeville in July and August 1991.

PRIVATE SPONSORSHIP

Increasing numbers of sports benefit from financial sponsorship from commercial organisations, and its importance as a source of funding is recognised by the Government and the Sports Councils. The estimated value of commercial sponsorship was £200 million in 1990. Motorsport and football receive the largest amounts of private sponsorship.

Sponsorship may take the form of financing specific events, or of grants to individual sports organisations or sportsmen and women. The Sports Aid Foundation and Sports Aid Trust raise and distribute funds from industry, commerce and private sponsors in order to assist the training of talented individuals; grants are awarded on the recommendation of the governing bodies of sport. The Scottish and Welsh Sports Aid Foundations and the Ulster Sports and Recreation Trust have similar functions. Sponsorship advisory services are run by the Central Council of Physical Recreation.

Successive governments have negotiated voluntary agreements with the tobacco industry to regulate tobacco companies' sponsorship of sport, the last one having come into force in 1987. This is designed to bring about a reduction in spending by tobacco firms on sports sponsorship and introduces a ceiling on promotional activity. It prohibits sponsorship of events where a majority of the participants are under 18 years of age or which are designed to appeal mainly to spectators under 18. It bans the depiction of any participants in a sport in media advertising, and imposes strict controls on siting of signs at televised events and on the size of health warnings on these signs.

POPULAR SPORTS AND RECREATIONS

Some of the major sports and recreations in Britain are described below. The increased provision of sports centres has improved opportunities for participating in indoor sports such as basketball, volleyball, fencing, judo, karate and other martial arts, gymnastics, squash, table tennis and shooting. Almost all outdoor sports have continued to gain in popularity, including such 'high-risk' activities as rock-climbing and sub-aqua diving. The number of people enjoying the recreational amenities of the countryside, rivers and coastline is also growing.

Sportsmen and women may be professionals (paid players) or amateurs. Some sports—like hockey and rowing—are amateur, but in others the distinction between amateur status and professional status is less strictly defined, or does not exist. The Amateur Athletic Association, for example, allows payments to be made into trust funds held by many top-ranking athletes.

Angling

The most popular country sport is angling, and there are about 4 million anglers in Britain. Many fish for salmon and trout, particularly in the rivers and lochs of Scotland and in Wales. In England and Wales the most widely practised form of angling is for coarse fish such as pike, perch, carp, tench and bream. Separate organisations represent game (salmon and trout), coarse and sea fishing clubs in England, Wales, Scotland and Northern Ireland.

The National Federation of Anglers in England organises national championships for coarse fishing and enters a team in the world angling championships. England won the world team event in 1987 and 1988 and the individual title in 1989 and 1990. Most coarse fishing is let to angling clubs by private owners, while those fishing for trout and salmon may rent a stretch of river, join a club, or pay for the right to fish by the day, week or month. Coastal and deep-sea fishing are free to all, apart from salmon and sea trout fishing, which is by licence only.

Association Football

Association football was first developed and codified in England during the nineteenth century.

Association football is the largest spectator sport and one of the most popular participation sports.

It is controlled by separate football associations in England, Wales, Scotland and Northern Ireland. In England over 335 clubs are affiliated to the English Football Association (FA) and 42,000 clubs to regional or district associations.

The Football Association, founded in 1863, and the Football League, founded in 1888, were both the first of their kind in the world.

In England and Wales the full-time professional clubs play in four main divisions consisting of 93 clubs and organised by the Football League. A number of leading clubs have been discussing the possible formation of a separate premier league from the 1992–93 season. In Scotland there are three divisions, with 38 clubs, belonging to the Scottish Football League.

In Northern Ireland, 14 semi-professional clubs play in the Irish Football League. During the season, which lasts from August until May, over 2,000 English League matches are played; total attendances reached 20 million in 1990–91, having risen for the fifth consecutive year.

The annual competitions for the FA Challenge Cup, the Rumbelows League Cup, the Tennents Scottish Cup, the Skol Cup (formerly the Scottish League Cup), the Irish Cup and the Welsh FA Cup are organised on a knock-out basis. The finals are played at Wembley Stadium, London; at Hampden Park, Glasgow; at Windsor Park, Belfast; and at the National Stadium, Cardiff.

The Sports Councils have made grants available to a number of clubs and local authorities to enable them to modernise or expand football facilities in areas of urban deprivation. Grants for various improvements such as all-weather pitches are also made throughout Britain by the Football Associations and the Football Trust, a body financed by the football pools companies (see p 452). The Government has reduced pool betting duty on the understanding that the revenue forgone by the Government is given to the Football Trust to be used for ground improvements.

Athletics

Amateur athletics is governed in England by the Amateur Athletic Association (which, formed in 1880, was the first national governing body for athletics) and by the Women's Amateur Athletic Association.

Scotland, Wales and Northern Ireland have their own associations. International athletics and the selection of British teams are the concern of the Amateur Athletic Association, which also administers coaching schemes. For the Olympic Games and the world and European championships one team represents Britain.

Athletics is attracting increasing numbers of participants, both men and women, in part because of the success of British competitors and the wide coverage of athletics events on television.

The London Marathon, which takes place every spring, draws leading runners from all over the world and is a mass-participation event (more than 23,000 runners took part in 1991).

Many British athletes, especially middle-distance runners, have enjoyed distinguished reputations: in 1954, for example, Dr (now Sir) Roger Bannister became the first man to run a mile in under four minutes. More recently British athletes won six silver and two bronze medals at the 1988 Olympic Games in Seoul, Korea. At the Commonwealth Games held in Auckland in 1990, England, Wales, Scotland and Northern Ireland competed separately and between them gained 16 gold medals for athletics. At the World Athletics Championships staged in Tokyo in August and September 1991, British athletes won gold medals in the women's 10,000 metres and the men's 4 x 400 metres relay. In August 1991, Britons held world records in the 800 metres (Sebastian Coe), the mile (Steve Cram), the decathlon (Daley Thompson) and the 4 x 200 metres indoor relay (Linford Christie, Darren Braithwaite, Ade Mafé and John Regis).

Badminton

The sport of badminton takes its name from the Duke of Beaufort's country home, Badminton House, where badminton was first played in the nineteenth century. Badminton is organised by the Badminton Association of England and the Scottish, Welsh and Irish (Ulster branch) Badminton Unions. There are also English, Welsh and Scottish schools badminton associations. Around 4 million people are estimated to play the sport in Britain. From 1992 badminton will become a full Olympic sport.

Basketball

Basketball is played, mainly indoors, by both men and women. There are about 1,000 registered clubs and the sport is played in most secondary schools and many other institutions. In all, over 1 million people participate and the sport's popularity has been increasing rapidly. The English Basket Ball Association is the governing body of the sport in England, and there are similar associations in Wales, Scotland and Northern Ireland. The leading clubs play in the National Basketball Leagues, and the main events of the year are the Coca-Cola National Cup Finals and the Carlsberg Basketball Championships, both staged in London.

Bowls

Bowls has been played in Britain since the thirteenth century. The game of lawn bowls is played on a flat green. In the Midlands, the north of England and north Wales a variation called crown green bowls is played, so named because the centre of the green is higher than its boundaries. Lawn and crown green bowls are mainly summer games; in winter indoor bowls takes place on synthetic greens and is growing in popularity. Once regarded as a pastime for the elderly, bowls is increasingly enjoyed by adults of all ages.

About 4,000 lawn bowling clubs are affiliated to the English, Scottish, Welsh and Irish (Northern Ireland Region) Bowling Associations, which, together with Women's Bowling Associations for the four countries, play to the rules of the International Bowling Board. Other associations, including the English Bowling Federation, are not under the Board's control. The British Crown Green Bowling Association is the governing body of crown green bowls, and has 2,500 affiliated clubs.

The outstanding player in recent years has been David Bryant, who has won three world singles championships. Richard Corsie was the winner of the World Indoor Singles title in 1991.

Boxing

Boxing in its modern form dates from 1865, when the Marquess of Queensberry drew up a set of rules eliminating much of the brutality that had characterised prize-fighting and making skill the basis of the sport. Boxing is both amateur and professional, and in both strict medical regulations are observed.

All amateur boxing in England, including schoolboy, club, association and combined services boxing (in the armed forces), is controlled by the Amateur Boxing Association. There are separate associations in Scotland and Wales, and Northern Ireland forms part of the Irish Boxing Association. The associations organise amateur boxing championships as well as training courses for referees, coaches and others. Teams take part in international meetings including the Commonwealth and Olympic Games, and European and World championships. Richard Woodhall won a bronze medal in the light-middleweight class at the 1988 Olympic Games.

Professional boxing is controlled by the British Boxing Board of Control. The Board appoints inspectors, medical officers and representatives to ensure that regulations are observed and to guard against overmatching and exploitation. British boxing has a distinguished record and at various times British boxers have held European, Commonwealth and world championship titles. Dave McAuley is the current International Boxing Federation (IBF) world flyweight champion and Chris Eubank is the World Boxing Organisation (WBO) world super-middleweight champion. Duke McKenzie has won world titles at two different weights and is currently holder of the WBO bantamweight world title.

Chess

Chess is growing in popularity and England now ranks second among chess-playing nations, having taken silver medals at the last three chess Olympics. Scotland, Wales and Ireland are separately represented. There are local chess clubs and leagues throughout Britain and the game is widely played in schools and colleges. Important domestic competitions include the British Championships (for all ages), the National Club Championships, the County Championships and the Leigh Grand Prix. The Hastings Chess Congress, dating from 1895, is the world's longest running annual international chess tournament.

The governing bodies of the game are the British Chess Federation (responsible for England and for co-ordinating activity among the home nations), the Scottish Chess Association and the Welsh and Ulster Chess Unions.

Cricket

Cricket is among the most popular of summer sports and is sometimes called the English national game, having been played as early as the 1550s. Among the many clubs founded in the eighteenth century is the Marylebone Cricket Club (MCC), which continues to frame the rules of the game. The Club is based at Lord's cricket ground in north London, the administrative centre of the world game. Men's cricket in Britain is governed by the Cricket Council, consisting of representatives of the Test and County Cricket Board (representing first-class cricket), the National Cricket Association (representing club and junior cricket), the Minor County Cricket Association, the Scottish Cricket Union, the Irish Cricket Union and the MCC.

Cricket is played in schools, colleges and universities, and in cities, towns and villages amateur teams play weekly games from late April to the end of September. Throughout Britain there is a network of league cricket contested by teams of Saturday afternoon players.

The main competition in professional cricket is the Britannic Assurance County

Championship of three-day and four-day games played by 17 county teams. There are also three one-day competitions—the Benson and Hedges Cup, the National Westminster Bank Trophy, and the Refuge Assurance League, played on Sundays. Some of the best supported games are the annual series of five-day Cornhill Insurance Test matches played between England and a touring team from Australia, India, New Zealand, Pakistan, Sri Lanka or the West Indies. A team representing England usually tours one or more of these countries in the British winter. Texaco Trophy one-day international games also attract large crowds. A World Cup competition takes place every four years, with some of the smaller cricketing nations as well as the major countries competing; the next one will be staged in Australia and New Zealand in 1992.

Cricket is also played by women and girls, the governing body being the Women's Cricket Association, founded in 1926. Women's cricket clubs have regular local fixtures, usually played at weekends, and may participate in the national league and club knock-out competitions. There are regular county matches as well as an area championship and a territorial competition. Test match series and a World Cup competition are played, with both major and minor cricketing nations taking part.

Curling

The ice sport of curling originated in Scotland, where it is now played by men and women almost exclusively on purpose-built rinks indoors. The governing body of the sport in Scotland is the Royal Caledonian Curling Club, which was formed in 1838; it has over 22,000 members. Curling is played in 24 other countries, including England and Wales. European and World championship competitions take place annually.

Cycling

Since the 1970s there has been a resurgence of interest in cycling, both as a means of transport and as a sport and recreation, and this has led central and local government to make greater provision for cycling. Activities include road and track racing, cycle speedway, time-trialling, cyclo-cross, mountain biking, touring, bicycle polo and bicycle moto-cross.

The British Cycling Federation is the governing body for cycling as a sport, with 900 affiliated clubs. The Cyclists' Touring Club, formed in 1878, is the governing body for recreational and amenity cycling and represents cyclists' interests in general. The Scottish Cyclists Union controls the sport in Scotland.

Equestrianism

Equestrian activities include recreational riding, show jumping and carriage driving. The art of riding is promoted by the British Horse Society, which is concerned with the welfare of horses, road safety, riding rights of way and training. It runs the British Equestrian Centre at Stoneleigh in Warwickshire. With some 52,000 members, the Society is the parent body of the Pony Club and the Riding Club movements, which hold rallies, meetings and competitions culminating in annual national championships. Leading horse trials, comprising dressage, cross-country riding and show jumping, are held every year at Badminton (Avon), Windsor (Berkshire), Gatcombe Park (Gloucestershire), Bramham (West Yorkshire), Burghley House (Lincolnshire), Blair Castle (Tayside) and Blenheim Palace (Oxfordshire).

Show jumping is regulated and promoted by the British Show Jumping Association, which has over 17,000 members and 2,800 shows affiliated to it. The major show jumping events each year include the Royal International Horse Show at the National Exhibition Centre, Birmingham; the Horse of the Year Show at Wembley in London; the Olympia International Show Jumping Championships in London; and the Hickstead Nations Cup and Derby meetings at Bolney in West Sussex.

The authority responsible for equestrian competitions (other than racing) at international and Olympic level is the British Equestrian Federation, which co-ordinates the activities of the British Horse Society and the British Show Jumping Association. British equestrian teams have an outstanding record in international competitions. The British three-day event team gained a silver medal at the 1988 Olympic Games; Ian Stark won the silver medal and Virginia Leng won the bronze medal in the three-day individual competition. At the World Equestrian Games held in Stockholm in 1990 Great Britain gained one gold, four silver and one bronze medal.

Field Sports

British field sports include hunting (on horseback and on foot), fishing, shooting, stalking, falconry and coursing. Fox hunting on horseback with a pack of hounds is the most popular British hunting sport, and there are 341 registered packs of hounds of all kinds in Britain.

Game shooting as an organised sport probably originated in the late eighteenth century, and takes place in many parts of Britain. Game consists of grouse, black-game, ptarmigan, partridge and pheasant, species which are protected by law during a close season, when they are allowed to breed on numerous estates supervised by gamekeepers. It is necessary to have a licence to kill game and a certificate issued by the police to own a shot-gun.

The British Field Sports Society looks after the interests of all field sports. Public opposition to field sports is considerable and is organised through such bodies as the League Against Cruel Sports.

Golf

Golf originated in Scotland, where for centuries it has carried the title of the Royal and Ancient Game. The oldest golf club in the world is the Honourable Company of Edinburgh Golfers. The Royal and Ancient Golf Club, the ruling authority of the sport for most of the world, is situated at St Andrews on the east coast of Scotland. Golf is played throughout Britain and there are golf courses near most towns, a few of them owned by local authorities.

The main event of the British golfing year is the Open Championship, one of the world's leading tournaments. Other important events include the Walker Cup and Curtis Cup matches for amateurs, played between Great Britain and Ireland and the United States, and the Ryder Cup match for professionals, played between Europe and the United States. Among the leading British professional players are Nick Faldo, Sandy Lyle and Ian Woosnam.

Sandy Lyle won the United States Masters golf tournament in 1988, Nick Faldo was the winner in 1989 and 1990, and in 1991 Ian Woosnam took the title. Laura Davies became the first British woman, in 1987, to win the United States Open Championship for women.

Greyhound Racing

The racing of greyhounds after a mechanical hare, one of Britain's most popular spectator sports, takes place at 36 major tracks operating under the same rules. Meetings are usually held three times a week at each track, with at least ten races a meeting. The rules for the sport are drawn up by the National Greyhound Racing Club, the sport's judicial and administrative body. The representative body is the British Greyhound Racing Board.

There about 50 mainly small tracks which operate independently. Like the major tracks, they are licensed by local authorities.

Gymnastics

Gymnastics is divided into four main disciplines: artistic or Olympic gymnastics, rhythmic gymnastics, sports acrobatics and general gymnastics. Both men and women compete in artistic gymnastics, although the apparatus used differs. Men use the floor, pommel horse, rings, vault, parallel bars and horizontal bar, while women exercise on the vault, asymmetric bars, beam and floor. Rhythmic gymnastics is for women only and consists of routines performed to music with ribbon, balls, clubs, hoop or rope. Sports acrobatics is gymnastics with people rather than apparatus. General gymnastics is non-competitive and is available to all age groups and to people with special needs.

In recent years the sport has increased in popularity, particularly among school-children, and there are now about 1,000 clubs with some 79,000 members. The British Amateur Gymnastics Association is the governing body for men and women gymnasts in Britain; the Welsh, Scottish and Northern Ireland Associations are affiliated to it, and the independent English and British Schools' Gymnastic Associations are under its control.

Highland Games

Scottish Highland Games, at which sports, dancing and piping competitions take place, attract large numbers of spectators from all over the world. The sports include tossing the caber, putting the weight and throwing the hammer. Among better-known Highland Games are the annual Braemar Gathering, the Argyllshire and Cowal Gatherings and a meeting at Aboyne.

Hockey (Field and Indoor)

Variants of hockey have been played in Britain for at least five centuries. The modern game was started in the nineteenth century by the Hockey Association (of England), which was founded in 1886 and acts as the governing body for men's hockey. Parallel associations serve in Scotland, Wales and Northern Ireland. Throughout England there are 820 men's hockey clubs, many with junior sections. Large numbers of schools also play the game; 500 are affiliated to the Hockey Association. Cup competitions and leagues exist at national, divisional or district, and club levels both indoors (six-a-side) and outdoors, and there are regular international matches.

The controlling body of women's hockey in England is the All England Women's Hockey Association (founded in 1895), to which are affiliated some 950 clubs and about 2,500 schools; separate associations regulate the sport in Scotland, Wales and Northern Ireland. League,

county, club and school championships for both outdoor and indoor hockey are played annually in England. The first international women's hockey match took place in 1896. Regular international matches are played, one of which is held each year at Wembley Stadium.

Men's and women's hockey are Olympic sports; at the 1988 Games the British men's team won a gold medal.

Horse Racing

Horse racing takes two forms—flat racing (throughout the year) and steeplechasing and hurdle racing (normally from August to early June). The Derby, run at Epsom, is the outstanding event in the flat racing calendar. Other classic races are: the Two Thousand Guineas and the One Thousand Guineas, both run at Newmarket; the Oaks (Epsom); and the St Leger (Doncaster). The most important steeplechase and hurdle race meeting is the National Hunt Festival Meeting held at Cheltenham in March. The Grand National, run at Aintree, near Liverpool, is the world's best-known steeplechase and dates from 1837.

The Jockey Club administers all horse racing in Britain. Its rules are the basis of turf procedure and it also licenses racecourses. Racing takes place on most days, excluding Sundays, throughout the year. About 13,000 horses are in training. British thoroughbreds continue to be a source of the world's best bloodstock.

Ice Skating

Ice skating became popular in Britain in the late nineteenth and early twentieth centuries and takes three main forms: ice dancing, figure skating and speed-skating. The governing body for the sport is the National Skating Association of Great Britain, founded in 1879. Participation in ice skating is concentrated among the under-25s. There are over 55 ice rinks in Britain, a relatively small number compared with many other European countries. In spite of this, British couples have won the world ice dance championship 17 times.

Judo

Judo, an individual combat sport derived from the ancient Japanese art of ju-jutsu, is growing rapidly in popularity in Britain, as a sport and general fitness training method and self-defence technique. Men and women take part in judo at all levels. Dennis Stewart won a bronze medal in the under-95-kg class at the 1988 Olympics, and at the Commonwealth Games in Auckland in 1990 England won 14 gold and two bronze medals and Scotland one gold, three silver and four bronze medals. Recent leading British exponents of the sport include Karen Briggs, Brian Jacks, Neil Adams, Neil Eckersley, Ann Hughes and Diane Bell. More than 900 judo clubs are registered with the British Judo Association, which is the official governing body of the sport throughout Britain.

Keep Fit

Keep fit classes aim to improve stamina, strength and suppleness through a variety of fitness and creative movement activities. The Keep Fit Association, formed in 1956, receives funding from the Sports Council to promote physical fitness and a positive attitude to health in England. Its national certificated training scheme for keep fit teachers is recognised by local education authorities throughout Britain. Autonomous associations serve Scotland, Wales and Northern Ireland.

Martial Arts

A broad range of martial arts, mainly derived from Japan, the People's Republic of China, Taiwan, Hong Kong and Korea, has been introduced into Britain during the twentieth century. It includes karate (the most popular of the martial arts), kung fu, aikido and kendo. Following the increase in interest in the 1960s and 1970s, the Martial Arts Commission was established in 1977 to develop and control martial arts and maintain high standards of safety. The Commission is made up of representatives from 16 national governing bodies, the Sports Council and the education and local authority sectors. It has 130,000 affiliated members.

Motor and Motor-cycle Sports

Motor racing and rallying, and motor-cycle racing, are popular spectator sports in Britain. The governing body for four-wheeled motor sport is the RAC (Royal Automobile Club) Motor Sports Association. The Association issues licences for a variety of motoring competitions and organises the Lombard RAC Rally, an event in the contest for the World Rally Championship, and the British Grand Prix, held at the Silverstone racing circuit as part of the Formula One World Motor Racing Championship.

British car constructors including Lotus, McLaren and Williams have enjoyed outstanding successes in Grand Prix racing, and Britain has had six world champion motor racing drivers. The British driver Nigel Mansell has won a total of 21 Grand Prix races. Other popular types of motor sport include autocross, drag racing and karting.

Motor-cycle sport, governed by the Auto-Cycle Union in England and Wales and the Scottish Auto-Cycle Union and Motor Cycle Union of Ireland (in Northern Ireland), caters for all forms of competition on two, three or four wheels, from low-speed trials to Grand Prix road racing. The major events of the year are the Isle of Man TT races, the British Road Race Grand Prix, the Ulster Grand Prix and other world championship events for trials, moto-cross, speedway and track racing. The Auto-Cycle Union provides off-road training by approved instructors for riders of all ages.

Mountaineering

All forms of mountaineering, which includes hill-walking and rock-climbing, are growing in popularity. There are around 100,000 rock-climbers and 700,000 hill-walkers, whose representative body is the British Mountaineering Council; separate bodies serve Scotland and Ireland.

Britain can claim to have invented the sports of rock-climbing and alpine-climbing.

The first recorded rock-climbs in Britain were made more than 100 years ago, and the Alpine Club, founded in 1857 and based in London, is the oldest mountaineering club in the world. British mountaineers have played a leading role in the exploration of the world's great mountain ranges.

Two national centres for mountain activities are run by the Sports Council: one at Plas-y-Brenin in north Wales and the other at Glenmore Lodge near Aviemore in Scotland. Popular areas for rock-climbing are south-west England, the Peak District of Derbyshire, the Lake District in north-west England, Wales and the Highlands of Scotland.

Britain's best-known mountaineer is Chris Bonnington, who has climbed Everest and led many successful expeditions throughout the world. Other influential British mountaineers include Doug Scott, Joe Brown, Don Whillans, Johnny Dawes and Lord Hunt.

Climbing on artificial structures is gaining in popularity and has developed into the sport of competition climbing. The first competition world climbing champion was Simon Nadin, who took the title in 1989.

Netball

Netball was introduced into England in 1895. It was first developed in the United States as an outdoor exercise. More than 60,000 adults play netball regularly in England and a further 1 million participants come from schools. The sport is played almost exclusively by women and girls both indoors and outdoors.

The All England Netball Association, formed in 1926, is the governing body for the sport in England. The English Schools' Netball Association is responsible for the sport in schools. Scotland, Wales and Northern Ireland have their own governing bodies.

Rowing

Rowing is taught in many schools, colleges and rowing clubs (including women's clubs) throughout Britain. The governing body of the sport in England is the Amateur Rowing Association; similar bodies regulate the sport in Scotland, Wales and Ireland. There are about 500 rowing clubs, and each year over 300 regattas and head races are held in England, Wales and Scotland under Association rules.

The University Boat Race, between eight-oared crews from Oxford and Cambridge, has been rowed on the Thames almost every spring since 1836. The Head of the River Race, also on the Thames, is the largest assembly of racing craft in the world, with more than 420 eights racing in procession. At the Henley Regatta in Oxfordshire, founded in 1839, crews from all over the world compete each July in various kinds of race over a straight course of 1 mile 550 yards (about 2·1 km).

The National Water Sports Centre at Holme Pierrepont, near Nottingham (see p 438), has a rowing course of Olympic 2,000-metre standard, as does Strathclyde Park in west-central Scotland. Britain won the gold medal in the men's coxless pairs at the 1988 Olympic Games. At the World Championships held in Vienna in August 1991 British rowers gained two gold medals.

Rugby Football

Rugby football takes its name from Rugby School, in Warwickshire, where it is believed to have originated in 1823. Since 1895 the game has been played according to two different codes: rugby union (a 15-a-side game) is played by amateurs and rugby league (a 13-a-side game) by professionals as well as amateurs.

Rugby union is played under the auspices of the Rugby Football Union in England and parallel bodies in Wales, Scotland and Ireland. Important domestic competitions include the divisional and county championships in England; the league and national club knock-out competitions in England and Wales; and the National League and Inter-District Championships in Scotland. The Five Nations Tournament between England, Scotland, Wales, Ireland and France is contested each year, and overseas tours are undertaken by the national sides and by the British Lions, a team representing Great Britain and Ireland. In 1987 teams from 16 countries competed for the first time in a world cup competition held in Australia and New Zealand. The final rounds of the next one will be staged in Britain and France in October and November 1991.

Seven-a-side rugby union has a strong following. Tournaments include the Middlesex Sevens, which is held every year at Twickenham.

Rugby league, played mainly in the north of England, is enjoying unprecedented popularity as a spectator sport. The governing body of the professional game is the Rugby Football League, which sends touring teams representing Great Britain to Australia, New Zealand and Papua New Guinea; annual matches are also played against France. The Challenge Cup Final, the major club match of the season, is played at Wembley Stadium in London.

The amateur game is governed by the British Amateur Rugby League Association. Matches between England and France are held each year and tours are arranged to Australia and New Zealand. A national league consisting of ten leading clubs was formed in 1986, and a second division came into existence in 1989.

Sailing

Sailing has always been popular in Britain, and the Royal Yachting Association, the governing body for the sport, has more than 70,000 members and 1,500 clubs and classes. Sailing in dinghies, motor yachts, windsurfers, powerboats and cruisers takes place at clubs throughout Britain. At the 1988 Olympics Mike McIntyre and Bryn Vaile gained a gold medal in the 'Star' class.

Skiing

Skiing takes place in Scotland from December to May and also at several English locations when there is sufficient snow. The five established winter sports areas in Scotland are Cairngorm, Glencoe, Glenshee, the Lecht and Aonach Mor, all of which

have a full range of ski-lifts, ski-tows and chair-lifts as well as professional instructors.

Over 115 artificial ski-slopes are also in constant use throughout Great Britain, and interest in cross-country skiing has been increasing. Britain has nearly 300 ski clubs, and it is estimated that 1·5 million people take part in the sport.

The governing body of the sport is the British Ski Federation, and there are separate national councils for England, Scotland, Wales and Northern Ireland.

Snooker and Billiards

The character of the present game of billiards was established in Britain at the end of the seventeenth century. Snooker, a more varied game invented by the British in India in 1875, has greatly increased in popularity and become a major spectator sport as a result of heavy television coverage of the professional tournaments. It is estimated that between 7 and 8 million people now play the game. British players have an outstanding record in snooker and have dominated the major professional championships. The main tournament is the annual Embassy World Professional Championship, held in Sheffield. British winners include Steve Davis (1981, 1983, 1984, 1987, 1988 and 1989), Joe Johnson (1986), Dennis Taylor (1985), Alex Higgins (1972 and 1982), Stephen Hendry (1990) and John Parrot (1991). Mike Russell won the World Professional Billiards Championship in July 1991.

The controlling body for the non-professional game is the Billiards and Snooker Control Council, which holds the copyright of the rules. The World Professional Billiards and Snooker Association is responsible for professional players, and organises professional events.

A growing number of women play snooker and billiards. Their representative body is the World Ladies Billiards and Snooker Association, with around 250 members. A women's world snooker championship is played every year in London, and the World Masters event, staged in Birmingham, embraces men's and women's singles and doubles as well as mixed doubles. The Embassy World Professional Championship will be open to women from 1992.

Squash Rackets

Squash rackets originated at Harrow School in the 1850s. Separate governing bodies are responsible for the sport in England, Wales, Scotland and Ireland. The governing body in England for men's and women's squash is the Squash Rackets Association, formed in 1989.

Squash enjoyed a period of very rapid growth during the 1970s and remains a popular sport. There are 9,250 squash courts in England, and the estimated number of players in Britain is 2·6 million. The main tournament is the British Open Championship. England currently holds the world title for women's team squash.

Sub-Aqua

Underwater activities include wreck and reef exploration, underwater photography, marine life study and nautical archaeology. The British Sub-Aqua Club is the governing body for all underwater techniques. It promotes safe diving, training, science and sport. The Club is the largest of its kind in the world, with over 40,000 members and more than 1,250 branches in Britain and overseas.

Swimming

Swimming is enjoyed by millions of people in Britain, many of whom learn to swim at public baths, schools or swimming clubs. Instruction and coaching are provided by qualified teachers who hold certificates awarded by the Amateur Swimming Associations in England, Wales, Scotland and Northern Ireland, to which nearly 2,000 clubs are affiliated. Northern Ireland forms part of the Irish Amateur Swimming Association. The Associations control swimming, diving, synchronised swimming and water polo championships and competitions.

For major international competitions, such as the Olympic Games and the World and European Championships, England, Scotland and Wales compete together as one team under the auspices of the Amateur Swimming Federation of Great Britain. At the 1988 Olympics, Britain won a gold, a silver and a bronze medal. Nick Gillingham currently holds the short-course world record for the 200-metres breastroke.

Table Tennis

The origins of table tennis are uncertain, but it developed in Britain from around the middle of the nineteenth century, becoming an Olympic sport in 1988. In addition to being one of the most popular indoor sports for young people, it is played by a broad age range of adults, with men outnumbering women. Requiring relatively simple and inexpensive equipment, table tennis is played in schools, youth clubs and private clubs. Britain's leading professional player is Desmond Douglas.

The governing body for men's and women's table tennis in England is the English Table Tennis Association, to which some 8,000 clubs are affiliated. There are separate governing bodies in Scotland, Wales and Northern Ireland.

Tennis

The modern game of tennis originated in England in 1872 and the first championships were played at Wimbledon in 1877. The controlling body in Great Britain, the Lawn Tennis Association, was founded in 1888; Northern Ireland forms part of the Irish Lawn Tennis Association.

The main event of the season is the annual Wimbledon fortnight, widely regarded as the most important tennis event in the world. This draws large crowds, with the ground at the All England Club accommodating around 30,000 spectators. There are also national and county championships and national competitions for boys' and girls' schools. The Federation Cup tournament involving women's teams from leading tennis nations was held in Nottingham in July 1991.

Tenpin Bowling

Tenpin bowling is played at some 1,500 indoor bowling centres throughout Britain. More than 25,000 people belong to the sport's governing body, the British Tenpin Bowling Association.

Volleyball

Volleyball was established in Britain in the 1950s, having first been played in the United States at the end of the nineteenth century. The number of registered players in Britain grew substantially in the 1980s, with men at first far outnumbering women; today, of the total of 25,000 registered players, about 11,000 are women. Volleyball is popular among schoolchildren and university and college students. Mini-volley is a version of the game adapted to the abilities of children under 13. Although volleyball can be played outdoors, it is normally played in indoor sports halls.

The English Volleyball Association (formed in 1971), the Scottish Volleyball Association (formed in 1964), the Welsh Volleyball Association (re-established in 1981) and the Northern Ireland Volleyball Association (formed in 1970) act as the sport's governing bodies for both men and women.

GAMBLING

Various forms of commercial betting and gaming are permitted in Britain under strict regulations. In 1990–91 the total money staked, excluding gaming machines, was estimated at £10,000 million.

Betting takes place mainly on horse or greyhound racing, and on football matches, usually through football pools. Racing bets may be made at racecourses and greyhound tracks, or through some 10,000 licensed off-course betting offices which take about 90 per cent of the money staked. A form of pool betting—totalisator betting—is organised on course by the Horserace Totalisator Board (HTB). Bookmakers and the HTB contribute a levy to the Horserace Betting Levy Board, which promotes the improvement of horse breeds, advancement of veterinary science and better horse racing.

The Foundation for Sport and the Arts was set up by the pools promoters in 1991 to channel funds to benefit athletics, sport and games (and the arts). The pools promoters will pay the Foundation amounts equivalent to a proposed reduction in pool betting duty in addition to other donations collected by them.

Gaming includes the playing of casino and card games, gaming machines and bingo. There are 120 licensed casinos operating in Britain, 21 of them in London. An estimated 3 million people, mainly women, play bingo in commercial bingo halls.

In addition, legislation allows local authorities and certain other bodies to hold lotteries.

Appendix 1

METRIC CONVERSIONS FOR BRITISH WEIGHTS AND MEASURES

Length

	1 inch	= 2·54 centimetres
12 inches	= 1 foot	= 30·48 centimetres
3 feet	= 1 yard	= 0·914 metre
1,760 yards	= 1 mile	= 1·609 kilometres

Area

	1 square inch	= 6·452 square centimetres
144 square inches	= 1 square foot	= 929·03 square centimetres
9 square feet	= 1 square yard	= 0·836 square metre
4,840 square yards	= 1 acre	= 0·405 hectare
640 acres	= 1 square mile	= 2·59 square kilometres

Capacity

	1 pint	= 0·568 litre
2 pints	= 1 quart	= 1·136 litres
4 quarts	= 1 gallon	= 4·546 litres
8 gallons	= 1 bushel	= 36·37 litres
8 bushels	= 1 quarter	= 2·909 hectolitres

Weight (Avoirdupois)

	1 ounce (oz)	= 28·35 grammes
16 oz	= 1 pound (lb)	= 0·454 kilogramme
14 lb	= 1 stone (st)	= 6·35 kilogrammes
112 lb	= 1 hundredweight (cwt)	= 50·8 kilogrammes
20 cwt (2,240 lb)	= 1 long ton	= 1·016 tonnes
2,000 lb	= 1 short ton	= 0·907 tonne

Double Conversion Tables for Measures and Weights

(Use the figures in the central column with those to the left or right, depending on which conversion is required. For example, 1 centimetre = 0·394 inch, and 1 inch = 2·540 centimetres.)

Centi-metres		Inches	Metres		Yards	Kilo-metres		Miles	Hec-tares		Acres
2·540	1	0·394	0·914	1	1·094	1·609	1	0·621	0·405	1	2·471
5·080	2	0·787	1·829	2	2·187	3·219	2	1·243	0·809	2	4·942
7·620	3	1·181	2·743	3	3·281	4·828	3	1·864	1·214	3	7·413
10·160	4	1·575	3·658	4	4·374	6·437	4	2·485	1·619	4	9·884
12·700	5	1·969	4·572	5	5·468	8·047	5	3·107	2·023	5	12·355
15·240	6	2·362	5·486	6	6·562	9·656	6	3·728	2·428	6	14·826
17·780	7	2·756	6·401	7	7·655	11·265	7	4·350	2·833	7	17·298
20·320	8	3·150	7·315	8	8·749	12·875	8	4·971	3·237	8	19·768
22·860	9	3·543	8·230	9	9·843	14·484	9	5·592	3·642	9	22·239
25·400	10	3·937	9·144	10	10·936	16·093	10	6·214	4·047	10	24·711

Kilo-grammes		Av. Pounds	Litres		Pints	Litres		Gallons
0·454	1	2·205	0·568	1	1·760	4·546	1	0·220
0·907	2	4·409	1·136	2	3·520	9·092	2	0·440
1·361	3	6·614	1·705	3	5·279	13·638	3	0·660
1·814	4	8·818	2·273	4	7·039	18·184	4	0·880
2·268	5	11·023	2·841	5	8·799	22·730	5	1·100
2·722	6	13·228	3·409	6	10·559	27·276	6	1·320
3·175	7	15·432	3·978	7	12·319	31·822	7	1·540
3·629	8	17·637	4·546	8	14·078	36·368	8	1·760
4·082	9	19·842	5·114	9	15·838	40·914	9	1·980
4·536	10	20·046	5·682	10	17·598	45·460	10	2·200

THERMOMETRICAL TABLE

$0° \text{ C} = 32° \text{ F}$
$100° \text{ C} = 212° \text{ F}$

To convert degrees Fahrenheit into degrees Celsius: subtract 32, then multiply by $5/9$; degrees Celsius into degrees Fahrenheit: multiply by $9/5$, then add 32.

BANK AND PUBLIC HOLIDAYS IN BRITAIN, 1992

Wednesday 1 January	New Year's Day
Thursday 2 January	Bank Holiday (Scotland only)
Tuesday 17 March	Bank Holiday (Northern Ireland only)
Friday 17 April	Good Friday
Monday 20 April	Easter Monday (England, Wales and Northern Ireland only)
Monday 4 May	Early May Bank Holiday
Monday 25 May	Spring Bank Holiday
Monday 13 July	Orangeman's Day (Northern Ireland only)
Monday 3 August	Bank Holiday (Scotland only)
Monday 31 August	Summer Bank Holiday (England, Wales and Northern Ireland only)
Friday 25 December	Christmas Day
Monday 28 December	Extra day because Boxing Day falls on a Saturday

CURRENCY

The unit of currency is the pound sterling divided into 100 new pence (p). There are seven coins: £1; 50p; 20p; 10p; 5p; 2p and 1p.

Bank of England notes are issued for sums of £5, £10, £20 and £50.

Appendix 2

GUIDE TO SOURCES
The principal official periodical sources used in the preparation of this edition are given below:

Chapter 1: Land and People
Social Trends, Population Trends, Regional Trends, General Household Survey, Family Expenditure Survey

Chapter 3: Overseas Relations
British Aid Statistics, British Overseas Aid, Arms Control and Disarmament Quarterly Review, Developments in the European Community

Chapter 4: Defence
Statement on the Defence Estimates

Chapter 5: Justice and the Law
Criminal Statistics, England and Wales; Criminal Statistics, Scotland

Chapter 7: Education
Education Statistics for the United Kingdom

Chapter 8: Planning, Housing and Urban Regeneration
General Household Survey, Housing and Construction Statistics

Chapter 9: Environmental Protection
Digest of Environmental Protection and Water Statistics

Chapter 11: National Economy
United Kingdom National Accounts (the 'Blue Book'), *Employment Gazette*

Chapter 12: Industry and Commerce
United Kingdom National Accounts (the 'Blue Book'), *Monthly Digest of Statistics*

Chapter 13: Manufacturing Industry
Size Analyses of United Kingdom Businesses, Business Monitors, United Kingdom National Accounts (the 'Blue Book'), *Monthly Digest of Statistics, Employment Gazette*

Chapter 14: Construction and Service Industries
Size Analyses of United Kingdom Businesses, Employment Gazette, Business Monitors

Chapter 15: Energy and Natural Resources
Digest of United Kingdom Energy Statistics, Development of the Oil and Gas Resources of the United Kingdom (the 'Brown Book'), *United Kingdom Minerals Yearbook*

Chapter 16: Agriculture, Fisheries and Forestry
Agriculture in the United Kingdom

Chapter 17: Transport and Communications
Transport Statistics, Great Britain

Chapter 18: Employment
Employment Gazette, New Earnings Survey

Chapter 19: Public Finance
Financial Statement and Budget Report

Chapter 21: Overseas Trade
Monthly Review of External Trade Statistics, United Kingdom Balance of Payments (the 'Pink Book'), *Business Bulletins*

Chapter 25: Television and Radio
BBC's *Annual Report and Accounts*, IBA's *Annual Report and Accounts*

Full purchasing details of British Government publications can be obtained from the annual list *Government Publications* issued by Her Majesty's Stationery Office (HMSO), which has agents overseas. The list includes all Bills and Acts of Parliament and the official parliamentary report *Hansard*, White Papers, annual reports, reports of official committees and most publications of government departments including the Central Statistical Office, which publishes a *Guide to Official Statistics*. HMSO also sells in Britain many titles published by international organisations such as the United Nations, the European Community and the Organisation for Economic Co-operation and Development.

A Catalogue of British Official Publications not Published by HMSO, published by Chadwyck-Healey, lists the more specialised departmental publications. Details of this and other commercial publications are available from bookshops or, overseas, from the British Council.

Index

Items are indexed under England, Northern Ireland, Scotland or Wales only where they are matters peculiar to these countries; otherwise they are indexed under the relevant subject headings.

Bold type in a sequence of figures indicates main references.

Acknowledgments for photographs
SCF/Fritz Curzon (between pp 70 and 71). Architectural Heritage Fund (facing p 230). RNLI (between pp 294 and 295). Shell (facing p 295). Environmental Picture Library/Martin Bond (facing p 295). CLIVE BARDA/London (between pp 358 and 359). Phil Starling: The National Gallery (facing p 422). The British Council (facing p 423).

Cover illustration by Bob Murdoch.

Written and prepared by Reference Services, Central Office of Information.

Printed in the United Kingdom for HMSO
Dd 295018 C200 12/91

ASPECTS OF BRITAIN

This new series covers all aspects of Britain's physical, economic and social structure, including its role in world affairs.

It provides factual, objective briefing on government policy and other developments—an ideal source for students, specialists, the media and others who need to be kept up to date.

Produced alongside and complementing *Britain Handbook*, widely looked on as one of the most useful reference books in Britain, the series is also backed up and kept up to date by the *Survey of Current Affairs*, a monthly journal of record and long-term reference source.

There are titles on major institutions such as the Monarchy and Parliament, urgent concerns such as the environment and defence, and Britain's position on important world issues. There will be separate books on Wales, Scotland and Northern Ireland.

The first titles are:

The Monarchy · Parliament · Organisation of Political Parties · Parliamentary Elections Women in Britain · Ethnic Minorities

Each book is illustrated in colour and contains reading lists and useful addresses.

For a free leaflet giving more details about this series, write to:

HMSO Books, Dept B, FREEPOST, Norwich NR3 1BR.

ASPECTS OF BRITAIN

Parliament

SURVEY OF
CURRENT AFFAIRS

For over 40 years this monthly publication has provided factual, objective coverage of government policy and legislation. Drawing on a variety of official and other reliable sources, the *Survey of Current Affairs* provides comprehensive coverage of British policy on recent issues, making it an ideal source of information for students, specialists, the media and others interested in finding out the facts about Britain and its policies. Its easily accessible style and handy format make it an attractive source of information.

The *Survey of Current Affairs* is a perfect complement to the *Britain Handbook* and the *Aspects of Britain* series, and updates and expands on the issues covered by these publications. It is distributed worldwide and is available in Britain from HMSO. Subscription includes both a six-monthly and an annual index, and there is a binder to hold 12 issues and the two indexes.

For a free leaflet giving more details about *Survey of Current Affairs*, write to: **HMSO Books, Dept B, FREEPOST, Norwich NR3 1BR.**

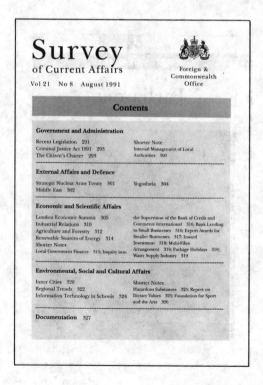

Survey
of Current Affairs

Foreign &
Commonwealth
Office

Vol 21   No 8   August 1991

Contents